Research into the Genealogy and Origin History of the Fridinger Families of *Medieval* Europe and into *Colonial Southern* America.

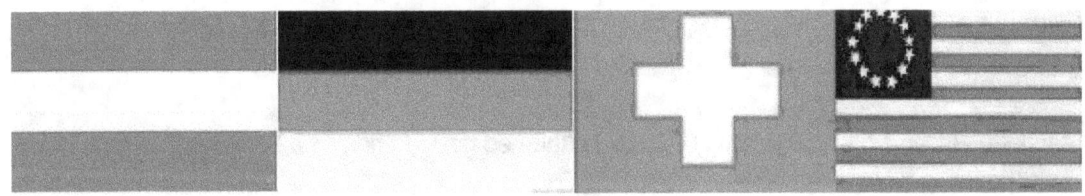

Fridingen/Frydingen/Fridinger/Fridingē/Fridigē/
Friding/Fryding/
Frydig/Fridig/Fridy/Fryday/Friday

Compiled by J.S Friday

October 2015

The Swabian Connection – Expanded Edition

The Genealogy and History of the Friday Families from Switzerland, Colonial and Southern America.

The Genealogy and History of the Fridiger Families from Germany, Austria, Switzerland, Colonial and Southern America.

Research into the Genealogy and History of the Frydig/Fridig Families Switzerland, Colonial and Southern America.

Research into the Genealogy and History of the Friding|Frydig Families in Medieval Europe and into Colonial Southern America.

Research into the Genealogy and Original History of the Fridinger Families of *Medieval* Europe and into ***Colonial Southern*** America.

100 Copies of the 1st Edition were self published in 2003 and distributed nationwide.

The 2nd Edition (Text Version) was produced in October 2003

The "Swabian Connection" & the "Schweiz Connection" editions were produced in the Fall of 2012.

Provided a copy to the Library of Congress Local History & Genealogy Collection on 1-20-2003. Provided a copy to the South Carolina Department of Archives & History in May 2003.

Printed in the United States of America

Epigraph

To understand the past is to understand the present.

Your ancestry is resonant. It precludes your history that you are part of that person's genealogy.

Genealogy clues should not be taken lightly, as they sometimes will reveal the most details.

Saving history starts with digging up, documenting by publishing that knowledge for others.

Genealogy is Mythology until one has documented an ancient ancestor.

$$P + T + (R/I) = D$$
[Patience + Time + Research divided by Insight = Discovery/Breaking down brick walls].

The best discovery is one in which a historical record changes your perception and warms your brain with fullfilness.

Got Ancestry?

Who's archiving and documenting your Ancestral family History?

~1782 - "You Dutchmen are celebrated for fine gardens; let us go and look at yours". Mr. Friday, you are a friend to your country. Remain so. We have not conquered it yet, and never will, and your name will yet be honored, while those of your countrymen who are with us will be despised." I gladly record the patriotism of Mr. Friday, in fulfillment of this prediction. by Colonel Maxwell "British Army" to John Fridig [Friday] (1743).

There is no better History lesson than one from your own ancestors.

Foreword

I ask for the indulgence for all who read this book as I sit here and write this, to place their name before ancestors before them. I like you have a stake in history one steeped in roots too far gone for those who can recall from just lore alone. I have a personal yet almost mystical reason for writing this. As Jeff writes he feels as if his ancestors speak to him. The morning I was asked to write another forward, I had an interesting experience. My wife seemed like she was in a frantic dream, I laughed rolled over and went to sleep as I heard her as if she was scared or whatever was in her dream. Upon waking up she told me about a man who she saw staring out where we have a window, but had a light a glow all around him he was white, older and she described him with a smile. It seemed great. That morning upon arising I had the text in which Jeff asked me to write another foreword. I have kept this sometime, between me and my wife before even writing this. Like Jeff he can tap into and guide where he needs to go. Although schooled with an M.S. in Project Management, I think this undertaking is difficult and doesn't fit me. He takes to it like it is his reason for being, here on earth. I and my family have taken so much joy in his work, his endeavor, and passion. I am especially grateful for this work, the identity, how our past projected in the future and who we are today. Everyone has a story but ours is just that "ours" we share in his writings. I started looking into this genealogy in 2002. It ultimately led me to different sources but once I emailed Jeff I got note back that went to it something like this "Hello Cousin". If that can't make a man feel great, I don't know what could. I know like myself you will be blessed by what you find here. I know that his heart has poured over this like Jeff's other works. Read the lines understand your history, he has done the work, please pick it up, inspire, ponder, and give wonder as how someone can take such different paths in our history to show us a clear guide by which we have come. My family had at one point stated many different oral histories some correct and some just that, oral history. Jeff has made it his clear duty to put our past in perspective. I stand all amazed by what he has done and would thank him to the end of the earth, as he has given you and identity and a past to pull from. Take it or leave it, you come from great stock. With great pleasure I give another great piece that we can work with, and that my relative Ophelia Friday would be surely proud of and look upon us all with a gaze of happiness and love. I truly think Jeff can tap into or has a guide that surely leads him the right way. Respectfully, ~ Brian Evans II

Preface

As a young man, I did some preliminary research on the Friday's background. What I had heard and found was the Friday's came from Germany. Many relatives had suspicions that the name was originally "Freytag" from Germany. This was not the case with this family, at least in the last 500+ years. While the German families "Freytag" where close in proximity with original Southern Colonists and Swiss like so many other nationalities in the new world, the Friday line that is documented are originally from Switzerland and did speak German like Martin Fridig and son Jacob who arrived in South Carolina in February 1735. Going back further in time, this Frydig's line could have easily migrated from Germany/Austria/Italy via the Roman Empire to Switzerland in the 15th century or much earlier than 13th century.

The case with the Freytag's in North Carolina, which have some of the exact names as the Fridig/Friday families and movements through southern America, their lineage does not cross through this Swiss-American Friday bloodlines. The Freytag's mainly began their start in North Carolina/Pennsylvania and the Fridig's in Charleston, Saxe Gotha and Orangeburg, South Carolina. This research is documenting the Fridig/Frydig/Fridy/Fryday/Friday Swiss-American family. Fridig was never Freytag/Fretag in Europe. Fridig became Friday/Fryday on board the ship William on the way to Carolina, so no Freytag research is necessarily needed, but has been done for fact-finding. I have spent the last ten years researching the Fridig's and I expect the search will continue. This book was written to help dispel rumors; give researchers a guide in further understanding and to open the doors for new records and connections. As with any research, I consider this compilation book as work in progress.

In October 2009, I decided to do another lookup for Frydig in the available online Swiss Records and found Gwer Fryding in a 1586 land transaction[1]. Fryding is not Fridig, but an original/former (Friding 1433,1437) name while Frydig/Fridig (1500's) is a later Swiss conversion with a character being dropped. The DNA sampling backed up the case there was more information available and tracked further back in time.

Based on the Historical Research, DNA sampling showed my Haploptype/Haplogroup going back 26000 years BCE to the location of Kiev, Germany[2] and before that to Afrika, I will comment later on this Ancestral Race. The Fridingers' (Fridingische men) can be generalized with many skills and characteristics: They have children with Brown, Blonde or Reddish hair, musically inclinded, Medium Build and Height, Strong Men, Fisherman, hard working, some religiously spiritual and some not, but all love their family and are a proud stock.

The books title was a combination of previous titles, however more to indicate the additional research in the Middle Ages where it had NOT been done by any American researchers for this family. Most of the Swiss researchers have also ignored this family due to an assumption from prior documented research that the "Families died out or the connections lost". This is just a researchers old excuse and the failure to dig deeper.

Introduction

During the research process I encountered lots of people with brick walls, researchers who could only look at the black and white details and also some researchers with extreme insite. The values for the insite I have kept and paved the way in this research. 1) When people migrated they usually came with family or neighbors. 2) Surnames can be written in a variety of forms (even in the same generation). 3) Try to locate all family members when researching, not just your primary line.

In 1291 the foundation of the Swiss Confederation with three rural communities (Schwyz, Uri and Unterwalden) made an alliance to protect their freedoms against encroachments by would-be overlords (German/Austrian and Northern Swiss nobles). The 1300-1400's saw the confederacy expand to a loose confederation with both rural and urban members. While the Swiss were undermining the nobility (1386 @ Lucerne and 1388 Näfels near Glarus) wars, I'm sure the serfs and lesser nobles were migrating into Switzerland to enjoy the new spirit of freedom. The Hapsburgs did not recover from these two wars[3]. In 1415 Aargau was conquered by the confederates from the Austrians. Peter Friding | Frydig family quietly moved into Frutigen/Adelboden before 1433. The Zurich civil war occurred shortly afterwards from 1443-1446. The Swabian war occurred in almost the full year for January through September of 1499 which was the Swiss rejection of the Reichstag of 1495. The Fridingen castles and many other Southern German Noblemen castles would be burned in 1499 by the 8000 Swiss in the Swabian region.

This book is the continuation of further research in the middle ages via German Latin Archive documents, research on surname Etymology (forms) and DNA of the parallel Haplogroups to locate the origin of Peter Friding (~1403) or Gwer Frydig (1535) one or both progenitors of this family history.

In the mid 1730's some Frydig's/Fridig's and other families left Switzerland either because of religious persecution or the search for new opportunities as described in the Purry's Pamphlet (1731) and Hans Jacob Riemensperger brochure (1740) to attract migration to Saxe Gotha Township in Carolina.

Two families arrived in Carolina @ Charlestown in 1735; Hans Frydig (1690) and Martin Frydig (1689) families. These two men may have been cousins and but no information has been found to show a relationship between the parties. Hans "John" (1690) had one boy and one girl. They had children but soon died out with one male surname (John) surfaces in 1785, but no Caucasian references after William Friday. Martin Frydig (1689) had 4 boys, 3 girls and maybe others. All children but one were born in Switzerland, they all came to Carolina and prospered. During the early 1800's many Friday's like George (1787), Godfrey (1801) Henry (1760), Emanuel (1792), Frederick (1754), Samuel (1802) and other's left South Carolina. This book will document the entrance into Carolina, the descendants of these Fridig's in South Carolina and follow them to Georgia, Alabama, Mississippi, Louisiana, Arkansas, Texas, Oklahoma and California.

Some assumptions & facts have been made:

- The previous research of Genealogists is 90% accurate.
- The route of the Friday's through the southern states can be followed.
- The transcriptions from Orangeburgh, SC "Book of Records" is correct.
- Documented sources of Census, Land Grants, Birth, Marriage, Burials, Cemetery, Tax, Manuscripts, SC Archives, Swiss Bibles, Book records, Family Records and Archives of various states are correct.
- Freidig, Frydig, Fridig, Friding, Fryding, Fridang, Fritig, Freijdig, Fridey, Freidig or Freitag name came from Germany to Switzerland (between 1200-1400's) and they associated with and spoke Swiss German. Frydig/Fridig surname became then Friday/Fridy/Fryday in the New World. Fridig is pronounced a variation of Fri-dee, Fry-dee, Fri-dic-er/ Frew-dic or Free-dic. The translation of Friday in Swiss-German is Friitig. Freidig is pronounced Free-dic which is similar as Friitig.

- Friding|Frydig surname & family comes from 2 possible families von Fridingen (1180 – 1560's) or von Torelen/Torla/Türelen/Törler "Urner family" (1257-1650) concluded from 2009-2012 research.
- Swiss and Tirol {Austrian} dialects tend to shorten names.
- German scripts/books can be translated with a certain degree of accuracy by online translators.

Document Format: You may notice some records for the living have been commented out. For example,.. Barbara (W_____) would have shown the maiden name, but does not. This is to protect privacy of the living descendants. Many descendants would like to see the data, but many have requested to have it the information scrubbed.

On the main ancestors there will be a header following their name such as:

Tom Friday (son of Jim, grandson of Steve, John, William). It will read as son of Jim, grandson of Steve, and so forth (great-grandsons...etc..) The format will cascade as far back as the ancestral line has been documented. Occasionally you may see an (*) astericks on certain names of Fridays that have very little documentation, or unknown to the main ancestral line.

****This concludes the finale for this series!!! If you would like to continue the research as more European records come available use these books for 2012 as reference to write another book to further archive and document connections to this ancient family lieneage.****

Contact this group http://groups.ancestry.com/site/fridig to track the latest information.
Gedcom Database http://wc.rootsweb.ancestry.com/cgi-bin/igm.cgi?db=timemachine

Table of Contents

Surname Naming Conventions,Variations,Placenames & Etymology

The variations of names in language can be associated with the time period and geography of Germany, Switzerland(Cantons), Tirol, Austria and even in German/Swiss borders who also speak French. The majority of the early placenames for Southern Germany (Swabia/Hegau) and Northern Switzerland have their origin between the year 816 (*St. Gallen*) and 1092 (*Fridinga*) +/- 100 years. The Abbots of St. Gallen Switzerland[4] have surnames beginning by 1077. Middle High German (MHG=MHD) in some instances had longer sounding words. This period starting 1100 and ended about ~1500. High German (Hochdeutch) is the language used today and even some Germans can't pronounce the old language. "In Switzerland they speak Swiss German which is completely different. Swiss German has its own pronunciation, many different words, its own grammar, and most Germans have difficulty understanding this funny language[5]". "The German-speaking Swiss write standard German". There is no Swiss German official language. Swiss German is spoken as a casual (emails, magazines, street talk etc..) informal German, where as High German is used in formal (Legal, Politics speeches etc..) settings. "The Swiss can also speak standard German very well, but to them it's a foreign language that they have to learn how to use when they start school (Eldrid.ch 2012)." Swiss German words frequently are written & pronounced totally different from other Cantons and their German counterparts (Greuzi=Guten Tag=Good Day"Hello". Swiss German (Schweizerdeutsch) is a branch of upper German called Alemannic. Also know as High Alemannic (Berndeutsch & Zurichdeutsch) comes from a branch of German. There are High Alemannic dialects that have preserved the ending –n which has been dropped in most Upper German dialects. Schwabisch and Baseldeutsche are both under Alemanische German. This maybe a reason Peter Friding {Frydig} (~1403) migrated to Bern and is shown with a later family name variation when he was documented in Frutigen in 1433. In MHD the –n is called the weak declenasion, all other nouns may be said to belong to the strong declension[6]. The "en" ending is defined as plural MHD and the "e" a singular MHD. "Masculine

The Swabian Connection – Expanded Edition

names of persons ending in a consonant take es in the Gen and e or en in the Dat and Acc. Feminine names of persons ending in a consonant take e in the Gen Dat and Acc (Wright 1888: pg 14)". The Masculine pronoun is a Distinction Accusative form that would be **Fridinge(n), Friding, or Fridige.** In the case of Fridig/Frydig, the "ig" is always pronounced "ic" (like Konig or bartig), except in Austria and some local dialects of Germany the "ig", is pronounced as in English "dig"[7]. Free-dig is unnatural to German ears (Forvo.com: Peter Figila 2012). The german letter "y" (=ü) does not have an English pronunciation, but possibly 'ew" when we hear Frydig currently spoken. Frydig {Frew-tig} is perhaps Frutigen Switzerlands way of making Peter's origin become Frutigische? After a while of reviewing, you may notice some of the names starting to blend (ie., Friedingen to> Fridinger to> Fridinge to> Friding or Fridige or Freidig). Researching the Etymology for Friding{Frydig} names that maybe possible I came across many variations and documented the following:

Fridy name referenced from Fridig/Friday in South Carolina via Thomas E **Fridy** (1825) descendants.
Peter Fride {also P Flick}[8] is listed as an Official Magister and Sekretar around 1420, 1439-1440 in Passau & Augsburg, Germany but no relation known to **Fridy** in South Carolina 1820's. In Bern[9]: vrida, Friden in the fridy 1533. fridi archer 1519 Friden good to 1529. Fridy Manttenn 1533. by the fridi student about 1525. the frid Stelly 1533.

Friday has been used worldwide in many English speaking countries, included native American tribes in Alaska. **Fridig** became **Friday** by 1800 in South Carolina in the Southern United States. According to the 1990 Census Bureau the name "**Friday**" 4,970th most popular last name (surname) in the United States; frequency is 0.002%; percentile is 63.163. According to the 1990 Census Bureau the name "Fryday" is the 84,915th most popular last name (surname) in the United States; frequency is 0.000%; percentile is 90.113.
Pronunciation of Surname: (Swiss German/Colonial "Frydig/Fridig/Freidig" to Anglicized "Friday/Fridy/Fryday" transition 1735+)
- On September 17th, 1736 **Hans Freidig {Frey-dic}** is written as receiving a land plat of 200 acres in Berkely Co, Carolina.
- On February 2nd 1740 Martin and son Jacob Fridig (**listed as Fritig**) **{Fry-tig/deg / Free-teeg/teg}** German Speaking inhabitants of Saxe Gotha bear witness to Hans Jacob Riemensperger brochure to attract migration to Carolina.
- The March 16th, 1748/49 petition of **Martin Fredagh {Free-dag/dac}** was written by the English court writer.
- On May 18th 1749 **Martin Fryday** (1689) is recorded in the Common Journal for petitioning for the ferry on the Congaree at Saxe Gotha.
- The **Fridy** family descended from **Thomas W Fridy** (1825) pronounces their surname swiftly as **{Fri-dee}**.
- December 2nd 1750 Rev. John Giessendanner writes the **Hans George frydie {fry-dee}** name as he hears it an understands it.
- On September 10, 1814 **Gabriel Frideg {Fri-deg}** (1752) has a plat of land surveyed for David Shotts.
- The 1880 census taker of Natchitoches, Louisiana wrote William Friday's (1827) name as **{Fridy}** with "no pause" on the 2nd syllable on the last half of the name.
- My father Richard also pronounced the name Friday **{Fri-dee/Fry-dee}** as if it is was a like a one syllable word and pronounced with the "a" being silent.
- Dallis Ann Friday Lauffenburger also confirmed their last name being pronounced **{Fri-dee}** with her father George Robert Friday (1937).
- In the 1976 book Placenames of Bern by Paul Zinsli the native name **Fridig** in Frutigen as **Freidig** is pronounced **Fridig**.
- In 2009, **Sebastian Freidig** advised that his uncle **Freidig** was from Switzerland and they pronounced their name **{Frei-dic}**, Frei like liberty.

The Swabian Connection – Expanded Edition

Fridays Dream Point - is the landing just below Briar Creek. The origin of the name is unknown. [See NSC, viii:17 The **Friday** Family also operated a ferry on the Congaree near what is now Columbia.] (Nueffer, Claude 1972)

(*) Fryg s. Frei/Frei/Frey/Fry/Frigen/Vrigie - Hans Frei 4/1472, Claus Fryg burger to Constanz[10] 1412 listed with Ulrich Fridingen. Thomas Frey (Fryg) Canocia to Constanz ~1343. Aygeltlngen 4/1383 Landrichter Hans Fryg von Stalringen listed with von Bodmen Ael. Hans Fryg and Kuni Fryg von Reken Mittwoch nach St Gallus 10/1428. Erhard Fryg von Augsburg[11], Suldnervertrag mit Konstanz 7/1403. Bregenz 4/1463 Uolin Fryg von Ragaz and Haini Fryg.

(*) Freytag/Fridag/Fritag have also been found in Germany & Switzerland and used for both a surname and day of the week. Hermann **Fritac** plebannus in Altmannshofen in 1188. Vriedach earliest records is one of **Wecelo Vriedach**[12] in 1198 located in the Archives of Kappenburg[13], Wesfalen, Germany. **Nicolaus Vriedach**[14], milites {soldier} appears in Minden, Germany (1241-1253) south of Schildesche on November 1246. Nicholaus also appears a year before in December 1245 as **Nicholaus Fridag** from the same book, then later appears in Wietersheim (record in Munster) as **Nicholaus Vrydach** (d+1287) in 1275. **Ecbertus Vriedach** appears in a Minden church records 1253-1265. Next comes **Otto Vriedach**[15] in Schildesche near Minden, (Northern) Germany in 1266-1288. **Theodericus Vrydach**, dictus **Johannes** and priest/dictus **Everhardus von Vrydach** appear 1309-1332 in Kamene[16]. Another **Diderich Vriedach** von Kamen records in the Katherinen church in Dortmund of Bovekinkhus in 1341. Nurnberg (1362) **Herman Fritag**, Conrad Geyger and others. Wilhelm Vrydach and Meynrich Vrydach in appear in a church record in Dortmund or Munster Germany in 1362. **Henz Fritag** appears in Baden, Constanz, Germany by 1371. The coat of arms for **Heinrich Fritag** in Basel Switzerland is a large star over a double layer of 3 mountains[17]. (1403) July 7th Walthern **Fritag** von Lenzburg, Aargau, Switzerland. In the book "Urkundenbuch der Stadt Basel" there is a brief record for a **Peter Fritag (~1386)** from Solothurn or Basel, Switzerland dating to 1416. The town of Rohrbach, Oberaargau, Bern, Switzerland has a duplicate coat of arms. **Fridag** used as a surname frequently in Berlin about the 1600's and commonly used as a day of the week. **Fritag/Freytag** is listed (~1400's) in many German monastery documents as the day of the week.

Fritig was listed for Jacob and Martin **Fridig** in 1740 for the Hans Jacob Riemensperger Brochure to attract migration to Saxe Gotha, Carolina[18]. The Alemannisch South Baden website list the word **Freytag** as a leisurely spelling as **Friddig or Frittig** – the website also list the day of the week as "**Fridig**"[19]. South Baden, Germany is the area were **Fridig** was documented as **Freidingen**. This is the only German locality listing **Fridig** as **Friday** for the day of the week. In Switzerland, Friday is spelled Frittig/Fritig. In Southern Baden, Germany, Friday is **NOT** spelled Freitag, **but is spelled Friddig or Frittig.** Their website (http://www.badische-seiten.de/alemannisch/lexikon.php) will actually list the day of the week as **Fridig** with date and time when visiting on a Friday.

(*) Fratting (Fredigen) 1251 in Moravia in Austria bordering Czeck Republic.

(*) Friden s. Frydin/Friethen/Vrethen/Vrede/Wreden/Vretheim/Vrethe/Wrethem from Alfeld, Germany[20] (near Hanover in Northern Germany). Brother Konrad & Ekbert von Freden resign tithes in Sorsum (Wennigsen, Germany) in 6/1219 (Hirzel 1896: 685). Brother Ekbert & Walter 1261, Gerhard 1264-68 with brother Konrad 1296-1310 other Friden names written as Vrethen, Vrede, Wreden, Vretheim, Vrethe and Wrethem[21]. Jenni Friden (Johann Frieden) has the earliest reference in Frutigen Bern in (1415) January 10th.

(*?) Urner family von Toernlon (Toernlen, Toerlen, Darelen) **Türelen or Törler: a branch of it Fridig** (1450? - ca.1550/1650). The Urner familie wappen is described as Silver, wrought gilt, chased, engraved with the arms of Urner{Uri} family[22]. Urner is synonymous with Uri - ie., Urner Alps=Uri Alps. The canton of Uri, Switzerland now uses (bull's head caboshed sable, langued

9

gules and noseringed) as their coat of arms with the origin dating between 1231-1243. Regarding the origin of the bull-emblem is the legend that the head of another, "Ure" (wild ox) represents what the first Alemannic settlers chose because they had their land as "ur" (wild) possessed[23]. In the Uri, Schweiz State Archives surnames documented and appeared as a derivative of : **Fridig (Friding, Fridung, Friden)** via typed notes, copies of articles (1443-1650)[24]. Werni **Fridig**(von Isenthal) in St. Jacob at the Sihl 1443. Anniv Seedorf 1470, Werni, werner buochers son and Jenni his brother and mother Machthilt (Matilda). **Martin** Kirchenvogt von Seedorf 1470, witness 1519. **Martin Friden** 1470 Kilchmeyer to Seedorf. **Ruedy Frytag/Fritag (Fridig)** 1499 vor Stockach is the first and only reference to Frytag. **Werni Friden** 1471 Attinghausen(Schrift 1501) **Gredi/Grett** Peters **fridigs** wirtin(land lady) was peter Pfisters Tochter(daughter) in Altdorf. This is believed to be **Martin Fridigs** wife **Grett Wallcher**. **Marti Fridig** (1518) May 3rd Isenthal. **Erni Fridig** and hausfrau 1522 Silenen(south of Altdorf). Spitalvogt in Altdorf 1564-1567 was **Heini Fridig. Heinrich** Council, Land clerk, a member of society 1599. The same reference mentions Toernlon (Toernlen, Toerlen, Darelen): Hand written notes (1257-1650), extract from the HBLS [25]. The earliest **von Toerlen** is **Rudolph** (~1237)[26]. Therese Metzger emailed(Oct 2010) to say that in the Historisch Biographischen Lexikon der Schweiz is mentioned only: **Friding/Fridung/Friden** that extinct in 1650. Therese's comments: "It was a branch of the old Urner family 'von Toernlon' - most probably from a son with the name **Friden (=Friedrich)"**. My thoughts: I have only found one single record that shows a first name Friedrich going to surname Freidige(=the Brave) who was Landgraf von *Thüringen,*Markgraf von *Meißen* & *Tuto* between (1257 † 1324). There was a Burkhart von tornlon, Anna sin wirtin(landlady), Klaus von torlen - Heini **fridig** wass Kuenratz sun from torla etc[27]. Toerlen is also v. Turlen[28]. One final reference puts this group surname of **Fridig** back toward Uri, Switzerland found in the book "Historisches Neujahrsblatt By Verein für Geschichte und Altertümer von Uri" in which itr describes **Türelen or Törler: a branch of it Fridig**[29] (1450? - ca.1550). This is Torler Alpes or Tyroler/Tyrol/Torle, Upper Switzerland/Lower Tyrol, Austria. Backing up this Tirol connection is another reference from "Der Landammann in den schweizerischen Demokratien Uri, Schwyz, Unterwalden" which states that "**Heini Fridig** wass Kuenratz sun from torla"[30]. Kuenratz (=Konrad/Conrad). The brief description appears to be Tirol dialect which if very different German with many possible intonations in the language for similar german words. This Torle location is not Torla Spain, but another word for Torle, Austria (SSE of Kempten, Germany, NNW of Innsbruck, Austria and NNE of Switzerland) or the better location being TURLEN or TOERLEN which is in Knonau in the district of Affoltern in the canton of Zürich, Switzerland[31]. There is also a Heinrich **Fridung** (~1360) {Burgergraf (Count) for Tyrol, Austria in 1511} and Conrad **Fridung** (~1388), however im unsure this was the same family, at least the Uri archives don't have them recorded. So, is Frydig from Torla? Yes, Heinrich Frydig (~1540) father Conrad (~1502) was from Torla, however if Conrad/Konrad was the son of Werner Friding/Fridig (~1420) it is most likely this lineage origin goes deeper over the border into Germany from Basel, Switzerland or into Tirol, Austria. Von Torla/Toerlen didn't occur to the 1450's so Werner Friding/Fridig origins are probably of SouthernDeutchland(Hegau) or NorthernSchweiz(Thurgau/Aargau) Fridinger families. Friding is a Swiss based deriviative of the ministerial family von Fridingen beginining in mid 1300's(14th century) by Urlich Friding (Fridingen/Fridinge/Frydingen).

Fridig/Friden/Friding/Fridung descendants from Uri/Torla:

First Generation
1. **Werner BUOCHERS**.

   Werner married **Machthilt**.

   They had the following children:

+   2   M   i.   **Werni Werner FRIDIG FRIDING** was born ~1420 and died ~1471.

       3   M   ii. **Jenni BUOCHERS** "Johann?".

Second Generation

2. **Werni Werner FRIDIG/FRIDIG/FRIDING** (Werner) was born ~1420 in Basel, Switzerland Or Underwalden, Tirol, Austria. He died ~1471 in Uri, Switzerland.

He had the following children:

+   4   M   i.   **Marti FRIDIG** was born ~1450 and died ~1528.

    5   M   ii.   **Peters FRIDIG(Pfisters)** was born ~1460. He died ~1502.

> L. Anniv. Attinghausen (Schrift 1501)+ Gredi/Grett Peter fridigs wirten(hosts) was Peter Pfisters Tochter in Altdorf.
> Note: Is this really a Peter Fridig? Actually Peter Pfisters!!

+   6   M   iii.   **Cuenrats ernis FRIDIG V TORLA** was born ~1502 and died ~1545.

Third Generation

4. **Marti FRIDIG** (Werni Werner FRIDIG FRIDING, Werner) was born ~1450 in Isental, Switzerland. He died ~1528 in Uri, Switzerland.

Marti married **Margaret WALLCHER** "Gret". Gret was born ~1453.

They had the following children:

    7   F   i.   **Verena FRIDIG** was born 1489 in Altdorf, Uri, Switzerland.

> Verena married **Andreas ASCHWANDEN** on 1508 in Attinghausen, Uri, Switzerland.

    8   M   ii.   **Richi FRIDIG** was born ~1472 in Isental, Switzerland.

    9   M   iii.   **Michael FRIDIG** was born ~1470 in Switzerland. He died ~1513.

    10   M   iv.   **Ruedi FRIDIG** "Reudy" was born ~1479. He died ~1501. **Ruedy** married Katrina and had children. Frytag, Ruedy , blieb vor Stockach 1499. Sch 15 Pfingsttagen

6. **Cuenrats ernis FRIDIG V TORLA** "Erni?" (Werni Werner FRIDIG FRIDING, Werner) was born ~1502 in Torla. He died ~1545.

Erni? married **Jta FRIDING** "Ita?", daughter of FRIDINGS.

They had the following children:

+   11   M   i.   **Heinrich FRIDIG** was born ~1540 and died ~1600.

    12   F   ii.   **Katrina FRIDIG** .

Fourth Generation

11. **Heinrich FRIDIG** (Cuenrats ernis FRIDIG V TORLA, Werni Werner FRIDIG FRIDING, Werner) was born ~1540 in Seedorf, Uri, Switzerland. He died ~1600.

Heinrich married **Anna TROSCH**.

They had the following children:

    13   F   i.   **Richentza FRIDIG** .

(*) Fridung/Fridunc/Fridunc von Zäringen(Zeringen)

Raben Fridunc von Zäringen appears in 1124(?). Konrad Fridung/Frydung was a Kuchenmeister (Kitchen Master) in Austria from 1414-1439. Konrad Fridung also has a coat of arms with a Crown[32] dated 4/13/1434 documented in Austria. Conrad Fridung was in Fragenstein near Tirol in

1464. Heinrich von Fridung is a Burgergraf (Count) for Tyrol, Austria in 1511. Conrad Fridang is mentioned many times in Schaffhausen, Switzerland records. In the Uri, Suisse State Archives surnames documented and appeared as a derivative of: Fridig (Friding, Fridung, Friden) via typed notes, copies of articles (1443-1650). Fridung/Fridunc is belive to originate from the house of Zäringen of which also is a Bird Free Standing. Zäringen is believed to originate from the Alaholfinger family(Erchanger Fridingen family).

Fridung, Andres b: ~1368 in Germany d: ~1401
Fridung, Berchtold b: ~1456 in Kempten,Germany? d: ~1487
Fridung, Conrad b: ~1388 in Austria d: ~1464 in Innsbruck,Austria
Fridung, Hanns b: ~1495 d: ~1526
Fridung, Heinrich b: ~1360 in Austria
Fridung, Heinricus b: ~1404 d: ~1444
Fridung, Johannes b: ~1436 d: ~1467
Fridung, Mann b: ~1548 in Kempten,Allgäu,Bavaria,Germany? d: ~1579
Fridung, Raben b: in Germany
Fridung, Ulrich b: ~1429 d: ~1460
Fridung, Walter Pfeffpler b: ~1395 d: ~1421

Fryding/Friding 1333/1335/38/1362/1418/1427-37 The 1st mention of **Friding** was in Vienna , Austria 1333 when Virich "Ulrich" **Friding** (Fridingen) was named in a document with Bishop Chünrat von Freising. This same Ulrici de Fridingen or latin Ulricus de **Fridinge** was related to B Niclaus, the Kaplan of Constanz[33]. There is a Dorf(village) location called **Friding** which is NiederBaiern(North Bayern) near Regensburg.

Other occurences of **Friding**: Albrecht der Schench v. Friding (Frieding) February (1336) in Stayn/ Stein, Austria. This Albrect is also Albrecht der Schenk von Verthouen[34] Feb 5th (1325) signet sealed [† S.] ALBERTI • DE • FRIDI[nG.] or Albrect Aidem[35] and wife Elsbet recorded Nov 17th (1325). Albrect der Schench **Friding/Verthouen** (~1306) has leaves surrounding a Horse as his Signet located in Stein/Stayn, Austria. Albrect der Schench **Friding/Frieding/Verthouen** has green leaf branches similar to the Count of Andech state coat of arms. Steyr(Austria) (1338) Dec 17th Konrad Suntheim sold to Bischofe Konrad von Freising, with Vlreich von Gruenburch, her **Hainreich von Honburch,** her **Volreich von Friding**, her Marquart Prevhauen, her Ot der Schek, her Chuonrat der Zauchinger, & Chuonrat (von) Pvechawe (MO:675). Urlich **Friding(Freidig)** von Baden (1347) May 10. Oetting near Bayern (1363) Dec 19th **Heinrich von Friding** (~1343) , Hans den Wegstorfer, Fridlin von Graben, **Uellin de Chling** (Clinger?) and many others[36] near Leuchtenberg, Bavaria, Germany (Bayerische) just west of Austria. Fryding/Freyding (*dicitur Frydius*) mentioned in Charter Caroli IV in 1377 in Cronica Mindensi[37]. In a Zurich Switzerland archives document for March 22, 1411 brother Ulrich (~1379) & Johann Fridingen (~1371) dispute was resolved – their names mentioned gebruder/brothers **Friding**[38].

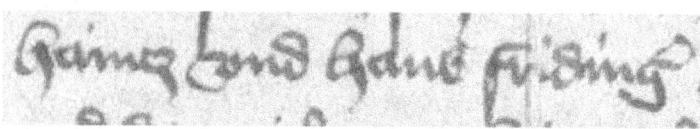

Johannes von Seon appears in Zurich document (March 22, 1411) helping with the dispute between brothers "**Friding**" Ulrich and Johannes von Fridingen "knights" all names Hohenkrahen/Fridingen(Hegau) registered[39]. This Zurich document appears misdated since only two men that are alive are Ulrich III (D. 1362?) and Johannes V (d. 1398?) OR Ulrich IV (d. 1417) and Hans VI (d. 1414). This 1411 dispute <u>may</u> have been the origins of **Peter Friding** (~1403). Translated from German to English "**Friding**" is translated as Fridingen. In the book "Vierteljahrsschrift for arms, seal and Genealogy Volume 16", von **Friding** is from hohen-krayen in vicinity of Fridingen, Singen, Germany. Kloster Einsiedeln urkunden[40] 1418 Mar 23rd assignment of Lehenhof Bongarten(Baumgarten dist Gottlieben) to Heinz and Hans Friding: Heinz (Haintz) Gugoch and his wife Verena, daughter of Cuoni Wintzen, both of Wiesholz (Wisholtz) give the court Bongarten from, which is a part of their fief of the Monastery of St. Katharinental and the Land of Bürkli Tegenhart and **Heinz (Haintz) Friding** borders, the brothers **Heinz (Haintz)** and **Hans Friding**, both of Wiesholz. Conrad Stähelinn and Walter (Wältin) Keller of

Ail(?) Attended as a consultant and arbitrator. Baumgarten occurs from the Bailiwick from the Herren(Lords) von Klingen in the monastery of Munsterlingen. **Heinz (Haintz/Haintzer) Friding** (~1395) & **Hans Friding** (~1398) **Fridinger** brothers beide(both) von Wiesholz located

near Ramsen, Switzerland just south from the German border south of Singen. Three records appear to show Hans and Haintz as children of a Klinger/Klingen(berg) or Keller mother and a Fridinger father:

1st) 1425 Cunral Uffhover to Tengen county judge in Unterklettgau brings a lengthy process betw **Ulrich Clinger**(der Junge, son of Walter Klingen?) and **Heinrich Fridinger** because of Kelnhofs to Wisholz to discharge **Clinger** what the Court refers[41].

2nd) Elizabeth von Fridingen father-n-law was named **Heinrich (Heintzel) Klingenberg** (~1306) and Albrecht her husbands brother was named Hans von K (Knobloch 1905:303). This indicates a Klingen(berg) female sister(?) to Ulrich v K or Albrecht v K had children with either Konrad III F (~1374), Heinrich X F, Heinrch XI F or another von Fridingen male. Fridingen @ Singen is only 11 miles from Wiesholz, Ramsen, Schaufhausen, Switzerland.

3rd) 1416 Jan 15th a record shows Konrad von Fulach in Schaufhausen exchange of serfs Henny Frener in Klosters St. Katharinental (KAE:26.25). Verena von Fulach was the 2nd or 3rd wife of Konrad von Fridingen.

4th) Sept 4th 1425 Before the court of the monastery of St. Agnes in Schaffhausen in the yard of St. Agnes, **Henry Friedinger** appears and opens up that he had prozessirt with the wife **Margaretha Klinger(Keller)** and their heirs because of its long half Kelnhofes to Wisholz that her but, as heir deceased brother Künzli Keller, who had previously owned the farm, the law of succession had been awarded. It takes place thereon the surrender of the rod to the attention of the woman and her heirs. Margaretha a widow with children by Sept 15th 1425.

Cuonrat von Friding (Fridingen @ Krahen) 1427.

Cuonrat **Friding** is listed in the Schaffhausen Switzerland archives on a documents dated 1422-28. A few more interesting records are found for Cleggöw/Klettgau in Schaffhausen archives[42]:

- Item VIII 1/2 ß Hensli Brimelwer gen **Kuontzenberg** und gen Fützhain zuo dem **Friding'** von des puntz wegen, quarta feria Quasi Modo. 1427-28
- Item VII ß Clewin Endingern gen **Kuontzenberg** zuo dem **Friding'**, in herzemanen uff ain fritag in der Osterwuchen. 1427-28
- Item VI ß Weltin Suter gen **Kräygen** und gen **Kuontzenberg** zuo dem **Fridinger** ... Misericordia Domini. 1427-28
- Item III ß Henslin Brimelwer gen **Kräygen** zuo **Cuonrat von Fridingen**, als wir im geantwurt hand von sins wibs fünfhundert guldinen wegen. 1427-28
- Item X ß dem Baldinger gen **Kräygen** (Zell und Costentz = gestrichen) zuo **Cuonrat von Friding'**, mit ainer antwurt, als er uns geschriben hatt, den Räntzen sicher ze sagen, und gen Zell zuo dem burgermaister, als er uff dz schriben herabkam, und gen Costentz mit I brief. 1427-28.

Werner **Fryding/fridyng/Fridiger/Fridig** (~1420) from Basel Switzerland and now living in Isenthal ,Sihl, & Uri, Switzerland by 1443 -fought in the Zurich war 1440-43. Conrad **Friding** (~1439) appears in a loan via Innsbruck, Austria in 1469. Jorg Freiding (~1475) who is a painter from Tirol, Austria in Rattenburg working for Emperor Maximiliian in 1505. Marti Friding (Fridig) (~1450) in Seedorf and Isenthal 1480-1500. Sebastian **Freyding** (~1504) in Untrasried, Ostallgäu, Bavaria, Germany in 1534. Christianus Rormeyer **Friding** (~1534) is a student @ Universität Freiburg in Breisgau, Germany in 1554. Johannes Fridingen (~1458) son of Rudolp is listed as **Friding** in the University of Tubingen in 1510. The University indexes consistently shows a transition of surnames changing coming out of the late middle ages period. In the Uri, Suisse State Archives surnames documented and appeared as a derivative of : **Fridig (Friding, Fridung, Friden)** via typed notes, copies of articles (1443-1650)[43]. In a 1506 document relating

13

to an interheritance of Prince Abbot of Kemptens wife Dorothea Awerin/Ower, Felictia von **Friding** was written[44]. She was a Rotenstein married to Conrad **Fridingen (~1476)**. The archive Index of the document also states she was **Felictia von Fridingen**. Christianus Rormeyer **Friding** (~1534) is a student @ Universität Freiburg in Breisgau, Germany in 1554. In the 1888 book "Vierteljahrsschrift für Wappen, Siegel und Familienkunde, Volume 16" **von Friding** is listed on Hohen-Kräyen. German: **von Friding** auf Hohen Krayen Jn b. ein w Schrägbalken darüber ein g. Löwe gk H Straußenfederbusch hd: b g. Translated: "**of Friding on High Krayen** Jn b. a w g diagonal bar over it a lion ostrich plume gk H hd: bg". Right below this reference also describes Fridingen. This is where ministerial knights **Fridingen/ger** family came to power. In the book "The brotherhood book of the Abbey of Reichenau" located in Germany just above the Swiss border the names **Luit Frid and Luit Fridinc** occur[45]. This is possibly Luitfrid Hirsheck (d.1040/~1135) or a later generation? Fridinc is concluded as Fridingin[46]. Katherine Fridingen (~1486) is listed in a Cronical of Augsburg book[47] (record dated 1523) as **Catherine Friding** with her soon to be husband Dr. Prygion and the daughter(?) of Hans Fridingen (1467) XI . Gwer **Fryding** (Fridig) uses in (1586) on a Swiss land record fief transfer. **Friding|(Frydig)** identified for Peter Friding (~1403) in Frutigen, Switzerland in 1433 & 1437 from the Bern research[48] of Hans Wandfluh in 1952. **Frydig** is being identified as the later familie surname (abt early 1500's?), **Friding** is the name as he came into the canton of Bern. **Frydig** is pronounced today as **Frew-dic** (ENHG/EMHG) ,however I don't think much has changed in pronunciation for this name Frydig in Frutigen, Switzerland. The german letter "y" (=ü) does not have an English pronunciation, but possibly 'ew" when we hear Frydig currently spoken. The "ig" is pronounced as "ich". In Austria and some local dialects of Germany the "ig", is pronounced as in English "dig"[49]. An 1828 Italian gazette has **FRIEDINGEN 0 FRIDING** city of reg ciré Wurtemberg Black Forest bai and from NE 2 1 1 4 1 4 The Tuttlingen and 6 SE from Rotweil on the left bank of the Danube Sound of silk yarn and has 1,000 inhabitants[50]. Over a dozen books prior to the 19th century having **Friding** listed as this same Suabian/Swabian village. Albert Bernhardt Faust wrote in his book Volume II of "List of Swiss Emigrants in the Eighteenth Century to American Colonies" that Hans Freydig (1690)(*) of Frutigen immigrated to America in 1735[51]. "No further news of him seems to have reached this country as of 26 Dec. 1750. He falls heir to a legacy of 75 crowns and his relatives here request that this property be given to them, since Freydig had said that he would give up his right to the legacy. The government, however, refuses this request on the grounds that the family circumstances of the emigrant are not known and that sufficient time has not elapsed for him to be declared missing. The interest on the capital, however, may be divided annually among the relative. This family name, which is common in the district of Frutigen Bern, Switzerland, is officially written **Frydig**.

Katharina v. Fridingen (~1508) the daughter(?) of Hans Fridingen IX (~1467) married Dr. Paulus Constantinus Prygion (Phrigion) (~1483) a Doctor and has her name recorded in the 1520's as **Catharina von Friding**[52] from the Augburg Chronicles in Schwaben dated 1595/96. A later book published in 1773 on this Cronicle has her listed as Catharina von Fridingen. Between the 1340's-

1470's Conrat, Buchorn Claus, Schag Hans, Henrich and Erhardus use **Fryding/Fridang** in Germany, Austria and Switzerland. An 1855 Topography and History book records the marriage of Anna (Grunenberg) to Wilhelm **von Friding**[53] (Fridingen) in 1434 along with other familiar names Mülinen, Grimm, Luternau etc... So, does **Frydig** comes from **Friding**? Yes, in Frutigen/Adelboden, and Thurgau in the 1500's. The Swiss (Frutigen & Uri) and Western Tirol did an Aposcope on the letter "n" and in the case of Frutigen switch the "i"(=ee) to a "y"(=ew) on some surnames and words shortening the word/pronounciation. Friding in 1433 and (Frydig=Frew-dic) later developed into the late 15th century and common thereafter. Peter or his father reduced their name to Friding, then his descendants in Frutigen/Adelboden continued the tradition with Frydig in their own dialect change.

Frieding/Freiding / Freyding {vrye ding} 1003, 1123 is used in Germany, Austria and Switzerland. In a Bamberg document[54] for Heinrich II, Fridinga **(Frieding)** is mentioned (1003) September 9th. **Frieding** was established in 1123 in a deed of gift of the Count of Andechs, Luitfried von Frutinnen served in the donation as a witness. The above word "Fridinga" referenced for Friding are either for the Fridingen location or Fridingen family. **Friding** (Frieding, Pfaffing, Austria) is also a town listed in Autrech{Austria}. There is also a village in Pempfling, Bayern, Germany, located SSW of Cham called **Frieding**. Another town of Frieding is listed in the Andechs, Upper Bavaria, Starnberg, Germany. **Frieding** (first documented as *Frutinnen* in 1123 A.D.) is listed as a a petite ville/town de "Allegmagne de les Souabe{swab} same as Schwaben/Suabia{swa-bea}, Germany in many Geographical reference books. In the book "Die Traditionen des Stiftes Polling, Volume 41" **Frieding** (Gem. Andechs, LK, Starberg, Germany), Frutingen: Pertholdus Kisse de - TR.53. Other spellings for **Frieding** are Frouetingen, Vrouttingen, Vrouting or Fruittingen. The **Frieding** coat of Arms is actually from Count Andechs which is a green leaf branch over a lion. Albrect der Schench **Friding/Verhoven** (~1306) has leaves surrounding a Horse as his Signet located in Stein/Stayn, Austria. Albrect der Schench **Friding/Frieding** has green leaf branches similar to the Count of Andech state coat of arms. Fryding/**Freyding** (*dicitur Frydius*) mentioned in Charter Caroli IV in 1377 in Cronica Mindensi[55]. There is a Jager/Jobst **Freiding** in upper Bayern around 1410. Jorg **Freiding** (~1475) was a painter in Rattenburg or Tirol, Austria for Emporer Maximillian in 1505. In the book "Geschichte der Stadt und Universität Freiburg im Breisgau, Volumes 7-9 By Heinrich Schreiber 1859" listed a John **Freiding** (~1484) from Kempten, Germany in 1514. In the book "Urkundenbuch der Stadt Braunschweig: 1361-1374" **Freiding** is pronounced **{vrye-ding}**. So is Frieding s. Fridingen? Not really it has it's own distinct identity in Bayern west of Starnberg, Germany (SSW of Munich).

Fridig {Free-dic(CH)/**Free-dig**(AT)**}** for the most part the surname "Fridig" is developed in Uri in the 1450's, then Fridig/Frydig in Frutigen/Adelboden during the 1500's. There are a few records prior to common usage heading in that direction: **(1401)**[56] **Fridig(en)** (Tengen,Germany), **Fridig (1444)** (Bregenz/Radolzell, Germany)[57] pronounced **{Free-dic}**[58] / **Peter Friding{Frydig} (1433 & 1437)** (Frutigen, Switzerland)[59] pronounced **{Free-ding**[60] & **Frew-dic**[61]**}**. **Fridingē** & **Fridigē** dated abt 1411-17 vom Arlberg wappenbuch **(1394-1430)** in Thal,Tirol, Austria[62] pronounced **{Free-ding**[63] or **Free-ding-ee MHD?}** & **{Free-dic-a**[64] or **Free-dig-ee MHD?}/ Fridig** (Türelen or Törler, Switzerland) **(1450?-1550)**[65]. The following in the same parchment handscript: **Ulrich vö Fridingē** (~1386) , **Hans vö Fridigē** , **Hans vö Fridigē** , **Cunrat vö Fridigē** (~1384), Heinrich **vö Fridingē** (~1330-d1403) Agatha Westerstetten of his marital/legitimate housewife. Dated between 1411-1417 comparing other role descriptions. Heinrich Fridinger (~1330) was already in Tirol (as purggrafen/burggraf)[66] around ~1385 so his family was at the right place at the right time for inclusion in this wappenbook. The wappenschild(COA's) of **Fridingē** painted for **Jorg von Fridingē** (Fridingen) (~1453) and **Johannes von Fridingē** (Fridingen) (~1458) were recorded in the 1483 Richental book for the Council of Constanz[67] . **Fridig** is 1st record mentioned in 1401 for Ruedolf von **Fridig(en) [Fridingen] (~1328/~1378)** in the monastery for St. Michaels in Tuegen(Tengen), Germany OR Vienna, Austria. Another St. Michael church is in Bosingen, Germany (NNE of Singen)[68]. The closest coat of arms and different variation appears in 1394-1430 Arlberger Armorial for the Abbey of St. Christopher (est 1386) in Thal, Tirol, Austria transcribed **Fridingen as fridigē** & **fridingē** in Tyrol/Tirol[69]. The 2nd oldest record is mentioned in Frutigen, Switzerland in 1433 & 1437 under the name **Peter Friding{Frydig}**[70]. The reference is re-recorded in 1952 in the Bernese journal of history and local history organized by the Historical Society of the Canton of Bern, the State Archive of Berne, Switzerland. In a 1941 book "Irkundenbuch der Abtei Sanct Gallen, Volume 6 by Kloster St. Gallen" for the Abbey @ St. Gallen, Switzerland indexed the following: **Fridingen (s.) Fridig** (ldkr Rudolfzell, von Hanns Wilhelm auf Krayen (High Crows), vogt zu Bregenz(Austria) (1444)[71.] This Hanns Wilhelm mentioned is Hans Wilhelm **Fridingen** (~1408). **Werni/Erni/Werner Fridi(n)g** (~1420), **Marti Fridig** (~1450) and **Richi Fridig** (~1472) are from Isenthal, and Seedorf, Switzerland who settle in Uri, Schwyz Canton of Switzerland[72]. **Werner Fridig** is also shown to come from

Underwalden, Tyrol, Austria[73]. **Werner Fridiger** is also shown to come from Basel[74]. **Werni fridyng** von Isental 1443. In the book "Archivum Heraldicum volume 36-37", **Heinrich Frydig** 1564-67 coats of arms is being decribed (no physical specimen): Under empty banner and small heart in somewhat raw cartouche an oval coat of arms with 3 stars over three-mountians[75]. This is similar to the **Heinrich Fritag** 1452 coat of arms which is a large star over a double layer of 3 mountains. In the 1881 book "Deutsches Wörterbuch Volume 1", **Fridig** means quietly made quiet and listed under the word **Freidigen** which means enclosure or a fence surrounding a sege[76]. In the Uri, Suisse State Archives surnames documented and appeared as a derivative of : **Fridig (Friding, Fridung, Friden)** via typed notes, copies of articles (1443-1650)[77]. The same reference mentions Toernlon (Toernlen, Toerlen, Darelen): Hand written notes (1257-1650), extract from the HBLS [78]. Therese Metzger emailed(Oct 2010) to say that in the Historisch Biographischen Lexikon der Schweiz is mentioned only: **Friding/Fridung/Friden** that extinct in 1650. It was a branch of the old Urner family 'von Toernlon' - most probably from a son with the name Friden (Friedrich). There was a Burkhart von tornlon, Anna sin wirtin(landlady), Klaus von torlen - Heini **fridig** wass Kuenratz sun from torla etc[79]. Toerlen is also v. Turlen[80]. One final reference puts the name of **Fridig** points back toward Uri, Switzerland found in the book "Historisches Neujahrsblatt By Verein für Geschichte und Altertümer von Uri" in which itr describes **Türelen or Törler: a branch of it Fridig**[81] (1450? - ca.1550). This is Torler Alpes or Tyroler/Tyrol/Torle, Upper Switzerland/Lower Tyrol, Austria. Backing up this Tirol connection is another reference from "Der Landammann in den schweizerischen Demokratien Uri, Schwyz, Unterwalden" which states that "**Heini Fridig** wass Kuenratz sun from torla"[82.] Kuenratz is same as Conrats/Conrad. The brief description appears to be Tirol dialect which if very different German with many possible intonations in the language for similar german words. This Torle location is not Torla Spain, but another word for Torle, Austria (SSE of Kempten, Germany, NNW of Innsbruck, Austria and NNE of Switzerland) or the better location being TURLEN or TOERLEN which is in Knonau in the district of Affoltern in the canton of Zürich, Switzerland[83.] The earliest **von Toerlen** is **Rudolph** (~1237)[84]. This **Heini Fridig** could be Heinrich **Fridung** (~1360) Burgergraf (Count) for Tyrol, Austria in 1511} and Conrad **Fridung** (~1388), however Heinrich appears to be older than Conrad vs the document reference. There is a Heinrich **Fridingen** (~1348) who was Burgraf over Tyrol in 1380, who was married to Agatha Westerstetten (~1349), however no scenario exist for Heinrich being a son of Konrad. Konrad Fridingen III (~1374) had a two illegitimate children Burkhard (~1423) and Konrad (~1409) and may have had others[85]. There is a another **Heini Fridig**, however his name was Freidinger. In 1380 **Heini Freidinger** (~1360) (from Freudigen b. Oberburg)[86] is recorded in Fraubrunnen monastery as a farmer[87]. In another book it says **Heini Freidinger** is established at Grafenried (1.3miles from Fraubrunnen) around 1380 (P.Zryd, Grafenried p. 10). As a surname "**Freidig**" he now lives, for example, the top Simmen valley - the name of ... the Simmen Valley - The name of the hamlet, an Alemannic settlement with the-ingen suffix, with the people of Freido has is phonetically nearer the joy and so firmly naturalized[88]. **Fridig** was used the last time in the U.S Census records in the 1800 Lexington, Fairfield & Orange Counties of South Carolina[89]. **Martin Fridig's** (1689) ancestral family lived in Adelboden, Switzerland from 1500-1674 above the Engstligen River. Martin's father **Peter Fridig** (1649) moved to Frutigen, Switzerland around 1675. **Frydig** is documented in the Swiss family name book in the Swiss Federal Archives to have their Heimatort "Town of Origin" or *commune d'origine,* of that being from Frutigen, Kandergrund, and Oberwil, Switzerland. Frutigen, Kandergrund and Oberwil are in the Canton "state or district of the Swiss Confederation" of Bern[90]. So, in conclusion **Türelen or Törler s. Fridig** (1450? - ca.1550) is an Invented/Un-natural derivative, however Peter **Friding{Frydig}** in Frutigen 1433 & 37, Heini **Freidinger (Freidig)** in Grafenried/Fraubrunnen 1380 & Ulrich **Fridingen {Friding\Freidig}** in Argau 1341 are natural/un-invented derivatives. The loss of the n in Fridingen may have occurred since Swiss German dialects have gone through the Alemannic n-aposcope in phonology{linguistics in sounds}, which led to the loss of final –n in words such as **Friding/Freidig/Fridig "Fridingen"** (standard German Freidingen/Fridingen). Aposcope {apokoptein} "means *cutting off, away from to cut* is the loss of one or more words from the end of a word, and especially the loss of an unstressed vowel"[91].

The Swabian Connection – Expanded Edition

Arlberger Armorial for the Abbey St. Christopher (est 1386) at Thal, Tirol, Austria. Estimated handscripted between 1411-1417.

Fridingen figd. 44v

The 44v side is filled with very coarse coat of arms drawn by Ulrich von Fridingen and below four times the simple shield for two Hans, a Konrad and Heinrich von Fridingen. The shapeless figure of the helmet is supposed to represent the split of white and black feather book. - At the village center Constance in Baden Fridingen still stand the remains of the castle Fridingen. They were once Fridingen v. ministeriales the Counts of Kyburg, and therefore a cause arms to hers anklingendes (consistently/uniformly). Already in 1198 was Herman v. Fridingen. Bishop of Constance. - The Squire Ulrich, a knight Hans and knight Konrad were Rudolph's the young sons, while another Hans brother Ulrich and Heinrich (+1403), the son of Henry Knight, the elder brother Rudolf was v. Fridigen.

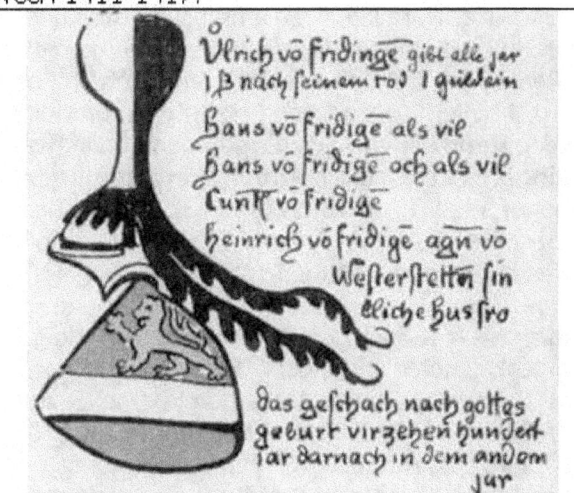

Ulrich vö Fridingē (~1386) Give all the year 13 after his one golden rod.
Hans vö Fridigē so many
Hans vö Fridigē oh so many
Cunrat vö Fridigē (~1384)
Heinrich vö Fridingē (~1330) Agatha Westerstetten of his marital/legitimate housewife. nested on the birth of god fourteen hundred year after that in the next year Anno 1402.

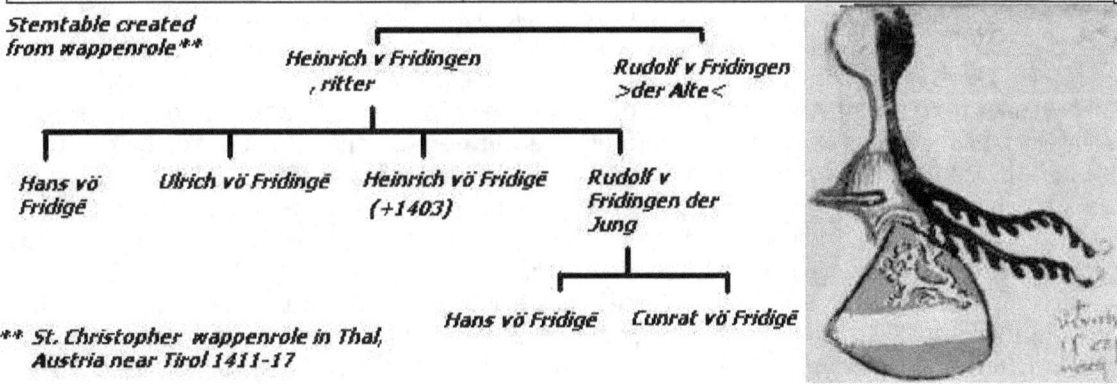

Stemtable created from wappenrole**

Heinrich v Fridingen, ritter — Rudolf v Fridingen >der Alte<

Hans vö Fridigē | Ulrich vö Fridingē | Heinrich vö Fridigē (+1403) | Rudolf v Fridingen der Jung

Hans vö Fridigē | Cunrat vö Fridigē

** St. Christopher wappenrole in Thal, Austria near Tirol 1411-17

Note: There is no Konrad son of Rudolf the young in Doblers book. Also, there is no combination of brother Hans, Ulrich, Heinrich and older brother Rudolph. This appears to be the Krahen or Bussen line of Fridinger (Dobler 1986: pg 451/4), however Ulrich and Rudolph is missing from either line in that time period. The missing Ulrich appears to reiterated in Dobler book with no index reference to Westerstten or Fridingen. Here is the translation: "Henry and Agatha's son Hans has after the death of the father's one-half of the tithes in Beisendorf, but already in 1347 had been to Adelaide by Blumberg pledger. This is mentioned as 1398 (April 22), his cousins **Ulrich** and Hans sell the other half of Krahen with his consent to Hans Murer of Schaffhausen by 116 pounds Pfenning (Dobler 1986: p403)." "The Westerstetten Fridinger incidentally had a double bond: Elizabeth, a sister **Ulrich**, Johann and Konrad to Krahen has to be an unknown time

- 1417 - from the Co-insurers in the settlement of 1398, Friedrich von Westerstetten participating Insurers (Dobler 1986: p 403)." Another document which appears a new Konrad neffew to Agatha: von Nortenberg. (Nortenberg im Baveria district court Rottenburg.) The N., usually Küchenmeister N. called, were a branch of the Küchenmeister of Rottenburg. Küchenmeister Anna N. and Margaret of Friedingen, sisters, born of Westerstetten, 1377th Leopold N, the log Holy Roman Empire Küchenmeister, and Dietrich Fuchs of the city of Constance, that because of the 900 U Heller, **Konrad von Friedingen** for their f dear Aunt Agatha (!) Of Westerstetten, widow of **Heinrich von Friedingen** heritage in the coin out of town, has to have **Conrad von Friedingen** and his cousin **Rudolf von Friedingen** then compared that the latter should include the money 1420 (Knobloch 1919 : 248). **Note:** Küchenmeister translates to Chef's/Kitchenmaster. This crest (1411-1418) wappen(COA) has a Crest of White/Black plumage divided as if the family or rights come from "von Riedern".

Freudigen {frodiga} (1389) Freudigen {froidiga} **von Freidingen** 1389 **freidigen, Freidigen** as noted in the book "Ortsnamenbuch des Kantons Bern, alter Kantonsteil, Volume 1, Part 1".There is a town in Oberburg, Berne, Switzerland named **Freudige(n)** documented from 1402-1435. In 1380 **Heini Freidinger** (~1360) (from **Freudigen** b. Oberburg)[92] is recorded in Fraubrunnen monastery as a farmer[93]. In another book it says **Heini Freidinger** is established at Grafenried (1.3miles from Fraubrunnen) around 1380 (P.Zryd, Grafenried p. 10). As a surname "**Freidig**" he now lives, for example, the top Simmen valley - the name of ... the Simmen Valley - The name of the hamlet, an Alemannic settlement with the-ingen suffix, with the people of Freido has is phonetically nearer the joy and so firmly naturalized[94]. So, does **Frydig** come from **Freudigen**? Possibly, however no other surname records appear with this Swiss spelling Freudige in the 14th or 15th century to later become **Frydig. Frydig** actually starts to appear in the 1500's in Frutigen/Adelboden. In Bern[95]: **Freudigen** {froidiga} **von Freidingen** 1389, from the amicable **freidigen, Freidingen, Froidingen 1529, froudigen, Frudingen, frydigen 1531, frouwdingen 1574**[96] as noted in the book "Location, names, of the Canton of Bern, old part of the canton: documentation and interpretation Volume 1, Part 1". This appears to be a mistake but would be fabulous if true: 1466 **Friedigen**, a beautiful Baueruhof, 3 houses and 1 bunk, KG. Oberburg, A. Burgdorf. Older topographer from this mistake can be the nobles of **Freudigen** over **Friedingen** derived as Wilh(elm). **Freudingen** of 1390, by Marg(aret) **Freudingen**, Baroness to Schenkenberg[97]. In a Kloster Church (St. Andrews in Chur or Kappel in Zurich) in Northern Switzerland is painted some wappenschild for (Hartmann or Hans) v Baldegg, (Heinrich) v Gessler, (Gotfried) v Hunonberg and wife (Margarete) v Fridingen. Fridingen wappen(coa) is painted as v. **Friedingeu**[98]. The eu is pronounced "oi", like English oil, so "Free-ding-oi" is this pronounced. In (1371) March 25th records the Hunenberg family in the Cistercian kloster Abtei Cappel in Zurich canton (Hitz 1850: 20) which is probably the more exact location for these wappen artifacts and the year of death for Margaretha von Friedingen. Does **Friding** comes from **Freudigen**? Yes, kind of, it's one step Germanische or Schweiz from **Fridingen/Frydingen. Freudigen** is extremly rare surname spelling, not a typical Schweiz(Swiss) or German standard surname for **Fridingen.**

Fridiger/Frediger was 1st recorded in October 920 a.d. at the St. Gallen Switzerland monastery of an end of contract for Erchanger **Fridiger** (~873)[99]. Erchangers family is also known as the **Alaholfinger**. Fridiger is again mentioned as a monk in the Zurich records and the St. Gallichse (St. Gallen), Switzerland monasteries from 968, then again in 1028 – this maybe part of the Lake Constanz, Germany circuit of monsteries.The name also occasionally referenced in documents referring back to the Fridingen family from Germany and this is where the serf descendants (non-ritters/non-vogt's) would drop the "en" and start using this name. Bischop Herman II (Hirscheck) in 1179 is being described as a gentleman of the **Fridigen** in Hegau[100]. Conrad **Fridiger** (Fridingen) is mentioned in a 1894 German book "Communications of the Association for history and archeology in Kahla und Roda", of which Conrad owned the monastery in Roda, Germany and has sold it some years before 1334[101]. **Fridiger, Hainrich (~1273)** is shown in an Ulm monastery as Fridiger in Oct 1369. Johanne **Fridiger** (Fridingen) is written as the Burger of Dresden in 1454 located in the German book "Urkundenbuch der Städte Dresden und Pirna" published in 1875[102]. The same names are referenced for the people of Chief Fridigern/King Fridigern {frit'-i-gern} of the Visigoths {Anfuhrer of the West Goths} Duke Fridigern (in Gaul @ the Danube) during the Roman invasion at Adrianople in 378 A.D. Also known as **Fritigern/Fridiger**[103]. In the book "History of Christian names" is says King Fritigern derives his named from **Fridiger** {spear of peace}[104]. He died in 380 A.D. It is un-certain is this Chief **Fridigern** is related to Fridingen, possible, however 450 years will pass when Erchanger comes on the scene @ Hohentwiel. In the book "Urkundenbuch der Städte Dresden und Pirna" list Johanne **Fridiger** (~1424) is also listed as Frediger/Fridinger/Freidiger[105]. Hainrich von Fridigen (Fridingen)(~1273) is shown in an Ulm, Germany monastery as Fridigen in Oct 1369 of which described the Westersteten family estate records of Heinrich von W[106]. Heinrich **Fridinger** (Fridingen) is also found as Fridinger[107] and Castle Count {Burggrafen} in Tirol, Austria in 1385. Ulrich der **Freidiger** (Fridingen) (~1304) is listed as a witness in the Aargau, Switzerland archives for the Abbey Konigsfelden which was sold by Rudolph von Wicken on February 3rd 1340[108]. In an Archaeology book Ottilia (Emershofen) Fridingen and her son Johanne Fridingen (~1458) are both listed as the surname **Fridigen**[109]. In a book describing 15 century soldiers in Freiburg Germany, a Werner **Fridiger** (~1420) comes from Basel, Switzerland which is located on the Southern West Side of the German border[110]. Werner is also listed a Friding[111] and Fridig[112] in some Swiss records.

Fraidig/Fraydig/Fraydiger/Frayding/Frayding/Fraydinng is 1st mentioned in 1285 in Pfeffinger, Germany referred to Mr Wehrner **Fraydig**, Knight married to Agnes[113]. **Hanns (~1505), Stefan (~1545), Martinus (~1469)** in 1499 {Campidona diocese}[114] and **Konrad Frayding** appear in the Kempten, Germany area which is east of Lake Constance. Konrad was a serf with children[115]. This is believed to have occurred in St. Michaels Church in the same town. 2nd mentioned in 1399 is a **Claus Frydinger (Fridingen)** (~1369) von Bickelsperg in Wurtemburg, Germany[116]. 3rd mentioned is **Hans Frydinger** (~1384) in Cermona living in Konstanz, Germany. In the book "Renaissancekultur und antike Mythologie By Bodo Guthmüller, Wilhelm Kühlmann" Bernhard **Fraydiger** (Freidinger) (1499) has a coat of arms as the Red Pegasus in 1544 living in Dresden, Germany[117]. **Hanns Frayding** (~1505) has a coat of arms with two swords crossing over 3 mountains {dreiburg} in Kempten, Germany in 1535[118]. In the book "Die Matrikel der Universität Leipzig: Register By Universität Leipzig, Georg Erler" is shows Bernhard **Fraydinger** surname is the same (s.) as **Freidiger/ Fredinger/ Freidinger/ Freydiger**[119].

Descendants of Leon Leonhardt FRIDINGER/FRAYDINGER/FREYDINGER

First Generation

1. **Leon Leonhardt FRIDINGER/FRAYDINGER/FREYDINGER** was born 1510 in Bretten, Baden, Germany.

   Leon married (1) **Margarete HARTMANN** on ~1540. Margarete was born ~1510.

   They had the following children:

        2   F   i.   **Appollonia FRIDINGER** was born ~1541+ in Bretten, Baden, Germany.

                    Appollonia married **Markus SAYLER** on 5 Sep 1569 in in Bretten.

        3   M   ii.   **Leonhard FRIDINGER** was born ~1540.

                    Leonhard married **Mary ELFRIEDA** on ~1565.

        4   F   iii.   **Anna FRIDINGER** was born ~1540+.

Anna married **Martin FEGER** on 7 Feb 1566 in Bretten.

  5 M iv. **Bernhardt FRIDINGER** was born ~1540+. He died 28 Jan 1601.

        Bernhardt married **Barbara WÜRTZ** on 27 Jan 1567.

  6 F v. **Margaretha FRIDINGER** was born ~1550.

        Margaretha married **Simon HEYLER** on 24 Jan 1570 in Bretten.

+ 7 M vi. **Hans FRIDINGER** was born ~1545+ and died ~1598.

+ 8 M vii. **Eberhard FREIDINGER** was born ~1550+ and died 24 Mar 1624.

Leon also married (2) **Catherine N**.

They had the following children:

  9 M viii. **Lienhard FRIDINGER/FRAYDINGER** was born 25 Mar 1566.

Second Generation

7. **Hans FRIDINGER** (Leon Leonhardt) was born ~1545+. He died ~1598.

Hans married **Sybilla FARMER/BAUER/BAUR** on 15 Oct 1571 in Bretten.

They had the following children:

  10 F i. **Anna FREYDINGER** was christened 13 Jun 1578 in Bretten, Karlsruhe, Baden, Germany.

  11 M ii. **Leonhard FREYDINGER** was christened 13 Jun 1578 in Bretten, Karlsruhe, Baden, Germany.

  12 F iii. **Margaretha FREYDINGER** was christened 8 Oct 1579 in Bretten, Karlsruhe, Baden, Germany.

  13 F iv. **Justina FREYDINGER** was christened 26 Apr 1583 in Bretten, Baden, Germany.

+ 14 M v. **Hans Johann FREIDINGER** was born ~1572 and died 7 Oct 1631.

8. **Eberhard FREIDINGER** (Leon Leonhardt) was born ~1550+. He died 24 Mar 1624.

Eberhard married (1) **Barbara HAU** on 7 Sep 1582 in Bretten. Barbara died ~7/7/1595.

Eberhard also married (2) **Margaret DECKER**, daughter of Michael DECKER, on 7 Jul 1595.

They had the following children:

  15 M i. **Leonhard I FREIDINGER** was christened 8 May 1583.

  16 M ii. **Leonhard FREIDINGER** was christened 4 Oct 1584.

  17 F iii. **Barbara FREIDINGER** was christened 17 Oct 1585.

  18 M iv. **Johann I FREIDINGER** was christened 25 Jun 1587.

  19 M v. **Eberhard FREIDINGER** was christened 9 Mar 1589.

  20 M vi. **Johann II FREIDINGER** was christened 11 Jul 1591.

  21 M vii. **Christian FREIDINGER** was christened 24 Dec 1592.

Eberhard also married (3) **Katharine RIED**, daughter of George RIED and Magdalena WUNDERER, on 13 Sep 1597 in Bretten. Katharine was christened 6 Jan 1578.

They had the following children:

  22 F viii. **Katherina FREIDINGER** was born 1560 and was christened 2 Jul 1598.

The Swabian Connection – Expanded Edition

23	M	ix.	**Leonhard FREIDINGER** was christened 8 Feb 1601.
24	F	x.	**Anna FREIDINGER** was christened 26 May 1602.
25	M	xi.	**George FREIDINGER** was christened 16 Jan 1608.
26	M	xii.	**Balthasar FREIDINGER** was christened 19 Nov 1612.
27	M	xiii.	**David FREIDINGER** was christened 30 Jan 1614. He died 10 Feb 1614.
28	M	xiv.	**Johann Eberhard FREIDINGER** was christened 25 Oct 1618. He died 21 Aug 1622.
29	F	xv.	**Margarete FREIDINGER** was christened 26 Jan 1621.
30	F	xvi.	**Magdelene FREIDINGER** died 27 May 1631.

Third Generation

14. **Hans Johann FREIDINGER** (Hans FRIDINGER, Leon Leonhardt) was born ~1572 and was christened 13 Jun 1572 in Bretten, Baden, Germany. He died 7 Oct 1631.

Hans married (1) **Christina BEYSCHLEG** on 21 Feb 1597/1598 in Bretten, Baden, Germany.

They had the following children:

31	M	i.	**Hans George FREIDINGER** was christened 14 Jan 1598/1599.
32	M	ii.	**Martin FREIDINGER** was christened 25 Jan 1600/1601 in Bretten, Karlsruhe, Baden, Germany.
+ 33	M	iii.	**Hans Leonhard Lenart FREIDINGER** was born 27 Sep 1601 and died 18 May 1688.

Hans also married (2) **Margarete FEGERT** on 22 May 1604. Margarete was born ~1576.

Hans also married (3) **Catherina WAGNER** on 18 Aug 1612 in Bretten, Baden, Germany. Catherina was born ~1576.

Fourth Generation

33. **Hans Leonhard Lenart FREIDINGER** (Hans Johann FREIDINGER, Hans FRIDINGER, Leon Leonhardt) was born 27 Sep 1601 and was christened 27 Sep 1602. He died 18 May 1688.

Hans married **Christina WINTER** on 1638 in Bretton, Karlsruhe, Baden, Germany. Christina was born 1 Jan 1607/1608. She died 28 Feb 1676/1677.

They had the following children:

34	F	i.	**Catherina FREIDINGER** was christened 11 Jan 1636/1637.
35	F	ii.	**Anna Maria FREIDINGER** was christened 22 Dec 1639.
36	F	iii.	**Anna Maria FREIDINGER** was christened 1 Apr 1641.
37	M	iv.	**Hans Linhard FREIDINGER** was christened 16 Sep 1642.
38	M	v.	**Hans George FREIDINGER** was christened 19 Apr 1644.
39	F	vi.	**Margaretha FREIDINGER** was christened 14 Sep 1645.
40	F	vii.	**Elizabetha FREIDINGER** was christened 23 Sep 1652.
+ 41	F	viii.	**Catherina FREIDINGER** was born 17 May 1638 and died 21 Jun 1719.
42	M	ix.	**Hans Adam FREIDINGER** was born 5 Apr 1641. He died 1694 in Bellheim, Or Rheinpfulz, Germany.

Hans married **Margaretha KREBBUHL** on 15 Sep 1674. Margaretha was born 1645.

Fifth Generation

41. **Catherina FREIDINGER** (Hans Leonhard Lenart FREIDINGER, Hans Johann FREIDINGER, Hans FRIDINGER, Leon Leonhardt) was born 17 May 1638 and was christened 17 May 1638. She died 21 Jun 1719.

   Catherina married **Johann Conrad DORWARTH OR THORWART** on 23 Jul 1668.

   They had the following children:

43	F	i.	**Anna Barbara DORWARTH OR THORWART**.
44	M	ii.	**Johann DORWARTH OR THORWART**.
45	M	iii.	**Catharina DORWARTH OR THORWART**.
46	M	iv.	**Hans Ulrich DORWARTH OR THORWART**.
47	F	v.	**Anna Maria DORWARTH OR THORWART**.

Fridigen {latin 1185, 1259}/**Fridingin** 1200/**Frydigen** appears in St. Gallen monastery recorded in Latin for the family name dating over several centeries from 890-1500's. The 1909 Italian geographical society it list **Fridingen** as **Fridigen**. HERMANN VS DI GRA CONSTANT **ECCL** EPC **(Hermann Fridingen)** listed in the Salem Abbey as Episcopi de Fridigen[120]. Bischop Herman II (Hirscheck) in 1179 is being described as a gentleman of the **Fridigen** in Hegau[121]. In a document for Esslingen[122] dated November 4th 1287 or 1401(on back) has **Rudolf von Fridigen ze Tengen**. Either date would have an available Rudolf, although Rudolf IX Fridingen was

married to Clara von Tengen. In the book "Allgemeine Weltgeschichte" Hans Wilhem (~1408) is listed as von **Fridigen**[123]. In the book "Muenchner Wappenrolle Herold" list a Coat of Arms of von **Fridigen** of which is sourced is the "Kemptner Wappen und Zeichen" of 1963 which was published from Kempten, Bavaria, Allgau, Germany. Felecitia von Rottenstein wife of Conrad von **Fridigen** was born in Kempten, hence Conrad maybe the Coat of Arms for von **Fridigen.** In the 1967 book "Frühneuhochdeutsches Glossar", **Fridigen** is defined (german= friedlichen Zustand versetzen) and translated as peaceful state enable/restored[124]. In the 1991 book "Archeologia e storia della produzione del vetro preindustriale" **Otillia von Emershofen**, wife of **Rudolph Fridingen** (~1438) is listed as Otillia von **Fridigen**[125]. In the 1900 book "Ulmisches Urkundenbuch im Auftrage der Stadt Ulm: Bd. Die Reichsstadt" for the family of Westersteten, **Hainrich Fridigen**[126] (men of Austellerinnen{Austria}) was a siegler on the document of Seflingen{Soflingen} monastery in Ulm,Germany as was Cunrat Phalhain recorded October 31, 1369. Notice as the records show more in the Tyrol {Tee-roll} area or Austrian in nature the names are mutated/altered from their original spellings. This was **Heinrich Fridingen** (~1330) married to Agatha Westerstetten (~1349). In the 1801 book "Allgemeine Weltgeschichte, Volume 94" list another **Fridingen**[127] as Hannsen Wilhelm **Fridigen** (~1408) is located at Crayen **(Hohen-krahen)** and also list his relative William Gessler. In the book "Argovia, Volumes 5-6" has a latin monstery record in 1513 which was written Ursule de **Fridigen**[128] (~1439), wife of Johanne Luternow/Luternau and Ursula was the daughter of Wilhelm **Fridigen** (~1408). In 1342 the **Ulrich Fridingen** a canonicum of Constance was listed in latin as **Ulricum de Fridigen** (~1304) for a transitory debt closure[129]. In an Archaeology book **Ottilia (Emershofen) Fridingen** and her son **Johanne Fridingen** (~1458) the Abott of Bebenhausen are both listed as the surname **Fridigen**[130]. **Frydigen** is written in a few Swiss records for the Fridingen men in the 1500's. Rudolph von **Frydigen** (~1462) in Sumiswald, Switzerland[131] and decribing the Landcomthur in Elsass & Burgundy around 1515 and Lord Franz von **Frydigen** (~1504) German Order{Deutschordens} and acting head of the house Hitzkirch[132] around 1534. In the 1978 book "History of Orangeburg County, South Carolina" has **John Frydig** (1690) wife listed as Margaret **Frydigen** formerly Mrs. Bollerin. Rudolff von **Frydingen** dem Alteren (~1382/~1412) Riedlingen document located in Zurich archives dated (1439) February 3rd. This is why I believe the Swiss made their own interpretation, pronunciation and reduction/derivative of the surname Friding in 1433 and {Frydig=Frew-dic} later developed into the late 15th century and common thereafter.

Freidig/Freidige/Freydig {vreidec} appears by 1341/1347[133]. **Freidig**, {vreidec/vreidic} the word[134], not surname is (mhd – Middle High German 1050-1350) and has several meanings (apostate, **volatile, reckless**, wild, **defiant, arrogant, bold**, courageous, **cheerful**, and **cheerfully**)[135] . Freidig is listed as a family name between 1331-1378 in Baden, Germany and Aarau, Switzerland. Ulrich Freidig (~1304) was Mayor of Aarau, Baden, Switzerland in 1341. In the same reference Ulrich and wife Adelheit are listed as Freidingen – The Freidig Familiewappen (COA) is located in the City of Baden, Swiss archives. Many surname variations occur for Ulrich in the same canton of Aarau sources[136]: 2x Ulrich **Freidige** April 8th 1331, 1x Uellin(Uoli) **Fredinger** Jan 28th 1332, 2x Ulrich **Freidigo** & 1x Ulrichs **Freidigen** July 6th 1334, 1x Uolrich der **Freidger** Feb 3rd 1340, 4x Ulrich **Freidig** March 16, 1341, 4x Ulrich **Freidig** April 15th 1341,1x Ulrich **Friding** May 10th 1347, 3x Ulrich **Freidig** December 2nd 1348 (with Johannes Seon who married Anna von Bonstetten)[137]. There are also Freydig's who have home- rights in Lenk in the district of Ober-Simmenthal" which is Heini Freidinger who later went by Freidig in 1380. Reviewing the Etymology it appears the Swiss scribe is moving further away from Fridinge(n) starting around 1340. In 1380 Heini Freidinger (~1360) (from Freudigen b. Oberburg, Bern)[138] is recorded in Fraubrunnen monastery as a farmer[139]. In another book it says Heini Freidinger is established at Grafenried (1.3miles from Fraubrunnen) around 1380 (P.Zryd, Grafenried p. 10). Therefore, we would rather back close to the Old German personal name Freido (see Förstemann 2, p. 513, and Socin, p. 223, "the outcast"). As a surname "Freidig" he now lives, for example, the top Simmen valley - the name of ... the Simmen Valley - The name of the hamlet, an Alemannic settlement with the-ingen suffix, with the people of Freido has is phonetically nearer the joy and so firmly naturalized[140]. In the book "News Archive for Saxon History v16-18" it describes Freidig as a derivative of Freide whose original Bedeutungtransfnga, apostata - a similar transition, as expressed in the words of warrior, was originally established sva exul, extorris - are gradually transformed into that of a brave hero has: it means much , bold, and courageous. Count Frederick I (1257-1323) had a permanent nickname "Der Freidige" meaning the brave. He is also called Freidigen but his surname was to be constantly preserved, later, often in the form of "joyful", but that long without one. His platte grave is located in the Church of St. George in Eisenach, Germany. Bernhard Freydiger/Freidinger (1499) secretary of Dresden, Germany is listed as Freydig in the book "Zeitschrift für Rechtsgeschichte vol6". Bernhard's Coat of Arms is a Red Pegasus with 2 stars over it by 1544. See image later under Coats of arms. So, is Freidig s. Fridingen? Yes ,it really depends on where the person is from, the time period with which the dialect is properly used for Friedingen/Fridingen. Southern Germany(Hegau, Swabien & Constanz area) and Northern Switzerland (Aargau, Thurgau, Upper Bern, Uri etc..) & Western Tirol Austria origins would be origins of Fridingen between ~1300 through about 1500. The Dresden reference would be a stretch(4x the distance from Singen to Freudigen in Bern), but not improbable due to easy travel capacity. Bernhard is believed to be yet another lineage which moved north above Prage and south of Berlin.

So, in conclusion Heini **Freidinger**(later Freidig) in Grafenried/Fraubrunnen 1380 and Ulrich **Fridingen {Friding\Freidig}** in Argau 1341 are natural/un-invented derivatives.

First Generation (also called **Friding, Freidige, Fredinger, Freidigo, Freidigen, der Freidger**) son? of Heinrich Fridingen VII (~1275).

1. **Ulrich FREIDIG** was born ~1304 in Germany. He died ~1356 in After 1356.

     Ulrich married (1) **Adelheid BLUMENBERG(?)**. Adelheid was born ~1305 in Germany OR

The Swabian Connection – Expanded Edition

Austria.

They had the following children:

    2 F   i. **Gertrude FREIDIG** was born ~1325.

Ulrich also married (2) **Ida or Ita**. Ida was born ~1305.

They had the following children:

    3 F   ii. **Anna FREIDIGE** was born ~1320. She died ~1360?.

    4 F   iii. **Margaret FREIDIG** was born ~1322.

Note: Ulrich was probably the son of Heinrich VII von Fridingen (~1275) or one of the Bussen line that migrated to Lenzburg 1338 (Rudolf Fridingen) or other areas Baden in Aargau. Son(?) of Heinrich Fridingen VII (~1275) OR Johannes Fridingen II >der Altere< vogt to Kussaberg. It's very possible this is Ulrich Friding(en) II (~1304) the Domherr of Konstanz before his position if they were allowed to marry. This Johannes (~1302) vogt to Kussaberg (1341) and Ulrich Friding (~1304) in Baden[141] (1347) are found in the same document one page apart (Huber 1878 : 31,32). Then, Ulrich would be another son to Johannes Bertchtolt von Fridingen (~1280). So is Ulrich II von Friding (~1304) Domherr to Konstanz the same person as Ulrich Freidig (~1304)? It appears so, unless this is a cousin taken the similiar name and living the same years. The only other Ulrich I von Fridingen in the family is the Probst in Beuron in 1202.

(*?) Freide/Friden/Freiden was used infrequently but is a surname and also translated to the word Peace. In the Uri, Suisse State Archives surnames documented and appeared as a derivative **of** : Fridig (**Friding, Fridung, Friden**) via typed notes, copies of articles (1443-1650). **Konrad Fridung/Frydung** was a Kuchenmeister {Kitchen Master} in Austria from 1414-1439. It is very possible **Friede/ Friden/ Freiden** is a derivative and family of Fridingen, however no records have been located.

(*) Friedfertigen is also referred to as Fredige/Freidig. **Friedfertigen** is mentioned as the name Duke Frederich dem Fredige/Freidig of Thuringen, Germany. It's English definition is another word for more peaceable/peaceful or peace. The earliest name is referenced to Heinrich dem Friedfertigen born 1411, then a 2nd Ludwig v. des Friedfertigen born in 1478.

Fridinge {Fry-dinge} (1192/1324/1343/1410's/1483) appears latin as early as ~1192 for Hermanannus de **Fridinge (Fridingen)** II (~1153) in a book for the Annals Dei Parae Matris a Benedictine monastery in Helevtia[142]. Hermannus I the pre-decessor(?) wappenshild is present of that like Kyburg (divided with double lion) – Herman II (~1153) does not have arms recorded. Bishop dominus **Ulrich de Fridinge** (~1304) L solidos is re-recorded in latin and the index also records him as Friedingen[143]. His siegel stamp recorded on (1358) April 14th a Propst for St. Stephan in Constanz -
+S.VLRICI.DE.FRIDINGE.CN.ECCE.9STANT. He is also recorded as the distinguished **Ulricum de Fridigen**[144] a canonical Constanz in 1342. (Ulricus de Fridinge 1324, Ulr de Fridinge 1343) was already being used in Constanz NNW of Aargau/Aarau (south of Germany) Ulrich Freidige 4-1331 etc. In 1394-1430 the monastery Abbey of St. Christophe in Arlberger Thal in Tirol, Austria transcribed **Fridingen** as **fridigē** & **fridingē** in Tyrol/Tirol[145]. The following in the same parchment handscript: **Ulrich vö Fridingē** (~1386) , **Hans vö Fridigē** , **Hans vö Fridigē** , **Cunrat vö Fridigē** (~1384), **Heinrich vö Fridigē** (~1330-d1408) Agatha

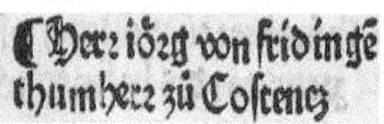

Westerstetten of his marital/legitimate housewife. Dated between 1411-1417 comparing other role descriptions. The wappenschild (COA's) of **Fridingē** painted (1483) for **Jorg von Fridingē** (Fridingen) (~1453) <left< and **Johannes von**

Fridingē (Fridingen) (~1458) >right> were recorded in the 1483 Richental book for the Council of Constanz[146]. So, I believe this was the step before dropping the "e" and "en" when their unrecorded children became serfs or one level below lesser nobles. Notice that as these names were recorded outside of Germany's common ground and into monasterial islands like Konstanz, St. Gallen in the corner of Northern Switzerland and Western Tirol - these "men in cloth" surnames take a latin tone and become shortened slighty with a long **ēē**.

Froutingen/Vroutingen/Vrotingen/Fruting/Frieding is written in the book "Monumentorum boicorum collectio nova, Volume 7 " under the Abbott Wernhero in 1180-83 where Ortwin (~1158) and Berthold Froutingen/Vroutingen (~1155) where they are believed to live on Pfaffenhofen, Baden-Württemberg, Germany. In the the book "Festgabe Alois Knöpfler zur Vollendung des 60. Lebensjahres: gewidmet " these two brother are listed as Frieding. In the book "Das Bistum Augsburg: Die Benediktinerabtei Benediktbeuern" Ortwin and Berthold surname is listed as Fruting.

Fruttiger/Fruttingen/Frutingen/Frutinger/Frithuger – Ulrich is listed in the Abbey St. Urban as **Fruttiger/Frutinger** in September 1294. The book "Allgemeines Eydgenössisches oder Schweitzerisches Lexicon" says the **Frutingen** race comes from St. Urban {Lucerne, Switzerland} in 1398. **Frutingen:** Pertholdus Kisse de - TR.53.

(*) Frutig/Fruting was determined by some modern researchers as being the **Frydig** name. It is believed most **Frutig/Fruting** names come from **Frutigen**, Switzerland. No lineage can be found associated with **Fruting**. A DNA sample could confirm. **Fruting**, Jakob is actually derived from **Frutingarten {Fruting-Garten}.**

Fritingen/Frittingen/Freitingen in the book "Archiv für die Geschichte der Republik Graubünden, Volume 1" Theodor von Mohr writes of the "Castle Steinsburg was bought in 1209 by Bishop Albert of Reinh {Reichenau?} of Cur **Fritingen**." This is none other than Albert **Fridingen** (~1156) of the Reichenau monastery. In the book "Monumenta Boica, Volume 31, Issue 1" Ortwin and Berthold **Freitingen** were a mendicant friar or a lay brother in a monastery or priory in Wasserburg(?) or Diessen Germany in 1170. In the book "Johannes von Müller sämmtliche Werke, Volume 17" **Frittingen** is pronounced **{Ffraith-in-gen}** for **Frutigen**, Switzerland.

Fraudheuger (~1667) believed to come from **Freidig/Freidiger** via the book "Neuhart chronicle vol 4" came out of Lenk, Berne Canton, Switzerland from **Johannes Fraudheuger** husband of Barbara Jacki.

Fridinger {frid'-ing-er} {latin 1200,60,68,1273}[147] was also used synomously with **Fridingen**. The "er" suffix on the end of a name would indicate "one who" as an occupational name or as Origin. One who **Fridings** or **Fridinger** (from **Fridingen**). In the Salem church records Heinrich **Fridingen** (~1170) is recorded on April 13, 1200 as **Heinrico Fridingen** {*H. dictus Fridinger*} described in the book "Wirtembergisches Urkundenbuch: 1138 - 1212, Volume 2". Also, in the Salem church records Conrad **Fridingen** (~1234) is recorded in latin as **Cünrado dicto Fridinger** on February 16, 1268 described in the book "Zeitschrift für die Geschichte des Oberrheins, Volume 37". In March 7th 1268 **Cünrado dicto Fridinger** is shown in the Salem monastery in Hohentengen, Germany (WO : 2761). H. Dicto **Fridinger** (Heinrich Espasingen? ~1236), Cvhradus et Hainricus, dictus Struze, de Wartunberch kloster Salem, Ber. de Sunthusen, H. de Sunthain, etc in Geisingen April 13th (1273) (WO : 796). As the last traces of old **friedingischer** rights can be found later in the Swiss lakeside {Untersee} among the place names still in the **Freidinger** @ Mannenbach-Salenstein (c. 1355) and in a wooded area east of

Steckborn (1378)[148].

Note: Salenstein (Canton of Thurgau, Switzerland) is in the same vicinity of Mannebach. Von Salenstein (Konrad von Salenstein 1291. Heinrich & Eberhard von Salenstein w/Hildebold von Steckborn 1227, Konrad von Wartenberg, Berthold von Krahen 1215). Eberhard & Burkhard von Salenstein, Ritter Heinrich von Steckborn, Albert von Riedern, Berthold von Krahen, and Eberhard Schenk von Salenstein 1230/36/40) has come up a few times referencing von Fridingen/Krahen familie records. Rudolphus advocatus de Fridingen III (~1247) appears in a Feldbach church selling Gerlikon fief with Burch de Salustein and Cunr de Salustein and Cunr Hiuneberc on November 5th (1275). In Aarau, Uellin Fredinger Jan 28th 1332. In the Irkundenbuch Abbey (1379-1411) St. Gallen, Switzerland Rudy {Rudolph} Fridinger is vogte of Romanshorn in December (1403). In Tobel, Mitglieder Convent (1558), Thurgau, Switzerland Hans Fridinger is written. In the book "Die Matrikel der Universität Wien, Volume 2, Part 2" it list Fridunger same as **Fridinger**. Rudolph Fridingen (~1445) and his brother Johannes Fridingen (~1458) {Bebenhausen Abbot} is listed in the Univerity of Tubingen149 attendance records as **Fridinger** from the year 1482/88. The University student indexes during the later 1400's to early 1500's seem to affectively identify the family conversions toward the end of the middle ages and begging of the Renaissance period. In the book "Urkundenbuch der Abtei Sanct Gallen, Volume 3" Fridinger is the same as Fridingen. In 1380 Heini **Freidinger** is recorded in Fraubrunnen monastery as a farmer150. In another book it says Heini Freidinger is established at Grafenried (1.3miles from Fraubrunnen) around 1380 (P.Zryd, Grafenried p. 10). Therefore, we would rather back close to the Old German personal name **Freido** (see Förstemann 2, p. 513, and Socin, p. 223, "the outcast"). . As a surname "**Freidig**" he now lives, for example, the top Simmen valley - the name of ... the Simmen Valley - The name of the hamlet, an Alemannic settlement with the-ingen suffix, with the people of Freido has is phonetically nearer the joy and so firmly naturalized[151]. Burckhart **Fridinger** (~1423) son of Konrad Fridingen (~1374), Vogt to Yestetten (Jestetten, Germany) listed in the Zurich archives Sept 24, 1453.

Fridingen/Freidingen/Freydyngen/Frydingen {Fri-ding-en latin=Vridingen} NHG(DE) established ~850/861 @ Tuttlingen, Baden-Württemberg, Germany on the Danube river and was granted city right around 1370 and founded by the Dukes of Hohenburg. 35.2 km or 21miles south is Fridingen (now Friedingen) ~1180/1190 where this family had beginnings is located between Singen, Steisslingen(Steißlingen) and south of Beuren an der Aach, Germany in the Hegau. The pronunciation sounds like the n is getting lopped off, the "g" has an "h?" along with it, the "d" alternately used as a "t" for a pronunciation like {Fri-dig-hen/Fri-tig-en} in New High German(NHG). Friedingen a more modern word(NHG) for the same name & is pronounced {Free-ding-en} and also sounds like {Free-tig-en} (Forvo : 2012). The parchment documents available on Monasterium.net for these early monastery records (1184-1287) list **Fridingen** (not Friedingen as in the transcribed notes and Dobler's book) as the actual written name. Fridingen is actually mentioned earlier in a monastery record in (786) June 29th describing King Charles(Charlemagne) & Brother-in-Law Gerold carry monastery under mountain fortress below Fridingen (WO:93). "The name "People of **Frido**" Fridingum (Friedingen @ O.A Tuttlingen) is mentioned in an 861 deed of donation from the monastery of St. Gallen, Switzerland. Pro Frido means "for keeping of the peace" , hence a surety alone may be a "fredum". **Friddo** was mentioned as the origin of many names {**Fridinc, Frede, Freid, Friede, Fritto etc..**} including **Fridingun** by 850 (name for Hohentweil castle) in the 1856 book "Altdeutsches Namenbuch,

Volume 1 By Ernst Wilhelm Förstemann". In 1371 is is first described as a town. It was sold to to the Duke Leopold of Austria in 1380. The Original village (**old Fridingen/alt Fridingen**) is mentioned in the St. Martin monstery. **Alt-Fridingen** referred to as the old/ancient ruin locations of **Fridingen** including one on the Danube built by Count von Hohenberg. Aelter/Alter is also referred to Elder or Older ones as an example **{Hans der** Aelter **von Fridingen/**Hans the Elder from/of **Fridingen}**. In a Lindau document dated April 20th 1395, **Ulrich Frydingen** (from Singen) and others are documented in Latin[152]. In the Zurich archives the town of Rudlingen/Riedlingen **Rudolph Frydingen** (Fridingen) (~1412) was listed as a mediator for Henry Randegg on Feb 3rd 1439.. **Ulrich Frydingen** (Constanz Diocese Bishop) has wappenshild Black/Gold recorded wappenbuch in St. Gallen about ~1459 which is the Alt/Older(actually new) form of Fridingen. Rudolph Fridingen XII (~1462) Landkomthur the Bailiwick of Alsace-Burgundy is listed as "Rudolph von **Frydingen**" in the Basel Archives citizens document with Ludwig Rüschach[153] in 2/13/1537. Johannes Fridinger (~1464) was indexed as **Frydinger**, Joh de Walcshuet[154]. Walshut is a town in Germany, also where his father Friedrich F was living. The Ingeram Codex of the former library Cotta has Alt-Fridingen coat of arms "Gold & Black divided" as alt **Frydingen**[155]. February 14, 1488 Eitelhans and Hans Thuring von Friedingen Siegels as "**von Frydingen zu Hohenkrayen**". Eitelhans von **Friedingen** (~1386) to Hohenkrahen, witness - also listed in the Basel archives on Feb 7th. Seat at Burg Friedingen, Kr.Konstanz has this Wappen (Lion **von Frydingen** & Per Pale **aldt Frydinge**) between 1400-1486 recorded in Saint Gallen Armory[156] Codex #305. Hanns Grym vonn **Frydingen** (~1466) recorded with both spellings[157] in (1536) October 19th. Eberhard Doblers 1986 books documents the family names as "Friedingen", however only two major histories show Fridingen spelled as "Friedingen". First is the book Kindler von Knobloch band 1-3 and the second is the notes section for Monasterium.net for Church parchment records. However the monasterium physical document images have the familie names as "Fridingen".

Vridingen {latin 1202,51,59}/**Fridingun** {lat}/ **Fridingerus/Fridingeram/Fridingera/ Fridingero** is occasionally latin for **Fridingen**. In 1243 **Hainricus [Heinrich]** and **Conradus [Conrad] Fridingen** are both listed in latin in the Kreuzlingen monasteries. **Heinrich Vridingen** is shown in Constanz, St. Peter Monastery in 1275. **R. de Vridingen** is shown as monachas of Salem in 1259 found in Baden-Wurtemburg archives. **Ite/Ita von Klingen-Fridingen** (~1239) was listed as **Ite de Vridingen** in a monastery transaction giving her Dowry to the monastery Klingenthal, Switzerland in 1261. In the book "The brotherhood book of the Abbey of Reichenau" located in Germany just above the Swiss border the names **Luit Frid** and **Luit Fridinc** occur[158]. This is possibly Luitfrid Hirsheck (d.1040/~1135) or a later generation? **Fridinc** is concluded as **Fridingin**[159]. In a monastery devotional record book written by Robert Turner in Latin records Clara **{Tengen?}** with the following surnames **Fridingerus/Fridingeram/Fridingera/ Fridingero**[160] wife of **Rudolph Fridingen** (~1368)

HohenFridingen {ho-en-frid-ing-en}[161] or **Burg Friedinger/Friedingen** Castle established about ~1090 sits near **Friedingen**, Singen Konstanz, Baden-Wurttenburg, Germany near Radolfzell over looking Lake Konstanz/Constance. Occasionally referenced as **Oferdingen (On=fridingen)** or **Friedingen (Hohenfriedingen=High Fridingen)**. In the book "Indicatore di storia svizzera, Volume 2" is list the same name **Honfridinga** or **Onfridinga. villa Fridinga {alt-fridinga}**. In the book "Indicatore di storia svizzera, Volume 2" is list the same name **Honfridinga or Onfridinga. villa Fridinga {alt-fridinga} (Frieding/Friding)** originated in 1090 in (**Fridengen**, B.A. Radolfzell, Germany) and is certain the ancestral home of the Hegau/Hegowe aristocracy recorded in Schafhausen, Switzerland. In 968 the Knight Niclas von **Fridingen** was in a tournament in Trier (NNW of Suabia) . Margaret Elrbach/Gessler (~1372) wife of Baron Hans **Fridingen** (~1371) claimed her husband Hans (deceased ~1417) came from the Hegauer Generation dating from the 12th century. The **Fridingen's** began documenting changing their names differently in the 1400's. Occasionaly written **Fredyngen/Freydyngen, Friudingen, Fridiger, Fridinger** or **Fridingun** in the Monasteries.

(Freidinger/Fridiger/Friding/ Frydig/Fridig) after the conflict from serfdom/trials/feuds came to an end. Wilhelm, Martin, Johannes, Rudolp, Margarathea, Ytelhanss , occasionally were documented as **Frydingen** during the 1400's. In a 1922 book for the Abbey @ St. Gallen, Switzerland indexed the following: **Fridingen s. Fridig** (ldkr Rudolfzell, von Hanns Wilhelm auf Krayen {Castle High Crows}, vogt z Bregenz{Austria} (1444) [162.]. The "**s.**" documented between two names means same as. This was Wilhelm **von Fridingen** (~1408). In the book "Die gaugrafschaften des almannischen Badens" the name comes from **Friedingen**, B.-A. Konstanz. **Fridinga.** = der Familie d. **Frido.** In a Latin Parchment dated June 25th, 1406 in Zurich Switzerland for the dispute of 5 monateries, the Abbot Goetfrid Ruit list **Freidingen** as **Fridingerus Frydingeri.** In the book "Römische quellen zur Konstanzer bistumsgeschichte zur zeit der Päpste By Karl Rieder" it describes the village of **Fridingen** as **Friudingen & Frudingen** of **Ulricus (Ulrich) Friding/Fridingen** in Konstanz, Germany in 1356. Other names synonymous with the same family are **v Hirscheck** (1043-1260's), **v Eichstegen** (1093-1096), **v Kiburg, v Tengen** 1080/1185, **v Markdorf** 1134, **v Stetten** 1158, **v Espasingen (Aspesingen)** 1135-1273, **v Winterthur, v Bregenz, v Burglen** 1176, **v Krahen, v Bussen, v Gailingen** 1087, **v Schwandorf** 1225-1288, **v Busslingen/Bueslingen** 1101 & 1185, **v Mahlspuren/Mahlspüren** 1091, **v Pfullendorf** 1058?, **Westendorf** 1289 & 1292 and **v Hohenfels** 1135?.

Hohen-Kraen/Krayen/Krähen {ho-en-kra-en} (Krahen, slang for crow) **HohenKrahen** (est before ~920) located @ Mulhausen, Singen Germany. In 1200 as **Creigin** or **Creien** (craig=steep rock) a hill top volcanic fortress established (~1180-90) mountain built by **Freidinger** Nobles is (17.4km) 27 minutes away from **HohenFriedinger** Castle (mentioned above) to the East North East in Mühlhausen-Ehingen, Konstanz, Germany. This castle is also know as Craien/Kraen/Krahen/Kraehen/Kroyen/Krayen/Kraen. The Hohentwiel castle can be seen from this view. Krayen is not the same as the castle Hohentwiel which Erchanger sat from between 850-920 a.d. **Hans Fridingen (~1371)** and children occupied the castle for many years. In the 1888 book "Vierteljahrsschrift für Wappen, Siegel und Familienkunde, Volume 16" "**von Friding**" is listed on Hohen-Krayen. German: **von Friding auf Hohen Krayen** Jn b. ein w Schrägbalken darüber ein g. Löwe gk H Straußenfederbusch hd: b g. Translated: "**of Friding on High Krayen** Jn b. a w g diagonal bar over it a lion ostrich plume gk H hd: bg". Right below this reference also describes Fridingen. This is where **Fridingen/ger** family came to power. In the History article Castles & Places in Baden-Wurtemburg. Castle Rock High Crows in Hegau by Frank Buchali list the Knights called **Creglin** in the 12th century regarding Hohenkrahen. The following were Krahener familie name variations recorded over 250 years. **Herungus de Chregin od. Chreginge** {lat} (1158)[163], vir ingenuus Diethalmus **de Craige** (1192), **Tiethelmus de Creie**[164] (=Diethelm) (1194), **Liutold Creigin** (~1188-1208)[165] s. **Krahen**[166], Liutold Creigen/Chreigin image left from latin parchment 1208. vir ingenuus Diethalmus de **Craige** (1192), **De Craien Henrico** et fratre eius **Hermanno** (1191),**Heinrico de Kreien** & **Hermanno de Kreien** (1194)[167], **de Crage** (1225)[168], Bertholdus dapifer **de Crage** (1225), D. nobilis homo de **Craeigin** & Burron et in **Vridingin** {lat} (9/1228)[169], Johannes miles de **Cragin** (1238)[170], Hainricus de Vridingin **advocatus de Craegen** (1240)[171], **advocatus de Creige** (1261), **Rvdolfo de Kraigin** {lat} (1267) [172], **Kreigen** (1272), **C. der voget von Cregen** (1280),**Craiger** (1280), **Hainrico advocato de Cragen** {lat} (1288)[173], **Kraygen** {lat=Kreign}[174] (1307), quondam Gtfridus de **Kreyen** (1310), **Krayger** (1334)[175], **Konrad Kray/Kraey/von Krayg**[176]**/Kreyg/Kreyer** (1381-97)[177] **Kragen** (1392)[178], **Kräygen** (1402)[179], Hans Wilhelm von Frydingen zu **Kriyen** (1427), Cnrat und Hans Wilhelm von Frydingen zu **Cragen** (1433), **Kray** (1450)[180] were many names associated in various records for the **Krahen** family a side branch of **Freidingen** and also researched by Maria Shreibler in her 1947 book "Der Friedinger Familie" and Bernhard Dobler's book in 1986 "Berg & Herrshaft HohenKrahen in Hegau".

Hohentwiel (Hontes, slang for Houten – twiel=rock) castle sits upon an extinct volcano fortress established in 914 located in Hegau, Singen, Konstanz, Germany 20 miles from Lake Constanz. Earlier referenced as **Onfridinga** by **914** with **Erchanger** in possession. In the book "Geschichte von Hohentwiel" **Erchanger** and his brother **Berchtold** are in possession of Hohentwiel castle by 893. "The name "**People of Frido**" is mentioned in an 861 deed of donation from the monastery of St. Gallen, Switzerland. **Friddo** was mentioned as the origin of many names {**Fridinc, Frede, Freid, Friede, Fritto** etc..} including **Fridingun** {named for Hohentweil castle in 850 a.d} in the 1856 book "Altdeutsches Namenbuch, Volume 1 By Ernst Wilhelm Förstemann".

Fridlingen is interpreted also the same as **Fridingen**. **Fridlingen** is listed as a town from **Suabia {swa-bea}, Germany** in many Geographical reference books. **Fridlingen** is also in Mosnang, Switzerland 2 hours west of St. Gallen.

Fridingon(904),Fridungin/Freidungen/Frudingen(1358,1442)/Fridunger/Freydung/Fri dung is a maybe another spelling or term ocassionaly in Latin for **Freidingen/Fridingen**. **Fridingon** in Ingelheim (904) June 15th King Louis (IV) returns to the priest Isanrich donated by King Charles, and later for his part in the uprising Bernard Fiscus confiscated estates to the intercession of Archbishop Hatho (Mainz) on the same, and confirmed at the same time one of these goods because Isanrich the monastery of Reichenau received Prekarei Treaty- Ruodhoho, venerable man, at that time, the abbot of the monastery, with the consent of the brethren there serving God, some things belonging to the monastery, located in the village surnamed himself to day life of its charter under precarious received: this is the **Fridingon** (Freidingen, Langenenslingen 78km NNE of Singen) 8 mansions in Zuiualtun (Zwielfalten) 2 in Gouuigon (Gauingen) 4 in Heingon(Hayngen) half (WO : 274). Very few if any old references exist except in later books. I believe this to be a pre-cursor to **Fridung.** In the book "Die Matrikel der Universität Wien, Volume 2, Part 2" it list **Fridunger** same as **Fridinger**. In the latin book "Römische quellen zur Konstanzer bistumsgeschichte zur zeit der Päpste By Karl Rieder" it describes the village of **Fridingen** as **Friudingen & Frudingen** of Ulricus (Ulrich) **Fridingen** in Konstanz, Germany in 1356 & 1358[181]. In 1404 the Abbot of Erhardus/Eberhard Freydang(~1384-1455) has listed many nobles including Jacob **Frudingen (Fridingen)** (~1359)[182.] **Fridung** used by Conrad/Kunratz **Fridung** a kitchen master confirmed his coat of arms as **Fridung** on Nov 17, 1430 in Ulm, Germany. It is also used as **Fridang** in the written Abott records. An 1866 book called "The law glossary: being a selection of the Greek, Latin, Saxon, French, Norman, and Italian sentences, phrases, and maxims" shows **Fryderinga, Frithing, Fridung,** and **Friderung** defined as expeditionis apparatus. " The fitting out of an expedition:" "Going out to war:" or a military expedition at the king's command: the refusal to do which was punished by fine at his pleasure. Vide *Leg. Hen.* 1, c. 10. In the Uri, Suisse State Archives surnames documented and appeared as a derivative of : **Fridig (Friding, Fridung, Friden)** via typed notes, copies of articles (1443-1650)[183]. Heinrich von **Fridung** is a Burgergraf (Count) for Tyrol, Austria in 1511. In 1414 Catherine of Burgundy,Duchess of Austria, her Doctor was named Conrad **Fridungen**[184] – this is believed to be Conrad **Fridingen** (~1384) III who had Illegitamate children.

(*) Fridang/Frydang 1353/ Frydag/ Frydank/Freidank 1233/Fridank/Vridag 1300/ Vrigdach/Vryedach used in various Abbot's and Monasteries. **Freitel{Freyel}** Hans Freytl appears in the 12th century, then becomes **Freidank Freyel** by 1381 in Erbeng[185]. **Fridang** used in Schaffhausen,Switzerland and naturalized in 1392. Konrad confirmed his arms in St. Martini/Martinum Ulm, Germany in 1430. **Fridang von Elrich** is in Erfurt, Germany in 1355. **Heini Fridank von Rheinegg** recorded in St. Gallen between 1421-1425. **Henrich Fridang** mentioned in Frankfurt, Germany in 1376. In 1353 a **Hartmude Frydang** is shown in the Frankfurt, Germany archives. Earlier records exist in Frankfurt during 1336-43. **Jeckel Frydang** appears also in the Frankfurt records later in 1380. **Freidank** appears as early as 1233 in reformation documents. The Widow of Heinrich **Vridag** is mentioned in Recklinghausen, Germany in 1300. Conrad **Fridang** is mentioned many times in Schaffhausen, Switzerland records between 1418 & 1433.

Frickinger/Frickingen/Frikkinger/Friggingen 1158/Frichingen/Friking/Fricken/ Fricke/Vrickingen ~980-1090 [**Frickingersche** - oldest coat of arms in Nordlingen] is used mostly in Eastern Germany/West Austria, however the Fridingen's are believed to be associated with the same group and surnames are interchangeable depending on locale. The nobles of **Frickingen** are undoubtedly descendants of the late Grafen (Count) Regilo in 988, his son Berchtold Frickingen died 1090 a monk from St. Blasien monastery recorded in the book "Freiburger Diözesan-Archiv, Volume 29". Frickingen in the village B.-A. Ueberlingen. Comes Burchardus de Frickinga in 1094, April 21st 1101 Burcardi comitis de **Rammesheim/Rammeshem** is called. Albertus and his son of Burchardus Vrickingin around 1135 (Knobloch 1898: 182). **Früeckhingen/Fruckingen** established around 1630's coming from the previously mentioned reference. The **Fricktal** Coat of Arms matches the **Frickingen** right side up leaf, although **Frickingen** has 1-3 roots on it's leaf. In the book "Die gaugrafschaften des alamannischen Badens" shows **Frickingen**, B.-A. Ueberlingen. Frikingen. = der Familie d. **Fricho aus Frideco. Frickingen {Frickinga}** 1094 Germany established by Berchard von **Ramsheim** recorded in Kloster Allerhl in Schauffhausen. It is located east 30 miles from Friedingen, Singen, Germany and separated between the Uberlingen See. (~1140) Fridechingin (Frickingen) Rŏdbertus de Biscingen, Eberhardus de Binezwangen, and many others (WO:497). Ritter Conrad and Sidfrid Frickingen is called in 1184 renounces what they did to the monastery @ Salem, by way of exchange given for a half hide and 4 Juchert in Falchinsteige the immediately preceding knights be Included in the deed of 1189 (Salem Abbey 1881: 47). Albrecht der Frickinger siegelstamp wappen **1357** from Frickingen[186].

Note: Act of **Ramsen (Rammisheim/Ramsberg)** in Hegau was established 1096 of which *Gerungo comite de Stulingen* (Stühlingen) signed with *Udalrici comitis de Rammesperch* by the deeds and gifts of Friderun with her son Marquard to the monastery Rinaugia in Eggingen. Adalbert and Heinrich v Ramsen 1100 were sons of Heinrich v Hirscheck (~1053) (Dobler 1986: 447). Urlichs son was Rudolf von Pfullendorf/Ramsberg of which the Pfullendorf(Stoffeln) came from another Herman d. A. von Hirscheck (~990-1044). Hegau Count Ludwig Pfullendorf-Ramsberg (to Stoffeln) was in possession of Hohenstofflen in 1067. Burchard v Ramsheim (v. Frickingen) was the brother[187] to Ludwig d. j. Graf in Unterseegau in Hegau 1101, v Stoffeln/v Pfullendorf 1116, both were sons to Ulrich v Ramsberg Hegaugraf 1080.

(Gero son or brother of Hermann A v. Hirscheck? ~990 or Ulrich Bregenz (d.~1045) First Generation
1. **Gero** died ~1118. (=Gerold?)

    (-17 May [1080/1110], bur Kloster Petershausen). Graf von Pfullendorf.

    He had the following children:

\+   2 M   i. **Ludwig PFULLENDORF STOFFELN** died 28 Jan 1135.

Second Generation
2. **Ludwig PFULLENDORF STOFFELN** (Gero) died 28 Jan 1135.

    He had the following children:

\+   3 M   i. **Ulrich v RAMSBERG** died ~1090.

Third Generation
3. **Ulrich v RAMSBERG** (Ludwig PFULLENDORF STOFFELN, Gero) died ~1090.

    Ulrich married **Adelheid**.

The Swabian Connection – Expanded Edition

They had the following children:

+   4 M   i. **Burchardus v RAMSHEIM FRICKINGEN** was born ~1061 and died ~1172.

+   5 M   ii. **Ludwig d. J. UNTERSEE V STOFFELN V PFULLENDORF** was born ~1064 and died ~1117.

Fourth Generation

4. **Burchardus v RAMSHEIM FRICKINGEN** (Ulrich v RAMSBERG, Ludwig PFULLENDORF STOFFELN, Gero) was born ~1064. He died after ~1101.

      B.   GRAFEN von FRICKINGEN und RAMMSEN

5. **Ludwig d. J. UNTERSEE V STOFFELN V PFULLENDORF** (Ulrich v RAMSBERG, Ludwig PFULLENDORF STOFFELN, Gero) was born ~1064. He died ~1117.

    Lodewicus comes de Stofiln

    He had the following children:

       7 M   i. **Ulrich**.

       8 M   ii. **Ludwig**.

+   9 M   iii. **Rudolf PFULLENDORF RAMSBERG I** was born ~1134 and died ~1180.

Fifth Generation

9. **Rudolf PFULLENDORF RAMSBERG I** (Ludwig d. J. UNTERSEE V STOFFELN V PFULLENDORF, Ulrich v RAMSBERG, Ludwig PFULLENDORF STOFFELN, Gero) was born ~1134. He died ~1180.

    Rudolf married **Adelheid**.

    They had the following children:

+   10 M   i. **Rudolf PFULLENDORF II**.

Sixth Generation

10. **Rudolf PFULLENDORF II** (Rudolf PFULLENDORF RAMSBERG I, Ludwig d. J. UNTERSEE V STOFFELN V PFULLENDORF, Ulrich v RAMSBERG, Ludwig PFULLENDORF STOFFELN, Gero).

    Rudolf married **Elisabetha**.

    They had the following children:

     11 F   i. **Ida PFULLENDORF**.

          Ida married **Albrecht HAPSBURG**.

(*?) **Frick(e)/Frickh/Fricho/Friko** is used in Germany, Austria and Switzerland before 900 A.D to present day. The Coat of arms also has 3 stars like the **Frydig** coat of arms. The are 22 locations(places) between German, Austria and Swiss that have a prefix of Frick.

(*) **Fluckinger/en & Flickinger/Flickingen** coat of arms resembles **Fridung** coat with wide open spread wings. The Authors DNA markers also match <u>some</u> of **Johannes Flickingen** descendants markers who migrated to Pennsylvania from Switzerland. DNA evidence suggest there is a Most Recent Common Ancestor before thousands of years ago in Germany with much mutation. FTDNA Flickinger[188] DNA research project has a haplogroup of **R1b1a2,** which is not of the Friding line. There is a Hensli {Johann} **Fluckingen** from Madiswil, Oberaargau, Bern, Switzerland before 1414. Albrecht Flickinger's website http://www.flickinger-albrecht.de/ shows a **Flickinger** is the same as **Fluckinger/en.** Albrecht also found other associated names are **Flügelsperch 1347, Fluglung 1326[189], Flügelau 1317, Flügelau 1310[190], Frügelsberg**

1374, Flüglingen 1266, and **Flüglinge 1200**[191]. Lord Nicolas Duke Kropf-Brinker has found the earliest record going back to **Chunradus Strouma der Fluegelingen** zu Gunzenhausen **946 AD** (Conrad III of Prussia).

Wartenburg connection - Then the nobles of **Wartenberg** called initially after their first seats Lords of **Geisingen** 1112 Conrad de Gisingen other hand, appears already in 1138 Conrad of **Wartenberg** known, the nobles of the 12th century took their name from their respective seats shall have so this Conrad 1112-1138 based of **Geisingen** on the enemy, **Wartenberg**, we moved to be barely walk astray if we declare the same for the builders of this mountain stronghold for if the latter stood before him she would have served his race certainly for dwelling so would this race is named after the **Wartenberg** same is true called themselves the lords of Hemen same initially after her former residences of Narrows first Berthold called by Engen to 1189 also **de Hewen** only towards the end of the 12th century so the castle **Hewen** built **Furstenberg** is a little older because 1175 was the feasts which until then had belonged to the Counts of Zollern conquered by the Duke Berthold of Zähringen.[192] The earliest cross-reference between Lowenberg and Fridingen (originally Hirscheck) is the **Konrad Furst von Konzenburg** (~1192) or **Furst von Hirscheck** (*Hirseg, Hirschegg, Hirseck*)[193] who sat on the Burg **Hirscheck**[194] in 1239, another known as Konrad von Wartenberg (Hainrici de Wartinberc 1239, Wartenberg/Wartenberc 1257, Wartunburch 1273[195], C. de Wartenburc 1278) and his brother Heinrich in the 1200's. The **Konzenberg/Wartenberg{berc} /Hirscheck** connection is re-affirmed and written in latin via the Salem Monastery where all parties are established and siegel signed C. PRINCIPI **HIRZECCHE (Hirscheck)** in 1239[196.] In 1248 a St. Gallen record with **Heinrico de Wartinberc** and 3rd reference note to 1249 in **Geisingen** show Hainricum de **Wartinberc,** Cunrado et Bertoldo fratibus de **Gisingen**, H. de **Gisingen** and **Gerungo de Cinbern** – signer **Lord Heinrich von Wartenberc** seal with **Lion(Lowen)** S.H. DE. WARTENB'C[197]. The same was 1257 (negotiatied to **Fridingen**) a fief von Konrad genannt Habse, which of these **Konr. von Wartenberg** hatte, in exchange for two acres in Grindelbuch (Ebend. 2, 81). The coat of arms/wappen shield for **Luenberger/Lowenberc** also resembles the Fridingen shield with the yellow Lion standalone and occasionally a Blue background. The earliest single lion siegelstamp is for Heinrich de Lowe Berc in 1293. Heinrich von **Fridingen** III (~1180) in Geisingen (1200) was believed to be married to a Wartenberg(?). **H. dicto Fridinger** signed a document in **Geisingen** between Cunradus et Hainricus, dictus Struze, de **Wartunberch** (owners of Salem kloster) in April 1273. Struze (Strauss) maybe a totally different family history. Konrad **Wartenberg** was located at **Geisingen** for a period of time 1257-1273. Rudolph **Fridingen** and way of exchange the same he did in 1257 called negotiated to **Fridingen** blessed is not far from one fief of Konrad Habse, the latter had by Konrad von **Wartenberg (Cunrado de Wartenberc)** (situm on **Fridingen** & eclessie in Salem)[198] in exchange for two acres in Grindelbook. Eberhard Dobler also had a question marked wether **Fridingen** were cousins to **Wartenberg**. These are probably Wartenburg brothers from Hirscheck-Konzenburg whom came from the family Furst von Hirscheck. **Conrad von Fridingen** I (~1214) married Ita von Clingen daughter of Ulrich Clingen of which he or his son Ulrich Clingen is mentioned in a monastery record with Ulrich dicti de **Lowenberc** (?) and Heinrich Sweindorf (**Krahen**? ~1258?) on May 23 1273 recorded in the Frauenkloster in Feldbach[199]. The place Geisingen after which Mr. Conrad called is certainly no other than the Donaueschingen Baden districts associated **Geisingen** according to which one named in the 15 century **Fürstenberg** line the **Geisinger**. The father and the brother of Conrad leads a certificate mentioned in 1095 miles to Cuno et de Gisingen fdii eius Bertholdus et Conradus give the monastery St. Georgen in the Black Forest quid haberunt apud Parmam rupibus in 1249 are the brothers Conrad and Berthold of Geisingen witness on a deed of the Abbot of St Gallen on the waiver of the lords of **Wartenberg** on their claims to the Runsthaler tithe. A line of nobles of **Geisingen** moved to the **Wartenberg**.

Furst & Konzenburg connection – Furst v. Hirscheck-Konzenberg (1239,1268,1300-1342)-Furstenstein(1211) {Bertold}. The earliest cross-reference between Fridingen & Hirscheck (originally **Hirscheck-Nendingen**). Even the rich tradition of Auer was Nendingen

(Nendincist a.d. person name itself derives from again) of Count **Gerold** given to the monastery. Around the year 1000 is of him in fief to the counts of Nellenburg of these occurred in the related to them were **Fursten**{princes} of **Hirscheck-Konzenburg** mountain and by them to their relatives with von Wartenberg vogtei set and lay church tithes[200]. The 2nd earliest cross-reference between Lowenberg and Fridingen (originally Hirscheck) is the **Konrad Furst von Konzenburg** (~1209) or **Furst von Hirscheck** (*Hirseg, Hirschegg, Hirseck*)[201] who sat on the Burg **Hirscheck**[202] in 1260, another known as Konrad von Wartenberg (Hainrici de Wartinberc 1239, Wartenberg/Wartenberc 1257, Wartunburch 1273[203], C. de Wartenburc 1278) and his brother Heinrich in the 1200's. Of the Counts of Nellenburg the place came to the family Hirscheck-Konzenberg and from this to the kindred Lords of Wartenburg[204]. Abgeg: Konzenberg, 1239, the first time mentioned as Cunzenberg castle was probably of Konrad Furst v Hirscheck beginning of the 13th century as the center of Lord of Konzenberg. **Nendingen** would later come to be settled by sex{family tribe} of **Hirscheck to Konzenburg**[205]. His brother Heinrich was in the Deutchenorderhaus in Althausen[206]. Konrad **Furst** Siegelstamp in 1239 shows the **Hirscheck** coat of arms in the Salem Abbey[207]. In Bernard Doblers book he believed the Freherr **Furst von Hirscheck** was established under the son of **Heinrich d.J Hirscheck** (~1063-1120). This appears to be comfirmed in the following records. Konrad Furst von Hirscheck/Konrad von Konzenberg's wife was named Adelhild von Wartenburg in the 1200's[208]. The **Konzenberg/Wartenberg{berc}/Hirscheck** connection is re-affirmed and written in latin via the Salem Monastery where all parties are established and siegel signed C. PRINCIPI **HIRZECCHE (Hirscheck)** in 1239[209]. Recorded earlier in 1239 **Konzenberg** was **Konrad die Fursten/Conradus Fursto**, Ulrico de Steinhausen, Hainrici de Wartinberc - **Sigillum E PRINCIPI HIRZECCHE** and original latin document located in archives of Karlsruhe[210]. In 1260 Conrad **Furst** and his brother transferred to the Steinhaus of his father, Ulrich fief Balzhausen. "All these letters C. dictus Furst and his brothers said the notice below. Know all of you that we Vlrich Stainhuse of the fee in Balzhus, which his father had purchased a while he lived, with all its rights conferred by a liberal for his possession. And in the concession fee, both free, should not arise in the future can be a challenge, to present letters, we gave our seal protection strengthened" (WO:2272). C. dictus **Furst** - Siggillum PRINCIPVM DE HIRS...E {Hirscheck}[211]. This is from the Familie **Furst von Konzenberg**. Another book confirms the connection to **Furstenberg** and **Wartenberg**: Noble of Fridingen occur and indeed the beginning, especially in connection with Hohenberg and Austria and later with Wirtemberg and **Furstenberg**[212]. In May of 1369 Count **Konrad von Furstenberg** and his wife Adelheid of Griessenberg called the bailiwick of the Bromshofen John Kupferschmid muddle which they have the brother **Ulrich and Heinrich von Lowenberg** (latin **Lönberg** 1369)[213] sold a 57 pound one shilling from Wil. Heinrich von Hirscheck was at North Althausen in 1086. From the counts Nellenburg the place came to the family of von **Hirscheck-Konzenberg** of this mountain and from this to the related neighboring lords von **Wartenberg**[214]. The place Geisingen after which Mr. Conrad called is certainly no other than the Donaueschingen Baden districts associated **Geisingen** according to which one named in the 15 century **Fürstenberg** line the **Geisinger**. The father and the brother of Conrad leads a certificate mentioned in 1095 miles to Cuno et de Gisingen fdii eius Bertholdus et Conradus give the monastery St. Georgen in the Black Forest quid haberunt apud Parmam rupibus in 1249 are the brothers Conrad and Berthold of Geisingen witness on a deed of the Abbot of St Gallen on the waiver of the lords of **Wartenberg** on their claims to the Runsthaler tithe. A line of nobles of **Geisingen** moved to the **Wartenberg**.

(1292) Albrecht der Schedel von Steußlingen übergibt dem Kloster Salem das Eigentumsrecht von Gütern(goods) to Grötzingen: Kloster Salem (1292) Cûnrat Hirisegge ze Westerndorf(Westendorf NNE of Kempten), **Hainrich and Cûnrat Hirisegge(Hirscheck)** represent the people (WO:5157).

Cuonrat Friding is listed in the Schaffhausen Switzerland archives on a document dated 1422-28. A few more interesting records are found for Cleggöw/ Klettgau in Schaffhausen archives[215]:
-Item VIII 1/2 ß Hensli Brimelwer gen **Kuontzenberg** und gen Fützhain zuo dem **Friding'** von des puntz wegen, quarta feria Quasi Modo. 1427-28

-Item VII ß Clewin Endingern gen **Kuontzenberg** zuo dem **Friding'**, in herzemanen uff ain fritag in der Osterwuchen. 1427-28

-Item VI ß Weltin Suter gen **Kräygen** und gen **Kuontzenberg** zuo dem **Fridinger** ... Misericordia Domini. 1427-28

-Item III ß Henslin Brimelwer gen **Kräygen** zuo **Cuonrat von Fridingen**, als wir im geantwurt hand von sins wibs fünfhundert guldinen wegen. 1427-28

-Item X ß dem Baldinger gen **Kräygen** (Zell und Costentz = gestrichen) zuo **Cuonrat von Friding'**, mit ainer antwurt, als er uns geschriben hatt, den Räntzen sicher ze sagen, und gen Zell zuo dem burgermaister, als er uff dz schriben herabkam, und gen Costentz mit I brief. 1427-28.

Note: This Konrad Fridingen III (~1384) has two illegitimate Fridinger heirs.

Hirscheck wappenschielde originally displayed seat Hirscheg, Kr. Saulgau, Baden-Wurtemburg, Germany. Also, {**Eichstegen**} @ Landkreis Ravensburg, Baden-Württemberg, Germany. Spelling variations include: Hirzescungen {Lat}, Hirscheck, Hirzegge, Hirseg, Hirsiger in Pfaffnau & Sursee, Switzerland maybe others.

Description: Rietstap blazons the arms of *Hirseg* as: *D'or, à un cerf de gueules, rampant contre une montagne d'azur, mouvant du flanc dextre.*

Or, a stag gules scaling the jagged side bendwise abased of a mountain issuant from dexter flank and base azure.

Translated: The Arms of Rietstap blazons Hirseg as:

Gold, a deer gules, rampant againsta mountain of blue, shifting the dextral side.

Note: The Hirscheck family origins (~1043) are prior to the Fridinger lieneage (1180-). From the Graf family of Winterthur came from the Lords of Hirscheck[216]. The earliest cross-reference between Lowenberg and Fridingen (originally Hirscheck) is the **Konrad Furst von Konzenburg** (~1209) or **Furst von Hirscheck** (*Hirseg, Hirschegg, Hirseck*)[217] who sat on the Burg **Hirscheck**[218] in 1260, another known as Konrad von Wartenberg (Hainrici de Wartinberc 1239, Wartenberg/Wartenberc 1257, Wartunburch 1273[219], C. de Wartenburc 1278) and his brother Heinrich in the 1200's. The **Konzenberg/Wartenberg{berc} /Hirscheck** connection is re-affirmed and written in latin via the Salem Monastery where all parties are established and siegel signed C. PRINCIPI **HIRZECCHE (Hirscheck)** in 1239[220.] The Hirsiger wappen occurs Pfaffnau & Sursee, Switzerland. A description of Single Deer {stag} over 3 dreiburgs {mountains}. Family 900 from the Canton Luzern familiewappens[221]. **Note:** appears repeated from the earlier Hirscheck surname? Eberhard Dobler shows Heinrich III v Fridingen as possbly married to v Wartenburg. Konrad Furst v Konzenburg(Hirscheck) married Adelheid v Wartenburg and their descendants move into Wildenstein(stain) by 1245. Wildenstein and Wildenfels are referenced to be the same families and location. Freiherren von Wartenberg were the Wildenfels vassals of the lords of Wildenstein (WO:1888)..

Konrad Furst I v. Hirscheck v Konzenburg

First Generation

1. **Konrad Furst I v. HIRSCHECK V KONZENBURG** was born ~1192. He died ~1239 in Konzenburg, Germany.

   Konrad married **Adelhildis v. WARTENBURG**, daughter of Conrad WARTENBURG D.A. Adelhildis was born ~1194.

   They had the following children:

+   2 M   i.   **Konrad II v. HIRSCHECK V WILDENSTAIN** was born ~1228 and died ~1277.

       3 M   ii.   **Heinrich v. HIRSCHECK V WILDENSTAIN** was born ~1229. He died ~1263.

Heinrich resided 1262 in Wildenstain.

Heinrich married **GUNDELFINGEN?**.

4 M iii. **Friedrich v. HIRSCHECK V WILDENSTAIN** was born ~1227. He died ~1263.

Friedrich resided 1245 - 1262 in Wildenstain.

Friedrich married **GUNDELFINGEN?**.

5 M iv. **R "Rudolph?" v. WILDENSTEIN** was born ~1230. He died ~1273.

Second Generation

2. **Konrad II v. HIRSCHECK V WILDENSTAIN** (Konrad Furst I v.) was born ~1228. He died ~1277.

Konrad resided 1262 in Wildenstain.

He had the following children:

6 M i. **Konrad III v. HIRSCHECK V KONZENBURG** was born ~1257. He died ~1345.

7 M ii. **Berthold HIRSCHECK** was born ~1258. He died ~1290.

8 F iii. **Margarete HIRSCHECK** .

Margarete was employed Priorin @ Dominikanerinnenklosters St. Maria in Gnadenzell (bei Gomadingen).

9 M iv. **Hermann v. FURST V KONZENBURG**.

10 M v. **Heinrich HIRSCHECK** was born ~1260. He died ~1293/1338.

Heinrich resided 1289 - 1292 in Westendorf. He was employed Kaufmann 1338 in Salmanswiler.

Lauenberg{latin}/Lewenberc(1197)[222], Luenberger/Löwenberg (1257,1346)/Kirche Lowenberg (1239)[223]/Lewenbergk (1241/48){latin}[224]/ Lowenberch (1267)/ Loemberg/Loiwenberc (1253,1277) / de Lowenberc (1253,1281) / Lowenberch/Leuberg (1291), Lönberg (1369) / Löemberg (1485) s. Lowenberg[225]

- Schwarzenbach (~815?) (**Wangen im Allgäu, BW, Germany**) **(A):** Charter established (815) June 26th. Ochsenhausen (1127) July 12th Adelbertus de Suarzzenbach in sancti Georgii in monasterio Hossenhusen with many others (WO:459). Ulm (1128) March 19th sancti Georii(St. George)mansum apud(remained in) **Suerzebach** mentioned with Ernist et frater eius Adelbertus de **Stuzelingin** (WO:461). Kloster Zwiefalten (~1150) matrona Halicha von Justingen or Steußlingen (WO:532). St. Gallen (~1230) July 13th Kloster Weisenau brothers Konrad and Heinrich Wartenburg transfer goods to "Tieringeshart" to Ritter **Ulrich von Schwarzenbach** genannt Hundsrücken in presense of Berthold monk nephew of our Salem and his brothers, Albert & Henry Bussenanc soldiers, Bertoldo de Burgelon and Henry de Guttingen soldiers (WO:1171). Geisingen (1273) April 13th Konrad & Heinrich genannt(called) Struz (dictus Struz) von Wartenberg (Wartunberch) presented & invited nobili viro Hermanno comite de Sulze, Ber. de Sunthusen, C. et C. de Gv̂tmetingin, H. de Sunthain et **H. dicto Fridinger** (fratribus Salem Cello/Ratolfzell), **Wernherus de Swarzenbach** & others (WO:796). Salem (1287) May 31st Siegler: Der Edle von Justingen (nobilis viri dicti de Justingin) testibus: **Wernhero dictates of Swarzenbach**, Rudolf dictates of Richenbach, Cûnrado dictate von Buch, item fratribus Eberhard supprior, Rudolf dictates of Giuttingin, Sifrido Custodes, Eberhard dictates of Stegboron(Steckborn), Anshelmus senior et Anshelmus iunior filius suus dicti de Justingin and others (WO:4549). Heiligenberg May 5th (1295) Graf Hugo von Werdenberg sold to its debt sake the monastery **Weißenau goods in Schwarzenbach** item bona dicta bar man quoque bona **dicta Zimbermann**: presentibus Cûnrado incurato sancte Christine, **Cûnrado nobili viro de Marthorf(Markdorf)**, Cûnrado notario nostro, Rûdolfo de Ramesperc, Cûnrado dicto Bumeler and a few others (MO:5660). The other Schwarzenbach is south of Zuzwil near Jonschwil, Switzerland.

- **Schwarzenbach (~779)** **(Jonschwil im Thurgau, Schweiz)** **(B)**: Konstanz (1213) Hainricus de Raprehtswilare(Rapperswil), Constantienses canonici; laici Ro^vdolfus de Steinah(Steinach), Egilolfus de Roschah(Rorschach), Liutholdus de Glatiburch, V^olricus dapifer de sancto Gallo, **Fridericus de Zu^vchinriet(Zuckenriet)**, Bertholdus miles de Anniwilaere(Andwil) (MO:1006). Kloster St. Johann und dem Johanniterhaus Bubikon das Kloster (1216) July 16th plebanis, Ber. de Burgelun, **W(alter) v. Schwarzenbach** (Gem. Jonschwil, Bez. Untertoggenburg), Friedrich v Z, **Heinrich u. B. v. Zuckenriet** (Gem. Niederhelfenschwil, Bez. Wil) and many others (MO:1036). (1221) **Eglolf u. Konrad v. Schwarzenbach** brudern (Gem. Jonschwil, Bez. Untertoggenburg). St. Gallen (1222) May 1st Heinrich v. Falkenstein, Lütold v. Krähen (nw. Singen BW 1222-1229), **Livtoldus de Swarcinbach/Lütold v. Schwarzenbach** (Gem. Jonschwil, Bez. Untertoggenburg 1222-1241), Rôrshach, Rosinberc and many others (MO:1095). Lütisburg (1228) Bishop Conrad of Constance notarized a comparison between the master of St. John Burkhard of Bubikon and the Count of Toggenburg : Eberhardus et Waltherus fratres carnales de Bichelnse(Bichelsee), **Leo de Hvckenriet**(Zuckenriet - Niederhelfenschwil, Wil), Chuno de Buches(Boschen?), Eppo de Secinchon(Zezikon – Münchwilen, TG), Chu^onradus Fantelinus et frater eius Heinricus de Lomeizß milites (Münchwilen, TG) and others (MO:1160). Kyburg (1241) **Lütold v. Schwarzenbach** (Gem. Jonschwil, Bez. Untertoggenburg 1222-1241). Tännikon (1257) June 15th Eberhard der alte und Eberhart der junge von Bichelnse, Arnold von Burgelon, Walther von Lantsberg, **Walth von Löwenberg**, Rudolf von Wilperg and others (Hitz 1854:22). Feldbach (1269) March 29th Berthold Abbot of St Gallen leaves the convent Feldbach the court in Thushein and the court in Sneith Sita juxta Gerlinkon which Burcard gennant(called) **Leo von Zuckenrieth** and his wife Elizabeth of his fief had and what Veltpach had bought for 96 silver marks testibus: Walthero capellano nostro dicto Lesti, H. viceplebano in Wile clericis, **Heinrico dicto Leone milite(Heinrich der Löwe soldier)**, V^olrico de Mose, Hartmanno de Brahsperch, Petro rectore scolarium in Wile and others (MO:1825). Toggenburg kloster Maggenöwe/ Maggenowe/ Maggenau (Magdenau) (1280) Feb 28th Cv^onrat von Mvnchwile (Münchwil, Kirchberg), **Heinrich der Zehender** (**Swarzenbach** & Hermuttingen (Ermatingen) & Gebsintal), Haertnit(Harnit) von Salwenstein, Eberhart II von Bichelnse(Bichelsee - Münchwilen TG 1252-1284), **Heinrich der Lo^ewe von Zucchenriet von ze Swarzenbach** for Graf Frederic von Toggenburg and others (MO:2044). Konstanz (1280) Mar 24th the counts Diethelm and Friedrich von Toggenburg give the monastery Magdenau own goods to Moos, Schwarzenbach and Gebsatal and Reichenauer fiefs Ermatingen, herre Heinrich Loewe of Zucchenriet of us hate ze

Swarzenbach, Henry from harrow ze Swarzenbach, and herre Cvonrat of Munchwile in Gebsatal, and Harnit of Salwenstein hate ze Ermvotingen, Hinder Wise the servant bruoder of Maggenovwe closter presence of Haertnit of Salwenstein and others (MO:2046). Schwarzenbach (1294) **Ulrich von Leuberg**{Vlricus miles dictus de Lo^enberch} sold the tithes into a creek Kloster Feldbach Oberbussnang, fief of the Monastery of St. Gallen, domini Eberhardi de Bvrgelon(Bürglen), testes Eberhardus I de Stechboron(Steckborn) monachus in Salem, **Waltherus von Loenenberch (Leuberg)** and others (MO:2349). (1295) December 30th Ulrich und her Walther die gebrûder (brothers) von Leuberg/Louwemberch (Löwenberg) waive any rights @ at Eigenmann, Henry Füchsli who entered the convent Diessenhofen stadt ze Swarzimbach (MO:2389). Wyl 1401, Ital Herrmann de Landenberg-Greifensee, chevalier de **Rod de Rosenberg-Zukenried**, de Rod de Breitenlandenberg, **Rod de Fridingen,** sous l arbitrage d Alb Blaarer, évêque de Constance (Muleller 1796:299).

Munchen (Mönch)/Munchenstein connection: The Hirscheck familie is believed to be the same line unto Conrad/Konrad **Furst von Munchen/Munchenstein** from **Lowenberg** in the 1373 & 1460's recorded in Canton Baselland, Basel, Switzerland[226]. From the Graf family of Winterthur came from the Lords of Hirscheck[227]. "Leonberg, earlier Lewinberch = Lowenberg, a named/called Wurttemburg, little town, by the Counts of Calw anno 1248 and founded by their coats of arms, the lions on the mountains. A rare example of the heraldic jerk effect on place names"[228]. Heinrich Lord to **Löwenberg** free knights will of his daughters Sophie Burggräfin and Catherine wife of **Mr. Conrad's Hapen of Munch of Münchenstein** knight vergabt for himself and his son Burkart v **Lowenberg** led 1346 at Kl Lützel names and arms after the **Munch v Münchenstein**[229]. Hans Thuring Mönch (~1390) von Lowenberg{also Muchenstein} married Magdalena von **Fridingen** (~1410) daughter of Ulrich Fridingen IV? Hans Wilhem Fridingen has a brother in law in **Lowenberg** around 1454, this would be Wilhem von Grunenburg. Hanns Thuring Jacob and Mathis, brothers the **Munch von Munchstein** called/named by **Lowenberg**[230] explained Gebruder that burger master's and komen council of Basel them Vermogen from agreeing to the dominion **Munchenstein Mütüts and Wartenberg** halp previously so hievor of ours in pfandswys to sy and according to the deed of purchase stebler under Basel werung have bezalt for fl and acknowledge it seal it over here for Hans Thuring lack halp mins insigels Michel Meyer of Basel and the other two brothers in May 19th 1515.

(*)*Landenberg non-connection*(**?**): The Landenberg family (Beringer, Walter etc) should not be confused with Leonberg (although many interesting associations) which appear in records for Münchwilen TG 1209-1267. Mühlebach (1209) June 24th Ebirhardus et Vualtherus carnales fratres de Bichilnsee, Ebirhardus de Burgilun, Walter II. v. Elgg (Bez. Winterthur ZH 1209-1216), Walter I. v. Bichelsee & Eberhard I v B (Bez. Münchwilen TG), Vuernherus plebanus de Stekkeborn, **Beringerus de Lanninberch/Beringer v. Landenberg (Alt-Landenberg**, Gem. Bauma, Bez. Pfäffikon ZH?), ältester bekannter Landenberger, Berchtold Fantelin (Pantlinus) and many others (MO:984). St. Gallen zu Tänikon (1257) June 12th Rudolf v. Güttingen, Eberhardus de Bichelnse(Bez. Münchwilen TG 1209-1262), **Walter I. v. Landsberg** (Gem. Balterswil, Bez. Münchwilen TG 1209-1267), aus dem Haus Bichelsee, nennt sich seit **1255 von Landsberg**, Walter III. v. Elgg (Bez. Winterthur ZH - 1252-1282), Klosterpropst Albrecht v. Ramstein 1246-1259, Berchtold v. Falkenstein 1244-1272, Magister Rudolf v. Eschingen and many others (MO: 1571). St. Gallen (1261) zu Tänikon January 31st Rudolf v. Eschingen (wohl Donaueschingen BW), Domherr v. Basel, 1247-1261, Berchtold v. Falkenstein, Eberhard I. v. Bichelsee, Wohl **Walter I v. Landsberg** (Gem. Balterswil, Bez. Münchwilen TG 1209-1267) and a few others (MO:1622). Wil zu Tännikon (1265) April **Walterus de Lantsperch** et Waltherus filius (sons) milites(knights) ministeriales in villa de Tennincon resign & surrender rights to monastery, Testibus: Magister Andreas de Willeberc, Eberhardus dapifer de Bichelnse, Cuonradus de Geisberc, Burchardus et Cuonradus fratres de Einwiler, Hugo de Eshenze milites, **Ulricus et Waltherus de Lonberc,** Diethelmus de Mose, H de Tusnanc, **Eberhardus de Loumeis**, Waltherus de Bunishoven, C de Curia.

DNA Research & Analysis
Haplogroup I2B1(=M223) {formerly I1c}

The I1C(I2B1) Haplogroup is now called M223. My personal advanced test was positive for SNP CTS6433 (=**I2a2a1c2a2**) which further defines the Friding/Fridig haplogroup according to ISOGG[231]. The CTS6433 SNP was formed 4,000 ybp years before presentThe concept for a Haplogroup is that between 13,000-14k years ago those families were closely related on the same tree branch of *Homo Sapiens*. DNA projects are trying to determine close proximity to the same family using distance comparison based on number of un-matched STR markers. "A Y-DNA haplogroup is defined[232] as all of the male descendants of a single person who first showed a particular SNP{pronounced Snip} mutation. A SNP mutation identifies a group who share a common ancestor far back in time, since SNPs rarely mutate. Each member of a particular haplogroup has the same SNP mutation". My Terminal SNP per Wayne Roberts(Group Co-Administrator of M223 @ FTDNA.com)= M223 --> CTS616, CTS9183 --> CTS10057, CTS10100 --> Z161 --> L801, Z76, Z183 --> CTS6433. However my research, I'm looking at very distant connections since the beginning of surnames, not how recent our ancestor was related from 1700-1800's as that distant scale indicates. If a family member test more more markers, say 67 or 111 the distance of 8-9 markers says "only possibly related" so the test is still trying to get a recent related match. The Genetic distance of our SC cousin Fridy is a Genetic distance of 7 for 26 markers which says we're NOT related based on FTNDA distant scale. So, we know we're related proved by Genealogical research. We should take this distant chart with somewhat a grain of salt or sliding scale. Even though significant time has passed and mutations exist on the distant scale for these families. I'm simply trying to determine an origin where these families were all related under the same paternal unmbrella in ancient times. *The comparitive families surname origins are my understanding and maybe only one perspective of the surname origins* due to researchers unable to look back further than their own brick walls. When there are surnames like Hughes, Smith, Godfrey, Marshall etc, there will be multiple origins and multiple haplogroups as evidence on these FTDNA surname projects have determined.

Fridig/Friding Surname DNA Project — Y-Chromosome STR Markers

I'm not sure why there is so much mutation (6) or mismatches between the two results Friday & Fridy, however when compared during a database search (Ybase.org, now FamilytreeDNA.org as of 4/19/2011) it is not enough to be so unique that our ancestral relationship does not show unrelated or separate blood-line. I can believe that the mutation of such results is because our ancestry was split off in the 1700's (nine generations ago) and we are the result of nine more generations into the future, thus, giving a total of eighteen generational differences for DNA to change and to manipulate away from the origin. If the Markers all were very exact, then the evidence would show we would have a very recent MRCA (Most Recent Common Ancestor), but in fact Gabriel Fridig (1728) is very far back in our Genealogy. Further explanation can be read at http://www.familytreedna.com/faq2.html#table1. The FTDNA web site for describing genetic distance markers[233] advises that if 6 or more mis-matched out of 37 markers then there would be no relation, however it also says to test additional family member to determine when the mutation took place. Since we know the entire family history we can safely say there has been a lot of mutations over the years.

The George Friday (1787) and Thomas W Fridy (1825) families I can confidently say are 100% related by Y chromosome passed from our South Carolina Fridig ancestors. George's grandfather would have been Gabriel and Thomas's great-grand father would have been Gabriel too.

Relativegenetics shows both Fridy and Friday Haplogroup {I1C} both being the same, now called I1b2a-Cont (Continental)[234]. I2B now being referred to as "**pre-Celto Germanic**"[235] Feb 2012.

This >map> below provided from Ancestry DNA results shows the likely migration pathways of our ancestors settling various spots along the way through Europe. This group shows the DNA distribution back to Northern Germany (circa ~25,000 years ago) southeast of Hamburg, south of Lubeck and north west of Berlin. "The I1C Haplotype is highest in German and Dutch populations (12% and 10% respectively) but with a generally broad distribution from the Volgas across to the British Isles (Relativegenetics.com 2006)."

A Ybase.org search reveals the following names & (Record ID's) on 19 markers: Cobb (W9LDM), Alcorn (B6WNE & 81B74), Watson (SPHM9), Kirk (DZZY7) Skorupowski (ICMU2)"Poland - Anglo Saxon" and Skidmore (X8COR & F8JVB) "Staffordshire , England" all showed up under Friday (me) and Fridy markers search. This scenario is called overlapping Haplotypes. These surnames were found to have a very high match of Markers on a Friday & Fridy haplotype search. Thse would be the same Haplogroup coming from North Europe through England, Ireland or Scotland many thousands of years ago and related to the same group split off some time ago near the last ice ages.

Conflicting surname Y results "Matching": It is my understanding that mutation does occur, so the Secondary names may have mutated in line with our family results or our surname may have once been theirs in origin back 14,000+ years or more. Another option would be they are actually heirs (someone cheated - Fridig male to [unknown female] and the descendant not actually aware of their real Y chromosome genealogy.

SMGF.org search Sorenson Molecular Genealogy Foundation website (done 5-27-2005) via 41504 markers reveals the following matches:
Pedigree Match#1 24/25 Markers – John Gibson Ammons (1813) – grandson of Catherine Friday (sister to Godfrey Friday) who was the daughter of Gabriel Fridig (1728). **Note:** It is believed the ancestor Michael Gabreal Ammons (1790) was actually an adopted son from the Fridig family.
Pedigree Match#2 22/24 markers - William Chapple (1834)
http://www.familysearch.org/Eng/Search/af/pedigree_view.asp?recid=2119435&familyid=0
Pedigree Match#3 22/24 markers - James Sullivan Williamson (1850)

The Swabian Connection – Expanded Edition

Pedigree Match#4 22/24 markers - Dale Sly (1881) d/o Christopher Slie/Sly (1650)
Pedigree Match#5 22/24 markers - Francis Crane Bidwell (1899) d/o Ira Mcleod Bidwell (1803)
Pedigree Match#6 22/24 markers - Hendrick Martin Bohne (1845) d/o Hans Bohne (1642)
DNA testing provided by www.relativegenetics.com

In 2010 additonal information was found on the FTDNA website for Leuenberger/Lybarger, Humphrey and Zimmerman, all of of which are Swiss origin. Both Luenberger and Zimmermann family names appear in Baden-Wurtemburg(Swabian), Germany in much earlier records where the Fridingen line occurs between 1100's- 1300's. Based on these names and the closeness of the DNA match they appear to be the same family before the 1200's, possibly further back to 900's or even earlier. In 2011, the German Lybarger family was found and was determined to come from the Schweiz Leuenberger family.

Lybarger/Leyenberger/Leuenberger s. Leonberg/Löwenberg
The Authors DNA Friding/Frydig Markers are close Leuenberger/Lybarger: 2nd best match found so far world wide 2012. All of these Leonberg 13th century references appear to come from Hirschecker in Thurgau origin of families. Hans Leuenberger (~1631) Orrenroth, Switzerland. Kit# N32240 or E5170. Once I dentified and made notice (via Genea Forum website) that my DNA markers were nearly identical to Leuenberger line the Leuenberger name reference disappeared from (Kit# E5170) the FTDNA Switzerland group. A few emails exchanged before this happened as Stephen Leunberger would not be able to assist as copyright issues and no further research can be identified or made available before 16th century until finalized. The Kit#E5170 disappeared from the FTDNA website after a week of discussion. I took a print screen of the record before the Leuenberger name was removed/ disappeared. All five Lybarger(Leyenberger) families (**Lee Hartshorne L, Robert L, John L, Larry L & George L**) and **Friding/Frydig** share a MRCA for 24+ generations @ 66.71% for 12 markers and a Genetic Distance‡ of 1. These results actually appear correct since the result should be about 40-50+ generations back before the 1100's with mutation rates considered. Randall L Lybarger confirmed CTS6433 SNP in 2014.

-Löwenberg connection(im Thurgau) s. Leuberg, Lönberg, Löwenberg
– "The Noble Leo Zuckenriet[236] built around 1228, the eponymous castle Leonberg (Leuenberg, Löwenberg, Lonberg, Leuberg). Immediately above the village near the hamlet Zuzwil Leuenberg hard on the St Gallishen frontier" (Rohn,Nater 1906 : 99).

Kloster St. Johann und dem Johanniterhaus Bubikon das Kloster (1216) July 16th plebanis, Ber. de Burgelun, **W(alter) v. Schwarzenbach**(Gem. Jonschwil, Bez. Untertoggenburg), Friedrich v Z (1213-1216), Heinrich u. B. v. Zuckenriet (Gem. Niederhelfenschwil, Bez. Wil) and many others (MO:1036). St. Gallen (1225) September 23rd E. et W. de Bichilnse, Diethalmi de Stainegge, B. de Burgilun, Eberhard I. v. Elgg (MO:1110). St. Gallen (~1230) July 13th Kloster Weisenau brother Konrad and Heinrich Wartenburg transfer goods to "Tieringeshart" to Ritter **Ulrich von Schwarzenbach** in presense of Berthold monk nephew of our Salem and his brothers, Albert & Henry Bussenanc soldiers, Bertoldo de Burgelon and Henry de Guttingen soldiers (WO:1171). Wil

The Swabian Connection – Expanded Edition

(1257) June 14th Eberhard I. und Eberhard II. von Bichelsee Zisterzienserinnen kloster Tänikon ask each other guarantor, among others hern **Walthern of Loewenberch (Walter v. Leuberg)**, hern Ruodolfen of Wilperch (Wildberg 1244-1259), hern Burcharten von Ainwille (Andwil 1257-1277), Cv°nraten den Giel (v Glattburg 1257-1280) with *abbet Berchtolts von sant Gallen* (v. Falkenstein 1244-1272) (MO:1574). Kasteln (1261) Count V. Hartmann of Kyburg certified that four brothers of Lieli sold with the consent of the Johanniterhaus Hohenrainstrasse an estate in Ermensee. Among the witnesses. . . **Wal. de Lowenberc** (MO:1674). Wil zu Tännikon (1265) April **Waltherus de Lantsperch (Landsberg)** et Waltherus filius (sons) milites(knights) ministeriales in villa de Tennincon resign & surrender rights to monastery(?) Testibus: Magister Andreas de Willeberc, Eberhardus dapifer de Bichelnse, Cuonradus de Geisberc, Burchardus et Cuonradus fratres de Einwiler, Hugo de Eshenze milites, **Ulricus et Waltherus de Lonberc(Leuberg),** Diethelmus de Mose, H de Tusnanc, **Eberhardus de Loumeis**, Waltherus de Bunishoven, C de Curia (MO:1748). Konstanz (1273) May 23rd Bischof Eberhard von Konstanz (Eberhard II. v. Waldburg 1248-1274) überträgt dem Zisterzienserinnenkloster Feldbach (Steckborn, TG) bisherige Lehen zu Zinseigen. Unter den Zeugen: . . . *V°lricus de Lowenberch* (**Ulrich v. Leuberg** (Zuzwil, Bez. Wil 1265-1302) (MO : 1917). **Conrad von Fridingen** I (~1214) married Ita von Clingen daughter of Ulrich Clingen of which he or his son Ulrich Clingen is mentioned in a monastery record with Ulrich dicti de **Lowenberc**(?) and Heinrich Sweindorf {**Krahen**? ~1258?} on May 23 1273 recorded in the Frauenkloster in Feldbach[237]. Wil/Hinwill (1277) Henry of Bernegg sold to the Hospitallers Bubikon possessions in Ringwil, **Swicher von Lo°wenberc**(Lueberg) die phahfen, Eberhart von Lomesse, Heinrichis des marsalchis and many others (MO:1277). Rorschach (1280) Rudolf and Eglolf of Rorschach certify that their disputes with the cousins of Rosenberg had been settled by arbitration. Conradt von Sultzberg, **Ruodolph von Löwinberg(Leuberg)**, Eberhard II von Burgulon, Heinrich der Strutz von Wertenberg(Wartenburg) and many others (MO:2051). Luzern (1281) Jan 28th *Friderich von Lowenberch* (Friedrich v. Leuberg from Zuzwil, Bez. Wil -1291) with Walter Iberg in Johanniterhaus Hohenrain, Hochdorf, Luzern (MO : 2057). Ramschwag (1291) June 15th, Ulrich von Ramschwag met his death towards dispositions in favor of the monastery of Salem and is making guarantor witnesses: Eberhard I. v. Steckborn, Swigger von **Loewenberch**/Swigger v. **Leuberg** and many others[238] (MO:2275). The earliest single lion siegelstamp is for Heinrich de Lowe Berc[239] in 1293. **+ SIGILLVM .HEINRICI.DE.LOW.BERC 1293.** Schwarzenbach (1294) Ulrich von Leuberg{Vlricus miles dictus de Lo°nberch} sold the tithes into a creek Kloster Feldbach Oberbussnang, fief of the Monastery of St. Gallen, domini Eberhardi de Bvrgelon(BürgLen), testes Eberhardus de Stechboron monachus in Salem, Waltherus von Loenenberch(Leuberg) and others (MO:2349). (1295) December 30th Ulrich und her Walther die gebrûder(brothers) von Leuberg/Louwemberch (Löwenberg) waive any rights @ at Eigenmann, Henry Füchsli who entered the convent Diessenhofen stadt ze Swarzimbach (MO:2389). Frauenfeld (Thurgau)/Schwarzenbach (1296) March 21st, Heinrich and Bertold of Wängi (from Münchwilen, Thurgau) and their mother sell the Johanniterhaus Tobel a vineyard on Immenberg with witnesses in Schwarzenbach[240]: Ulrich (1265-1302) & Walter v. **Leuberg** (Gem. Zuzwil, Bez. Wil), knights Walter & Swigger (1277-1296) v. **Leuberg** and Wilhelm v. Schwarzenstein (MO:2397). **Luenberg** is the family from which the modern **Leuenberger** I believe descend also the same area Peter von Fridingen resided and **Rûdolf von Fridingen VII (~1303)** beginning in 1333. Rudolph **Fridingen** and way of exchange the same he did in 1257 called negotiated to **Fridingen** blessed is not far from one fief of Konrad Habse, the latter had by Konrad von **Wartenberg** (situm on **Fridingen** & eclessie in Salem)[241] in exchange for two acres in Grindelbook. Eberhard Dobler also question marked wether **Fridingen** were cousins to **Wartenberg**. St. Gallen zu Wil (1324) Dec 8th Eberhart V von Bürglun der junge, ritter & frige, **Hainrich von Leonberg**, Franciscus der Bössche, **Johann von Leonberg**, for the Griessenberg family and many others (MO:3223).. Henricus 1312, 35th Heinrich Herre to **Lowenberg**, "Vrie and Knights" with wishes of his daughters Sophie Burggräfin and Catherine, wife of Mr. Conrad's Hapen of **Münch von Münchenstein**, Knight vergabt for himself and his f son Burkart v.

Lowenberg 1346 at Kl Lützel. Name and coat of arms then led the **Munch v. Münchenstein** W.: b. in a g. Lion of the tongue H.:. two horns with g. g. springs[242]. **Von Leuberg (LOeNBERG)** {Gules, a hunting bugle horn or furnished argent – drinking horns reversed}#288 on the Zurich >Wappenrolle> (~1335-40) strip II back page 6 and 5 above Wildenfels. "Noted 1269-1401, seat in Burg Leuberg, Wuppenau, Bz. Münchwilen, Thurgau)" (Clemmneson 2009:79). In October 1356 the Loewenberg castle @ Delemont in the Canton of Bern was ruined by an earthquake. Johannsen **Löwenberg** name shows up in the documents of Kloster/Church Fraubrunnen between the years 1312,1321,1331,1394,1396,1399 located in Switzerland[243]. Hans is a burger/citizen of Burgdorf (SSE of Fraubrunnen) between 1396-1399. Hans junior in Burgdorf by 1312. Ulrich von **Löwenberg** (~1340) and wife Anna are listed in the Comthur Registen records for Canton in Thurgau, Switzerland the same years as Rudolf von **Fridingen** (~1348) is Comthur for Tobel during the period between 1367-1371[244]. In May of 1369 Count **Konrad von Furstenberg** and his wife Adelheid of Griessenberg called the bailiwick of the Bromshofen John Kupferschmid muddle which they have the brother **Ulrich and Heinrich von Lowenberg** (latin **Lönberg** 1369)[245] sold a 57 pound one shilling from Wil. Heinrich von Hirscheck was at North Althausen in 1086. In 1478 which is in the possession of Konrad von **Leonberg** the Annex on Hallwyl since the second half of the 14 century lives in a burgerliche family name **Geisinger** leads the low prestige 1378 Zurich Should connected with the noble family of Geisingen?[246] **Heinrich** Lord to **Löwenberg** free knights will of his daughters Sophie Burggräfin and Catherine wife of **Mr. Conrad's Hapen of Munch of Münchenstein** knight vergabt for himself and his son Burkart v **Lowenberg** led 1346 at Kl Lützel names and arms after the **Munch v Münchenstein**[247]. Hans Thuring Mönch (~1390) von **Lowenberg(1426-28)**{also **Muchenstein**} married Magdalena von Fridingen (~1410) (Kindler von Knobloch 1991: 154) daughter of Ulrich Fridingen IV? The 15th century occurs the **Lords of Loewenberg**[248] members of a line of Baseishen (Basel) sex of **Munch von Munchenstein** which after the baronial race took its name and coat of arms and partly dropped the root name, such as Hans 1440/46, Conrad 1446, Hans Friedrich 1479 and Jacob A in 1521. So, from the data available the Leunberg lines appears to be from Schwarzenbach or Lowe Zuckenriet families with a Burgelon/Burgelun influence due to the Lion wappenshielde(COA) later for Lowenberg. The Wildberg family was also in Jonschwil by 1218. Another thought would be the Tänikon based Bichelsee family. This Stephen Leuenberger 2010 line also has closest DNA marker {from author} haplotype ever found. Hans Wilhem Fridingen has a brother in law in Lowenberg around 1454, this would be Wilhem von Grunenburg. This is further documented in the Rheinfelden stadt archives regarding a dispute from Henry Gessler and the aforementioned parties.[249] I do not see the Grunenberg's as the source of the Friding/Fridig name as Peter Friding (~1403) was already in Frutigen in a much earlier period and points the lineage elsewhere. Gwer Fridig (1535) also would have been noted as a Gessler if he was from this familiy.

Kit #	Paternal Ancestor Name/Project	Country	Haplo group	Dys 393	Dys 390	Dys 19	Dys 391	Dys 385	Dys 426	Dys 388	Dys 439	Dys 389 I	Dys 392	Dys 389 I	Dys 458	Dys 459	Dys 455	Dys 454	Dys 447	Dys 437	Dys 448	Dys 449	Dys 464	Dys 460	Ygata H4
	Luenberger Project																								
146751		Germany	I2a	13	24	16	12	14-14	11	13	13	13	11	32	16	8-10	11	11	25	15	20	30	12-14-15-15			
125027		Unknown C	I2b1	15	23	15	10	15-15	11	13	12	14	12	32											
125030		Unknown C	I2b1	15	23	15	10	15-15	11	13	12	14	12	32											
N49714	Wynigen, Bern, Switzerland	Switzerland	I2b1	15	23	15	10	15-15	11	13	12	14	12	32											
N32240	Hans Leuenberger, b. 163	Switzerland	I2b1	15	23	15	10	15-15	11	13	12	14	12	32	15	8-9	11	12	26	14	20	27	11-11-14-14	11	10	1
125031		Unknown C	I2b1	15	23	15	10	15-15	11	13	12	14	12	32	15	8-9	11	12	26	14	20	27	11-14-14-15			
125028	Nicolaus Leyenberger b.	Switzerland	I-CTS6433	15	23	15	10	15-15	11	13	12	14	12	32	15	8-9	11	12	26	14	20	27	11-14-14-15	11	10	1
89360	Nicholas Leyenberger	Germany	I2b1	15	23	15	10	15-15	11	13	12	14	12	32	15	8-9	11	12	26	14	20	27	11-14-14-15	11	10	1
E5170	S Leuenberger	Switzerland	I2b1	15	23	15	10	15-15	11	13	12	14	12	32	15	8-9	11	12	26	14	20	27	11-14-15-15	11	10	1
125029		Unknown C	I2b1	15	23	15	10	15-15	11	13	14	12	32	15	8-9	11	12	26	14	20	27	11-14-14-15				
e18777	Christoph Leuenberger	Rohrbach g	I2b1	15	23	15	10	15-15	11	13	12	14	12	31	15	8-9	11	12	26	14	20	27	11-11-14-14	10	10	1
B3411	Peter Friding, 1403 - afte	Switzerland	I-CTS6433	15	23	15	10	15-15	11	13	11	14	12	32	15	8-10	11	11	25	14	20	28	11-14-14-15	10	10	1

Ycaii	Dys456	Dys607	Dys576	Dys570	Cdy	Dys442	Dys438	Dys531	Dys578	Dyf395S	Dys590	Dys537	Dys641	Dys472	Dyf406S	Dys511	Dys425	Dys413	Dys557	Dys594	Dys436	Dys490	Dys534	Dys450	Dys444	Dys481	Dys520	Dys446	Dys617	Dys568	Dys487	Dys572	Dys640	Dys492	Dys565	DYS710	DYS485	DYS632	DYS495	DYS540
19-21	15	14	18	18	38-40	13	10	11	8	15-16	8	11	10	8	10	9	12	22-22	15	11	12	12	14	9	13	27	20	11	13	12	12	11	12	12	11					
19-21	15	14	18	19	36-37	13	10	11	8	15-16	8	11	10	8	10	9	12	22-22	15	11	12	12	14	9	13	27	20	11	13	12	12	11	12	12	11					
19-21	15	14	18	19	36-37	13	10	11	8	15-16	8	11	10	8	10	9	12	22-22	15	11	12	12	14	9	13	27	21	11	13	12	12	11	12	12	11					
19-21	15	14	17	22	37-37	13	10																																	
19-21	15	14	17	19	38-39	13	10																																	
19-21	14	14	17	20	34-40	12	10	12	8	15-16	8	12	10	8	10	9	12	22-22	15	11	12	12	13	9	14	27	20	11	14	12	12	11	12	12	11	31	13	8	15	11

Result: Genetic distance 1-5+ (19 of 24) markers defined by FTDNA: 20/25 You are not related and the odds greatly favor that you have not shared a common male ancestor with this person in excess of 2,000 years. All three Leuenberg families **(David L, William Nic L & Warner Ernest L jr)** and **Friding/Frydig** share a MRCA for 24+ generations @ 66.71% for 12 markers. These results actually appear correct since the result should be about 40-50+ generations back before the 1100's with mutation rates considered.

Löwenberg connection(*?)(*im Luzern & Basel*) s. {Leonberg/ Lowenberg/ Loewenberg}: The Earliest reference of this surname is July 29th, 1197 in Linaria Waide, Emperor Heinricus/Henry VI freed at the request of his followers **Rüdiger von Lauenburg** some people to serfs Waldau(Germany) and indistricts of Frederick Frose {Governor} of a portion of the taxes payable by them. The 2nd earliest reference to Lowenberg in the Synode of Breslau under the Bishop of Nanser in 1241/48. It's possible these two are separate non-related families as the Leonberg families in Thurgau appear unique. Jordanus Lownberch (~1237) appears in Burgdorf, Bern archives as early as 1257 beside Heinricus Stetelon. The earliest single lion siegelstamp is for Heinrich de Lowe Berc[250] in 1293 + **SIGILLVM .HEINRICI.DE.LOW.BERC 1293.** Notice the upright Lion like Kyburg/Fridingen wappenschield. The coat of arms/wappen shield for Luenberger/Lowenberc also resembles the Fridingen shield with the yellow Lion standalone and occasionally a Blue background. **Name variations include:** Lowenberg, Lowenberch, Lowenberc 1293. Note: Lion appear to come from an earlier familie, possibly the same as the Fridingen/Krahen line. Lenburg s. Leonberg (1249), a wurttemberger fief also has a lion as the wappen. Leuenberger, Leuenberg in Basel, Switzerland – 1932 with a description: Single lion upright over dreiburg {mountain}. Note: The Lion appears to come from an earlier Lowenberg familie, and prior to Lowenberg possibly the same as the Fridingen/Krahen line. Johannsen Löwenberg name shoes up in the documents of Kloster/Monastery Fraubrunnen between the years 1312,1321,1331,1394,1396,1399 located in Switzerland[251]. The Fraubrunnen monastery was founded by Count Hartmann IV. der Ältere und Hartmann V. der Jüngere von Kyburg[252] on the floor of the settlement Mulinen in 1246. In Sept 1267 there was a Peace agreement for Lowenberg in Murten between Count Rudolf von Habsburg Count in Alsace, and Margaret , the widowed countess of the older Kyburg[253]. This does not appear to be a merge of the family connection. Eberhard Dobler's research believed that Furst v Hirscheck Freherr Furst von Hirscheck was established under the son of Heinrich d.J Hirscheck (~1063-1120). In Wartenburg (March 1369) the brothers **Ulrich and Heinrich of Loenberg (also Lowenberg)** graciously gave Cunrat{Conrad} of Furstenburg and his wife Adelheid of Griessenberg[254] loans or gifts – document not fully understood. This family connection is made complete by a St. Gallen document which shows 2 consecutive entries mentioning both names in July 1268 (1st, The dean in Pfohren testifies bishop Eberhard von Konstanz on demands that the brothers prince of Hirschegg did without this rule opposite of Konrad von Wartenberg with exception of the Mannlehen, which one, and the noble people belonging to the rule, which another of the brothers reserves itself. 2nd, The four brothers Konrad prince of Konzenberg leave their castle Hirscheck a corner including everything belong to, with exception of the Mannlehen, which one of the younger brothers reserves itself, to their Oheim the brothers Konrad and Heinrich von Wartenberg.)[255] Hans Thuring Mönch (~1390) von Lowenberg(1426-28)(also Muchenstein) married Magdalena von Fridingen (~1410) daughter of Ulrich Fridingen IV? .

- Zimmer s. {Zimmern 1254/ Zimbern {Cinbern/Cimbern 1099-1254/ Ancencimbra 994/Zimer/Zymber/Zimmermann?/Cimbermann?}

There is a German word reference and University book for Zymer/Zymerman s. Zimmerman, Zimbermanus s. Zimmerman, Zimmer s. Zimmern, Zimmern s. Simmern[256]. John Carpenter head of the DNA website for Zimmermann understands that Zimmern is totally different than Zimmermann. His logic, Zimmern(=rooms) and Zimberman(=carpenter). I disagree, I believe it's in the Etymology, not the definition and they are from the same familie. My explaination using his logic. Mann(=husband), ie Husband of Zimmern.The University student indexes during the later 1400's to early 1500's seem to affectively identify the family conversions toward the end of the middle ages and begining of the Renaissance period. Wappen(coat of arms) from the Free Lords of Zimern seat @ HerrenZimmern Bosingen, Rottweil Germany formerly a fief of St. Gallen[257]. Notice the common theme of the Lion. Kloster St. Gallen (779) Flozoluestale(Flözlingen, Zimmern over Rottweil). Ancencimbra (HerrenZimmern in Bosingen) appears with Gebhard von Konstanz (~949) (brother to Liutfrifd von Winterthur) in Ingelheim (994) November 4 (WO:310). The Line of Hirscheck has beginnings from the Winterthur families. This Gebhard was also the founder of Petershausen in 983. Wernhervs & Manegoldus brothers de **Cimberin(Zimmern)** appears in a Rottweil document in 1099. Sigbodo de Cimberen (1163) in Wurzburg. Gerlaco plebano in Cimberen, Rudolfus sacerdos de Cymberen (1182) in Worms. Konrad Zimmern is the abott of Reichenau 1234-1255 and appears in many records with Fridingen family[258]. In 1248 a St. Gallen record with **Heinrico de Wartinberc** and 3rd reference note to 1249 in **Geisingen** show Hainricum de **Wartinberc,** Cunrado et Bertoldo fratibus de **Gisingen**, H. de **Gisingen** and **Gerungo de Cinbern** – signer **Lord Heinrich von Wartenberc** seal with Lion S.H. DE. WARTENB'C[259]. Konrad Zimmern appears with Heinrich v Fridingen (~1213) in the year 1254. About 1276 Rudolph Hewen, F(rederico) de nobili Wildenstain, Wer(nhero) **Cimber**holci, C. libero de Nuwenhausen etc (Kohlhammer 1885: 13). Oberndorf Nov 27th (1289) Eberhart von Lupfen, **Cûnrat von Zimmern** and **Wernher** sines brûders son hath given Abreht Schorpen von Oberndorf, Abreht Rihger, **Stainmar der zimmerman** and Ûlrich Schorp (MO:4843). The history[260] of the Lords of Wildenstein castle show half being owned by von Justingen and Zimmern. Was this Berthold v. J. zu Zimmern in 1308? Is this the start building of the Zimmern half in 1297? "Count Hermann von Schultz sold to Berthold and Heinrich von Justingen by 25 marks in silver following goods to Gösslingen: the hub because Luitpold and the Meier building of Zimmern." Werner v Zimmern seigelstamp in 1356 shown above. Another example is the Zimmern wappen/coat of arms with blue background & yellow lion standing/walking on a large battle axe[261]. Very similar wappen with the upright Lion instead walking axe on the same angle as the White Bend that of Fridingen. The History of Zimmern can be detected around 1080 in the orginal area of the Black Forest. Johannes Zimmern is recorded in the Swabian Knights in the league against Appenzeller document in 1407 with Heinrich von Randeck, Rudolph von Fridingen, Stephan von Gundelfingen & others.

- Zimmerman s. {Zimbermann/Cimberman/Carpentarius}: Hans Zimmermann (~1702) from Switzerland, Kit#53199 and Michael Zimmermann 1617 from Switzerland, Kit# 124510. *Multiple surname origins are believed to exist*. John Carpenter head of the DNA website for Zimmermann understands that Zimmern is totally different than Zimmermann. His logic, Zimmern(=rooms) and Zimberman(=carpenter). I disagree, I believe it's in the Etymology, not the definition and they are from the same familie. My explaination using his logic. Mann(=husband), ie Husband of Zimmern.The University student indexes during the later 1400's to early 1500's seem to affectively identify the family conversions toward the end of the middle

ages and begining of the Renaissance period. Some early references: Salzburg, Austria (1004) @ St. Peter, Rinhardus filius Friderici **carpentarii**. Kloster Zwettl, Austria (1156-71) Erchenbert von Gars, Otto von Stein und sein Sohn Konrad, Otto Grave, Ulrich Peier, **Hermann carpentarius**, Heinrich von Horn, and many others (MO:1451). Kreuzlingen (1243) March 8th Heinrich von Vridingen and son Heinrich & Conrad advocatias in Ruhinhusen et Beringen in bonis ecelesiae Crucelino: Arnoldus de Langinstain, et Chuno de Velpach, **magistro Eberhardo carpentario** and others. The earliest record for Zimmermann is (1249) March 1st Aarberg in Bern archives are testes: Ulrich Froburc, **Burchardus dictus Zimbermann** cives de Arberc and many others (Res Bernenses 1877 : 296). Again March 6th (1259) with Ulricus de Ulvingen. Other records: (1265) in Passau, Germany outside Munich on the Austrian border in the Monastery Niedernburg[262] as witnesses: **Chunrad der Zimmermann**, Perchtold der Zimmermann. Rohrdorf(?) 1265 Truchsess Berthold von Rohrdorf, Vîrico plebano de Meschilch testes: Wolfradus prepositus et Chûnradus concanonicus de Burron, decanus de Diethershoven, Dietho viceplebanus in Meschilch, clerici, Vîricus scultetus de Mulhain, Burchardus dictus Gerzeli, Berhtoldus Wipf, Chûnradus Lancenhoven, Chûnradus Torie, Hainricus Rispuhil, Chûnradus faber, Hainricus frater suus, **Ch{o}nradus carpentarius** and others (WO:2528). Altheim (1273) June 18th Dekan Albero von Binzwangen dispute Äbtissin Konvent von Heiligkreuztal and Schwester(sister) Judenta daughter of in memory of **Cûnradi carpentarii dicti Richart** and others (WO:3158). Salem (1287) Ritter Wernher genannt von Riedhausen (Riethusen) testibus: Burchardo ministro de **Marchdorf**, Friderico ministro de Kunigesegge, Bertoldo de Adanshoven, Hainrico de Meniwanch, Hermanno dicto Wizzige, Burchardo fratre eiusdem, magistro **Hainrico carpentario de Gugenhusen** and others (WO:4514). Oberndorf Nov 27th (1289) Eberhart von Lupfen, **Cûnrat von Zimmern** and **Wernher** sines brûders son hath given Abreht Schorpen von Oberndorf, Abreht Rihger, **Stainmar der zimmerman** and Ûlrich Schorp (MO:4843). Another record (1291) July 15th shows **Cunradi dicti Zimmerman** recorded with the Graf Albert von Hohenberg family in kloster Kirchberg in Schömberg or Rangendingen or Trillfingen (Trúhelfingen) Germany 107km North of Fridingen in Singen (WO:5115). The same record he Conrad may also be in Schömberg, Germany even closer to Fridingen and all 3 in hidden in the 1572 Swabian map. Heiligenberg May 5th (1295) Graf Hugo von Werdenberg sold to its debt sake the monastery Weißenau goods in Schwarzenbach item bona dicta bar man quoque bona **dicta Zimbermann**: presentibus Cûnrado incurato sancte Christine, **Cûnrado nobili viro de Marthorf(Markdorf)**, Cûnrado notario nostro, Rûdolfo de Ramesperc, Cûnrado dicto Bumeler and a few others (MO:5660).Kloster Kirchberg (1305) October 28th Cunrad **Zimmernman**[263] in a document for Graf Albrecht von Hohenberg and his brother Rudolf, Huban ze truhelvingen, hainrich Lubolt, burkart der kirchherre von zimmern, Dietcrich der tieringer der **kirchherre von fridingen** (Scheitlin:1862). In 1299 Werner von Zimmern{Zimberman 1292 & 1300} is the Johanniter in church records for Rottweil, Germany[264]. Eberhart der Zimmerman (~1284) in a Meskirch & Wildenstein[265] document dated Febr 1309. He is also listed with Anselm Wildenstain & his son from kloster Buren, Hainrich der Wilde and many more.. Meskirch is 31 miles NWW of Hohenkrahen. Wildenstain/stein familie at least from the 1260's comes from Hirscheck. Berhtolt der Zimmernmann is at Fortsetzung or Niederbaldingen in the same book in a doc dated May 1323 & Febr 1329. Other names Eberhard Spiznagel, Berhtolt der Garwe and Bertholt Spiznagel. Martin Zimmermann is in Zurich 1309-1320 at or about the same time as Anna Fridingen (~1301) who married Gotfried Mulner in 1336. They are together in a Charter document for Kloster Wurmsbach in (1309) May 5th. In 1330 Albrect Zimmern is recorded on an imperial tax record in the Church of St. Gallen[266.]

- Zurich archives: Glattbrugg (1347) March 10th Konrad Ammann von Wallisellen, Walter von Hunenberg, **Ulrich Zimmermann** witnesses Eberhard Stuki, Jakob Stuki und Stökli, der servants von Hünenberg (ZO:25116). Kyburg (1362) April 30th Margareth von Hunenberg wife of knight Walther Hünenberg, brothers **Ulrich und Burkart Zimmerman**, Eberhard Stuki, Rudi Sterch von Wallisellen and others (ZO:25114). Margaret von Fridingen (~1328) married Gotfried von Hunenberg (~1328) a relative of Walter von H. Zuirch (1349) March 15th **Chuonrat Zimberman von Kloten** a loan with many others (LO:273886). Wien {Vienna} (1370) **Heinrich Zimbermann** and many others (ZO:346317). Perugia (1932) November 26th Alberti Carpentarii, Euerardi Bruner, Henningi Huntpis and many others (MO:6919).

45

- **Lucerne archives:** Dulliken (1317) August 7th Ulrich von Zofingen and wife Hemma sale agreement with their children Conrad, Henry, Walter, Ulrich and Hemma apply the monastery of St. Urban, witnesses: Mr. Konrad, Vizepleban in Dulliken; Konrad von Buchegg; Johannes de Annwile, **Ulrich Zimmermann**, Heinrich Roto of Dulliken; Wernher von Buchen and Sigfrid, brothers, von Däniken (LO:1118664). Hitskirch (1350) Rudolf und Lütold von Aarburg, brothers sale, one in Twing Leimbach Located Schuppose that is cultivated by Bürgi Pflegel and Uli Zimermann for 6 1/2 Mütt cores, 2 bushels of oats, 10 urn on a pig, 60 eggs and 6 chickens at Henmann von Rubiswil, squire to 90 lb new Zofinger pennies. Witnesses: Johan Hesse, Heini von Buchholz, Johan von Engelwart (LO:1121460). Many more Zimmermanns are recorded from 1394-1448 and further. The Schaffhausen archives have **Zimbermann** listed the same as **Zimmerman** record in 1392[267]. Hans Zimbermann (Zimmermann) is record in the same archives in 1425. Walter Zimbermann {Zimmermann} in 1447. **Peter and Haman Freidinger** zimmermanns (=Carpenters) to Waldkirch[268] assumes the obligation November 12th (1449). The Zimmern'sche wappen/coat of arms in 1487 is described as the following: (two yellow lions in blue boxes with axes between the front sweetness, and a still on the helmets of red deer antler head with yellow and red breast)[269]. The wappen for Lord Wilhalm von NewHawser comtur(commander) to Kapfenburg 1535 is quartered with 2 Tuetonic crosses and 2 Lions on the Axe[270]. It is on the same page as Rudolf von Fridingen who also was had a Teutonic quartered wappen. The Zimmern Chronicle (1400-1500's) documents at least 13 bastard Zimmern children, of whom did take on other various surnames (Hurwhich : 270).

DNA Research from Darvin L Martin: "Just by looking at DNA comparisons between the Martin/Yoder/Zimmerman families and those closely related genetically[271], I have determined that my Martin/Yoder/Zimmerman families lived near Winterthur (in modern Canton Zurich) before they migrated west with the Kyburg expansion into Bern in the early 1200s. Prior to that, likely soon after 746, they came from Swabia (Martin:2010-12).

In summary, while we don't find a familie name origin around the 900's-1000's period where families are merging and being created under one name. We do know their origins are in the heart of Swabia in the very same records of the families of Winterthur, Bregenz, Hirscheck and Kyburg's appear. Konrad Zimmern was an employer to Heinrich von Fridingen during the 1230's. The Zimmern family were deeply rooted into Meskirch where the Gundelfingen and Wildenstein families also lived and whose origins are supposed to be from the Hirscheck familie.

Kit #	Paternal Ancestor Name	Country	Haplo group	Dys 393	Dys 390	Dys 19	Dys 391	Dys 385	Dys 426	Dys 388	Dys 439	Dys 389 I	Dys 392	Dys 389 ii	Dys 458	Dys 459	Dys 455	Dys 454	Dys 447	Dys 437	Dys 448	Dys 449	Dys 464	Dys 460	Ygata H4	Ycaii
	Schweiz Project	I2b1 (or new I2a2a) M223+, M284-, M379-, P78-, P95-																							
71356	Alfred Humphrey bo|	Switzerlan	I2b1	14	22	16	10	15-15	11	13	11	13	12	29	16	8-10	11	11	26	15	19	28	11-14-14-14	11 10	19-19
124510	Michael Zimmerman	Switzerlan	I2b1	14	23	15	10	15-15	11	13	11	13	12	30	15	8-9	11	11	24	14	20	28	11-14-14-15	11 9	18-21
6060	Hans Zimmerman, b	Switzerlan	I2b1	14	23	15	10	15-16	11	13	11	13	12	30	15	8-9	11	11	24	14	20	27	11-14-14-15	11 9	19-21
139725	Hans Zimmerman b.	Switzerlan	I2b1	15	23	15	10	15-15	11	13	11	14	12	32											
E5170	S Leuenberger	Unknown C	I2b1	15	23	15	10	15-15	11	13	12	14	12	32	15	8-9	11	12	26	14	20	27	11-14-15-15	11 10	19-21
B3411	Peter Friding, 1403	Switzerlan	I2b1	15	23	15	10	15-15	11	13	11	14	12	32	15	8-10	11	11	25	14	20	28	11-14-14-15	10 10	19-21

Dys456	Dys607	Dys576	Cdy	Dys 570	Dys 442	Dys 438	Dys 531	Dys 578	Dyf 395 S	Dys 590	Dys 537	Dys 641	Dys 472	Dyf 406 S	Dys 511	Dys 425	Dys 413	Dys 557	Dys 594	Dys 436	Dys 490	Dys 534	Dys 450	Dys 444	Dys 481	Dys 520	Dys 446	Dys 568	Dys 487	Dys 572	Dys 640	Dys 492	Dys 565	DYS710	DYS485	DYS632	DYS495	DYS540
14	14	18	20	33-39	12	10	11	8	15-16	8	11	10	8	10	9	12	21-22	15	11	12	12	13	9	12	27	20	11	13	12	12	11	12	12	11				
14	14	17	19	33-39	12	10	11	8	15-16	8	11	10	8	10	9	12	21-22	15	11	12	12	13	9	12	27	20	11	13	12	12	11	12	12	11	29	13 8	15	11
15	14	17	22	37-37	13	10																																
14	14	17	20	34-40	12	10	12	8	15-16	8	12	10	8	10	9	12	22-22	15	11	12	12	13	9	14	27	20	11	14	12	12	11	12	12	11	31	13 8	15	11

Result: Genetic distance 10+ (17 of 27) markers defined by FTDNA: >6 You are totally unrelated to this person. **Frederick Rusell Zimmerman** for ancestor Hans Z (1546) and **Jeff Friday** share a MRCA for 24+ generations @ 91.41% for 12 markers and a Genetic Distance≠0 from Friding/Frydig.

- Lybarger/Lyberger/Lybyer s. {Leyenberger/Leuenberger}:
Nicklaus Leyenberger the son of Benedikt Leuenberger from Bern, Switzerland who migrated to Pfalz, Germany[272]. Nicklaus migrated to Pennsylvania then to Frederick, Maryland[273]. The Directory of family associations show Lionberger the same name as the Leyenberger/Leuenberger family[274]. Lybarger researchers from Kaiserslautern, Germany found that Leyenberger would be a Swiss spelling as Leuenberger of which a Nikolaus Leyenberger family groups found in Brenschelbach and Volklingen, Germany[275]. "Also the Lybarger family was originated from Nicholas Leuenberger who moved to Germany from Berne Switzerland and became Lybarger[276]".

- Ritter s. {Rieder/Riederer/Riedrer/Reidern/Roder/Reeder}:
Michael Ritter ~1725 in Germany under Kit# N72434. Ritter shows in the same Haplogroup. Jacob Reeder (~1760)/Hans Adam Roder (~1645) shown in same haplogroup. Dachsberg, Riederer Ritter v., s. Riderer[277]. Descendent Jacob Reeder (~1760) Genealogy DNA test[278] of Hans Adam Roder (~1645) born in Berne, Switzerland. Variant spellings are described:
Reeder, Rader, Roeder, Roder, Retter, Reider, Reader, Ritter. Rudern s. Reidern/Riedirn/ Riederen[279] 1138-1185 burg in Frutwilen Canton of Thurgau, Switzerland. Ritter FTDNA group only showing 2 close matches out of 56 individuals.

N72434	Ritter	Michael Ritter (approximateoy 1725)	Germany	I2b1	14	23	15	10	15-16	11	13	11	14	12	3:
N34099	Reiter			I2b	15	23	16	10	14	16	11	13	11	14	12	32																			
N72434	Johann Ritter b. ca. 1740 in Baden, Germany, d. Germany			I2b1	14	23	15	10	15	16	11	13	11	14	12	32	15	8	10	11	11	25	14	20	27	11	14	14	14	12	11	19	21	14	14	17	18	

Friedrich Riederer/Reidrer (~1450) living in the small village of Muhlhausen in the Bodensee area describes the Rhetoric story of his serf family belonging to the Knights of Fridingen @ Hohenkrahen in 1476. His Coat of Arms left (white steel) is Lords of Fridngen and the right (black) is Lords of Steckborn[280]. Shield divided (in metal & black) with three eight pointed stars placed diagonally. Von Steckborn (*Stegborn*) was from Minisiterial of Reichenau noted in the years 1187-1332, named for Steckborn on the Untersee W of Konstanz (Zurich wappenrolle pg 8 & 23). Steckborn wappenshild is half Gold and Half Black exactly like the Alt-Fridingen wappenschilde. In Eberhard (Doblers 1986: 131) also realized this **"Fridingen" Black & Gold wappen comes from the extinct ministerial between Reichenau and Steckborn**, Switzerland occuring in the 14th century (1300's). Other names in this period: Ulrich Reidrer, Cunrado Reidrer, Liutfrid dictus Reidrer, Johannes Reidrer, Jakob & Klaus Riederer 1476. **The Riederer familie took half the wappenshilde from von Fridingen & half from von** Steckborn was from Ministerials of Reichenau noted in the years 1187-1332, on the Untersee W of Konstanz (Zurich wappenrolle pg 8 & 23). Steckborn wappenshild is Gold & Black split(per pale). As the last traces of old friedingischer rights can be found later in the Swiss lakeside (Untersee) among the place names still in the Freidinger @ Mannenbach (c. 1355) and in a wooded area near Steckborn (1378)[281]. Note: Salenstein (Canton of Thurgau, Switzerland) is in the same vicinity of Mannebach. (1171) March 15th Reichenau, monastery Salem estate in Sweindorf(Schwandorf) Hugo comes Tiuwingen(Tubingen) Eberhardus et frater(brother) Swicgerus de Rieden(Winterrieden) Rudolfus de Rammisperc signers: Ludewicus & Bertoldus de Lucelenstetin, Gerungus de Huneberc, Conradus de Bodimin, Conradus de Ramisberc, Rudolfus & Burchardus de Ramisberc and others[282]. Monastery Salem, Reichenau abbot @ Constanz (1194) May(?) Presentibus Wernh dec Hermanne prepos Eberh hospital Alberto cust Hermanno camer et fere toto Augensi capit Burch pleb SJoh Ridegero et Heinr et Herrn eiusd eccl canonicis Eberhardo pleb Inférions celle et Cônr eiusd eccl canon Wernhero pleb Superioris celle et Wernero canon eiusd eccl Constant eccl canoncis Ulr custode mag Alberone Cônr Rvdeg Rudolfo pleb de Celia (Ratolfi=Radolfzel) Rud pleb de Fridingen laicis Landoldo de Wincelun, Heinr de Kreien, Hermanno de Kreien, Bertoldo de Riederen, Alb fratre ei Eberh de Salunstein, Alb de Salenstein 1194 presid Rome Celestino Heinr[283]. Von Salenstein (Konrad von Salenstein 1291. Heinrich & Eberhard von Salenstein w/Hildebold von Steckborn 1227, Konrad von Wartenberg, Berthold von Krahen 1215). Eberhard & Burkhard von Salenstein, Ritter Heinrich von Steckborn, Albert von Riedern, Berthold von Krahen, and Eberhard Schenk von Salenstein 1230/36/40) has come up a few times referencing von Fridingen/Krahen familie records. Unknown location (1246) October 17th Swigerus miles de Gundiluingin, Hainricus de Gundelui[n]gin, Hilteboldus de Stekeborun, Ebirhardus pincerna de Salunstain, Albertus et Rûdolfus de Riedirn fratres, Cvnradus cellerarius, Cvnradus de Cella Ratolfi (=Radolfzell) and others (WO:1613). (1275) November 5[th] Rudolphus advocatus de Fridingen III (~1247) appears in a Feldbach church selling Gerlikon fief with Burch de Salustein and Cunr de Salustein and Cunr Hiuneberc.

[Ryter, Ritter] familie are in Frutigen between 1399-1432. Jenni Riter, Peter Riter von Richenbach and Jenni Riter (Wandflu 1952: 79). (Johann) Ryter, genannt{called by} von Wildenstein [Hans (**Ryter**) Wildenstein (II)] is in the Bern archives dated (1466) Feburary 16. Wildenstein origins are known to be from Hirscheck. Others: Jacob rhyter (1334) June 10 in Frankfurt. Peter Ryter in Nurenburg (1442) April 10. Ernst Hanse von Ryter in Meissen(?) (1390) June 5 and (1391) March 13. Ulrich Ryder in Ortenberg, Bayern 1433. Hans Rytter gen Grosshans (1476) July 21 and Yttal Hans Reyter, Ursula Rytterin, Anna Ryterin (1466) August 5 in Ulm, Germany.

- Jung s. {Jungingen? }: Heinrich Jung (1670) is believed to have been born in Dunzweiler,Zweibrucken,Germany which is 3 hours NNW of Singen, Germany.. The Jung surname origins are not known, however "Jung/Yung" is also describing the age of a "Young" man comparative to "Alt" describing an "Old" man. Many nobles used "der jung/der yunger" when documenting names. They could have come from any family referring to Jung including a family that posessed holdings of a church named Jung St. Peters as an example.

Cuonrat **Friding (Fridingen)** is listed in the Schaffhausen Switzerland archives on a document dated 1422-23. A few more interesting records are found for Cleggöw/ Klettgau in Schaffhausen archives[284]:

- Item X ß verzarten die knecht, als si in der nach[t] um stübi [Stubeten, geschlossene **Zirkel von Jünglingen** und Jungfrauen, gewöhnlich Altersgenossen : Schweizerisches Idiotikon 10,1190] von **Kreyen [Krähen = Hohenkrähen]** : Das Land Baden-Württemberg, Register Band VIII, Seite 301] komen, alz der schriber hinussgeschikt ward. 1420.

Burkhard Hohenfels was understood to be a son of Hermann d.j. Hirscheck (~1085) via Doblers research. During 1150-1190 Burkhard von Hohenfels is the canon of Constance/Konstance 1191 and after he died with no male heirs the Alt-Hohenfels castle (in Sipplingen) passed to his brother Wolf von **Jungingen**[285].

Konstanz 1415, a dispute between Graf Heinrich and Graf Egen von Furstenberg has Rudolf von Fridingen {Obmann=chairman} from Thengen/Tengen signing the document with Lienhart von Jungingen. No further affiliation found.

Before 1459, the Von **Jungingen** wappenshield has quartered Blue & White Checkered shield[286]. The Zurich wappenrolle shows a Blue Shield with a pair of scissors centered open.

- Brunner s. {Brun/Brunnen?/Brunnenfeld?/Brunnenvelt?}:

Brunner DNA kit# E9632 and kit# 169805 both i2b1 Haplogroup from Switzerland. The surname "Brunner" comes from German speaking countries like Germany, Switzerland, and Austria. Brunners, it is understood to be related to the job of working with water & wells[287].

- St. Gallen has the earliest record for Brunner is (956/957) **{Prunnon}=Brunner** North of Bregenz and East of Konstanz & Kisslegg just outside of Wangen Allgäu (WO | 289) . The next record[288] is (1181) May 5th Henricus de Rumesperch/ Henricus von Rumisperchwird von **Brunner**/Heinricus de Rovmesperch(Romisperch) grafen von Ronsberg with a few others like Bertholdo de Lupheim, Harthmannus de Baldelheim, Henricus de Veringen, Ludovicus de Helfinstein, Fridericus de Zollera, Swiggerus de Eichheim, Heinricus de Stetin (~1138) father of Von Krahen and Von Fridingen sons. Ronsberg/Rumesperch family have connections to Kloster Weissenau and Kloser Salem between 1185-1241. Rammesperch founded under the act of Rammisheim(Ramsen) in ~1096 with Gero Stuolingen and Udalrici Rammesperch both known to be from the Uldaricher familie. Brunner, Ramisperch, Stetin, and Zoller have a Swabian connection.

- St. Blasien (1189) June 29th *Bischof Hermann (II.) von Konstanz* (=Fridingen) and the abbott Manegold confirmed predcessor Ottonis(Otto) describing possessions in Burgilun and other locations, tithes to Imindingin, & Frikkingin(Frickingen) and other churches Stein, Buron, **Brunnon** etc (WO:696).

- In 1330 Burkhard Fridingen (~1288) that the clerical Fridingen parrochialem smaller orders, and appointed the ordinances of the age spread to the church of dioc attained by and at that time upon minoribus order and state lawful to set up parrochialem church about **Brunnen**[289].

- In 1349 Rudolf, Ulrich and Heinrich **Brunner** sold the Church of Oetenbach in Zurich – Councillors including Gottfried Mulner husband of Ann Fridingen (~1301) were in attendance[290].

- In 1403 Nikolaus **Brunner** became chaplan @ St. Conrad's in Constenz, Germany[291]. Ulrich Fridingen IV (~1386) agreed to be mayor & council for a year @ Constenz in 1402.

- In 1429 Rudolph & Johannes von Fridingen sells their serfs Anna **Brunner**, daughter of Berthold Weber also of Fridingen[292].

- Jenne Brunner, Peter and Hans Brunner in Bern[293] by 1418(?).

- The small village **Brunnen**hof is located a few miles from Hohenkrahen.

Kit #	Paternal Ancestor Name	Country	Haplo group	Dys 393	Dys 390	Dys 19	Dys 391	Dys 385	Dys 426	Dys 388	Dys 439	Dys 389 I	Dys 392	Dys 389 ii	Dys 458	Dys 459	Dys 455	Dys 454	Dys 447	Dys 437	Dys 448	Dys 449	Dys 464	Dys 460	Ygata H4	Ycaii
	Brunner Project																									
	I2 Brunner																									
159305	Joseph Brunner, 160	Germany	I2b1c	15	24	15	10	15-16	11	13	11	14	12	30	16	8-9	11	11	24	14	20	28	14-14-15-15	11	10	19-19
169805	Brunner	Switzerlan	I2b1	15	24	15	10	15-17	11	13	11	14	12	32	16	8-10	11	11	25	14	20	27	11-14-14-15	11	9	19-21
	I2 Brunner Gp B																									
224310	Chris Brunner, b. 18	Germany	I2b1	14	23	16	10	15-15	11	13	12	14	12	31	16	8-10	11	11	25	14	20	28	11-14-15-15	10	10	19-21
B3411	Peter Friding, 1403	Switzerlan	I2b1	15	23	15	10	15-15	11	13	11	14	12	32	15	8-10	11	11	25	14	20	28	11-14-14-15	10	10	19-21

Dys456	Dys607	Dys576	Dys 570	Cdy	Dys 442	Dys 438	Dys 531	Dys 578	Dyf 395 S	Dys 590	Dys 537	Dys 641	Dys 472	Dyf 406 S	Dys 511	Dys 425	Dys 413	Dys 557	Dys 594	Dys 436	Dys 490	Dys 534	Dys 450	Dys 444	Dys 481	Dys 520	Dys 446	Dys 617	Dys 568	Dys 487	Dys 572	Dys 640	Dys 492	Dys 565	DYS710	DYS485	DYS632	DYS495	DYS540
14	16	18	19	37-38	13	10																																	
14	14	17	18	35-40	12	10																																	
15	14	17	20	36-39	12	10																																	
14	14	17	20	34-40	12	10	12	8	15-16	8	12	10	8	10	9	12	22-22	15	11	12	12	13	9	14	27	20	11	14	12	12	11	12	12	11	31	13	8	15	11

Result: Genetic distance 5+ (19 of 24) markers defined by FTDNA: 5 20/25 You are not related and the odds greatly favor that you have not shared a common male ancestor with this person in excess of 2,000 years.

- Zender s. {Zander/Zahnder/Zehner/Zehender/Zehnder/Scehender/ Zechender}:

Gottfried Zender (Zänder), of Germany shows in the same Haplogroup with terminal SNP L1290(=I2a2a1c2a3). FTDNA test kit # 167020. "The home of this ancient race has no place in modern canton of Aargau, near the town of Aarau Originally perhaps noble servants of the Count de Rore are bearers of the name Zehender or Scehender and mine Santander as it was written in the sequence usually already in the XIII century in documents before the Erblehensbrief given to Bruck Zinstag for Galli 127Ö v in which Count Hartmann von Habsburg, the Noble Jacob Kienberg the fortress Kienberg and various others is invested even before Item a shed to Sarmeustorf located, the Zehender of Aarau, etc[294]. Already in 1270 appears in documents not, however, in Aarau a carrier of the name Scehender namely Wernher called Scehender as a witness in Langenthal with a donation of Knight Wernher von Luternau to the House Thunstetten in another document dated 16 September 1299 (SG VOL2 1907: 611)". Zehner/Zehender (1281) Professional name, he zehendaere to Middle High German Tenth Man. 25 coat of Arms located for various spellings in Schweiz cantons. (**latin=zechender/zehenderin** 1491)[295]. Zehenten is translated to the word tithes. " Zehender – "who levied the tithe ("Zehnten") for a landlord, a rural tribute (tax) of cattle, grain and fruit"[296]. (1101- 1122†)[297] **Gero Zehender**[298] abbt of Einsidlen(Einsiedeln - south of Zurich & Winterthur) in the canton of Schwyz, Switzerland under Graf von Freyburg in Ergaw(Aargau) (Hitz 1848:99). He built the *Tüfelsbrugg* (Devils Bridge) in Egg in 1117 which allowed the road to the nearby Einsiedeln. This is the same kloster in which the Kyburg/Winterthur, Lupfen, Stuhlingen, Lenzburg, Rapperswill & Toggenburg family from 1052-1173. Gero is a family naming tradition: Gerolt Hirscheck (~1022), Gerold v Buch v Tengen (~1060) and Gero Stulingen (~1047). Other sources show him being Gero Frohburg[299] brother to Ludwig and son of Wolfrad von Frohburg († 1095). If this record is incomplete, then we can move to Heinrich Zehender (moved from Schwarzwald to Thurgau) record which is located in Thurgau where Fridinger(Krahen), Steckborn, Salenstein, Leonberg records appear in the same time frame. Turicensis (1149) March 13th & 20th kloster " *Celle beati Martini/cellae B.Martini (=St. Martin)* " mountain @ Turigensis, Zurich, **Rudolf Cendare**[300](=Zeendar/Zender/Zehnder), Luitold Linden, Burchart Niger(=Schwarz) and many others unrecognized (Orell, Füssli 1856 : 144). (~1265) peasants Lutfrido namely Fridemanno, **Henry dictor Zehender** et **Sigewino** brothers were commemorrated by Otto von Eberstein Sr give goods of Bauern to the monastery Herrenalb auf (Bad Herrenalb in Schwarzwald) (WO:2529). See also Drescher family name originally from Herrenalb 1273 (WO: 3133) with similar wappen like Fridingen appearing (1389) in Mulhausen. St. Gallen (1275) August 24th Johannes Chuchimeister, **Chv°nrat der Zehender**, Chv°nrat uon Engeciswiler (Enggetschwil, Bez. Gossau), **Volrich der Burger**, Johann Ougeli and others (MO:1954). Rapperswil & St. Gallen (1276) May 1st H. Schubinger, **H Zehender**, Konrad Banwart, H. marschalci/Heinrich Marschall v. Rapperswil and many others (MO:1968). Toggenburg kloster Maggenowe (1280) Feb 28th **Heinrich der Zehender** (Swarzenbach & Hermuttingen (Ermatingen) & Gebsintal), Haertnit(Harnit) von Salwenstein, **Heinrich der Lo°we von Zucchenriet von ze Swarzenbach** for Graf Frederic von Toggenburg and others (MO:2044). (1300) Der Edle Heinrich von Brauneck & wife Alheid von Zweibrücken and others: also called **Siboto dicto Zehender** solves half of his goods yearly six sumerinos wheat and 70 pence. Also Siboto son of one of their goods paid Zehender maldrum wheat and eight ounces of coins. Gruningen & Zurich (1314) October 6th **Rûdolf der Zehender** von Berlinkon, Frid. von Toggenburg phleger ze Gru°ningen and others (MO:2903). Kloster Erbrach (1327) July 6th **Konrad Zehender** von Gänheim ("Gauenheim") has to inheritance. (1362) May 7th **Klaus Zehender** von Aarau , Shupose in Kagiswil. Rapperswil & Winterthur (1364) February 5th Peter v. Ebersberg, **Ru°din Zehender**, Ru°din Bo°tswiller and many others (MO:4918). (1370) March 29th Mechthild Zenderin and Marchtwart Zhender burger to Arowe, Nicolaus Zehender burger to Arowe. (1382) Markwart & Klaus Zehender von Aarau. (1402) June 9th Marquart Zehender von Aarau. (1386) January 10th, Wernherus Decimatoris (Zehender) of Pfullendorf clerk of the diocese of Constance notiarized & scribed a document for Johannes Gässler(Gaessler/Gessler?) von Bischofszell, Kirchherr von Niederhelfenschwil, unterstellt seine Kirche dem Schutz von Lütold Schenk III von Landegg (MO:1386_I_10). **Pfullendorf has the origins of Ulrdaricher family of which Hirscheck is also known. Zurich (1428) Guothans Zander, Hans Klinger, Walther Klinger and many others (ZO:393661). (1500) July 9th Magdelena Luternau married Marquand Zehender. (1491) Ulrich Luternau who married **Ursula Fridingen**, (latin=Marquardus **zechender/** Magdalena **zehenderin**) (Wyss 1884 : 161). Johannes{Jean} Zehnder of Echwyz Konventual of Engelberg became pastor of Sins after the early death Feers in the same way he died in 1542 elected. He was leader of the Tuetonic Order between 1535-1542. Zhender was pre-ceded before **Francois von Fridingen** 1542-1545. An interesting Coat of Arms for Zeender[301] is found 1657 in the Canton of Zurich Schweiz - it shows 2 females diaganoly quartered and 2 Golden Lions with a background of Blue (nearly identical to Hans von Fridingen (1500s) wappen with female). In the Canton of Thurgau a similar Zehnder wappen (of Aadorf formerly of Ettenhausen) is shown with 2 women holding wheats in both hands opposite of Golden Lions on a quartered shield[302] but without the divided line under the lions. Other name forms: Zehnder Zehcuder Zehenter Zehntner Zehander Zender or the like come Tenth Zehnder or elsewhere in the Black Forest in Baden Württemberg, in Switzerland and elsewhere before a family connection is not established (C. Winter:1901)

- Michael s. {St. Michaels} Names located in Germany, Tirol and Schweiz. FTDNA Kit# 65183 for Michaels with unknown origin. *Multiple surname origins are believed to exist.* Frankfurt & Kirche Würzburg (846) July 5th King Ludwig with many villas honoring *sancti Martin*(Saint Martin) and villa Helicbrunno(Heilbronn) in honore *sancti Michaelis*(Saint Michaels) (WO:194). (1015) santic Michaelis apud Babenbergk. (1075) Vivus abscessit - Quod 1075 factum ese probat Lambertus, qui eum sub h.a. abbatem S. Michaelis Bamb (=proves that it thinks Lambert, who have him under Abbot St Michael Bamberg. (1111-1125) Abt Wolfram des **St. Michaels klosters zu Bamberg**, Ebo zu Röttingen, Fridericus gener Ebonis de Sgegeuelt, Walchun de Chircheim, Arnolt de Wulsinheim, Heinrich filius Marcholfi, Luitolfus de Wisindorf et Eberhardus filius eius, Pliggerus et alii quam plures and a few others (WO:423). Speyer (1122) February 17th Bishop Bruno von Speyer allows that of Margrave Hermann and his wife Judintha enriched with goods and tenth St. Pancras Parish Church in Backnang in an Augustinian Canonicat, and built by the same Saint Michaels church was converted to a church. (1183) The 1st Wengen monastery church was in Ulm Michelsberg on the Swabian Alb. Verona (1186) Pope Urban III. takes the Episcopal Church in Augsburg said possessions in his protection and confirmed several of the person of the Bishop rightful rights – mentioned: Staphense(Insel mit der *St. Michaelskapelle im Staffelsee*, zur Gemeinde Seehausen am Staffelsee gehörig.) Mainz (1189) The Cardinal Archbishop Conrad of Mainz confirmed the happened by Günther bishop of Speyer Association of **St. Michael's** parish there to Backnang with the St. Pancras pen. München (1259) Oktober 9th **Vlricus comes de Wirtenberch**, Gebhardus comes de Hirzberch & others Saint Michelspurch Michelsburg (Ruine), St. Lorenzen, Trentino-Südtirol, Italien (WO:2247). Wengen"the meadows" @ Ulm (1270) Herr Ebo von Söflingen, **St. Michaels** messe(harvest), bishoffes von Augespurc/Bishop of Augsburg (Hartmann v Dillingen IV), Rûdolf von Horningen, der her Gerwik der Giusse, der Swarze von Sevelingen, brûder C. der gardian von Ulme, bruder Begern unsers closters brûder, bruder Ulrich] Leidolf, bruder C[unrad] von Winden (WO:2922) **Note:** Hartmann IV von Dillingen established the kloster @ Söflingen Abbey January 1258. (1272) September 29th was 1st mentioned in German text in Deutch *sant michaels tach*(Saint Michael Day) Konrad von Kalheim & Konrad von Wartenfels Hof zu Sidenfeld. Sept 29th is also the same day for the feast of St. Michaels the Archangel[303]. It may have its origins back to (1014) called Michaelmas[304] in England. Landau (1305) Graf Wernhart von Leunberch (Leonberg) give Chunrat von Tannberg, Wernhart von Hartheim und dessen Frau Alheit die Burg zu Tannberg als Lehen on *sant Michaels tach*(day) (MO:528). **Fridig** is 1st record mentioned in 1401 for Ruedolf von **Fridig(en)** [Fridingen] (~1328/~1378) in the monastery for **St. Michaels** in Tuegen(Tengen), Germany OR Vienna, Austria. Another St. Michael church is in Bosingen, Germany (NNE of Singen)[305].

- Arnold s. {von Arnold} Names located in Germany and Tirol, Austria. FTDNA Kit# 64997 for Jacob Arnold (1763) with German Pallantine origin. Kit# N76807 Peter Anold (1923) from Germany is 8+ steps from **Friding/Frydig**. *Multiple surname origins are believed to exist.*

Another group is from the British Isles per Darvin Martin 2012 are related. Arnold{Arnoldus} is associated with Swabian nobles in the monasteries before the 1100 including the Hirschecker and Binzwanger families. The Earliest record is in Speyer (1023) Knight **Arnold** to land and rights in Glattbach and Diefenbach (WO:332). On January 4th (1083) Heinrich & neffe(nephew) Heinrich von Hirscheck(Altshausen) witnessed a document with **Arnold von Binzwanger** with brother Manegold & Ludwig, Sigfridus et filius fratris eius Hermannus de Wilere and others at the kloster St. Georgen in Schwarzwald (Eberhard : 1964). Eschingen (1100) Burchardus comes Nellenburc monastery Salvatoris testes: Ludwicus comes Stoffeln, Hiltheboldus de Tannecho (Steinegg), Ruldofus de Dengen(Tengen), Burchardus de Dengen(Tengen), Gerungus & **Arnoldus Gothmatignen** and others (FU 1885:45). "Arnold die Freiherren & Herren von - It took several baronial as well as several of the knighthood belonging to families of the name which are partly in the Royal Prussian province of Silesia, partly located in the kingdoms of Bavaria is Aach in Tyrol a baronial family of that name, they seem sämmtlich of various agreements to be because they also various arms of the two oldest families of Arnold, one distinguishes the Silesian and Silesian possessed in the **Frankish**[306] Glogauschen Fürstenthnme goods wholesale and Little Leschen Läsgen also Seedorf and Seifersholz to Grünberg (Reichenbach 1836:141)." Rotenacker (1116) Lŏdewicus comes de Stofiln, Ŏdalricus comes de Gamutingin, Rŏdolfus comes de Bregantio, Rŏpertus de Grùminbach, Ernest, Adelbertus et Otto de Stuzzilingen, **Arnoldus de Hiltiniswilare,** Rupertus de Rieth(Rieden), Bertoldus et Cünradus de Tannegga(Steinegg) and others (WO:427). Nikolaus Arnold 1400 Pfarrkirche zu Toblach (Südtirol/Southern Tirol, Austria). Peter Arnold in Toblach anno 1427. Christoph 1470, Cunrad 1475 and sohns Johann & Andreas in Toblach. Johann George von Arnold Mundschenk und Oberst(Butler & Colonel) 1707 in Wissgrill, Austria.

Wappen described: " The coat of arms of the old Silesian family of Arnold is in a divided shield its prow and yellow is a tree aut a green mountains located is the poop is blue and tar n an erect tiger in one front paw holding a wreath. On the helmets are two wings, the white front bottom, black on top, above the rear yellow, blue below between the Tigers, but abbreviated below. The Franconian line is in the middle of the shield of an oblique golden bar its right side you can see below three red roses in a white field, and the top three stars on the helmets we notice two buffalo horns at their tips a star attached. In the middle of a crowned man image below is abbreviated and without arms whose clothing blan on the front, white on the posterior and is denoted with a star on the chest. From the crown of three ostrich feathers give the lienor would mean the other two red. Bio helmet covers are formerly white and red white and blue, the posterior. The rest of Mr. Von Arnold hexagonal golden star in a red field, and an equally complicated. Between buffalo horns on their helmets winning (Reichenbach 1836: 141-142)."

Kit #	Paternal Ancestor Name	Country	Haplo group	Dys 393	Dys 390	Dys 19	Dys 391	Dys 385	Dys 426	Dys 388	Dys 439	Dys 389 I	Dys 392	Dys 389 Ii	Dys 458	Dys 459	Dys 455	Dys 454	Dys 447	Dys 437	Dys 448	Dys 449	Dys 464	Dys 460	Ygata H4	Ycaii
Arnold Project																									
64997	Jacob Arnold10/22/:	Unknown	I2b1	14	20	15	10	15-15	11	13	11	13	12	31	15	8-10	11	11	26	14	20	26	11-13-14-15	11	9	19-21
44161	Arnold	Unknown	I2b1	15	23	15	10	15-16	11	13	11	13	12	30	16	8-9	11	11	25	15	20	28	11-11-14-15	11	10	19-21
N76807	Arnold Peter, b. 192	Germany	I2b1	15	23	15	10	15-16	11	13	11	14	12	31	15	8-9	11	11	26	14	20	27	11-14-15-15	11	10	19-21
7655	Arnold	Unknown	I2b1	15	24	15	10	15-16	11	13	11	13	12	30	16	8-9	11	11	25	15	20	28	11-11-14-15	11	10	19-21
155355	JAMES B. ARNOLD,b	Unknown	I2b1	15	24	15	10	15-16	11	13	11	13	12	30	16	8-9	11	11	25	15	20	28	11-11-14-15	11	10	19-21
235819	Arendall	Unknown	I2b1	15	24	15	10	15-16	11	13	11	13	12	30	16	8-9	11	11	25	15	20	28	11-11-14-15	11	10	19-21
24559	William Arnold b. ab	Unknown	I2b1	15	24	15	10	15-16	11	13	11	13	12	30	16	8-9	11	11	25	15	20	28	11-11-14-15	11	10	19-21
86757	Pulaski County, KY,	Unknown	I2b1	15	24	15	10	15-16	11	13	11	13	12	30	16	8-9	11	11	25	15	20	28	11-11-14-15	11	10	19-21
B3411	Peter Friding, 1403	Switzerlan	I2b1	15	23	15	10	15-15	11	13	11	14	12	32	15	8-10	11	11	25	14	20	28	11-14-14-15	10	10	19-21

Dys456	Dys607	Dys576	Dys 570	Cdy	Dys 442	Dys 438	Dys 531	Dys 578	Dyf 395 S	Dys 590	Dys 537	Dys 641	Dys 472	Dyf 406 S	Dys 511	Dys 425	Dys 413	Dys 557	Dys 594	Dys 436	Dys 490	Dys 534	Dys 450	Dys 444	Dys 481	Dys 520	Dys 446	Dys 617	Dys 568	Dys 487	Dys 572	Dys 640	Dys 492	Dys 565	DYS710	DYS485	DYS632	DYS495	DYS540
14	14	17	20	33-39	12	10	11	8	15-16	8	11	10	8	10	9	12	21-22	15	11	12	12	13	9	13	26	20	12	13	12	12	11	12	12	11					
14	14	19	17	31-37	12	10																																	
15	16	18	16	32-38	12	11																																	
14	14	18	17	31-37	12	10																																	
14	14	18	17	31-37	12	10																																	
14	14	19	17	31-37	12	10																																	
14	14	19	17	31-37	12	10	11	8	15-16	8	12	10	8	10	10 0		19-22	17	11	12	12	19	9	14	25	20	10	13	11	13	10	11	12	11					
14	14	19	17	31-37	12	10	11	8	15-16	8	12	10	8	10	10 0		19-22	17	11	12	12	19	9	14	25	20	10	13	11	13	10	11	12	11					
14	14	17	20	34-40	12	10	12	8	15-16	8	12	10	8	10	9	12	22-22	15	11	12	12	13	9	14	27	20	11	14	12	12	11	12	12	11	31	13	8	15	1

Result: Genetic distance 7 (17 of 24) markers defined by FTDNA: >6 You are totally unrelated to this person.

Ernest/Earnest s. {Ernest/Ernst von} *Multiple surname origins are believed to exist.*

Marchtal kloster (776) Stiozaringas(steußlingen) 1st mention the church of St. Martin (WO:73). Ernst herzog von Schwaben 1012-1015. (1043) June 16th regarding Rietilinis(Riedlings) estate Eberhard Constantiensis aecclesiae , Irmingarde, advocatis Heremanni (vogt Hermann Hirscheck), abott Folmarus and the following witnesses Oudalricus Prigantinus, Switker, Wezel, Swigger, **Ernest**, Gerolt, Ruger, Landolt, Otgoz, Lupreht, Sigipreht, Hartnit, Engilscalch, Enceli, Simpreht, Hunolt, Eppo, Ello, Alberich, and Episcopus Eberhardus (WO:345). Rotenacker (1116) Lŏdewicus comes de Stofiln, Ŏdalricus comes de Gamutingin, Rŏdolfus comes de Bregantio, Rŏpertus de Grùminbach, **Ernest, Adelbertus et Otto de Stuzzilingen**, Arnoldus de Hiltiniswilare, Rupertus de Rieth(Rieden), Bertoldus et Cünradus de Tannegga(Steinegg) and others (WO:427). Ulm (1128) March 19th sancti Georii(St. George)mansum apud(remained in) **Suerzebach** mentioned with **Ernist** et frater eius Adelbertus de **Stuzelingin** (WO:461). (1148) Originally from Altsteußlingen abbot of **Ernst von Zwiefalten** dies driven by religious enthusiasm, but he laid down his high office and participated in the Second Crusade. He fell into the captivity of the Saracens, who him in the city of Mecca in 1148 (?) Tormented horrible death.

Bosshard s. {Bosshart/Bosshard/Bossard?/Bossart?/Bouchard?/Bossardt/Boeshartin?} for Stephan Bosshard and his ancestor Hans Bosshard (1606) whom died March 30,1669. Most of these family members origin are from Winterthur, Schweiz. Also for Hugo Bosshard. Some names occurences: (962) Herzog Burkhard von Schwaben schenkt dem Kloster Einsiedeln (Meinradszell). (1020) Burkhard II, 1001-1022 Abt von St. Gallen. Allerheiligen Kloster (1092) Burkhard III. von Nellenburg. Baindt (1259) Werner Koch of Altdorf sold two meadows at Banpfen in Onriet**(Bossart)** by 7 marks of silver to the monastery Baindt & convent Winegarten. H. ministri de Rauenspurc, dominus **R. de Vridingen(Fridingen)** monachus de Salem, dominus Al. plebanus dominarum, dominus C. de Kilhain and others (WO:2257). In the area between the villages and the Schussen Schachen Baindt and Sulpach found today that so called, Föhrenried in which it is doubtful whether it can be considered a newer name for **Onriet as Bossart**[307] in **Württemberg(North of Kempten in Allgau)**. Würzburg In Konzil (1287) March 13th **Bouchardus Metensis**, Arnoldus Babenbergensis, Gebehardus Brandenburgensis and a few others with Erzbischof Sigfried von Köln (WO:4522). Würzburg (1288) May 21st **Burkhard (Bouchardus) von Metz**, Bischöfen Arnold von Bamberg , a few others with Bischof Mangold von Würzburg (WO:4670). Zurich (1381) March 11 Zurich in court of the knight and mayor Eberhart Mülner in Zurich appears Klaus Huber of the Rek Sattler of Zurich and defended against the claim of the Johans Rek and Jenni Förscher Regensperg of them that the two Melliker goods previously had offered to Buy to the on November 15, 1380 with the pins geschlofsenen Zurzach purchase agreement which was then confirmed to the clientele of Rüdiger von Grüningen, Heinrich Bruggli and Franz Kloter that said goods aforementioned claimants were offered for sale but not required recently. Siegler of parchment mayor Eberhart Mülner in Zurich witnesses Rud Moso, Nyclaus Wallse, **Klaus Bosshart**, Kunrad host Kunrad Huber, Merkli Frvo, Heinrich Götfrid. Jan 1st (1394) **Hartman Hunaberg called Wolf**, Schultheiss of Zurich, sits in judgment publicly

and draw up a certificate. The Zurich citizens Cueni Streler had the mayor and councilors lied to a story: He was of Wiedikon Arriving at Stukys Expectant between the field infirmary and Stukys stoking met a servant (in a black coat with new Blätzen) and did this the Kuntels the painter child removed. Streler under oath admits that he found the child when Ketzistürli, it brought to the town hall and there presented his lies have. It is therefore imprisoned by the Council and declared unfit certificate. At the request of his relatives, he can present his case before the mayors, where he vows to want to be good friend with the Zurich group. If he even wanted to raise claims against people of Zurich or people belonging to Zurich, he will make this apply only in the courts of his domicile. Hartman Hunaberg sealed. Witnesses Ruodolf Brun, Ruodolf Kilchmater the old, power Marti Ruodolf Hagnower, Frantz Kloter, Ruodolf Jsnach, Johans Amman, Peter of Lubegg, Peter Rapp, Uolrich Tunnbrunn, **Claus Bosshart**, Henry Berger, Jacob Gürtler, Heinrich Gumpost, Ruedi Metziner and other respectable people (ZO: 357098). Kloster Wurmsbach in Zurich March 31 (1394) Johans von Wengi (Wängi, Bez. Münchwilen TG), Rudger von Gruningen, Jacob Glenter der jung, Chuntzman Zoller, Hans Hert, Rudolf Trinkler, Chunr. Huber, Johans Amman, Markwart Frijo, Johans Hemerli, **Claus Bosshart** burgere(citizen) Zurich and a few others (MO:6649). Johans Wisso, Propst von St. Felix und Regula Zürich purchase goods, verurkundet, dass Ritter Wilhelm im Turn von Schaffhausen (1390) March 3 Witnesses: **Johan Amman** Vogt of the provost, Uolrich Friburger, **Nyclaus Bosshart** from Zurich, Johans Meiger of Hottingen and other respectable people (ZO: 356815). (1523) **Baschli Bosshard, Hans Bosshard, Peter Bosshart** (von Bärentschwyl?), **Welti Bosshart**, Peter Baumanns and others. Zurich (1525) Feb-July, **Marx Bosshard (s. Marxen Bossharten)** knecht(=servant) ,Ulrich Zwingli, Konrad Brunner von Zollikon and others. (1527) March 9 Saturday - BM and R to an unnamed country pastures, Vogtherr the forested areas of the monastery Petershausen. Request to appeal the **Hans Bosshard** Burgers to Winterthur, who entertain as steward of the monastery of the rectory Oberwinterthur, the same wood benöthigte not continue to deny[308]. (1528) Johannes Bosshart in der Grafschaft Kyburg (Oberwinterthur & Seuzach). (1532) Annli Bosshart. The Bosshard families of Zurich[309] have 6 different coat of arms, of which two are distincly different. The Bossard/Bassart family have 10 different COA's of which two Bossart's are like the Bosshard #3 (Altishofen) & #1 (Baar).

1. In Silver or Red, split up with black bottom with golden ball, sign board in reversed colors 1603 & 1860.
2. Riveted(reverse triangles) by silver and black 1863.
3. In blue silver rafters accompanied by three six-pointed silver stars (2, 1) 1937.

In comparing Y-DNA 25 marker results (Genetic Distance‡ of 1), the probability that **Mr. Stefan Bosshard** and **Friding/Fridig** shared a common ancestor within the last 24 generations @ 97.85%. In comparing Y-DNA 25 marker results (Genetic Distance‡ of 2), the probability that **Mr. Hugo Bosshard** and **Friding/Fridig** shared a common ancestor within the last 24 generation @ 92.05%.

Auman s. {Orman/Aumon/Ammon/Aumann/Awmann/Awemann/Amman/ Ouwamann/Owemann/} Kenneth Wayne Orman shows a MRCA for 24+ generations a 95.87% Genetic Distance‡4 steps from Friding/Frydig with 37 marker compare. Auman/Orman family were descendants from John M Auman (1710) from Germany. William Thomas Auman shows a MRCA for 24+ generations a 95.87% Genetic Distance‡4 steps from Friding/Frydig with 37 marker compare. Dr. George Luis Auman for ancestor Andrew Auman (1762) shows a MRCA for 24+ generations @ 95.87% Genetic Distance‡4 steps from Friding/Frydig with 37 marker compare & 98.38% GenDist‡5 on 67 markers. Definition of AM'Man (amtmann, amptman) in European nations a judge cognizance in civil cases, in France a notary[310]. In Germany Amt=Office, in Switzerland "Amman a civil officer invested with a certain branch of executive government magistrate justice of peace an Amman" [311]. Some early records for surnames above. Rorschach (~1260) Rv°dolf von Rorschach and brother Egilolue, Ru°doluen an Jacobe **hern Rv°doluis amman**, hern Heinrich von Valkinstein, hern Rv°dolue uon Guttingin, hern Heinrich uon Griezinberc, hern Arnolde uon Bivrgelon, hern Heinriche uon Rauinsburc, hern Egilolue von

Rosinberc, dim marschalke uon Valkinstein(Rudolf II. v. Falkenstein) and others (MO:1652). Goylake Glamorganshire (Wales) (1276) Jan 12th mortgage by Roger le Hastare of Kenefeg, of his wife's land at Goylake, for forty years to Margam abbey witnesses KENEFEG ROBERT HUGH vicar, priest of the Harding to WAREMOTH Llewelin tailoring **RICARDO le ORMAN** and many others. (MO:03070723). Rorschach in St. Gallen (1276) May 4[th] Rv°dolf von Rorschach vnd fro[v] Willibirch, **Gotfr. hern Rv°dolfes amman von Rorschach**, maeister Herman von Riedern (MO:1969). Stettfurt in Thurgau (1282) **meister Bertolt der elter amman**. Mühldorf Bayern (1311) Feb 28[th] Meinhart von Polling, Wolfel der Schu[e]tz, der[c] Gossenperger, der Schalihner, **Peter der amptman von Ering** and others (MO:345). Pfäffikon (1328) Jan 6[th] Ulrich der ältere von Hohenklingen & his Bruder Ulrich, Abt Johannes II. von Hasenburg von Einsiedeln, der **Heinrich Ammann von Diessenhofen** & Heinrich Wäleschinger von Steisslingen & sons (KAE:N67). Uberau, Rhienheim, Germany (1331) Graffen Wilhelm von Katzenelnbogen sold to **Hermann Aumann** charges that he had the Count of his court to Ueberau fief[312]. Kloster Aspach/Asbach in Passau, Bayern (1337) March 25th Albrecht von Uetzing und Chunrat sein Sohn, Otakcher von Utzing und Hainrich sein Sohn, **Chunrad der Aumann zu Ering** and others (MO:42). Mondeee (Austria) (1342) Feb 14th St. Valentines day, Christian Abt about Mondsee gives Otten of Dirnberg etc, Goods to Dirnberg and half the tithe to Wangach: **Ruether der Ammon**, hainrich von Chasten, Chunrat von went, hainrich von went, Chunrat Pachmair and others (MO:400). Schaffhausen Mar 1378 Heinrich von Randegk, Vogt und dem Rat von Schaffhausen, verkaufen verschiedene Mitglieder(Sell to various) der **Familie Ammann**, Johannes von Herblingen, **Wilhelm Ammann**, Konrad von Teufen, Johann Hün von Beringen, Jakob Brümsi, Johannes von Fulach and others (SH:1066). Jan 1st (1394) **Hartman Hunaberg called Wolf**, Schultheiss of Zurich, sits in judgment publicly and draw up a certificate. Hartman Hunaberg sealed. Witnesses Ruodolf Brun, Ruodolf Kilchmater the old, power Marti Ruodolf Hagnower, Frantz Kloter, Ruodolf Jsnach, **Johans Amman**, Peter of Lubegg, Peter Rapp, Uolrich Tunnbrunn, **Claus Bosshart**, **Henry Berger**, Jacob Gürtler, Heinrich Gumpost, Ruedi Metziner and other respectable people (ZO: 357098). **Cord Aumann** born (1480) in Bad Salzschlirf, Fulda, Hessen [313]. **Claus Aumann/Awmann** born (1520) in Bad Salzschlirf, Fulda, Hessen (RW:metzieder). **Peter Auermann** der ältere Kupferfchmied zu Freiberg (1518). Marburg (1580) Sept 30th **Johann (Henn) Aumann aus Oberhaun**, Reinhards von Baumbach and others (MO:1810). **Hans Auermann** (1619) in Steinmetz. Some Ormans migrated from Russia to Wales 1880's which was Simon Orman (1857) and family (Goodbrand 2010: X).

Kit #	Paternal Ancestor Name/Project	Country	Haplo group	Dys 393	Dys 390	Dys 19	Dys 391	Dys 385	Dys 426	Dys 388	Dys 439	Dys 389 I	Dys 392	Dys 389 II	Dys 458	Dys 459	Dys 455	Dys 454	Dys 447	Dys 437	Dys 448	Dys 449	Dys 464	Dys 460	Ygata H4	Ycaii
19333		Unknown	I2b1	15	23	15	10	15-15	11	13	11	13	12	31	15	8-10	11	11	25	14	20	28	11-14-14-15			
101181		Unknown	I2b1	15	23	15	10	15-15	11	13	11	14	12	32												
19332	Michael Auman 174(	Germany	I2b1	15	23	15	10	15-15	11	13	11	14	12	32	15	8-10	11	11	25	14	20	27	11-14-14-15	10 9	19-21	1
19374		Germany	I2b1	15	23	15	10	15-15	11	13	11	14	12	32	15	8-10	11	11	25	14	20	27	11-14-14-15	10 9	19-21	1
144599		Unknown	I2b1	15	23	15	10	15-15	11	13	11	14	12	32	15	8-10	11	11	25	14	20	27	11-14-14-15	10 9		
42741		Unknown	I2b1	15	23	15	10	15-15	11	13	11	14	12	32	19	8-10	11	11	25	14	20	27	11-14-14-15			
42710	Michael Auman b.18	Unknown	I2a2	13	25	16	11	14-15	11	13	13	13	11	30	18	8-10	11	11	25	15	20	31	12-14-15-15	10 10	21-21	1
304491	Michael Auman c.17	Germany	I2a	13	25	16	11	14-15	11	13	13	13	11	30												
305390	Georg Amann b abt	Germany	I2b1	14	23	17	11	14-15	11	14	11	13	12	29	14	8-9	11	11	26	15	20	28	11-13-14-14	11 10	19-19	1
B3411	Peter Friding, 1403	Switzerlar	I2b1	15	23	15	10	15-15	11	13	11	14	12	32	15	8-10	11	11	25	14	20	28	11-14-14-15	10 10	19-21	1

Dys456	Dys607	Dys576	Dys 570	Cdy	Dys 442	Dys 438	Dys 531	Dys 578	Dyf 395 S	Dys 590	Dys 537	Dys 641	Dyf 406 S	Dys 511	Dys 425	Dys 413	Dys 557	Dys 594	Dys 436	Dys 490	Dys 534	Dys 450	Dys 444	Dys 481	Dys 520	Dys 446	Dys 617	Dys 568	Dys 487	Dys 572	Dys 640	Dys 492	Dys 565	DYS710	DYS485	DYS632	DYS495	DYS540	DYS714	DYS716
14	14	17	21	33-40	12	10																																		
14	14	17	21	33-40	12	10																																	
14	14	17	21	33-41	12	10																																	
15	12	18	17	34-35	13	10	11	8	15-15	7	12	10	8	11	9	12	22-22	16	10	12	12	12	7	10	30	21	13	14	10	13	11	11	12	9	30	14	8	14	11	26 27
18	16	18	20	33-35	13	10																																	
14	14	17	20	34-40	12	10	12	8	15-16	8	12	10	8	10	9	12	22-22	15	11	12	12	13	9	14	27	20	11	14	12	12	11	12	12	11	31	13	8	15	11	24 27

Woolf/Wolfe s. {Wolf/Woolfe/Woolf, ram?,rat?,rich?,gis?,ger?} Louis Aubrey Wolf descendant of John Wolf (1828) from Arkansas, LA, MS via Kit# 128255 shows a MRCA for 24+ generations a 89.89% Genetic Distance‡3 steps from Friding/Frydig with 25 marker compare with a terminal SNP CTS6433(=I2a2a1c2a2). **Ronald Edward Wolf** via Kit N18435 shows a MRCA for 24+ generations a 70.47% for 12 markers. *Multiple surname origins are believed to exist*. Possible ancient connection and naming convention detailed herein. **Wolferat** II von Beringen graf v Altshausen (~983- †4-9-1065). In kloster Petershausen on the alter of St. Stephen prior to 1043(?) are four noble men who were killed together Wernher namely Hermann, Burchard and **Wolfarn**. Burkhard Hohenfels was understood to be a son of Hermann d.j. Hirscheck (~1085) via Doblers research. Hermannus de Madelespuron (~1067) Madelespuron (Mahlspuren/ Mahlspüren), near Witichiwilere (Wittichen), Germany - Record in St. Georgen kloster 6/1091 Hermann brother gave "marriage" Ruzella to **Wolfger** received in faith. During 1150-1190 Burkhard von Hohenfels is the canon of Constance/ Konstance 1191 and after he died with no male heirs the Alt-Hohenfels castle (in Sipplingen) passed to his brother **Wolf von Jungingen**[314]. Kloster Prüfening (1140) Regensburg, Berthold von Andechs, **Adalbero und Rutbert von Pochsberg, Egilof von Stein** und seine **Brüder Eggbert und Ulrich.** Bamberg (1154) Feb 3rd Eberhardus Salzburgensis archiepiscopus, Vdalricus comes de Lencenburc, Pertoldus comes de Thirol, Egeno comes de Vehingen; nobiles et liberi Marcwardus de Grunbach, Odalricus de Hurningen, Altman de Sigenburc, **Odalricus de Steine, Rubertus Wolf**, Regenoldus de Otelingen, **Adelbertus de Berge**, Heinricus de Otelohesdorf et frater eius Meingoz; Heinrich de Papenheim, Herman de Eische, Pillungus de Memestorf et Gundeloch frater eius, Eberhardus de Tunteuelt, Adelbertus de Vraha, **Otnandus de Burgelin** and others[315]. (1164) Egelofus des Steine, **Roupreth qui dicitur Wolf** & frater **Alphretus** (MGH:471). (1165) **Hans Wolf von Homburg** in tournament in Zurich documented in a book about the Hohgaus[316] - This comes after the section about von Fridingen family of which Homburg is also known as (Homburg, Honburg, Hohenburg, Huhenburch also Homberg in Schwabia). Augensis abbot of Sweindorf Salem @ Reichenau (1171) March 15th Eberhardus and frater(brother) Swicgerus de Reidin testes: **Gerungus de Hvneberc**, Rudolfus miles quidam de Rammisberc, confirmation Diethelmus (=Krenkingen) abbot in Sweindorf and others (FA 1885:64). Teuringen (1171) March 31st Manegoldus comes Veringen(Bieringen), with his children **Wolfrado** and Eberhard, Count Berthold of Zolre, Count Frederick of Zolre, Hainricus of Stöphe, **Bruno & Hainricus frater de Marhtdorf** with Albertus & Burchardis de Frichingen (Frickingen) with others as Heinrich von Bayern & Otto von Hasenwiler donate estate to Schwandorf and Rickenbach monasteries (WO:612). 1180 **Roudprecht Wolf de Pochsberch** and frater **Alphretus**. Bergatreute (1185) Herzog Welf exchange called goods between the monastery Adelberg and the Church in Echterdingen and this was done with the consent of and know it to **Hermann, bishop of Constance(=Fridingen),** and at the request of Berhtoldo(=Stetten), prelate of the church of the same, witnesses: Philip Sindiluingin (Sindelfingen) of the provost, Mangold of Otolfiswank, Ernist of Stüzelingin, Diet of Rauinsburk(Ravensburg) (WO:667) and others Hainr pleb de Schennins, Oulr de Obirndorf clericus, Albert de Bozwilre, Chounr de Sarmannesdorf, Chounr de Willare, Hainr prae bendar de Vilmaringen, Burch miles de Baden, **Walther de Hunoberg**, Hartm de Chienberg (REC 1895:122). (1191) Bischof Diethelm von Konstanz notarized accomplishment between Kloster Salem und Ulrich von Bodman Klosterhofes Madach, presentibus: Gothefrido et filio eius Manegoldo comitibus de Rordorph, **De Craien Henrico et fratre eius Hermanno**, Burchardo de Honuelfi(Hohenfel), **Chönone de Huneberc(Homberg)** and many others (SA 1881:69). Landesperc (1192) Ulricus de Sevelt, Hermanus de Pouckelon, Roudpertus de Ramesheim, **Kunradus & frater eius Heinricus de Mullhusen, Eberhardus Wolf** and others[317]. Westminster Middlesex, England (1210) William Wolf (MO: 320209). (1214) Lupi (**die Wolfe** die rittere) in Ellenhardi Argentinesis Annales. Perg or Petoviam/Pettau (Slovenia south of Austria) (1235) July 8th Herr Hermann, bruder Otto, **Heinrich von Wolf** and others in Deutchen Orders (MO:230). Beuron (1253) April 22nd **Wolfradus** provost sancti Martini in Burron, Ebirhardo Nellinburc and present soldiers **Walther and Hainrico de Wildenvels** which begins on this side of the Danube, on the border Wildenstein near Fúhlenthal(Füllehaus) and Oberhusen, stretching himself up to the cliff, which is called Sperberloch(near Friedingen @ Danau/Danube) and others (WO:1183). Reichenau March 31st (1254) Domherr Burkhard von Bräunlingen, R. nobilis senior de Hewon, **Wolf dictus Wakerniz**, C. de Tierberch, H(einrich) advocatus de Craien(Krähen) (MO:1506). (1260) March 1st Lüttich (Belgium) **Eberhard v Wolf** (MO:550). Hettingen (1267) August 30 Count **Wolfrad {** *Wolfradus***} of Veringen** the Elder and his sons **Wolfrad** and Henry and Earl Mangold of Nellenburg approve the sale called possessions in Wilflingen which knight Heinrich von Gundelfingen had worn them as a fief, against other they applied to fiefs there at the monastery Heiligkreuztal - Arnold Wildinvelz, Aeinsilino de Wildinstain et **Rvdolfo de Kraigin**, Hainricus et Swiggerus fratres(brothers), filii predicti(sons of the said) Hainricus senior miles de Gvndiluingin, Anshelmo de Iustingin(Justingen) (WO:2704). **Rogerus le Wolf** 1314-15 Liskeard(Lisquiret) Burough England, **Richardus Wolf** 1337 Plymton Burrough England[318]. (1353) Herman the elder von Landsberg, bailiff in Thurgau and Aargau, and his son Herman's younger, named Griffense have asked of Mayor, Council and citizens of Zurich, the release of her imprisoned cousin Arnolt of Landsberg, son of the late Beringer of Landenberg, so that with the help of his friends can come to an agreement with Zurich. If this does not materialize, they agree that it 24 to June again into captivity to return or to pay 130 MS. Guarantors Heinr. of Rusegg, Johans of Frowenvelt, Egbrecht Goldberg, Heinr. of Wagenberg, Uolrich Gyel, **Hartman of Huneberg called Wolf**, and Peter of Huneberg called stork. Arnolt of Landsberg agrees to keep his cousins and the guarantor harmless. It sealed the 2 Herman von Landsberg, the 7 guarantors and Arnolt v. Landsberg (ZO:272251). (1390) Goetfrid von Hünenberg, Ritter, und seine Söhne Heinrich, Kirchherr von Merenschwand, **Hartman, genannt Wolf,** und Johans Uolrich verkaufen die Vogtei Knonau mit allen Rechten und Zubehören für 110 Pfund Pfennig an die Brüder Goetfrid von Hünenberg, Kirchherr von Rohrdorf, und Peter, genannt Storch (ZO:346339). Ttanslation: Goetfrid Hünenberg, knight, and his sons, Henry, Kirchherr of Merenschwand, **Hartman called Wolf,** and Johan Uolrich sell the Bailiwick Knonau with all rights and accessories for 110 pounds penny to the brothers Goetfrid Hünenberg, Kirchherr of Rohrdorf, and Peter, called stork. Jan 1st (1394) **Hartman Hunaberg called Wolf**, Schultheiss of Zurich, sits in judgment publicly and draw up a certificate. The Zurich citizens Cueni Streler had the mayor and councilors lied to a story: He was of Wiedikon Arriving at Stukys Expectant between the field infirmary and Stukys stoking met a servant (in a black coat with new Blätzen) and did this the Kuntels the painter child removed. Streler under oath admits that he found the child when Ketzistürli, it brought to the town hall and there presented his lies have. It is therefore imprisoned by the Council and declared unfit certificate. At the request of his relatives, he can present his case before the mayors, where he vows to want to be good friend with the Zurich group. If he even wanted to raise claims against people of Zurich or people belonging to Zurich, he will make this apply only in the courts of his domicile. Hartman Hunaberg sealed. Witnesses Ruodolf Brun, Ruodolf Kilchmater the old, power Marti Ruodolf Hagnower, Frantz Kloter, Ruodolf Jsnach, **Johans Amman**, Peter of Lubegg, Peter Rapp, Uolrich Tunnbrunn, **Claus Bosshart**, Henry Berger, Jacob Gürtler, Heinrich Gumpost, Ruedi Metziner and other respectable people (ZO: 357098). 1413 **Hans Wolf** @ Radolzell near Constanz in same records as **Wolf von Wolfurt** & **Ulrich von Wolfurt to Bonndorf** 1419. **Wilimus Wolf** 1433 Suffolk Count England. Vorarlberger (1501) Feb 26th **Hans Wolf**, Untervogt & Rat (VLU:4627). (1534) Nov 12th Christophel von Schinen & **Konrad Wolf**, Prädikant(preacher) zu Gachnang (KAE:249). 1546-1553 **Wolf von Homburg** with Hans von Fridingen @ Hohenkrahen. George Wolf von Wildenstein (~1590's). Orangeburg, Orange Co, SC (1840) Martin Friday, his neighbors were William Yon (1770-80), Jeremiah Hainsworth (1760-70), Henry Young, Robert Argrove, Effa Yon, Martin Argrove, William H. Corbett (1810-20) John Brown, Elizabeth Sally, John Corbett, Martin Bolen (1790-1800) and John A Sally. The Corbett, Fanning's and more Yons lived further down. On the other side of Martin lived Jacob Stroman (1791), Redick Sojourner (1791), Elisha Tyler (1790-1800), **John Wolfe** and Henry Smoke (~1805).

Kit #	Paternal Ancestor Name	Country	Haplo group	Dys 393	Dys 390	Dys 19	Dys 391	Dys 385	Dys 426	Dys 388	Dys 439	Dys 389 I	Dys 392	Dys 389 II	Dys 458	Dys 459	Dys 455	Dys 454	Dys 447	Dys 437	Dys 448	Dys 449	Dys 464	Dys 460	Ygata H4	Ycaii Dys456
	Woolf Project																								
128255	John Wolf c1828 MS	Switzerlan	I2b1	15	23	15	10	15-15	11	13	11	14	12	32	15	8-10	11	11	25	14	21	27	11-14-14-15	10 10	19-21	15
SMGF	Lawrence Wolf 1811	Baden,Ger	I2b1	14	23	15	10	15-15	11	13	11	14	12	32	16	8-10	11	11	25	14	20	27	11-14-14-15	11 10	19-21	14
B3411	Peter Friding, 1403	Switzerlan	I2b1	15	23	15	10	15-15	11	13	11	14	12	32	15	8-10	11	11	25	14	20	28	11-14-14-15	10 10	19-21	14

Dys607	Dys576	Dys 570	Cdy	Dys 442	Dys 438	Dys 531	Dys 578	Dyf 395 S	Dys 590	Dys 537	Dys 641	Dys 472	Dyf 406 S	Dys 511	Dys 425	Dys 413	Dys 557	Dys 594	Dys 436	Dys 490	Dys 534	Dys 450	Dys 444	Dys 481	Dys 520	Dys 446	Dys 617	Dys 568	Dys 487	Dys 572	Dys 640	Dys 492	Dys 565
15	17	18	35-42	12	10	12	8	15-16	8	12	10	8	10	9	12	21-21	15	11	12	12	13	9	14	27	20	11	13	12	12	11	12	12	11
14	17	19	33-40	12	10	11	8	15-16	8	12	10	8	10	9	12	21-22	15	11	12	12	13	9	14	26	20	11	13	12	12	11	12	12	11
14	17	20	34-40	12	10	12	8	15-16	8	12	10	8	10	9	12	22-22	15	11	12	12	13	9	14	27	20	11	13	12	12	11	12	12	11

DYS710	DYS485	DYS632	DYS495	DYS540	DYS714	DYS716	DYS717	DYS505	DYS556	DYS549	DYS589	DYS522	DYS494	DYS533	DYS636	DYS575	DYS638	DYS462	DYS452	DYS445	Ygata A1	DYS463	DYS441	Yggaat 1	DYS525	DYS712	DYS593	DYS650	DYS532	DYS715	DYS504	DYS513	DYS561	DYS552	DYS726	DYS635	DYS587	DYS643	DYS497	DYS510	DYS434	DYS461	DYS435
29	13	8	15	11	24	28	16	11	11	11	11	13	9	12	11	10	11	12	31	10	13	22	13	11	10	20	15	23	9	23	12	12	14	26	12	21	18	13	16	18	9	12	11
31	13	8	15	11	24	27	16	13	11	12	11	12	9	12	11	10	11	12	32	10	12	22	13	11	11	23	15	24	9	23	14	12	14	28	12	21	18	13	15	17	9	12	11
31	13	8	15	11	24	27	16	13	11	12	11	13	9	12	11	10	11	12	30	10	12	22	14	11	10	19	15	22	9	23	14	12	14	29	12	2◇	8	12	15	17	9	12	11

An FTDNA administrator John Ozment comparison of Wolf & Friding markers. John O is a descendant of John Wolf.

John Wolf and Lawrence Wolf — 36 mutations

John Wolf and Peter Friding — 30 mutations

Peter Friding and Lawrence Wolf — 25 mutations

Segrest s. {Segrist/Sigrist/Sigriste} Ueli Siegrist shows a MRCA for 24+ generations a 91.41% Genetic Distance‡0 steps from Friding/Frydig with a 12 marker compare. Claude Harvey Segrest Jr. for ancestor Hand Joggi Sigrist from Rünenberg, Switzerland. Ben H Segrest & Claude Segrest shows a MRCA for 24+ generations a 97.85% Genetic Distance‡1 steps from Friding/Frydig with a 25 marker compare. Other family name variations in German are supposed to occur (Siecrist, Siegrist, Siegerist, Sigeris, Sigeris, Siegeriss, Sigerist, Sigriz), but none found when searching the german & latin texts. Sacrist {lat} is defined an official in charge of the sacred vessels, vestments, etc., of a church or a religious house. (1187) Konrad (called Conrad Sacristan), Canon and Sacristan of Freising Church, wrote in the year 1187 a deed of the same collection, in which he also recorded some historical information about the bishops of Freising. Jettenhausen (1250) Jan 19th Ritter Hermann von Raderach "An der Egge" bei Ravensburg in Kloster Weisenau, Heinrico de Valchenstein, **Berhtoldo sacristan**, canonicis minoris Augie and others (WO:1743). **Cunradus sacrista** de Endingen Griesheim 1261, **Heinrico Sacristo** uxor Gertrude in the monastery Saint Blasii in the black forest under Abbas Arnoldus 1271, Hugo **sacrista** de Hunzebach 1274, Chonrat **der sigriste** Klingnau 1277, Hugo Johannes **des sigeristen** sun Gressweiler 1280, Chûnrat **der sigeriste** Riehen 1285 = Cunrat **Sigrist** von Rihen 1291, Wernherus **sacrista** de Tullikon 1286, **Ülrich Sigriste** Kleinbasel 1290, Hetzelo de Otlikon filius sacriste 1291, C.dictus **Sacrista** 1295, Diethelmus filius **sacriste** ville Otlikon 1297, Rûdolf **der Sigeriste** Freiburg 1299, **Heinricus dictus Sigriste** civis minoris Basilee 1300 (Helbing & Lichtenhahn 1903:496). Burg Andelfingen (1312) Rudolf von Lindenberg in kloster Wettingen with **Burkart der sigrist**, **Heinrich der keller**, Jacob der wirt, Heinrich v. Wespersbühl (1289-1324) Cv⁰nrat des vogtes sun von Aha(Aach near Singen) (MO:2835) from the Aargau Aarau Archives. Arbon(in Thurgau) (1332) Rudolf, Bishop of Constance and Pflegler of the monastery of St. Gallen, and the chapter of St. Gallen give the priest **Jacob Sigrist** (*herr Jacoben dem Sig(re)sten*) the Salvator and the Lady Chapel in the Abbey, with interest from the court and the Hause Blasenberg tenths to mountain (MO:3493). Kloster Klingental (1337) Hedwig witwe(wife) of **Johann Sigriste** von Egringen (BS: 841084). Zurich (1341) Duke Louis of Teck, imperial judges to Kufstein, commanded the cities of Zurich, Constance, Schaffhausen and St.

Gall, **Heinrich von Tengen**(IV 1296-1348 in Singen, BW) owned farm and church tax Küsnacht to protect - **Chvenrat Berchtold**, den man nennt den{is called the} **Sigrist** buwet and the church set ze Kuessenach (MO:3791). Heilgenberg Kloster (1344) Jakob Wegner, Chuonrat Walasseller, Heinrich Wigand, Heinrich Wiler, Jacob Revel, Zürcher Bürger; Johans Wisso, **Ruodolf Sigrist**, Burkart Grosman, Chuonrat Tallinger, Heinrich Borre von Höngg (ZO:344289). Heinrich Sigrist is in Bern canton by (1348) Johannes von Bubenberg the Schultheiss, Council and two hundred of the city of Bern decided that the Commander of the Knights who fled to the house Buchsee Bern Eigenmann(proper man?) **Heinrich Sigrist** again may take the attention (BA:33688). St. Gallen (1359) Rudolf of Rorschach, Kirchherr to Rorschach, and his brother Rudolf, Kirchherr to Herisau, give **Nicholas Sigrist(Sigristen)** von Hemberg grain of interest from the farm Weggenwil , Ulrich Sarri/Saerri and others (MO:4605). Zurich (1370) Růedgern and Burkart Sigristen gebrůdern(brothers) von Vegschwil . Many Sigrist follow in the archives after **Burkard Sigrist** in 1372. Zuirch (1379) Ritter Eberhart Mülner, Schultheiss von Zürich , **Albrecht Sigrest** und Jenni, dessen Sohn (ZO: 346951). (1387) Küni Keller von Fulau verpfändet(pledge) an Abt Kuno von St. Gallen(Kuno v. Stoffeln) den Zehnten(tithes) zu Zünikon - Cûnraten den Saler schulthaissen ze Winterthur and **Hainrichen Sigrist** {S'.HAINRICI.DCI.SIGGRIS} burger ze Frowenfeld(in Thurgau) (MO:6172). Konstanz (1395) the Constance Stadtammann a notarized agreement between **Hans Sigrist** der **zimbermann** burger ze Constanz, Eglolf of Rorschach and their wives(Hans+Katherine & Eglolf+Ursel) on the one hand and on the other hand Henry von Dettighofen of the annual interest of two houses in Constance (MO:5818). Lichensteig (1406) **Hans Sigrist** and Ulrich Merkli von Schwiz, William von Monfort von Tettnang and others. Diessenhofen (1408) Nov 18th **Ulrich Sigrist**, Hofmeister(steward) des Klosters St. Katharinental just south east of Ramsen & Weisholz where the **Friding** brothers (Hans & Heintz) were living by 1418 (KAE:26.24). Heinrich Sigrist von Buchhorn 1463 in Thurgau. **Henry Sigrist** was a passenger on the same ship William for captain William Vitery (1735) with **Martin Fridig** and other passengers. **Henry Seacrest** listed as a soldier under Captain Henry Giesendanners Company & Lt. John Wolf (Nov 1781) in South Carolina.

Berger s. {Berger/Burger/Burgar} – Glen Eric Berger on ancester Ernest Berger (1806) from Baden Germany shows a MRCA for 24+ generations @ 96.96% via a Genetic Distance‡12 from Friding/Frydig on 25 markers. Some possible ancient connections listed. Winterthur (1249) Mar 8th graf Ulrich von Berg Berga, Heinrich von Burgau, presentibus Ruperto dco de Tannenvels, Waltero Thithelario, **Bur de Hohinvels** and others. Constanz (1260) September 22nd Heinrich von Bankholzen(Radolzell), **Ulrich Burger** von St. Gallen (Volric dicto Burgaer) & Egelolfo de Valkenstain II (MO:1642). St. Gallen (1275) August 24th Johannes Chuchimeister, **Chv°nrat der Zehender**, Chv°nrat uon Engeciswiler (in Gossau), **Volrich der Burger**, Johann Ougeli and others (MO:1954). (1282) *Graf Ulrich von Berg* (**Ûlrichus comes de Berga**) Hainrichus dictus Sanze faber de Ehingen possessiones quasdam in **Vrikkingen**, testes: Chûnradus Zeho, Dietrichus Liutholdus, Diethrichus Bergerius, Chûnradus pannicisor cives in Ehingen (WO:3982). Wien (1285) **Willibald Berger** @ Wiener Schotten klosters (MO:1285 3). (1286) **Cunrat von Basel der Berger** (KK 1898: 45). De Basilea family has roots in Esslingen & Ravensburg dating back to 1276 (WO:3386). Konstanz (1291) Jan 30th *Der Edle Konrad von Wartenberg, Ritter, schenkt* Testes: magister **Johannes de Basilea** canonicus sancti Stephani and others (WO:5025). Schaller/Scalarii may also have a conection to Basil/Baseler family in the mid 1200's. St. Gallen (1305) Jan 24th Ulrich von Elgg, Stadtammann von St. Gallen, Henricus dei gratia abbas(Ramstein) monasterii sancti Galli, **Henricum dictum Berger**, ego presentibus confiteor (MO:2621). Jan 1st (1394) **Hartman Hunaberg called Wolf**, Schultheiss of Zurich, sits in judgment publicly and draw up a certificate. Hartman Hunaberg sealed. Witnesses Ruodolf Brun, Ruodolf Kilchmater the old, power Marti Ruodolf Hagnower, Frantz Kloter, Ruodolf Jsnach, **Johans Amman**, Peter of Lubegg, Peter Rapp, Uolrich Tunnbrunn, **Claus Bosshart**, **Henry Berger**, Jacob Gürtler, Heinrich Gumpost, Ruedi Metziner and other respectable people (ZO: 357098).

Hover/Hoover s. {Huber/Huober/Hueber} - Mr. Joel Cook Huber Kit# 256881 for ancestor from Netherlands & Kit# B6743 from Switzerland, shows a MRCA for 24+ generations a 92.39% Genetic Distance‡2 steps from Friding/Frydig with a 25 marker compare. Three Hoover families (Ralph M Hover, H. Hoover & B.K. Hoover) shows a MRCA for 24+ generations a 70.47% Genetic Distance‡1 step from Friding/Frydig with a 12 marker compare. Other family name variations in German & Switzerland: **Heinricus dct H** 1273 Burger in Pfullendorf (Knobloch:142). Klosterneuburg (1277) Mar 25th Marquard von Pillichdorf verkauft an Dietrich von Kahlenberg Gülten zu Enzersdorf. **Heniricus III Huober** Elggensis 1283- Nov 1289 Eclessia in Constanz. Baindt (1288) Der Edle Eberhard von Gundelfingen, Kirchherr zu Ebersbach, schenkt dem Kloster Baindt auf Bitten seiner Schwester, Äbtissin daselbst, die Brüder Berthold und **Rudolf, Söhne Konrad Hubers (Hubarii)** zu Ebersbach, und Heinrich, Sohn Konrad Mageblins zu Atzenberg, nachdem sein Bruder Ulrich sel (WO:3839). Isny in Allgäu (1297) Hainr et Cûn dictis Huber and many others (WO:5966). Chaepfing (1299) Jan 3rd Heinr v. Ried (Ridnern), Heinrich bei dem Bach (Pach) & Sohn Konr zu Kapfing (Chaepfing), **Heinr der Huber (Hü-) zu Kapfing** und seine Söhne Heinr und Ainweig, and many others (MO:1299). Salzburg (1307) June 25th **Konrad dem Huber von Mühldorf** and others (MO:1307). Klosters Raitenhaslach(East of Munich) (1312) **Frid(reich) der Huober**, F(ridreich) Darm, Ch(unrat) der probst von Pfæffing, Ch(unrat) der Puntschuoh and many others (MO:1312). Zurich (1340) Ritter Heinrich der alte von Tengen und Junker Heinrich von Tengen, Sohn des verstorbenen Chuonrat von Tengen, **Burkart der Huober** von Bullach and others (ZU: 273899). Zurich (1341) **Johans von Fridingen, Ritter, Vogt** und Pfleger zu Küssaberg (-perg), urkundet, dass Johans, Sohn des verstorbenen Berchtolt in dem Bache von Tuengen, Kaplan der Kapelle St. Michael zu Tuengen, und Schwester Anna, seine Schwester, mit deren Vogt Heinrich von Immodingen dem Kloster Rheinau eine halbe Hube zu Dankstetten. Die erwähnte halbe Hube wird von Lutolt von Aichain bebaut. Siegel von J. von Fridingen, Johans und Heinrich von Immadingen. Zeugen: Cuonrat der Keller von Rheinheim, Johans der Huober, Wernher der Schmid, Berchtold der Bekko, Hainrich der Halder, Ruodolf Wigli, Johans sein Sohn, Johans Verro, Heinrich Roto, Johans Roto and others (ZO: 274315) Zurich (1342) Uolrich Hueber and others (ZU: 274367). Stein am Rhein (1343) May 8th Bertold der Huber, gesessen zu Oehningen (SH:660). Zurich (1381) March 11th Zurich in court of the knight and mayor Eberhart Mülner in Zurich appears Klaus

Huber of the Rek Sattler of Zurich and defended against the claim of the Johans Rek and Jenni Förscher Regensperg of them that the two Melliker goods previously had offered to Buy to the on November 15, 1380 with the pins geschlofsenen Zurzach purchase agreement which was then confirmed to the clientele of Rüdiger von Grüningen, Heinrich Bruggli and Franz Kloter that said goods aforementioned claimants were offered for sale but not required recently. Siegler of parchment mayor Eberhart Mülner in zurich witnesses Rud Moso, Nyclaus Wallse, KlausBosshart, Kunrad host Kunrad Huber, Merkli Frv o, Heinrich Götfrid. Zurich Wappen Silver schield with Red Hirsch(deer) http://www.chgh.net/heraldik/h/hu/hubers.htm. There are other coat of arms with grapes in the divide surrounded by Glue, Gold and Black. Others with Golds Stars and a mountain. Others with the Black letter H on a Gold background over a Mountain.

Kit #	Paternal Ancestor Name/Project	Country	Haplo group	Dys 393	Dys 390	Dys 19	Dys 391	Dys 385	Dys 426	Dys 388	Dys 439	Dys 389 I	Dys 392	Dys 389 II	Dys 458	Dys 459	Dys 455	Dys 454	Dys 447	Dys 437	Dys 448	Dys 449	Dys 464	Dys 460	Ygata H4	Ycaii
87354	(Hover)	Switzerlar	I-M223	13	23	15	10	15-15	11	13	11	14	12	32	15	8-10	12	11	25	14	20	27	11-14-14-15	10	10	19-2:
256881	Johan Huber, b.1705 d.	Netherlan	I-M223	13	23	15	10	15-15	11	13	11	14	12	32	15	8-8	12	11	25	14	20	27	11-14-14-14	11	10	19-2:
B6743	Georg Huber	Switzerlar	I-M223	14	23	15	10	15-15	11	13	11	13	13	32			14									
B7054	Hoover	Germany	-	14	23	15	10	15-16	11	13	11	14	12	32	15	8-9	11	11	25	14	20	28	11-14-14-15	11	9	19-2:
N75412	John Huber	Germany	I-M223	14	23	15	10	15-16	11	13	11	14	12	32	16	8-10	11	11	25	14	21	28	11-14-15-16	12	9	19-2:
H2232	John Hoover	Unknown	I-M223	14	23	16	11	15-16	11	13	11	13	12	29	13	8-10	11	11	26	15	20	28	11-13-14-15	10	10	19-1:
65636	Huber	Switzerlar	I-M223	13	23	16	10	15-15	11	13	11	14	12	32	15	8-9	11	11	25	14	20	28	11-14-14-15	11	10	19-2:
N37972	John Huber, born 1751	Unknown	I-M223	14	23	15	10	14-15	11	13	11	14	12	32	15	8-9	11	11	25	14	20	28	11-14-14-15	11	10	19-2:
E4399	(Huber)	Unknown	I-M223	14	23	15	10	15-15	11	13	11	14	12	32												
303230		Unknown	I-M223	14	23	15	10	15-15	11	13	11	14	12	32	15	8-8	11	11	25	14	20	28	11-11-14-14	11	10	19-2:
167492	(Hoover) N. C.	Germany	I-CTS643	14	23	15	10	15-15	11	13	11	14	12	32	15	8-9	11	11	25	14	20	28	11-11-14-14	11	10	19-2:
182965	Hoover, Indiana	Unknown	I-M223	14	23	15	10	15-15	11	13	11	14	12	32	15	8-9	11	11	25	14	20	28	11-14-14-15	11	10	19-2:
161761	(Huber)	Switzerlar	I-M223	14	23	15	10	15-15	11	13	11	14	12	32	15	8-9	11	11	25	14	20	28	11-14-14-15	11	10	19-2:
253212	Jcob Huber b abt 1660	Switzerlar	I-M223	14	23	15	10	15-15	11	13	12	14	12	32												
B3411	Peter Friding, 1403 - af	Switzerlar	I-CTS643	15	23	15	10	15-15	11	13	11	14	12	32	15	8-10	12	11	25	14	20	28	11-14-14-15	10	10	19-2:

Kit #	Dys456	Dys607	Dys576	Dys 570	CDy	Dys 442	Dys 438	Dys 531	Dys 578	Dyf 395 S	Dys 590	Dys 537	Dys 641	Dys 472	Dyf 406 S	Dys 511	Dys 425	Dys 413	Dys 557	Dys 594	Dys 436	Dys 490	Dys 534	Dys 450	Dys 444	Dys 481	Dys 520	Dys 446	Dys 617	Dys 568	Dys 487	Dys 572	Dys 640	Dys 492	Dys 565	DYS710	DYS485	DYS632	DYS495	DYS540	DYS714
87354	15	14	20	19	35-40	12	10																																		
256881	15	14	19	18	34-34	12	10																																		
B6743							10																																		
B7054	15					13	10																		13			13													
N75412	15	14	18	20	34-35	11	10	11	8	15-16	8	11	10	8	10	9	12	21-21	15	11	12	12	15	9	14	27	20	11	13	12	12	11	12	12	11						
H2232	17	15	17	20	31-36	13	10	11	8	15-16	8	11	10	8	11	9	12	21-22	15	11	12	12	17	9	14	25	21	8	13	12	13	11	12	13	11	29	14	8	15	11	23
65636	15	15	17	19	34-38	13	10																																		
N37972	15	15	17	19	34-38	11	10	11	8	15-16	8	11	10	8	10	9	12	21-21		11	12	14	9		13	28	20		13	12	13	11		12	12	11					
303230	15	15	18	21	35-35	14	10	11	8						10	9	12	21-21							13	28	20		13	12	13	11		12	12	11					
167492	15	15	17	20	35-38	13	10	11	8	15-16	8	11	10	8	10	9	12	21-21	15	11	12	12	14	9	13	28	20	11	12	13	11	12		12	11						
182965	15	15	17	20	35-37	12	10																																		
161761	15	15	17	19	33-38	13	10																																		
B3411	14	14	17	20	34-40	12	10	12	8	15-16	8	12	10	8	10	9	12	22-22	15	11	12	12	13	9	14	27	20	11	14	12	12	11	12	12	11	31	13	8	15	11	24

Hain s. {Hayn/Hainen?/Heyne} for **Andrew Hain** descendant of Christian Hain b.1751 shows a MRCA for 24+ generations @ 91.41% via a Genetic Distance‡0 from Friding/Frydig on 12 markers. Some early References for Hain/Hayn: Rittergut, 1175 **Herren von Hain**. (1185) Petrus er Hermanns de **Hägens**, (1216) Rudolfus Bruneslaus und Dippoldus **Hagane** fratres und ihre Schwester Lucia schenken dem Kloster Zelle, (1270) Heinemanus miles de **Hägen**, (1285) Wilhelmus de Indagine guardiaus in Dresden, (1287) **Volkmarus de Hayne** miles, (1288) **Henricus de Hagin** miles, Germany (1385) Feb 20th Rüdiger (Rutiger) **vom Hain** (vom Hayne) and many others (MO:77). Wien (1361) Deutschmeister Bruder Philipp von Bickenbach, beurkundet im Kapitel zu Frankfurt das Ergebnis der Visitation, die durchgeführt worden war durch **Johann v. Heyn Komtur zu Marburg**, Bruder Heinrich Pfarrer zu Munerstad [Münnerstadt], Bruder Johann v. Rotenstein Komtur zu Bückein [Beuggen] und Ulrich Pfarrer zu Rothenburg. Zugegen: Bruder Ulrich v. Tetingen Landkomtur zu Elsaß, Bruder **Reinhart Hycin Landkomtur v. Biesen und Utrecht**, Bruder Adam v. Talhusen Landkomtur v. Westfalen, Bruder Boppe v. Hennenberg Komtur zu Zwinfurt [Schweinfurt], Bruder Heinrich v. Rickenberg Komtur zu Straßburg, Bruder Johann v. Liningen Komtur zu Wiesenburg [Weißenburg] und many others (MO:2094). Sachsenhausen (1361) Aug 10th **Reinher gen. Huon** (MO: 2095). Wien (1367) Feb 5th Gerhard v. Ysbach, Heinrich Slume, Johann Schicke und die anderen Schöffen von Kudenkoven [Küdinghoven] beurkunden, daß Frau Trutelant, Witwe(Widow) des **Ritters Johann v. Lewenberg**, ihr Sohn Heinrich, Katharina, Abdissa zu Zijsendorp, und Grete, ihre Tochter, dem **Reinhard Hayn, Vizekomtur zu Biesen**, ihren Hof zu Roylstarp verkauft(sold) haben (MO:2186). Wien (1406) Mar 18th Revers des Gerlach v. Redelnheim an **Johann v. Hayne, Komtur zu Sachsenhausen** (MO:2830) and Komtur zu Frankfurt in (1408).

Gersper/Gerspach s. {Gersbach/Gerstburger} Name References: St. Blasien (1166) mentions ęcclesia(church) **Gerisbac**, quam nobilis homo Chönradus de Hussinchilcha(Hoßkirch) hereditario(rights of inheritance)(WO:603). In (1173) Foligno document mentions Gerispach

Schopfheim in Baden, Germany. Sankt Blasien (1189) Herman von Konstanz (=Fridingen) Confirmed St. Blasien goods lastly mentions *Gerispach et alias ęcclesias quas racionabiliter possident* (WO:696). Engelszell (1303) Rüdiger von Haichenbach, Hausfrau & Sohn Chadolt, sell to Bischof Wernhart von Passau, Ulrich Gerstberg Geigersperch (Geisberger), Ulrich von Chlenow/Ulrich Klenauer and many others (MO:1303). (1305) Lobenstein Vlrich von Gersperch, wernhart der Graspech, urkunden in Reideck (MO:1305). Casper Gersperg (1433) Schaufhausen. Ursula Humpysen (Humpeisen) @ Castle Schloss Gersperg (Girsperg) (1533) in Zurich or Graubunden. William C Gersper for ancester Peter Gasper from Baden, Germany is confirmed **CTS6433>Z171-** which appears to be his terminal SNP.

Spory s. {Spori/Spöri/Sporri} Name References: Worms, Germany (1142), **Cunradusi Spore** and many others (WO:502). Weißenau (1275) May 8th, Cunrado de Marhdorf(Markdorf), **Cûnrado Sporer,** Cûnrado Sporli de Tetenang civibus de Ravensburg and many others (WO:3324) Ravensburg (1281) March, **Conradi Sporarii(Conradus Sporarius),***Kloster Schussenried* (Sorech) mentioned and others (WO:3894). Basel, Schweiz (1356) June, Cuonrat von Eptingen genannt (called) **Sporer.** Berne, Schweiz (1415) June, **Peter Spöri** and others (BE:61000). Schauffhausen (1455) **Pesti Sporin** and others. Basel, Schweiz (1456) April, **Hans Spor** and others (BS:845672). Lucerne, Schweiz (1477) March, **Rudolf Spöri**, Cllewi Huber, Rudi Wolf and others (LU:1118849). Berne, Schweiz (1510) May, **Heinrich Spöre (Spori)**, Landschreiber and others (BE :40545). Bäretswil, Zurich (1538) Spörri. Boltingen, Berne (1659) Spori. Baltenswil, Bassersdorf, Zurich (1731) Spörri. Confirmed CTS6433 - J Michael Spory for ancestor Phillip Jacob Spory (1833) from Hamburg or Darmstadt, Germany. Family probably migrated from Switzerland into Germany then on to America similar to the Leunbergers migration. FTDNA M223 Y-Clan page shows Spory closer to English variant families possibly due to ancient line (+2K ya MRCA). 19 commons markers @ first 30 marker, no match appearing on FTDNA so mutation rate is high or MRCA is very distant.

- Alternate ancient German/Schweiz families with same Haplotype s. {Auman, Backer/Bacher, Battenfield, Baumann, Berger, Bosshart, Cohen, Drescher?, End, Ernest/Earnest, Fedinger, Foeller, Fricke/Frick, Gerspach/Gersbach, Gruhl/Grule, Hughes?/Hew?/Huse?, Hoffman, Humpiss?, Hain, Landwehr, Lortschter, Rettig/Reddick, Lambertus, Juenemann, Marti/Martin, Medlhammer, Nieman, Pushel/Puschel, Schall, Switzer, Schmidt, Unterberg, Struze/Strauss, Waalkes, Wolf/Woolf (=ram,rat,rich,gis,ger,furt?)}
Names located on Germany and Switzerland groups on the FTDNA website.

a. **Gruhl s. Grule/Gruel** for James Gruhl on 11 markers. Other name variations: *Gruhl*(e), Grul(e), Grull(e), Gruel(e), Grül(le), Ghrule, Gruhll, Grulh, Grhull, Gruell, Grüel, Grühl, Groln[319]. Wien (1309) Nikolaus Gruel and others (MO:1290).
b. **Baumann (s. Buman) familie** – FTDNA Kit#223141 I2B1 haplogroup. Johannes Bauman d. 1798 Halifax, PA. Baumen family's earliest references are in Aargau, Switzerland for Melchior Baumann (~1526). Interestingly enough, Franz Ludwig Baumann has been writing histories on Allgaus since before 1974 including that of frequently referenced Hans Fridingen familie in that southern area of Swabia. The 1795 wappen(coa) for Hn v BAUMANN is a pale horizontal divide with Deer Horns on top with a woman above the Helm and arms (as deer antlers) outstretched. Similar to Hirscheck and Fridingen combined. Other Bumans located in Zimmerburg, Switzerland was Peter Buman (~1420) and Uli Bumann 1393.
c. **Frick** coat of arms if a Red Wolf standing with white background found in Argau on Ulrich I von Frick in 1277.
d. **Lambert s. Lamb/Lambertus** (latin=Lambertus/Lanpertum) (~976-1018) was a Bishop of Constanz, Germany in 995-1018 and St. Petershausen during the period before Hermann von Hirscheck donates to the monastery. Lambertus listed in a document (995) August 27th with

Gebhard von Konstanz son of Gerald & Imma. (1015) santic Michaelis apud Babenbergk. (1075) Vivus abscessit - Quod 1075 factum ese probat **Lambertus**, qui eum sub h.a. abbatem S. Michaelis Bamb (=proves that it thinks **Lambert**, who have him under Abbot St Michael Bamberg. Petershausen Cronicles describing Bishop Lambert taking away goods from the monastery that Gebhard II had built to Bamberg: "Vengeance of God upon Lampertum. But the decision was not left unpunished, that Lampertus obstinately into the holy place hath offended. For the term of his life when he was told he approaching, began to overstate it bred worms, which are called human lice, so that no talent could be rescued by them. Mostly for the families as well as in the Rhine in the bath with baths, as imminent passion tamed somewhat, but in the same water from a swarm of bees both ears of each frame as a pile of ants proceeded until the League exalavit spirit engine (MGH: 641)." The FTDNA Lambertus Admin wrote me in Feb 2013 and advised that the connection between Friding is probably greater than 600 years to the Lambertus family of which comfirmed the above data.

James L Lambert shows a MRCA for 24+ generations @ 89.81% via a Genetic Distance‡2 from Friding/Frydig on 25 markers. **Ed Lamb** shows a MRCA for 24+ generations @ 90.82% via a Genetic Distance‡2 from Friding/Frydig on 25 markers.

e. **Unterberg** is a town located in Tyrol,(Southern) Austria. In 1370 Heinrich Unterberg at the time Castle Richter in Eger[320], Germany (1061). Also, known as Egerland. George von Unterberg/Vunterberg (~1334) & Frits/Friczel der Elsenbeck/Elsenpekch were recorded[321] near Steyr, Austria in May 1364.

f. **Humpiss (Huntpiß) familie** - An undocumented(?) Barbara von Friedingen died in 1553 at the Kloster Grabdental[322] (in Waldberg?) and buried beside Appolonia Hundbissin von Waltrams in 1535. This maybe the Barbara von Fridingen (~1458) that married Anton von Emershofen in 1479, which is also the same year as a Fridingen feud. There is another record for Barbara married to ItelHans Huntpiß citizens of Ravensburg 1516-26 (Kindler von Knobloch a 0 II 164). Most Humpis familie comes from Ravensburg or Waldberg, Germany before 1424 but earliest records Frick I Humpis in 1334 LandVogt over Schwaben.. An epitaph of Frederick Humpis Waltram († September 28, 1559) and his wife Anastasia of Sirgenstein († October 19, 1587). Crest of Humpis Waltram and Sirg of Sirgenstein, on the sides of the crest with a **Coat of Arms Fridingen** in stone[323]. Jacob Hunbiss von Waltrams is in a record for Hohenkrahen with Wolf von Homburg, Hans Konrad von Bodman and more in 12/1549. On the same page is mentioned: Among the debt will also have a - certainly on of history goes back to Hans Fridingen - annuity of 80 guilders for the benefit of the wife, Barbara, Fridingen, which accordingly - as a nun is Heligkreutzal in 1549/50 were still alive (Dobler 1986: 290). Another record[324] shows Marcus Auw married to Magdelena von Fridingen and their daughter married Frederico Hundpiss de Waltrams who has another son Frederic who married Anastatia de Sitgenstein (Görlinus 1662 : 140).

g. **Strauss s. Strazza/Struze/Straze** - Fabian **Strauss** died before 1621. Kit# 224453 Haplogroup I2B1 under the The Strauss Y-DNA Research Project. Straß, near Pfullendorf, Germany. The Hirschecker family owned property @ Pullendorf before 1180. Based on research it appears Straus is a much earlier than the Uldaricher/Geroldonen Frankisch(?) Connection(?) a line that starts in Austria than Swabia. Some ancient name references: Austria (1004) All Christians know that the two brothers Gotescalehus and Engilscalchus with his wife Richkarda handed her estates to strazza on the altar of St. Peter, witnesses are delivered to the altar. Megingoz de sure, Piligrimus and his cousin Chinradus and Henry of Schalheimin, Liutwinus provost, Wolfram of offinwanch, Witigo de suriheimin, **Heinrich of strazza**. Salsburg, Austria (1004) **Engilscalchus de Strazza** testes: Pabo de Albin, Engilpreht et liuttold et Heinricus de Albin, **Dietmar de strazze**. Austria (1004) **Engilscalchus de Strazza** in Salzburg uxor wife Ekkarde had proprety @ Scugine. Hilzingen (1050) Adelbero de Engin et filii eius Burchardus et Bertoldus Liutoldus et Röpertus de Fusibach, Hoch de Miringen, Landoldus de Wiuzelun, Adelbertus de Swercin, et Arnaldus frater eius Richolf us de Banchelsho ven 0 et Foccho et Rödulfus filii sui Egilwarth de Calpfen, Chöno de Seolvingen et Sigefredus frater eius **Adelbertus de Strazza**, **Tuto de Honstetin**, Wipertus de Hönerhusin and others. Klosters Allerheiligen (1080) March 1st Graf Burkhard von Nellenburg, Abbot Wilhelm von Hirsau, Gerolt de Tengin, Gerolt de Buch, **Adelbreht de Strazza** and others (SH:576). Stein Klosters Allerheiligen (1092) February 26th

63

Graf Burkhard von Nellenburg, **Hartwic de Strazza**, Benno de Speicchinga, Diethalm de Tochimburc, Dieterich comes de Biurgeliun(Nellenburg), Herimann de Egga and others (SH:576). Worms (1179) Cv̂hradus pincerna, Arnoldus dapifer de Rötenburc, **Volcmarus Struzo advocatus Goslariensis** and many others (WO:635). Konstanz (1258) Walthero de Ramestain, Berhtoldo de Bvssenanc, **Hainrico de Straze**(Gachnang, Thurgau, Schweiz), Rv̂perto de Tannenvelse, **V̂lrico de Straze** militibus (WO:2192). Ehingen (1263) March 8th Egelolf von Stvezelingin Schwestern(sisters) Mechthilde und Willibirg, Swiggerus senior de Gundiluingin, Wernherus de Stv̂ezelingin, **Ulricus de Straze** and others (WO:2429). Geisingen (1273) April 13th **Konrad** and **Heinrich called Struze**(von Wartenburg), leave the monastery of Wartenberg Salem ownership of the church and other Bolstern called at the request of the tenant farms since it mortgaged. Testibus: Hermanno comite de Sulze. Ber. de Sunthusen. C. et C. de Gv̂tmetingin. H. de Sunthain et **H(einrich). dicto Fridinger(Fridingen)**. De fratribus vero de Salem Hainrico cellerario maiore, Nos **Wernherus de Swarzenbach**, Bernherus, dictus Haller, Wetzlo et Burcardus, and others (WO:796). **Struze/Strauss** in (1273) is believed to come from Heinrich and Konrad von Wartenburg both related by marriage or from the Furst von Hirscheck families. Rorschach (1280) Rudolf and Eglolf of Rorschach certify that their disputes with the cousins of Rosenberg had been settled by arbitration. Conradt von Sultzberg, Ruodolph von Löwinberg(Leuberg), Eberhard II von Burgulon, **Heinrich der Strutz von Wertenberg** (Wartenburg) and many others (MO:2051). Also the largest STRAUSS family of South Africa descends from **Georg Friedrich STRAUSS** (1697-1749). Wappenschilde as an Osterich bird dating back to 1297 Heinrich Struze de Phule. Kloster Niedernburg @ Passau (1430) Anne of Ramsperg, the monastery Dechantin Niedernburg, and waitress Ursula of Ramstorff certify that **Mertein Strauss** and his wife Elspet her brother and brother Kristan Weiss of Great Tungasting and others (MO:423).

h. **Martin s. Marti/Martin.** FTDNA Kit# 254226, 192021, & 158503 for Christian Martin 1669-1748 & David Martin 1691 - 1784 of Switzerland. Marchtal Kloster (776) **sancti Martini** in Stiozaringas(Altsteußlingen) (WO:73). Fridugis (d. 834) "fri-du-zhi" (Fredegisus, Fridigis, Fridugisus, Fredegis, Fredugis) born in England, deacon @ York and left for France 796, appointed ~804 as deacon for St. Martin of Tours by Charlemagne[325]. Mentioned Martinskappelle (cappella superior) to Petershausen (1129) October.

i. **Backer s. Bacher** - Robert P Bacher for ancestor George Bacher in Neckarelz, Baden, Germany shows a MRCA for 24+ generations at 92.03% via Genetic Distance‡2 from Friding/Frydig on 25 markers. They have 3 COA's: One in Obwalden and the other two in Valais (Munster & Sitten). The one from Sitten is similiar to the Fridingen and Steinegg wappen here described: In blue silver links oblique wavy beam, accompanied by the figure of two silver lilies. Salzburg, Austria (1404) **Fridel Pacher**, der Hainrice Nikel and many others (MO:1404).

j. **Medlhammer s. Medilhaimer.** Andreas Medlhammer for ancestor Vitus Medilhaimer (d. 1671) in Velburg, Bavaria shows a MRCA for 24+ generations @ 91.59% via a Genetic Distance‡0 from Friding/Frydig on 25 markers. Berndorf, Salzburg, Austria (1664) **Stephan Medlhammer** to Schwabenwaldt and Hanns Schörgenstötter to Clain-Höpfling (MO:1512).

k. **Landwehr s. Landwehr** for **Michael Allen Landwehr desendant** of Herr von Neiman (~1800) Baden, Wurrtemburg, Germany shows a MRCA for 24+ generations @ 91.41% via a Genetic Distance‡0 from Friding/Frydig on 12 markers. Landwehr defined is bascially a grove Hedge barrier/boundary or natural walls/fences, trench landscape for military defense by preventing outsiders from crossing dating back to the early roman period in Europe. Niedenstein @ Kassel (1474) der Landwehr(lantwere) is translated as "the militia" (MO:9). Neumünster @ Wurzberg (in norther Bavaria) March 24th (1550) Johann Scheffner, Johann Erbar, Michael Landwehr, Georg Prosamer, Peter Koch, Leonhard Weinmann, Martin Glaser, Valentin Hofmann, Martin Hermann, gesessen zu Harthausen (MO:65).

l. **Pushel s. (Puschel/Pueschel/Puzchil/Pusschel/Puschil/Püschel/Püßel/Pewschel/Peuschel/Büschel)**[326] for Stephen Gerald Pushel shows a MRCA for 24+ generations @ 96.96% via a Genetic Distance‡1 from Friding/Frydig on 25 markers. Ducemburgensis ~1160 Johannes Georgius Puschel decanus in Herzogenburg (MGH:428). (1375) November 19th Otto, pastor of St.

Veit im Pongau (Pongowe), represents a pen letter from the Foundation one week exhibition in Goldegg by 2 Marchart dem Pründlinger blessed dedicated, Corporal of the gold Eggern and appropriate goods to Voithub St. Veit in the parish Marchart der Pründlinger blessed and Chunrat sein Prueder and **Hansel der Püschel be Aydem** formerly of the ze rehten loans had habent and habent the tan by the Pründlinger. Würzburg (1408) January 8th **Hermann Peuschel** von Iphofen sold an annual Leibgeding (MO:5339). (1427) October 16 Urfehdebrief of Chuntz Veit Bassaw, Schuhknecht Zwettl, who had been due to death worthy offense in prison. Seal Witnesses: Hans the Puschel, Hans the Gewder (MO:1047a). (1434) **Henne Puschel der junge** (Neumeister 1976:73). (1471) March 21st **Erasm Puschel** Pflegler to Nusdorff whether Traysem, and Dorothy, his wife, sell, Prior Bartholome and the Carthusian convents to Axpach their part in a meadow Genant dŷ Sternŷn (MO:390). Andechs (1521) **Jörg Puchlär**, Richter zu Andechs, verkauft an Christoph Ritter von **Pochsberg**, Abt zu Andechs (BO:1521). Salzburger (1605) **Christoph Püschel**. Rich nobility from 11.20.1635 for **Matthew Püschel** on Bogendorf, Mayor in Schweidnitz (German/Prussian province of Silesia). Wappenschilde COA described as a chevron surrounded by 3 flowers quartered by Black Furstenburg with a lion in between two horns on the crest[327].

m. **Nieman s. Nieman** for **Richard Lewis Nieman** shows a MRCA for 24+ generations @ 88.79% via a Genetic Distance‡2 from Friding/Frydig on 25 markers.

- Alternate ancient Scottish/Irish/English/Normandie(France) families with same Haplotype s. {Bowers, Bidwell, Chandler,Godsey, Hughes, Enos/Hennot, Jones (Wales), Marshall, Maynard, Paige, Penrose, Rose, Shazell, Schly/Sly, Stirling/Sterling, Stewart/Stuart }

- Humphrey s. {Humpfrey/Humphroy/Humfri/Unfridus/Hunfridus/Humfrid}:
Alfred Humphrey (1840) born in Switzerland. Humphrey appears in many English records and limited German records. Although there is a spelling listed as **Humpruee in Thurgau Switzerland** during the 1600's. Other spellings in Schweiz: Hundbrüh, Humprü, Humprüe, Humprüq(en), Hundbrüg, Hundbruh, Hundprüg s. Hundbrüh, Hund-prie, Hundprü, Hundprüe, Huntbruh, Hunt-prew, Huntprüe, Georg Huntprüg, Bürger zu Steckborn (Rohr 1990:166).

   If not German/Schweiz then possibly English & Welsh Origins: Unfrey, also Humphrey from the Welsh name AP-Humphrey when became Bumphrey (Bardsley 1901:122,408). Carls de Grossen son was named Humfried I(markgraf of Rhatien & Istrien) around 800 with a grandson Humfried II (Zurichgau graf) (Fickler 1859:18). Another look into France and Southern England for Hutto, found in (Feudal Cambridgeshire) Croydon 1086 a Humphrey (Unfridus of Eudo the sewer) also in Winepol 1086 (**Anslevilla** of Eudo the sewer), another record for him Hunfridus de Anslevilla (under-tenant of Eudo), a juror Erningford hundred. Also in these records Humphrey the arch deacon of Salisbury[328]. Eude or Eudo is French for the German word "Odo" whom was Bishop of Bayeux/Earl of Kent and the Half Brother to William the Conquerer(Saxon line restored with Edward the confessor 1042). William & **Humphrey** Ancelville(Ansleville) were subtennants of Rojjer de Montgomeri in Hampshire and held 2 houses and a garden under Eudo @ Domesday (Ballard 1904 : 21). Ansleville is Anneville-en-Saire(=Manche community in Normandie) (Keats-Rohan 1999 : 70). According to *Domesday Descendants*, this was land which had been forfeited by William de Ansleville to the de La Haye family. "They are supposed to have been both the sons of **Samson** d 'Ansneville (b4 ~1050) and in that case the extreme parsimony of the King towards them is difficult to explain unless indeed we accept the conjecture that their father came to England with them and was the Equarius guidam regis (Bedfordshire f 218) or the Samson (Staffordshire f 247) inscribed as holding directly of the King. The Annevilles may be traced in Hampshire Bedfordshire Somersetshire &c to the end of the reign of Henry II. At that time Alured d Anneville was assassinated in the latter county. In the reign of King John we find Jordan d'

Anneville, whose wife, Beatrice de Lacy, granted ten acres of land at Elmedon to the Knights Templars"[329] . In the parish of Waltham Kent is the hamlet and green of Hanville so called after the family of Handville or Handheld whose habitation was close to it Several of them lie buried in this church they afterwards removed (Murray 1889:31). Duke William in 1061 gave **Samson Anneville** of his squire and the abbot of Mont Saint Michel half of the island of Guernsey in equal portions to load Samson d Anneville and his heirs to the squire service near his person and his successors when they come in to the island load off ten pounds of relief oath of fealty and all other services due to the Duke and Duchy of Normandy[330]. Another Humphrey occures in the same area: Descendant of Richard Muri (~1032) of Bohun, Normandy. **Humphrey de Bohun** 1071-1093 constable to the King of England - St. Martin @ Marmoutier & St. George @ Bohun. 1134 Charter of Henry I addressed to the archbishop of Rouen - **Humphrey de Ansgervilla** Testibus: **Unfridus de Bohon** and many others. Walter Fitz Humfrey quarterly & sable COA during the 3rd Crusade (1191) from England to the Holy Land (Dansey:134). The Baron seals of Humphrey{Humfridi} de Bohun in 1301 looks like a Kyburg COA with 6 lines 3 split by the diagonal bar – arms dates back before 1240. This line of Bohun has many Humphreys beginning in Normandie before 1130 and ending in 1361. Heinrici de Bohen daughter Matilda married Anselm Marshall {Ancelmo filio et hæredi Willielmi le Mareschall} Earl of Pembroke in Dec 1245. Humphrey de Bohun, Earl of Hereford & Essex, England (1276-1321). A Humfry line[331] occurs by William Humfry born before ~1543 Frior's Manor, Little Sampford, Essex, England. Humphrey Humpreys, Bishop of Hereford, England (1701-1712). Is this Bohun family also the same Gundelfingen from Swabia? So, the question is where does the Humphrey surname become intact? Are the Humfried from Swabia the same as the group from England?

- Hutto s. {Huttow/Hottow/Huto/Otto?/Hotoft/Hotot 1066-1630}: Hotot appears to be the origin of Hutto. The 1st Otto is Ottonis in Aachen (817) June 4th in the Kloster Salem for Kaiser Ludwig (WO:149). Huttos' origin are Lower Palantine Germany and Basel, Switzerland. The 2nd Otto is Kaiser (Emperer) Otto I in (961) May 17th in Worms. There was a Huto II in St. Gallen[332] Switzerland. This Bishop Hatto, even Hato, Hotto and Otto allegedly belonged to the family of the Counts of Sulgen[333]. There is also a Hutto I an Abbott on the Island of Reichenau in Lake Constanz, Germany which was a hot spot for the Fridingishe family. Huodo II appears in 1034. Markgraf Huodo (d. 993) appears in North Thuringen, Germany documents between 979-992. Huodo s. Hudo[334]. The Town of Hutiwil von Norden was at one time first called in the middle of the 9th century as Huttiwilare = hamlet of Hutto[335]. Brixen in Tirol,Austria (1075-90) **Der Frei Hatto** swapped the Brimer church under bishop Altwin for goods in Ekki and other testes Actum Glanhosen/Glanahouen. However, Huddo is in exact vacinity of Fridingen families @ Reichenau, Germany. There maybe a Hutto connection to Hattingen (=Hatto). This following record points back to an earlier family connection between Binzwanger-Sigmaringen (Hattingen) familie and the Hirschecker familie: On January 4th (1083) Heinrich & neffe(nephew) Heinrich von Hirscheck(Altshausen) witnessed a document with Arnold von Binzwanger with brother Manegold & Ludwig and others at the kloster St. Georgen in Schwarzwald (Eberhard | 1964). "Count Berchtold Hattingen gave the monastery of Reichenau entries for 973 Hattingen[336], but appears to be much older" "The name Hattingen means something like "settlement of Hatto" (Wilimski : 1973). The names Hatto, Haddo, Hatho, Hato, Hetto go back (Birlinger : 1878). "The name of our town was originally Hatingen (1208) or Hätingen (1264), ie with a long a, as the unadulterated dialect today says. O. v. Ehrenberg has derived the name of the short form of a personal name Hato or Hatu = battle, see Hadubrand, the Germanic first name[337]". In the words of the personal name Hatto = Heddo =der Krieger/Warrior[338].

However more likely is the Hutto family from the same Hautot's (pronounced "ow-tow") origin of Seine-Maritime or Normandie, France where Hautot is a placename. "Hotot family originated in Normandy Bailiwick of Rouen, where the land is located near Hotot Valley Corbon in the country of Auge & Bishop Bridge between the city of Caen" (Frères 1866:779). Also, mentioned in Domesday Book of 1086 as *Hotoft*[339](in Lincolnshire, England). Hotoft meaning Anglo-Norse place name : Old English *hoh* "decline", "slope" and Old Norse *topt* "site of a house"[340]. Same name as the <u>Hottot</u>; Hotot (f. e. <u>Hotot-en-Auge</u>) ; Hautot (former *Hotot*. f. e. <u>Hautot-sur-Seine</u>) in Normandy[341]. Unclear wether Jean de Houdetot (Veauville parish families) signer of Houdetot in Caux (1034) Normandie during the war with William the Conqueror is related to Hotot although later (1219) there is a Pierre de Hotot @ church tithes of Foville/Fauville. While searching for Humphrey connections: (Feudal Cambridgeshire) Croydon 1086 a Humphrey (Unfridus of Eudo the sewer) also in Winepol 1086 (**Anslevilla** of Eudo the sewer), another record for him **Hunfridus de Anslevilla** (under-tenant of Eudo), a juror Erningford hundred. Also in these records Humphrey the arch deacon of Salisbury[342]. Eude or Eudo is French for the German word "Odo" whom was Bishop of Bayeux/Earl of Kent and the Half Brother to William the Conquerer. **William & Humphrey Ancelville(Ansleville)** were subtennants of Rojjer de Montgomeri in Hampshire and held 2 houses and a garden under Eudo @ Domesday (Ballard 1904:21). Ansleville is Anneville-en-Saire(=Manche community in Normandie) (Keats-Rohan 1999:70). According to *Domesday Descendants*, this was land which had been forfeited by **William de Ansleville** to the de La Haye family. "They are supposed to have been both the sons of **Samson** d 'Ansneville (b4 ~1050) and in that case the extreme parsimony of the King towards them is difficult to explain unless indeed we accept the conjecture that their father came to England with them and was the Equarius guidam regis (Bedfordshire f 218) or the Samson (Staffordshire f 247) inscribed as holding directly of the King. ~1060 "Notification that one of the nobles named Hugh Tale both gave to Holy Trinity the tithe of Sanreith and that Walo a oca wno afterwards possessed that land gladly conirmed the gift their successor **Osbern de Ansevilla** admitted to the fellowship of the abbey has himself confirmed their gift. [Signa] Hugonis Talebot; Walonis de la Roca; **Osberai de Ansevilla; Osberni de Hotot** Testes: Gulbertus de Ou; Osbertus de Albertivilla; Heddo de Canaan; Rodulfus filius Hermeri; Rodulfus de Pauliaco; Osbernus filius Goiffredi de Ou; Gozelinus de Alladio" (Round 1899:24). The author of the History of the Royal Abbey of Saint Pierre de Jumièges after reporting provisions of the agreement which we give the text adds such is the origin of the **manor of Hauville** land that **William and Osberne Hautot/Hotot** had data the abbey in 1073 in the scope of a fief which had been alms to the year 1056 by Gilbert Crespin he was given the name of abbot Court in the course of time Edict J abbot (Lestringant 1916: 146). Some noble names within England or France: **Osberni de Ansleville, Osberni de Hotot 1060**, The **Sire de Hotot/Sire d'Asneville (brother to Samson?)** en Auge, is appointed governor to Val-de-Saire from among the knights who astistoient their Duke William the Bastard, to the conquest of England in 1066 and many others on the Dive's roll: **Honfroi d'Ansleville, Guillaume d'Ansleville, Raoul de Hauville, Hugue de Hoto** & **D'Houdetot**. Guillaume et Osberne de **Hautot** 1080, Hugh de Hotot 1086 sub tenant under Countess Judith, William Hotot 1129/1130 son of Wiliam I de Albina-Brito, Willemus de Hotot 1148 @ Norman place-name called Hotot/Hautot[343], Charter of Hugh -Richard du Hommet @ Rouen 1160, Gislebertus de Hotot 1164, Haman de Hotot (1168-90), Roger de Hotot 1172 @ Clermont, Guillaume du Hommet Connetable du Normandie des 1175, Charter of Richard I (1190) June 8th Testibus: Ricardo de Humeto, Nicholoa de Hotot, Thomas de Hotot, Thoma de Otot ~1200, Guillaume du Hommet Barons de Normandie assemblerent a Rouen en 1205, cirencester Gloucestershire (England) Henrico Hotot (Aug 1 1209), Peiere de Hotot 1214, Lichfield Staffordshire (England) Ricardo Hotot (July 22 1236), Henry de Hotot 1237, Roger de Hotot 1247, Robert de Hotot 1284 & 1294, Fulco de Hotot de Botlesford 1271, Thomas & Radulfo de Hotot 1286, Sir vincent hutot {*azure seme of tencelles gold has a silver lion*}[344] – "Nicolas Hotot, fl.1302, o.s.p.m., S.Hotot, son of Jean and Luce d'Harcourt. He commanded a ship in 1295 in the fleet of his cousin Jean d'Harcourt. Hotot-en-Caux or Hautot-sur-Mer, dep Seine-Maritime, arr Dieppe, can Offrainville" (Clemmensen 08:28), theologien professuer Raoul de Hotot 1308, Thomas de Hotot (1309) Seigneur du Hommet, doctuer Radolphus de Hoitet 1310, William de Hotot/Hotos 1330's(?) >English Parliamentary Roll> COA, Richard de Hotot 1337 & 1339, Jean de Hotot ~1356, monsr Robt Hotot {azure a cross patonce argent between four roses or}[345] possibly Robert Hotot, Kt., JP and on commissions in Suffolk between 1386-1398. The same arms were borne by Robert Hotot (fl.1298-

67

1326) of Turvey & Stagsden in Beds. The cross is formy in the older and was probably blazoned eslargie, which may be tranlated as either patonce or formy (Brault EB 157)" (Clemmensen 08:79). Nicholas Hawto/Hawte(Hawe in Ashmole) COA>> bore @ the siege of Rouen 1418 bend azure 3 Lions passant[346]. Thomas & Robert 1463, and Sier de Hotot 1630 en Normandie[347]. Sir William Hawte of Kent had a quatered arms with cross, per pale azure with gules and Lion passant found in the Arundell Roll. Many Yonn/Yon and Hattow/Hottow marriages have connections between Orangeburg, SC and Bolbec, France - Isaac Yon (1640) and Judith Hautot (1638) married in 21 October 1657 in Lintot ER, Seine-Maritime, France. Martin Friday (1783), David Friday (1776), Daniel Friday (1813) and some of their descendants lived near the Hutto family in Orangeburg, SC, however no marriages were known. No affiliation found during the 1800's. So, the questions come forward: Were the Hotot/Anneville family originally related from England/France centuries before (746 end of Franks control of Swabia) **Samson** d 'Ansneville (b4 ~1050) or did they migrate recently in from Swabia prior to the 1066 Norman invasion of England by William the Conquerer?

Kit #	Paternal Ancestor Name	Country	Haplo group	Dys 393	Dys 390	Dys 19	Dys 391	Dys 385	Dys 426	Dys 388	Dys 439	Dys 389 I	Dys 392	Dys 389 Ii	Dys 458	Dys 459	Dys 455	Dys 454	Dys 447	Dys 437	Dys 448	Dys 449	Dys 464	Dys 460	Ygata H4	Ycaii
	Hutto Project																								
259744	John Bailey, b. 1810	Unknown	R1b1a	13	24	14	10	11-14	12	12	12	13	13	29	18	9-10	11	11	25	16	18	29	14-15-16-17	10	11	19-23
130890	Andrew Hutto, b c	Unknown	J2	12	25	15	10	12-15	11	16	12	12	11	28	15	8-9	11	11	28	16	19	29	13-15-15-19	11	10	19-20
56942	George Hutto b.c.17	Unknown	I2b1	15	23	15	10	15-16	11	13	11	13	12	30	15	8-9	11	11	25	14	20	27	11-14-14-16	11	9	19-21
241367	George S. Hutto, b	Germany	I2b1	15	23	15	10	15-16	11	13	11	13	12	30	15	8-9	11	11	25	14	20	27	11-14-14-16	11	9	19-21
181842	William H D Hutto, b	Unknown	I2b1	15	23	15	10	15-16	11	13	11	13	12	30	15	8-9	11	11	25	14	20	27	11-14-14-16	11	9	19-21
90677	Isaac Hottow/Hutto	Unknown	I2b1	15	23	15	10	15-16	11	13	11	13	12	30	15	8-9	11	11	25	14	20	27	11-14-14-16	11	9	19-21
94981	Jason Hutto b 1820	Unknown	I2b1	15	23	15	10	15-16	11	13	11	13	12	30	15	8-9	11	11	25	14	20	27	11-14-14-16	11	9	19-21
119090	John Castleberry Hu	Unknown	I2b1	15	23	15	10	15-16	11	13	11	13	12	30												
62876	George S. Hutto, b.	Unknown	I2b1	15	23	15	10	15-16	11	13	11	13	12	30	15	9-9	11	11	25	14	20	27	14-14-14-14	11	9	19-21
62610	John Andrew Jacks	Unknown	I2b1	15	23	15	10	15-16	11	13	11	13	12	30	15	8-9	11	11	25	14	20	27	11-14-14-16	11	9	19-21
58463	David Hutto, b.c. 17	Unknown	I2b1	15	23	15	10	15-16	11	13	11	13	12	30	15	8-9	11	11	25	14	20	27	11-14-14-16	11	9	19-21
68634	Nicholas Hutto b 18	Germany	I1	14	22	14	10	13-14	11	14	11	13	11	29	15	8-9	8	11	22	16	20	31	13-14-15-15	10	10	20-21
83411	Peter Friding, 1403	Switzerlan	I2b1	15	23	15	10	15-15	11	13	11	14	12	32	15	8-10	11	11	25	14	20	28	11-14-14-16	10	10	19-21

Dys456	Dys607	Dys576	Dys 570	Cdy	Dys 442	Dys 438	Dys 531	Dys 578	Dyf 395 S	Dys 590	Dys 537	Dys 641	Dys 472	Dyf 406 S	Dys 511	Dys 425	Dys 413	Dys 557	Dys 594	Dys 436	Dys 490	Dys 534	Dys 450	Dys 444	Dys 481	Dys 520	Dys 446	Dys 617	Dys 568	Dys 487	Dys 572	Dys 640	Dys 492	Dys 565	DYS710	DYS485	DYS632	DYS495	
15	15	21	17	34-36	11	12	11	9	15-16	9	10	10	8	10	10	12	23-23	17	10	12	12	16	8	12	22	19	13	12	11	13	11	11	12	12					
13	14	16	17	36-38	12	9	11	8	15-17	8	12	10	8	10	9	12	21-23	16	11	12	12	16	8	12	23	20	12	12	11	14	10	13	12	11					
14	14	17	18	31-38	13	10																																	
14	14	17	18	31-38	13	10																																	
14	14	17	18	31-38	13	10																																	
14	14	17	18	31-38	13	10																																	
14	14	17	18	31-38	12	10																																	
14	14	17	18	38-38	13	10																																	
14	14	17	18	31-38	13	10																																	
14	14	16	20	35-35	12	10																																	
14	14	17	20	34-40	12	10	12	8	15-16	8	12	10	8	10	9	12	22-22	15	11	12	12	13	9	14	27	20	11	14	12	12	11	12	12	11	31	13	8	15	1

Result: Genetic distance 9+ (15 of 24) markers defined by FTDNA: >6 You are totally unrelated to this person. Joel H Hutto descendant of George H confirmed CTS6433>Z171- SNP in 2014.

- Humes s. {Hume/Home/Holmes?} William Leroy Humes, David Decker Humes & Larry Frank Humes for ancestor Thomas Humes ~1760 Ireland shows a MRCA for 24+ generations @ 72.80% via a Genetic Distance‡2 from Friding/Frydig on 25 markers. Ryan David Holmes for ancestor Moses Holmes Sr ~1751 from Ireland to New York then Canada shows a MRCA for 24+ generations @ 90.95% via a Genetic Distance‡2 from Friding/Frydig on 25 markers. Some surname origins and mentions: Many surname forms are found in the early records: Hum, Hom, Heum, Hoome etc. Scotland, "Hume which gives Sirname to that Great Family and was formerly the Residence of the Earls of Hume whose strong Castle there is now demolished"[348]. "The Homes are said to be descended from the **Saxon princes of Northumbria**, through Cospatrick I, Earl of Dunbar (d. 1081)"[349]. Cospatrick fled to Scotland from Northern England in 1066, carried with him the Edger Atheling, the heir to the Saxon line and his two sisters Margarete and Christina (Hume 1903:34). Hume comes from the latin word for land (Hume 1903: 6). Patrick de Home coat of arms right comes from Dunbar coat of arm in Red background[350]. In my opinion this appears to be a very early family prior to 700 a.d due to the 72% percentile shown on the DNA Tip report for distance. "These individuals (CTS6433) <u>do not appear to be descended from the ancient Home/Hume lines from Scotland</u> and may have obtained their surnames via a Non Paternal Event (NPE), such as taking the surname of the wife, straight surname change, illegitimate birth, adoption, etc (James R Hume 2014)".

Kit #	Paternal Ancestor Name/Project	Country	Haplo group	Dys 393	Dys 390	Dys 19	Dys 391	Dys 385	Dys 426	Dys 388	Dys 439	Dys 389 I	Dys 392	Dys 389 II	Dys 458	Dys 459	Dys 455	Dys 454	Dys 447	Dys 437	Dys 448	Dys 449	Dys 464	Dys 460	Ygata H4
	Hume/Home Project																							
150558	Andrew Hume b.1690, Du	England	I-CTS6433	14	23	15	10	15-15	11	13	11	14	12	32	15	8-10	11	11	25	14	20	27	11-11-14-14	11 10	1
117885	Moses Holmes, b. 1751-1	Unknown C	I-M223	15	23	15	10	15-15	11	13	11	14	12	32	15	8-10	11	11	24	14	20	28	11-14-15-15	11 10	1
148361	Thomas Humes b.c. 1760	Ireland	I-CTS6433	15	23	15	10	15-15	11	13	11	14	12	32	15	8-10	11	11	25	14	20	27	11-11-14-14	11 10	1
200759		Unknown C	I-CTS6433	15	23	15	10	15-15	11	13	11	14	12	32	15	8-10	11	11	25	14	20	27	11-11-14-14	11 10	1
B3411	Peter Friding, 1403 - afte	Switzerlan	I-CTS6433	15	23	15	10	15-15	11	13	11	14	12	32	15	8-10	11	11	25	14	20	28	11-14-14-15	10 10	1

Ycaii	Dys456	Dys607	Dys576	Dys 570	Cdy	Dys 442	Dys 438	Dys 531	Dys 578	Dyf 395 S	Dys 590	Dys 537	Dys 641	Dyf 406 S	Dys 511	Dys 425	Dys 413	Dys 557	Dys 594	Dys 436	Dys 490	Dys 534	Dys 450	Dys 444	Dys 481	Dys 520	Dys 446	Dys 617	Dys 568	Dys 487	Dys 572	Dys 640	Dys 492	Dys 565	DYS710	DYS485	DYS632	DYS495
19-21	14	14	17	20	31-38	12	10	11	8	15-16	8	11	10	8	10	9	12	22-22	15	11	12	12	13	9	13	26	20	12	13	12	12	11	12	12	11			
19-21	16	14	16	17	35-41	11	10																															
19-21	14	14	17	20	31-36	12	10	11	8	15-16	8	11	10	8	10	9	12	22-22	15	11	12	12	14	9	13	26	20	12	13	12	12	11	12	12	11	33	13 8	15
19-21	14	14	17	20	31-37	12	10																															
19-21	14	14	17	20	34-40	12	10	12	8	15-16	8	12	10	8	10	9	12	22-22	15	11	12	12	13	9	14	27	20	11	14	12	12	11	12	12	11	31	13 8	15

- Eno/Enos 1700[+] s. {Henne 1401/de Henne/ Hennot/ Henno/ Hannot /Hanot}

DNA.ancestry.com results for Donald Q Eno (MRCA=7gen), Charles Timothy Enos (MRCA=19gen), Mark Imler Eno (MRCA=25gen). Some surname origins and mentions: (906) Tarrif rates for Ostland, Markgrafen Aribo zu Raffelstätten (over Austria) who took the oath: Salaman, Reinolt, Gerolt, **Henno**, Humperht, and many others mentioned (MO:906). St. Remy de Sens, France, Cartulaire général de Yonne (May 1234) **Gilo de Henot** and others (MO: 2360415). Robert de Hennot 1239 in Normandie[351]. Richard Hennot 1249 in Wiltshire. Robert de Hennot 1433 in France[352]. France (1159) **S. Henot, sacristæ** (=St. Enos, the sacristy) documented in Cartulaire de Saint-Cyr de Nevers (MO:02270112). "The first of the name of whom we have authentic record was Collard Henno, of Mons (the capital of the ancient county of Hainault), whose presence at the reception of Burghers, in Valenciennes, is given in the Registry of Burghers of that city under the date of February 7, 1463" (Leach:1934). COA described as: Azure, a chevron argent, two estoiles d'or in chief, crescent argent in point. A Tuetonic names book has the following: Old Germ- Anna, Anno, Enno, Hanno, & Henno 5th century. English- Anne Hann Hanna Hanney Henn Henney. Modern German- Hanne Henne. French –Anne, Anne, Hanna, Hanna, Harry, Henne, Henno & Enne (Ferguson 1864: 289). Francois Anould Hannot 1661. "Hainault or HAINAUT" is the French name of the Belgian province which is called Henegouw in Flemish and Hennegau in German names signifying the gau or district on the River Haisne Haine or Henne, called Hagna in the tenth century The oldest forms of the name Hainault are Hagnauvum terriiorium and Hainan pagus both dating from the seventh century" (Taylor 1898: 140).

Kit #	Paternal Ancestor Name	Country	Haplo group	Dys 393	Dys 390	Dys 19	Dys 391	Dys 385	Dys 426	Dys 388	Dys 439	Dys 389 I	Dys 392	Dys 389 Ii	Dys 458	Dys 459	Dys 455	Dys 454	Dys 447	Dys 437	Dys 448	Dys 449	Dys 464	Dys 460	Ygata H4
	Eno/Enos/Hennot																								
Ancestry.com	Donald Q Eno - 9		I2b1	15	23	15	10	15-15	11	13	11	14	12	32	15		11	11	25		20	27	11-14-14-15	10 10	
	Charles Timothy Enos - 16		I2b1	15	23		10	15-15	11	13	11	14	12	32	15		11	11	25		20	27	11-14-14-15	10 10	
	Mark Imler Eno - 31		I2b1	15	23		10	15-15	11	13	11	14	12	32	15		11	11	25		20	27	11-14-14-15	10 10	
B3411	Peter Friding, 1403	Switzerlan	I2b1	15	23	15	10	15-15	11	13	11	14	12	32	15	8-10	11	11	25	14	20	28	11-14-14-15	10 10	

Ycaii	Dys456	Dys607	Dys576	Dys 570	Cdy	Dys 442	Dys 438	Dys 531	Dys 578	Dyf 395 S	Dys 590	Dys 537	Dys 641	Dys 472	Dyf 406 S	Dys 511	Dys 425	Dys 413	Dys 557	Dys 594	Dys 436	Dys 490	Dys 534	Dys 450	Dys 444	Dys 481	Dys 520	Dys 446	Dys 617	Dys 568	Dys 487	Dys 572	Dys 640	Dys 492	Dys 565	DYS710	DYS485
19-21					10																																
19-21					10																																
19-21					10																																
19-21	14	14	17	20	34-40	12	10	12	8	15-16	8	12	10	8	10	9	12	22-22	15	11	12	12	13	9	14	27	20	11	14	12	12	11	12	12	11	31	13

- Page s. {Paige/Page/Pagham/Pagenham/Pageham}:
Page DNA kit for Norman Hugh Page and ancestor being Sir Richard Page (~1330) exact markers with no steps between 25/37 markers. 15 other Page familys are inluded in this Y-DNA match with 0 steps. "Probably the earliest record for the Page family was 1151/1157 for John de Pagham the 4th bishop & dicoese of Worcester, England" (Cutter 1913:454). "The arms of all these Page families bear a resemblance to each other and doubtless they were all descended from the same ancestor The origin of the name of Page as a family cognomen may be found in Rymers Foedera Acts of the Kings of England in 41st Henry III AD 1257 when it appears that Hugo de Pageham of Ebor York was a bearer of dispatches from Edward King of England to the King of Spain and thus being Letter Bearer or Page he became known as Hugo Page de Pageham[353]" (RCM Page 1883:15). Sir Gregory Page of England had sons whom came to America after 1600.

- Biddulph s. {Bidwell/Biddall/Biddell/Biddle}
Robert James Bidwell & Richard Francis Bidwell for ancestor Richard Bidwell (~1606/1620) shows a MRCA for 24+ generations @ 91.41% via a Genetic Distance‡0 from Friding/Frydig on 12 markers. A New York writer said the Bidwell family came from England and is derived from a Saxon name Biddulph[354] meaning war wolf. One of the oldest castles is Biddulph built in Norfolk County, England in 1066 the same years as the William the Conqueror. It is said one of Williams generals married the Biddulph heiress and of that time and assumed her name". Many names are derived from this Saxon Biddulph, the ones being used are Bidwell, Biddle, Biddell (Cutter 2009:378). Thomas de Biddulph of Staffordshire coat of arms during the 1300's was vertical Eagle covering the shield. Another arms was 3 soldering irons in sable.

- Chandler s. {Chandelier/Candelarius/Chaundeler }
Eddie Chandler for ancestor John Chandler (~1600) St. Margertes, Westminster, London England. Also Dean Wade Chandler for ancestor Henry Isham Chandler (~1811) both show a MRCA for 24+ generations a 91.33% Genetic Distance‡2 steps from Friding/Frydig with a 25 marker compare. Other Chandlers show about the same: Chris Chandler 97.72%, Ronald Ewing Chandler 91.85% and Michael David Chandler 91.33% for 25 markers. Other family name variations in England & Normandie occur (Chandler, Chandlier, Chandeler, Candelarius, etc). The name Chandler defined as a maker of candles or French for chandelle[355]. Matthew le Candeler/le Chaundeler in St. Clements 1274, Nicholas Chandeler and his nephew John Wymund de Stenhale London 1283, William le Chandeler 1285, *Gilbertus Candelarius*, a monk of Préaux in the fourteenth century, Adam le Chandeler 1290,1309, Reginald le Chandiler living at St Michael le Quern and William his son 1290, Richard Chandler of St. Ives(?) approached Richard Swift[356] of Over for a wager in 1316, Stephen Chandler wife Margaret was Nurse for Edward II in France 1324, John Swyft alias Chandler canon of Salisbury 1390, Roger Mymmes Roger de 'chandeler' St. Alphage, Cripplegate. Mentions cousin John le Chandeler in Jwerielane 1351, John Chaundeler rector of Werbelington 1391, John Chaundeler treasurer of Salisbury, England 1394, Jehan le Chandelier 1452-58 Normandie, Godefridus Candelarius 1499, Gulliame de Chandlier (+1502) sculptor Dijon France. COA image from Chandler Hotel>> prior to 1775 by Herald College of England described as Azure Checkered(occasionaly Red) Three Lions Pasant in Argent bend, Gules (Pelican nursing young with her Blood).

- Bratly s. {Haugen/Helfenstein?}

William George Bratly for ancestor Peder Andersen Haugen c1646 Beitstad, Norway shows a MRCA for 24+ generations a 100% Genetic Distance‡4 steps from Friding/Frydig with a 37 marker compare. Bishop Haugen(Hugo) of Wirzburg buried in St. Peter 990ad. Some research in 1644 shows Haugen in Alemagne[357] with the similar coat of arms as the Hefenstein family. "DIË HAUGEN en Alemagne coupé de gueules sur argent, a un demy Eléphant rampants contourné de l'un en l'autre la taille dégoutant du sang". Translated: Die Haugen in Alemagne Gules and Argent, a demy Elephant bypassed crawling from one another in the size of blood disgusting. I believe the Hefenstain was part of the early Gundelfingen line of which is a parallel line to Hirschecker. Giengen (1171) May 1st comes Otto de Chirberg, **Ludewicus comes de Helphenstein**, Degenhardus de Helonsten, Folenandus de Stuophe, **Diemo et Godefridus frater eius de Gundelfingen** and others (WO:613). Many German records show Haugen a 1st name as early 1318 into the 1600's. Another records shows a farmstead Haugen near Glomma[358] in SE Norway which has Viking age burials prior to 900ad.

a. Orville Edward Bowers for ancestor George Bowers (1590) Scotland shows a MRCA for 24+ generations @ 88.79% via a Genetic Distance‡2 from Friding/Frydig on 25 markers.
b. Aaron Marshell/Marshall for ancestor John Marshall (~1596) Isle of Wright , England shows a MRCA for 24+ generations @ 89.39% via a Genetic Distance‡2 from Friding/Frydig on 25 markers. De **maarschalk** {Lat. *Marscalcus* of *Marescalcus campi*} Field Marshall or commander in chief.
c. **Sly s. {Sly/Schly 1327}** - Richard Allen Sly for ancestor Jenkins Sly (~1783) from Scotland(?) MRCA for 24+ generations @ 100% via a Genetic Distance‡4 from Friding/Frydig on 37 markers. The Sly family settled in New York prior to 1809. Some ancient history on the name: **Peter Sly and Willaim Sly** (Village of Hemingford Abbots), **William & Richard Sly** (Village of Hadden), in the County of Huntingdonshire (1327). **John Sly** and wife Cristina of Hemingford Abbotts (Godmanchester) 1362. John Sly and his wife Margarete in Hemingford Abbots in (1439) November 11th. **William Sly** played "a fool of fashion" in a Tudor & Stuart play called "The Malcontent" in (1604) (Taylor & Francis 1961:234). Register of Baptisms of the French Protestant Refugees Settled at Thorney (1703-4) Jan 28 Jeremie f d'Abraham Ris et Damoiselle Dorothee Peirson, n Jan 19 T Les Sieurs Charles Whinyeats et **Walter Sly**; Madame Susanne Peirson femme de Monsr Ralph Peirson escuyer. (1704-5) Walter Sly femme is shown to be Madame Susan Peirson. Before 1718 **Walter Sly** married 2nd Susan Dundalk (from Ireland) – other family members **Peirson Sly, John Sly**, another Walter Sly of which they are living @ the Isle of Ely (Cambridge). (1720) **Mr Walter Sly** on the jury for the Manor of Thormey Abbey (Warner 1879:250).
d. **Sterling s Stirling/Starling** : Charles John Sterling jr for ancestor John Sterling 1798 Londonderry, Ireland had a MRCA for 24+ generations @ 89.34% via a Genetic Distance‡2 from Friding/Frydig on 25 markers. William Roy Sterling MRCA for 24+ generations @ 91.44% via a Genetic Distance‡2 from Friding/Frydig on 25 markers. Paul Noel Starling MRCA for 24+ generations @ 57.88% via a Genetic Distance‡2 from Friding/Frydig on 25 markers.
e. **Hughes s. Hew/Hewe/Huse** for **Randall Lamar Hughes, Dr. William Daniel Hughes and Richard Hughes** shows a MRCA for 24+ generations @ 97.17% via a Genetic Distance‡4 from Friding/Frydig on 37 markers. Kit# 141096 Reddick Hughs, b.c. 1795, Johnston County, N.C. *Multiple surname origins are believed to exist in different countries.*
Some possible English & French origins: Hugues was a popular first name, so this maybe conicidence. "mesire **hue** de bauchei d'or a un fer de moulin de gheules tur
1 O G cross moline **Hugues** (IX) de Baucay, d.<1309, S.Baucay (Baussay-le-Noble, dep Vienne, arr & can Loudun, cne Mouterre-Silly) & Champigny-sur-Veude, son of Guy (d.1270) and Emma Dm.Blou & Champigny, served in Aragon 1285 and in Flanders 1304. He inherited Baucay from his uncle **Heugues** (VIII, d.1270)" (Clemmensen 08:28). Thomas Hughes 1287 near Bath, England[359].

Some possible <u>Germanic</u> name origins: Rom (1098) *Husechirche/* Hosskirch/Hoßkirch (WO:386). (1151) Reimbert von Murecke abte @ St. Paul(Austria) testes: **Wernher de Huse**, Otto de Liebeniz, Heinricus de Melnich, Heinricus de Wizze, et Gotscalcus de Goᵞnowitz, Engelscalcus de Murekke and others (MO:1151). Ulm (1226) exists for which the surety **Rv̊dolfus de Hewe** of how such a noble man, if said **Rv̊dolfus de Hewe** (Hohehhewen) natural pay debts, and John de Dirbehein, Burchard of Hohinburc testes: H. comes de Dilingen, E. dapifer de Walpurch, C. et E. pincerne de Winterstetin, Dieto de Rauinspurch and others (WO:1079). Innichen (1269) Heinrici de Welfsperch nec non Swikeri de Richenberch, Heinrico canonico Frisingensi, Chvnrado decano Inticensi, Hermanno et Wernhardo canonicis sancti Andree Frisingensis, **Vlrico de Huse** and many more (MO:102). Neutoggenburg (1270) Friedrich II & Diethalmus counts of Toggenburc(Toggenburg), Wecilo dictus Schnoede "Dienstmann=service man" and said **Rvodolfus vamme Huse(Husen)** town of Wile all the presents inspectors greeting (MO:1857). Matrei (in Osttirol) (1271) **Härtung v. Haus (Huse)** and many others unrecognized (MO:1271). Konstanz (1309) January 31st Wilhelm von Steinach(Rorschach) und sein Sohn Wilhelm verkaufen dem Heiliggeistspital St. Gallen den Hof Achen. Cûnrat von Bûchegge, **Johans Vᵒlriche vom Huse** ritter, her Hartman der Munche von Basel pfaffe, Walther von Honberch(Ravenburg, BW), Hainrich der Giger and others (MO:2714). Lengenfeld, Austria (1334) Ulrich, at the church to Lengenfeld, leaves the convent Imbach 2 Pfenning Gülte that **Ulrich der Hew** had been giving him a paddock and an orchard whose property is now entitled to the monastery to Lengenfeld and his wife (MO:214).

Kit #	Paternal Ancestor Name	Country	Haplo group	Dys 393	Dys 390	Dys 19	Dys 391	Dys 385	Dys 426	Dys 388	Dys 439	Dys 389 I	Dys 392	Dys 389 II	Dys 458	Dys 459	Dys 455	Dys 454	Dys 447	Dys 437	Dys 448	Dys 449	Dys 464	Dys 460	Ygata H4	Ycaii
	Hughes Project																								
179632	George Hughes	Unknown	I2b1	15	23	15	10	15-15	11	13	11	13	12	30	15	8-10	11	11	25	14	20	29	11-14-14-15	11	9	19-21
183828		Wales	I2b1	15	23	15	10	15-15	11	13	11	13	12	31	15	8-10	11	11	25	14	20	28	11-14-14-15	11	9	19-21
141096	Reddick Hughs, b.c.	Unknown	I2b1	15	23	15	10	15-15	11	13	11	13	12	31	15	8-10	11	11	25	14	20	28	11-14-14-15	11	9	19-21
250619	John Hughes	Wales	I2b1	14	23	15	10	15-17	11	13	11	14	12	32												
212482	John Hughes	Wales	I2b1	14	23	15	10	15-17	11	13	11	14	12	32	17	8-9	12	11	25	14	20	27	11-14-14-15	11	10	19-21
258788	John Hughes b. - d.	Wales	I2b1	14	23	15	10	15-17	11	13	11	14	12	32	17	8-9	12	11	25	14	20	27	11-14-14-15	11	10	19-21
B3411	Peter Friding, 1403	Switzerlan	I2b1	15	23	15	10	15-15	11	13	11	14	12	32					15	14	20	28	11-14-14-15	10	10	19-21

Dys456	Dys607	Dys576	Dys570	Cdy	Dys 442	Dys 438	Dys 531	Dys 578	Dyf 395 S	Dys 590	Dys 537	Dys 641	Dys 472	Dyf 406 S	Dys 511	Dys 425	Dys 413	Dys 557	Dys 594	Dys 436	Dys 490	Dys 534	Dys 450	Dys 444	Dys 481	Dys 520	Dys 446	Dys 617	Dys 568	Dys 487	Dys 572	Dys 640	Dys 492	Dys 565	DYS710	DYS485	DYS632	DYS495
14	13	17	19	34-40	12	10																																	
14	14	17	19	34-40	12	10																																	
14	14	17	20	35-40	12	10	11	8	15-16	8	11	10	8	10	9	12	21-22	15	11	12	12	13	9	13	28	20	11	13	12	12	10	12	12	11				
15	13	17	19	34-39	12	10																																	
15	13	17	19	34-40	12	10																																	
14	14	17	20	34-40	12	10	12	8	15-16	8	12	10	8	10	9	12	22-22	15	11	12	12	13	9	14	27	20	11	14	12	12	11	12	12	11	31	13	8	15

f. **Rose s. Rose** for **Kennth J Rose** (Kit# 6926 ancestor= ThomasR (Ann Leonard) 1806 Bucks Eng to MA 1837) **& Steven M Rose** (Kit# 25798 ancestor= Walter W R 1881 (m Florence Lycett 1909) ENG) shows a MRCA for 24+ generations @ 90.99% via a Genetic Distance‡2 from Friding/Frydig on 25 markers.

g. **Penrose** for Raymond Penrose for ancestor Michael Penrose b1811-12 in Kilanenn (Killinierin) County Wexford Ireland d1888 in Lindsay, Ontario Canada shows a MRCA for 24+ generations @ 97.52% via a Genetic Distance‡4 from Friding/Frydig on 37 markers. Ray presumes "Michael's family was probably part of the emigration from Cornwall in 1750-52 at the time Cromwell put down the Irish revolt". A family of Penrose dates back before 1066 to Sithney[360], Cornwall, England. The Coat of arms prior to 1531 is "Ermine on a bend azure three roses or but subsequently the blazon was as noted above on tablet and window of St.Sithuinus" (Leach/Penrose 1903:3). Also in crest was a Loo trout an emblem of Chasity for this Cornish family. In Pennsylvania, Sarah (Owen) Biddle wife of James Penrose had a son named Clement Biddle Penrose (1771) who married Ann H Bingham[361]. <- Pointing out the Biddle(Bidwell?) and Penrose connection Friding/Frydig has to both names genetically.

- Distant Related I2B1 within a large Surname HG of non-I2B1 members.
Surname projects that have "a" matching Haplogroup.
a. Frey/Fry/Fray (3 of 73) only produced 3 in Haplogroup I2B1 out of 73 individuals.
b. Ritter/Reitter/Ridder produced only 1 result for I2B1 Johann Ritter ca. ~1740 in Baden, Germany out of 49 individuals.
c. Godfreu/Godsey (5 of 35), Green/Greene (12 of 331), Hurst (2 of 78), Murphy (4 of 284), Martin (12 of 505), Schroeder/Shrader (1 of 25), Schwarts/Schwartz (2 of 72), Arnold (5 of 86), Woolf (5 of 142).
d. Bishop/Bischoff (3 of 50) most of the group is R1b1a2. 1 exact match @ 12 markers Kit#234825 for Paul D Bishop. Boling/Bolin (6 of 60) (most R1b1a2), Stewart/Stuart (11 of 750)
e. Stumpf/Stumb s. Bistumb?(2 of 16).
Source: Family Tree DNA Surname Project results.

- Not Y-DNA Related in over 13k-14, 000+ years to Haplogroup I2B1.
Surname projects that have no matching Haplogroups.
a. Flick/Fleck/Fleek produced 0 results for I2B1 out of 10 individuals.
b. Flückiger/Flickinger produced 0 results for I2B1 out of 7 individuals from Switzerland and Austria.
c. other families with no related members: Bean, Geiger, Garvin, Zehner, Towler/Toler, Schwarcz, Marks, Jumper/Schumpert, Otto, St. Germain, Ammerman, Shuler/Schüler(Bern), Altman, and Ernst (Prussian)..
d. Friede produced 0 results as G-M377 for ancestor Friede born (1747).
Source: Family Tree DNA Surname Project results.

- Family Surname Related/Associated , Not Y-DNA Related - possible marriage
or known relatives or connections in Genealogy. *Surname Count(Haplogroup)*
I Haplo families: Rauls/Rawls 2(I1-M170), Hinton shows mostly in I1 and R1b1b2, Wooten 5+(I1-M253 & R-M269), Heinrick Goats/Guess (I-L126), Wyss/Weiss (I1-M170), Richard Odum (1727) (I1A2B->Z138),
G Haplo families: Pou 2(G),
J Haplo families: Roll/Rolls 2(J-CTS7683),
R1 Haplo families: Thomas Ammons 1(R-L47), Hinton shows mostly in I1 and R1b1b2, Selfe/Selfe 10(R-M269/R-L48), Spillman 4(R1....), Hapsburg/Krise 18(R-L2), Berryman, Berry (most R1b1b2), Bledsoe 3(R1B1), Blue/Blaw, Bolling/Bolin 1(most R1b1a2), Brodie (R-M269), Ray (R-L21), Gregg/Grigg 20+(R-M269/R-L48), Schüler +4(E1b1b1), Strothers 20(R1....), Suddeth 10(R1...), Geiger/Gyger 5(E, R1 & T), Weber 1(R1b1a2a1a1b3), Yaun/Yawn 1(R1b1a2), Mann 1(R1b1a2), Odum 6(R1....), Ray 1(R1b1a2), Salley/Sali 2(R1b1a2), Corbett 1(R1b1a2), Dreyer/Dryer 6(R-M269), Faust 1(R1b1a2), Brodie 1(R1b1a2), Odom 6(R1..), Spielmann/Spillman 6+(R-M269), Summerour 4(R1....), Wooten 5+(I-M253 & R-M269).

- Family Surname Related/Associated , I2 Y-DNA Related - possible marriage or
known relatives or connections in Genealogy. *Surname Count(Haplogroup)*. Surname
projects that have "a" matching Haplogroup.
I2 Haplo families: Joseph Adrian Odum (1880) 1(I2a2b1), Murphy (4 of 284), Stewart/Stuart (11 of 750).

In summary, while there is no method from which FTDNA does an ancient determination of family origins, they can organize the ancient groups called Haplogroups. From there we can get a reasonable scale of distance, however much better to use a known ancestor to determine the rate of mutation like the Fridy vs Friday known MRCA connection of Gabriel Fridig (1728). One surprise was the Ammons family which appears as another Fridig descendant adoption some time around the 1780's during the ending of the American Revolutionary war in South Carolina. Not so much of a surprise was the world wide surname variation of Zimmermans/Carpenters, Arnolds,

Greens, Schwartz, Ritter and other families show that these surnames were produced from unique families not related to each other in many thousands of years. The biggest surprise and confirmation was the Leonberg/Leuenberger connection which is believed to occur in the 11th – 12th century in Schwarzenbach or Steusslingen (in Swabia) to the von Burglen/von Steusslingen(?)/von Lowe/Zuckenriet families south into Thurgau, Switzerland. The Fridingen/Krahen family along with Zehnder, Leonberg, Redierer were all in the area on the Southern Shores of the Bodensee (Fridinger @ Mannennach, Steinegg, Salenstein etc, later Wil & Lowenberg etc..) Canton of Thurgau, Schweiz from the 12th-14th century.

I2B1(=M223) Haplogroup from FTDNA projects
(Additional surnames variations & possible ancient family connections)

Alpine Y-DNA project

I2□M223□Z161□L801□CTS1977 Emmental Bern cluster

118941	Welty	Ulrich Walti	Switzerland	I-M223	14	23	15	10	13-15	11	13	11	14	1?
120371	Baumgartner	Niklaus Baumgartner, 1674, Trub, Canton Bern	Switzerland	I-CTS1977	14	23	15	10	13-15	11	13	11	14	1?

I2→M223→Z161→L801→CTS6433→Z78→Z171→L1196→Z190* ● Central Europe? ■ BigY

158503	Martin	Christian Martin 1669-after 1748, Emmental Bern	Switzerland	I-Z190	14	23	15	10	15-16	11	13	11	13	1?

I2→M223→Z161→L801→Z183→CTS6433 candidate ► confirm, check CTS1977

B3411	Friday (Fridig/Frydig)	Peter Friding (~1403) Ramsen?→Frutigen CTS6433	Switzerland	I-CTS6433	15	23	15	10	15-15	11	13	11	14	1?

I2→M223→Z161→L801→Z183→CTS6433* candidate ► consider Geno 2.0 to confirm

E13136	Cravarezza	Franco Cravarezza, b. 1949, Asti, Piemonte	Italy	I-M223	14	23	15	10	15-15	11	13	12	14	1?

I2→M223→Z161→L801→Z183→CTS6433→L1201+ ● Rhine V./C.Germany? (C.European?)

65183	M.	Nienburg, Lower Saxony, Germany	Germany	I-CTS1977	14	23	15	10	14-15	11	13	11	14	1?
124510	Zimmerman	Michael Zimmerman 1617 - 1677, Steffisburg, Bern	Switzerland	I-M223	14	23	15	10	15-15	11	13	11	13	1?

Anglo - Saxon (Germanic) Y-DNA project

Group : I-CTS6433 / DYS 390=23

B3411	Peter Friding (~1403) Ramsen?→Frutigen CTS6433	Switzerland	I-CTS6433	15	23	15	10	15-15	11	13	11	14	12	32	15	8-10	11	11	25
205736	Isaac Tynes, b. ca 1710 d. 1763 (VA) of UK origin	United Kingdom	I-CTS6433	15	23	16	10	15-15	11	13	11	14	12	30	15	8-10	11	11	26

Denmark I2 Y-DNA project

I2-M223 Branch Z161+ Germanic

64043	Jørgen ERIKSEN of Aalborg Amt, DK	Denmark	I-Z171	12	23	15	10	15-16	11	13	11	15	12	32	15	8-10	11	11
N22636	Jakob Andersen (c1900-), Toxwærd, Præstø Amt, DK	Denmark	I-Z166	14	23	14	10	15-15	11	13	11	14	12	31	15	8-9	11	11
172582	Kanters 1959, Vanløse, Danmark	Denmark	I-CTS1977	14	23	15	10	14-15	11	13	11	14	12	32	15	8-8	11	11
194590	Ola Trulsson Sø-Eik,c.1612, Nannestad, AKR	Norway	I-CTS6433	14	23	15	10	15-15	11	13	11	15	12	33	15	8-10	11	11
N16957	Rasmus Jensen (1824-1888) Skanderborg A., DK	Denmark	I-M223	14	23	15	10	15-16	11	13	12	14	12	32	15	8-10	11	11
181751	William Rose, ca.1720-1795, Francis Moore Rose	Unknown Origin	I-M223	15	23	15	10	14-15	11	13	11	13	12	31	16	8-10	11	11
259263	Gustaf Uddesson Ullman 1685-1755 Kristinehamn (S)	Sweden	I-Z165	15	23	15	10	14-15	11	13	11	14	12	31	15	8-10	11	11
B3411	Peter Friding (~1403) Ramsen?→Frutigen CTS6433	Switzerland	I-CTS6433	15	23	15	10	15-15	11	13	11	14	12	32	15	8-10	11	11
N20850	Niels Hammer, b.c.1620, Viborg, Viborg Amt, Denmar	Denmark	I-CTS6433	15	23	15	10	15-15	11	13	11	14	12	33	14	8-9	11	11
110829	Lauritz Pedersen, b. 1767, Erristø, Vejle, Denmark	Denmark	I-Z171	15	24	15	10	15-15	11	13	12	14	12	33	15	8-10	11	11

Haplogroup I Y-DNA Project
I2 M223>Z161>CTS6433

I2 M223 Branch I2-Z161, CTS6433 Anglo-Norman

173448	England	I-Z78	14	23	15	10	14-14	11	13	11	14	12	32	15	8-10	11	11	25	14	20	29	11-14-14-15		11	9	19-21
86529	Netherlands	I-CTS6433	14	23	15	10	15-15	11	13	11	14	12	31	15	8-10	11	11	25	14	20	27	11-14-14-14		11	10	19-21
18187	Portugal	I-CTS6433	14	23	15	10	15-16	11	12	11	14	12	31	15	8-10	11	11	26	14	20	29	11-14-14-15		11	10	19-19
95801	Scotland	I-CTS6433	15	23	15	10	15-15	11	13	11	13	12	31	15	8-10	11	11	25	14	21	27	11-13-13-15		12	11	19-21
B3411	Switzerland	I-CTS6433	15	23	15	10	15-15	11	13	11	14	12	32	15	8-10	11	11	25	14	20	28	11-14-14-15		10	10	19-21
141784	Unknown Origin	I-CTS6433	16	23	18	10	13-15	11	13	12	14	12	32	15	8-9	11	11	25	14	20	27	11-15-15-15		10	10	19-21

Switzerland DNA Project

I2a2a (xI2a2a1), M223+, M284-; could be I2a2a2 or I2a2a3; need to test Z161 and L701

71356	Alfred Humphrey born approx 1840, Switzerland	Switzerland	I-M223	14	22	16	10	15-15	11	13	11	13	12	29	16	8-10	11	11	2
124510	Michael Zimmerman 1617 - 1677, Steffisburg, Bern	Switzerland	I-M223	14	23	15	10	15-15	11	13	11	13	12	30	15	8-9	11	11	2
223141	Johannes Baumann b.1752 d. 1798 Dauphin co Pa	Switzerland	I-Z77	14	23	15	10	15-15	11	13	11	13	13	30	15	8-10	11	11	2
139725	Hans Zimmerman b. 1546 Switzerland	Switzerland	I-M223	15	23	15	10	15-15	11	13	11	14	12	32					
B3411	Peter Friding (~1403) Ramsen?→Frutigen CTS6433	Switzerland	I-CTS6433	15	23	15	10	15-15	11	13	11	14	12	32	15	8-10	11	11	2
E5170	need earliest known paternal ancestor info	Unknown Origin	I-M223	15	23	15	10	15-15	11	13	12	14	12	32	15	8-9	11	12	2

I-M223 Y-Haplogroup Project (partial list)
1.2.2.1.1.1.2- M223>...>L801, Z76, Z183>CTS6433* (Cont2a)

Kit	Surname	Description	Location	Haplo						
25835	Stirling	James Stirling b. about 1780	Scotland	I-M223	15	23	15	10 14-15	11	13
144233	Stirling	(William Stirling, 1834 - 1925)	Scotland	I-M223	15	23	15	10 14-15	11	13
201831	Terry	Harrison Terry b1846 Crystal Springs, Copiah Co MS	United Kingdom	I-CTS6433	15	23	15	10 14-15	11	13
35606	Mitchell	unknown grandfather, Dundee Scotland 1888	Unknown Origin	I-M223	15	23	15	10 14-15	11	13
58200	Quarterman	Robert Quarterman	Unknown Origin	I-M223	15	23	15	10 14-15	11	13
163236	Roberts	Tho.Roberts b.c1555 Wales?or AlgernonSydneyRoberts	Unknown Origin	I-M223	15	23	15	10 14-15	11	13
173851	Peterson	Anton Pedersen,15/02/1855-02/11/1942 DEN	Denmark	I-M223	15	23	15	10 14-15	11	13
121053	Jones	John Jones b.1750 Albemarle Co,VA d. Giles Co,TN	Unknown Origin	I-M223	15	23	15	10 14-16	11	13
46040	Jones	Lewis H. Cole b. 1844 Giles Co., TN (Jones NPE)	Unknown Origin	I-M223	15	23	15	10 14-16	11	13
130080	Wood	William Wood b. 1737 VA d. 1804 Randolph Co. NC	Unknown Origin	I-M223	15	23	15	10 15-15	11	13
N18915	Smith	Smith b. 1803 VA; Parents also born VA.	Unknown Origin	I-M223	15	23	15	10 15-15	11	13
81462	Marshall	Aaron(son of John m. Eliza Ferrel)Marshel Marshall	England	I-M223	15	23	15	10 15-15	11	13
95801	Galloway	Galloway, Coatbridge, Scotland	Scotland	I-CTS6433	15	23	15	10 15-15	11	13
N10920	Galloway	Andrew Galloway 1777 - 1851 m Rachel Mustard 1785	Scotland	I-M223	15	23	15	10 15-15	11	13
193177	Renshaw		England	I-M223	15	23	15	10 15-15	11	13
25570	Sterling	John Sterling, 1798, Londonderry, Ireland	Scotland	I-M223	15	23	15	10 15-15	11	13
N76491	Stavroulis	Stavroulis	Greece	I-M223	15	23	15	10 15-15	11	13
N32756	Lake	Stephen Lake, b c1828 NY, d 1862 Calhoun MI	Unknown Origin	I-M223	15	23	15	10 15-15	11	13
216807	STARLING	STIRLING OF CASTLECARY STIRLING TO CAMBRIDGE-ESSEX	Scotland	I-M223	15	23	15	10 15-15	11	13
187087	Schall		Germany	I-M223	15	23	15	10 15-15	11	13
N64950	Fisher	John Fisher b.1793	Unknown Origin	I-M223	15	23	15	10 15-15	11	13
234606	Breugem	Heyndrick Claesz. van Leeuwen, b.1490, d.1550	Netherlands	I-M223	15	23	15	10 15-15	11	13
N58526	Gilbert	John Gilbert b. abt. 1877 Germany	Unknown Origin	I-M223	15	23	15	10 15-15	11	13
N95946	Muncherian		Turkey	I-M223	15	23	15	10 15-15	11	13
321350	Ferris	Ezra Ferris, b. 1820 and d. 1906	Unknown Origin	I-CTS10057	15	23	15	10 15-15	11	13
182047	Watson	Evan Thomas Watson, b. 1759 VA	England	I-M223	15	23	15	10 15-15	11	13
30070	Whitfield	George Carter-Tabb	Unknown Origin	I-M223	15	23	15	10 15-15	11	13
117885	Holmes	Moses Holmes, b. 1751-1761, N.Y., d. N.B. Canada	Unknown Origin	I-M223	15	23	15	10 15-15	11	13
148361	Humes	Thomas Humes b.c. 1760 Ireland	Ireland	I-CTS6433	15	23	15	10 15-15	11	13
N7692	Bidwell	John Bidwell, b. 1620, d.1687	England	I-M223	15	23	15	10 15-15	11	13
B3411	Friday (Fridig/Frydig)	Peter Friding (~1403) Ramsen?->Frutigen CTS6433	Switzerland	I-CTS6433	15	23	15	10 15-15	11	13
46386	Hain	Christian Hain, b.1751 ???????	Germany	I-M223	15	23	15	10 15-15	11	13
128255	Wolf	John Wolf c1828 MS-c1878 Bradley Co AR (CTS6433)	Switzerland	I-CTS6433	15	23	15	10 15-15	11	13
20386	Maynard		England	I-M223	15	23	15	10 15-15	11	13
N102216	Maynard	William MAYNARD, abt.1783 - bet.1861/1871	England	I-M223	15	23	15	10 15-15	11	13
206068	Berckmans	Ghislenus Berckmans 1860-1943	Belgium	I-M223	15	23	15	10 15-15	11	13
158607	Harris	Robert H Harris, 1828-1903, Botetourt, VA	Unknown Origin	I-M223	15	23	15	10 15-15	11	13
32980	Graves	Gen. 133, Joseph Graves of MA, b. 1699	England	I-M223	15	23	15	10 15-15	11	13
325319	Павловић	Душан Павловић, b 1890, Врање	Serbia	I-M223	15	23	15	10 15-15	11	13
N20850	Hammer	Niels Hammer, b.c.1620, Viborg, Viborg Amt, Denmar	Denmark	I-CTS6433	15	23	15	10 15-15	11	13
277485	Connell	William James Connell, b 1715 and d. 1780 (NPE)	Scotland	I-M223	15	23	15	10 15-15	11	13

German Language Area DNA Research Project (partial list)

Kit	Surname	Description	Location	Haplo										
167020	Zänder	Gottfried Zender, Germany	Germany		15	22	15	10	15-16	11	13	11	14	11
56121	Rosenbeck	john henry rosenbeck	Denmark	I-M223	15	22	16	10	15-16	11	13	11	14	12
63907	Moote		Unknown Origin	I-M223	15	23	14	10	15-16	11	11	11	13	12
271159	Staver	Charles Stoeber, b. 1817	Germany	I-M223	15	23	15	10	14-15	11	13	11	13	12
259263	Ullman	Gustaf Uddesson Ullman 1685-1755 Kristinehamn (S)	Sweden	I-Z185	15	23	15	10	14-15	11	13	11	14	12
189395	Shutt		Germany	I-M223	15	23	15	10	14-15	11	13	12	14	12
224453	Strauss	Georg Friedrich STRAUSS (1697 - 1749)	Germany	I-M223	15	23	15	10	14-15	11	13	11	14	12
188536	Miller	Abraham Miller b1700 d1725>>John C. m.Ogden 1887	Germany	I-M223	15	23	15	10	14-16	11	13	11	14	12
245086	Kleylein		Germany	I-M223	15	23	15	10	15-15	11	13	10	13	12
N88253	Michel	MICHEL	Unknown Origin	I-M223	15	23	15	10	15-15	11	13	11	13	12
144628	Waalkes	Waalko Waelkens, 1555, Emden, Germany	Germany	I-Z185	15	23	15	10	15-15	11	13	11	13	12
N93580	Wacker		Germany	I-M223	15	23	15	10	15-15	11	13	11	14	12
143090	Bacher	Georg Bacher, germany, Neckarelz, baden	Germany	I-M223	15	23	15	10	15-15	11	13	11	14	12
317893	berger	Ernst berger b.1806 and d. 1869	Germany		15	23	15	10	15-15	11	13	11	14	12
B3411	Friday (Fridig/Frydig)	Peter Friding (~1403) Ramsen?->Frutigen CTS6433	Switzerland	I-CTS6433	15	23	15	10	15-15	11	13	11	14	12
46386	Hain	Christian Hain, b.1751 ???????	Germany	I-M223	15	23	15	10	15-15	11	13	11	14	12
N51991	Stumb	Joseph Stumpff, 1730 - 1817	Germany	I-M223	15	23	15	10	15-15	11	13	12	14	12
125028	Lybarger	Nicolaus Leyenberger b. Abt 1660 Switzerland	Switzerland	I-M223	15	23	15	10	15-15	11	13	12	14	12
89360	Lybarger	Nicholas Leyenberger,	Germany	I-M223	15	23	15	10	15-15	11	13	12	14	12
267583	Ottenbrite	Josef Ottenbreit, b bef 1840, Bukowina	Germany	I-M223	15	23	15	10	15-15	11	14	11	14	12
N2137	Battenfeld	John Conrad Battenfeld, 1819 Rennertehausen, Hesse	Germany	I-M223	15	23	15	10	15-15	11	14	11	14	12
159162	Shuman	John Shuman b. abt 1764 near Philadelphia	Germany	I-M223	15	23	15	10	15-16	11	13	11	14	11

The Viking Y-DNA Project

I2 M223 Branch Z161+, CTS6433+

Kit	Description	Location	Haplo												
229793	Joseph Franklin Porter, b 1803 Ireland d 1871 NC	Ireland	I-M223	13	23	14	10	16-16	11	13	11	14	12	31
N3171	George Worsham, 1620, Henrico Co., VA	England	I-M223	13	23	15	10	15-15	11	13	12	14	12	31
49021	Thomas Lawrence d 1628 Tarleton Lancashire England	England	I-CTS6433	14	23	15	10	15-15	11	13	11	13	12	30
31248	John Andrew Crockett, b. 1775, TN	Unknown Origin	I-CTS6433	14	23	15	10	15-15	11	13	11	14	12	31
77830	Hans Nilsson born c.1740 Tegneby Tanum (O), Sweden	Sweden	I-CTS6433	14	23	15	10	15-15	11	13	11	14	12	30
22066	Henry Sewell of the Severn River, MD, b. ca. 1730	Unknown Origin	I-Z190	14	23	15	10	15-15	11	14	11	14	12	30
364799	Wm Jasper Wolfe ca 1844 AR ca 1881 Carroll Co, GA	Unknown Origin	I-CTS6433	14	23	15	10	15-15	11	13	11	14	12	32
194590	Ola Trulsson Sø-Eik,c.1612, Nannestad, AKR	Norway	I-CTS6433	14	23	15	10	15-15	11	13	11	15	12	33
80999	Charles Walls	England	I-CTS6433	14	23	15	10	15-16	11	12	11	14	12	31
18187	Emmanuel (Antonio) Anthony 1735 PT-1792 SC USA	Portugal	I-CTS6433	14	23	15	10	15-16	11	12	11	14	12	31
82516	Francisco Bernardo Cavalcanti de Mello d1821	Brazil	I-CTS6433	14	23	15	10	15-16	11	13	10	13	12	29
177954	John Chandler, 1600	United Kingdom	I-Z166	15	23	14	10	15-15	11	13	11	13	12	31
5559	MacLea South	United Kingdom	I-Z166	15	23	15	10	15-15	11	13	11	14	12	32
B3411	Peter Friding (~1403) Ramsen? zu ->Frutigen	Switzerland	I-CTS6433	15	23	15	10	15-15	11	13	11	14	12	32
128255	John Wolf c1828 MS-c1878 Bradley Co AR (CTS6433)	Unknown Origin	I-CTS6433	15	23	15	10	15-15	11	13	11	14	12	32
N124123	Mr. Nicholas Partridge b. bef 1690 d. 1756 or bef	Unknown Origin	I-CTS6433	15	23	16	10	16-17	11	13	12	14	12	32
N52116	Neil McGugan, b.c. 1750, North Knapdale, Argyll	Scotland	I-CTS6433	15	23	15	11	14-15	11	13	11	14	12	32
205736	Isaac Tynes, b. ca 1710 d. 1763 (VA) of UK origin	United Kingdom	I-CTS6433	15	23	16	10	15-15	11	13	11	14	12	30

CTS6433+ SNP DNA migration Map
(*SNP formed 4000 ybp*[362])

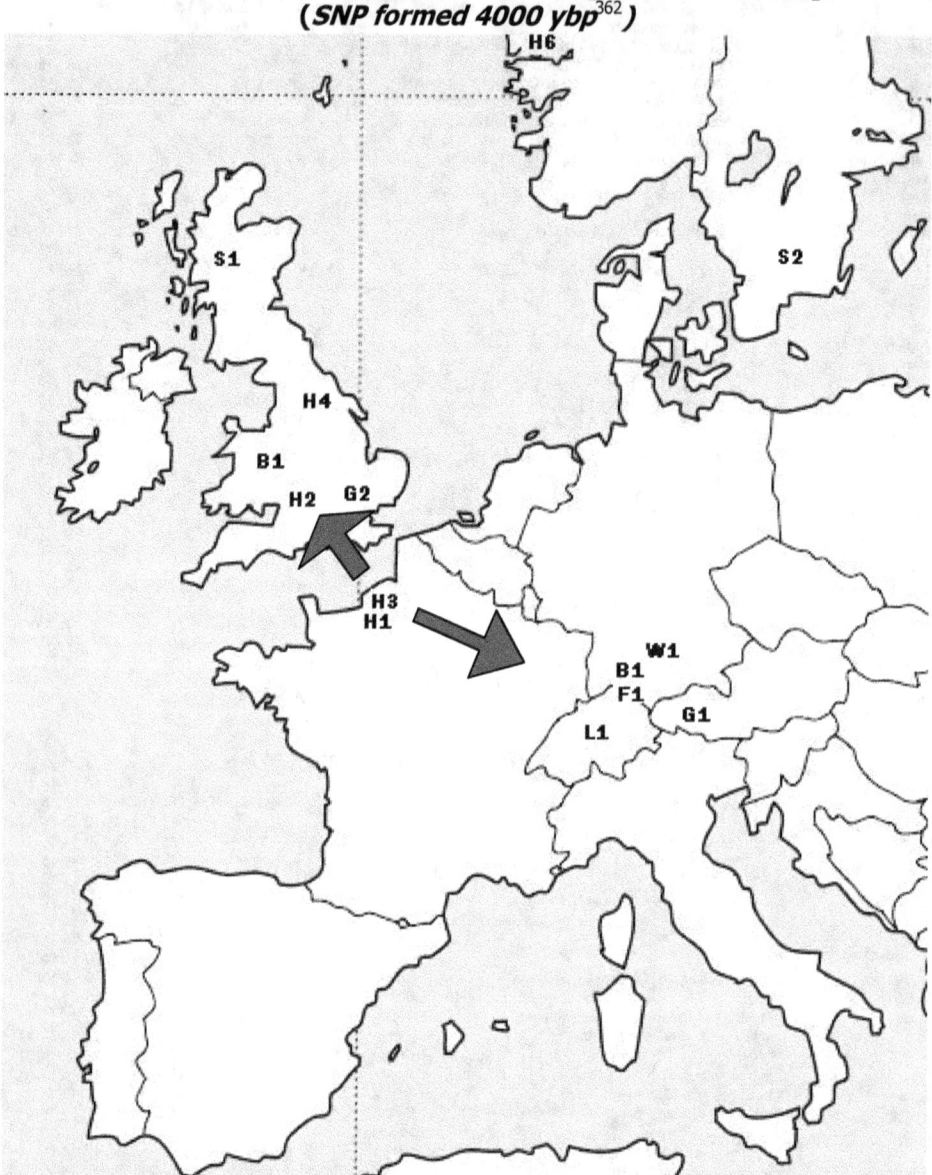

The Fränkische(Francorum) lineages

-Norse/Swedes/Scandinavian Fränks

H6 – (*Bratly s. Haugen***) Peder Andersen Haugen c1646 Beitstad, Norway** confirmed **CTS6433+.** Surname Data shows Haugen as Allemanic German, 1st name as far back as 990a.d

S2 – (*Carlin s. Andersson/Anderson?***)** Truls Andersson for ancestor from Tolånga(1703?) &/or Skivarp (1780) confirmed **CTS6433+.**

S2 – (*Sigard s. Carlin***)** Carl Lennart Siguard for ancestor Carlin from Malmö (1913) confirmed **CTS6433+.**

The Swabian Connection – Expanded Edition

S2 - (Falk s. Nilsson/Nilson?) Kit#77830 Hans Nilsson born c.1740 Tegneby Tanum (O), Sweden confirmed CTS6433+.

S2 – (Trulsson s. Trulsson) Kit#194590 Ola Trulsson Sø-Eik (1612) Nannestad, AKR confirmed CTS6433+.

S2 – (Öhrström s. Öhrström) Anders Öhrström from Tolånga (1738) confirmed CTS6433+.

- Briton/Scots/Picts/Saxons Fränks

S1 – (Sly s. Schly) Richard Allen Sly for ancestor Jenkins Sly (~1783) from Scotland(?) - *Predicted CTS6433.* Surname Data shows Peter Sly and Willaim Sly (Village of Hemingford Abbots), William & Richard Sly (Village of Hadden), in the County of Huntingdonshire (1327).

G2? or G1? (Graves s. Greaves) John (1730) from Virginia and George Graves for ancestors from England. Surname data shows: Zwettl, Austria (1156-71) for Otto Grave. Hackney, Westminster, England (1231) for Aliciam de la Grave.

H2 – (Hughes) Randall Lamar Hughes for ancestor Reddick Hughes confirmed CTS6433+**, Dr. William Daniel Hughes and Richard Hughes from Scots/Irish or Wales.** Surname Data shows Thomas Hughes 1287 near Bath, England. Hughes a popular English & French 1st name Hughes and also Hews/Huse a German Austrian origin of 1151.

B1 – (Bidwell s. Biddulph) Robert James Bidwell & Richard Francis Bidwell for ancestor Richard Bidwell (~1606/1620) from England - *Predicted CTS6433.* Surname Data shows name Biddulph during reign of William the Conquerer in 1066 around Norfolk county, England.

H1 – (Enos s. Hennot) Donald Q Eno, Charles Timothy Enos & Mark Imler Eno ancestry believed from England. *Predicted CTS6433.* Surname Data shows Henot 1234 in France and Hennot 1239 in Normandie. A Northern German & Ostland document mentions a 1st name Henno dating to 906.

H3 – (Hutto s. Hottot) Joel Hutto for ancestor George Hutto apear 18th century French Hugenot (Swiss/German) confirmed CTS6433+>Z78-. Surname Data shows Haudetot dating to 1034 in Normandie, then Hotot moving into England around the mid 1200's..

H1 to H4 - (Humes s. Home/Hume) Larry Frank Humes for ancestor Thomas Humes ~1760 Ireland confirmed CTS6433+>. Surname Data shows ancient Scotland and Normandie.

Others:
William **Sample** (1700) confirmed CTS6433+. **Karle** confirmed CTS6433+. Kit#N124123 Patridge for ancestor Nicholas **Partridge** (1690) confirmed CTS6433+. Kit N23744 **Johnson** from Aberdeen, Scotland confirmed CTS6433+. (**Hurtt s. Hurt**) Kit# 40100 for ancestor William **Hurt** Sr (1614) Bristol, UK confirmed CTS6433+.

- Alemmani/Germania Fränks

F1 – (Fridig s. Friding(er/en) Jeff Friday for ancestor Peter Friding (~1403) confirmed CTS6433+>Z78-. Surname Data shows line originates from Hirschecker Bregenz familie from Hegau/Swabia prior to 1043 in Swabian Hegau, then some families later migrate into Switzerland by the 1300's. This Bregenz family descends from Gerold (d. 799) brother in law to Charlegmagne who is recorded as Alamannian noble who served the Frankish king.

L1 – (*Lybarger s . Leyenberger*) Lee Lybarger for Nicholas Leyenberger (~1660). confirmed CTS6433+. Surname data shows Canton of Bern 1500's and Germany later. Familie origins believed to be Leuberg/Lowenberg Thurgau nobles after 1200's and Swabia prior to Swabia 1180.

F1/H2 – (*Aumon s. Orman/Auman/Amann?/Ammon?*) Dr. George Luis Aumon for Ancestor Andrew Auman (1762). *Predicted CTS6433.* Surname data shows Wales or Northern Switzerland in the late 1200's depending on which branch split from which location.

B1 – (*Gersper s. Gerspach / Gersbach/Gerstburger*) William Gersper for ancestor Peter Gerspacher of Baden 1834. Term SNP actually CTS4336+. Surname data shows 1st reference in St. Blasien in Baden-Wurtemburg in the Black Forest. 3rd reference *Gerispach* under Hermann von Konstanz(=Fridingen) in 1189.

W1 – (*Wolf s. Hunenberg or Homburg or Poschberg*) Louis Aubrey Wolf for ancestor John Wolf (1828) confirmed CTS6433+>Z78-Y4955-,S2364-. Surname data shows Rubertus Wolf in Bamberg 1154. Hans Wolf von Homburg in Zurich 1165. Roudprecht Wolf de Pochsberch 1180. Believed to be closely related to Hirscheck prior to 1043.

B1 – (*Hoover s. Huber*) Joel Cook Huber for ancestor Huber from Netherlands. B.K.Hoover ancestor Hoover from N.C confirmed CTS6433+>Z78-. Surname data shows Heinricus dct H 1273 Burger in Pfullendorf. Baindt (1288) Brüder Berthold und **Rudolf, Söhne Konrad Hubers (Hubarii)** zu Ebersbach. Many others Huber familiy appearing in Switzerland.

L1 – (*Spory s. Spörri/Sporri/Spori*) J Michael Spory for ancestor Phillip Jacob Spory (1833) from Hamburg or Darmstadt, Germany confirmed CTS6433+. Surname data shows Canton of Bern in 1415 and many other surname possible origins in Southern Germany. Migration route maybe similar to that of Lybarger family.

B1 – (*Hain s. Hayne/Hagin?*) Mr. Andrew Hain for Christian Hain 1751? *Predicted CTS6433.* Surname data shows **Herren von Hain** 1175 in Rittergut,Germany. Many locations throughout Germany into the 1400's.

F1/L1 (*Segrest s. Sigrist/Sigriste*) Mr Claude Harvey Segrest for ancestor Hand Joggi Sigrist. *Predicted CTS6433.* Earliest surname references appear to be Sacristan/Sacrista from the year 1187 in Southern Germany & Northern Switzerland.

? – (*Berger s. Berge?/Berger?/Heilgenberg?/Leuenberger?*) Glen Eric Berger on ancester Ernest Berger (1806) from Baden Germany. *Predicted CTS6433.* Surname data shows **G1 (*Bishop s. Bischoff*)** from Ancestor Martin Bischoff 1595-1661 Austria confirmed CTS6433+.

Others:
Sachs for ancestor Carl Sachs (1932) confirmed CTS6433+. (*Clubb s. Klopp*) Kit#N119895 for ancestor Peter Clubb/Klopp (1711) confirmed CTS6433+. *Morreale* Kit#N126045 for ancestor Giuseppe Morreale born in Sicily (1831) confirmed CTS6433+. (*Hartig s. Althörnitz/Hartigové(Czech)*) Kit#141784 for ancestor William **Hartig** (1827) confirmed CTS6433+.

Coats of Arms (Wappenschildes/Wappen Heraldik)

Coats of arms came in many forms Personal, Monastery/Kirchen(Church),Tournament societies, Order "Emblems" of Knighthoods[363], Villages, City and Stadts(States). In the monastery or church records they were called Wappenseigels(Coat of Arms Seals) used to wax stamp authentication. They were used in the original form to apply a piece of clothing called a surcoat for Knights or Monks(Monch) surname emblem over the Armor so other Knights would know who they were fighting & know who their comrades were. Flags/Banners with the coat were carried into battle on a long stave, on their horses or used during a tournament (in times of peace). They may also carry a shield with the same emblem as their loyalty of their Family/ Village/Kingdom or Crown. They were also used as the Village or Kingdom identification of family or origin and many monasteries also have them, both of which are typical in Germany & Swiss cantons. These were placed on the walls of the fortress entrances, decorations internally about the structures & final destinations above their tombs Grabplatten(Grave Plates). Some researchers books suggested as families were married their coat of arms would change {quartering by marriage ancestry}. Based on the Bishops of Contanz/Konstanz the arms didn't start adding multiple{+3} families coats of arms{on one shield} until the late 1500's. Only the very High Nobles (Herzog, Konig, Burgraff, etc) quartered their Wappens by families ancestry shown examples in the St. Gallen Switzerland codices. That has not been with the case as many Fridingen women (Margarete v Fridingen (~1328)[364] {Hunenberg}, Ursula v Fridingen (~1439)[365] {Luternau} took their paternal fathers coat of arms to their grabplatten. The earliest dated family Wappenschildes found in Southern Germany was the that of the familie Nellenburg (889) and Furstenburg (1030) as referenced in the Zuricher Wappenrolle amendment notes[366]. Gebhard I, a Bishop of Konstanz shown the

earliest in 875[367], however if you review the actual parchment from 820-900's the siegels are images of roman heads starting with like Karl de Gross (~747). It's not until about 1099 we start to see images of Bishops full bodied sitting with their Holy Staff. See left image[368] siegelstamp for Bishop Hermann II (=Fridingen) von Konstanz for 1184. The 1st earliest known physical familie wappensiegel is for Graf Albert von Dillingen dated 1193 located in the Munich archives (WO:1934). The 2nd earliest known physical familie wappensiegel is (1208) recorded as Rodolfi de Tierstein (Thierstein)[369] in Frienisperg monastery near Fricktal (Frick), Schweiz which is Golden shield with a Red Doe on a

Green Dreiburg (similar to Hirschecker). The wappensiegels/ wappenschild start replacing a persons image from the 1210's through 1220's and become the familie siegelstamp of choice. See right image of Graf Mangold von Nellenburg wappenseigel dated (1220) also found in Abbey of St. Gallen Codex[370]. Reviewing this Zuricher wappenrolle updates 1st noted date of the highest period of wappen (COA) occurrences appeared between 1130–1280 and then continuing and trickling down by the 16th century. Almost anyone could be recorded with an arms – The Richental's Chronik des Konzils(Council) to Konstanz, Germay (1414-1418) had the following recorded: Clergy, Popes, Cardinals, members of conclave, Bishops, Abbotts, Canons, Religious Orders, Universities, Kings, Electors, Dukes, Princely counts, Counts, Barons, Ternionen, Imaginary Realms and Towns. Jorg Fridingen (~1464) is listed as a Canon(of Konstanz) while Johannes von F, Cunrat von F & Ulrich Hainrich von F are listed under "Untitled Nobles". The (COA's) & Sieglestamps would start to being recorded (sketched or painted) in the mid 1300's via scribes in monasteries on what is refered to a wappenrolle "Armorial" on parchment and then later placed in a book. The Zuricher wappenrolle is the oldest known coats of arms of high and low nobility of the Middle Ages in existence dating to between 1335-1345. The Coats described below primarily come from SudDeutchland, Northern Half of Switzerland, Eastern Austria & Tyrol. The following coat are arms are presented in case of etymology/DNA variations possibilities that are not known and for your enjoyment between the variations of similar surnames in southern Germany, Eastern Austria and Northern Switzerland.

The Swabian Connection – Expanded Edition

Hanns Frayding (German) ~1535

Origin Displayed: Kempten, or Legau, Germany for **Hanns Frayding** (~1505) in 1535.

Spelling variations include: **(*) Fraidig**, **Fraydig**, **Frayding**, **Frayding**, **Fraydinng** and maybe more.

Description: Two obliquely crossed over a hunting Spies Dreiburg - without color.

Source: Kemptner Wappen und Zeichen Eduard Zimmermann[371], Kempten, Verlag für Heimatpflege, 1963

Note: Fraydig/Frayding/Frayding/Fraydinng is 1st mentioned in 1285 in Pfeffinger, Germany referred to Mr Wehrner Fraydig, Knight married to Agnes. This is believe to occurred in St. Michaels Church in the same town. Hanns (~1505), Stefan (~1545), Martinus (~1469) and Konrad Frayding appear in the Kempten, Germany area which is east of Lake Constance. Konrad was a serf with children.

Freitag (Schweiz) ~1798

Origin Displayed: Luzern, Switzerland - formerly Fribourg

Spelling variations include: **(*)** Frutig, Freitag, Fretig, Freteg, Fruting (extinct since ~1798).

Description: Oranges or Orange Apples on Green Leaf Tree with Blue sky on a mountain. Family 629.

Legal Verbiage:
The above-mentioned illustration from the collection of public records Luzern takes place without guarantee. With it no official registration and no legal protection are connected. Archives can vouch neither for quality nor correctness of the provided coats of arms. The Swiss coat of arms right does not offer special protection for family coats of arms. However they are subject to the usual regulations of copyright."

Note: It is inconceivable that Frydig/Frydig (after being Freideg 1st) is a variation of Freitag.

Source: http://www.staluzern.ch/cgi-bin/wappen.pl?06/0660.jpg

Fridang (German) ~1332

Origin Displayed: (~1332) Franfurt, Germany, Austria or Switzerland

Spelling variations include: (*) Fridang, Frydang, Fredang, Freidank, Frydank, Vrydanke, Vridang, Fridanus and maybe others.

Description: Red with White checks.

Image Source: http://www.wappenbuch.com/imagesE/E124.jpg

Note: Conrad Fridang is mentioned many times in Schaffhausen, Switzerland records as Fridang/Fredank/Fredach. **Fridang** was naturalized in Schaffhausen in 1392.

Fridung (Schweiz/German) ~1430

Origin Displayed: (~1430) Uri, Switzerland for Konrad Fridung.

Spelling variations include: (*?) Fridung, Fridunc, Frydang, Fredang, Freidank, Frydunk and maybe others.

Description: Wings on White Background, Bird pirched on top of Helmet. Believed to be designed from Herzog of Savoye/Savoyen..

Image Source: http://www.wappenbuch.com/imagesE/E124.jpg

Note: Konrad Fridung also has a coat of arms with a Crown[372] dated 4/13/1434 documented in Austria. Heinrich von Fridung is a Burgergraf (Count) for Tyrol, Austria in 1511. Conrad Fridang is mentioned many times in Schaffhausen, Switzerland records. The Frickingen coat of arms has wings surrounding a leaf with 3 roots above the helmet. The Flickingen coat of Arms is a double wing set as the above wappen displays. Walter III von Halwill (~1226) & Berchtold Halwill I (~1247) of Argau, Switzerland has the same double wings Siegel in 1256, then 1277[373] and is continually repeated until 1575 with Burkhart von Halwill (~1545). In the Uri, Suisse State Archives surnames documented and appeared as a derivative of: **Fridig (Friding, Fridung, Friden)** via typed notes, copies of articles (1443-1650). Fridung/Fridunc is believe to originate from the house of Zäringen of which also is a Bird Free Standing. Zäringen is believed to originate from the Alaholfinger family.

Freidinger (German) ~1544

Origin Displayed: (~1544) Meissen, or St. Dealer, Germany for Eberhard Fraydinger **{alias Fraydinger/Freidinger/en}**

Spelling variations include: Fraydinger, Freidinger, Freydinger, Freydiger, Freidiger, Freudiger and maybe others.

Description: Red Pegasus with two stars.

Image Source: http://www.freidinger.de and Renaissance culture und antike Mythologie By Bodo Guthmüller.

Note: Leonard Freidinger is also believed to use this Wappen and be the son of Bernhard. A 2nd Tengen wappen is shown in the Zuricher Wappenrole a White Unicorn with a Red background recorded 1335/1345. Tengen family is understood to come from the Hirscheck. The name Friedinger and (COA) is also listed as the common fridingischen shield Gold Lion walking the white bend with the background of light blue for Winterthur[374].

Fridingen/Krähen (German/Schweiz) ~1250's-1500's

375

Zurich wappenrolle parchment created by an unknown cronicler[376] about 1335-1345. Clients and Artist are unknown. The 1860 re-issue of the book says Fridingen (Klettgau). There were no Fridingen in Klettgau during the mid 1300's, howerver this is a stones throw from Constanz or Hohenkrahen. The only records @ Klettgau were Cunrat{Conrad} Friding(en) (~1384) relating documents in Schaufhausen 1422-1428 or Heinrich Fridinger XI (~1385) von Wiesholz[377] in 1425 & 1428.

Wappenschild(Coat of Arms) of friedingische form being used under the name Goffris von Kreugen by 1307. Gotfrid von Krahen (~1277-1307) husband of Katherine Bodman sits on HohenKrahen with the blue shield with golden lion before 1307. Votive painting 16th century and probably and older copy of the picture found at the New Castle Bodman. This was probably a memorial painting since 7 family members including Gotfried died in the Old castle when it burned by a lightning strike[378] on October 17, 1307.

Origin Displayed: before ~1250 Fridingen, near Singen, Germany or Mulhausen, Hohenkrahen, Radolfzel, or Klettgau, Germany and various parts of Southern Germany, Western Austria and Northern Switzerland. In 1250, Johannes von Kraege {Krahen} uses this same symbol as his Siegelstamp.

Spelling variations include: Fridingen/ Friedingen/ Friedinger[379] 1855?/Frydinge/ Krahen/ Kraege/ Kraegen 1250, Friedingeu ~1371 Schweiz, fridigē & fridingē in Tyrol/Tirol[380] 1394-1430, fridingē 1483 Konstanz[381], von frÿdingen 1470 St. Gallen[382], Frydingen or Alt ~1500-40 SudDeutchland[383],& maybe others.

Description: Azure{Blue} a bend argent and in chief a lion rampant; above the helmet a plume of white feathers. Around the mid 1400's the feathered crest became colored Gold and Black (von Steckborn rights).

Source: Top Left - Zuricher Wappenrolle Roll of Arms 1335/45. Right - Hans Ingeram Codex & Scheibler Armorial in 1696.

Note: It is believed this shield comes from the Burglen/Bürglen (1176) familie of which the Fridingen's were familie. In a 16th century a Codex for SudDeutchland this Black & Gold wappen(COA) is correctly identified as "Frydingē or Neu"[384] and the Blue Lowen wappen as "Fridingen or Alt".

Alt-Frydingen{aldt/neu frÿdingê} (German/Schweiz) 1355-1535

(1428/1459)	von Steckborn (1187-1332)	
Wappenbuch des Ulrich in St. Gallen.	reconstructed by Author.	Siegel Heinrichs von Fridingen. 1428.

Origin Displayed: Fridingen, Germany or St. Gallen & Steckborn, Switzerland (dating 1355-1459[385]).

Spelling variations include: Frydingen/Friedingen/Fridingen/Fridungen/Fridingen/Frydinge {older arms} aldt frÿdingê[386] St. Gallen 1470, fridigē & fridingē in Tyrol/Tirol[387] 1394-1430, Fridingen[388] 1483 Konstanz, neu-Frydingē ~1500-40 SuDeutchland[389], von Steckborn & maybe others.

Description: Black & Gold (Half & Half) lack of Lion on Blue via Hans Ingeram Codex 101[390] . Colors shown in reverse (Gold & Black) in the early 1500's wappenbuch for Anton Tirol[391].Since about 1410 led members of the sex of Fridingen this coat of arms (in addition or alternatively to the above "Lion Crest") is the reason for this is unclear[392]. See explantion below.

Note: Reinold von Fridingen (~1061) and his brother Folcmar de Fridingen (~1059) von Nendingen shows their wappen split in gold & black in 1089 during the property of Martinsweiler gifts donated to the monastery of St. Georgen[393], Königsfeld, Schwarzwald, Germany. This was added later during the 1300's to the wappen Hegau tribe/sex of Fridinger, which originally only had the border golden Lion on a silver diagonal bar. It was 1st thought the Fridingen lost track of their ancestry & used the 1089 St. Georgen reference to add this to their schield. However in E Dobler book (pg 131) also realized this comes from the extinct ministerial between Reichenau & Steckborn, Switzerland. Ulricus de **Fridinge**[394] de solidos {Ulrich Fridingen II (~1304)} in 1355, Heinrich von Fridingen (~1385) shows this wappenshilde in 1428. Johannes von Fridingen "Abbott" (~1458) has the Gold and Black (top right quarter & bottom left quarter) on his wappen at Bebenhauser monastery. His brother Rudolph von Fridingen (~1445) "Compthur" also has the same Gold & Black in the bottom left quarter of his arms. Von Hewen wappen has the same colors (Black over Gold horizontally)[395]. Friedrich Schenk von Wartenburg aud Bohem {Bohmen} ~1337? also is shows with an exact Black and Gold schield[396]. This wappen should be called Neu/New-Fridingen, not Older-Fridingen. It's becomes a 2nd Generation design until the Quartered 3rd Shield is created in the late 1400's. In a 16th century a Codex for SudDeutchland this Black & Gold wappen(COA) is correctly identified as "Frydingē or Neu"[397] and the Blue Lowen wappen as "Fridingen or Alt".

Fridingen {quartered} (German) 1400's-1560's

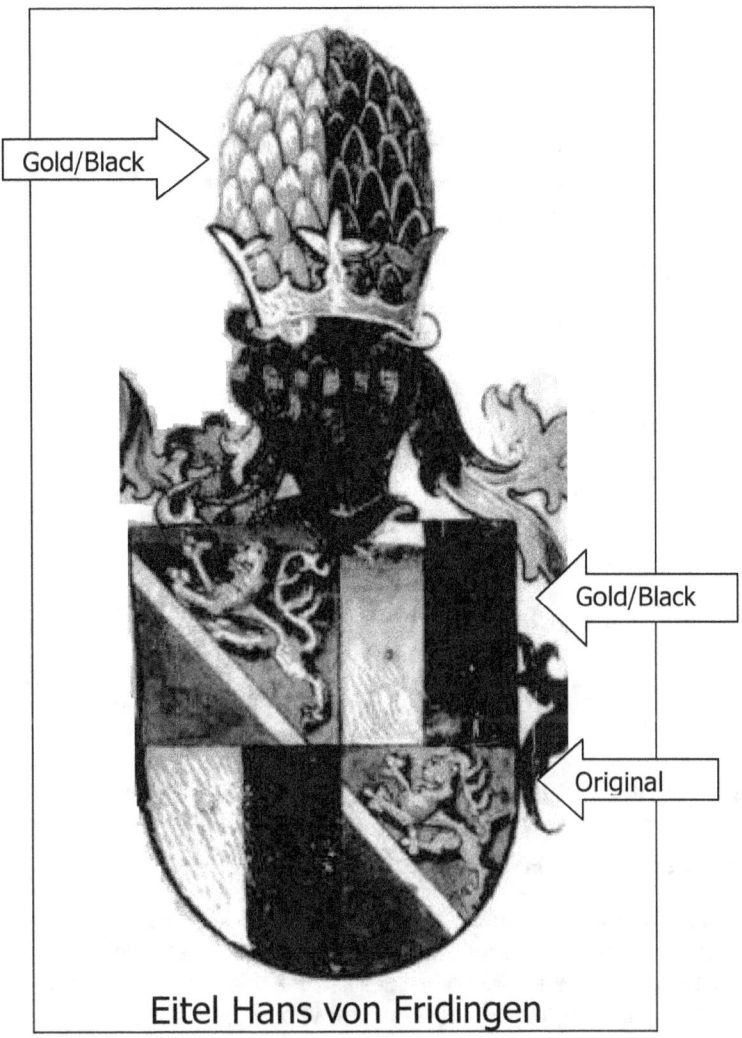

Gold/Black

Gold/Black

Original

Eitel Hans von Fridingen

Origin Displayed: Quartered in Southern Germany and Northern Swiss from about 1350's to 1560's. Mostly in the newer generations (1400's+).

Spelling variations include: Fridingen 1483 Hochen Burg to Konstanz[398]/Frydingen/Frydinge, {unquartered} fridigē or fridingē in Tyrol/Tirol[399], Krahen/Kraegen and maybe others.

Description: Blue and White with Lowen quartered across the Gold & Black {von Steckborn}. Occasionaly the wappenschilde is shown with the Neu-Fridingen Schilde on the bottom and the Black & Gold crest over head. Eitel Hans F, Rudolph v F, Hans v Fridingen and many others used the New-Fridingen quartered. Rudolph Fridingen the Landkomtur der Ballei Elsaß-Burgund des Commander of Deutschen{Tuetonic} Ordens has his Coat of Arms(Bl. 76v (69v) uniquely quartered with Alt-Fridingen, New-Fridingen & the Teutonic Cross (Black over white)[400]. The bottom left corner is Brown and Gold the Alt-Fridingen/Old-Fridingen familie. Upper left and Lower right is a White background with Black Crosses which is from the Teutonic Order which Rudolph was Commander for 4 years. Helmet is Orange and a Plume of white feathers above the Helmet with a cross.

Heinrich Frydig/Fridig (Austrian/Schweiz) ~1480-1560

Reconstructed by Author

Origin Displayed: Schächenthal, Switzerland, Munzen, Uri or Tyrol, Austria 1480-1560's.

Spelling variations include: Frydig, Fridig, Friden?, Friding?, Fridung?

Incomplete Description: Unter leerem Spruchband und kleinem Herz in etwas roher Kartusche ein ovales Wappen mit 3 Sternen uber Dreiburg. In einigen diser Bucher ist der Name Heinrich Frydig handschriftlich eingetragen. Ob diser der Trager des wohl selbst angefertigten Holztempels war. Lasst sich nicht ermitteln, da dessen Familienwappen unbekannt ist. Heinrich Frydig war 1564-67 Sturze eines einmal gekuppelten Fensters war in erhabener Arbeit ein nach rechts[401].
Translation from German: Under empty banner and small heart in somewhat raw cartouche an oval coat of arms with 3 stars over dreiburg {three mountains}. In some this Bucher is handwritten registered the name Heinrich Frydig. Whether this was the Trager probably of the wood temple even made. Cannot be determined, since its family coat of arms is unknown. Heinrich Frydig was 1564-67 fall of a once coupled window was in raised work to the right.
Source: Archivum heraldicum, Vol 36-37 By Schweizerische Heraldische Gesellschaft 1922.

Note: The physical wappen {Coat of Arms} has been reconstructed from the above source and similiar Oferdingen, Fricke or Eilenburg wappen all of which have three stars. It is also similiar to the **Fritag** wappen which is one star over a double layer of 3 mountains. To see in color visit the Friday family website. Located in the Berne archives are: Frydig familiewappen[402] in Frutigen arms appears by 1800 and Freidig familiewappen in Lenk appear by 1815. These are near duplication wappen described as 2 Red Stars over a Bird sitting on a mountain with 1 tree on each side of the bird. Andrear Fridig (Achwanden) husband of Verena Fridig has "Wappen der Fridig" 3 Sterne{stars} uber Dreiberg{mountains} in Munz(en), Uri Switzerland archives circa 1555/60.

The Swabian Connection – Expanded Edition

Alberti De Frieding/Friding (Austrian) ~1278-1325

Origin Displayed: siegel/signet for Freiding/Fryding/Friding, Stein/Stayn, Austria 1200's.

Spelling variations include: Freiding, Frieding, Fryding, Friding, Verthouen maybe others.

Description: A Horse head in Shield surrounded by Peace Branches on either side.

Source: Fridingen Adler buch by Maria Scheiber

Note: A siegel also represents the duplication of a coat of arms, however no coat of arms has been found for Alberti der Schenk von Friding. Freiding @ Andechs, Starnberg, Germany coat of Arms from 1803(?) appears to come from Friding via the Leaf and Branch >image right>. The village arms also has a gold lion (rampant) over Blue background under a peace branch or green Limb from an Olive Tree. The Gold Lion may also come from earlier familie of Fridingen of which Albrecht is supposed to descend. Freiding 1st mentioned as Frutinnen in 1123 a.d[403]. This Albrect is also Albrecht der Schenk von Verthouen[404] Feb 5th (1325) signet sealed [† S.] ALBERTI • DE • FRIDI[nG.] or Albrect Aidem[405] and wife Elsbet recorded Nov 17th (1325). No children are known to this marriage.

There were 7 other notables specifically using Friding surname:
1) Ulrich Friding (Fridingen) (~1304) vogt to Baden, Argau, Switzerland in 1347.
2) Conrad Friding (~1439) appears in a loan via Innsbruck, Austria in 1469.
3) Peter Friding (~1403) residing in Frutigen, Switzerland in 1433 & 1437.
4) Jorg Freiding (~1475) who is a painter from Tirol, Austria in Rattenburg working for Emperor Maximiliian in 1505.
5) Heinrich Friding (~1343) near Leuchtenberg, Germany or Wien{Vienna}, Austria.
6) Heinz (Haintzer) Friding (~1395) & Hans Friding (~1398) Fridinger brothers, beide(both) von Wiesholz located near Ramsen, Switzerland just south from the German border. Kloster Einsiedeln urkunden[406] 1418. Fridingen @ Singen is 11 miles from Wiesholz, Switzerland.
7) Gwer Fryding (1535/1564) land transfer from "Pleiken" {Bleiken?}, Switzerland (43 miles west of Adelboden) or from Pleicken, Wattwil, Saint Gallen, Switzerland in 1586.
8) Sebastian Freyding (~1504) in Untrasried, Ostallgäu, Bavaria, Germany in 1534..
9) Christianus Rormeyer Friding (~1534) is a student @ Universität Freiburg in Breisgau, Germany in 1554.
9) Werner Fryding/Fridiger/Fridig (~1420) born in Basel Switzerland and now living in Isenthal , Sihl, & Uri, Switzerland by 1443. Fought in the Zurich war 1440-43.

Note: Damian Fridinger's personal coat of Arm's takes the olive branch on the right side of the shield and a double divided line <u>as if he was not sure</u> if his ancestry is from Fridingen or the Friding family.

Damian Fridinger (German/Austrian) 1553

(COA) Reconstructed..

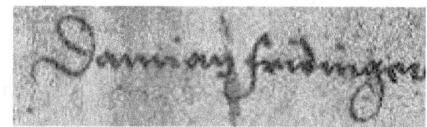

Origin Displayed: Wien(Vienna), Austria ~1553. Son of Dr. Wolfgang Fridinger?

Spelling variations include: Fridinger or Frydinger.

Description: A Green Branch/Limb from Olive Tree held by hand with a double bend of Gold on a Black Background. A similar description is also found in a book for Sebastian Friedinger (and brothers Erasmus, Andreas, Johann and Wolf Fridinger) for the house Austria in wars against the Turkish hereditary enemy carried out services and in particular Sebastian for its activity of many years in the war chancellery the knight-moderate aristocracy with the following coat of arms: Split signs, in front divided by black and Gold five times diagonally left, in the back a geharnischte hand with yellow sleeve, a branch of oil grows holding in the black field from the lower corner. Stechhelm also black-golden bulge; Kleinod. three Straußenfedern, the two outside silver, the middle black; Covers black-golden[407]. The arms above is adorned with Black and White feather plummage including a knights helm above the shield.

Source: Neues Jahrbook - Heraldisch-Genealogische Gesellschaft "Adler". Maria Scheiber

Note: The Coat of Arms for Damian Fridinger 1553, Andreas Fridinger and Freiding @ Andech all carry the Peace or Olive Branch originating(?) from Albrecht/Alberti der Schenk Friding/Verthouen siegla in ~1305. The Gold Lion may also come from earlier familie of Fridingen of which Albrecht is supposed to descend. Damian Fridinger's personal coat of Arm's takes the olive branch on the right side of the shield and a double divided line <u>as if he is not sure</u> if his ancestry is from Fridingen or Friding family.

The Swabian Connection – Expanded Edition

Names & Events Index of the European Middle ages

All of Switzerland and it's cantons left the Holy Roman Empire (eventually recognized) in 1648. After finding Gwer's Frydigs land transfer in 1586 with his surname listed as Fryding, this got me to look for more name variations by searching Swiss archives, German & Austrian internet search engines. The Luzern, Bern, Schaffhausen, Zurich Cantons, German, and Austrian archives or books have the following names and events found with various dates:

Terminology:

Vogt or Vogtei (*advocatus*)= land overlord for military protection(lord protectors), mostly nobility and knights.

Mönch (Monk) = obvoiusly the lords servants typically noble sent to a monastery for higher learning.

Nonne (Nun) = female version of a monk, also comes from noble families.

Mitgründer = co-founder

Gründerkreiss = founders circle/members circle

Gründer = founder

Domherr = Canon of the cathedral

Truchseß – trustees usually over a castle

Propst = ordinary priest

Charter = parchment record date of establishment (Act) usually a monastery or village.

Pfarrei = rectory parish priest office

Deutchorden = Deutch "German" Order Tuetonic Knights

Komtur/Compthur = Commander of Tuetonic Knights

Graf = Count

Bischop = Bishop and highest position was at Konstanz, Germany

Kloster = monastery

Burgraff = Castle Count appointed

Abt/Abbtei = Abbot head elder over a Monastery.

Edelknecht = noble servant, squire(armiger), not yet a knight or nobleman.

Rat(he)=council member

Camer/camerarius = Chamberlain

Laicus=layman

Provost(propositus)= a constable or reeve ; a warden (of a church).

pleb(Plebano)=from the parish

filii(filio)=child of

frat(fratres)= brothers of, or actually brothers

Pincerna=butler

Cust(custodes)=watchemen

Dictus = having been said,referred to

Pfleger = Guradian, Trustee

Milites=Ritter(Knight)

Nobiles(Edelfreie Nobility)=Free Noble/Free Herr(Free Baron/Masters/Lords)

Names	Location	Year	Job/Event
Fridingun/Findingen 1st mentioned	Fridingen @ Danubian{Danube}, Germany	June 786	King Karl & brother-in-law Count Gerold carry monastery under mountain fortress below Fridingen
Fridingun 2nd Mentioned (Hohentwiel castle)	Fridingun @ Tuttlingen, Germany	June 850/861	June 24th in St. Gallen monastery record donation of goods

The Swabian Connection – Expanded Edition

Erchanger (~873) & Berchtolt Fridingen brothers (~878)	Hohentwiel, Germany	893	Posession of Hohentwiel Castle
Erchanger (~873) & Berchtolt Fridingen (~878)	Hohentwiel, Germany	912	Construction of Castle Hohentwiel
Erchanger Fridingen (~873)	Constanz, Baden-Württemberg,Germany?	914	at Castle Onfridinga, Hohenfridingen , (feu/feudal) Fridingen
Erchanger Fridingen (~873)	Hohentwiel, Germany	915	Duke of Swabia (915-917) & Residence
Erchanger Fridingen (~873)	Germany	917	death record
Erchanger Fridingen (~873)	Langdorf,Germ. St. Gallen or Freunfeld,Thurgau,Switz	920	ends contract w/St. Gallen
Niclas von Fridingen (Abensburg?)(~938)	Trier, Germany	968	Tournament @ Trier
Ulrich von Fridingen (~938)	Merseburg, Germany	968	Tournament @ Merseburg
Fridiger (~938)	Zurich, Switzerland	968	Monk=monastery record Kirchenprovinze
Count Regilo Frickingen	Heiligenberg, Germany	988	Grafen/Count - Established Frickingen line
Fridiger (~996)	Campitona village near Constanz, Germany or St. Galliiches {St. Gallen}, Switzerland	1026	Monk=monastery St. Galliiches or Campitona village near Constanz, Germany
advocatis Heremanni (vogt Hermann Hirscheck)	Petershausen kloster	6/1043	regarding Rietilinis(Riedlings) estate Eberhard Constantiensis aecclesiae
Gerolt(Hirscheck) and brother Hereman (Hirscheck)	Petershausen kloster	1058	donation (Owiltingen in Linzgau) from Swiggerus who married Adelheid (sone named Gotteschalk)
Eberhard & Burkhard von Nellenburg, Heremanni de Hoinstetin	Kloster St Salvator und Allerheiligen zu Schafhausen	1087	Kloster St Salvator und Allerheiligen zu Schafhausen
Folkmar de Fridingen (~1059)	Martinweiler, Germany	1089	gifts of Monastery of St. George in Schwarzwald (black forest)
Act of Fridingen by Bertold Zollerin(?) /Zaringen(?)	Germany	1090	Act of Fridingen
Fridingen (latin=*Fridinga*) established	Reichenau, formerly St. Gall monastery	1090	charter
Berthtold von Frickingen (~1060)	St. Blasien, Klingnau, Switzerland or Schwarzwald, Germany	1090	died, son of Count Regilo
Graf(Count) Burchard von Nellenburg son of Eberhard and Ita Nellenburg	Kloster Allerheiligen	4/1090	Count Burchard of Nellenburg renewed and notarized his parents and his donations to the monastery of All Saints.
Hermannus de	Madelespuron	6/1091	Hermann brother gave

Madelespuron (~1067)	(Mahlspuren/Mahlspüren), near Witichiwilere (Wittichen), Germany. Record in St. Georgen kloster.		"marriage" Ruzella to Wolfger received in faith.
Reinold Fridingen (~1061)	Talheim, Tuttlingen, Germany	1095	
Heinricus de Ebenwilare (~1063)	Kloster Allerheilgen, Schweiz	1096/ 1105	Traditional Sancto Salvator(Holy Saviour) & Dicitur in his villa Mówinheim
Hineirch von Hirschegg/Heinrici de Hirzisegge (~1063)	Petershausen kloster, Constanz, Germany	12/1121	Obituary Algovia(Algau), Germany. Buried in Peterhausen
Ortwin & Liutfrid Frietingen/Fruotingen/Fre utingen		1130	
Heinrici de Evenwilare (Ebenweiler)	Worms or *Klosters Allerheiligen to Schaffhausen*, Germany	4/1145	Estate record
Herimmani (~1085?) & wife	Worms or *Klosters Allerheiligen to Schaffhausen*, Germany	4/1145	Uxor in Sweindorf & Stuzelingen
Hermannus(=I Mahlspuren?) & frater (brother) Burchardus (=Hohenvels?)	Speier or Stuzelingen or Salem kloster, Germany	8/1152	Presbiter de Stuzelinge
Hermann von Fridingen	Salem, Konstanz, Germany	~1155	Kloster Domherr
Herungus de Chregin/Chreginge (~1105) = (Krahen)	Aach or Constanz, Germany	1158	Ministerialen konstanzische Domherr
Hilegarde de Fridingen	Hallwill/Ala-ville, Thurigin, Constantiensis, Germany	1165-85	Uxor for Wilhelmus in Ludis
Heremanus de Madilsburron, Heinricus de Tengin	Kloster Allerheiligen in Schaffhansen	1167	Nomination of individuals
Ortwin & Berthold Frietingen/Vroutingen/Fri ding(en) (~1141)	Wasserburg, or Diessen, Germany	1170	frater under Abott Wasserburg/Diessen?
Ortwin & Berthold Froutingen/Vroutingen/Fri ding(en) (~1141)	Pfaffenhofen, Baden-Württemberg, Germany	1180	frater under Abott Wernhero
Hermanno de Vridingen with Hainrich de Vrichingen and others	Constanz, Germany	April 1181	Records under Berthold von Bussnang bishop.
Hermann >de Fridingen< (~1153)	Constanz, Germany	1183	thru 1189 - Bishop
Albert Krieger	Cella sancte Mariȩ, St. Märgen, Black Forest	1185	quod vocatur
Hermann von Hirzekke(Voitsberg?)	Vierfeld bei Pressburg	May 1189	Crusades under Freidrich
Freidingen's on Hohenkrahen	Muhlhausen, Hohenkrahen, Germany	1190	Hohekrahen Castle rebuilt by Friedingen nobles

Diethelm de Craien (~1098)		1192	witness on a charter of Henry VI
Kunradus & frater eius Heinricus de Mullhusen	Landesperc	1192	Charter of Landesberc
Tiethelmus de Creie (~1098)	Constantie (Constanz, Germany)	1194	Efringen record
Rudolph Fridingen (~1164), Heinrico de Kreien (~1170), Hermanno de Kreien (~1153)	Kloster Salem @ Reichenau, Constanz, Germany	1194	Salem Kloster Archives
Rudolph Fridingen (~1164)	Kloster Salem @ Reichenau, Constanz, Germany	1194	
Hans Friedrich von Fridingen (~1167)	Nuremburg, Germany	1197	Tournament in Nuremburg
Fridingen ministerial familie	Castle Krahen, Germany	1200	familie in posession of Castle Craien
H. de Fridingin	St. Gallen	~1200	Income records of monastery
Heinrich Fridingen	Geisingen,Germ or Kloster Salem @ Reichenau, Constanz,Germany	1200	Salem monastery record
Heinricus de Vridingen	Göggingen, Germany	1202	Testes for Beringero milites in Meschilchi feudom habetat in Hohinberc.
Albert of Reinh {Reichenau?} Fritingen/Fridingen (~1156)	Steinsberg Castle, Weiler, Sinsheim, Baden, Germany	1209	Bishop, Purchased Castle Steinsberg
gennant H. Cellensis Advocatus	Radolfzell, Germany	1209	Vogt
Heinrico aducato de Fridingen	Dorfisberc	1212	Vogt
Heinrich de Fridingen	Schina (Scheinen) & Ratholfi (Radolfzell), Germany	1215	Vogt
Lütold v. Krähen	St. Gallen charter	6/1208	confratrem
Swiker & Conrad von Mühlhausen	Volkolderode	Sept 1223	contract
Diethelm v. Krähen	Salem Kloster @ Reichenau, Constanz, Germany	9/1228	Ecclesie
Heinricus de Vridingen	Reichenau, Germany	1230	advocatus
Johannes miles de Cragin fatetur (~1217) and domina Ita	Kreuzlingen, Thurgau	1238	Fathers estates in Tegerwiller(Tägerwilen) & Haiminhovin (Heimenhofen in Allgau or Andwil)
Heirich, dem vogt von Kraehen w/sohn Heinrich & Konrad	Castro Craegen	1240	Vogt to Krahen
Heinrich von Fridingen	Constanz, Germany	Mar 1243	Vogt to Fridingen
Hainricus de Vridingen and	Kreuzlingen, Thurgau	Mar 8	advocatias in Ruhinhusen et

sons Heinrich & Conradus		1243	Beringen in bonis ecelesiae Crucelino
Cvnradus de Cella Ratolfi{Radolfzell}(=Fridingen)	Radolfzell, Germany	Oct 1246	Neufrach(?) Reichenau Gundelfingen urkunden
Chunradus Vridingen (~1234)	Creigen/Hohenkrahen, Germany	1/1251	Advocate to Vridingen
Rudolph Fridingen (~1228)	Kloster Salem @ Reichenau, Constanz, Germany	1258	monachus - Prince Bergisches deed book V, 96
Alberti {Albertus} Fridinger – A....HIRSAVGIENSIS. Same Albertus des Ergeczingen des Bozzinger(Baisingen?) Both from area of Rottenberg.	Hirsau, Germany	Apr 6, 1260	Hirsau Kloster Monastery North of Black Forest
Heinricus de Vridingen	Reichenau, Constanz, Germany	9/1260	Dictus advocatus de Ratolfi Cell (Radolfzell)
Conrad Fridingen (~1234)	Creigen/Hohenkrahen, Germany	May 6 1261	Deceased record - Advocate to Creigen & Fridingen – Basel Stadt Archives
Ita von Klingen-Fridingen (~1239)	Creigen/Hohenkrahen, Germany	May 6 1261	Dower given to Klingenthal Monastery in Switzerland – Basel Stadt Archives
Hainricus advocatum de Vridingen	Kreuzlingen, Thurgau	1262	monastery record @ Richlinshusin
Conrad Fridinger (~1234)	Kloster Salem @ Reichenau, Constanz, Germany	3/1268	Salem monastery record
Conrad dco Fridinger (~1234)	Hohentengen (Diengen), Germany	3/1268	Testibus record
Cünrado/Conrad Fridingen (~1234) or Cûnrado dicto Fridinger	Hohentagen, Tubingen, Germany	3/1268	Hohentagen monastery record
H dicto Fridinger	Geisingen, Germany	Apr 1273	Cünradus et Hainricus dictus Struz fratres de Wartvnberch kirch in Bolstern
Rudolphus advocatus de Fridingen III (~1247)	Kloster Feldbach, Switzerland	11/1275	Sell of Gerlikon fief
Burkhart milite dicto de Fridingen (~1246)	Salem, Gründelbuch,Germany below Fridingen (at Donau)	1/1276	Fief purchased Kloster Salem and Resignation. milite(=Ritter/Knight)
Rudolfus de Fridigen	St. Märgen, Schwarzwald	1284	diaconus
Rudolf Fridigen {Fridingen} (~1259)	Esslingen or Tengen, Germany	11/1287	Monastery record
Rudolf Fridingen (~1259)	Fridingen, Radolfzell,	1289	Vogt to Fridingen

The Swabian Connection – Expanded Edition

	Germany		
Hilmarus Fridinger	Praha, Česká	1292	Národní archive
Ulrich Frutinger (~1264)	St. Urban Monastery, Luzern, Switzerland	1294	monastery record, had two sons 7 wife
Her Hainrich der Vogt von Vridingen	Schaufhausen	April 1296	Bailiwick of 2 Huben in Buech (im Hegau)
Heinrich de Fridingen (~1267) advocat(i d)e fridi(ngen)	Reichenau, Constanz, Germany	Oct 1297	Advocate, Ulm Stadt Archives
Hiltmar Fridingerus (Fridinger) (~1268)	Prag(Prague, Czech Republic)	April 1299	Meinhardi & Tausentmark family record
Peter Frutigen (~1295)	Sion (or Sitten), Canton Valais, Switzerland	1300	1300?
Pillung Hiltmar Fridingerus (Fridinger) (~1268)	Prag(Prague, Czech Republic)	8/1302	Burgers to Prag
Rufen Frutinger(n) (~1280)	Thun, Obersimmental, Switzerland	1303	Purchase of two achers
herr Heinr. der vogit von Fridingen	Diessenhofen, Thurgau	6/1306	Vogte to Fridingen
Gotfried von Krahen (~1277)	Hohenkrahen, Germany	1307	Death, votive Painting from 16th cent located in Neu Bodman Schloss.
Eberhard von Hohen-Fridingen (~1281)	Ravensburg, Germany (btwn Constanz & Kempten)	1311	Tournament in Ravensburg
Peter Frutingen(r) (~1295)	Interlaken, Switzerland	1316	Monk?
Peter Frutingen (~1295)	Frienisberg,Seedorf, Aarberg,BE, Switzerland	1325	Prior=monastic superior
Heinrich Rudolf v Friedingen for Hug de Muller & his wife Mechtild	Bohringen (Konstanz), Germany	1325	Letter about the Muhle=Mill
Albert Fridingen (~1306) son of Eggehard von Fridingen (~1275)	Sindelfingen, Germany	11/1326	Kanon=Eclesiastic law maker?
Uolricus von Freidingen (~1304)	Interlaken, Switzerland	1327	witness to property sale @ Goldbach near Burgdorf
Burchardi de (Burkhart) Fridingen (~1246)	Constanz, Germany	2/1330	clerici @ Constanz Diocese and Brunnen, Germany
Ulrici de Craien (Fridingen @Hohenkrähen)	Fridingen & Muhlhausen & Constanz, Germany	2/1330	clerici @ Constanz Diocese. Petition with Mulhusen (Mahlhausen).
Heinrich and Rudolf von Fridingen	Swartzwald, Germany	June 1332	Apply offsets via Hertzog Albrecht & Ott
Růdolf von Fridingen VII?, w/Eberhard Eppenstein	Wil, Thurgau, Switzerland	1333	Hainrich von Honburg komendúr(comthur) des huses ze Tobel
Johanne Freidinger (~1302)	Frienisberg, Seedorf (Bern), south of Aarberg, Canton of Bern, Switzerland	2/1332	Friar/brother in Kloster/Church Frienisberg
Uellin(Ueli) Fredinger	Aaurau, Switzerland	1/1332	Burger to Arowe
Růdolf von Fridingen VII	Tobel, Münchwilen,	1333-	Comentúr, Konvent des

(~1303)	Thurgau, Switzerland	1371	Ordens
Albrecht/Albert der Schench Friding = S. AL[BERT]I • DE • FRIDInG (~1306)	Stayn/Stein, Austria	2/1336	Burgraf=castle count half the parish church St. Nyclas to his late wife Elspet
Rudolph Fridingen (~1294)	Lenzburg, Aargau, Switzerland	June 1338	thru 1358 Kaplan=Chaplan
her Volreich von Friding & Hainreich von Honburch	Steyr, Austria	Dec 1338	Konrad Sunthaim sell to Bischofe Konrad von Freising
Joannis/Joannes (Johannes) Fridingen	Kussaberg, Germany	1339	Euitas & Praefecti
Ulrich der Freidiger (Fridingen) (~1304)	Aargau, Switzerland	Feb 1340	Aargau Archives witness Abbey Konisfelden being sold. Pfaff
Johann Hans Fridingen (1310)	Küssachberg (Kussaberg), Germany	1341	Vogt=Governer
Ulrico (Ulrich) Fridingen	Kastell, Thurgau, Schweiz	2/1340	Pfaff
Ulrico (Ulrich) Fridingen (~1304)	Constanz, Germany	1341	clerici @ Constanz Diocese
Ulrich Freidig von Aarau w/daughter Gertrud	Aarau, Schweiz	3/1341	Samnung
Rudolph Fridingen (~1328?)	Sundgau(Suntgowe), Germany	June 1341	Vogt=Governor & Pfleger=keeper of church
Rudolph Fridingen (~1328?)	Friedingen,Singen (Hohentwiel),Germany or Singen, Mühlhausen-Ehingen, Germany	1341	Landvogt
Johann d. A von Fridingen	Kussaberg, Germany	5/1341	Ritter(knight)
Johann Hans Fridingen (~1302)	St. Blaise monastery	6/1341	Vogt & Obmann zu Küssachberg
Johans von Fridingen	Zurich, Swiss Archives	7/1341	Ritter, Vogt & Pfleger
Ulricum de Fridigen (~1304)	Constanz, Germany	2/1342	canonicum contance/domherrn
Rudolf von Fridingen VII (~1303)	Johanniterhauses Tobel, Bez. Münchwilen, Thurgau	April 1342-71	Komthur
Johann von Friedingen	Rheinau, Zurich, Switzerland	1343	Vogt zu Küssaberg - annual ground rent on the goods of John Wänninger Rheinau in favor of the monastery Rheinau
Ulrico de Fridingen	Constanz, Germany	3/1343	Praefect in Radolfzell/domherren
ritter **Heinrich von Fridingen (~1306) & wife Ursula**	Kalchrain, near Feldbach, (Thurgau), Switzerland from Weinzinsen, Germany	July 1346	Sell wine interest in Feldbach kloster.
Heinrich & Rudolph v Frid... ritter, Adelheit v Blumenberg Heinrichs v Frid...	Constanz, Germany	Jan 1347	tithes to Buessendorf and Giltlein
Ulrich Friding/Freidig (~1304)	Baden, Aaurau, Switzerland	5/1347	Will of Weibel at Belliken, Switzerland
Conrad Frutinger (~1280)	St. Urban Monastery,	1347	monastery record

	Luzern, Switzerland		
Conrad Frutinger (~1280)	Haus Roggwyl, Ober-Aargau, Switzerland	1347	Pfleger=Nurse or keeper of church
Margarete v. Freidingen-Hunenberg (~1328)	Cham, Zug, Switzerland	1348	Donation of New Alter
Ulrich Freidig (~1304)	Baden, Aarau, Switzerland	12/1348	Payment to Samnung
Elsbeth Tochter des Johann von Fridingen des jungen Wittwe des Burkart von Hohenvels	Hornstein archives in Binningen	1350	Vor Graf Eberhard von Nellenburg Landgraf etc
Hermann Frutinger (~1321)	Augsburg, Germany	1351	
Ulrich Fridingen	Frauenfeld, Switzerland	5/1351	domherr
Růdolf von Fridingen VII	Tobel, Münchwilen, Thurgau, Switzerland	6/1351	comentúr
Heinrich von Fridingen	Singen,Germany	1352	Goods to Singen
Alter/older Fridingen place name called Freidinger	wooded area near Lakeside Untersee @ Mannenbach, near Steckborn, Thurgau Canton, Switzerland	1355	Last traces of alter/older fridingen rights place name Freidinger
Ulrico {Ulrich} Fridingen (~1304)	Bologna, Italy	Sept 1355	Student in Bologna
Heinrich von Mülhausen presents Alberti von Freising	Gemona, Italy	Nov 1355	Clerico in Moguntine(Mainz, Germany)
Růdolf von Fridingen	Tobel, Thurgau, Schweiz	Jan 1356	Comentúr to Tobel in Thurgau
Ulrico {Ulrich} Fridingen (~1304)	Constanz, Germany	Sept 1356	clerici @ Constanz Diocese
Elizabeth Fridingen & Albert Klingenburg	Constanz, Germany?	1357	marriage record
Conrad Fridingen (~?)	Radofzell, Germany	1357	Burgermeister=Mayor
Peter Frutinger (~1328)	Thun, Obersimmental, Switzerland	1358	Guardian of the Barfüsser to Burgdorf
V°lrich von Fridingen +S.VLRICI.DE.FRIDINGE.C N.ECCE.9STANT & Peter Herr to Hewn	St. Stephan in Konstanz, Germany	4/1358	Propst
Ulrich von Fridingen	St. Stephan in Konstanz, Germany	6/1358	Propst
Ulricus de Fridingen w/Conradus Johannis de Ravenspurg	Brisgau, Zovingen or Constanz, Germany	June 1359	archidiacontanum
Hans der Friedinger	Schaufhausen	April 1360	Sold baut(building) to Johannes Benz, Bürger von Diessenhofen
Růdolf von Fridingen, Ludwig v Hornstein, Itel v Stadion	Salzburg, Austria	Feb 1362	Herzon Rudolph & bruder Friedrich of Austria and many others.
Růdolf von Fridingen VI (Fridinger)	Vorlanden(Foreland Austria of Hapsburgs)	Mar 1362	Rat(he)=member of council, parsonage to St Michael in

			Vienna.
Heinrich von Friding (~1343)	St. Thomastag, Oetting? Germany	Dec 1363	Bayern, or Oetting, Germany
Rufen Frutinger(n) (~1280)	Thun, Obersimmental, Switzerland	1363	
Peter von Fridingen (~1308)	Wil & Lommis, Thurgau, Switzerland	Nov 1364	Estate @ Lommis
Růdolf von Fridingen VII	Tobel, Münchwilen, Thurgau, Switzerland	Nov 1367	Comthur to Tobel
Johannes von Friedingen (~1343)	St. Urban, Luzern, Switzerland	May 1370	Estate record Heinrich Wigh of Aach
Johannes von Friedingen (~1343) & Johannes von Kragen	St. Michaels, Switzerland	May 1370	Estate record Heinrich Wigh of Aach
Růdolf von Fridingen VII	Tobel, Münchwilen, Thurgau, Switzerland	1371	Comthur to Tobel
Ernst Fridingen (~1343)	Esslingen,Germany	1374	Tournament in Esslingen
Rudolf von Fridingen der Alte zu dem Bussen gesessen	Bussen, Germany	1380	
Heinrich Fridingen (1347)	Merano, Tyrol, Austria	1380	thru 1395 Burgraf/Kellermeister=Castle Graf & Winemaker
dominus Hainricus dictus Fridinger (~1347)	Meran, Tirol, Austria	Apr 17th 1380	Burggraf
Heini Freidinger (Freidig) (~1347?/1360)	Abtei Fraubrunnen, Bern, Switzerland	1380	farmer, planting at monastery Fraubrunnen
Hugg von Frindigen	Reichenhall, Germany	July 1382	Salzburg archives
Claus Fridingen (~1369)	Constenz, Germany	1385	S. Stephan
Heinrich Fridinger (1347)	Meran, Tirol, Austria	1385-87	Burggraf
Rudolf von Friedingen	Togendorff	1387	
Haintz(Heinrich) von Mülhausen w/ Hainrich von Randegge voigt & others	Schaffhausen, Switzerland	Mar 1387	contract
Hans von Fridingen gessen to Krähen	Liechtenstein	April 1390	Signers to Truchsess Johann von Waldburg document.
Rudolf von Fridingen, Edelknecht	Stuggart, Wurtemburg, Germany	April 1392	Edelknecht in Toggendorf vogte to Bussen
Ernst Fridingen (~1343)	Schaffhausen, Switzerland	1392	Tournament in Shaufhausen
herr Ulrich of Fridingen, hans Fridingen, Rudolf von Fridingen, Heinrich and Ruodolff his sons	Germany	Dec 1392	St. George Banner
Ursula Fridinger	St. Agnes at Öhningen, Schaffhausen.	May 1394	Serf Admission to monastery St. Agnes
Ulrich von Fridigen	Lindau, Germany	Apr 1395	Ritter=Knight
Rudolph Fridingen (~1328/~1378)	Schaffhausen, Switzerland	1398	Sold Monastery St. Agnes
Rudolph Frutinger (~1368)	St. Urban Monastery,	1398	Abott

	Luzern, Switzerland		
Claus Frydinger/Fridinger (~1369) von Bickelfperg	Bickelsperg, Germany	1399	
Landenberg-Greifensee, , **Rod de Rosenberg-Zukenried, Rod de Fridingen,** Alb Blaarer	Wyl, Thurgau	1401	Related to Eliz Schwarzzin a' Fridingen uxor to Wilhelmus Blaarer de Wartensee?
Rudolph Fridig(en) {Fridingen} (~1328/~1378)	St. Michael, Tuegen{Tengen}, Germany or Vienna, Austria	1401	1st reference for Fridig
Ulrich Fridingen (1328? OR ~1379?)	Constenz, Germany	1402	Burgermeister & Rath to Costentz
Rudi (Rudolph) Fridinger (~1378)	Romanshorn, Thurgau, Switzerland	Dec 1403	Vogtei
Ulrich Fridingen (1328? OR ~1379?)	Constanz, Germany	8/1403	Abend Asumpt doc for Cunrat Schallenburg
Rudolf v. Fridingen d. Ä.	Tubingen, Baden-Württemberg,Germany	Nov 1403	Frena Kburg (Kyburg) sell their festivals Schalksburg to her uncle Gf. Eberhard v. Wirtemberg.
Ulrich Fridingen (1328? OR ~1379?)	Constanz, Germany	1/1405	Knight, Burgermeister & Rath: contract to Constanz
Rudolf von Fridingen	Engen, Germany	Feb 1405	Vogt to Engen
Itel Fridinger (~1386)	St. Blasien, Klingnau, Switzerland	1406	Propst
Clara Schmerlin uxor Uolrici de Fridingen militis , sepulta sub vestibulo .	Constanz, Germany	3/1406	Uxor – Diocese record.
Ulrich Fridingen (~1328) wife Clara Schmerlin	Constanz, Germany?	1406	death record - Constantiensis group of monastery records
Fridingerus Frydingeri {Latin for Friedingen}	Zurich, Switzerland	1406	Goetfrid Ruti referee dispute of 5 abbots -Latin Parchment
Rudolf von Fridingen	Engen, Germany	4/1406	Vogt
Rudolf von Fridingen	Engen, Germany	May 1407	Vogt to Engen
Rudolph Fridingen der jung (~1378)	Konstanz, Germany	1407-9,1412	-1412. (Hauptmann)=Captain of St. George Shields ritterschaft/knight hood - Zurich Archives
Ulrich, Rudolf der Junge & Johannes von Fridingen	Konstanz, Germany	Oct 1407	Member of St. George Shields ritterschaft/knight hood - Zurich Archives
Eytel/Itel Fridinger (~1386)	Klingnau, sancti Blasiia in Nigra Sylva(Swarzwald)	Aug 8, 1407	Propst
Rudolf von Fridingen der Jünger	Constanz, Germany	Oct 1407	Ritterschaft in Schwaben
Johann von Fridingen	Pfit (Ferrette, Haut-Rhin, Alsace, France?)	1408	Vogt to Pfirt
Rudolf von Fridingen , Heinrich von Fridingen &	Waldsee, North of Konstanz, Germany	June 1408	Member of St. George Shields ritterschaft/knight hood -

The Swabian Connection – Expanded Edition

many other families..			Zurich Archives. Rudolph= hauptleut(Hauptmann/Captai n)
Hans Wilhelm Fridingen	Holland, Germany	1409	Vogt=Governer
Margaret von Gessler-Fridingen (~1372)	Brugg, Aargau, Switzerland	1408-9	Purchased house to comply with Bernese.
Hans von Fridingen VI (~1371)	Botzberg, Aarau, Switzerland	6/1409	Steuermeyern(Tax/Revenue officer?)
Heinrich Fridingen (~1378), Rudolf von Fridingen	Schwaben, Germany	Feb 1409	St. George Shields ritterschaft/knight hood
Rudolf von Fridingen der Jünger	Ulm or Innsbrooke, Austria	Nov 1409	Urkunden with Graf v Wirttemburg & Hertzog Friedrich Osterrich, Steyr, Krain.
Hans von Fridingen Gemahlin(wife) Margaretha Gessler	Heiligkreuztag im Herbst	Sept 1410	Ritter, & Vogt to Phirt
Ulrich (~1379) & Johann Fridingen (~1371)	Krayen, German or Zurich, Switzerland	1411	feud of brothers resolved. Zurich document
Ulrich v Fridingen	Konstanz, Germany	9/1411	Siegler with Bentz Schmid von Sigmaringen
Ulrich Fridingen	Konstanz, Germany	1411	Statthalter (Governor) of PrinceBishop.
Itel Fridinger	St. Blasier, Klingnau, Aargau, Switzerland	1411	Propste
Rudolf von Fridingen	Tengen, Germany	1/1412	confesses that he settled down to Tengen
Ulrich v Fridingen	Konstanz, Germany	4/1412	Knight & Vogt to Bishop Otto of Constanz
Ulrich v Fridingen	St. Urban kloster(?)	5/1412	Knight, Mayor and Aldermen to Costentz a mercenary contract .
Ulrich v Fridingen & Hans Von Fridingen w/ Hans Thüring Mönch	Liestal, Basel, Switzerland	7/1412	Accord with Herzog Friedrich von Österreich
Hans von Fridingen	Agram, Constanz	Oct 1412	Tax payment to Martini
Heinrich von Fridingen wife Adelheid Blumenberg(Blumeneck) (d. 1403)	Busendorf(Biesendorf), Engen, Germany	1413	Zehnten to Busendorf
Rüdolff von Fridingen, Landenburg, Rüdolff v Rosenberg v Zukkenriett and others	Wil, St. Gallen, Switzerland	Jan 1413	St. gallen accord
Johann von Fridinger/en	Chur, Switzerland	Sept 1413	Tax payment to Martini
Hans Frydinger /Johann v. Friedingen/ Johann Fridinger	v. Pfullendorf u. Isny(in Allgau), Germany	1/1414	Steuern = Steward
Hensli (Johann) Flückinger	Madiswil,Oberaargau,	1414	Amtsmann=official man

(~1384)	Bern,Switzerland/Grunenberg		
Rudolf von Fridingen der Jung IX	St. Urban, Switzerland	5/1414	
Rudolf von Fridingen	Konstanz, Germany	Jan 1415	St. Augustinerordens
Knights of Fridingen	Blumegg, Germany	1415	Knights of Friedingen the rule Blumegg, village Fützen, the village Kommingen..
Rudolphus Fridingen and filius(children) Heinrich and Rudolpho	Daugendorf, Germany	1415	Rights to Villa Daugendorf via Zwifaltenfis abbot Wolfhardus Lapide in Suevia.
Heinrich and Rudolf Fridingen (brothers)	Blumegg, Stuhlingen, Germany	1415	buy 1415 Herrschaft Blumegg and sell them at 1432's Monastery St Blaise(in Swarzwald).
Ulrich von Fridingen	Konstanz, Germany	3/1415	Ritter=Knight . Salary of 300 Guldens to servant
Konrad von Fridingen	Konstanz, Germany	3/1415	Salary of 500 Guldens to servant
Götz Schultheiss & Haintzmann von Mülhausen	Schaufhausen, Switzerland	May 1417	Purchase contract between their wall
Heinrich & Rudolf sons of Ruedolf Fridingen (~1378)	Blumembeck, Germany	Dec 1417	purchase of castle Blumembeck
Rudolphus Fridingen	Daugendorf, Germany	1418	Late Candidate to Zwifaltenfis
Konrad Fridingen (~1384) & Ritters Konrad des Schwarzen	Kraen/Krahen, Hohentwiel, Germany	2/1418	purchase of Goods to Duchtlingen, siegel missing.
die Brüder Heinz (Haintz) & Hans Friding von Wiesholz. The brothers Fridinger	Weisholz near Ramsen, Schaufhausen, Switzerland	3/1418	Kloster Einsiedeln record
Heinrich Truschess (=Fridingen)	Castle Diesenhofen, Germany	1419	Truschess=trustee
Ulrichen von Fridingen	Nurnberg or Schaufhausen, Switzerland	May 1420	Ritter
Rudolph Fridingen (~1378)	St. Nikolaus Church, Lausheim, Germany	1421	Pfleger=Keeper of church
Hans Wilhelm Fridingen (~1408)	Shenkenburg, Switzerland	1421	
Ritter Konrad von Friedingen & der Kaplan Stalvringer	Mühlhausen	May 1421	Exchange against an estate to Beringen
bruders Heinrich & Rudolph von Frindingen	Marchtal, Baden-Wirtemburg, Germany	April 1422	Kloster Marchtal
Rudolf v. Fridingen	Gerolseck/Sulz/Wirtimberg	1/1423	Mediation between the rule of Wirtemberg (hosts) and Wolf v. Geroldseck
Verena von Friedingen des Rates, des Wilhelm Imthurn (als Vogt der Frau	Kloster Allerheiligen	April 1423	Hof zu Jestetten

Verena) & des Konrad von Fulach.			
Heinrich Friedinger & Frau Margaretha Klinger	Kloster St. Agnes in Schaffhausen	April 1425	Court addressing farm record succession previously owned by Künzli Keller
Heinrich Fridinger von Wiesholz (XI ~1385?) ? with Ulrich Klingen der junge	Wiesholz, Ramsen, Switzerland	1425	Schaufhausen records
Ernst Fridingen (~1343)	Constanz, Germany	1425	landvogt=overlord guardian secular justice territory rulers
Ulrich Klingen der junge vs Heinrich Fridinger von Wisholz	Schaffhausen	July 1425	District Court in Unterklettgau Law Suit against **Heinrich Fridinger von Wisholz** (did not appear)
Margaretha Klingerin	Kloster St. Agnesen, Schaffhausen	Sept 1425	invested Margaretha Klingerin the widow and children, as heirs of salvation Künzli basement, with a half portion of the Kelnhofes to Wisholz.
Cunrat von Friding (Fridingen) III (~1384)	Kraygen (Krahen), Germany	1427-28	Familie Kuontzenberg records in Schaufhausen relating to Constanz.
Hans Konrad von Fridingen nephew of abbot Friedrich von Wartenberg	Radolfzell, Germany	1427-1453	Neffe(neffew)
Hainrich von Fridingen XI (~1385)	Klettgau, Switzerland	1428	Summa totalis in dem pund im Cleggöw. Schaufhausen records
Heintzen gen Kräygen & Götz Schulth[aiß], von Cuonraten von Fridingen	Schaufhausen, Switzerland	1428	to apply a tag from the Tettingers, dominica post Nicolay. Schaufhausen records
Margaret Erlbach/Gessler-Freidingen (~1372)	Shenkenburg, Switzerland	1431	sold Castle Shenkenburg & rights to Baron Thüring of Aarburg.
Rudolff & Cunrat von Fridingen	Nurnberg, Germany	5/1431	Pfalsburger citizens bailiwick of Swabia
B? v. Fridingen	St. Blasien, Klingnau, Switzerland	1432	Purchased Kloster St. Blasien
Brother Heinrich and Rudolf von Fridingen & cousin Conrad Fridingen	St. Gallen Archives	12/1432	Fief for village Ebetingen
Peter Friding [Frydig] (~1403)	Frutigen, Switzerland	1433 & 1437	Citizen/Family in Frutigen
Fren Fridingerin	Webergasse near Schaufhausen, Switzerland	1437	Steuerbuch(tax book)
Knights of Fridingen	Hohenlupfen,Stühlingen im Landkreis Waldshut in Baden-Württemberg, Deutschland	1437-1439	Knights of Friedingen the rule castle Hohenlupfen end 1439.
Johannes Fridiger (~1424)	Dresden, Germany	1441	1454 Burger=Citizen

The Swabian Connection – Expanded Edition

Werner Fryding/Fridiger/ Fridig (~1420)	Born Basel, Swiss/Isenthal & Uri, Swiss	1443	
Werner Fryding/Fridiger/ Fridig (~1420)	Sihl, Switzerland	1443	
Hans Wilhelm Fridingen (~1408)	Bregenz,Germany(over the border to Switzerland)	1444	Vogt=Governer
Hans Wilhelm Fridingen (~1408)	Lucern, Switzerland	11/1446	Lucern message from Confederates
Haman Fredinger with son-n-law Peter	Waldkirch, Germany	11/1449	Zimmermanns=Carpenters
Conrad Fridingen (~1442?)	Chur, Switzerland	1451	Stadtvogt @ Castle Haldenstein
Burckhart Fridinger/en (~1423)	Yestetten (Jestetten, Germany)	9/1453	Vogt=Governer
Klas Frutinger (~1434)	Munchen, Germany	1454	Burger=Citizen
Konrad Fridinger Jkr (~1420)	Radolfzell, Germany	1454-1465	Burgermeister (Ammann)
Hans Johannes Fridingen (~1428)		1458	Seckelmeister?
Hans (Johann) Frieden	{Rebgütern to Oberhofen}, Berne	1467	Burgerin to Berne
Conrad Fryding (~1439)	Innsbruck, Austria	1469	Loan
George von Fridingen III (~1458)	Ammerswyl, Lenzburg, Aargau, Switzerland	1471	Church Kleriker/Pfarrer
Stephan de Fridingen (~1442)	Alpirsbach, Schwarzvald, Germany	1471	Monch
Rudolp (~1445) & Martin Fridingen (~1454)	Kressbach. German (South of Tubingen)	1472	thru 1478. Mortgaged Castle Kreßbach
Konrad Fridinger	Radolfszell, Germany	2/1475	Bürgermeister
Hans Itelhaus (~1449) Hans Thüring von Fridingen (~1452)	Schaffhausen, Switzerland	1476	sale of Holy Spirit Hospital at Schaffhausen
Veit von Fridingen	Wien, Austria	6/1477	Deutschordenskandidaten
Georgius (Jorg) Fridingen (~1458)	Tubingen, in Basel, Switzerland	1478	Student Basiliensis @ Tubingen University
Conrat von Fridingen	Chur, Canton of Graubunden, Switzerland	8/1481	Vogt to Chur
Herr(=Lords) von Fridingen	Konstanz, Germany	1482,84	Member of St. George Shields ritterschaft/knight hood - Zurich Archives
Stefan Fridingen (~1442)	Wittnau, Germany	1482	Propst=senior official ecclesial management
Rudolph Fridingen (~1445)	Tubingen, Germany	1482	thru 1488 - Student @ Tubingen University
Jorg von Fridingē (Fridingen) (~1453)	Constanz	1483	Wappen in Ulrich Richental Concilium zu Konstanz
Johannes von Fridingē (~1458)	Constanz	1483	Wappen in Ulrich Richental Concilium zu Konstanz
Martin Fridingen II & Rudolf Fridingen XIV	Castle Bussen, Germany	1483	
Bartholomew Fridingen (~1485)	Fridingen, Constanz, German	1485	Priest @ Fridingen, Germany

Bernhard Fraydiger/Freidinger (~1458)	Dresden, Germany	1486	1558 Sekretär(y)
Simon Fridingen (~1458)	Berne, Switzerland	1488	a monastery in Bern, Switzerland
Rudolf von Fridingen	Beuggen	1490	Hofmeister später Landkomthur
Johanne (Jean) Fridinger	Waldshut, Germany	1490	Student in Bologne/Bologna
Georg von Fridingen	Beuggen	1492	Hauskomthur
Hans Thuring Fridingen (~1452)	Kraen/Krahen, Hohentwiel, Germany	1492	Letter from Confederation
Simon von Friedingen (~1463) {Symoni de Fridingen}	Muri, Aargau, Switzerland	1493	Pfarrer confirmation elected decan.
Simon Fridinger	Chur, Switzerland	1494?	Dekan?
Elsin Grefin von Frauenfeld, Widow of Hanns von Fridingen under Dienerin des Nicolaus, Bischofs zu Tripolitan	Basel, Switzerland	2/1495	Dienerin des Nicolaus, Bischofs to Tripolitan
Rudolp (~1445) & Martin Fridingen ~1454)	Kressbach, German (South of Tubingen)	1497	Sold Castle Kreßbach
Richi Fridig (~1472)	Isental, Uri, Switzerland	1500	or 1512. Havoc in Seedorf church.
Marti Fridig (~1450)	Isental, Uri, Switzerland	1500	or 1512 Chappel Owner
Michael Fridig (~1470)	Isental, Uri, Switzerland	1500	or 1512
Ernst "Benedict?" von Fridingen (~1469)	Friedingen & Hohenkrahen in Singen and Baden-Wuerttemberg, Germany	1501	Innsbuck, Austrian archive letter to Hohenkrean
Jorg Freiding (~1475) {Fridingen?}	Rattenberg, Austria	1505	Maler=Painter
Felictia von Friding {Rotenstein-Fridingen} (~1446)	Kempten, Germany	1505	Kempten Archives Inheritance record for Dorothea Awerin.
Conrad Fridingen (~1444)	Eyrs, Schlanders, Italy (SSE of Innsbruck & Tirol, Austria)	1506	Richter= Judge
Henz Fluckingen (~1477)	Rohrbach, Switzerland	1507	Home and yard purchase - Berne, Switzerland archives
Hans Johannes Fridingen (~1467)	Freyenthurn, Kärnten, Austria	1511	or 1532
Heinz Fridig (~1472)	Nuremburg, Germany	1512	
Bauer Fridig (~1473)	Nuremburg, Germany	1512	
Johannes Fridinger	Constanz, Germany	1512/13	Under Roman Curtisan Theobald Huoter
Ursula Fridingen-Luternau (~1446)	Aarau, Argau, Switzerland	1513	
Hans Grimm von Fridingen (~1466)	Schlatt, Germany	1520	
Johannes Fridinger	Constanz, Germany	Jan 1521	Bischöflicher Official & Rath? to Zurich.
sons of Martin Friedingen	Duchtlingen, Baden-	1522	Bill of Sale for Guardians

(~1454)	Wurttemberg, Germany		
Nicklaus Fruting {Frutig} (~1495)	Moosseedorf, Berne, Switzerland	1523	
Hans Grimmen Fridingen (~1458)	Constanz, Germany	1524	Brother n law to Marcus von Knoringen
Hans Johannes Fridingen (~1467)	Constanz, Baden-Württemberg, Germany	1525	Hofmeister (Steward)
Hans Johannes Fridingen (~1467)	Eggen, near Waldburg, Germany	1528	or 1529 Landvogt (Governor)
Hans Johannes Fridingen (~1467)	Kraen/Krahen, Hohentwiel, Germany	1534	
Sebastian Freyding (~1504)	Untrasried,Ostallgäu,Bavaria, Germany	1534	bill of sale
Hanns Frayding (~1505)	Unterallgäu in Bavaria, Germany	1535	Gerichtsammann=Court Ammann to Legau
Burger **Erasmus Fridinger**	Weymer, Austria	Oct 1535	Urger sale of 1/8 des Winter-Hammers Haus
Rudolp Fridingen (~1445)	Altshausen, Ravensburg, Baden-Württemberg, Germany	1537	Coat of Arms @ Tuetonic Castle Altshausen
Bartholoma Frydinger	Muhlhausen, Germany	1539	Kaplan
Franz Fridingen (~1519)	Hitzkirch, Lucerne, Switzerland	1542	thru 1546 Compthur/Leupreister
Sebastian Freyding (~1504)	Untrasried,Ostallgäu,Bavaria,Germany	1542	bill of sale
Jorg Fridingen (~1472)	Hohen Geroldseck, Germany	1544	Vogt=Governer
Franz von Fridingen	Mülhausen 1549, Mainau 1549 – 54	1544	Hauskomthur
Dorothy Fridingen (~1510)	Tubingen, Germany	1552	Uxor for Siegmond H Hertneck (~1507)
Cristianus Rormeyer Friding (~1534)	Universität Freiburg in Breisgau, Germany	1554	Student
Benedit Fruting {Frutig} (~1530)	Trachselwald, Emmental, Bern, Switzerland	1558	thru 1560 Vogt=Governer
Sebastian Fridingen (~1533) son of Damian Fridingen[408]	Graz, Austria	1558/59	Student @ Graz school
Rudi (Rudolf) Frieden von Waltwil	Berne, Switzerland	1564	
Agnes Frydiger (~1536)	Basel, Switzerland	1566	
Gwer Fryding [Frydig/Fridig] (1535/1564)	land transfer from "Pleiken" { Bleiken bei Oberdiessbach?), Switzerland (43 miles west of Adelboden) or from Pleicken, Wattwil, Saint Gallen, Switzerland.	1586	5-30-1586 Land fief Transfer
Simon Friedinger (~1563)	Waldkraiburg, Germany?	1593	Pfarrvikar (Assistant Pastor)
Barbel Fridinger (~1602)	Thurgau, Switzerland	1602	thru 1637
Peter Freidinger von Stockstadt	Stockstadt, Germany	1479-1584	Schiffer=Boatsmen/Sailer/Skipper

The Swabian Connection – Expanded Edition

Des Fridingen in The Middle Ages

The Middle Ages(Mittelalter) technically began in the 5th/6th century and ended in the 15th century. Before the Holy Roman Empire, there was King/Duke/Chief **Fridigern (~352)** who rose up as a Peaceful leader of the Visigoths for a better life for his people across the Danube to Thrace. In the book "Italy and her Invaders" it describes Fridigern as embracing Christianity (Head of the Christian party) and friendship with Rome.

In the book "Alemannien and the Nordan" it describes the Fridingen nobles in the 7th century who set themselves apart and established a half dozen inhumation barrows separated from others and on the outskirts of the row grave cemetery (on the Danube river) near the AltFridingen ruine. Inhumation barrows are graves dug out with rock built around them.

When Charlemagne (742-†814) (Frankish King) came into power 768, one of his Paladins(soldiers) and brother-in-law Gerold (~730-†795) played a significant role in integrating Bavaria into the Frankish[409] Kingdom. Some consider Gerold's line as part of Alaholfing families, however many reseachers cite Geroldonen & Uldaricher lines as being Frankish(Francs) Allemanic[410] lineage in Schwabia and Thurgau. One being that Gerold was Graf in Middle Rhein area implying a Franconian origin[411]. Singen (787) Feb 15th Bishop Aginao awarded frankish Ato the Deacon @ St. Gallen with possessions in Schlatt, Mühlhausen, Ehingen, Weiterdingen, Welschingen, Gundihhinhova etc. "In 910 Burchard Hunfridinger from Raetian (descendant of Hunfried I von Rhathien ~775) married Hitta daughter of Ulrich V(?) and Burchard had attempted to become Duke, but he was killed in 911 and his son exiled. The Hunfridingers were the opponents[412] of the Uldaricher families. The Brothers Erchanger and Berchtold sought to take his place (Jeep 2001 | 227)". Duke Erchanger Fridingen (~873) Pfalzgraff and his brother Berchtold (~876) came into possession Hohentwiel castle presumably with the castle already there or built by 914. Erchanger was the Duke of Swabia from 915-917. He caused a conflict with King Conrad and was supposedly be-headed in 917. These two brothers were thought to have begun the official line of Fridinger nobility. However, Fridingen place name is actually mentioned earlier in a monastery record (786) June 29th describing King Charles Martell (Uncle of Karl de Grosse) & Brother-in-Law Gerold carry monastery Beuron under mountain fortress below Findingen/Fridingen on the Danube (Danubian) (RI:272). This is also about the time period Muhlhause is recorded Mulinusa 787 & Mulinhusa 976. The celebration of 1150 year old festival occurred in 2011 for the Stadt(=State) of Fridingen @ Donau records the year in (861). Erchanger (~873) and his family come from a noble family race called Ahalolfings or Alaholfings (=Alaholfinger) in the area of Alemannia (the center being Reichenau with a diameter 200-400 miles). The Ahalolfings rose in the Carolingian empire to posess lands in Alemannia, Bavaria, Franconia and Italy. An older relative named Berthold was a co-founder of the Reichenau abbey in 724. Richardis the daughter of Erchanger married Charles the Fat. The Ahalolfings supposedly died out in 973 with Berthold III. Herzog Hermann I von Schwaben (†949) the fränkischen ancestor of the wife of Hermann d j von Mahlspuren (Dobler 1986:17). In 983 Gebhard (949) (son of Ulrich von Bregenz) Bishop of Konstanz established the Monastery called St. Petershausen (in Constanz) which would later be the burial location of Eppo von Heilgenberg (=Ebberhardt IV von Nellenburg)[413] and wife Tota/Touta along with Hermann d .A von Hirscheck with wife Perhterad. "Also Eppo von Heiligenberg (also Eppo de Sancto Monte, Eberhardus advocatus Petrishusensis, comes de Nellenburg, de Potamo)[414] and his wife Touta at the altar of St Peter buried in the same church above the altar, their portraits are painted on the wall to the likeness of the man are verses in the inscription and the portrait of the woman. In addition it is on the same wall is a grave writing on Hermann von Hirzisegga (Hirscheck) and his wife Perchterada. On the other side of the church at the altar of St Stephan four noble men who were killed together Wernher namely Hermann, Burchard and Wolfarn[415]." "Bishop Conrad, the small Augsburg annals came only generally call a Swabian most probably from the nobles families of Hirscheck, but it is here, as we noted here take occasion, not to think about Hirscheck in the Bregenz Forest (Brown

II, p 103) but at Hirscheck (Hirzisegga) at Alshausen in Wirtemberg top official Saulgau where the ruins of the castle Hirscheck can still be seen, on which also lived beyond doubt that Hermann von Hirzisegga, what good about the year 1040 the monastery Petershausen considerable bequeathed (Chron Petershus u. Staelin I 595) probably the Hirschecker Conrad and Rudolph came with the bishop, Walter 1133 1150 to Augsburg sons of one of the Palatinate photographers Mangold of Dillingen was the founder of Anhausen[416]." "(1056) Eberhard Nellenburg - Eberhardo ppo Annone eiusdem aecclesiae presbytero herimanno advocato[417] {translated= Eberhard (e?)ppo not the same church, the priest called herimanno} (=Hermann Hirscheck)." The notes identify this as Hezelo von Wald(d.1088) son Hermann(d.1094), however I have his birth about (~1050-70) so this would be Herman Hirscheck (~996) or his son(?) Hermann (~1030). "Werner von Winterthur married the daughter Irmengarde de Nellenburg, the daughter of Ebberhardt von Nellenburg. "Hermann der Ältere von Hirscheck (@ Altshausen) donated to the reign of Emperor Conrad II (1024-1039) the monastery Petershausen (near Konstanz) as a relic acquired in Agaune arm of a martyr of the bäischen Legion, gave also his brother, the monk community assets Allmannsweiler and in Winnenden, Hermann and his wife Bertha, their final resting place in Petershausen[418]". Their epitaph: *Perhterat aetherii Herimanque perennia regni Petri suscipite precibus bona Gregoriique ,Vos et vestra decens post debita sabbata proles Istinc octavam speratis adire beatam.* Translated: Perhterat Herimanque ethereal realm of perpetual support requests Gregoriique good, you and your offspring to rest due after becoming the eighth quarter you expect to go happy. In 1060 the brothers (Hirscheck) Hermann and Gerold give their possession to Mimmenhausen/Miminhusin(Nimwendusin), Reute/Ruti(Reute be Meersburg), Esscherichsweiler and Neufrach/Niuviron(Neuffern/Neufra in Riedlingen) from Petershausen. Translated from Latin to English: "Gerold and his brother gave up at times like these Pr Herimannus Miminhusin, Ruti, and Eschichiswilare Niuuiron, and he very reverently Gerold times Theodoric, abbot of the monastery conversed in the same very reverently until the death of his own, previously in the habit of a beard, and then to monks (Macklot 1848 : 135)". Arnold (Heilgenberg?) possibly a relative of Hermann did just a year at the abbey and in 1065 renounced (Herder 1873 : 240). Gerold gave his life to the monastery[419] and from this determined either Hermann or Arnold (=Heilgenberg?) comes the Hirscheck/Fridinger/Krahen lineage. Count Burchard of Nellenburg (son of Eberhard Nellenburg & Ita III) renewed and notarized his own and his parents Donations to the monastery of (*Allerheiligen in Schauffhausen*) All Saints 1090, which had been previously established (1087) June 2nd. At the request of Abbot William of Hirsau, the he can come to the Reformation the monastery, he renounced the right of all Advokatie and other privileges, giving the church the house Scafhusacum moneta publication, mercato etc. By an embassy to Pope Gregory VII, he looks to the monastery immunity, and confirmed the donations of his father, Eberhard (in the Monastery of All Saints on June 4, 1087). It also determines the Duke Bertold, the Courts and Bosinga Hemmental at All Saints assign Fridingen (1090) April 14 *convenientes in villa que dicitur **Fridinga**,* Ludewici legally filled my petition twice before witnesses Pilgrin de Hussinkirchun, Eberhardus de Justingin, Dietricus de Hundersingin, Adelbero de Singin, Wipertus de Walthusen, Wipertus de Hönerhusin, Egilwart de Chalfon, Rödolf de Tengin (grandson(?) of Heinrich Hirscheck(?)), Bertoldus de Beringin, Bertoldus of his son[420].

In 1089 Folmar von Fridingen is in Martinweiler at a tournament; this is recorded in the beginnings of the St. George's Monastery in the Black Forest. Come from local nobles before the brothers Folkmar, Adelbert and Eberhard free of Nendingen which the first and second witness one of Hesso von First{Furst} to Kloster St Georgen made foundation 6 April 1092, the second and third 17 January 1094 at St George's Monastery give property in Ettismeiler[421]. In 1092 Folkmar von Nendingen gave his property from Martinsweiler to the St. Georgen Monastery which is also the same year mentined the village name Nendingen. Folkmar is unknown to this family Hirschecker main line, but possible an earlier cousin before Hermann I von Hirscheck-Fridingen (~1135) or a Nellenburg descendant. Even the rich tradition of Auer was Nendingen (Nendincist a.d. person name itself derives from again) of Count Gerold given to the monastery. Around the year 1000 is of him in fief to the counts of Nellenburg of these occurred in the related to them were Fursten{princes} of Hirscheck-Konzenburg mountain and by them to their relatives with von Wartenberg vogtei set and lay church tithes[422]. However, Nendingen would later come to be settled by family Hirscheck family @Konzenburg[423]. In the St. Christopher monastery recorded the reference (1411-17) the familie von Fridingen came from the Ministerial and Grafen von Kiburg line which is an older reference to Adabert v Winterthur/Kiburg (~975) father to Hermann v Hirscheck (~996). The commonly referenced and more documented Kyburg lieneage comes from Adelheid v Winterthur/ Kyburg (~1050) daughter of Adalbert v Winterthur (~1020) who married Hartmann I von Dillingen (~1050).

This Hirschecker-Mahlspüren trunk lineage had a myriad of surnames appearing in charters or other monastery records prior to the 1200's. Three primary klosters/monasteries they were documented in: Petershausen 1043, 1058/60, 1084,1120/21 – St. Georgen 1083, 1091, 1101 and Allerheiligen 1090, 1145. Bueslingen (Büßlingen in Tengen,Germany) an occasionally used name for this family Hirscheck had the church Buesslingen as a sole possession in the monastery of Allerheiligen(All Saints) in Schaufhausen in 1145. After 1149 brought the nobles of Tengen claims the Bailiwick[424]. In 1183 comes the name Fridingen as a familie and surname. Krahen(Craegen) family name established between 1158-1194. Others names used before being established surname were Hirscheck (1043-1083), Gailingen (1087), Ramsen (1101), Busslingen (1101), Winterspuren (1101), Schwandorf (1131), Mahlspuren/Mahlspüren (1131), Espasingen (1135), Stetten (1130/1158) ,Hohenfels (~1130's) and Fridingen (1181,1190's+) Fridinger (1200's+). Salestetin & Reidern families I believe have beginning lineages from 1135, 58,60 to 1194/97 of Hermann v Stetten brothers. An Original document dated November 4th (1281) has Rudolf von Fridigen zu Tengen, although 2nd page has the 1401 date[425]. Mulhouse (BA Engen) passed 1338 the brothers Walter and Ulrich Baron of Hohenklingen the church to Mulhouse among Krähen serfs[426]. By 1401 Rudolph Fridingen has been referenced as Fridig(en) in St. Martin Monastery in Esslingen or Tengen(?).

In the Thal St. Christopher wappenrolle recorded (1411-1417) it appears this is a turning point for the Fridingen (Fridinge/Fridige) as they continue moving outside Hegau(Swabia) into Tirol Western Austria, the

Die v. f. waren einst Ministerialen der Grafen v. Kiburg und führten darum ein an das ihrige anklingendes Wappen. Bereits

dialects and spellings continue to change. The (1411-17) St. Christopher document reaffirms the families connections to Kiburg which would have been back prior to 1043 on the male Adelbert von Kyburg Uldaricher Lineage. In Weisholz near Ramsen, the Fridinger brothers Hans & Heinz Friding owning land in 1418 – this area in canton of Schaufhausen was originally part of the Hegou/Hegau of Swabia. It's my understanding during the mid 1300-1400's more population growth in Southern German and Northern Switzerland as a result the Noble children had to take various positions outside of their common homeland of Hegau in Swabia south into places like (Baden or Brugg in Aargau, Lommis, Thurgau, Tirol or Innsbruck Austria, Zug, Chum, Bern and Zurich etc..). Combined with Swiss waring with the German/Austrian Nobles (for autonomy) small or individual peasant/serf migrations to new lands meant new opportunities especially if you were against the Reichstag (Emperial Parliament) and expansion policies of Savoy to the west and Habsburgs to the east in 1323 of Switzerland. The Swabian Nobles and their Swiss descendants show a variation of Etymology and pronunciations as they become recorded in Schweiz(Swiss) and Austrian records. Bern became a permanent member of the Swiss Confederacy in 1353 (Schelbert 38:2007) and Frutigen part of Bern in 1400. Peter Friding (~1403) appears in Frutigen,Bern, Switzerland by 1433 & 1437. Peter F most likely a 2nd or 3rd generation Frei serf from the canton of Aargau, Thurgau or Schaufhausen(Ramsen/Weisholz) descendant of von Friding(er/en) familie. Hans Waldfluh said about Frutigen (translated from Schweiz to English): "From a number Ausburger it can be shown that these or their descendants settled in the city. Among them were some members of the gender gennant v. Kienthal, Truschen, Great, Kander Matter, Mullenberg, Falb (originally called Zumkehr Valw). The list of Ausburger our valley offers a scenic view of the development of naming. Smell a documentary of these people you meet infrequently or not at all, a numerical indication of the presence of her sex. Of the 122 recorded gender namen are still 40 in the Office Frutigen. If you think about it, what stood on the strength

109

of Swabia feet of the former family name, so that's a significant number to call. The disabled family names are those which still occur today in the valley. All persons without a location derived explicitly from Frutigen (Wandfluh : 1952)." In my opinion only a very few families actually would have an origin (derived explicitly) from Frutigen before (1400) the anniversary unification with Bern. Frydig/Fridig being this Friding descendants dialect and spelling change in Frutigen/Adelboden from the 1500-1700's. Another line of Friding /Fridig in Isental, Canton Uri, Switzerland from an Werni Fryding (Fridig) by 1420 born in Basel, Switzerland on the German border. This Fridig/Friding/Friden/Fridung lineage ends supposedly in the 1600's for the Uri Canton of Switzerland. In the 15th century, the Friedinger's lost lands and properties were lost through succession, inheritance and feudes, litigation disputes of economic and social influence, and had to gradually sell them off the village castle to the Lords of Bodman. Monasteries were also sold off too, and the descendants while moving in to Chaplan or Burgermeister type positions. Reviewing E. Dobler's Hirscheck stemtable, it is inconceivable that out of 67 (17 of clergy) Fridinger males from Hermann Hirscheck @ Petershausen in 1043 to Hugo von Fridingen in 1568 had no children, especially when some of those generations has between 5-7 children per family. By 1476 remained the Fridingen only a few pieces of property. The Fridingen led from Hohenkrahen raids/robbers by the surroundings until, on 12 November 1512 a 8000-strong punitive expedition of the Swabian League to stop the robbers. As a result, lost the track of the Friedingen name ceased after 1560 – Friedinger/Friding/Freidig/Fridig/Frydig would be the alternative lesser noble/feudal serf surnames in different time frames starting in the late 1300's, in *Frutigen/Adelboden* as Friding/Fryding in the mid 1400's and Frydig/Fridig in the early 1500's..

The Swabian Connection – Expanded Edition

Rudolf von Fridingen (~1462)

Stained glass pane: circa 1516/19 Rudolf von Fridingen (~1462) was the Comthur "Land controller" for many locations in Germany and Switzerland. His image was commissioned on the Bern Muenster Cathedral Church in Switzerland sometime between 1499-1535. The church began construction in 1421 and converted to Protestant with accepting the Reformation in 1528 as did most of Switzerland by that time. In Sudeutschland or Ravensburg, Germany Germany dating ~1530 there is a Coat of arms of the Swabian League united religious and secular estates.

The Description: Brown Crosses over White Background diagonally left to right. Fridingen Shield in upper right corner has the yellow Lion standing in the White Stripe between Blue backgrounds. The bottom left corner is Black Golden the Alt-Fridingen/Old-Fridingen familie. Upper left and Lower right is a White background with Black Crosses which is from the Teutonic Order which Rudolph was Commander for 4 years. Helmet is Orange. Plume of white feathers above the Helmet with a cross. (69v) herr rudolf von fridingen, Landescomentur der ballei in elses und burgundi (Rudolf von Friedingen, Landkomtur der Ballei Elsa-Burgund des Deutschen Ordens) und weitere 8 Komture. Translation: Bl 76v (69v) Mr Rudolf of Fridingen, Landescomentur elses in the Bailiwick and Burgundian (Rudolf von Friedingen, Alsace and Burgundy Komtur the Bailiwick of the Teutonic Knights) and a further 8 commanders. **Notable dates:1483** Education @ University of Tubingen,Germany. 1490 Hofmeister (später Landkomthur). 1497 Comthur to Sumiswald, Switzerland. 1500 Kommenthur to Sumiswald Sumiswald, Switzerland. 1501 Kommenthur to Hitzkurch, Luzern, Switzerland. Comthur (1503,1506,1508, 1512,1521) Koniz,Switzerland. 1506 Education @ Universität Tübingen, Switzerland. Land Meister/Magistrate 1522-1537 Elsass,Germany. 1525 LandComthur Altshausen, Ravensburg, Baden-Wurtemburg, Germany.

The Swabian Connection – Expanded Edition

Rudolf von Fridingen (~1462)	**Rudolf von Fridingen (~1462)**

circa 1516/19	circa 1516/19

The Black cross over white shield is the Teutonic Order of Arms which he was a Comthur over Koniz, Switzerland. The stained glass pane was commissioned before 1535 via the Deutchen Order of the Tuetonic Knights of which he was the leader at that time. His coat of Arms also has this Shield diagnoly with the Fridingen wappen. These panes are called the "Dance of Death" and is located in Muester St. Vincent Church Cathedral, Bern, Switzerland.

The Dance of Death was an allegory of universality and inevitability of death due to the popular thoughts of the Black Plague in the prior 14th century. He is also on Stained Glass windows in Sumiswald. The Church in Sumiswald shows him in knightly armor, bareheaded, his helmet at his feet, he kneels before the healing. Katharina covered his armor to his knees a walking white skirt with the black "Deutchen Order of the Cross". The above wall painting is also in Color and located on the Dominikaner Monastery in Bern, Switzerland[427].

The Fridingen Shield border Lion seems to prove a mixture origin of Winterthur, Kyburg, Dillingen & Burglen. Fridingen being an ancestor of Burglen comes the gold and blue colors, which could have responded to the Nellenburgische house colors a Gold background with 3 Blue half-deer antlers (possibly in black). The Buirglen/Burglen/Bürglen shield was 1st noted in 1176[428]. The family of Dillingen splits off: instead of the black box, one blue and Lion Doubled/Trippled, now turning to one Lion split. An image of Warmannus d. Dillingen et Kyburg (~1006) a Bishop of Konstance, Germany in 1026 has a quartered wappenschild with 2 Lowen(Lions) split between upper & lower portions of the white bend[429]. Ulricus I de Dillingen (~1081) also carries the wappen with a double Lion divided on blue dated 1111 . Hermann II de Fridingen (~1101) is shown on the same wappenschild diagram with one lion. The Burglen familie only has the single

The Swabian Connection – Expanded Edition

golden Lion across the entire shield of Blue. Hermann Hirscheck d. J (~1101) married the daughter of Graf Dietrichs von Bürglen-Nellenburg. From this line the HohenFriedingen & Burg HohenKrahen was established (~1170-1180) and resided under Heinrich I von Stetten a fridingische noble. An interesting note the wappen for Heinrich Lowenberg {*LOW BERG*} in 1293 is a single Lion like the Burglen wappen. Luenberger family is understood to come from Lowenberg line.

The following families names may have also influenced the shield design of von Fridingen/ Krahen: v Kiburg (gold & black with bend), v Dillingen (gold, black & blue & white with bend), v Stetten, v Espasingen (gold & black stag horns),v Nellenburg (gold w/3 blue stag horns) v Winterthur (white & red lions), v Bregenz (blue w/white moon & gold star), v Krenkingen (blue with red/white stripes), v Burglen (blue & gold lion) and possibly v Hirscheck/Hirseg(gold w/Stag on blue mountain). Hirscheck/Hirseg shield may have come later during 13-14th century. The following names (v Krahen, v Bussen, v Fridingen, v Tengen and v Hohenfels) could not have influenced since the shield would have been designed at the same time as the name being created. The surnames starting to be used at the same time between 1158-1180/90. Transcribed from Eberhard Dobler book from German to English: "The border Lowe seems to prove the origin of Winterthur. He puts in the arms of the Counts Winterthur-Kyburg (in black, a yellow bar Schrag, Lowen accompanied by the same branch) and about 1180 of them split off counts of Dillingen (instead of the black box, one blue; Lowen doubled). Warmannus Com d Dillingen et Kyberg bishop (1026) of Constance/Konstanz shows 2 gold Lions divided by white over 2 gold Lions with background of blue[430]. The yellow and blue colors of the coat of arms Fridingen Burgler and could have responded to the Brandenburg nelle house colors (1986)." Johannes von Krahen was using the signet before 1250. Gotfrid von Kreygen is shown with the Blue Lion shield by 1307(votive painting produced in the 16th century @ Castle Bodman)..

Origin of Fridingische Wappenschilde(COA) table:

Haus of Kyburg 1180.	Haus of Winterthur	Haus of Bürglen	Haus of Nellenburg

Ancestral von Dillingen	Herman d. A Hirscheck (~990) relatives: Brother-Werner I v Winterhur (~995) Father-Adalbert v Winterhur (~975) Grandfather- Liutfried v Winterhur (~945).	Dietrich von Burglen-Nellenburg or Eberhard v. Stetten (~1139) [Freiherren v Burglen] son/nephew of Hermann I von Fridingen (~1103)	daughter of Dietrich Nellenburg married ~1105 Hermann d. J. von Mahlspuren/Espasin gen (Hirscheck) (~1085)

Haus of Dillingen

Grafen von Dillingen ~1180

Von Tengen

~1050? Gerold v. Tengen, Son of Herman v Hirscheck?. (Tengen noted 1236-1359)

Von Fridingen/Krahen

~1184(?)-1250

1250-1500's

Muhlhausen (in Hegau), Germany

quartered schield –

Von Fridingen 1400-1500's

Muhlhausen-Ehingen, Germany

Von Steckborn in Thurgau 1187 - 1332

Alt-Fridingen or Neu-Fridingen 1355-1535

Bueren @ Aach , Singen, Germany – Donation of Diethelm v {Krahen-Fridingen} in 1228. Nephew to Diethelm v Krenkingen († d. 1206)

Many other coats of arms (wappenschilde) appear to replicate or have some characteristics of the Fridingische/Krahener {Burglen\Winterthur\Kyburg (*lack of lowe/lion or Schrägbalken/diagonal bar*)} form: wappenschilde images from the Zurich wappenrolle circa ~1340.

- **Bueren at Aach**, **Mulhausen, Bohringen** @ Radolfzell am Bodensee (1896) and **Mulhausen Ehingen** villages taken from Lords of Fridingen rights and donations. Understood, no issue.

- **von Bürglen (BViRGLEN)** {*Azure, a lion rampant or crowned gules, lack of bend*} #68 Zurich wappenrolle 4 & 5 up from Tengen & Hewen. FreiHerren (FreeLords) Eberhard von Stetten v Burglen (~1139) son of Hermann v Stetten/Espasingen (~1103) (Dobler 1986:448). Stein Klosters Allerheiligen (1092) February 26th Graf Burkhard von Nellenburg, **Hartwic de Strazza**, Benno de Speicchinga, Diethalm de Tochimburc,

Dieterich comes de Biurgeliun (Nellenburg), Herimann de Egga and others (SH:576). Constanz (1176) Herm prepos, Heinr dec, Frider de Nidingen, C de Foro, Ulr de Annvillare, **Heinr de Fridingen**, mag Albert, Hesso, Conr de Tegervelt, Gotefr de Rordorft, **Bruno et Hainr de Marchtorff**, Ölr de Willare, Hesso, **Hainr de Vrichingen, Burch et Hainr et Bertold Stateli**, Burch de Hohenburg, Chônr de Willare, Dieterici cum filiis Ebernandi, Thiethelm de Tochemburg, **Eberhardus de Burgelun** and many others (RE:116). Constantie (1183) bischof von C(=Hermann Fridingen) & äbten Dietpert von SBlasien & Gebhard von Petershausen, Chônr dec, ödalr cust, Hesso canon, Chônr de Thetingin, Hugo cellerar, Provinciales: **Eberh de Burgelun**, Diethelm de Snegginburc, **Berht et Chônr de Wilare**, Wecil et Chónr de Hugoldishovin, **Chônr de Anniwilare de monte, Rôd de Anniwilare fil domini Hessonis**, Hiltibold et Hugo fratr Bódeg, Hesso fil Ödilr, and a few others (REC 1895:121). Constantie (1194) Ödalr comes de Bergin, Ödalr de Klingin, **Ebirh de Burgilun, Tiethelmus de Creie(Krahen)**, Berhtold de Kalpfo and others (Wagner1895:128). Mülibach (1209) Albertus pleb de Wila, **Wernherus pleb de Stekkenboren**, Egilolfus pleb de Waldkilche, comes Diethelmus iun de Togginburch ,**Waltherus advoc de Klingin, Eberhardus de Burgilon cum filio s Berchtoldo**, Albertus de Bussenanch cum filio s Alberto Eudolfus Ulricus, Heinricus carnales fratr de Gütingen, Rudolfus et Heinricus carnal fratr de Wunninberch, Volcmarus de Geinwilare, Ebirhardus de Spiegilberch, Rudolphus de Steinache, Berchtoldus de Anniwilare, Fridericus et Wernherus de Schoninberch, Albertus de Heidoltiswilare cum filio s Wezilone Wezilo dapifer de Hugol tishoven Rudolfus de Winterthure, Chunradus Giel, Waltherus de Eilgau, Ebirhardus et Waltherus carnales fratres de Bichilnsee, Beringerus de Lamminberg, Egilolfus et Heinricus cam fratr de Valchknistein, Rudolphus de Bochislo, Arnoldus de Heitinowe, Berchtoldus Fantilie and others (RE:139). (1216) Diethelm I. v. Steinegg 1216-1256, **Berthold v. Bürglen** 1209-1244, abbott Rudolf v. Tengen 1198-1219 and many others (MO:1035). (1216) July 16th Kloster St. Johann und dem Johanniterhaus Bubikon das Kloster: **Ber. de Burgelun**, H de Arbun, F et H(einrich) et B de Zukenriet, R et H. de Gutting(en), W. de Swarcenbah(Walter Schwarzenbach) militibus and many others (MO:1036). Embriaci (1223) May 25th Chvnr de Schalchon, Chvnr de Tocchenburch, comes Werner de Honberch, Lvtold de Begensperch, Walter de Thegerveld, Arnold de Warta, **Bertold de Burgelon**, Werner et Chuno de Tuffen and many others (RE:156). St. Gallen (~1230) July 13th Kloster Weisenau brother **Konrad and Heinrich Wartenburg** transfer goods to "Tieringeshart" to Ritter Ulrich von Schwarzenbach in presense of **Berthold monk** nephew of our Salem and his brothers, Albert & Henry Bussenanc soldiers, **Bertoldo de Burgelon** and Henry de Guttingen soldiers (WO:1171). (1243) B et H thesaurariis, B eiusd loci, **R de Burgulun**. Constanz (1244) June 29th Walt de Ramstein, **Ul nobilius de Clingen, H. miles de Burgelon** and others. Tännikon (1257) June 15th Eberhard der alte und Eberhart der junge von Bichelnse, Albrecht von Bussenanch, Hainrich von Grizzenberg, **Arnold von Burgelon**, Walther von Lantsberg, **Walth von Löwenberg**, Rudolf von Wilperg and others (Hitz 1854:22). Rorschach (~1260) Rv°dolf von Rorschach and brother Egilolue, Ru°doluen an Jacobe hern Rv°doluis amman, hern Heinrich von Valkinstein, hern Rv°dolue uon Guttingin, hern Heinrich uon Griezinberc, hern **Arnolde uon Bivrgelon**, hern Heinriche uon Rauinsburc, hern Egilolue von Rosinberc, dim marschalke uon Valkinstein(Rudolf II. v. Falkenstein) and others (MO:1652). Kloster St. Johann und dem Johanniterhaus Bubikon das Kloster (1261) July 16th plebanis, **Ber. de Burgelun**, W(alter) v. Schwarzenbach(Gem. Jonschwil, Bez. Untertoggenburg), Friedrich (1213-1216)v Z, Heinrich u. B. v. Zuckenriet (Gem. Niederhelfenschwil, Bez. Wil) and many others (MO: 1036). Zurich (1264) Feb 11th **Rŭdolfi dicti de Burgilon** canonici Turicensis. Rorschach (1276) May 4th Rv°dolf von Rorschach vnd fro[v] Willibirch, Gotfr. **hern Rv°dolfes amman von Rorschach**, maeister Herman von Riedern (MO:1969). >Wappensiegel< dated September 8th (1293) for Eberhard von Burglen (MO:2319). St. Gallen zu Wil (1324) Dec 8th Eberhart von Bürglun der junge, ritter & frige, Hainrich von Leonberg, Franciscus der Bössche, Johann von Leonberg, for the Griessenberg family and many others. "The Fhrn. von Bürglen, noted 1176, seat in Bürglen (Bz. Weinfelden, can Thurgau), became extinct with the death of the three brothers, Eberhard (VI) d.1401, Albrecht, a citizen of Konstanz d.c1408, and Arnold, Komtur OT in Schönack 1393. The lands, worth 3000 gulden, went in half parts to Sax and to Kaspar von Klingenberg [873, K745]" (Clemmenson 2009).

115

- **von Steinegg/Staineg** {blue,wavy white bend engrailed, lack of lion} #135 Zurich wappenrolle. Castle Steinegg is in Huttwilen, District of Steckborn, Thurgau, Switzerland. (As the last traces of old friedingischer rights can be found later in the Swiss lakeside (Untersee) among the place names still in the Freidinger @ Mannenbach (c. 1355) and in a wooded area near Steckborn (1378)[431]. Salenstein (Canton of Thurgau, Switzerland) is in the same vicinity of Mannebach. St. Georgen monastery *Adelbertus de Salestetin*(=Salzstetten) 1092 & Alberti de Salestetin (1094) August 20th or previously researched found (doubtful von Salenstain) Adelbert or Albrecht von Salenstein in 1092 & 1094 charters of the monastery for St. Georgen (Black Forest). Rottweil (~1099) Hiltiboldus de Taneccho (Tennegg). Being in Rottweil records, is Hiltiboldus from Zimmern origin? Eschingen (1100) Burchardus comes Nellenburc monastery Salvatoris testes: Ludwicus comes Stoffeln, **Hiltheboldus de Tannecho** (Steinegg), Ruldofus de Dengen(Tengen), Burchardus de Dengen(Tengen), Gerungus & Arnoldus Gothmatignen and others (FU 1885:45). Rotenacker (1116) Lŏdewicus comes de Stofiln, Ŏdalricus comes de Gamutingin, Rŏdolfus comes de Bregantio, Rŏpertus de Grùminbach, Ernest, Adelbertus et Otto de Stuzzilingen, Arnoldus de Hiltiniswilare, Rupertus de Rieth(Rieden), **Bertoldus et Cünradus de Tannegga(Steinegg)** and others (WO:427). Bertoldus et Cünradus de Tannegga 1116 and des Berchtoldus de Tannecko 1123 in Wirtemberger (Durer 1899 : 449). Zartan (1145) **Berht de Steinegga**, Bernhard Steckboren Dec (1146). St. Blassi in Schwarzwald (1150) August 20th Eberhardis Nellenburch, **Bertoldus de Steinecko**, Ripertus de Mucheim (Mauchen in Stühlingen)[432], Burkardus de Wadinswilare and many others (Neugart 1795:82). Freiburg in Breisgau (1152) January 12th **Hiltebolt de Steinegge**. Maulbronn (1157) June 4th Cûnradus de Steinegge. Würzburg (1194) Jan 28th **Bertoldus de Steinecge et filius(son) Vlricus**. Monastery Salem, Reichenau abbot @ Constanz (1194) May(?) Presentibus Wernh dec Hermanne prepos Eberh hospital Alberto cust Hermanno camer et fere toto Augensi capit Burch pleb SJoh Ridegero et Heinr et Herrn eiusd eccl canonicis Eberhardo pleb Inférions celle et Cônr eiusd eccl canon Wernhero pleb Superioris celle et Wernero canon eiusd eccl Constant eccl canoncis Ulr custode mag Alberone Cônr Rvdeg Rudolfo pleb de Celia (Ratolfi=Radolfzel) **Rud pleb de Fridingen** laicis Landoldo de Wincelun, **Heinr de Kreien, Hermanno de Kreien**, **Bertoldo de Riederen**, Alb fratre ei Eberh de Salunstein, Alb de Salenstein 1194 presid Rome Celestino Heinr[433]. (1196) May 20th in Mainz, Emperor Henry VI. confirmed the purchase, making the Reichenauische porter, Berthold Maisere Ritter, the convent Maulbronn(Mulinbrunnen) transfers an estate in Weissach: comes Egono de Vraha, Eberhardus de Eberstein, **Bertoldus de Stainnekke** (Steinegg), Bertoldus Strubeche, Gumboldus de Vehingen, Reinhardus de Glatebhac (WO:752). (1216) Diethelm I. v. Steinegg 1216-1256, Berthold v. Bürglen 1209-1244, abbott Rudolf v. Tengen 1198-1219 and many others (MO:1035). Esslingen (1227) Abt Hildebold von Steckborn (Stegborn) abbot of Petershausen (WO:1099). Domaniums **Heinrich I von Tannegg** 1233-1248 acquired as the castle Kussaberg and gave Tannegg after he built a castle there (Herder 1902:7). Uznaberg May 27th (1260) Fridericus comes de Toggenburch, Diethelmus et Crafto(Diethalmus et Kraffo) testes: Jacobus de Bvole, Ebirhardus de Lovmeis 1255-1289, Bertoldus de Steinegge, Konrad Fantelin (Pantlinus) 1228-1261 and others (MO:1632). Von Salenstein (Konrad von Salenstein 1291. Heinrich & Eberhard von Salenstein w/**Hildebold von Steckborn** 1227, Konrad von Wartenberg, **Berthold von Krahen** 1215). Eberhard & Burkhard von Salenstein, Ritter Heinrich von Steckborn 1236, Albert von Riedern, Berthold Truchsess (Trustees) von Krahen and Konrad, and Eberhard Schenk von Salenstein 1230/36/40) has come up a few times referencing von Fridingen/Krahen familie records. Feldbach (1275) November 5 **Rudolphus advocatus de Fridingen** III (~1247) appears in a Feldbach church selling Gerlikon fief with Burch de Salustein and Cunr de Salustein and Cunr Hiuneberc(Hunoberg). Toggenburg (1280) Feb 28th Heinrich den Zehender, Haertnit von Salwenstein, Heinrich der Loewe von Zucchenriet von ze Swarzenbach for Graf Frederic von Toggenburg and others (MO:2044). (1300) Wolf von Steinegg (Stainegge). St. Verene @ Constanz (1330) February 7th Petitio Burcbardi de Fridingen clerici Constance & Brunnen with

Heinrico de Steinegg (Bulls 1908:239). St. Verene @ Constanz (1330) February 7th a petition from Ulrici de Craien (Fridingen @HohenKraen /Mulhausen) and Heinrico de Steinegg both canonico of Constanz an accord with Mulhausen[434] – probably the origin of Steckborn wappen quartered into the Fridingen family shield (Bulls 1908:239). November 29th (1351) Diethelm von Steinegg (d. 1358) Dompropst, Ulrich von Fridingen (~1304) Domherren, Heinrich Honburg and others @ Diessenhofen[435]. Ulrich v Friding & Diethelm v Steinegg worked together from the 1343-1358.

- **von Steckborn (Stegborn)** {*plume per pale*} von Steckborn, ministeriales of Reichenau, later Fhr., noted 1187-1332, named for Steckborn on the Untersee W of Konstanz (can Thurgau) (Clemmenson:173). #240 on the Zurich wappenrolle or HausZumLoch (~1300-6) wappenfries. 1st mentioned as Stecheboron in 843 @ Reichenau (WO:189). Steckborn (1146) Dec 11th Steckboren happened with Bernhard(=von Clairvaux) from Crozingen. Salem (1187) Hiltiboldus de Stecheboron, Vernherus de Welpach, Bertoldus de Lucelenstetin, Bertoldus de Reith, Otto Stozz, Albertus pincerna et alii. Kreuzlingen in Thurgau (1213) **Wernerus plehanus de Stechiboron, Conradus miles de Fricchingen** and others. Esslingen (1227) **Abt Hildebold von Steckborn (Stegborn)** abbot of Petershausen (WO:1099). Im Lager vor Böblingen (1243) Aug 13[th] F. comes de Zolre, Ottober[tol]dus dapifer de Walpurch, R(udolph) de Roschach and 2 sons, **H. iunior de Stechborun** and others (WO:1499). Ennbueren(?) (1246) Oct 17[th] Gundelfingen document Hainricus de Gundelui[n]gin et Hainricus de Friberc nobiles, Hainricus Senflinus, Burcardo Bosshin(Boschen 11/1246), Albero de Ertingin, Hainricus dictus *der Vesare*; de ministerialibus vero Augiensis ecclesie: **Hilteboldus de Stekeborun**, Arnoldus de Langinstain, Burcardus senior de Tetingin, **Ebirhardus pincerna de Salunstain**, Waltherus de Wellinberc, **Albertus et Rûdolfus de Riedirn** fratres, **Cvnradus de Cella Ratholfi (=Fridingen near Radolfzell)** and others (WO:1613). Neufrach(?) (1246) November 29[th] *Swigger von Gundelfingen und dessen Söhnen*, videlicet Hilteboldi de Stekeborun, Alberti de Riedirn, **Rv̊do[l]fi fratris sui et Eberhardi pincerne de Salunstain militum,** Hainrico et Hermanno dictis Sterren, Bertoldo Grivben, Burcardo Bosshen, Testes: Hainricus nobilis de Gundiluingin, Hainricus de Friberc, **Hilteboldus de Stekeborun**, Arnoldus de La[n]ginstain, Burcardus senior de Tetingin, Albertus de Riedirn, **Rv̊dolfus frater suus, Ebirhardus pincerna de Salunstain, Cvnradus de Cella Ratholfi(=Fridingen)** and others (MO:1617). Under Edberhard II von Waldburg (1248-1274) Castle Batrenhausèn with appurtenances from Hilpoldo of Steckboren (Herder 1902:7). Merspurc (1256) Sept 5th Berthol do decano de Sevelt, **Hilteboldo et Eberhardo filio suo de Stekborun, Walthero et Goezwino fratribus de Hohenvels**, Hainrico et Burkardo filio suo de Ramsberg, Friderico fil ei Burkardo de Oberridern,Ulírico de Oberriedern ,Vírico Burkardo et Hainrico de Urendorf and others (RE:219). Constanz (1261) B de Hohenvels ecclesie, Ita nobilis de Clingen notice of event died **C(onrad) aduocati de fridingen** testes: Dominus de Valchenstein, B Dominus de Annuwiler, Dominus de Heidelberch, Dominus **Hilteboldus miles de Stegboren**, Dominus Volricus, C de Tetinchon, siegel *Sororis ite de vridingen* (Hirzel 1873:358)[436]. diblus Salem & Weißenau (1267) Dec 22nd testibus: **Eberhardo de Stekborum milite**, Ulrico dicto Sralle, Cûnrado de Vrendorf and many others (WO:2641). Salem or Bebenhausen (1269) Ritter Wolfelin von Bonlanden (Wol. miles dictus, Wolf. miles de Bônlanden) Schwester(sister), der Gemahlin(wife of) des Walther von Hohenfels (Hohinvelse) Testes: Diepoldus nobilis de Bernhusen, Waltherus de Hohinvelse, Wer[nherus] dictus Tuzzer de Niuuinhusen, C. plebanus et Wer. Albus ibidem, G. dictus de Rote, item **Eberhardus monachus in Salem dictus de Stechkeboren**, and others (WO:2817). Salem (1287) May 31st Siegler: Der Edle von Justingen (nobilis viri dicti de Justingin) testibus: Wernhero dictates of Swarzenbach, Rudolf dictates of Richenbach, Cûnrado dictate von Buch, item fratribus Eberhard supprior, Rudolf dictates of Giuttingin, Sifrido Custodes, **Eberhard dictates of Stegboron (Steckborn)**, Anshelmus senior et Anshelmus iunior filius suus dicti de Justingin and others (WO:4549). (1298) herre bruder Cûnrat von Blûmenvelt luprister von Alshusen(Konrad von Schifferstadt Komtur), brûder **Eberhart von Stekebrûnnen** and a few others (WO:6152). February 7th (1330) a petition from Ulrici de Craien (Fridingen @HohenKraen) and Heinrico de Steinegg both canonico of Constanz an accord with Mulhausen[437] – probably the

117

origin of Steckborn wappen quartered into the Fridingen family shield. Will in Thurgau (1333) Der Komtur von Tobel(Hainrich von Homburg in Steckborn) tauscht mit Eberhard von Eppenstein, Bertoltes des Ammans, Lútolt der schenk von Landegge riter, **Brůdolf von Fridingen** and others (MO:3537). The (1411-1418) wappen(COA) @ St. Christoper kloster in Thal, Tyrol for Fridingen|Fridinge/Fridige has a White/Black crest plumage divided as if the family or rights come from Riedern. Friedrich Riederer/Reidrer (~1450) living in the small village of Muhlhausen in the Bodensee area describes the Rhetoric story of his serf family belonging to the Knights of Fridingen @ Hohenkrahen in 1476. Friedrich Riederer coat of arms (white steel) is Lords of Fridingen and the right (black) is Lords of Steckborn[438].

- **von Riedern (RIEFERN)** {*Horizontal four argents white and sable*}. #287 Riedern below #286 Salenstein on the Zurich wappenrolle. Black probably taken from Steckborn as did the New-Fridingen quartered wappenshield. von Riedern, Dienstmannen of Ab.Reichenau, noted 1174-1273, seat in Burg Riedern near Fruthwilen (Gem. Salenstein, Bz. Steckborn, can Thurgau). Castle ruins at Fruthweilen, above MannennBach District Steckborn The Riedrin of (Riedrin) were reichenauische ministeriales and probably kinsmen of the taverns of Salenstein with which they usually occur together[439]. Rotenacker (1116) Lödewicus comes de Stofiln, Ŏdalricus comes de Gamutingin, Rŏdolfus comes de Bregantio, Rŏpertus de Grùminbach, Ernest, Adelbertus et Otto de Stuzzilingen, Arnoldus de Hiltiniswilare, **Rupertus de Rieth(Rieden)**, Bertoldus et Cünradus de Tannegga(Steinegg) and others (WO:427). Kloster Salem Constanz (1169) Mar 10th Rôdolf de Sevelt, Waltherus de Clingin, **Burkardus de Obiriedin**, Burkhard jun de Frichingen, Bruno de Marhdorf, ministeriales Hesso de Annewilar, Rôd de Wilar and many others (RE 1895:113). Augensis abbot of Sweindorf Salem @ Reichenau (1171) March 15th **Eberhardus and frater(brother) Swicgerus de Reidin** testes: **Gerungus de Hvneberc**, Rudolfus miles quidam de Rammisberc, confirmation Diethelmus(=Krenkingen) abbot in Sweindorf and others (FA 1885:64). Dorfisperc (1174) Diethelmus (Krenkingen), Hugo de Langenstein, Rvdolfi de Riederen and others. Monastery Salem @ Reichenau abbot @ Constanz (1194) May(?) Presentibus Wernh dec Hermanne prepos Eberh hospital Alberto cust Hermanno camer et fere toto Augensi capit Burch pleb SJoh Ridegero et Heinr et Herrn eiusd eccl canonicis Eberhardo pleb Infèrions celle et Cônr eiusd eccl canon Wernhero pleb Superioris celle et Wernero canon eiusd eccl Constant eccl canoncis Ulr custode mag Alberone Cônr Rvdeg, Rudolfo pleb de Celia (Ratolfi=Radolfzel) **Rud pleb de Fridingen** laicis Landoldo de Wincelun, **Heinr de Kreien, Hermanno de Kreien, Bertoldo de Riederen, Alb fratre ei Eberh de Salunstein**, Alb de Salenstein 1194 presid Rome Celestino Heinr[440]. "Castle ruins at Fruthweilen meantime above Mannenbach District Steckborn of the Riedern (Riedrin) reichenauische ministerials and probably kinsmen of the taverns were Salenstein with which they occur mostly together. Have the same standard sequence is quite unclear since there is always repeating the same name in the family from 1194-1209 we find the three brothers Albert and Rudolf Berchtold often referred to a second-generation brothers, Albert and Rudolf which belong alongside the older Rudolf in a document of 1221 be called (Rahn, Haffter, Durrer:1899)" . Reichenau (1197) Bishop von Contanz(Diethelm v Krenkingen) von C abt von Reichenau, kirche Reichenau einen zehnt zu Gründelbuch Grindilbuch welchen Sigeband von Hugo von Wahingen, Hugo von **Rudolf von Fridingen**, Wernhero dec, Hermanne prepos, Ebirhardo hospitalis, provis A custode Herrn camer et aliis fratr nris ministeriales ceci nre aderant Hugo de Langenstein. **Alb pincerna et E et H fratres sui de Salunstein. Albert et B et R(udolph) fratr sui de Riedern,** Bertold de Wolmutigen (Wagner 1895: 129). Neufrach(?) (1246) Nov 29th videlicet Hilteboldi de Stekeborun, Arnoldi de Langinstain, Burcardi senioris de Thetingin, Alberti de Riedirn, Rvdo[l]fi fratris sui et Eberhardi pincerne de Salunstain militum, Swigerus senior videlicet de Gundeluingin, Swigerus et Vlricus milites et Swigerus laicus nondum miles fratres, filii sepedicti Swigeri, idelicet Cvnrado, Hainrico et Hermanno dictis Sterren, Bertoldo Grivben, Burcardo Bosshen, Testes: videlicet Eberhardus decanus; de militibus vero: Hainricus nobilis de Gundiluingin, Hainricus de Friberc, Hilteboldus de Stekeborun, Arnoldus de La[n]ginstain, Burcardus senior de Tetingin, **Albertus de Riedirn,**

Rv̊dolfus frater suus, **Ebirhardus pincerna de Salunstain,** Hainricus Senflinus, Bertoldus prior, Cv̊hradus cellerarius, **Cvnradus de Cella Ratolfi(=Fridingen)** et Hainricus de Bartilstain, Ego Fridericus Kamer[ar]ius de Thengin(Tengin) subscripsi and others (WO:1617). Swigerus miles de Gundiluingin (1246) Hilteboldus de Stekeborun, **Albertus et Rûdolfus de Riedirn** fraters(below Markdorf), Ebirhardus pincerna de Salunstain (WO:1613). Rorschach (1276) May 4th Rv°dolf von Rorschach vnd froᵛ Willibirch, Gotfr. hern **Rv°dolfes amman von Rorschach, maeister Herman von Riedern** (MO:1969). The (1411-1418) wappen(COA) @ St. Christoper kloster in Thal, Tyrol for Fridingen|Fridinge/Fridige has a White/Black crest plumage divided as if the family or rights come from Riedern. Friedrich Riederer/Reidrer (~1450) living in the small village of Muhlhausen in the Bodensee area describes the Rhetoric story of his serf family belonging to the Knights of Fridingen @ Hohenkrahen in 1476. His <Coat of Arms< left (white steel) is Lords of Fridingen and the right (black) is Lords of Steckborn[441]. Shield divided (in metal & black) with three eight pointed stars placed diagonally. Von Steckborn (*Stegborn*) was from Minisiterial of Reichenau noted in the years 1187-1332, named for Steckborn on the Untersee W of Konstanz (Zurich wappenrolle pg 8 & 23). Steckborn wappenshild is half Gold and Half Black exactly like the Neu/Alt-Fridingen wappenschilde. In Eberhard (Doblers 1986: 131) also realized this "Fridingen" Black & Gold wappen comes from the extinct ministerial between Reichenau and Steckborn, Switzerland occuring in the 14th century (1300's). Other names in this period: Ulrich Reidrer, Cunrado Reidrer, Liutfrid dictus Reidrer, Johannes Reidrer, Jakob & Klaus Riederer 1476. The Riederer familie took half the wappenshilde from von Fridingen & half from von Steckborn was from Minisiterials of Reichenau noted in the years 1187-1332, on the Untersee W of Konstanz (Zurich wappenrolle pg 8 & 23). Steckborn wappenshild is Gold & Black split(per pale). The modern (1939) wappen for the village of Reidern & Durschen in the canton of Glarus[442] is divided like Steckborn Gold and Black opposite colored stars on each side with the Gundelfingen/Justingen "spines" going up from the bottom in the middle of the shield.

- **von Salenstein (SALENSTAIN)** {*Per pale or and argent, a mount of 10 peaks couped vert*}. #286 on the Zurich wappenrolle above Riedern. In addition (Sale-, Salu-, Salo-, Salun-, Saulen-, Salle-, Salle-, Salwin-) (Boxler : 1991). von Salenstein, Dienstmannen of Reichenau, noted 1092-1372, seat in Gem. Salenstein (Bz. Steckborn, can Thurgau). Salenstein (Canton of Thurgau, Switzerland) is in the same vicinity of Mannebach. St. Georgen monastery *Adelbertus de Salestetin*(=Salzstetten) (1092) & Alberti de Salestetin (1094) August 20th or previously researched(doubtful von Salenstain) Adelbert or Albrecht von Salenstein in 1092 & 1094 charters of the monastery for St. Georgen (Black Forest). Constantie (1158) Testes: **Heinricus Habardus de Salwnstein,** ministeriales: **Burchardus de castro Homburch, Bertoldus et Arnoldns frater eius de Hioninberch,** Burchardus de Banchilhouen, Eberhardus marchsehaleus, Rudolfus de Wilare, **Herungus de Chregin (=Hermann Krahen),** Bertoldus de Husin and others (FU 1885:61). (abt 1160) Domcapitular **Heinrich von Salenstein** lived Constanz (Huber 1886:476). (abt 1174) Diethelm von Reichenau (Krenkingen) abbot for Kloster Salem leaves huben in Dornsberg & Sweindorf, Sweigerus Gundoluingen beneficio, Eberhardo uero Rudolphus Ramesberch habebat and others: testimonious Hermannus Spaikingen (=Espasingen?), **Eberhardus de Salustein,** Bertholdus de Hewen etc. Konstantie (1190) July 15th Bertholds von Engelberg, Liutold von Regenberg, Diethelm Constanz (Krenkingen), **Eberhart de Salwinstein et Heinr frat(er)** (Wagner 1895:125). (1194) May(?) Monastery Salem, Reichenau abbot Diethelm von Reichenau(Krenkingen) @ Constanz Burchardo dapifero de Rotinuelse, **Rodolfo uiro nobili de Fridingen,** Presentibus: Rudolfo pleb de Celia (Ratolfi=Radolfzel) **Rud pleb de Fridingen** laicis Landoldo de Wincelun, **Heinr de Kreien, Hermanno de Kreien, Bertoldo de Riederen,** Alb fratre ei **Eberh de Salunstein, Alberto de Salenstein** presid Rome Celestino Heinr and many others[443]. Mersburch (1219) Eberhards von Salzburg und Lütolds seines bruders von Regensberg, Rudegero Chimensi epo, Eberharde Salensi abb, ,Walthero et fratre s de Rotenlaim, et **Hainrico de Clingen** advoc Walthero de Tegervelt, and **Diethelmo de Crenchingen** (RE:150). Klosters in Gerlingen(?) (1226) Fridericvs comites de

Zolre, Werinhervs, milites de Richtenberch, Cônradus plebanus de Schonenberch, **Eberhardvs laicus de Sallestein** and others (WO:1072). Neufrach(?) (1246) October 17[th] *Ritter Swigger und seine Söhne von Gundelfingen,* Testes: Burcardo Bosshin, Hainricus de Gundelui[n]gin et Hainricus de Friberc, Hilteboldus de Stekeborun, **Eberhardvs laicus de Sallestein**, Albertus et Rûdolfus de Riedirn fratres, **Cvnradus de Cella Ratolfi{Radolfzell}** (=Conrad I von Fridingen) and others (WO:1613). Neufrach(?) (1246) November 29[th] *Swigger von Gundelfingen und dessen Söhnen,* videlicet Hilteboldi de Stekeborun, Alberti de Riedirn, **Rv̌do[l]fi fratris sui et Eberhardi pincerne de Salunstain militum, Burcardo Bosshen**, Testes: Hainricus nobilis de Gundiluingin, Hainricus de Friberc, Hilteboldus de Stekeborun, Arnoldus de La[n]ginstain, Burcardus senior de Tetingin, Albertus de Riedirn, **Rv̌dolfus frater suus, Ebirhardus pincerna de Salunstain** and others (MO:1617). Gottelieben (1258) Ul de Salunstain. St. Gallen Klosterarchiv Magdenau January (1259) Ulrich von Salenstein passes his wife Mia ownership in Ermatingen and Salenstein, Alberti electi Augiensis (Albrecht v. Ramstein) testes: the noble lords R. von Guting(en), Egil and R. de Rorscah, Hart de Niderndorf, Conr.de Lutgering(Liggeringen), Heine dictus Burziler said, Wernherus et R von Tunretun(Dürnten), Hilteboldus and Lutoldus de Gerlinkon and many others (MO:1597). Frauenklosters Tanikon (1270) October 13th Eberhardi dapiferi(stewards) de Bichelnse possessiones in Liboltsberg, Testes milites **Joh dapifer de Swendorf II (~1233)**, Cuno de Velthach, Heinr de Badewegin, **C de Salunstain** and others[444]. Eberhard & Burkhard von Salenstein, Ritter Heinrich von Steckborn, Albert von Riedern, **Berthold von Krahen**, and Eberhard Schenk von Salenstein 1230/36/40) has come up a few times referencing von Fridingen/Krahen familie records. (1275) November 5th Rudolphus advocatus de Fridingen III (~1247) appears in a Feldbach church selling Gerlikon fief with Burch de Salustein, Cunr de Salustein and Cunr Hiuneberc. Toggenburg kloster Maggenowe (1280) Feb 28th **Heinrich der Zehender** (Swarzenbach & Hermuttingen (Ermatingen) & Gebsintal), **Haertnit(Harnit) von Salwenstein**, Heinrich der Loewe von Zucchenriet von ze Swarzenbach for Graf Frederic von Toggenburg and others (MO:2044). Konstanz (1280) Mar 24th the counts Diethelm and Friedrich von Toggenburg give the monastery Magdenau own goods to Moos, Schwarzenbach and Gebsatal and Reichenauer fiefs Ermatingen, herre Heinrich Loewe of Zucchenriet of us hate ze Swarzenbach, Henry from harrow ze Swarzenbach, and herre Cvonrat of Munchwile in Gebsatal, and **Harnit of Salwenstein** hate ze Ermvotingen, Hinder Wise the servant bruoder of Maggenovwe closter presence of **Haertnit of Salwenstein** and others (MO:2046). St. Gallen for Kloster Feldbach (1282) September 23rd von Giel family properties Cholbrunne (Niederbüren, Bez. Wil), Willisperch (Iltisberg), molendini(mill) dicti Hainzinun (Herinessenmüli, u. Bez. Gossau) schûpozse Burron(Wohl Niederbüren, Bez. Wil) to Waltheri Lindenberch(Lindenberg, Gem. Niederbüren) family, Fridericus de Gundoluingen (Gundelfingen 1272-1283 Dekan), Eberh. de Bichelnse, Cunrado Salunstain and many others (MO:2095). Reichenau April 6th (1288) Heinrich des Älteren von Schmalegg (Smalnegge), Kirchrektors Albert von Bermatingen (Bermetingen) testibus: magistro C[onrado] dicto Phefferhart canonico ecclesie sancti Johannis Constantiensis, domino Lu{i}toldo canonico ecclesie Inferioris Celle dicto de Gerlikon, **Hainrico advocato de Cragen**, Rûdolfo filio suo, Hugone de Langenstain, Hainrico de Tetingen et **Cûnrado de Salunstain militibus** and others (WO:4654). Kloster Salem Reichenau (1297) Grafen Kirchberg, videlicet dominum **H de Fridingen (+s advocat(i d)e fridi(ngen))** dominum C villicum de Lutgeringen, dominum **C de Salunstain, et Eberhardum Pincernam de Salunstain** nostri monasterii ministeriales dictis abbati and others. Oct 1297 WappenSiegel >right> for Eberhard Schenk von Salenstain in 1297.

- **von Hattingen (HATINGEN)** {Gules, a bend argent – mans head hatted} #285 on the Zurich wappenrolle above Salenstein & Riedern. Like Kyburg color Red with Bend, lack of Lion. "von Hattingen, Dienstmannen of Reichenau, same stock as Vogt von Hattingen and Vogt von Mehringen, noted 1263-1412, seat in Hattingen (BA. Engen, Kr.Konstanz, B-W)" (Clemmenson:2009). "Count Berchtold Hattingen gave the monastery of Reichenau entries for 973 Hattingen[445], but appears to be much older" "The name Hattingen means something like "settlement of Hatto" (Wilimski:1973). On January 4th (1083) **Heinrich &**

neffe(nephew) Heinrich von Hirscheck (Altshausen) witnessed a document with Arnold von Binzwanger with brother Manegold & Ludwig and others at the kloster St. Georgen in Schwarzwald (Eberhard:1964). Hettingen occurs in the year 1096 Graf Adalbert I von Binzwanger-Gamertingen (von Hatingen)[446]. Eschingen (1100) Burchardus comes Nellenburc monastery Salvatoris testes: Ludwicus comes Stoffeln, Hiltheboldus de Tannecho(Steinegg), Ruldofus de Dengen(Tengen), Burchardus de Dengen(Tengen), **Gerungus** & **Arnoldus Gothmatignen** and others (FU 1885:45). The **Adelberti de Gamertingen** is in the same Shaffhausen document (1101) April 21st as **Herimanni de Böselingen (Büßlingen)** and his brother **Adalbert de Winterspuren**, Röperti de Hadolfingen(Hailfingen), **Adelberti de Werenswilare** and others (WO:409). So, was the Gamertingen familie from the Hirschecker line? Possibly, however further back before their ancestor[447] Wolferat II von Beringen graf v Altshausen (~983- †4-9-1065). Rotenacker (1116) Swiger and Erliwin de Gundeluingen (Gundelfingen), Ernest, **Adelbertus** and monk **Otto de Stuzzilingen** (~1070)(Steußlingen), **Ŏdalricus comes de Gamutingin, Rupertus de Rieth (Rieden)** and others (WO:427). Tissen Kellmünz (1128) March 26th Ernist de Stuzelingin (WO:462). St. Georgio(Georgen) (1138) Berthtoldus de Guotmatingen. Ulrich I married Adelheid Dillingen daughter of Hartmann von Dillingen and Adelheid von Winterthur-Kiburg. Ulrich II von Gamertingen-Achalm (†1150) (son of Arnold von G †1090) married Judith and their children were Ulrich III (†1166) the St. Gallen klostervogt, Graf Konrad I. (†v.1150) and Adelheid and Bertha[448]. The crest of Berthold von Hettingen (1150-1232) in the vestibule buried in the cathedral Zwiefalter, a red lion **in Gold**[449](Veringen wappen? form). Kloster Salem (1208) Heinricus sacerdos de Hatingen (Hettingen), **Heinricus & Wathi de Stuzelingen brothers** & Hermannus miles de Graneheim with Grafen **Heinrico de Warstein** and others (WO:828). Hartmannnus (Hartmann) plebanus in **Hettingen, Rudolphus miles de Hatingen** with Graf Gothfridus Sigemeringen (Sigmaringen) others in the Konvente of Bebenhausen (~1240). Hanricus plebanus de Hetingen in Veringen (1252). Walter von Hattingen (1262) March 18th with others in Waldkirch im Breisgau. Fridericus de Haetingen (1272) and others in document @ Bebenhausen. Hilteboldus minister de Hetingen with some familiars Burchardus de Jungingen, Eberhardus Jungingen, Anshelmus de Justingen and other in Heiligkreutal document (1272) Jan 12th (WO:3055). **Note:** The names Hatto, Haddo, Hatho, Hato, Hetto go back (Birlinger:1878). "The name of our town was originally Hatingen (1208) or Hätingen (1264), ie with a long a, as the unadulterated dialect today says. O. v. Ehrenberg has derived the name of the short form of a personal name Hato or Hatu = battle, see Hadubrand, the Germanic first name[450]". In the words of the personal name Hatto = Heddo =der Krieger/Warrior[451].

- **von Tengen** { *bend with fluer de lis, lack of lion*} shield appears to be a derivative of Fridingen/Krahen with a lowered bent bar and a fleur-de-lis attached to it. #72 unicorn and #324 yellow fleur-de-lis on the Zurich wappenrolle. Surname origins believed to come from Gerold/Gerolt von Tengen s. Gerolt de Buch who also signed and is the brother to Heinrich d. A Hirscheck (~1043) family in the Basel Rhein document on March 1st 1080. Klosters Allerheiligen (1080) March 1st Graf Burkhard von Nellenburg, Abbot Wilhelm von Hirsau, **Gerolt de Tengin**, Gerolt de Buch, Adelbreht de Strazza and others (SH:576). Act of **Fridingen** (1090) April 14th signers: Rudolf von **Tengin**, Eberhards de Justingen etc[452]. Act of **Schaffhausen** (1091) June 7th signers: Burchard de **Tengen**, Eberhart de **Tanchinga**, Eberhart de Raemesinga (Ramsen), Manegolt de Gundeliuga (Gundelfingen), The later reign Tengen goes to the families of our example **Hirscheck** back; the barons of Tengen descendants of Herman Hirscheck the elder (Dobler 1986: pg 23). Eschingen (1100) Burchardus comes Nellenburc monastery Salvatoris testes: Ludwicus comes Stoffeln, Hiltheboldus de Tannecho(Steinegg), **Ruldofus de Dengen(Tengen), Burchardus de Dengen(Tengen)**, Gerungus & Arnoldus Gothmatignen and others (FU 1885:45). (1135) B. de Rinhart donations to monastery S . Salvatoris at Schaufhausen teachings of these men who were present when they looked on all these events are some of the names of children stated that there was count Eberhard of Nellinburc of our party Odalricus comes de Ramisberc, Heinrich Landolus de Seoluingin, Gerhardus de Honnstetin, Eberhardus and his brother Adilbero de Tiuelo, **Heinricus & Ruodolfus** and grandson of **Herman Tengin**, **Hermannus de Aspisingin (Espasingen)**, Diethel de Lutegaringin, Uldaricus de Ramislei and his brother Ernist, Berhardus de Luoningin, Otto of Reginsberc, Bilgcrin Iestetin (Justingen) and many others[453]. Bueslingen (Büßlingen in Tengen, BW) occasionally used name for this family Hirscheck had the church Buesslingen as a sole possession in the monastery of Allerheiligen(All Saints) in Schaufhausen in 1145. After 1149 brought the nobles of Tengen claims the Bailiwick[454]. **Heinricus, comes de Tuingen(Tengen)** venue of Lodi with many others in the kloster of Edenheim in June (1161) (WO:587). Verona (1184) Bischof (Hermann) von Konstanz, Abt (Diethelm) von Reichenau, H(einrich) von Tengen (*nobilis vir H. de Tengen*) Kirche in Büßlingen (*ecclesia de Buselingen*) (RI:1202). (1181/1185) September 22 H.(=Heinrich) von Tengen in the church of Bueslingen with Hermann von Contanz(=Fridingen). Merishausen June 21st (1208) Rudolf von Güttingen contract and witnesses Liutoldum confratrem meum de Creigin(Lütold v. Krähen), R. de Tengin (**Rudolf v. Tengen**) Abott des Benediktinerklosters Allerheiligen in Schaffhausen, **A. de Chreigin(Krähen)**, Wernher v. Staufen and others in a St. Gallen document (MO:981). (1216) Diethelm I. v. Steinegg 1216-1256, Berthold v. Bürglen 1209-1244, abbott Rudolf v. Tengen 1198-1219 and many others (MO:1035). St. Gallen (1228) Truchsess(Steward) Ulrich and Ulrich dictus Blarer of St. Gallen in St. Gallen donate to a hospital, testes: Livtoldus decanus dictus de **Krêigen**, Berhtoldus de **Tengin** and many others (MO:1158). St. Gallen (1237) September 24th inspectorus, that Sir H(enry) and of his son Henry, the elder of the Tengin and C(unrad) with the unanimous consent of the Obertriet(Oberried) **L. quondam decani(Werk)dekan Lütold v. Krähen)** and a few others (MO:1264). (1246) Nov 29th videlicet Hilteboldi de Stekeborun, Arnoldi de Langinstain, Burcardi senioris de Thetingin, Alberti de Riedirn, Rv̌do[l]fi fratris sui et Eberhardi pincerne de Salunstain militum, Swigerus senior videlicet de Gundeluingin, Swigerus et Vlricus milites et Swigerus laicus nondum miles fratres, filii sepedicti Swigeri, idelicet Cvnrado, Hainrico et Hermanno dictis Sterren, Bertoldo Grivben, Burcardo Bosshen, Testes: videlicet Eberhardus decanus; de militibus vero: Hainricus nobilis de Gundiluingin, Hainricus de Friberc, Hilteboldus de Stekeborun, Arnoldus de La[n]ginstain, Burcardus senior de Tetingin, Albertus de Riedirn, Rv̌dolfus frater suus, Ebirhardus pincerna de Salunstain, Hainricus Senflinus, Bertoldus prior, Cv̌hradus cellerarius, **Cvnradus de Cella Ratolfi** et Hainricus de Bartilstain, **Ego Fridericus Kamer[ar]ius de Thengin(Tengin) subscripsi** (WO:1617). (1247) Anselm of Justingen vergabt its goods once in Wazzescaven (water makers), now called Heiligkreuztal, at the request of the Earl of Wolfrad Veringen and for his salvation's sake the nuns of that monastery – testes: Wol. de Veringen, **Hainrico milite de Stivzelingen**, Wezzelone milite de Brozzekeuen, H. milite dicto Velwen, **Wal. plebano in Diengen(Tengen)** (WO:1623). Winterture (1249) Jan 5th grafen Hartmann d ä und dem iü von Kiburg, **C et H de Tengen,** Ruod nob de Wart and many others (RE:198). Konstanz (1255) Cun von Tengen, des miles Arnold (REC: 214). Salem Konstanz (1268) March 7th **Cunrado dco Fridinger** (~1234) @ Hohentengen (Diengen), Germany with Heinrich von Veringen, Hainri dco Ramunc, the Biutzichoven familiy, and others sign documents in the church for kloster Salem[455]. Hohentengen (1272) June 24th Graf Mangold von Nellenburg transfers item to Heinrich Ramung von Schwarzach (dictus Ramunch de Swarza) testibus: **H[einrico] de Swaindorf**, Alberone et Ůlrico fratribus de Regenoltswiler, fratre H[einrico] dicto Strube converso de Salem (WO:3086). Hohentengen August 1st (1273) Graf Heinrich der Ältere von Veringen beurkundet, dass Heinrich, Konrads von Ursendorf Sohn Heinrich von Schwarzach (Swarzach) testibus: Mangoldo de Nellenburc, **Cunrado decano in Deggen(Tengen)**, Wern[hero] de Hundirsiggin, et H[einrico] filio eius, Alberto de Eberhartswiler et Ber. filio fratris sui, Ulrico et Alberto fratribus de Regnolf[s]wiler, **H[einrico] de Aspisiggen (Aespisingin/ Espasingen)**(~1236) and others (WO:3162). Mengen (1292) Heinrich von Schwarzach, Bürger in Mengen, presentibus videlicet honorandis viris **Cůnrado decano in Diengen**, Rud. plebano in Almswiler, Ůlrico dicto Turner, Æbelino dicto Hundu{i}bel, Bur. dicto Ru{i}de, **Æbelino fratre decani in Diengen** et . . villico de Swarzach and others (WO:5185). Zurich (1340) Ritter Heinrich der alte von Tengen und Junker Heinrich von Tengen, Sohn des verstorbenen Chuonrat von Tengen, Burkart der Huober von Bullach and others (ZU: 273899). Zurich (1341) Duke Louis of Teck, imperial judges to Kufstein, commanded the cities of Zurich, Constance, Schaffhausen and St. Gall, **Heinrich von Tengen**(IV 1296-1348 in Singen, BW) owned farm and church tax Küsnacht to protect - **Chvenrat Berchtold**, den man nennt den{is called the} **Sigrist** buwet and the church set ze Kuessenach (MO:3791). Siegel for Rudolf von Nordschwaben (family from Schopfheim) in 1343 and 1396 is shown with the same wappenshield as Tengen (Knobloch 1919:247). "Have inherited from the elder Hermann Hirscheck must also in the western Hegau rich possession, which focuses on high Stoffeln and Bibertal to lay up to Tengen. The later reign of Tengen Beispel is our opinion on the good families of Hirscheck back: the barons of Tengen descendants of Hermann the Elder. Also from this family came to our adoption of the subsequent possession of the Earls of Pfullendorf to more things with the mountain Stoffeln. As heirs of the Earl of Pfullendorf Hirschecker have - probably in the 3rd Quarter of the 11th century - at the High Stoffeln the first castle built where were apparently also their relatives still Tengener involved. Structurally closely connected "with the pfullendorfischen Hinterstofflen tengensche the castle was <Mittlestofflen>. With the founding of the castle pfullendorfishcen Hohenstofflen depends probably reflect the establishment of the parish Weiterdingen (St. Maritius), who also was struck Duchtlingen church. For the biggest part of Hermann's the Elder Hegau possession of Hirscheck but came to his heirs from the House of Lords of Tengen, which here and were able to build on a considerable Zurichgau rule (Dobler 1986:23)". The Conrad von Tengen familie name ended in the late 1440s(?) (Krieger 1904: 1155). Unicorn wappen siegel shown: 1239 >Siegel>Heinrich von Tengen, 1275 Heinrich & Konrad von Tengen, 1302 Heinrich v T, 1398 Clara v Tengen (wife of Rudulp v Fridingen) (Woeber 1898: 39). (1335) D. Eberhardus Baro a' Tengen[456] obituary 1347 wappen Unicorn with Red background.

- **von Stoffeln** {*lack of bend with 3 red lion legs*} similar to the 2 Kiburg red lions. #169 on the Zurich wappenrolle. **vô stösseln** {*lions head*} FreiHerren von Stoffeln noted 1100 (Stuggart wappenbuch:1022). (1058) Peterhausen donation (Owiltingen in Linzgau) from Swiggerus who married Adelheid (son named Gotteschalk) with the following witnesses Ottonis (Buchorn), Roudolf comes (de Pfullendorf fortasse sive de Achalm), Eberhart, Oudalrich, Adelbret, Hezo, Hezil, Adelolt, **Gerolt(Hirscheck)**, **Hereman(Hirscheck)**, Alwich, Adelbero, Ratolt, Hezel, Roudolf, and Marcwart[457]. (1064) February 23 recorded in latin {Annonis} Anno v. Steusslingen 1056-1075 Erzbischof v. Köln of which Anno von Busslingen 1131 was probably named after. Act of Ramsen (Rammisheim/ Ramsberg) in Hegau was established 1096 of which *Gerungo comite de Stulingen* (Stühlingen) signed with *Udalrici comitis de Rammesperch* by the deeds and gifts of Friderun with her son Marquard to the monastery Rinaugia in Eggingen. Adalbert and Heinrich v Ramsen 1100 were sons of Heinrich v Hirscheck (~1053) (Dobler 1986:447). Urlichs son was Rudolf von Pfullendorf/Ramsberg of which the Pfullendorf(Stoffeln) came from another Herman d. A. von Hirscheck (~990-1044). Hegau Count Ludwig Pfullendorf-Ramsberg (to Stoffeln) was in possession of Hohenstofflen in 1067. Burchard v Ramsheim (v. Frickingen) was the brother[458] to Ludwig d. j. Graf in Unterseegau in Hegau 1101, v Stoffeln/v Pfullendorf 1116, both were sons to Ulrich v Ramsberg Hegaugraf 1080. Rotenacker (1116) **Lǒdewicus comes de Stofiln**, Ŏdalricus comes de Gamutingin, Rŏdolfus comes de Bregantio, Rŏpertus de Grùminbach, Ernest, Adelbertus et Otto de Stuzzilingen, Arnoldus de Hiltiniswilare, Rupertus de Rieth(Rieden), Bertoldus et Cünradus de Tannegga(Steinegg) and others (WO:427). Tissen Kellmünz (1128) March 26th Ernist de Stuzelingin (WO:462). Worms & Kloster Allerheiligen (1145) item predium **Heinrici de Evenwilare**, also his wife and estate **Herimanni Sweindorf, Stuzelingen** and with others (WO:515). Speyer (1152) King Frederic I of Tubingen in Kloster Salem gave **Hermannus(=Stetten?)** presbyter(priest) de Stuzelinge(Altsteußlingen) et frater(brother) **Burchardus(=Hohenvels?)** similiter dicitur cum omnibus pertinentiis suis **Hohonbuch** (gave them the same with all its appurtenances) witnesses Vlrico comite de Lenzburch(Lenzburg) and a few others (WO:544). Ruck (1181) Cv̂hrado de Dachowe, Otdone comite de Chilberc(Kyburg), Eberhardo da Eberstein, **Adelberto de Stofelen**, Heinrico de Heimsheim, Cv̂hrado de Stamheim, Rv̂dolfo de Gvdingin(Guttingen), Hugone de Yhelingen, Friderico de Duzelingen in a document for

Pfalzgraf Hugo von Tübingen gifts for kloster(monastery) Herrenalb (WO:645). Merishausen June 21st (1208) Rudolf von Güttingen contract and witnesses Liutoldum confratrem meum de Creigin(Lütold v. Krähen), R. de Tengin (Rudolf v. Tengen) Abott des Benediktinerklosters Allerheiligen in Schaffhausen, A. de Chreigin(Krähen), **Wernher v. Staufen** and others in a St. Gallen document (MO:981). Meersburg (1260) Heinrich von Leonegg (Burg, s. Pfullendorf) wappenseigel stamp shown with Ram on 3 dreiburgs exactly like Burkhard von Ramsburg 1253 wappensiegel (Salem Abbey 1881 : 550).

- von Lommis s. Loumeissae 3/1214, Lomeisz 1228, Lomes 1255, de Loemeis 1265, von Loumeiz 1279, Lomeise 1280, Loemass, Loemmass 1344, Lomass 1364
{*wappen from von Tengen*} is exactly the same with 2 bends and a fleur-de-lis appearing in the Zurich wappenrolle. #434 in the Zurich wappenrolle and 2 after of Pont-en-Ogoz. Led by Tengen, introduced the emblem of Lommis, Ulrich von Tengen around 1339 a vassal of Reichenau and his wife Adelheid, daughter of Hermann Marschalk (Kindler von Knobloch 1919:35). Mülibach (1209) Albertus pleb de Wila, **Wernherus pleb de Stekkenboren**, comes Diethelmus iun de Togginburch ,**Waltherus advoc de Klingin, Eberhardus de Burgilon cum filio s Berchtoldo,** Albertus de Bussenanch cum filio s Alberto Eudolfus Ulricus, Heinricus carnales fratr de Gütingen, Berchtoldus de Anniwilare, Fridericus et Wernherus de Schoninberch, Albertus de Heidoltiswilare cum filio s Wezilone Wezilo dapifer de Hugol tishoven Rudolfus de Winterthure, Waltherus de Eilgau, Ebirhardus et Waltherus carnales fratres de Bichilnsee, Egilolfus et Heinricus cam fratr de Valchknistein, Rudolphus de Bochislo, **Berchtoldus Fantilie** and others (RE:139). From Toggenburg ministeriales (1209-1443), Berchtold gennannt fantelinus (Fantilin/ Pantlinus) (1209-1249), Uolricus de Cecinchovin(v. Zezikon) plebanus Loumeissae 3/1214, **Heinricus I de Lomeiz** and brother Chunradus Fantelinus 1228, Eber(hardus) de Lomes 1/1255-1289 in Kyburg, Konrad Fantelin (Pantlinus) 1228-1261, **Eberhart von Lomeise** 1280, Eberhard von Lommis 12/1358 Heinrich II v Lommis (1267-1285) in Wil, Thurgau, Switzerland. Lütisburg (1228) Bishop Conrad of Constance notarized a comparison between the master of St. John Burkhard of Bubikon and the Count of Toggenburg : Eberhardus et Waltherus fratres carnales de Bichelnse(Bichelsee), **Leo de Hvckenriet** (Zuckenriet - Niederhelfenschwil, Wil), Chuno de Buches(Boschen?), Eppo de Secinchon(Zezikon – Münchwilen, TG), **Chu°nradus Fantelinus** et frater eius **Heinricus de Lomeizß** milites (Münchwilen, TG) and others (MO:1160). Wil zu Tännikon April (1265) **Waltherus de Lantsperch** et Waltherus filius (sons) milites(knights) ministeriales in villa de Tennincon resign & surrender rights to monastery(?) Testibus: Magister Andreas de Willeberc, Eberhardus dapifer de Bichelnse, Cuonradus de Geisberc, Burchardus et Cuonradus fratres de Einwiler, Hugo de Eshenze milites, **Ulricus et Waltherus de Lonberc/Löuberg,** Diethelmus de Mose, H de Tusnanc, **Eberhardus de Loumeis**, Waltherus de Bunishoven, C de Curia (MO:1748). Kreuzlingen in Thurgau (1278) April 27th **Vlricus et Wernerus milites de Loewenberg,** presentibus praefato Decano Bernwardo viceplebano in Wile, **Rudolpho sacerdote vicario in Lommais**. Tannikon (1358) Dec 3rd Eberhart von Lommis gives Heinrich Keller right to heriditary and loan to Wil(in Thurgau) (Hits 1852:27). "Approximately in the same generation that follows the Krayger Burkhard II and the Canon, was Peter, another Friedinger belong, whose inclusion in the genealogy of the family are not possible. 1364 (November 30) sold in Wil (Canton St. Gallen) wife Elizabeth, "Peters Friedingen" happy marriage of the daughter and Hanigis Boschen marital bliss housewife, with her daughter Margaret the advocacy of an estate in Lommis. As the granddaughter of Margaret already deceased persons by Peter Fridingen, this must have been born approximately in 1300 / 1310th From the same generation of Hegauischen Fridinger is also the St. John Rudolf VII (Fridingen), from 1333 1371 in the Order branch not far from Wil and Lommis ravine is demonstrated. Perhaps it was he who had brought the resume its relatives of Peter Fridingen from Hegau here (Dobler 1986:107)." Lommis "von Lommis, toggenburger ministeriales, noted 1209-1443, seat in Lommis (Bz. Münchwilen, canton Thurgau, Switzerland) from Zurich wappen rolle (Clemmensen 2009: p 61). Lommis (Lommais, Lomas, Laumas, Loubmeisse, Loumais) is supposed to come from the nobles of Toggenburg[459]. The

Loomis DNA group on Ysearch.org did not have matching Haplogroup on any of the 7 "English/England" members as of 4/2012. **Note:** Elizabeth Bosche was the daughter of Eberhard von Lommis[460]. A document for Pfalsburger Nurenburg dated (Feb - Mar 9) 1431 list many signers including Jerge von Buchen, Houpt marschalk, der landcomentur in Eilsas, Jacop Eberhart & Jerge truschsesen(*trustees*)...Rudolff & Cunrat von Fridingen[461]. In Ulm, another Bayern document with Haupt Marschalk and Jorg von Gundolfing are signing side by side dated 1434. Rudolff von Frydingen dem Alteren (~1382/~1412) also signed in the Riedlingen document (1439) February 3rd with Houpt Marschalk who married Dorethee, Heinrich Randegg (~1365) who married Kunigande F (~1380), Ulrich Klingen and Hans Ulrich Stoffeln located in Zurich archives. Rudi Fridinger (~1378) the vogte of Romanshorn,Thurgau in 1403 of whom I'm thinking Eberhard is referring to other relatives in Thurgau.

- **von Ramschwag (RAMENSWAG)** {Argent, in pale two lions passant gardant gules crowned or silver}. #132 in the Zurich wappenrolle, 5 down from Fridingen and 3 above Steinegg/Staineg. Konstanz (1176) September 24[th] O[v]Iricus de Rammiswag(Ulrich I. v. Ramschwag in Haggenschwil, Thurgau), Swigerus de Glateburg (Swiger v. Glattburg), Ro[v]dolfus de Rorscach (Eglolf u. Rudolf v. Rorschach) and others (MO:971). H de Rameswag 1229-1244, Konrad v Ramschwag 1226-1244, Ulrich v Ramschwag 1265-1291.

- **Pundt {de Pont-en-Ogoz}** (heren vom punt) {*Blue Lion in bend*} in the Canton of Freiburg 12[th] century by Clemmenson. #432 in the Zurich wappenrolle and 2 ahead of Lommis. Origins probably came from Hartmannus von Chiburch (Kiburg). (1258) September 18th **Burchard Pont** >*Burchardum dictum Pônt*< dem Kloster Heiligkreuztal Testium: H. de Pivnt and others (WO:2189). The wappenbuch of Grunenberg 1480 has the identical wappenschield of Fridingen except the Lion is walking "in the white" vs "on the white". In the book "Grundriss der Genealogie, Volume 8" is shows der Pont-en-Ogoz wappen(COA) in Freiburg and der **Lommis** in Thurgau on the same page. #432 on the 1430 Zurich wappenrolle has them two apart on the parchment. Pont-en-Ogoz[462] – "Pfarrei Avry Bezirk Greyerz Schlosskapelle S Theodul Mem de Frib I p 2 Pfarrkirche Visitation 1453 Archives de la societe de history Fribourg I p 197". "Destruction is my Diger ago has generated Hertzog Wilhelm in Bavaria soliche spend on clothes and ross solicher Ristung his Gdn c Maximum number volckhs the schböbischen **Pundt** sent to you as you pulled in 2 days for **Hochenkräen** and bound and verprent wortten as one of the baby Christ zölt year 1512"[463]. 1512 is the destruction at HohenKrahen by the Swiss. Note: a Swiss Castle history says this wappen come from "a combination of the elements of the arms of the previous municipalities; the lion is taken from the arms of Le Bry, the bend from Avry and the pales from Gumefens"[464].

- **Fürst von Hirscheck (HIRSEG)** {Or, a stag gules scaling the jagged side bendwise abased of a mountain issuant from dexter flank and base azure} {lack of lion, stag walking mountain bend}. #346 in the Zurich wappenrolle two above Güttingen. (1058) Peterhausen donation (Owiltingen in Linzgau) from Swiggerus who married Adelheid (sone named Gotteschalk) with the following witnesses Ottonis (Buchorn), Roudolf comes (de Pfullendorf fortasse sive de Achalm), Eberhart, Oudalrich, Adelbret, Hezo, Hezil, Adelolt, **Gerolt(Hirscheck)**, **Hereman(Hirscheck)**, Alwich, Adelbero, Ratolt, Hezel, Roudolf, and Marcwart[465]. Petershausen (~1071?-1086?) Herimannus senior de Hirzisegga purchased arms Saint Maurice, Herimannus and his brother have two farms with in Alminishus and Winiden(Almannsweiler et Winnenden in praef Saulgau & Michelwinnaden prope Waldsee) (MGH:643). Michelwinnaden received the donation of the Lords of Hirscheck in the 11th century – the coat of arms for family Wielin was Yellow, Back & Yellow. Allerheiligen (1093) Dec 27th Gozpertus cum manu filii et advocati mei Alberici, Gerung de Stulinga, Diethalm de Tokkemburg, Erlewin et Sigefrid de Honsteti, **Liutolt de Eichsteiga**, Liutolt de Wilare(Ramsen?) and others. (1096) Gebehardus episcopus(bishop) et/& Heinricus de Ebenwilare(=Hirscheck) handed out traditional Sancto Salvatori(Holy Saviour) delivered to all the saints in the abilities of his village[466], which is called Mówinheim (Mauenheim) mansions (Wagner 1895:78). Schauffhausen (1096) June 1st **Heinricus de Ebinwilare, Cönradus de Eichsteiga, Eberharth de Höneburk(Homberg)** and others. Ebenwilare is SSW of Althausen and SSE of Eichstegen – Mauenheim Engin is west of Altshausen and NNW of Muhlhausen. Dieto of Eistegen married in 1153, divorced by Frederick Barbarossa Adela of Vohburg. The **Adelberti de Gamertingen** is in the same Shaffhausen document (1101) April 21st as **Herimanni de Böselingen (Büßlingen)** and his brother **Adalbert de Winterspuren**, Rŏperti de Hadolfingen(Hailfingen), **Adelberti de Werenswilare** and others (WO:409). Allerheiligen Worms & Kloster Allerheiligen (1145) item predium **Heinrici de Evenwilare**, also estate **Herimanni et uxoris eius in Sweindorf, Stuzelingen** and with others (WO:515). (1150) Item **Adelbertus** tradidìt in viculo **Werinswilare**(O.A Saulgau). Vor(About) 1163 Hermann der Aeltere von Hirschegg bringt einen 145 Thebäerarm aus S Maurice nach Petershausen (Stückelberg 1902:29). Altinbrugg (1162-1182) Testes: Bruno de **Mahrtorf**, Hugo palatinus de Tǔwingen, Ebirhardus de Tanne, Dieto de Rauinsburch, Bertholdus de F , Chŏno de Sumirŏwe, **Albertus frater eius(and his brother) Wezilo de Eigistegin**, Fridericus de Walpurch, Ortolfus de Smalunegge, Hermannus de Radirei and others (WO:589). Weingartern (1219) Ulrich von Weissenau, des marschall Anselm von Justingen, des truchsess Eberhard von Waldburg, des Conrad von Winterstetten, **Dieto von Eichstegen** and others (RE: 1011a). Weingartern (1220) Anshelmus de Iustingen, marscalcus, Eberhardus dapifer de Waltpurc, Covnradus de Winersteten, **Dieto de Eihstegen(Eichstegen)**, Bernhardus minister de Rauenspurc (WO:962). Salem (1222) Conradus de Wartinberc. Greisingen (1228) August 1st Burchardus de Kilhdorf decimas, quas fratres de Salem de manu nostra conpararunt in predio, quod advocatus de Suarzenberc (Konrad v Schwarzenberg s. Waldkirch) act in Gisingen presents Burchardo preposito, Hanrico de Lupfon(v. Lupfen), Hanrico de Wartenberc 1215-1251, Rudolfo de Ailekov (v. Elgg 1216-1228), Walthero de Alstetten (v. Altstätten 1213-1243), Walthero de Wiltperc (v Wildberg), Rudolfo de Hagenwilare (v. Hagenwil 1227-1264) (MO:1155). St. Gallen (~1230) July 13th Kloster Weisenau brother Konrad and Heinrich Wartenburg transfer goods to "Tieringeshart" to Ritter Ulrich von Schwarzenbach in presense of Berthold monk nephew of our Salem and his brothers, Albert & Henry Bussenanc soldiers, **Bertoldo de Burgelon** and Henry de Guttingen soldiers (WO:1171). **Konrad Fürst** wappensiegel[467] >right> dated 1236 found in the Salem Abbey. St. Gallen (1230) Konrad & Heinrich von Wartenberg. Wendlingen (1237) May 24th Graf Egeno von Aichelberg übergibt den Nonnen zu Boos (Baindt), our own sisters and their heirs confer the name of Hainrico von Ebenwilar, ministerial and faithful, and not Minister Conrad von Ebersbach (WO:1334). Aichelberg (1238) May 17th Dienstmann (Ministry) Heinrich von Ebenweiler (WO:1362). Booz(Baindt/Bewnde/Buende) (~1237/8) mentioned **Konrad von Schussenried, Heinrich von Ebenweiler** and other neighbors through which the sisters were persecuted and harassed[468]. Konzenberg (1239) Conrado/Konrad Fursto deceased husband of Vdelhildis(v. Wartenburg) buried @ Salem with advice of friends and grandfather, the lords of the Hainrici Wartinberc. In presence of these H Wartinberc of grandfather, Vlrico subcellarer of Salem, Walther grangario, Cv̂hrado versa Livtfrido parish of Nendingen, Gerone of Waltinstein, Bilgerino of Tutelingin, Hvgone of Meringen, Vlrico of Steinhv̂sen, Cv̂hone Hainrico and his brother, and a medical clerk Cv̂hrado Meschilh. Seal of our fathers strength: S*igillum* . C . PRINCIPI . . .HIRZECCHE (WO:1373). Villingen (1244) Cvnradus aduocatus de Swarzinberc, Cvonrado seniore de **Wartinberc** et Hainrico filio and others (MO:1358). (1245) November 15th The brothers **Konrad and Heinrich von Wartenberg** pass their wealth Kunegundehaus, fief of John of Ringgenburg to their ancestors and their soul salvation. At the monastery Baindt (WO:1568). John von Eichstegen handed in 1250 for the purpose of founding of the monastery his castle Eichstegen-Löwental and accessories to the Dominicans in Constance. Rotenmünster (1254) . Rudolph **Fridingen** and way of exchange the same he did in 1257 called negotiated to **Fridingen** blessed is not far from one fief of Konrad Habse, the latter had by Konrad von **Wartenberg** (situm on **Fridingen** & eclessie in Salem)[469] in exchange for two acres in Grindelbook. Villingen (1258) May. Meersburg (1260) Heinrich von Leonegg (Burg, s. Pfullendorf) wappenseigel stamp shown with Ram on 3 dreiburgs exactly like Burkhard von Ramsburg 1253 wappensiegel (Salem Abbey 1881 :550). (1260) **Konrad Fürst** and his brothers transferred from the Ulrich von Steinhaus whose paternal fief Balzhaus (WO:2272). "All these letters C. dictus Furst and his brothers said the notice below. Know all of you that we Vlrich Stainhuse of the fee in Balzhus, which his father had purchased a while he lived, with all its rights conferred by a liberal for his possession. And in the concession fee, both free, should not arise in the future can be a challenge, to present letters, we gave our seal protection strengthened" (WO:2272). Konrad, Heinrich and Friedrich (deer-**Hirschsiegelestamp**[470] 1262) brothers von **Wildenstain** 3/1262. Hettingen (1267) August 30 Count Wolfrad {Wolfradus} of Veringen the Elder and his sons Wolfrad and Henry and Earl Mangold of Nellenburg approve the sale called possessions in Wilflingen which knight Heinrich von Gundelfingen had worn them as a fief, against other they applied to fiefs there at the monastery Heiligkreuztal - Arnold Wildinvelz, Aeinsilino de Wildinstain et **Rvdolfo de Kraigin**, Hainricus et Swiggerus fratres(brothers), filii predicti(sons of the said) Hainricus senior miles(ritter/soldier) de Gvndiluingin, Anshelmo de **Iustingin**(Justingen) (WO:2704). In 1263 Heinrich von Gundelfingen has a **{Hirschsiegel}**. Geisingen (1268) July, the four brothers **Konrad Fürst of Konzenberg** left their mountain castle Hirscheck together with all appurtenances, with the exception of male fief, which reserves one of the younger brothers to. Their uncle, the brothers Konrad and Heinrich von Wartenberg (WO:2792). St. Gallen (1270) Hainricus Wartinberc. Geisingen (1273) April 13th Konrad & Heinrich genannt(called) Struz (dictus Struz) von Wartenberg (Wartunberch) presented & invited nobili viro Hermanno comite de Sulze, Ber. de Sunthusen, C. et C. de Gvtmetingin, H. de Sunthain et **H. dicto Fridinger** (fratribus Salem Cello/Ratolfzell), Wernherus de Swarzenbach & others (WO:796). Geisingen (1278). Konrad v. Wartenberg 1215-1278 and Heinrich gen. **Struz v. Wartenberg** 1242-1284 (MO:1570). Villingen (1281) January 13th. Salem (1290) Nov 17th **Cünradus nobilis dictus der Fürst de Cünzenberch** waived the right of ownership of his posessions, **Hainrico dicto der Furste** and others. (1292) Albrecht der Schedel von Steußlingen übergibt dem Kloster Salem das Eigentumsrecht von Gütern(goods) to Grötzingen: **Cûnrat Hirisegge ze Westerndorf, Hainrich and Cûnrat Hirisegge(Hirscheck)** represent the people (WO:5157). Konstanz (1300) May 25th. Konstanz (1301) September 23rd Cûnradus dictus **Furst de Kûnzemberg** (Konrad Fürst v. Hirscheck zu Konzenberg) (MO:2357). Schattbuch (1335) August 31st **Cunrat der Furst von Cuntzenberg** Landrichter zu Schatbuch in der Grafschaft zum Hailigenberg (disputes between) Hainrich dem Frien(der Frige) von Sunnenberc & Kloster Salmanswiller (FU 1885:129). Schattbuch (1338) August 10th **Cunrat der Furst von Cuntzenberc** Landrichter zu Schatbuch (express to) **Bruder Hainrichen** dem Kaufman von Salmanswiller (FU 1885:407). Schattbuch (1341/43) May 21st Cunrat der Furst von Cuintzenberg, seigel C PRINCIPIS DE KWNSENBERCH.

- von Ainwile (Andwile) located an hour east of **Bürgeln** in Thurgau {Argent, a stag's head couped gules} {lack of lion, stag torso with Bear/Wolf, similiar to Hirscheck}. #113 on the Zurich wappenrolle. Two down from the Kallenburg wappen #115 a Green Linden tree upright with white background while Clingen(Hohenklingen) wappen #52 is a Green Oak tree up right with yellow background found on the Zurich wappenrole. Kallenburg #115 is directly next to Clingenberg(Klingenberg) #116 {per pale Black/White} on the Zurich role. Petershausen (1060) Chapel St Johannes Baptiste **Wolferad von Wilare** gattin Gotistiu filius **Sigifridus** under bishop Otto (1071-1080) Ogglehausen in parish Iudintunberc, **Burgweiler in HohenZollern** MGH:642). St. Georgen Kloster (1083) Jan 4th Heinrich & neffe(nephew) Heinrich von Hirscheck(Altshausen) witnessed a document with **Arnold von Binzwanger** with brother Manegold & Ludwig, **Sigfridus et filius fratris eius Hermannus de Wilere** and others in Schwarzwald (Eberhard : 1964). Stein Klosters Allerheiligen (1092) February 26th Graf Burkhard von Nellenburg, **Hartwic de Strazza**, Benno de Speicchinga, Diethalm de Tochimburc, Dieterich comes de Biurgeliun(Nellenburg), Herimann de Egga, **Toto de Wilare**(Radolfzel or Ramsen) and others (SH:576). Worms (1145) Redditus manegoldi et uxoris eius ac filie in **Wilare**. Kloster

Salem Constantie (1158) Testes: **Heinricus Habardus de Salwnstein**, ministeriales: Burchardus de castro Homburch, Bertoldus et Arnoldns frater eius de Hioninberch, Burchardus de Banchilhouen, Eberhardus marchsehaleus, **Rudolfus de Wilare, Herungus de Chregin (=Hermann Krahen),** Bertoldus de Husin and others (FU 1885:61). Königstuhl (~1160) **Herimanno de Marcdorf** with Duke Welf VI passing the Kloster St. Blasien to Nendingen, **Nahthilt, filias Operti de Wilare apud Ravinspurch** with others (WO:582). Cruceline (1166) Apr 8th Laici seculares: **Bruno de Marhdorf**, Eberhardus mariscalcus, **Berhtoldus de Wilare**, Ortwinus, **Hesso Marquart** and others (RE 1895:112). Constanz (1169) Mar 10th Otto & interfuerunt advocatus eiusdem ecclesiae **Fridericus de Wildinstein**, Rôdolf de Sevelt, Waltherus de Clingin, Burkardus de Obiriedin, Burkhard jun de Frichingen, **Bruno de Marhdorf, ministeriales Hesso de Annewilar**, **Rôd de Wilar** and many others (RE 1895:113). Constanz (1175) September 24th Diakon **Berthold von Andwil (Bertoldum diaconum de Annenwillare)** later *domherr von Constanz* 1192-1213 (MO:929). Conradus et Rudolfus de Annewillare Ministerialen 1176. Constanz (1176) Herm prepos, Heinr dec, Frider de Nidingen, C de Foro, **Ulr de Annvillare, Heinr de Fridingen**, mag Albert, **Hesso**, Conr de Tegervelt, Gotefr de Rordorft, **Bruno et Hainr de Marchtorff**, **Ölr de Willare, Hainr de Vrichingen,** Burch et Hainr et Bertold Stateli, Burch de Hohenburg, **Chônr de Willare**, Dieterici cum filiis Ebernandi, Thiethelm de Tochemburg, **Eberhardus de Burgelun** and many others (RE:116). (1180) Aug 22nd Hainr de Winterture et fil suus Rödolf et fr suus **Chônr et Rod de Annenwillare**, Hainr Statili, Hainr Havenare, Hiltebolt Havenare ministeriales comitis Chônrat Scade Bert pincerna, Chônr de Liebenberg, Ölr de Wurmenhuse, Alb de Slate, and others. Constanz (1181) April 2nd Zehten zu Schlatt , **Hermanno de Vridingen**, Ölr de Hugone, **Hainr de Vrichingen, Hessone, Bert et Chônr de Willare, Hainr Staetilin** and a few others. Constantie (1183) bischof von C(=Hermann Fridingen) & äbten Dietpert von SBlasien & Gebhard von Petershausen, Chônr dec, ödalr cust, **Hesso canon**, Chônr de Thetingin, Hugo cellerar, Provinciales: **Eberh de Burgelun**, Diethelm de Snegginburc, **Berht et Chônr de Wilare**, Wecil et Chônr de Hugoldishovin, **Chônr de Anniwilare de monte zu Berg, Rôd de Anniwilare fil domini Hessonis**, Hiltibold et Hugo fratr Bódeg, Hesso fil Ödilr, and a few others (REC 1895:121). Bergartirutin (1185) Oulr de Cilicgou, **Chounr de Willare**, Walther de Hunoberg, and many others. Salem Constanz (1189) Diethelm von Konstanz , Rudolphus resignation, Conradus de Tegerueld, Wernherus de Stophen ,Conradus de Tettingen, **Bertoldus de Annewilare** ,Albertus de Walpurc, Ministeriales: Wernherus de Arbona et filius eius Rodolfus, **Rodolfus de Annewilare**, Conradus de Castello, Hilteboldus de Zurich and others (SA:65). Würzburg (1192) June 7th **Hermanni de Fridingen Grindelbûch, Adelberti et filii eius Burchardi de Frikingen, Hermanni de Marcdorf** et aliorum plurium, comes **Burchardus de Hohenberc, R˘oberti et Bertholdi de Aha Dorfisberc, Marquardus dapifer de Anewilære** and many others (WO:726). (1193) May 13th Gerungus et Cunradus frater eius de Sulegeu testes: Otto Frisingen, Cuno de Minzenberc, Otto de Hurwin, **Marcquardus de Anwilre** and others (SA:74). Thurgau (1196) Nov 25th Marquardi Crucelinesis , Testes: **Heinricus de Annewilare, Baldebrehtus de Annwilare** and others[471]. Konstanz (1199) June 11th Diethelmus, dei gratia Constantiensis episcopus , W. videlicet de Stoufin et **M. de Anwiler**, canonicos Constantienses testes: C. de Tegervelt, W. de Arbun (WO:769). Konstanz (1200) *Bischof Diethelm von Konstanz*, Testes: Wernherus de Stôfin, Hugo cellerarius, **Marquardus** frater suus, Vlricus de Castil, **Berhtoldus de Annuviler**, Rûdigerus de [Ra]tirshouena, Cunradus de Gundelfingen and others (WO:793). Mülibach (1209) Albertus pleb de Wila, **Wernherus pleb de Stekkenboren**, Egilolfus pleb de Waldkilche, comes Diethelmus iun de Togginburch ,**Waltherus advoc de Klingin, Eberhardus de Burgilon cum filio s Berchtoldo**, Albertus de Bussenanch cum filio s Alberto Eudolfus Ulricus, Heinricus carnales fratr de Gütingen, Rudolfus et Heinricus carnal fratr de Wunninberch, Ebirhardus de Spiegilberch, Rudolphus de Steinache, **Berchtoldus de Anniwilare**, Fridericus et Wernherus de Schoninberch, Albertus de Heidoltiswilare cum filio s Wezilone Wezilo dapifer de Hugol tishoven Rudolfus de Winterthure, Chunradus Giel, Waltherus de Eilgau, Ebirhardus et Waltherus carnales fratres de Bichilnsee, Beringerus de Lamminberg, Egilolfus et Heinricus cam fratr de Valchknistein, Rudolphus de Bochislo, Arnoldus de Heitinowe, Berchtoldus Fantilie and others

(RE:139). Thurgau (1236) Henricus eps testatur quod **Berhtoldus miles ecclesiae Const ministerialis dictus de Annewilare** cum uxore sua Judinta et filia sua Heilwiga praedium suum in Buoche monasterio in Crucelin. Constanz (1241) June 11th H. de Raprehtiswilere, et **H. de Höhinvels**, Constantiensibus canonicis, Vl. de Haidilberch , **Ber. de Annewilere** and others (WO:1451). Constanz (1242) July 11th *Ritter Albero von Spielberg samt seinen Kindern,* presentibus viris in Cristo B. de Hohinuels, **Ber. de Annewile**, Vl. de Bertisshuss, C. de Hugultischouen et R. de Staze(Strass) militibus and others (WO:1475). Constanz (1248) Dec 16th **Walther v Clingen vogt der kirche Bischofzeil, Ulrich von Klingen bruder Walthers**, Peregrinus et Cunradus Ymbria, prepositi dns **Hugo de Clingen**, Waltherus Dihtelarius, Heinricus de Straze, Waltherus de Rammstein canonici Constant, nobil vir Hein de Rosenegge, C de Steine, **Bertoldus et Bertoldus de Annewiler** and others (RE:198). Bregenz to Constanz (1251) Jan Egilolfo de Valckenstein, Ruodolpho de Hasinweiler, Walthero de Ramestein, Heinrico de Straze, **Heinrico de Clingenberg, Baldeberthus de Aneweiler**, magistro Walcone, Ruperto de Tannenvelse and others (RE:203). Engen or Constanz (1251) Mar 13th Friedrich v Wildenstein , Hiltebold v Steckborn (Stekiboron), **Bertold v Andweil (Annewiler)**, Hug v Oftringen and others (RE:204). Konstanz (1251) July 1st comiti Vl. de Wirtenberc, **Ber. de Annewilare senior** and others (WO:1824). Gottlieben (1255) Nov 16th Bertoldus de Hohinvels, **Baldepertus de Annewiler, Hainr de Straze,** Cînr pleb de Diengen, C nob de Louffen, Frid Hoenburc, Cvnr de Schônowe, Alb de Castello milites and others. 1255 **Baldebert Andwile domherr zu Constanz**. Constanz (1261) B de Hohenvels ecclesie, **Ita nobilis de Clingen** notice of event died **C(onrad) aduocati de fridingen** testes: Dominus de Valchenstein, **B Dominus de Annuwiler,** Dominus de Heidelberch, Dominus Hilteboldus miles de Stegboren, Dominus Volricus, C de Tetinchon, siegel *Sororis ite de vridingen* (Hirzel 1873:358)[472]. Conrad I v Fridingen's nephew **Rudolph III v F** appears in the 1267 document with **Arnold von Wildenfels.**

- von Heidegg s. Heideck, Haidegkh, Haydegg, Hewdegg, Heydegg the "von Heideck" #402 in the Zurich wappenrolle ~1340 which is half/half split very much like {Alt-Frydingen/Neu-Frydingen Black & Gold shield} however in Yellow right half and Blue Left Half {Yellow & Blue per pale}. "Von Heideck vassals of Gr.Kyburg noted 1185-1552, Truchsessen of Gf. Lenzburg, has their seat Burg Heidegg near Gelfingen & Hirzkirch (Hochdorf canton Luzern, Switzerland) (Clemmensen 2009: pg 72). Konrad, Gotfried and Hiltpold von Heidegg are already in canton of Bern @ Interlaken[473], Switzerland by 1312.

- Heideck Not as much the same as Fridingen, the Lords of Heideck{*lat* Haydegg}[474] {Freidloh 1139-1159 & brother Ulrich 1159-1169} a shield with 3 Horizontal bars (Red on Top, White through the middle and Blue on bottom. The Lords of Heideck, whose family seat was at (2.5km north of) Trochtelfingen in Hohenzollern, are most likely a different line of the Lords of **Hirscheck** (Dobler 1968:65). More the same as von Krenkingen, Dielthelm von Fridingen/Krahen mother was a Krenkingen and his Sieglestamp "Krenkingen" shown as a Bishop of Constanz. "There are reasons to believe that the ratio of the ancestors of Reichenau Friedingischen zue was well ahead of time Diethelms already tight. By the feudal possession of the monastery Lichen Kellhofs Friedingen in which they had taken over after our acceptance of the Nelleburgen castles around 1105/1110, the family stood in a fiduciary relationship to the abbey. On the island, ruled as abbot since 1139 Herron{Lords} two of Heideck, Friedloh/ Frideloh (1139-1159) and after him his brother Ulrich (1159-1169). The Lords of Heideck, whose family seat was at Trochtelfingen in Hohenzollern, are most likely a different line of the Lords of **Hirscheck**. The two abbots of Reichenau in front of Dielthelm Krenkingen are then relatives of Mahlspuren been (Dobler 1986:65)."

 - von Wildenstein (WILDENSTAIN) {*White bend, lack of lion "with three triangular teeth on each edge argent" with 2 swans}* #120 on the Zurich wappenrolle and same strip as #128

The Swabian Connection – Expanded Edition

Fridingen. Wildenstain come of these barons is thus, we see only through their seals that on the romantic rocks Wildenstein Castle in Baden Danube valley,three very different families who all are indiscriminately followed by the same named on each other, the oldest of the same was as their label to show the Fursten{Prince} of Hirscheck the second to the Barons of Justingen the third to the Barons von Wartenberg but this genealogical significance[475]. The Zurich wappenrolle has Wildenstein wappen and the Fridingen wappen(COA) painted on the same strip of parchment. **Ruthard v Wildenstein** 1165 Domherr in Konstanz. Constanz (1169) Mar 10th Otto & interfuerunt **advocatus eiusdem ecclesiae Fridericus de Wildinstein**, Conradus et vir ingenuus **Burchardus iunior de Frichingin** Testes: Conradus advocatus Constantiensis et filius eius Arnoldus comes, **Rodolfus de Seuelt, Waltherus de Clingin**, Burkardus de Obiriedin, **Burkardus iunior de Frichingin, Bruno de Marhdorf** canonici maioris ecclesiae: Heinricus decanus, Heinricus praepositus ecclesiae s Stephani, Ortolfus, Conradus, Ulricus, Eberhardus sacerdos de Bodimin, Conradus et Marcholfus sacerdotes, ministeriales **Hesso de Annewilar, Rodolfus de Wilar** cives and others (FU:63). Worms January (1179) Vogt Volkmar Struzo (von Wildenstein) von Goslar, Ulrich von Speyers and others (RI:2479). Turin (1186) March 27th Hermannus(=Fridingen?) Monasteriensis episcopus, Odo Taurinensis episcopus, Ruodolfus imperialis aulae prothonotarius, Iohannes praepositus Sancti Germani in Spira, Conradus marchio Montis Ferrati, Bonifacius frater eius, Willelmus marchio de Palodio, Bertoldus dux Meraniae, **Henricus de Wildenstein**, Ulricus de Gudenberc, Guichardus frater burgun de Magdeburc and many others (RI:1186). (1210) siegler bei abt Eberhard von Petershausen für **Adilgoz miles von Wildenstein** die vogtei von Bichtlingen (Birchtlingen) nach graf Mangolds von Eordorf. (1211) Agolt von Wildenstein and many others (RE:140). Kreuzlingen in Thurgau (1243) March 8th **Hainricus de Vridingen** duo fiilii eius **Hainricus et Cuonradus** advocatiam in Richinhusen(Ruhinhusen), Friderico de Thengen, **Burchardo de Wildinstein,** warandi: **Hainricus et Conradus de Vrídingen filii Hainrici** and many others[476]. Friderico de Wildenstain 11/1245, Konrad , Heinrich and Friedrich(deer-Hirschsiegelestamp[477] 1262) brothers von Wildenstain 3/1262, Alshelmus de Wildenstain 8/1263 (teeth-sieglestamp478 1263) & 1278 & 1296. Some Wildenstein nobles: It appears these Hirscheck-Wartenberg brothers Friedrich, Conrad and Heinrich move to Wildenstein about 1245 (WO:1568). Engen or Constanz (1251) Mar 13th **Friedrich v Wildenstein , Hiltebold v Steckborn (Stekiboron), Bertold v Andweil (Annewiler)**, Hug v Oftringen and others (RE:204). Linz (1253) June 5th Walter von Kallenberg der Ältere und **Heinrich von Wildenfels** goods to Irrendorf, Testes: Otto et Hainricus de Hohinberc, **Arnoldus de Wildenuelsi**, Wolfrado preposito de Burron, Ego **Fridericus de Wildensten** (WO:1888). Salem (1253) Dec, die brüder Walther & Rüdiger v Kallenberg (Kallenberc). Constanz (1263) Mar 11th **Conrad, Heinrich und Friedrich brüdem von Wildenstein**, others présentions: Rvdolfo de Rinegge, Cünrado de Castel, Hainrico de Burgelon, et Cünrado de Shonenowe, multibus Diethalmo de Guttingen, Rudolfo de Shulzberg, Vírico et Walthero fratribus de Castel, **Vírico et Cünrado de Urendorf**, et Alberto de Vrikingen and others (RE: 236). Hettingen (1267) August 30 Arnold Wildinvelz, Rvdolfo de Kraigin, Aeinsilino de Wildinstain, Hainricus senior miles de Gvndiluingin, Anshelmo de **Iustingin** (Justingen) (WO:2704). In 1263 Heinrich von Gundelfingen has a {Hirschsiegel}. Dates provided by Baden-Wurttemburg Ukendenbuch archive[479]. Augsburg (1272) Ludwig von Dillingen Archidiakon, **R.(=Rudolph?) et F.(=Friedrich) de Wildenstein** and many others (MO:192). "For the same reason we identify with the Bussener Henry VIII that knight **Heinrich of Fridingen**, the (1308) May 22nd at the castle HohenFridingen of ratification, which he Stalinshube in Kaltenbach - north of Stammheim (Thurgau) - the Diessenhofen Burger Henry Muller silver was sold at 11 Marks, after it had been about him can be free of the Lord **Anselm of Justingen** as property. On the Bussener line also includes the mention is **Anselm of Justingen** after father Heinrich Rudolph had already done this in 1294 with a paid Heligkreuztal witness support (Dobler 1986:398)." Other surnames by wappenschilde: von Scheller {bend of teeth}to Werthenau oder von Wildenstein 15th century[480]. von Falkenstein[481] {deer on burg} Bertoldus de Valkenstein 1288, Friedrich von Wildenstein 1262. Flecke von Schmiechen[482] {horned

The Swabian Connection – Expanded Edition

goat} herren v Justingen-Steuslingen, Heinrich der Fleck ritter 1311. 1397/98 John of Zimmern gets one half of the castle Wildenstein as a fief, the other office, for the administration.

- von Wildenfels (WILDENVELS) {Per pale argent and sable, issuant from the line of division a demi-lion passant gardant gules} #233 on the Zurich wappenrolle and 5 down from Loenberg/Leuberg. Beuron (1253) April 22nd **Wolfradus** provost sancti Martini in Burron, Ebirhardo Nellinburc and present militibus(soldiers) **Walther and Hainrico de Wildenvels** which begins on this side of the Danube, on the border Wildenstein near Fúhlenthal (Füllehaus) and Oberhusen, stretching himself up to the cliff, which is called Sperberloch(between Brunnen & Friedingen @ Danau/Danube) and others (WO:1183). Linz (1253) June 5th Walter Kallenberg der Ältere and **Heinrich von Wildenfels** sell their goods to stray village to the monastery Beuron by 14 marks. **Otto et Hainricus de Hohinberc**, Wolricus Buzzo et **Arnoldus de Wildenuelsi, Ego Fridericus de Wildensten** and others (WO:1188). Constanz (1263) Mar 11th Conrad, Heinrich und Friedrich brüdern von Wildenstein, others présentions: Rvdolfo de Rinegge, Cünrado de Castel, Hainrico de Burgelon, et Cünrado de Shonenowe, multibus Diethalmo de Guttingen, Rudolfo de Shulzberg, Vírico et Walthero fratribus de Castel, **Vírico et Cünrado de Urendorf**, et Alberto de Vrikingen and others (RE: 236). Constanz (1263) April 11th presentibus: Ebirh de Winterstetin, Hainr de Clingenberc, Baldebrehto de Anewilär, **Burch de Hohenvelse, Berhtoldo de Wildenvelse**, magro Vir de Hiltelvingen, Walt de Kirchain clericis, Hainr de Kavenspurch, Priderico de Sumerôwe and many others(RE:237). Hohentengen (1265) Graf Mangold (M.) von Nellenburg (in Nellinburch) überträgt (transferimus) dem Kloster Salem, Testes: **H. et Ar. fratres milites de Wildinvelsi**, H. de Rordorf, Wezilo de Rischach, F. de Maghinbůch, C. monacus de Veringin, H. conversus de Bu{e}ningin and others (WO:2513). Konstanz (1265) Feb 13th **Bertoldo de Wildenvels**, Cvhrado de Gvnde/ingen (Gundelfingen) and others (WO:2545). Hettingen (1267) August 30 Count **Wolfrad {*Wolfradus*} of Veringen** the Elder and his sons Wolfrad and Henry and Earl Mangold of Nellenburg approve the sale called possessions in Wilflingen which knight Heinrich von Gundelfingen had worn them as a fief, against other they applied to fiefs there at the monastery Heiligkreuztal - **Arnold Wildinvelz, Aeinsilino de Wildinstain** et **Rvdolfo de Kraigin**, Hainricus et Swiggerus fratres(brothers), filii predicti(sons of the said) Hainricus senior miles de Gvndiluingin, Anshelmo de Iustingin(Justingen) (WO:2704). Konstanz (1268) July 18th Ulrichs und seiner brüder Eberhard uud Bertold edler von Gundelfingen, testes: **B. de Wildenvels**. Konstanz 1269 July 18th transfers at the request of the brothers Ulrich, Eberhard and Berthold von Gundelfingen the German home Altshausen the village Ebersbach testes: H[artmannus] comes in Grůningen, **Ber[tholdus] de Wildenvels** and others (WO:2869). 1271 **Berthold von Wildenfels** Canonicus zu Konstanz No 470 is shown with wappensiegle as a *Fleur-de-lis*. 1272 Ber[toldus] de Wildinvelsi, 1276 diaconus Berchtoldi de Wildenfels, 1278 **Wal[therus] et H[einricus] dicti de Wildenvelze** fratres, Beuron (1292) **Heinrich und Ulrich von Wildenfels**, Brüder **Walters**, leisten dem Kloster Bürgschaft (WO:5241). **Note:** Early origins appear to form from Walthero Klingnau brother to Ita v Klingen who married Conrad I v Fridingen, his brother was Heinrich v F. In the same year 1253 Walther Kallenberg appears with Heinrich v W. The Kallenburg wappen #115 is a Green Linden tree upright with white background while Clingen(Hohenklingen) wappen #52 is a Green Oak tree up right with yellow background found on the Zurich wappenrole. Kallenburg #115 is directly next to Clingenberg(Klingenberg) #116 Split per pale Black/White on the Zurich role. Conrad I v Fridingen nephew Rudolph III v F appears in the 1267 document with **Arnold von Wildenfels**. Even further back the Wildenvels name may originate from **Waltherus de Hohenvels (~1206)** with a Ulrich v Clingenberg & Heinrich v Markdorf connection in 1226.

- von Gundelfingen (GVNDELFINGEN) {*bend "with spines" lack of lion, swans head betwn 2 angle bars tipped with peacock feathers*} . #74 on the Zurich wappenrolle and 2 down from #72 Tengen. (*lat* Gundolvingen) noted 1068, extinct 1546, seat Gundelfingen (Munsingen, Baden Wurtemburg). In the Codex diplomatic book for the Salem abbey has **Gundelfingen, Wildenstain** and **Steusslingen** all using these siegelstamps (spines or tooth style). The First Barons of Gundelfingen were so successful they divided into three Lordships and lines (ZC 2: 367). Mainz in kloster Oberstenfeld (1016) Grafen Adelhart & son Heinrich with witneses Odelricus, cancellarius regis Heinrici, Wecel, Gerbertus, Vmmo, Gerbertus, Heinricus, **Diemo, Swiggerus**, clerici, Adelbertus et fratres eius Eberhardus, Burchardus, Ropertus, Otto de Glasehusen, Heinricus, filius comitis Hecelonis, Ello, Hacelin, Gumpertus de Rota, Hitto (WO:327). (1043) June 16th regarding Rietilinis(Riedlings) estate Eberhard Constantiensis aecclesiae , Irmingarde, advocatis **Heremanni (vogt Hermann Hirscheck),** abott Folmarus and the following witnesses Oudalricus Prigantinus, **Switker**, Wezel, **Swigger**, Ernest, **Gerolt**, Ruger, **Landolt**, Otgoz, Lupreht, Sigipreht, Hartnit, Engilscalch, Enceli, Simpreht, Hunolt, Eppo, Ello, Alberich, and Episcopus Eberhardus (MGH:643-4). Peterhausen (1058) transactions from (Owiltingen in Linzgau) to St. Georgen from **Swiggerus** who married Adelheid (son named Gotteschalk[483]) with the following witnesses Ottonis (Buchorn), Roudolf comes (de Pfullendorf fortasse sive de Achalm), Eberhart, Oudalrich, Adelbret, Hezo, Hezil, Adelolt, Gerolt(Hirscheck), Hereman(Hirscheck), Alwich, Adelbero, Ratolt, Hezel, Roudolf, and Marcwart[484]. (1093) December 27 in monastery Allerheiligen, Gerung de Stulinga (Stuhlingen)(~1096) and Burchardus comites de Nellenburg with others[485]. In (1100) there is a **Billung of Gundelfingen (Pillunc de Gundolvingen)** finished in a traditional instrument of the Benedictine monastery of St. Ulrich and Afra in Augsburg[486]. In a Badischen archives list **Swikerus de Gundelfingen** with Bertholdus de Chilchperg and others in (1105) February 26 (Dumge 1836:27). They{Gundelfingen} have the same origin as the nearby Justingen (Clemmenson 2009:47). Some Justingen nobles: Rotenacker (1116) **Swiger** and **Erliwin de Gundeluingen (Gundelfingen)** in the same document **Ernest, Adelbertus** and **monk Otto de Stuzzilingen** (~1070) (Steußlingen), Ŏdalricus comes de Gamutingin (WO:427). Otto von Steußlingen was the grand nephew von Anno (Steußlingen or Busslingen?). **Rudolph v Gundelfingen** 1145 Domherr in Konstanz. Kloster Zwiefalten (~1150) matrona Halicha von Justingen or Steußlingen (WO:532). Ulm February (1157), Friedrich forces the brothers **Swigger** and **Henry von Gundelfingen** to suit their relatives Richenza(Hirschbühl), wife of Burggraf Konrad von Augsburg court for the provision of her estranged heritage of her grandfather, Reginhart von Dapfen (Tapheim) and her brother Konrad(son of Hartwig von Altenbeuren) (RI:436). (1157) Weildorf (1163) **Swiggero de Gundeluingen** in villa Wildorf, Rudolphus de Rammesperc, Adelbertum de Dilignen, **Heinricus de Gundeluinge**, Brononis de Marchdorf et Adelberti, fillii Burchardi de Frichingen and others (WO:595). Giengen (1171) May 1st comes Otto de Chirberg, Ludewicus comes de Helphenstein, Degenhardus de Helonsten, Folenandus de Stuophe, **Diemo et Godefridus frater eius de Gundelfingen** and others (WO:613). Donauwörth May 7th (1171) **Diemo de Gundeluingen**, Cònradus pincerna, Henricus marshalcus (MO:615). Burg Stauffen (1181) May 25th Billungus de Justingin, **Rûpertus de Gundelfingin**, Ludewicus comes de Helfenstein and others (WO:650). (1187) **Cuonradus de Gundolvingen** archidiaconus . Buorron (1192) Dec 15th **Chonr de Gundelfingen, Burchard de Hoenburc et Chónr** frat(er), Heinr Statelinus(=Stetin?) and many others (Wagner 1895:126). Konstanz (1200) *Bischof Diethelm von Konstanz*, Testes: Wernherus de Stöfin, Hugo cellerarius, Marquardus frater suus, Vlricus de Castil, Berhtoldus de Annuviler, Rûdigerus de [Ra]tirshouena, **Cunradus de Gundelfingen** and others (WO:793). (1228) Prefentibus **Swikero de Gundelvingen et Hermanno filio** eius. Anselm von Justingen 6/1216, Anselm jung (son) & Alt (father) v J 1264, Anselm v J 3/1266, Anselm v. J 1269, Anshlmus de Justingen 1278, Anselm von Justingen 1281/82, Anselm von Wudenstein (Wildenstein) 1283, Anshalmo de Wildinstain. Justingen et de Wildinstain 2/1283. Some Gundelfingen nobles: Godefirdus frater de Gundelfingen 5/1171-72, Rupertus de Gundelfingin 5/1181, Ulrich and Son Ulrich v Gundelfingen 1220, Ritter Heinrich von Gundelfingen 8/1267, Heinrich v Gundelfingen 4/1269, Ulrich, Eberhard & Berthold Gundelfingen 7/1269, Konrad Gundelfingen 3/1270 (siegelstamp[487] 1279), Ulrich von Gundelfingen (dictus de Gundolfingen) 2/1279, Degenhart von Gundolfingen 7/1280. (1246) October 17th Swigerus miles de Gundiluingin, Hainricus de Gundelui[n]gin, Hilteboldus de Stekeborun, Ebirhardus pincerna de Salunstain, Albertus et

Rûdolfus de Riedirn fratres, Cvnradus cellerarius, Cvnradus de Cella Ratolfi (Krahen?) and others (WO:1613). Meersburg (1272) Dec 26[th] Eberhardus von Konstanz, Cunradus and Heinrich von Gundelvingen, **Hermannum dictum Boschin** and children of his sister Adilhaidem wife of Gruiben their children Hainrico, Cûnrado, Hainrico, Hermanno et Berhtoldo (SA 1881: 73). Hainrichus de nobilis vir de Gundulfingen[488] has a siegelstamp {deer stag jumping east} in 1274. Saint Gallen Konstanz (1280) Eglolf V. of Steusslingen lets the Johanniterhaus Bubikon a courtyard. First witness. . . ago herr Friderich von Gvndolvingen (1246-91) (MO:2053). Gundelfingen (1289) April 27th Bernold called Staufen certifies that he in 1285 with the consent of his wife Agnes his two inhabited by farmers Hartnid and Dieterich farms in Harthausen: Siegler Herr **Degenhard von Gundelfingen** (Gundelvingen) laicus, Herr Berchtold von Schaumburg (Schaunburc) testes: Heinricus dictus de Staufen, Berhtoldus de Butelspach et de Heinricus Westendorf(Hirschegg) (WO:4788). **Note:** Act of Ramsen (Rammisheim/Ramsberg) in Hegau was established 1096 of which *Gerungo comite de Stulingen* (Stühlingen) signed with *Udalrici comitis de Rammesperch* by the deeds and gifts of Friderun with her son Marquard to the monastery Rinaugia in Eggingen. Adalbert and Heinrich v Ramsen 1100 were sons of Heinrich v Hirscheck (~1053) (Dobler 1986: 447). Urlichs son was Rudolf von Pfullendorf/Ramsberg of which the Pfullendorf (Stoffeln) came from another Herman d. A. von Hirscheck (~990-1044). Rotenacker (1116) **Adelbertus et Otto de Stuzzilingen**, Lödewicus comes de Stofiln, Rödolfus comes de Bregantio, Röpertus de Grùminbach and others (WO:427).

- von Steußlingen In the Codex diplomatic book for the Salem abbey has **Gundelfingen, Wildenstain** and **Steusslingen** all using these siegelstamps (spines or tooth style). "Anno had 5 brothers and 2 sisters. Anno's brother Werner, Archbishop of Magdeburg from 1063-1078 took his mother by that then took her tomb in Magdeburg Cathedral. His brother, Haymo was Probst in Cologne. The 3rd Brother, Walter fell in 1080 in Westphalia Erwitte. Anno's fourth brother Adalbero founded the house Steußlingen-Arnstein in Saxony. His older brother, Otto von Steußlingen is the progenitor of, remaining in the house Steußlingen descendants, as well as the families **Justingen and Gundelfingen**. Otto von Steußlingen Grandnephew of Anno, born around 1070, died between 1140/50. Between the years 1118 and 1128, Otto went to Jerusalem for the second time, he brought the Monastery Zwiefalten with relics. Ernst von Steußlingen Possibly a son of Otto was Ernest von Steußlingen, abbot of the monastery Zwiefalten 1141 - 1146, the high scholarship and extraordinary life of piety is attributed. Seriously on 2 Crusade, was captured and towed to Mecca. Since he could not deny his faith, he was killed horribly. The body was ransomed and buried in the city of Antioch. In the 17th century employed attempts to achieve sainthood Ernst went under in the 30-year war. In Zwiefalten he was still revered as a saint."[489] Ulm (1128) March 19th sancti Georii(St. George)mansum apud(remained in) Suerzebach mentioned with Ernist et frater eius Adelbertus de Stuzelingin (WO:461). Tissen Kellmünz (1128) March 26th Ernst de Stuzelingin (WO:462). Worms (1145) April-May Klosters Allerheiligen, the estate of Heinrici de Evenwilare(Ebenweiler), Herimanni {Mahlpsuren, husband to Burglen-Nellenburg} and the estate of his wife in Sweindorf and Stuzelingen (Steißlingen) and with the others (WO:515). (1138) Otto von Steußlingen Schenk von auf der Rückkehr Seine defendants nach Jerusalem dem Kloster Zwiefalten , His brothers Ernst and Adelbert. Their sister Juta(Touta) is married Gerung von Rietheim , their daughter is Adelheid (WO:13). (~1150) Recording that the **Noble matrona Halicha of Justingen or Steußlingen** has to their salvation sake vergabt to the Monastery Zwiefalten 10 Mark Silver. Speyer (1152) kloster Salem, **Ernst von Altsteußlingen (Stuzelinge)** donated with the consent of his wife and his sons farms Tiefenhülen (Tufenhuluwe) and Bremfeld and the priest and his brother **Herman von Altsteußlingen**, Burchard Hohonbuach the yard (RI:130). Altorf December 25th (1179) Herzon Frederic von Schwaben, **Rödolfo de Phullindorpf,** ducis Welfonis **testes: comes** Rödolfus de Phullindorpf. comes Bertolfus de Berge et frater suus comes Ödalricus, **Albere de Frichingen** et frater suus Burchardus, Chûnradus de Shûzenriet, Dieto de Rauinisburch, Fridericus de Walburch, Eberhardus de Tanne et frater suus Bertolfus, Rödolfus de Bröion, Burcardus de Bodemen et eius

Ôlricus, Harthmannus de Chilhberc comes, Gôtefridus de Roredorf, **Ernest de Stôzeligen**, **Rûdolfus de Gôttigen**, **Heinricus de Marhtorf** and others (WO:641). Ulm (1183) Diethelmus Augensis abbas, **Diemo de Gundilvingen, Burchardus comes de Hohinberc(Hohenburg), Cv̂nradus de Scuzinriet, Ernist de Stuzzelingen** and several others (WO:661). Bergatreute (1185) Herzog Welf exchange called goods between the monastery Adelberg and the Church in Echterdingen and this was done with the consent of and know it to Hermann, bishop of Constance(=Fridingen), and at the request of Berhtoldo(=Stetten), prelate of the church of the same, witnesses: Philip Sindiluingin (Sindelfingen) of the provost, Mangold of Otolfiswank, **Ernist of Stüzelingin**, Dieto of Rauinsburk(Ravensburg) (WO:667) and others Hainr pleb de Schennins, Oulr de Obirndorf clericus, Albert de Bozwilre, Chounr de Sarmannesdorf, Chounr de Willare, Hainr prae bendar de Vilmaringen, Burch miles de Baden, **Walther de Hunoberg**, Hartm de Chienberg (REC 1895:122). Verona March 4th (1185) **Albert & his sons Burchardi de Frikingen**, Herimanni de Marchdorf, Ex traditione **Hermanni de Fridingen Grindilbuch** cum pertinentis suis, Ex largitione Alberti, Burchardi itemque Heinrici, Alberti, Burchardi Frichingen Reintinhasila cum appenditiis, from the generosity of **Ernistonis Stuzelingen** and his sons and others (WO:671). Zisterzienserkloster Herrenalb (1186) November many Speyer nobles, **Otto von (Alt-) Steußlingen (Der unter den Zeugen genannte Otto von (Alt-) Steußlingen** (Kanoniker/Canon von Speyer), Albertus *Caluus* and many others (RI:3028). Bischof Ulrich von Speyer certifies that the exchange-called possessions had been definitely concluded between him and the Count Palatine Rudolf from Tübingen for the purpose of construction of the monastery Bebenhausen, in the presence and with the consent of the Emperor Frederick and his son, as the then protective stewards of his church (1188) testium: **Ottonis de Stuzelingen**, Albertus de Mezzingen, Waltherus de Ûtenbrugge, Albertus de Sackis(Hohensax), Sviggerus de Aichain (WO:683). Ulm (1215) June 20th König Friedrich II and kloster Lorche testes: Anselmus marscalcus de lustingen(Justingen), Bertoldus de Druhcpurc, **Albertus de Stivcelingen** (*Stuzzilingen* = Altsteußlingen), Bertoldus de H[un]delahc, Dieto de Rauensburc, Berengerus de Rauenstein, Euerhardus dapifer de Tanne, Conradus de Tanne, Conradus et Bertoldus de Stovphen et alii quam plures and others (WO:880). Reichssachen (1228) Albert and his sohn sohn Ernst and Egelolf von Steusslingen of them lehnrührige possessions which Henry of Thalhofen sold the monastery Steingaden (RI:11033). Ehingen (1243) April 29th **Albertus de Stuzilingen** gennant **Schädel** leaving his possessions in Andelfingen he wore by Count Hartmann of Dillingen in fief, the sisters in Heiligkreuztal – witnesses H. de Gundoluingen (Gundelfingen), **E. et A. de Stuzilingen** and others (WO:1493). (1247) Anselm of Justingen vergabt its goods once in Wazzescaven (water makers), now called Heiligkreuztal, at the request of the Earl of Wolfrad Veringen and for his salvation's sake the nuns of that monastery – testes: Wol. de Veringen, **Hainrico milite de Stivzelingen**, Wezzelone milite de Brozzekeuen, H. milite dicto Velwen, Wal. plebano in Diengen(Tengen) (WO:1623). (1253) Konvent von Heggbach, Rudolf Maselheim & his heairs sold goods, Grafen Ulrich von Schelklingen testes: Rudigerus de Shalkelingen, Albertus Kimo, H. Mvskunig, H. de Husen, **H. de Stuselingen** milites and others (WO:1872). Gottlieben (1254) March 10th C. de Erlbach, R. de Ephingen, dominus H. de Hvsen, **H. de Stuzzelingen**, C. notarius, H. minister in Ehingen and others (WO:1927). Ehingen (1263) March 8th Egelolf von Stvezelingin Schwestern(sisters) Mechthilde und Willibirg, Swiggerus senior de Gundiluingin, **Wernherus de Stv̂ezelingin, Ulricus de Straze** and others (WO:2429). >Wappensiegel> for Egilof von Steusslingen dated 1263 (Weech 1881:451). Gutenberg (1285) Dezember 10 Edlen Albert Noble Schedel and Eglolf his son Steußlingen. (1292) Albrecht der Schedel von Steußlingen übergibt dem Kloster Salem das Eigentumsrecht von Gütern(goods) to Grötzingen: **Cûnrat Hirisegge ze Westerndorf** (Westendorf NNE of Kempten), **Hainrich and Cûnrat Hirisegge(Hirscheck)** represent the people (WO:5157). (1299)

- von Justingen {*deer on mountain, Hirscheck form*}. Steußlingen & Gundelfingen have the same origin coat of arms as the nearby **Justingen** (Clemmenson 2009:47). Justingen 1st appears in (1090) April 14th with **Eberhardus de Justingin**, Rudolph de Tengin and others signing the Act of **Fridingen**. The Justingen wappen(COA) appears in two forms. Justingen the state (COA) for the district of Shelkingen has a blue background with 4 white barbed teeth on each side very similar to von Wildenstein and the Hirschecker stag form. The Justingen wappen(COA) appears in two forms. Justingen the state (COA) for the district of Shelkingen has a blue background with 4 white barbed teeth on each side very similar to von Wildenstein. Donations of H Rinhart to St. Salvatories in Schafhausen signers 1135: Bilgerin de Jestingin(Justingen), Hermannus de **Aspisingen(Espasingen)**, Eberhard de Nellinburc, Odalricus comes de Ramisberc(Ramsen), Heinricus grandfather to Rudolfus de Tengin, Udalricus of Ramislei(Ramsen) and his brother Ernist and others[490]. Kloster Zwiefalten (~1150) matrona **Halicha von Justingen or Steußlingen** {uxor} wife of N. Margret of Esteten (WO:532). Burg Stauffen (1181) May 25th Billungus de **Justingin** and Rûpertus de Gundelfingin. (1207) Bischof Werner von Konstanz, Let it be known, therefore, as well present as to posterity, that, Some have free man, **Anselm of Ivstingen**(Justingen), Mahthilde with their mother, a kind of Witingen estate in the village, he had owned with the right of patronage of the church that it can freely Stein (WO:825). Ulm (1215) June 20th Vlricus de Helfanstein(Helfenstein), comes Egeno de Vrahc et filius suus, **Anselmus marscalcus de Iustingen(Justingen)**, Bertoldus de Druhcpurc, Albertus de Stivcelingen(Altsteußlingen) and others (WO:880). **Anselm Marschall von Justingen** (1216) June 24th (knight on horse wappenshilde) - the ReichshofMarshal Anselm of Justingen adopt the monastery Salem all prerogatives, which he had to speak at the mill roof stowage under his castle Justingen (WO:904). Nürnberg (1219) Nov 2nd Herzog Friedrich von Rothenburg donates good testes: Eberhardus Salzpurgensis archiepiscopus, Eberhardus et Vlricus comites de Helfinstein, Heinricus de Nifa, **Anshalmus de Iustingin**, imperialis aule marscalcus, **Cunradus de Clinginberc, imperialis aule pincerna** and many others (WO:943). (1247) **Anselm of Justingen** vergabt its goods once in Wazzescaven (water makers), now called Heiligkreuztal, at the request of the Earl of Wolfrad Veringen and for his salvation's sake the nuns of that monastery – testes: Wol. de Veringen, , Wezzelone milite de Brozzekeuen, H. milite dicto Velwen, Wal. plebano in Diengen(Tengen) (WO:1623). Domherren Hermann von Justingen in Pongau (Salzburg, Austria) 1252, Anselm jung (son) & Alt (father) v J 1264, Anselm v J 3/1266, Anselm v. J 1269, Anshlmus de Justingen 1278, Anselm von Justingen 1281/82, Anselm von Wudenstein {Wildenstein} 1283, Anshalmo de Wildinstain..Justingen et de Wildinstain 2/1283. Some Wildenstein nobles: Friderico de Wildenstain 11/1245, Konrad , Heinrich and Friedrich(deer-Hirschsiegelestamp[491] 1262) brothers von Wildenstain 3/1262, Alshelmus de Wildenstain 8/1263 (teeth-sieglestamp[492] 1263) & 1278 & 1296. **Note:** Hermann I von Fridingen provides good and donations to Steißlingen and Schwandorf in 1140 (Dobler:54). Worms (1145) April-May Klosters Allerheiligen, the estate of Heinrici de Evenwilare(Ebenweiler), Herimanni {Mahlpsuren, husband to Burglen-Nellenburg} and the estate of his wife in Sweindorf and Stuzelingen (Steißlingen)and with the others (WO:515). The book Die Kultur der Abtei Reichenau says the Steißlingen (O.-A. Ehingen), a tribe with Justingen and Gundelfingen) had in 1356 with the Wartenberg share[493]. However having a Hirscheck wappen form being used in Friedrich Wildenstein 1262 (Elk/Deer on Mountain) and Hainrichus 1274, Heinrich Gundelfingen 1263 (Deer jumping east) would point toward an earlier Hirscheck origin Herman Hirscheck (~990) or a brother Gero(Gerolt) rather than a Ulrich Bregenz (d. ~ 1045) descendants. Burkhard Ramsberg has also the same Hirscheck form (Ram on Mountain) in 1253.

- **von Brunnenvelt** *(double bend ,lack of lion)* crescent on each tip a tuft of cock feathers von Brunnenfeld, ministeriales, noted 1274-1411, seat in Brunnenfeld (Bz. Bludenz, Vorarlberg). #203 on the Zurich wappenrolle, 2 down from Tengen in list. Liutfridus de Briulingen 1108—1122 procurement of goods in St. Peter, Aasen and Gundelfingen (Krieger 1904: 266) . 1132 the Free noble Heinrich von Staufenburg not bequeathed upon entering the monastery of St. Georgen, among others. In the Incarnation of the Lord 1132, a certain knight named Heinrich von Staufenberg, was born free and noble, the holy day of Pentecost [29 May] monk at the monastery of St. George. He handed but on the altar of orgenannten martyr his goods: in Owingen and Ousingen Mansi, in Bettighofen [Betechoven] and Mimmenhausen [Mimminhusen], Steingart et/and **Bräunlingen (Pruwelingen)**, in Klengen and over Achen [Ouberach], what makes the sum total of 41 Mansi. These are the witnesses: Arnold of Wolfach Bruno and Konrad von Hornberg [Hornberch] and many others. To Bräunlingen Briulingen Brülingen Pruwelingen Bringilingen acquired early on the Abbey of Reichenau property you owned there was a Kelnhof of it the foundation of the parish of one of the oldest parishes were founded all over the neighborhood a Reichenau curtis has belonged to the Church of St George in the upper cell Abbot Diethelm (=Krenkingen) sold 1181. Even before 1150 was also the monastery of All Saints in Schaffhausen to **Bräunlingen** posession. Of their patronage went to the diocese of Constance bez the Archdiocese of Freiburg in 1181, the prince mentioned plebanus Cunradus de **Brulingin** (Lintz 1897:148). December (1181) Bertoldus Constantiensis, monasterii St. Blasii et **Heinricum plebanum de Frichingin**, Hugoni de Bollingin, Odarlico sic canonico, Wernero de Singin et Cunrado de **Brulingin** presentibus in Radolfzell, Testes (=signers) nostro **Hermannus (Fridingen?)**, Ortolfus de v canus Albero magister scholarum Odalricus praepositus St. Stephani also of Salem Marcwardus s Odalrici Gebehardus of the parish priests of the House of **Cunradus Brulingin,** Cunradus Leffingin of Henry of Stamiheim, **Hiltibolt de Stulengin, Burcardus of Ramisberc**, Werner of Arbun, Diethalm Snegginburc of the acts of 1181, however, are presiding in the Roman See, the most holy Pope Alexander the third of this name most of the reign of Emperor Frederick and his 28 year of the reign of his son Frederick and a noble leader Swabians[494]. In the 12th century gives his own property there Liutfridus de **Briulingen** Totam. The ministeriales Duke Conrad of Zähringen 1152 included **Reginhardus de Briulingen 1239**, the ministeriales **Rodulfus de Brulingen** and **Henricus de Notingesten** called. Feldkirch (1312) May 22 Herr **Rudolf von Ramsperch, Gerunk von Brunnenvelt, Gerunk von Notgenstain**, Nuwenburk familie and others[495].

- **von Hohenfels (***lat* **HOHENVELS)** {like heidegg but Horizontal, Per fess vert and argent, lack of lion}. Located NW of Überlingen. #189 on the Zurich wappenrolle. Established via an Undocumented Charter for Burkhard von Hohenfels (~1104) after ~1135-1150 from the son of Hermann Hirscheck der Jung (~1085). **Walter v Hohenfels** 1148 Domherren in Konstanz. Speyer (1152) King Frederic I of Tubingen in Kloster Salem gave **Hermannus (=Stetten?)** presbyter(priest) de Stuzelinge (Altsteußlingen) et frater(brother) **Burchardus(=Hohenvels?)** similiter dicitur cum omnibus pertinentiis suis Hohonbuch (gave them the same with all its appurtenances) witnesses Vlrico comite de Lenzburch(Lenzburg) and a few others (WO:544). (1191) Bischof Diethelm von Konstanz notarized accomplishment between Kloster Salem und Ulrich von Bodman Klosterhofes Madach, presentibus: Gothefrido et filio eius Manegoldo comitibus de Rordorph, **De Craien Henrico et fratre eius Hermanno, Burchardo de Hohenvelsi/Honuelfi(Hohenfel), Chönone de Huneberc(Hunoberg)** and many others (SA 1881:69). Regensburg (1205) Aug 30th Alb grf v Dillingen, Tiedo v Ravensburg, **Conr v. Hohenfels** and many others (RI:35). Regensberg (1211) Imma wife of ritter **Rihperus von Hohenfels** (MO:9999). Constanz (1212) ritter **Walther von Hohenvels, Hermann prepos de Burron** and many others (RE:142). Nürnberg (1215) December 10 **Chvͦnradus de Hôhenvels** , Arnoldus de Schoenvelt, Hermannus marchio de Baden, Heinricus de Giselingen, Albertus de Stovfe(Staufen) and others (WO:887). Uberlingen (1226) October 28th Burckhardo milite de Ramsperg, Pfullendorf mentioned with **Burchardus et Waltherus de Hohenvelse**, H. de Malspuren(=Hermann IV Mahlspüren), H. comes de Wartstain, **C. de Marchdorff senior** and others (WO:1082). **Burchardus et Waltherus de Hohenvelse** in Weingarten (1226) November 6 for King Heinrich for the *Klosters Weißenau* with some common familiars **Hartmannus comes de Dilingen**, Werinherus comes de **Chiburch(Kyburg),** Manegoldus comes de Nellenburch, Ludewicus comes de Castello, Hainricus de Nifen, Fridericus de Truheldingen, Bilgerinus de Hvrewen, Heberhardus dapifer de Walpurc, Cvͦnradus et Heberhardus pincerne de Wintirstetin, **Burchardus de Hohenburch, Rodolfus et Burchardus de Ramesberc** and others (WO:1083). Winterstetten in Burgkapelle (1241) **Gozwinus de Hohenvelse**. Militibus(=ritter/knights) Walter v. Hohenfels (nw. Überlingen BW) 1248-1282; Göswin Hohenfels 1241-1278 (MO:1570). Constanz (1241) June 11th H. de Raprehtiswilere, et **H. de Höhinvels**, Constantiensibus canonicis, Vͦl. de Haidilberch, **Ber. de Annewilere** and others (WO:1451). Constanz (1242) Jan 21st Hil de Shinon, Rud de Hasinwilare, AI de Bolle, Walth Thihtelario, Walth de Ramstain, et **Hainr de Hohinvels** Const canonici priori de Cappella (RE:178). Constanz (1242) July 11th *Ritter Albero von Spielberg samt seinen Kindern,* presentibus viris in Cristo. **B. de Hohinuels**, **Ber. de Annewile**, Vl. de Bertisshuss, C. de Hugultischouen et R. de Staze(Strass) militibus and others (WO:1475). Constanz (1245) Feb 2nd Alb de Bolli, Ottino Rüd W Dihtelarius, **H fil Liutfridi et Hainr de Hohenvels**, Lutold de Schilberch canonici & otherss (RE:185). Winterthur (1249) Mar 8th graf Ulrich von Berg Berga, Heinrich von Burgau, presentibus Ruperto dco de Tannenvels, Waltero Thithelario, **Bur de Hohinvels** and others. Konstanz (1250) Feb 16th *Hermann von Raderach genannt Gnifting* ego Hermannus de Raderay, Rodolfo de Hewin et fratribus suis, Conrado de Valchenstein, **Petro de Hohenburc**, Henrico de Sconneche, Bertoldo de Rordorf, **Waltero de Hohenuels**, Vlrico de Clinginberch, **Hainrico camerario de Marhdorf** and others (WO:1746). Gottlieben (1255) Nov 16th **Bertoldus de Hohinvels**, Baldepertus de Annewiler, Hainr de Straze, Cînr pleb de Diengen, C nob de Louffen, Frid Hoenburc, Cvnr de Schônowe, Alb de Castello milites and others. Merspurc (1256) Berthol do decano de Sevelt, **Hilteboldo et Eberhardo filio suo de Stekborun, Walthero et Goezwino fratribus de Hohenvels**, Hainrico et Burkardo filio suo de Ramsberg, Friderico fil ei Burkardo de Oberridern,Ulírico de Oberriedern ,Vírico Burkardo et Hainrico de Urendorf and others (RE:219). Constanz (1257) June 9th Cùnrado de Tierberg, viris nobilibus **Cunrado de Wartenberg et Hainrico fratre suo dco Struz**, Hainrico de Valkenstain, Hainrico de Gnezeuberg, Amoldo de Biurgelun, Bertholdo de Hohenegge, Bertholdo de Rordorf dapiferis, Hainrico de Ravenspurg, **H et Eber de Stekborun**, **Wal et Goezwino de Hohenvels** militibus de fratribus de Salem (RE:223). Kloster Klingenthal in Basel (1261) Ita des Vogts Konrad von Fridingen Witwe, Bertholdus de Hohenvels, Testes: B dominus de Annuwiler, dominus de Heidelberch, dominus Hilteboldus miles de Stegboren, C de Tetinchon ille de Raeitershoven and others (URK V1:293). Constanz (1261) **B de Hohenvels ecclesie**, Ita nobilis de Clingen notice of event died **C(onrad) aduocati de fridingen** testes: Dominus de Valchenstein, **B Dominus de Annuwiler**, Dominus de Heidelberch, Dominus **Hilteboldus miles de Stegboren**, Dominus Volricus, C de Tetinchon, siegel *Sororis ite de vridingen* (Hirzel 1873:358)[496]. Uberlingen (1262) Wolfraduf ivnior de Veringen, Maedelingi de Marhdorf, nobili viro Oswaldo de Marhdorf , **Walthero et Goezwino fratribus de Hohenvels**, Jacobo de Hunberg and many others. Salem or Bebenhausen (1269) Ritter Wolfelin von Bonlanden (Wol. miles dictus, Wolf. miles de Bônlanden) Schwester(sister), der Gemahlin(wife of) des **Walther von Hohenfels (Hohinvelse)** Testes: Diepoldus nobilis de Bernhusen, **Waltherus de Hohinvelse**, Wer[nherus] dictus Tuzzer de Niuwinhusen, C. plebanus et Wer. Albus ibidem, G. dictus de Rote, item **Eberhardus monachus in Salem dictus de Stechkeboren**, and others (WO:2817). Konstanz (1271) December 22, **Bertoldus** keeper and his brother said the scholar **Burcardus Hohenvels**. Konstanz (1276) May 19 **Bertoldo de Hohenvelse** preposito. Basel (1276) June 20th **Goiswin von Hohinfelse**. Heinrich v H was brother to Konrad von Hohenfels Herr zu Reipoldskirchen (d.1369). Kastell in Thurgau (1340) Feb 4th Bischof Nikolaus von Konstanz, Eberhard von Sulzberg, pfaf **V°lr. von Fridingen**, herr **Walther von Hohenuels** ritter, and others (MO:3736).

- **von Clingen (AltenKlingen)** {Sable billety or, a lion rampant argent crowned or} #51 on the Zurich wappenrolle. The Kallenburg wappen #115 is a Green Linden tree upright with white background while Clingen(Hohenklingen) wappen #52 is a Green Oak tree up right with yellow background found on the Zurich wappenrole. Kallenburg #115 is directly next to Clingenberg(Klingenberg) #116 {per pale Black/White} on the Zurich role. **Hugo v Klingen** 1110 Domherr von Konstanz. Kloster Salem Constanz (1169) Mar 10th Otto & interfuerunt **advocatus eiusdem ecclesiae Fridericus de Wildinstein**, Rôdolf de Sevelt, **Waltherus de Clingin**, Burkhard jun de Frichingen, **Bruno de Marhdorf**, Heinr dec Heinr prepos ceci, Conradus et Marcholfus sacerdotes, ministeriales **Hesso de Annewilar, Rodolfus de Wilar** and many others (RE 1895:113). Constanz (1175) Rud com de Phullindorf, **Walth et Olr de Chlinga** and many others (RE:116). Bergartirutin (1185) **Oulr de Cilicgou**, Chounr de Willare, Walther de Hunoberg, and many others. Constantie (1194) Ödalr comes de Bergin, **Ödalr de Klingin**, Ebirh de Burgilun, **Tiethelmus de Creie(Krahen)**, Berhtold de Kalpfo and others (Wagner1895:128). Wildenvels

137

name may originate from **Waltherus de Hohenvels** (~1206) with a **Ulrich v Clingenberg** & Heinrich v Markdorf connection in 1226. Mülibach (1209) Albertus pleb de Wila, **Wernherus pleb de Stekkenboren**, Egilolfus pleb de Waldkilche, comes Diethelmus iun de Togginburch ,**Waltherus advoc de Klingin, Eberhardus de Burgilon cum filio s Berchtoldo**, Albertus de Bussenanch cum filio s Alberto Eudolfus Ulricus, Heinricus carnales fratr de Gütingen, Rudolfus et Heinricus carnal fratr de Wunninberch, Ebirhardus de Spiegilberch, Rudolphus de Steinache, Berchtoldus de Anniwilare, Fridericus et Wernherus de Schoninberch, Albertus de Heidoltiswilare cum filio s Wezilone Wezilo dapifer de Hugol tishoven Rudolfus de Winterthure, Chunradus Giel, Waltherus de Eilgau, Ebirhardus et Waltherus carnales fratres de Bichilnsee, Beringerus de Lamminberg, Egilolfus et Heinricus cam fratr de Valchknistein, Rudolphus de Bochislo, Arnoldus de Heitinowe, Berchtoldus Fantilie and others (RE:139). Mersburch (1219) May 8th Eberhards von Salzburg und Lütolds seines bruders von Regensberg, Rudegero Chimensi epo, **Eberharde Salensi** abb, Walthero et fratre s de Rotenlaim, et **Hainrico de Clingen** advoc Walthero de Tegervelt, and **Diethelmo de Crenchingen** (RE:150). Nürnberg (1219) Nov 2nd Herzog Friedrich von Rothenburg **donates good testes:** Eberhardus Salzpurgensis archiepiscopus, Eberhardus et Vlricus comites de Helfinstein, Heinricus de Nifa, Anshalmus de Iustingin, imperialis aule marscalcus, **Cunradus de Clinginberc, imperialis aule pincerna** and many others (WO:943). Constanz (1220) Rüdiger von Raetterschen (Rátirshovin),Vlrich Episcopaliscelle prepos, Heinr de Raprehtiswilere, Heinr de Domo,Heinr fll Liutfridi, Hiltibold de Shinun, **Ulr advoc de Clingin, Dieth de Creigin**, Wezilo dapifer Cunr marscalcus Cunr pincerna, **Heinric de Clingenberch** Marq scultetus Constant (RE:151). Constanz (1220) July 29th Waltherus de Botenleim et Lùtoldus frater s Hainricus camerar, Heinricus de Baperhswiller, Hilteboldus de Shina, Heinricus fil Lùtfridi, Burchardus de Castello, Heinricus Figulus, Otteno, **Heinricus de Clingen** and others (RE:152). Speyer (1233) Konrad von Nordenberg, das Drittteil der Vogtei zu Gebsattel testes: Hermannus marchio de Baden, Conradus pincerna de Lympurg, **Waltherus pincerna de Klingenberg**, Conradus de Weinsperg and others (WO:1245). Constanz (1248) Dec 16th **Walther v Clingen vogt der kirche Bischofzeil, Ulrich von Klingen bruder Walthers**, Peregrinus et Cunradus Ymbria, prepositi dns **Hugo de Clingen**, Waltherus Dihtelarius, Heinricus de Straze, Waltherus de Rammstein canonici Constant, nobil vir Hein de Rosenegge, C de Steine, Bertoldus et Bertoldus de Annewiler and others (RE:198). Konstanz (1250) Feb 16th Hermann von Raderach genannt Gnifting ego Hermannus de Raderay, Rodolfo de Hewin et fratribus suis, Conrado de Valchenstein, **Petro de Hohenburc**, Henrico de Sconneche, Bertoldo de Rordorf, **Waltero de Hohenuels, Vlrico de Clinginberch, Hainrico camerario de Marhdorf** and others (WO:1746). Bregenz to Constanz (1251) Jan Egilolfo de Valckenstein, Ruodolpho de Hasinweiler, Walthero de Ramestein, Heinrico de Straze, **Heinrico de Clingenberg**, Baldeberthus de Aneweiler, magistro Walcone, Ruperto de Tannenvelse and others (RE:203). Constanz (1261) B de Hohenvels ecclesie, **Ita nobilis de Clingen** notice of event died **C(onrad) aduocati de fridingen** testes: Dominus de Valchenstein, B Dominus de Annuwiler, Dominus de Heidelberch, Dominus **Hilteboldus miles de Stegboren**, Dominus Volricus, C de Tetinchon, siegel *Sororis ite de vridingen* (Hirzel 1873:358)[497]. Conrad I v Fridingen's nephew **Rudolph III v F** appears in the 1267 document with **Arnold von Wildenfels**. Pfäffikon (1328) Jan 6th **Ulrich der ältere von Hohenklingen** & his Bruder Ulrich, Abt Johannes II. von Hasenburg von Einsiedeln, der **Heinrich Ammann von Diessenhofen** & Heinrich Wäleschinger von Steisslingen & sons (KAE:N67). Kloster Klingental (1337) Hedwig witwe(wife) of **Johann Sigriste** von Egringen (BS: 841084). Mulhouse (BA Engen) passed 1338 the brothers **Walter and Ulrich Baron of Hohenklingen** the church to Mulhouse among Krähen serfs[498].

- von Markdorf (MARTDORF) {like Kyburg/Stoffeln,Frickingen & Fridingen, Lowe/Lion alone, Argent, a lion statant gardant gules, virgins head.}. #151 on the Zurich wappenrolle. "Fhr. von Markdorf al. Marktdorf al. Martdorf, noted 1134, seat in Markdorf (Kr. Überlingen, B-W). "The arms, a leopard statant, derived from von Ravensburg, were changed to the present from spikes of a wheel, and noted into the 16th century" (Clemmensen:2009). Maracdorf established 817. Bamberg(?) 1111-25 Abt Wolfram des St. Michaelsklosters testes: Fridericus gener Ebonis de Sgegeuelt, Walchun de Chircheim,

Arnolt de Wulsinheim, **Heinrich filius Marcholfi** and Luitolfus de Wisindorf (WO:423). (1129) Konrad von Zwiefalten and his wife Matilda(=Markdorf?) donate goods to an estate near the village of Marchtorf(Markdorf) Kloster Ochsenhausen for their annual Memorial (WO:466). **Hermann v Markdorf** (~1083) Free Lords (FreiHerren) to Markdorf and co-member to Kloster Salem 1134/1137 and son(?) of Heinrich d.j Hirscheck (~1063). "In the year 1141 a Knight is called **Heinrich von Eichstegen**. Uberlingen (1153) September 23rd Stabilimus insuper ei ut. Her(mannus)(=Fridingen? Domher), **Heinricus de Marchdorph, Cunradus de Schussenriet** and many others (WO:559). Konstanz (1155) **Hermanni de Marcdorf** beside Adelberti & Burchardi de Fricchingen, comes Rûdolfus de Phullendorf, Ŏdalricus de Lenzeburc in Kloster Salem and others (WO:558). Königstuhl (~1160) **Herimanno de Marcdorf** with Duke Welf VI passing the Kloster St. Blasien to Nendingen, **Nahthilt, filias Operti de Wilare apud Ravinspurch** with others (WO:582). Weildorf (1163) Swiggero de Gundeluingen in villa Wildorf, Rudolphus de Rammesperc, Adelbertum de Dilignen, Heinricus de Gundeluinge, **Brononis de Marchdorf** et Adelberti, fillii Burchardi de Frichingen and others (WO:595). Cruceline (1166) Apr 8th Laici seculares: **Bruno de Marhdorf**, Eberhardus mariscalcus, **Berhtoldus de Wilare**, Ortwinus, Hesso Marquart and others (RE 1895:112). Kloster Salem Constanz (1169) Mar 10th **Waltherus de Clingin**, Burkardus de Obiriedin, Burkhard jun de Frichingen, **Bruno de Marhdorf**, Heinr dec Heinr prepos ceci and many others (RE 1895:113). Teuringen (1171) March 31st Manegoldus comes Veringen(Bieringen), with his children Wolfrado and Eberhard, Count Berthold of Zolre, Count Frederick of Zolre, Hainricus of Stŏphe, **Bruno & Hainricus frater de Marhtdorf** with Albertus & Burchardis de Frichingen (Frickingen), with others as Heinrich von Bayern & Otto von Hasenwiler donate estate to Schwandorf and Rickenbach monasteries (WO:612). Altdorf (1179) December 25th Duke of Swabia V. Friederich confest that and the conditions under which the advocacy of said possessions of the monastery Kreuzlingen with Duke of Welfonis - Testes: Hainricus de Rûmesberch, comes **Rŏdolfus de Phullindorpf(Pfullendorf)**, comes Bertolfus de Berge et frater suus comes Ŏdalricus, **Albere de Frichingen(Frickingen) et frater suus Burchardus**, Chûnradus de Shûzenriet, Dieto de Rauinisburch, Fridericus de Walburch, Eberhardus de Walhse, **Eberhardus de Tanne**(Tennecho?) et frater us Bertolfus, Rŏdolfus de Brŏion, Burcardus de Bodemen et eius Ŏlricus, Bertolfus de Rithusen, Lanfridus abbas Campidonensis, Harthmannus de Chilhberc comes, Gŏtefridus de Roredorf, **Ernest de Stŏzeligen**(Altsteußlingen), Rûdolfus de Gŏttigen, **Heinricus de Marhtorf** (WO:641). **Bruno de Mahrtof**, Albertus & Wezilo de Eigistegin (Eichstegen) "relatives or descendants of Konrad/Luitold v E?", Dieto de Rauinsburch (Ravensburg) for Altinbrugg (1162-1182) in the Kloster Kreuzlingen (WO:589). Konstanz June 20th (1183) Kloster Salem, **Hermanni de Marcdorf**, from the generosity of Ernistonis Stuzelingen and his sons, Ex traditione **Hermanni de Fridingen Grindilbuch** cum pertinentis, Heinrici, Alberti, Burchardi Frikingen Reintinhasila, Uldraicus comes de Chiburc(Kyburg), Hartmannus come de Chilperc(Kyburg), scilicet **Wartinberc** and others (WO:663). Verona March 4th (1185) Albert & his sons Burchardi de Frikingen, **Herimanni de Marchdorf**, Ex traditione **Hermanni de Fridingen Grindilbuch** cum pertinentis suis, Ex largitione Alberti, Burchardi itemque Heinrici, Alberti, Burchardi Frichingen Reintinhasila cum appenditiis, from the generosity of Ernistonis Stuzelingen and his sons and others (WO:671). Überlingen Kloster Weingarten (1187) September 23rd Erzbishop Konrad von Mainz, Bishop Otto von Bamberg, Abt **Diethelm von Konstanz (=Krenkingen), Heinrich von Markdorf** and many others (RI:3103). St. Blasien (1189) June 29th *Bischof Hermann (II.) von Konstanz* (=Fridingen) and the abbott Manegold confirmed predcessor Ottonis(Otto) describing possessions in Burgilun and other locations, tithes to Imindingin, & **Frikkingin(Frickingen)** and other churches Stein, Buron, **Brunnon** etc (WO:696). Würzburg (1192) June 7th **Hermanni de Fridingen Grindelbûch, Adelberti et filii eius Burchardi de Frikingen, Hermanni de Marcdorf** et aliorum plurium, comes **Burchardus de Hohenberc, Rˇoberti et Bertholdi de Aha Dorfisberc, Marquardus dapifer de Anewilære** and many others (WO:726). (1200) Rudolphus plebanus de Marcdorf. Tobel, Thurgau (1207) May 28th Conrad Spirensis, Rudolph Haspburg, Frideriuc Zolre, **Herm de Marchdorf** and others. Dieto de Eihstegen kloster in Weissenau in Ravensburg/Weingarten

(1220) with Anshelmus de Iustingen(Justingen), Bernhardus minster de Rauenspurc (WO:962). Uberlingen (1226) October 28th Burckhardo milite de Ramsperg, Pfullendorf mentioned with **Burchardus et Waltherus de Hohenvelse, H. de Malspuren(=Hermann IV/HeinrichIII Mahlspüren), H. comes de Wartstain**, C. de Marchdorff, senior **H. comes de Wartstain** and others (WO:1082). The Eichstegen wappen(COA) for Ravensburg landkreis is the identical Hirschecker wappen (Elk/Deer climbing mountain facing West) as it probably should be as the Burg(Castle) Hirschegg was there. In (1236) **Konrad v Markdorf** uses a wappensiegel with the bladed wheel >right> (Weech 1881:255). Konstanz (1250) Feb 16th Walthero de Hohinvels, **Hainrico camerario de Marhdorf**, Walthero de Hohinvels, Vlrico de Clinginberch and others (WO:1747). By 1250 Markdorf receives city rights[499] from the Lords of Markdorf. Nagold (1251) Graf Burkhard von Hohenberg gives him the hereditary entitled advocacy of a farm in the village astray by his parents and his salvation's sake the Beuron, **H. de Machtorf** (WO:1793). 1255 0 de Marthorf . Markdorf (1266) Cv̂hradus nobilis de Marchdorf (WO:2617). Meersburg (1284) Hevenkoven(Hefigkofen) family in Kloster Salem testibus: Rv̂dolfo de Oberriedern, Cunrado de Maenlinshoven, dicto **Ekol de Marchdorf**, domino Ůlrico abbate, fratre Hainrico cellerario de Isenina, fratre **Eberhardo de Stekeboron** and a few others (MO:4275). Salem (1287) Ritter Wernher genannt von Riedhausen (Riethusen) testibus: **Burchardo ministro de Marchdorf,** Friderico ministro de Kunigesegge, Bertoldo de Adanshoven, Hainrico de Meniwanch, Hermanno dicto Wizzige, Burchardo fratre eiusdem, magistro **Hainrico carpentario de Gugenhusen** and others (WO:4514). Tuttlingen (1290) Janaury 29th **Konrad von Wartenberg** nobilis et miles transmits the monastery Feldbach a tithe to Hemmenhofen fief from the monastery of St. Gall, testes: Eberhardus de Stekboran monachus in Salem, Ber. de Hemenhofen, H. dictus Gaisler(Gessler?), Walth dictus Karrer de Martorf (Markdorf) and others (MO:2228). Heiligenberg May 5th (1295) Graf Hugo von Werdenberg sold to its debt sake the monastery Weißenau goods in Schwarzenbach item bona dicta bar man quoque bona dicta Zimbermann: presentibus Cv̂nrado incurato sancte Christine, **Cv̂nrado nobili viro de Marthorf(Markdorf)**, Cv̂nrado notario nostro, Rv̂dolfo de Ramesperc, Cv̂nrado dicto Bumeler and a few others (MO:5660). (1328) VLRICI. OSWALDI. DE. MARCTORF leapord shield (Knobloch 1919:28).

- **von Frickingen (FRIKINGEN)** {like Kyburg, Stoffeln, & Bürglen, Lowe/Lion alone, Argent, a lion statant}. Wappensiegel found for Albrecht der Frickinger zu Frickingen in the Furstenberg archives Feb 1357 #547. (1157) Weildorf . Sevelt(Selfeld/Sevelth) (1158/1165) April 17th Waltherus de Sevelt, **Herm, Arnold, Arnold, Eberh, Berctold, Heinr, Gerold, Alb, hii omnes de Steten**, Eberh de Mulnhoven, **de Friggingen Burchard, Albert** and others (RE 1895:107) (WO:601). (1163) Swiggero de Gundeluingen in villa Wildorf, Rudolphus de Rammesperc, Adelbertum de Dilignen, Heinricus de Gundeluinge, Brononis de Marchdorf et **Adelberti,** fillii **Burchardi de Frichingen** and others (WO:595). Konstanz @ Salem (1165) Waltherus de Seuelt(Seefelden), Albertus. hii omnes de Stetin, **De Frikingen Burcardus. Albertus** and many others first named (WO:601). Kloster Salem Constanz (1169) Mar 10th Walt Clingin, **Burkhard jun de Frichingen**, Bruno de Marhdorf, and many others (RE 1895:113). Teuringen (1171) March 31st Manegoldus comes Veringen(Bieringen), with his children **Wolfrado** and Eberhard, Count Berthold of Zolre, Count Frederick of Zolre, Hainricus of Stöphe, Bruno & Hainricus frater de Marhtdorf with **Albertus & Burchardis de Frichingen (Frickingen)** with others as Heinrich von Bayern & Otto von Hasenwiler donate estate to Schwandorf and Rickenbach monasteries (WO:612). Constanz (1176) **Heinr de Fridingen**, Conr de Tegervelt, Gotefr de Rordorft, **Bruno et Hainr de Marchtorff**, Ölr de Willare, **Hainr de Vrichingen, Burch et Hainr et Bertold Stateli**, Burch de Hohenburg, Chônr de Willare, Dieterici cum filiis Ebernandi, Thiethelm de Tochemburg, **Eberhardus de Burgelun** and many others (RE:16). Altorf December 25th (1179) Herzon Frederic von Schwaben, Rŏdolfo de Phullindorpf, ducis Welfonis testes: comes Rŏdolfus de Phullindorpf. comes Bertolfus de Berge et frater suus comes Ŏdalricus, **Albere de Frichingen et frater suus Burchardus,** Chûnradus de Shûzenriet, Dieto de Rauinisburch, Fridericus de Walburch, Eberhardus de Tanne et frater suus Bertolfus, Rŏdolfus de Brŏion, Burcardus de Bodemen et eius Ŏlricus, Harthmannus de Chilhberc comes, Gŏtefridus de Roredorf, Ernest de Stŏzeligen, Růdolfus de Gŏttigen, Heinricus de Marhtorf and others (WO:641). Constanz (1181) April 2nd Zehten zu Schlatt , **Hermanno de Vridingen**, Ŏlr de Hugone, **Hainr de Vrichingen**, Hessone, Bert et Chônr de Willare, **Hainr Staetilin** and a few others. Constanz (1181) April 17th **Heinrich von Frickingen**, Hiltibolt Stulingen, Burcard de Ramisberc and many others (REC 1895:119). Konstanz June 20th (1183) Kloster Salem, Hermanni de Marcdorf, from the generosity of Ernistonis Stuzelingen and his sons, Ex traditione **Hermanni de Fridingen** *Grindilbuch* cum pertinentis, **Heinrici, Alberti, Burchardi Frikingen** *Reintinhasila*, Uldraicus comes de Chiburc(Kyburg), Hartmannus come de Chilperc(Kyburg) and others (WO:663). Verona March 4th (1185) **Albert & his sons Burchardi de Frikingen, Herimanni de Marchdorf**, Ex traditione **Hermanni de Fridingen Grindilbuch** cum pertinentis suis, Ex largitione Alberti, Burchardi itemque Heinrici, Alberti, **Burchardi Frichingen** *Reintinhasila* cum appendicitis, from the generosity of Ernistonis Stuzelingen and his sons and others (WO:671). Konigsstuhl (1185) Lvdewicus comes de Sigemeringen, Henricus marchio de Rvmesperc, **Henricus comes de Wartstein, Burchardus comes de Hohenberc** et frater eius comes Fridericus, **Ernest de Stuzelingen, Burchardus et Albertus frater eius de Frichingen**, Hartmannus et Conradus de Mimenhusen and others (FU 1885:71). St. Blasien (1189) June 29th *Bischof Hermann (II.) von Konstanz* (=Fridingen) and the abbott Manegold confirmed predcessor Ottonis(Otto) describing possessions in Burgilun and other locations, tithes to Imindingin, & **Frikkingin(Frickingen)** and other churches Stein, Buron, **Brunnon** etc (WO:696). Albrecht der Frickinger zu Frickingen >wappensiegel> dated Feb 1357. (1227) pleban Rudolph von Frickingen to kloster Salem.

- **von Wartenburg (WARTENBERG)** genant **Straus/Struz** {like Kyburg/ Stoffeln/ Rameschwag/ Frickingen/ Wildenfels/ Fridingen & Markdorf Lowe/Lion alone, Argent, a lion statant gardant gules}. #156 on the Zurich wappenrolle. Five down from Markdorf and Thirteen from Stoffeln. Strazz located in 3 possible places: Straß, Argenbühl, RV, or Straß, Kißlegg, RV, or Straß, Wangen im Allgäu by 1050,1092,1242 Strass, Gachnang, Kt. Thurgau, Schweiz. Austria (1004) All Christians know that the two brothers Gotescalehus and Engilscalchus with his wife Richkarda handed her estates to strazza on the altar of St. Peter, witnesses are delivered to the altar. Megingoz de sure, Piligrimus and his cousin Chinradus and Henry of Schalheimin, Liutwinus provost, Wolfram of offinwanch, Witigo de suriheimin, **Heinrich of strazza**. Salsburg, Austria (1004) **Engilscalchus de Strazza** testes: Pabo de Albin, Engilpreht et liuttold et Heinricus de Albin, **Dietmar de strazze**. Austria (1004) **Engilscalchus de Strazza** in Salzburg uxor wife Ekkarde had proprety @ Scugine.. Hilzingen (1050) Adalbero de Engin, Liutoldus et Ropertus de Fusibach, Hoch de Miringen, Landoldus de Winzelun, Adelbertus de Suercin, Richolfus de Banchelshoven, Egilwarth de Calpfen, Chöno de Seolvingen, **Adelbertus de Strazza**(Strass bei Gachnang,Thurgau), **Tuto de Honstetin,** Wipertus de Hönerhusin, Gozpertus de Liutcgcringen, Alberich de Biberaha[500]. Klosters Allerheiligen (1080) March 1st Graf Burkhard von Nellenburg, Abbot Wilhelm von Hirsau, Gerolt de Tengin, Gerolt de Buch, **Adelbreht de Strazza, Pico de Stetin** and others (SH:576). Kloster Weingarten (1090) comite Marquardo de Schwarzache, comite **Berchtoldo de Wartenberc**, comite Hartmanno de Veringen and others (WO:367). Stein Klosters Allerheiligen (1092) February 26th Graf Burkhard von Nellenburg, **Hartwic de Strazza**, Benno de Speicchinga, Diethalm de Tochimburc, Dieterich comes de Biurgeliun(Nellenburg), Herimann de Egga, **Toto de Wilare**(Radolfzel or Ramsen) and others (SH:576). Schauffhausen (1150) Adelberto comite de Heigirloch, Reginboto de Utinwilari, **Adelbertus de Strazza** and others[501]. Uberlingen (1153) September 23rd Otto, Babenbergensis episcopus, **Heinricus de Marchdorph, Cunradus de Schussenriet** and many others (WO:559). Worms (1179) Cvhradus pincerna, Arnoldus dapifer de Rŏtenburc, Hartmannus comes de Kircperc et eius frater Otto comes, comes Bertoldus de Berga et eius frater comes Vĥricus, **Volcmarus Struzo**

advocatus Goslariensis and many others (WO:635). Altdorf (1179) December 25th Duke of Swabia V. Friederich confest that and the conditions under which the advocacy of said possessions of the monastery Kreuzlingen with Duke of Welfonis - Testes: Hainricus de Rûmesberch, comes **Rŏdolfus de Phullindorpf (Pfullendorf)**, comes Bertolfus de Berge et frater suus comes Ŏdalricus, **Albere de Frichingen(Frickingen) et frater suus Burchardus**, **Chûnradus de Shûzenriet**, **Dieto de Rauinisburch**, Fridericus de Walburch, Eberhardus de Walhse, **Eberhardus de Tanne**(Tennecho?) et frater us Bertolfus, Rŏdolfus de Brŏion, Burcardus de Bodemen et eius Ŏlricus, Bertolfus de Rithusen, Lanfridus abbas Campidonensis, Harthmannus de Chilhberc comes, Gŏtefridus de Roredorf, **Ernest de Stŏzeligen**(Altsteußlingen), Rûdolfus de Gŏttigen, **Heinricus de Marhtorf** (WO:641). Ulm (1183) **Diethelmus Augensis abbas,** Diemo de Gundilvingen, Burchardus comes de Hohinberc, **Cv̂nradus de Scuzinriet**, Ernist de Stuzzelingen and several others (WO:661). Bockenheim (1196) **Wernerus de wartenberc** and others (MO:435). (1200) Decanus de Ebingen in partibus domini de **Lupfen et de Wartenberg** (WO:776). Konstanz (1205) Apr 6th Diethelm(=Krenkingen) bishop of Constance gets the happened one of the brothers Konrad and Beringer foundation of the monastery Schussenried through the mediation of a settlement with the heirs of the same **Konrad von Wartenberg**, **milites Chŏnradus et Beringerus**, Albertus prepositus de Sindiluingin, Wernherus de Stŏifin; ministeriales accepti domini regis Philippi: Fridericus dapifer de Walpurch and Heinricus de Smalineæge (WO:811). (1215) Bischop Otto Freising bought a castle in Wartenberg MO:126). (1220) The during her life happened one of the noble brothers Konrad and Bernger von Schussenried, by their heirs, the **brothers Konrad and Heinrich von Wartenberg** but contested foundation of the monastery Schussenried is maintained by a comparison between the said heirs and the monastery (WO:954). Geisingen (1228) August 28th presentibus: Burchardo de Kilrchdorf preposito concerning the tithes that from his own hand from the advocate of the Suarzenberc to the same monks in the praesidium of Salem, **Hanrico de Lupfon, Hanrico de Wartenberc**, Rudolfo de Ailekov, Walthero de Alstetten, Walthero de Wiltperc, and Rudolfo de Hagenwilare MO:1155). St. Gallen (~1230) July 13th Kloster Weisenau brother Konrad and Heinrich Wartenburg transfer goods to "Tieringeshart" to Ritter Ulrich von Schwarzenbach in presense of Berthold monk nephew of our Salem and his brothers, Albert & Henry Bussenanc soldiers, **Bertoldo de Burgelon** and Henry de Guttingen soldiers (WO:1171). Constanz (1242) July 11th *Ritter Albero von Spielberg samt seinen Kindern*, presentibus viris in Cristo B. de Hohinuels, Ber. de Annewile, Vl. de Bertisshuss, C. de Hugultischouen et **R. de Staze(Strass) militibus** and others (WO:1475). Villingen (1244) Cvnradus aduocatus de Swarzinberc, Cvonrado seniore de **Wartinberc** et Hainrico filio and others (MO:1358). (1245) November 15th The brothers Konrad and Heinrich von Wartenberg pass their wealth Kunegundehaus, fief of John of Ringgenburg to their ancestors and their soul salvation. In 1248 a St. Gallen record with **Heinrico de Wartinberc** and 3rd reference note to 1249 in **Geisingen** show Hainricum de **Wartinberc,** Cunrado et Bertoldo fratibus de **Gisingen**, H. de **Gisingen** and **Gerungo de Cinbern** – signer **Lord Heinrich von Wartenberc** seal with **Lion(Lowen)** S.H. DE. WARTENB'C[502]. Constanz (1248) Dec 16th Walther v Clingen vogt der kirche Bischofzeil, Ulrich von Klingen bruder Walthers, Peregrinus et Cunradus Ymbria, prepositi dns Hugo de Clingen, Waltherus Dihtelarius, **Heinricus de Straze**, Waltherus de Rammstein canonici Constant, nobil vir Hein de Rosenegge , C de Steine, Bertoldus et Bertoldus de Annewiler and others (RE:198). Bregenz to Constanz (1251) Jan, Egilolfo de Valckenstein, Ruodolpho de Hasinweiler, Walthero de Ramestein, **Heinrico de Straze**, Heinrico de Clingenberg, Baldeberthus de Aneweiler, magistro Walcone, Ruperto de Tannenvelse and others (RE:203). The same was 1257 (negotiatied to **Fridingen**) a fief von Konrad genannt Habse, which of these **Konr. von Wartenberg** hatte, in exchange for two acres in Grindelbuch (Ebend. 2, 81). Rudolph **Fridingen** and way of exchange the same he did in 1257 called negotiated to **Fridingen** blessed is not far from one fief of Konrad Habse, the latter had by Konrad von **Wartenberg** (situm on **Fridingen** & eclessie in Salem)[503] in exchange for two acres in Grindelbook. Eberhard Dobler also had a question marked wether **Fridingen** were cousins to **Wartenberg**. Heinrich von **Fridingen** III (~1180) in Geisingen (1200) was believed to be married to a Wartenberg(?). **H. dicto Fridinger**

signed a document in **Geisingen** between Cunradus et Hainricus, dictus Struze, de **Wartunberch** (owners of Salem kloster) in April 1273. Konrad **Wartenberg** was located at **Geisingen** for a period of time 1257-1273. Neuffen (1269) Feb 2nd **Ûlrico dicto Struz et Arnoldo** filiastro suo (WO:2827). **Conrad von Fridingen** I (~1214) married Ita von Clingen daughter of Ulrich Clingen of which he or his son Ulrich Clingen is mentioned in a monastery record with Ulrich dicti de **Lowenberc** (?) and Heinrich Sweindorf (**Krahen**? ~1258?) on May 23 1273 recorded in the Frauenkloster in Feldbach[504]. Konstanz (1258) Walthero de Ramestain, Berhtoldo de Bvssenanc, **Hainrico de Straze**(Gachnang, Thurgau, Schweiz), Rvperto de Tannenvelse, **Vlrico de Straze** militibus (WO:2192). Geisingen (1273) April 13th *Die Gebrüder Konrad und Heinrich genannt Struz* (dictus Struz) *von Wartenberg* (Wartunberch) (WO:3149). Konstanz (1291) Jan 30th *Der Edle Konrad von Wartenberg, Ritter, schenkt* Testes: magister Johannes de Basilea canonicus sancti Stephani and others (WO:5025). Konrad von Wildenstein (Wartenberg) 1326 wappen siegel to >right>. Friedrich Schenk von Wartenburg aud Bohem (Bohmen) ~1337? also is shows with an Black and Gold schield similar to Steckborn[505].

- Marshall s. Marshall/Mareschall/Marascalus - John Marshall(nephew of William Marshall/Mareschall earl of Pembrooke and Longueville in Normandy) of Camden, England during the 1191 Crusades(Siege of Acre) carried a coat of arms almost identical to Justingen and Gundefingen golden barbed teeth with a red back ground (Dansey:78). **Marschall von Basel** {*bend with teeth, lack of lion*} similar to Wildenstein. Gotfried von Krahen (~1277) sister Agnes von Kreyen (~1280) married Jacob Marschalk. Agnesa was the uxor to Johannes Marschalci armiger de Basilea in 1310 (Kindler von Knobloch 1919:31). #473 on the Zurich wappenrolle. There are many other **Marschalk families**: **Werner Marschall von Markdorf** 1182 abbot of Weingarten, Marschalk von Zimmern (Hohenberg/ HohenZimmern/ Wartenberg) Ow familie 1200, Marschall von Staufen 1161. Ulm (1215) June 20th Vlricus de Helfanstein(Helfenstein), comes Egeno de Vrahc et filius suus, **Anselmus marscalcus** de Iustingen(Justingen), Bertoldus de Druhcpurc, Albertus de Stivcelingen(Altsteußlingen) and others (WO:880). Anselm Marschall von Justingen (1216) June 24th (knight on horse wappenshilde) - the Reichshof Marshal Anselm of Justingen adopt the monastery Salem all prerogatives, which he had to speak at the mill roof stowage under his castle Justingen (WO:904). (1219) William Marshall of Pembroke effigy is a knight with a large Lion covered shield. Marschall von Hohenberg, Marschall von Neurenbürg 1353, Marschall von Delsberg, Marschall von Falkenstein 1244, Marschall von Bleideck, Marschall von Pappenheim, and Marschall von Dettikofen 1264 (Herren von Gundelfingen). >Seal> for William Le Marshal, Earl of Pembroke England dated ~1301. It appears Henry VII marshcall Anselm Marshall von Justingen wappensiegel was adopted(?) by the Marshall family of England during Anselms negotiations there in 1234. Heinrici de Bohen (of Herefordiæ, England) daughter Matilda married Anselm Marshall {Ancelmo filio et hæredi Willielmi le Mareschall} Earl of Pembroke in Dec 1245. Wil/Hinwill (1277) Henry of Bernegg sold to the Hospitallers Bubikon possessions in Ringwil, Swicher von Lo[v]wenberc(Lueberg) die phahfen, Eberhart von Lomesse, **Heinrichis des marsalchis** and many others (MO:1277). A document for Pfalsburger Nurenburg dated (Feb - Mar 9) 1431 list many signers including **Jerge von Buchen, Houpt marschalk**, der landcomentur in Eilsas, Jacop Eberhart & Jerge truschsesen {*trustees*}...**Rudolff & Cunrat von Fridingen**[506]. In Ulm, another Bayern document with **Haupt**(Haubt) **Marschalk** (to Pappenheim) and Jorg von Gundolfing are signing side by side dated 1434.

- Hans Hage vogte to Trugent(?) in 1483 also has the wappen of Tengen[507]. The book Richental, Ulrich (von) Concilium zu Konstanz Augsburg: Anton Sorg, 2 Sept. 1483 rolle had so many schields that take this form I stopped documenting. Similar arms (bend is green and background is white lacking blue) is the wappen for Jürgen von Neuhausen, Hauskomtur in Matgnaw in 1483. It also identified in the index is this note "The family was noted 1243-1704, and their seat was in Neuhausen auf den Fildern (Kr.Esslingen, B-W). He is noted as from England and in the Order of St.John by Justinger (p.247).

143

- **Tum / Thun** (also Tunn, Tum, Tono) {*blue shield white bend, lack of lion*}, almost identical to Fridingen shield. Origin Ministerial bishops of Trient around 1145. Wappen identified for Simon von Tum around 1350 Schloss Bragher, he died in 1420. Located in the Arlberger Tirol book[508]. Werner von Thun 1146 was the son of Konrad Zaringen or Ulrich von Kyburg (d.1127) in the Canton of Bern. Thun was part of the Kyburger misteriales[509].

- **von Paulschwiller** unidentified. {*white bend bust lack of lion, man ch. arms with cap*} (Clemmenson 2009:219).

- **von Vomdeg** {*white bend lack of lion, bust of queen ch. arms betw bull's horns*} "von Windeck, noted in Schwaben and Alsace. A Jacob von Windeck is noted for being at the tournament in Heidelberg with the Wolf society (Kruse R 429) (Clemmenson 2009:238).

- **von Weiler** unidentified. {*Red bend lack of lion*}. Similar arms used by Heideck [859]. (Clemmenson 2009:237).

- **von simmatingen** {*bend lack of lion pitcher filled with ostrich plume*} von Sulmentingen, noted 1225, named from the Burg Obersulmentingen, Kr. Biberach (Clemmenson 2009:239).

- **von Lindow {***bend lack of lion bend ch. fleur-de-lis 2 wings per fess*} von Lindau, noted 1310, seat in Lindau, present Hof Lintdenthal and with Gerichtsrecht im Nordenstedt, nr Wiesbaden (Hessen). Lindau is associated with many **Fridingen** records from the late 1400's.

- **von ruchneg und vom stain vom liectenberg** {*bend lack of lion, 2 wings each ch.*} extinct 1922) and to Ostheim (Kr. Mellrichstadt, UFr.). Later they belonged to RRC Rhön-Werra. von Ruchnegg al. Raueneck, noted 13C, extinct 1550, seat Burg Raueneck (Kr.Ebern, OFr.). The regensburger ministeriales Lichtenberg has Ar-Gu in ING:62. (Clemmenson 2009:256). Stein family is associated with Fridingen records during early 1400's.

-**von reytzenstain und von der grünsack und von wildenstain** {*bend lack of lion, 2 wings each ch. Bend*} von Reizenstein, branch of von Grüne, franconian Uradel, seat at Burg Reitzenstein (Kr. Naila, OFr.) Two brothers in 1398 together with a von Wildenstein acquired the nearby Burg Selbitz.

- **von der Grünsack**, not identified, but probably also a branch of von Grüne. von Wildenstein, bavarian Freiherr, a branch of von Grüne (Clemmenson 2009:256). Wildenfels is also Wildenstein few associated record w/**Fridingen**.

- **von Langenow** {*bend lack of lion. ball of wool betw bull's horns*} seat at Burg Langenau nr Nassau, Wurttemburg, Germany (Kr. Lorelei, R-P). (Clemmenson 2009:278). Diethelm von Krenkingen sells Langnau(in Zurich) property about 1221 (Dobler 1986: 69).

- **von Flachsland** {*bend lack of lion. plume of feathers*} alsatian Uradel, noted 1185-c.1780, with seat at Flachsland bei Bollwiller nr **Mulhouse** (dep Haut-Rhin), and lands in Sundgau. (Clemmenson 2009:305).

- **von Möhringen, Hugo (s. Meringen/er)** {*bend lack of lion*} wappenseigel March 25th (1324). Ach in Hegau

Legend:
MO = Monasterium.net(http://www.mom-ca.uni-koeln.de/mom/search) : Charter number
WO = Wubonline.de : Charter number

Dates provided by Baden-Wurttemburg Urkendenbuch archive[510].
FU = Fürstenbergisches Urkundenbuch 1885
MGH = Monumenta Germaniae Historica www.mgh.de/dmgh/indices?q= : Page Number
RI = Regesta Imperii http://www.regesta-imperii.de/regesten/suche.html : Number
AO= Archivesonline http://www.archivesonline.org/search.aspx : ID Number
RW = Rootsweb:database http://wc.rootsweb.ancestry.com/

Fridinger / Krahen Sieglestamp

- Inverted colors to show shadowing & detail Bronze engraved seal used by Johannes von Krahen with the same fridingengishce Lion on a beam and Shield by 1250 and he is a Trustee(=Steward) of HohenKrahen. [Sigillum Johan]NIS + DE + KRAEGE + M[ilitis] . This translated is his stamp/signature Johan of Kraege Knight. Kraege is the location of HohenKrahen castle. Werner Siebler on behalf of the States Monument office found this broken fragment (above) on the Northwestern slope of Hohenkrahen in 1985[511]. Note: Militis or Miles is translated to Knight/Soldier.

- Black & White drawn from wax impression image found in Eberhard Dobler book "Burg und Herrschaft Hohenkrahen im Hegau 1986".

A wax impression using the Seal Stamp of the Bronze fragment. The impression emphasizes some type of hard strike and blow on the seigel/seal which caused the inevitable break.

Burg HohenKrahen circa ~1180/90

Postcard image of HohenKrahen(High Crows) castle and mountain. HohenKrahen was established between 1180-1190. West side of the Mountain Krahen. Also, near the location where the bronze Siegel Stamp was found in 1985. The Krahen/Fridingen family held the castle from 1180 through 1512.

Burg Krahen ~1180/90 - 1512

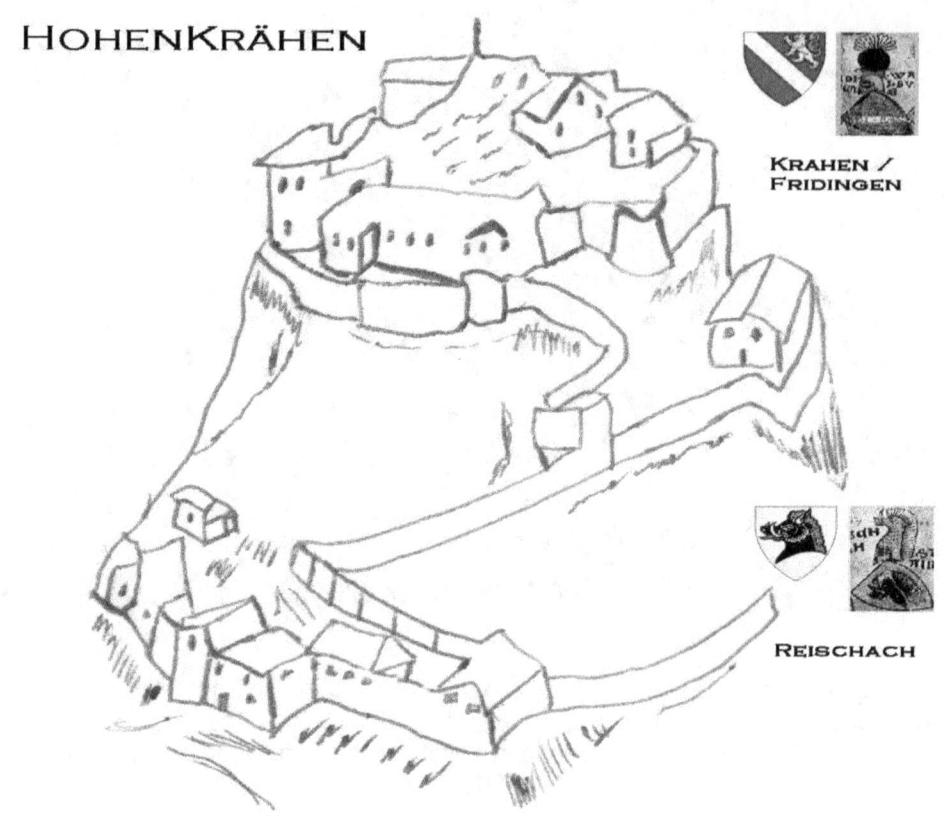

Sketch image of HohenKrahen(High Crows) castle and mountain from architecture plans & images. The Krahen/Fridingen family held the castle from 1180 through 1512(*confiscation*). [512]. Reischach familie was on the mountain during the late 1480's through early 1510's.

The Swabian Connection – Expanded Edition

Fridingen Schlössle ~1170/80 - 1499/1512

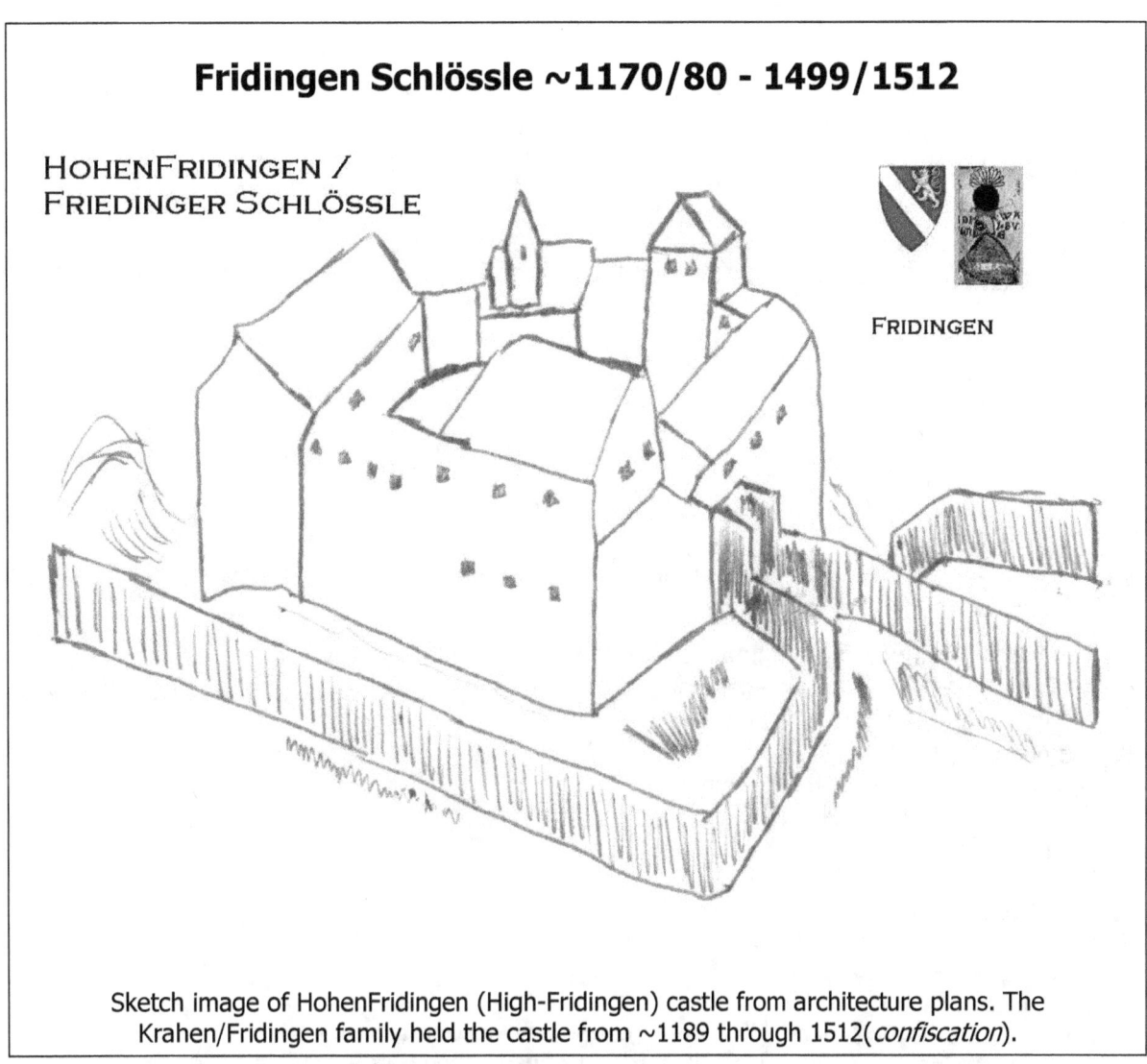

HOHENFRIDINGEN /
FRIEDINGER SCHLÖSSLE

FRIDINGEN

Sketch image of HohenFridingen (High-Fridingen) castle from architecture plans. The Krahen/Fridingen family held the castle from ~1189 through 1512(*confiscation*).

The many seals of the house of Fridingen's. Notice most carry the Lion {Lowe/Rampant} walking the Line and/or the Helmet with the Plume of Feathers {Gold & Black}. Heinrich and Hans appear to carry the alt-Fridingen wappen which is Black and Gold occurring in the early 1400's from the old friedingischer rights can be found in the Swiss lakeside (@ Untersee) among the place names still in the Freidinger @ Mannenbach @ Salenstein (c. 1355) and in a wooded area east of Steckborn (1378)[513]. Many arms feather plumes are split Black & Gold even though the Black & Gold shield may not be present. Notice Gottfrid's Black & Gold plume crest above a possible throwback as I'm not aware of (Black & Gold) being present in 1307.

| Siegel Rudolfs von Fridingen des Jüngeren. 1398. | Siegel Heinrichs von Fridingen. 1428. | Siegel Rudolfs von Fridingen. 1428. | Siegel Wilhelms von Fridingen. 1430. |

| Siegel Jakobs von Fridingen. 1432. | Siegel Stefans von Fridingen. 1472. | Siegel Friedrichs von Fridingen. 1476. | Siegel des Hans von Fridingen. 1535. |

The following people have gone under the name Fridingen/Krahen:

Fridingen, Adelbert b: ~1075 in Martinsweiler [Morzeneswilere],Germany d: in Nendigen,Germany

Fridingen, Adelwart b: ~1130 in Germany

Fridingen, Agatha b: ~1512

Fridingen, Albert b: ~1156 in Germany d: 1210

Fridingen, Albert b: ~1240/70 d: ~1330

Fridingen, Anna

Fridingen, Anna b: ~1301 in Zurich,Switzerland d: ~1349 in After 1349

Fridingen, Anna b: 1522

Fridingen, Anne b: ~1580 in Germany

Fridingen, Appolonia b: ~1429

Fridingen, Barbara b: ~1458

Fridingen, Bartolomeus b: ~1485 in Fridingen,Hohentwiel,Germany d: ~1538

Fridingen, Benedict Ernst b: ~1469 d: ~1518 in Hohenkrahen,Germany (Castle High Crows)

Fridingen, Berchtolt b: ~876

Fridingen, Bernhard b: ~1458 in 13 Oct 1499 Meissen,Germany d: ~1559

Fridingen, Berthold b: ~1060 in St. Blasien,Waldshut district,Baden-Württemberg,Germany

Fridingen, Bertold b: ~1141 d: ~1204

Fridingen, Brigita b: ~1452

Fridingen, Burchardus b: ~1064

Fridingen, Burckhart b: ~1423 in Germany OR Switzerland d: ~1454

Fridingen, Burkard b: ~1246 in Germany d: ~1276

Fridingen, Burkart b: ~1298 d: ~1330

Fridingen, Burkhard b: ~1157

Fridingen, Catherina b: ~1508

Fridingen, Conrad b: ~1234 d: ~1269

Fridingen, Conrad b: ~1384 in Fridingen,Germany d: ~1460?

Fridingen, Conrad b: ~1444 d: 1512

Fridingen, Cordula b: ~1453

Fridingen, Dorethea

Fridingen, Dorothea b: ~1400 in Germany

Fridingen, Dorothea b: ~1505 d: ~1561

Fridingen, Dorothea b: ~1510 d: ~1553 uxor for Siegmond H Hertneck (~1507)

Fridingen, Eberhard b: ~1076 in Martinsweiler [Morzeneswilere],Germany
Fridingen, Eberhard b: ~1281 in Germany
Fridingen, Eberhard b: ~1440
Fridingen, Elsbeth
Fridingen, Elsbeth b: ~1350 in Germany d: ~1371
Fridingen, Elsbeth Von b: ~1320 in Reichenau,Hohenzollern,Wuerttemberg-
Hohenzollern,Germany d: ~1350
Fridingen, Erchanger b: ~873 in Germany d: ~917
Fridingen, Ernst b: ~1343 in Fridingen,Germany
Fridingen, Folmar Folkmar b: ~1059 in Germany d: ~1095 in Nendingen,Germany
Fridingen, Franz b: ~1519 d: ~1554 in After 1554
Fridingen, Freidrich b: ~1238
Fridingen, Friedrich b: ~1388 d: 1425
Fridingen, Gertrude
Fridingen, Hanns b: ~1371 in Germany d: ~1414
Fridingen, Hans b: ~1405
Fridingen, Hans Albrecht b: ~1135 in Germany
Fridingen, Hans Friedrich b: ~1167 in Germany
Fridingen, Hans Grimmen b: ~1458 d: 1528 in Or ~1543
Fridingen, Hans Johann b: ~1428 in Switzerland d: ~1459
Fridingen, Hans Johannes b: 1467 in Germany d: 1546 in Switzerland
Fridingen, Hans Thüring b: ~1452 in Switzerland d: ~1492 in After 1492
Fridingen, Hans Wilhelm b: ~1408 in Fridingen,Germany d: ~1476
Fridingen, Heinrich b: ~1170 in Germany d: ~1230
Fridingen, Heinrich b: ~1267
Fridingen, Heinrich b: ~1306
Fridingen, Heinrich b: ~1348 in Germany d: 1395 in Schwaben,Fridingen,Germany
Fridingen, Heinrich b: ~1430 d: ~1489
Fridingen, Herman II b: ~1153 in Germany d: 1191
Fridingen, Hildegard von b: ~1145
Fridingen, Hugo b: 1305? in Germany d: 1377
Fridingen, Hugo b: 1480 in Freiburg,Germany d: ~1555
Fridingen, Irenaeus Gretlin
Fridingen, Itelhaus Eytel b: ~1386 d: ~1476
Fridingen, Jakob b: ~1359 d: ~1448
Fridingen, Johann Hans b: ~1310 d: ~1370
Fridingen, Johannes b: ~1424 in Germany
Fridingen, Johannes "Pre-reformer" b: ~1458 d: 21 DEC 1534
Fridingen, Johanns "the Cook" b: ~1376 in Fridingen,Germany
Fridingen, John the young b: ~1260
Fridingen, Jorg Georg b: ~1462 d: ~1544 in After 1545
Fridingen, Josef b: ~1477? in Wien,Austria
Fridingen, Katherina b: ~1512 in Germany
Fridingen, Klsbeth b: ~1335
Fridingen, Kunigunda Anna b: ~1369 in Staufen,Freiburg,Baden-Wet,Germany d: 1417
Fridingen, Kunigunde b: ~864
Fridingen, Liutfrid b: ~1100 in Austria?
Fridingen, Liutfrid b: ~1125 d: ~1180
Fridingen, Magdalena von b: ~1428 in Loewenberg,Preussen d: ~1445
Fridingen, Margaret b: ~1328
Fridingen, Margarete b: ~1440 in Germany
Fridingen, Margaretha
Fridingen, Margaretha Magdelena
Fridingen, Martin b: ~1454

The Swabian Connection – Expanded Edition

Fridingen, Martin b: ~1454 in Germany d: ~1522 in After 1522
Fridingen, Niclas b: ~938 in Germany
Fridingen, Ortwin b: ~1140 in Germany d: ~1204
Fridingen, Paulus b: ~1495 in Ebingen,Germany d: ~1530
Fridingen, Petrus Hamma b: ~1483
Fridingen, Reinold b: ~1061 d: in Talheim bei Tuttlingen,Germany
Fridingen, Roderich b: ~1838
Fridingen, Rudolf von b: ~1445 in Fridingen,Germany d: ~1530 in Switzerland?
Fridingen, Rudolph b: ~1259 in Tengen,Germany d: ~1359
Fridingen, Rudolph b: ~1328 in Germany OR Schaffhauser,Switzerland d: ~1404
Fridingen, Rudolpho b: ~1164 in Fridingen,Germany d: ~1258
Fridingen, Ruodolffen Junger b: ~1378 in Tengen,Germany d: ~1460
Fridingen, Sibilia b: ~1508
Fridingen, Simon von b: ~1463 d: ~1494
Fridingen, Stefan b: ~1442 d: ~1490
Fridingen, Ulrich b: ~1406 d: ~1465
Fridingen, Ulrich Hans b: ~1379 in Liebburg,Switzerland d: ~1429?
Fridingen, Ulrich von b: ~938 d: ~969
Fridingen, Uolricus IV b: ~1304 in Germany d: ~1356 in After 1356
Fridingen, Ursula b: ~1446 in Switzerland d: ~1513 in Aarau,Argau,Switzerland
Fridingen, Vrena Verena b: ~1406
Fridingen, Walter S
Fridingen, Ytelhansen Eitel b: ~1449 d: ~1489
Fridinger, Andrae b: ~1550 in Austria d: ~1626
Fridinger, Appollonia b: 1541 in Bretten,Baden,Germany
Fridinger, Benedictus b: ~1704 in Austria
Fridinger, Claus b: ~1369 in Bickelfperg,Germany d: ~1400 in After 1399
Fridinger, Damian
Fridinger, Erasmus
Fridinger, Hiltmar b: ~1281 in Prag,Czech Republic
Fridinger, Jacob b: ~1276 in Prag,Czech Republic
Fridinger, Leon Leonhardt b: 1510 in Bretten,Baden,Germany
Fridinger, Nicolaus b: ~1313 in Prag,Czech Republic
Fridinger, Sebastian b: ~1533 in Austria d: ~1564
Fridinger, Simon b: ~1563 in Wien,Austria
Fridinger, Thomas
Fridinger, Wolfgang b: ~1523 in Wien,Austria d: ~1553
Krahen, A von b: ~1188 d: ~1208
Krahen, Agnes von b: ~1280 d: 1323
Krahen, Bertold II. von d: 1266?
Krahen, Bertold von b: ~1185 d: ~1248
Krahen, Diethelm de von b: ~1172 in Germany d: SEP 1228
Krahen, Gotfried von b: ~1277 d: ~1307
Krahen, Heinrich II. von b: ~1170 in Germany d: ~1230
Krahen, Hermann III. von b: ~1171 d: ~1194
Krahen, Johannes I.von b: ~1217 d: 1256
Krahen, Judenta von
Krahen, Liutfrid von b: ~1180 d: ~1228
Krayger, Konrad der b: ~1352 d: ~1382
Krayger, Liutpold b: ~1375 d: ~1383

The following people have gone under the name **Friding/Fridig surnames..**
Friding/Verthouen, Albrecht/Alberti der Schenk b: ~1306 d: ~1336
Friding, Christianus Rormeyer b: ~1534 in Germany d: ~1555

The Swabian Connection – Expanded Edition

Friding, Conrad b: ~1392 in Germany OR Schaffhauser,Switzerland d: ~1432
Friding, Elizabeth
Friding, Gerg b: ~1559 in Germany. Daughter Anna Friding christened Jan 17 1584 in Planntenhardt,Wurtemburg, Germany. Gerg married Catharina.
Friding, Haintzli b: ~1395 in Wiesholz,Schaufhausen,Switzerland d: ~1426
Friding, Hans b: ~1398 in Wiesholz,Schaufhausen,Switzerland d: ~1419
Friding, Gret
Friding, Heinrich b: ~1343
Friding, Heinrich b: ~1599
Friding, Johann Jakob
Friding, John b: ~1484 in Kempten,Germany d: ~1515
Friding, Jorg b: ~1475 in Austria? d: ~1506 in After 1505
Friding, Maria b: 24 FEB 1636 in Uesslingen,Thurgau,Switzerland
Friding, Ulrich b: ~1303 d: ~1334
Friding, Peter b: ~1403 d: died after ~1438 in Frutigen/Adelboden, Switzerland
Friding, Verena b: ~1537 in Grossnoechstetten,Bern,Switzerland
Friding Freyding, Sebastian b: ~1504 d: ~1542
Friding Freyding, Conrad b: ~1439 in Innsbruck,Austria? d: 1470 in After 1469
Freidig, Anna b: 1529 in Kriegstetten,Soleure,Swiss
Fridig, Richi b: ~1472 in Isental,Switzerland
Fridig, Marti b: ~1450 in Isental,Switzerland d: ~1528 in Switzerland
Fridig, Heinrich b: ~1540 in Uri,Switzerland
Fridig, Heinz b: ~1472 in Germany
Fridig, Bauer b: ~1472 in Germany

Name Legend:
d. Ä = der Ältere (the elder)
d. J = der Junge (the young)

Genealogy of the Hirscheck/Krahen/Fridinger lineage
(stem table research started by Eberhard Dobler 1986)

First Generation

1. **Gerold d. Ä** was born ~710. He died 795.

   Gerold married **Imma**, daughter of Hnabi. Imma was born ~736. She died 798 in Aachen, Nordrhein-Westfalen, Deutschland.

   They had the following children:

   2 M i. **Hadrien/Adrien d' ORLÉANS** was born ~755. He died 10 Nov 821.

   Hadrien/Adrien married **Waldrat der VIDONEN** . Waldrat was born ~760. She died ~825.

   3 F ii. **Hildegard de VINZGAU** was born ~757. She died 30 Apr 783 in Thionville, Lorraine, France.

   Hildegard married **Karl der GROßE,CHARLESMAGNE** "The Great". The Great died 814.

The Swabian Connection – Expanded Edition

+   4 M   iii. **Ulrich I** died 807.

     5 M   iv.   **Gerold II**.

     6 M   v.   **Uto/Voto** was born ~788. He died 803.

     7 M   vi.   **Megingoz** was born ~765. He died ~796.

     8 M   vii. **Erbio** was born ~756. He died ~793.

Second Generation

4. **Ulrich I** (Gerold d. Ä) died 807.

    He had the following children:

        9 M   i.   **Ulrich II** was born ~781. He died ~815.

+   10 M   ii.   **Ratbert** was born ~780 and died ~817.

        11 M   iii. **Bebo** was born ~783. He died ~804.

        12 M   iv.   **Gerold** was born ~782. He died ~804.

Third Generation

10. **Ratbert** (Ulrich I, Gerold d. Ä) was born ~780. He died ~817.

    He had the following children:

+   13 M   i.   **Ulrich III** died 896/900.

Fourth Generation

13. **Ulrich III** (Ratbert, Ulrich I, Gerold d. Ä) died 896/900.

    He had the following children:

+   14 M   i.   **Ulrich V ?** died 27 Sep 894/926.

Fifth Generation

14. **Ulrich V ?** (Ulrich III, Ratbert, Ulrich I, Gerold d. Ä) died 27 Sep 894/926.

    Ulrich married **Perehheide** on 886/890.

    They had the following children:

        15 F   i.   **Irmintrud** was born ~870. She died ~894.

        16 F   ii.   **Persehdrud** was born ~869. She died ~887.

+   17 M   iii. **Keroldus** was born ~870 and died ~887.

Sixth Generation

17. **Keroldus** (Ulrich V ?, Ulrich III, Ratbert, Ulrich I, Gerold d. Ä) was born ~870. He died ~887.

   He had the following children:

	18	M	i. **Burchart BREGENZ**.
+	19	M	ii. **Adalhart v BUCHORN**.
+	20	M	iii. **Ulrich V v. BREGENZ** was born ~920 and died 10 Aug 955.

Seventh Generation

19. **Adalhart v BUCHORN** (Keroldus, Ulrich V ?, Ulrich III, Ratbert, Ulrich I, Gerold d. Ä).

   Adalhart was employed Graf in Buchorn.

   He had the following children:

	21	M	i. **Richere BUCHORN**.

20. **Ulrich V v. BREGENZ** (Keroldus, Ulrich V ?, Ulrich III, Ratbert, Ulrich I, Gerold d. Ä) was born ~920. He died 10 Aug 955.

   Ulrich resided in Bregenz, Austria.

   Ulrich married **Dietburg/Thietburga ZAHRINGEN**. Dietburg/Thietburga died 9 Aug 949.

   They had the following children:

+	22	M	i. **Ulrich VI v BREGENZ** was born ~938 and died ~969.
	23	M	ii. **Marquard** was born ~948. He died ~999.

   Marquard was employed Graf 998 in Goldenshuntar?.

+	24	M	iii. **Liutfried v. WINTERTHUR** was born ~945.
	25	M	iv. **Gebhard v. KONSTANZ** was born 9 Aug 949. He died 27 Aug 995.

   Gebhard was employed Bischof 979 - 995 in v. Konstanz. He was employed Grunder 983 in v. Peterhausen.

Eighth Generation

22. **Ulrich VI v BREGENZ** (Ulrich V v. BREGENZ, Keroldus, Ulrich V ?, Ulrich III, Ratbert, Ulrich I, Gerold d. Ä) was born ~938. He died ~969.

   Ulrich resided 968 in Grießwärtel, Germany. He was employed Ritter=Knight 968 in Grießwärtel, Germany. He was employed Grafen=Count in Bregenz, Germany.

   He had the following children:

+	26	M	i. **Ulrich BREGENZ** died ~1045.

24. **Liutfried v. WINTERTHUR** (Ulrich V v. BREGENZ, Keroldus, Ulrich V ?, Ulrich III, Ratbert, Ulrich I, Gerold d. Ä) was born ~945.

   He had the following children:

+	27	M	i. **Adalbert v. WINTERTHUR V. KYBURG** was born ~975 and died 8 Sep

1030.

28 M   ii. **Werner v. KIBURG** was born ~980. He died 1030 in Rebell.

Ninth Generation

26. **Ulrich BREGENZ** (Ulrich VI v BREGENZ, Ulrich V v. BREGENZ, Keroldus, Ulrich V ?, Ulrich III, Ratbert, Ulrich I, Gerold d. Ä) died ~1045.

He had the following children:

      29 M   i. **Marquand BREGENZ** was born ~1075.

+   30 M   ii. **Ulrich BREGENZ** died ~1097.

+   31 M   iii. **Gero STUHLINGEN-KLETGAU-ALPGAU** was born ~1047 and died ~1122.

+   32 M   iv. **Ludwig HEGAU** was born ~1047 and died 28 Jan 1135.

27. **Adalbert v. WINTERTHUR V. KYBURG** (Liutfried v. WINTERTHUR, Ulrich V v. BREGENZ, Keroldus, Ulrich V ?, Ulrich III, Ratbert, Ulrich I, Gerold d. Ä) was born ~975. He died 8 Sep 1030.

He had the following children:

+   33 M   i. **Werner I. v. WINTERTHUR** was born ~995 and died 22 Aug 1040.

+   34 M   ii. **Hermann v. HIRSCHECK D.Ä I** was born ~996 and died ~1044.

      35 M   iii. **Gerold?** was born ~997. He died ~1044.

Tenth Generation

30. **Ulrich BREGENZ** (Ulrich BREGENZ, Ulrich VI v BREGENZ, Ulrich V v. BREGENZ, Keroldus, Ulrich V ?, Ulrich III, Ratbert, Ulrich I, Gerold d. Ä) died ~1097.

Ulrich married **Berhta RHEINFELDEN**.

They had the following children:

      36 M   i. **Rudolph BREGENZ**.

31. **Gero STUHLINGEN-KLETGAU-ALPGAU** (Ulrich BREGENZ, Ulrich VI v BREGENZ, Ulrich V v. BREGENZ, Keroldus, Ulrich V ?, Ulrich III, Ratbert, Ulrich I, Gerold d. Ä) was born ~1047. He died ~1122.

Gero was employed Graf 1067 in v Pfullendorf v Klettgau 1067. He was employed Graf 1071 in Alpgau.

Gero married **Berht** "Bart".

They had the following children:

+   37 M   i. **GERUNG v STÜHLINGEN** was born ~1069 and died 1124.

32. **Ludwig HEGAU** (Ulrich BREGENZ, Ulrich VI v BREGENZ, Ulrich V v. BREGENZ, Keroldus, Ulrich V ?, Ulrich III, Ratbert, Ulrich I, Gerold d. Ä) was born ~1047. He died 28 Jan 1135.

Ludwig was employed Hegaugraf 1067 in Graf. He was employed Abbot 1131 in Reichenau Abbot, Konstanz, Germany.

He had the following children:

+   38   M   i.   **Ulrich v RAMSBERG** was born ~1060 and died ~1090.

+   39   M   ii.   **Ernist RAMSEN** died ~1135.

33. **Werner I. v. WINTERTHUR** (Adalbert v. WINTERTHUR V. KYBURG, Liutfried v. WINTERTHUR, Ulrich V v. BREGENZ, Keroldus, Ulrich V ?, Ulrich III, Ratbert, Ulrich I, Gerold d. Ä) was born ~995. He died 22 Aug 1040 in Bohemia.

Werner married **Irmengard NELLENBURG**. Irmengard was born 990. She died 1053.

They had the following children:

    40   M   i.   **Werner II.** was born ~1000. He died 18 Jun 1053 in during the Battle of Civitate.

+   41   M   ii.   **Adalbert v. WINTERTHUR** was born ~1020 and died 18 Jun 1053.

    42   M   iii.   **Liutfried** died 22 Aug 1040 in In Bohemia.

    43   M   iv.   **Hermann** was born ~1020. He died 8 Apr 1065.

         Hermann was employed Abott 1051 - 1065 in Einsiedeln, Schwyz, Switzerland.

34. **Hermann v. HIRSCHECK D.Ä I** (Adalbert v. WINTERTHUR V. KYBURG, Liutfried v. WINTERTHUR, Ulrich V v. BREGENZ, Keroldus, Ulrich V ?, Ulrich III, Ratbert, Ulrich I, Gerold d. Ä) was born ~996. He died ~1044.

Hermann was employed vogt Jun 1043 in Peterhausen.

Hermann married **Perhterad** "Bertha" in Peterhausen.

They had the following children:

+   44   M   i.   **Hermann HIRSCHECK** was born ~1030 and died ~1058.

    45   M   ii.   **Gerold / Geroldus HIRSCHECK** "Geroldo" was born ~1022. He died ~1058.

Eleventh Generation

37. **GERUNG v STÜHLINGEN** (Gero STUHLINGEN-KLETGAU-ALPGAU, Ulrich BREGENZ, Ulrich VI v BREGENZ, Ulrich V v. BREGENZ, Keroldus, Ulrich V ?, Ulrich III, Ratbert, Ulrich I, Gerold d. Ä) was born ~1069. He died 1124.

GERUNG was employed Graf 1089 - 1099 in Stülingen.

GERUNG married **Cuniza TOGGENBURG** on 1093. Cuniza died ~1135.

They had the following children:

    46   M   i.   **Berthold v STÜHLINGEN**.

    47   M   ii.   **Ludolf v STÜHLINGEN** was born ~1104.

    48   M   iii.   **Volknant v STÜHLINGEN** was born 1105.

38. **Ulrich v RAMSBERG** (Ludwig HEGAU, Ulrich BREGENZ, Ulrich VI v BREGENZ, Ulrich V v. BREGENZ, Keroldus, Ulrich V ?, Ulrich III, Ratbert, Ulrich I, Gerold d. Ä) was born ~1060. He died ~1090.

Ulrich was employed Graf 1080 in Hegau.

Ulrich married **Adelheid**.

They had the following children:

+   49   M   i.   **Burchardus v FRICKINGEN V RAMSHEIM** was born ~1064 and died ~1102.

+   50   M   ii.   **Ludwig d. J. UNTERSEE V STOFFELN V PFULLENDORF** was born ~1064 and died ~1117.

39. **Ernist RAMSEN** (Ludwig HEGAU, Ulrich BREGENZ, Ulrich VI v BREGENZ, Ulrich V v. BREGENZ, Keroldus, Ulrich V ?, Ulrich III, Ratbert, Ulrich I, Gerold d. Ä) died ~1135.

He had the following children:

    51   M   i.   **Ernest RAMMISHEIM** was born ~1137. He died ~1167.

41. **Adalbert v. WINTERTHUR** (Werner I. v. WINTERTHUR, Adalbert v. WINTERTHUR V. KYBURG, Liutfried v. WINTERTHUR, Ulrich V v. BREGENZ, Keroldus, Ulrich V ?, Ulrich III, Ratbert, Ulrich I, Gerold d. Ä) was born ~1020. He died 18 Jun 1053.

He had the following children:

    52   F   i.   **Adelhaide WINTERTHUR KYBURG** was born ~1050. She died ~1125.

          Adelhaide married **Herman DILLINGEN**. Herman was born ~1050. He died 16 Apr 1120.

          Herman was employed Graf/Comte 1074 in Dillingen.

44. **Hermann HIRSCHECK** (Hermann v. HIRSCHECK D.Ä I, Adalbert v. WINTERTHUR V. KYBURG, Liutfried v. WINTERTHUR, Ulrich V v. BREGENZ, Keroldus, Ulrich V ?, Ulrich III, Ratbert, Ulrich I, Gerold d. Ä) was born ~1030. He died ~1058.

He had the following children:

+   53   M   i.   **Heinrich v HIRSCHECK D.Ä** was born ~1043 and died ~1091?.

+   54   M   ii.   **Hermann HIRSCHECK** was born ~1050 and died ~1080.

+   55   M   iii.   **Gerold v BUCH V TENGIN** was born ~1060 and died ~1085.

Twelfth Generation

49. **Burchardus v FRICKINGEN V RAMSHEIM** (Ulrich v RAMSBERG, Ludwig HEGAU, Ulrich BREGENZ, Ulrich VI v BREGENZ, Ulrich V v. BREGENZ, Keroldus, Ulrich V ?, Ulrich III, Ratbert, Ulrich I, Gerold d. Ä) was born ~1064. He died ~1102.

Burchardus resided 1094 - 1101 in Frickingen.

He had the following children:

+   56   M   i.   **FRICKINGEN** .

50. **Ludwig d. J. UNTERSEE V STOFFELN V PFULLENDORF** (Ulrich v RAMSBERG, Ludwig HEGAU, Ulrich BREGENZ, Ulrich VI v BREGENZ, Ulrich V v. BREGENZ, Keroldus, Ulrich V ?, Ulrich III, Ratbert, Ulrich I, Gerold d. Ä) was born ~1064. He died ~1117.

Ludwig was employed 1095 in im Unterseegau. He was employed 1101 in Hegau 1101 v Stoffeln v Pfullendorf.

Ludwig married **Ms**.

They had the following children:

> 57 M i. **Ulrich**.

> 58 M ii. **Ludwig**.

+ 59 M iii. **Rudolf PFULLENDORF RAMSBERG I** was born ~1134 and died ~1180.

> 60 M iv. **Arnold PFULLENDORF** died ~1165.

> Arnold married **Elizabeth**.

53. **Heinrich v HIRSCHECK D.Ä** (Hermann HIRSCHECK, Hermann v. HIRSCHECK D.Ä I, Adalbert v. WINTERTHUR V. KYBURG, Liutfried v. WINTERTHUR, Ulrich V v. BREGENZ, Keroldus, Ulrich V ?, Ulrich III, Ratbert, Ulrich I, Gerold d. Ä) was born ~1043. He died ~1091?.

Heinrich was employed Grunderkreis in St. Georgen, Austria. He resided 1083 - 1091 in St. Georgen, Austria.

He had the following children:

+ 61 M i. **Hermann HIRSCHECK D.Ä** was born ~1067 and died ~1102.

> 62 M ii. **Adalbert de WINTERSPUREN** was born ~1071. He died ~1102.

> > Adalbert resided 1100 in v. Ramsen. He resided 1101 in v. Winterspuren.

> 63 M iii. **Heinrich v. RAMSEN** was born ~1070. He died ~1100.

> > Heinrich resided 1100 in v. Ramsen.

> 64 M iv. **Arnold v. EGGENWILER** was born ~1061. He died ~1091.

> > Arnold was employed Monch=Monk 1091 in St. Georgen, Austria.

+ 65 F v. **Ruzela HIRSCHECK** was born ~1061 and died ~1092.

54. **Hermann HIRSCHECK** (Hermann HIRSCHECK, Hermann v. HIRSCHECK D.Ä I, Adalbert v. WINTERTHUR V. KYBURG, Liutfried v. WINTERTHUR, Ulrich V v. BREGENZ, Keroldus, Ulrich V ?, Ulrich III, Ratbert, Ulrich I, Gerold d. Ä) was born ~1050. He died ~1080 in or 1084.

He had the following children:

+ 66 M i. **Heinrich HIRSCHECK D.J.** was born ~1063 and died Dec 1121.

> 67 M ii. **Liutold EICHSTEGEN** was born ~1064. He died ~1093.

+ 68 M iii. **Konrad EICHSTEGEN** was born ~1066 and died ~1096.

55. **Gerold v BUCH V TENGIN** "Gerolt" (Hermann HIRSCHECK, Hermann v. HIRSCHECK D.Ä I, Adalbert v. WINTERTHUR V. KYBURG, Liutfried v. WINTERTHUR, Ulrich V v. BREGENZ, Keroldus, Ulrich V ?, Ulrich III, Ratbert, Ulrich I, Gerold d. Ä) was born ~1060. He died ~1085.

Gerolt was employed 1080 in von Buch. He was employed Monch 1084 in Peterhausen.

He had the following children:

> 69 M i. **Burchardt TENGEN** was born ~1070. He died ~1112.

+ 70 M ii. **Rudolph TENGEN** was born ~1071 and died ~1135.

Thirteenth Generation

56. **FRICKINGEN** (Burchardus v FRICKINGEN V RAMSHEIM , Ulrich v RAMSBERG, Ludwig HEGAU, Ulrich BREGENZ, Ulrich VI v BREGENZ, Ulrich V v. BREGENZ, Keroldus, Ulrich V ?, Ulrich III, Ratbert, Ulrich I, Gerold d. Ä).

He had the following children:

+   71 M   i.   **Aldelbert FRICKINGEN** was born ~1141 and died ~1172.

+   72 M   ii.   **Burchardus FRICKINGEN** was born ~1139.

59. **Rudolf PFULLENDORF RAMSBERG I** (Ludwig d. J. UNTERSEE V STOFFELN V PFULLENDORF, Ulrich v RAMSBERG, Ludwig HEGAU, Ulrich BREGENZ, Ulrich VI v BREGENZ, Ulrich V v. BREGENZ, Keroldus, Ulrich V ?, Ulrich III, Ratbert, Ulrich I, Gerold d. Ä) was born ~1134. He died ~1180.

Rudolf married **Adelheid**.

They had the following children:

+   73 M   i.   **Rudolf PFULLENDORF II**.

      74 M   ii.   **Gottfried RAMSBERG**.

      75 M   iii. **Arnold PFULLENDORF**.

61. **Hermann HIRSCHECK D.Ä** (Heinrich v HIRSCHECK D.Ä, Hermann HIRSCHECK, Hermann v. HIRSCHECK D.Ä I, Adalbert v. WINTERTHUR V. KYBURG, Liutfried v. WINTERTHUR, Ulrich V v. BREGENZ, Keroldus, Ulrich V ?, Ulrich III, Ratbert, Ulrich I, Gerold d. Ä) was born ~1067. He died ~1102.

Hermann resided 1087 in v. Gailingen. He resided 1091 in v. Mahlspuren. He resided 1101 in v. Busslingen.

He had the following children:

+   76 M   i.   **Hermann HIRSCHECK D.J.** was born ~1085 and died ~1145.

      77 M   ii.   **Heinrich v. SCHWANDORF** was born ~1087. He died ~1132.

                  Heinrich was employed Monch=Monk 1131 in Beuron. He resided in v. Schwandorf.

      78 M   iii. **Anno v. BUSSLINGEN** was born ~1089. He died ~1131.

                  Anno resided 1131 in v. Busslingen.

      79 M   iv. **Berthold v. ESPASINGEN** "Bertoldi" was born ~1086. He died ~1107.

                  Bertoldi resided 1106 in v. Espasingen.

65. **Ruzela HIRSCHECK** (Heinrich v HIRSCHECK D.Ä, Hermann HIRSCHECK, Hermann v. HIRSCHECK D.Ä I, Adalbert v. WINTERTHUR V. KYBURG, Liutfried v. WINTERTHUR, Ulrich V v. BREGENZ, Keroldus, Ulrich V ?, Ulrich III, Ratbert, Ulrich I, Gerold d. Ä) was born ~1061. She died ~1092.

Ruzela married **WOLFGER** on 24 Jun 1091 in Wittichen, Germany.

They had the following children:

      80 M   i.   **Alberich WOLFGER V. ESPASINGEN** was born ~1076. He died ~1108.

66. **Heinrich HIRSCHECK D.J.** (Hermann HIRSCHECK, Hermann HIRSCHECK, Hermann v. HIRSCHECK D.Ä I, Adalbert v. WINTERTHUR V. KYBURG, Liutfried v. WINTERTHUR, Ulrich V v. BREGENZ, Keroldus, Ulrich V ?, Ulrich III, Ratbert, Ulrich I, Gerold d. Ä) was born ~1063. He died Dec 1121 in Algovia, Germany and was buried in Petershausen, Konstanz.

Heinrich resided 1083 in von Hirscheck. He resided 1096 in von Ebenweiler.

Heinrich married **Richinza**.

They had the following children:

+   81   M   i.   **Hermann von MARKDORF** was born ~1083 and died ~1160.

         82   M   ii.   **Furst von ? HIRSCHECK**.

         83   M   iii.   **Konrad v HIRSCHECK** was born ~1103. He died 24 Oct 1167 in Augsburg, Germany.

                      Konrad was employed Bischof 1152 - 1167 in Augsburg, Germany.

         84   M   iv.   **Rudolph I HIRSCHECK** was born ~1103. He died ~1135.

68. **Konrad EICHSTEGEN** (Hermann HIRSCHECK, Hermann HIRSCHECK, Hermann v. HIRSCHECK D.Ä I, Adalbert v. WINTERTHUR V. KYBURG, Liutfried v. WINTERTHUR, Ulrich V v. BREGENZ, Keroldus, Ulrich V ?, Ulrich III, Ratbert, Ulrich I, Gerold d. Ä) was born ~1066. He died ~1096.

He had the following children:

+   85   M   i.   **Heinrich EICHSTEGEN** died ~1142.

70. **Rudolph TENGEN** (Gerold v BUCH V TENGIN, Hermann HIRSCHECK, Hermann v. HIRSCHECK D.Ä I, Adalbert v. WINTERTHUR V. KYBURG, Liutfried v. WINTERTHUR, Ulrich V v. BREGENZ, Keroldus, Ulrich V ?, Ulrich III, Ratbert, Ulrich I, Gerold d. Ä) was born ~1071. He died ~1135.

He had the following children:

+   86   M   i.   **Heinricus? TENGEN** was born ~1132 and died ~1167.

Fourteenth Generation

71. **Aldelbert FRICKINGEN** (FRICKINGEN , Burchardus v FRICKINGEN V RAMSHEIM , Ulrich v RAMSBERG, Ludwig HEGAU, Ulrich BREGENZ, Ulrich VI v BREGENZ, Ulrich V v. BREGENZ, Keroldus, Ulrich V ?, Ulrich III, Ratbert, Ulrich I, Gerold d. Ä) was born ~1141. He died ~1172.

He had the following children:

         87   M   i.   **Heinrich FRICKINGEN** died ~1182.

72. **Burchardus FRICKINGEN** (FRICKINGEN , Burchardus v FRICKINGEN V RAMSHEIM , Ulrich v RAMSBERG, Ludwig HEGAU, Ulrich BREGENZ, Ulrich VI v BREGENZ, Ulrich V v. BREGENZ, Keroldus, Ulrich V ?, Ulrich III, Ratbert, Ulrich I, Gerold d. Ä) was born ~1139.

He had the following children:

         88   M   i.   **Heinrich FRICKINGEN** "Heinrico" was born ~1159. He died ~1179.

73. **Rudolf PFULLENDORF II** (Rudolf PFULLENDORF RAMSBERG I, Ludwig d. J. UNTERSEE V STOFFELN V PFULLENDORF, Ulrich v RAMSBERG, Ludwig HEGAU, Ulrich BREGENZ, Ulrich VI v BREGENZ, Ulrich V v. BREGENZ, Keroldus, Ulrich V ?, Ulrich III, Ratbert, Ulrich I, Gerold d. Ä).

Rudolf married **Elisabetha**.

They had the following children:

89   F   i.   **Ida PFULLENDORF**.

Ida married **Albrecht HAPSBURG**.

76. **Hermann HIRSCHECK D.J.** (Hermann HIRSCHECK D.Ä, Heinrich v HIRSCHECK D.Ä, Hermann HIRSCHECK, Hermann v. HIRSCHECK D.Ä I, Adalbert v. WINTERTHUR V. KYBURG, Liutfried v. WINTERTHUR, Ulrich V v. BREGENZ, Keroldus, Ulrich V ?, Ulrich III, Ratbert, Ulrich I, Gerold d. Ä) was born ~1085. He died ~1145.

Hermann resided 1131 in v. Mahlspuren. He resided 1135 in v. Espasingen.

Hermann married **Ms BURGLEN-NELLENBURG**, daughter of Dietrich von BURGLEN-NELLENBURG, on ~1105.

They had the following children:

+   90   M   i.   **Heinrich Habardus(?) HIRSCHECK DE SALENSTEIN** was born ~1105 and died ~1161.

     91   M   ii.   **Eberhard HIRSCHECK** was born ~1106. He died ~1136.

     92   M   iii.   **Liutfried HIRSCHECK** was born ~1105. He died ~1136.

     93   M   iv.   **Arnold v STETTEN** was born ~1130. He died ~1159.

         Arnold resided 1158 in v. Stetten.

+   94   M   v.   **Burchard HOHENFELS** was born ~1104 and died ~1167?.

     95   M   vi.   **Adalbert HIRSCHECK** was born ~1107. He died ~1136.

+   96   M   vii.   **Hermann I. v STETTEN V. ESPASINGEN** was born ~1103 and died 1183.

81. **Hermann von MARKDORF** (Heinrich HIRSCHECK D.J. , Hermann HIRSCHECK, Hermann HIRSCHECK, Hermann v. HIRSCHECK D.Ä I, Adalbert v. WINTERTHUR V. KYBURG, Liutfried v. WINTERTHUR, Ulrich V v. BREGENZ, Keroldus, Ulrich V ?, Ulrich III, Ratbert, Ulrich I, Gerold d. Ä) was born ~1083. He died ~1160.

Hermann was employed Co-founder in Salem Monastery, Germany.

He had the following children:

     97   M   i.   **Bruno MARKDORF** was born ~1143. He died ~1172.

+   98   M   ii.   **Hainricus MARKDORF** was born ~1151 and died ~1187.

85. **Heinrich EICHSTEGEN** (Konrad EICHSTEGEN, Hermann HIRSCHECK, Hermann HIRSCHECK, Hermann v. HIRSCHECK D.Ä I, Adalbert v. WINTERTHUR V. KYBURG, Liutfried v. WINTERTHUR, Ulrich V v. BREGENZ, Keroldus, Ulrich V ?, Ulrich III, Ratbert, Ulrich I, Gerold d. Ä) died ~1142.

He had the following children:

+   99   M   i.   **Wezilo de EIGISTEGIN** died ~1182.

86. **Heinricus? TENGEN** (Rudolph TENGEN, Gerold v BUCH V TENGIN, Hermann HIRSCHECK, Hermann v. HIRSCHECK D.Ä I, Adalbert v. WINTERTHUR V. KYBURG, Liutfried v. WINTERTHUR, Ulrich V v. BREGENZ, Keroldus, Ulrich V ?, Ulrich III, Ratbert, Ulrich I, Gerold d. Ä) was born ~1132. He died ~1167.

He had the following children:

     100   M   i.   **Rudolph II v. TENGEN** was born ~1165. He died 1235.

         Rudolph was employed Abbott 1198 - 1219 in Allerheiligen, Schaffhausen, Switzerland.

+   101   M   ii.   **Heinrich II v. TENGEN** was born ~1166 and died ~1238.

Fifteenth Generation

90. **Heinrich Habardus(?) HIRSCHECK DE SALENSTEIN** (Hermann HIRSCHECK D.J., Hermann HIRSCHECK D.Ä, Heinrich v HIRSCHECK D.Ä, Hermann HIRSCHECK, Hermann v. HIRSCHECK D.Ä I, Adalbert v. WINTERTHUR V. KYBURG, Liutfried v. WINTERTHUR, Ulrich V v. BREGENZ, Keroldus, Ulrich V ?, Ulrich III, Ratbert, Ulrich I, Gerold d. Ä) was born ~1105. He died ~1161.

He had the following children:

102   M   i.   **Albert v. SALENSTEIN** was born ~1160. He died ~1198.

103   M   ii.   **Eberhard v. SALENSTEIN** was born ~1160. He died ~1198.

104   M   iii.   **Heinrich v. SALENSTEIN** was born ~1160. He died ~1198.

94. **Burchard HOHENFELS** (Hermann HIRSCHECK D.J., Hermann HIRSCHECK D.Ä, Heinrich v HIRSCHECK D.Ä, Hermann HIRSCHECK, Hermann v. HIRSCHECK D.Ä I, Adalbert v. WINTERTHUR V. KYBURG, Liutfried v. WINTERTHUR, Ulrich V v. BREGENZ, Keroldus, Ulrich V ?, Ulrich III, Ratbert, Ulrich I, Gerold d. Ä) was born ~1104. He died ~1167?.

He had the following children:

+   105   M   i.   **Burchardus HOHENFELS** was born ~1161 and died ~1192.

96. **Hermann I. v STETTEN V. ESPASINGEN** (Hermann HIRSCHECK D.J., Hermann HIRSCHECK D.Ä, Heinrich v HIRSCHECK D.Ä, Hermann HIRSCHECK, Hermann v. HIRSCHECK D.Ä I, Adalbert v. WINTERTHUR V. KYBURG, Liutfried v. WINTERTHUR, Ulrich V v. BREGENZ, Keroldus, Ulrich V ?, Ulrich III, Ratbert, Ulrich I, Gerold d. Ä) was born ~1103. He died 1183.

Hermann resided 1158 in v. Stetten. He resided 1169 in v. Espansingen. He resided in v. Friedingen.

Hermann married **NN**.

They had the following children:

+   106   M   i.   **Heinrich I. von STETTEN** was born ~1138 and died May 1181.

107   M   ii.   **Herman II FRIDINGEN** was born ~1133 in Germany. He died 1192.

Herman resided 1181 in v. Friedingen. He was employed Imperial Bishop 1183 - 1189 in Constanz, Baden-Württemberg, Germany, Holy Roman Empire. He resided 1183 - 1191 in Lake Constanz, Germany.

108   F   iii.   **Ms HIRSCHECK**.

Ms married **Rudolph von GUTTINGEN**, son of Adelheid. Rudolph was born ~1154. He died ~1208.

109   M   iv.   **Arnold von STETTEN** was born ~1138. He died ~1159.

+   110   M   v.   **Eberhard von STETTEN V. BURGLEN** was born ~1139 and died ~1177.

111   M   vi.   **Gerold von STETTEN** was born ~1139. He died ~1176.

Gerold resided 1176 in v. Burglen.

+   112   M   vii.   **Berthold von STETTEN V. BÜRGLEN** was born ~1139 and died ~1209.

113   M   viii.   **Albert von STETTEN** was born ~1138. He died ~1159.

98.   **Hainricus MARKDORF** (Hermann von MARKDORF, Heinrich HIRSCHECK D.J. , Hermann HIRSCHECK, Hermann HIRSCHECK, Hermann v. HIRSCHECK D.Ä I, Adalbert v. WINTERTHUR V. KYBURG, Liutfried v. WINTERTHUR, Ulrich V v. BREGENZ, Keroldus, Ulrich V ?, Ulrich III, Ratbert, Ulrich I, Gerold d. Ä) was born ~1151. He died ~1187.

He had the following children:

114   M   i.   **Hermann MARKDORF** was born ~1168. He died ~1192 in Or ~1225.

+   115   M   ii.   **Conrad MARKDORF Sr** was born ~1185 and died ~1228.

99.   **Wezilo de EIGISTEGIN** (Heinrich EICHSTEGEN, Konrad EICHSTEGEN, Hermann HIRSCHECK, Hermann HIRSCHECK, Hermann v. HIRSCHECK D.Ä I, Adalbert v. WINTERTHUR V. KYBURG, Liutfried v. WINTERTHUR, Ulrich V v. BREGENZ, Keroldus, Ulrich V ?, Ulrich III, Ratbert, Ulrich I, Gerold d. Ä) died ~1182.

He had the following children:

116   M   i.   **Dieto de EIGISTEGIN** died ~1221.

101.   **Heinrich II v. TENGEN** (Heinricus? TENGEN, Rudolph TENGEN, Gerold v BUCH V TENGIN, Hermann HIRSCHECK, Hermann v. HIRSCHECK D.Ä I, Adalbert v. WINTERTHUR V. KYBURG, Liutfried v. WINTERTHUR, Ulrich V v. BREGENZ, Keroldus, Ulrich V ?, Ulrich III, Ratbert, Ulrich I, Gerold d. Ä) was born ~1166. He died ~1238.

He had the following children:

+   117   M   i.   **Konrad I v. TENGEN** was born ~1212 and died 1275.

118   M   ii.   **Reinhard TENGEN** was born ~1191. He died ~1240.

Reinhard was employed Dompropst 1211 - 1240 in Strassburg.

119   M   iii.   **Heinrich III v. TENGEN** was born ~1217. He died ~1250.

120   M   iv.   **Bertholdus TENGEN** was born ~1208. He died ~1229.

Bertholdus was employed Domherr v. Konstanz 1228 in Konventual v.St. Gallen.

Sixteenth Generation

105.   **Burchardus HOHENFELS** (Burchard HOHENFELS, Hermann HIRSCHECK D.J., Hermann HIRSCHECK D.Ä, Heinrich v HIRSCHECK D.Ä, Hermann HIRSCHECK, Hermann v. HIRSCHECK D.Ä I, Adalbert v. WINTERTHUR V. KYBURG, Liutfried v. WINTERTHUR, Ulrich V v. BREGENZ, Keroldus, Ulrich V ?, Ulrich III, Ratbert, Ulrich I, Gerold d. Ä) was born ~1161. He died ~1192.

He had the following children:

+   121   M   i.   **Chv°nradus de HÔHENVELS** was born ~1185 and died ~1216.

106.   **Heinrich I. von STETTEN** (Hermann I. v STETTEN V. ESPASINGEN, Hermann HIRSCHECK D.J., Hermann HIRSCHECK D.Ä, Heinrich v HIRSCHECK D.Ä, Hermann HIRSCHECK, Hermann v. HIRSCHECK D.Ä I, Adalbert v. WINTERTHUR V. KYBURG, Liutfried v. WINTERTHUR, Ulrich V v. BREGENZ, Keroldus, Ulrich V ?, Ulrich III, Ratbert, Ulrich I, Gerold d. Ä) was born ~1138. He died May 1181 in After May 1181.

Heinrich resided 1158 in v. Stetten. He resided 1170 - 1180 in Burg Friedingen.

He had the following children:

+   122   M   i.   **Heinrich II. von KRAHEN** was born ~1170 and died ~1230.

+   123   M   ii.   **Hermann III. von KRAHEN** was born ~1171 and died ~1194.

+   124   M   iii.   **Rudolf I. von FRIDINGEN** was born ~1164 and died ~1258.

      125   M   iv.   **Ulrich von FRIDINGEN** was born ~1172. He died ~1202.

> Ulrich was employed Propst Bueron 1192 - 1202 in v. Friedingen.

110.   **Eberhard von STETTEN V. BURGLEN** (Hermann I. v STETTEN V. ESPASINGEN, Hermann HIRSCHECK D.J., Hermann HIRSCHECK D.Ä, Heinrich v HIRSCHECK D.Ä, Hermann HIRSCHECK, Hermann v. HIRSCHECK D.Ä I, Adalbert v. WINTERTHUR V. KYBURG, Liutfried v. WINTERTHUR, Ulrich V v. BREGENZ, Keroldus, Ulrich V ?, Ulrich III, Ratbert, Ulrich I, Gerold d. Ä) was born ~1139. He died ~1177.

He had the following children:

      126   M   i.   **Eberhard v. BURGLEN** was born ~1161. He died ~1182.

112.   **Berthold von STETTEN V. BÜRGLEN** (Hermann I. v STETTEN V. ESPASINGEN, Hermann HIRSCHECK D.J., Hermann HIRSCHECK D.Ä, Heinrich v HIRSCHECK D.Ä, Hermann HIRSCHECK, Hermann v. HIRSCHECK D.Ä I, Adalbert v. WINTERTHUR V. KYBURG, Liutfried v. WINTERTHUR, Ulrich V v. BREGENZ, Keroldus, Ulrich V ?, Ulrich III, Ratbert, Ulrich I, Gerold d. Ä) was born ~1139. He died ~1209.

He had the following children:

+   127   M   i.   **Berchtold BÜRGLEN** was born ~1179 and died ~1245.

115.   **Conrad MARKDORF Sr** (Hainricus MARKDORF, Hermann von MARKDORF, Heinrich HIRSCHECK D.J. , Hermann HIRSCHECK, Hermann HIRSCHECK, Hermann v. HIRSCHECK D.Ä I, Adalbert v. WINTERTHUR V. KYBURG, Liutfried v. WINTERTHUR, Ulrich V v. BREGENZ, Keroldus, Ulrich V ?, Ulrich III, Ratbert, Ulrich I, Gerold d. Ä) was born ~1185. He died ~1228.

He had the following children:

      128   M   i.   **Hainrico camerario de MARKDORF** was born ~1224. He died ~1251.

      129   M   ii.   **Oswaldus de MARKDORF** was born ~1225. He died ~1256.

117.   **Konrad I v. TENGEN** (Heinrich II v. TENGEN, Heinricus? TENGEN, Rudolph TENGEN, Gerold v BUCH V TENGIN, Hermann HIRSCHECK, Hermann v. HIRSCHECK D.Ä I, Adalbert v. WINTERTHUR V. KYBURG, Liutfried v. WINTERTHUR, Ulrich V v. BREGENZ, Keroldus, Ulrich V ?, Ulrich III, Ratbert, Ulrich I, Gerold d. Ä) was born ~1212. He died 1275.

Konrad married **Adelheide**. Adelheide died 1264.

They had the following children:

+   130   M   i.   **Konrad TENGEN** died 1318.

      131   M   ii.   **Heinrich TENGEN** was born ~1245. He died ~1291.

Seventeenth Generation

121.   **Chv°nradus de HÔHENVELS** (Burchardus HOHENFELS, Burchard HOHENFELS, Hermann HIRSCHECK D.J., Hermann HIRSCHECK D.Ä, Heinrich v HIRSCHECK D.Ä, Hermann HIRSCHECK, Hermann v. HIRSCHECK D.Ä I, Adalbert v. WINTERTHUR V. KYBURG, Liutfried

v. WINTERTHUR, Ulrich V v. BREGENZ, Keroldus, Ulrich V ?, Ulrich III, Ratbert, Ulrich I, Gerold d. Ä) was born ~1185. He died ~1216.

He had the following children:

+   132   M   i.   **Waltherus de HOHENVELSE** was born ~1206 and died ~1258.

      133   M   ii. **Burchardus HOHENVELSE** was born ~1206.

122.   **Heinrich II. von KRAHEN** "Heinricus" (Heinrich I. von STETTEN, Hermann I. v STETTEN V. ESPASINGEN, Hermann HIRSCHECK D.J., Hermann HIRSCHECK D.Ä, Heinrich v HIRSCHECK D.Ä, Hermann HIRSCHECK, Hermann v. HIRSCHECK D.Ä I, Adalbert v. WINTERTHUR V. KYBURG, Liutfried v. WINTERTHUR, Ulrich V v. BREGENZ, Keroldus, Ulrich V ?, Ulrich III, Ratbert, Ulrich I, Gerold d. Ä) was born ~1170 in Germany. He died ~1230.

Heinricus resided 1202 in Creagen, Hohenkrahen, Germany. He was employed Advocate 1215 in Shina/Sienne, Germany.

Heinricus married **KRENKINGEN**, daughter of KRENKINGEN.

They had the following children:

      134   M   i.   **Diethelm de von KRAHEN** was born ~1172 in Germany. He died Sep 1228.

                       Diethelm was employed Bishop listed under Krenkingen 15 Jul 1190 - 1206 in Konstanz, Germany.

                       Diethelm married **Adelheid / Adelhaide**.

      135   M   ii. **Liutfrid von KRAHEN** was born ~1180. He died ~1272.

                       Liutfrid was employed Monch=Monk 1208 - 1228 in St. Gallen, Switzerland. He was employed Dekan/Dean in St. Gallen, Switzerland.

      136   iii. **A von "Adilheid " KRAHEN** "Adelbert? or Adilheid?" was born ~1188. Adelbert? or Adilheid? died ~1208.

      137   F   iv. **Judenta von KRAHEN** died ~1283.

                       Judenta married **Abtissin LINDAU**.

123.   **Hermann III. von KRAHEN** (Heinrich I. von STETTEN, Hermann I. v STETTEN V. ESPASINGEN, Hermann HIRSCHECK D.J., Hermann HIRSCHECK D.Ä, Heinrich v HIRSCHECK D.Ä, Hermann HIRSCHECK, Hermann v. HIRSCHECK D.Ä I, Adalbert v. WINTERTHUR V. KYBURG, Liutfried v. WINTERTHUR, Ulrich V v. BREGENZ, Keroldus, Ulrich V ?, Ulrich III, Ratbert, Ulrich I, Gerold d. Ä) was born ~1171. He died ~1194.

He had the following children:

+   138   M   i.   **Bertold von KRAHEN** was born ~1185 and died ~1248.

124.   **Rudolf I. von FRIDINGEN** "Rudolpho" (Heinrich I. von STETTEN, Hermann I. v STETTEN V. ESPASINGEN, Hermann HIRSCHECK D.J., Hermann HIRSCHECK D.Ä, Heinrich v HIRSCHECK D.Ä, Hermann HIRSCHECK, Hermann v. HIRSCHECK D.Ä I, Adalbert v. WINTERTHUR V. KYBURG, Liutfried v. WINTERTHUR, Ulrich V v. BREGENZ, Keroldus, Ulrich V ?, Ulrich III, Ratbert, Ulrich I, Gerold d. Ä) was born ~1164 in Fridingen, Germany. He died ~1258.

Rudolpho resided 1194 in Kloster Salem, Germany.

He had the following children:

+   139   M   i.   **Heinrich III. von FRIDINGEN** was born ~1180 and died ~1251?.

140 M ii. **Hermann IV. FRIDINGEN** was born ~1179. He died ~1226.

+ 141 M iii. **Konrad Furst I v. HIRSCHECK V KONZENBURG** was born ~1192 and died ~1239.

127. **Berchtold BÜRGLEN** (Berthold von STETTEN V. BÜRGLEN, Hermann I. v STETTEN V. ESPASINGEN, Hermann HIRSCHECK D.J., Hermann HIRSCHECK D.Ä, Heinrich v HIRSCHECK D.Ä, Hermann HIRSCHECK, Hermann v. HIRSCHECK D.Ä I, Adalbert v. WINTERTHUR V. KYBURG, Liutfried v. WINTERTHUR, Ulrich V v. BREGENZ, Keroldus, Ulrich V ?, Ulrich III, Ratbert, Ulrich I, Gerold d. Ä) was born ~1179. He died ~1245.

He had the following children:

+ 142 M i. **Heinrich BÜRGLEN** was born ~1222 and died ~1271.

143 M ii. **Arnold BÜRGLEN** was born ~1220. He died ~1250.

Arnold was employed Dompropst 1240 - 1249 in Strassburg.

130. **Konrad TENGEN** (Konrad I v. TENGEN, Heinrich II v. TENGEN, Heinricus? TENGEN, Rudolph TENGEN, Gerold v BUCH V TENGIN, Hermann HIRSCHECK, Hermann v. HIRSCHECK D.Ä I, Adalbert v. WINTERTHUR V. KYBURG, Liutfried v. WINTERTHUR, Ulrich V v. BREGENZ, Keroldus, Ulrich V ?, Ulrich III, Ratbert, Ulrich I, Gerold d. Ä) died 1318.

He had the following children:

144 M i. **Konrad TENGEN** died 1321.

Eighteenth Generation

132. **Waltherus de HOHENVELSE** (Chv°nradus de HÔHENVELS, Burchardus HOHENFELS, Burchard HOHENFELS, Hermann HIRSCHECK D.J., Hermann HIRSCHECK D.Ä, Heinrich v HIRSCHECK D.Ä, Hermann HIRSCHECK, Hermann v. HIRSCHECK D.Ä I, Adalbert v. WINTERTHUR V. KYBURG, Liutfried v. WINTERTHUR, Ulrich V v. BREGENZ, Keroldus, Ulrich V ?, Ulrich III, Ratbert, Ulrich I, Gerold d. Ä) was born ~1206. He died ~1258.

Waltherus married **BONLANDEN**, daughter of BONLANDEN.

They had the following children:

+ 145 M i. **Göswin v HOHENFELS** was born ~1221 and died ~1292.

146 M ii. **Bertholdus HOHENFELS** was born ~1239. He died ~1280.

147 M iii. **Heinrich de HÖHENVELS** was born ~1226. He died ~1246.

138. **Bertold von KRAHEN** (Hermann III. von KRAHEN, Heinrich I. von STETTEN, Hermann I. v STETTEN V. ESPASINGEN, Hermann HIRSCHECK D.J., Hermann HIRSCHECK D.Ä, Heinrich v HIRSCHECK D.Ä, Hermann HIRSCHECK, Hermann v. HIRSCHECK D.Ä I, Adalbert v. WINTERTHUR V. KYBURG, Liutfried v. WINTERTHUR, Ulrich V v. BREGENZ, Keroldus, Ulrich V ?, Ulrich III, Ratbert, Ulrich I, Gerold d. Ä) was born ~1185. He died ~1248.

Bertold married **Ita Schenk von CASTELL**.

They had the following children:

+ 148 M i. **Johannes I.von KRAHEN/CRAGIN** was born ~1217 and died 1256.

139. **Heinrich III. von FRIDINGEN** (Rudolf I. von FRIDINGEN, Heinrich I. von STETTEN, Hermann I. v STETTEN V. ESPASINGEN, Hermann HIRSCHECK D.J., Hermann HIRSCHECK D.Ä, Heinrich v HIRSCHECK D.Ä, Hermann HIRSCHECK, Hermann v. HIRSCHECK D.Ä I,

Adalbert v. WINTERTHUR V. KYBURG, Liutfried v. WINTERTHUR, Ulrich V v. BREGENZ, Keroldus, Ulrich V ?, Ulrich III, Ratbert, Ulrich I, Gerold d. Ä) was born ~1180. He died ~1251?.

Heinrich was employed Vogt 1201 in Radolfzell, Germany. He was employed Vogt 1240 in Krahen, Germany.

Heinrich married **WARTENBERG?**.

They had the following children:

+ 149 M i. **Heinrich IV von FRIDINGEN** was born ~1213 and died ~1271?.

+ 150 M ii. **Konrad I von FRIDINGEN** was born ~1214 and died May 1261.

    151 M iii. **Rudolf II von FRIDINGEN** was born ~1218. He died ~1259.

               Rudolf was employed Monch=Monk 1258 in Salem Monastery, Germany.

141. **Konrad Furst I v. HIRSCHECK V KONZENBURG** (Rudolf I. von FRIDINGEN, Heinrich I. von STETTEN, Hermann I. v STETTEN V. ESPASINGEN, Hermann HIRSCHECK D.J., Hermann HIRSCHECK D.Ä, Heinrich v HIRSCHECK D.Ä, Hermann HIRSCHECK, Hermann v. HIRSCHECK D.Ä I, Adalbert v. WINTERTHUR V. KYBURG, Liutfried v. WINTERTHUR, Ulrich V v. BREGENZ, Keroldus, Ulrich V ?, Ulrich III, Ratbert, Ulrich I, Gerold d. Ä) was born ~1192. He died ~1239 in Konzenburg, Germany.

Konrad married **Adelhildis v. WARTENBURG**, daughter of Conrad WARTENBURG D.A and Agnes von FLAMBORN?. Adelhildis was born ~1194.

They had the following children:

+ 152 M i. **Konrad II v. HIRSCHECK V WILDENSTAIN** was born ~1228 and died ~1277.

    153 M ii. **Heinrich v. HIRSCHECK V WILDENSTAIN** was born ~1229. He died ~1269.

               Heinrich resided 1262 in Wildenstain. He resided 1268 in Esslingen, Germany.

               Heinrich married **GUNDELFINGEN?**.

    154 M iii. **Friedrich v. HIRSCHECK V WILDENSTAIN** was born ~1227. He died ~1263.

               Friedrich resided 1245 - 1262 in Wildenstain.

               Friedrich married **GUNDELFINGEN?**.

    155 M iv. **R "Rudolph?" v. WILDENSTEIN** was born ~1230. He died ~1273.

142. **Heinrich BÜRGLEN** (Berchtold BÜRGLEN, Berthold von STETTEN V. BÜRGLEN, Hermann I. v STETTEN V. ESPASINGEN, Hermann HIRSCHECK D.J., Hermann HIRSCHECK D.Ä, Heinrich v HIRSCHECK D.Ä, Hermann HIRSCHECK, Hermann v. HIRSCHECK D.Ä I, Adalbert v. WINTERTHUR V. KYBURG, Liutfried v. WINTERTHUR, Ulrich V v. BREGENZ, Keroldus, Ulrich V ?, Ulrich III, Ratbert, Ulrich I, Gerold d. Ä) was born ~1222. He died ~1271.

He had the following children:

    156 M i. **Arnold BÜRGLEN II** was born ~1232. He died ~1285.

+ 157 M ii. **Eberhard BÜRGLEN** was born ~1237 and died ~1285.

Nineteenth Generation

145.   **Göswin v HOHENFELS** (Waltherus de HOHENVELSE, Chv°nradus de HÔHENVELS, Burchardus HOHENFELS, Burchard HOHENFELS, Hermann HIRSCHECK D.J., Hermann HIRSCHECK D.Ä, Heinrich v HIRSCHECK D.Ä, Hermann HIRSCHECK, Hermann v. HIRSCHECK D.Ä I, Adalbert v. WINTERTHUR V. KYBURG, Liutfried v. WINTERTHUR, Ulrich V v. BREGENZ, Keroldus, Ulrich V ?, Ulrich III, Ratbert, Ulrich I, Gerold d. Ä) was born ~1221. He died ~1292.

Göswin married **Judenta**.

They had the following children:

    158   F   i.   **Adelheid HOHENFELS** died ~1333.

                   Adelheid married **Konrads v RAMSCHWAG**.

148.   **Johannes I.von KRAHEN/CRAGIN** (Bertold von KRAHEN, Hermann III. von KRAHEN, Heinrich I. von STETTEN, Hermann I. v STETTEN V. ESPASINGEN, Hermann HIRSCHECK D.J., Hermann HIRSCHECK D.Ä, Heinrich v HIRSCHECK D.Ä, Hermann HIRSCHECK, Hermann v. HIRSCHECK D.Ä I, Adalbert v. WINTERTHUR V. KYBURG, Liutfried v. WINTERTHUR, Ulrich V v. BREGENZ, Keroldus, Ulrich V ?, Ulrich III, Ratbert, Ulrich I, Gerold d. Ä) was born ~1217. He died 1256.

He had the following children:

+   159   M   i.   **Johannes II. von ESPASINGEN** was born ~1233 and died ~1270.

    160   M   ii.   **Bertold II. von KRAHEN** died 1266?.

149.   **Heinrich IV von FRIDINGEN** (Heinrich III. von FRIDINGEN, Rudolf I. von FRIDINGEN, Heinrich I. von STETTEN, Hermann I. v STETTEN V. ESPASINGEN, Hermann HIRSCHECK D.J., Hermann HIRSCHECK D.Ä, Heinrich v HIRSCHECK D.Ä, Hermann HIRSCHECK, Hermann v. HIRSCHECK D.Ä I, Adalbert v. WINTERTHUR V. KYBURG, Liutfried v. WINTERTHUR, Ulrich V v. BREGENZ, Keroldus, Ulrich V ?, Ulrich III, Ratbert, Ulrich I, Gerold d. Ä) was born ~1213. He died ~1271?.

Heinrich married **BODMAN?**.

They had the following children:

+   161   M   i.   **Heinrich V. von FRIDINGEN** was born ~1243 and died ~1281.

+   162   M   ii.   **Rudolf III. von FRIDINGEN** was born ~1247 and died ~1299.

+   163   M   iii.   **Konrad II. von FRIDINGEN** was born ~1241 and died ~1281.

150.   **Konrad I von FRIDINGEN** (Heinrich III. von FRIDINGEN, Rudolf I. von FRIDINGEN, Heinrich I. von STETTEN, Hermann I. v STETTEN V. ESPASINGEN, Hermann HIRSCHECK D.J., Hermann HIRSCHECK D.Ä, Heinrich v HIRSCHECK D.Ä, Hermann HIRSCHECK, Hermann v. HIRSCHECK D.Ä I, Adalbert v. WINTERTHUR V. KYBURG, Liutfried v. WINTERTHUR, Ulrich V v. BREGENZ, Keroldus, Ulrich V ?, Ulrich III, Ratbert, Ulrich I, Gerold d. Ä) was born ~1214. He died May 1261.

Konrad resided 1268 in Hohentengen, Germany.

Konrad married **Ita KLINGEN**, daughter of Ulrich KLINGEN and Ita von TEGERFELDEN. Ita was born ~1239. She died ~1262.

They had the following children:

    164   M   i.   **Heinrich WILDENVELS** died ~1254.

    165   M   ii.   **Walthero WILDENFELS** died ~1254.

166 M iii. **Arnold WILDENFELS** was born ~1248. He died ~1268.

152. **Konrad II v. HIRSCHECK V WILDENSTAIN** (Konrad Furst I v. HIRSCHECK V KONZENBURG, Rudolf I. von FRIDINGEN, Heinrich I. von STETTEN, Hermann I. v STETTEN V. ESPASINGEN, Hermann HIRSCHECK D.J., Hermann HIRSCHECK D.Ä, Heinrich v HIRSCHECK D.Ä, Hermann HIRSCHECK, Hermann v. HIRSCHECK D.Ä I, Adalbert v. WINTERTHUR V. KYBURG, Liutfried v. WINTERTHUR, Ulrich V v. BREGENZ, Keroldus, Ulrich V ?, Ulrich III, Ratbert, Ulrich I, Gerold d. Ä) was born ~1228. He died ~1277.

Konrad resided 1262 in Wildenstain.

He had the following children:

167 M i. **Konrad III v. HIRSCHECK V KONZENBURG** was born ~1257. He died ~1345.

168 M ii. **Berthold HIRSCHECK V WILDENSTAIN** was born ~1258. He died ~1290.

169 F iii. **Margarete HIRSCHECK**.

Margarete was employed Priorin @ Dominikanerinnenklosters St. Maria in Gnadenzell (bei Gomadingen).

170 M iv. **Hermann v. FURST V KONZENBURG**.

171 M v. **Heinrich HIRSCHECK** was born ~1260. He died ~1339.

Heinrich resided 1289 - 1292 in Westendorf. He was employed Kaufmann 1338 in Salmanswiler.

157. **Eberhard BÜRGLEN** (Heinrich BÜRGLEN, Berchtold BÜRGLEN, Berthold von STETTEN V. BÜRGLEN, Hermann I. v STETTEN V. ESPASINGEN, Hermann HIRSCHECK D.J., Hermann HIRSCHECK D.Ä, Heinrich v HIRSCHECK D.Ä, Hermann HIRSCHECK, Hermann v. HIRSCHECK D.Ä I, Adalbert v. WINTERTHUR V. KYBURG, Liutfried v. WINTERTHUR, Ulrich V v. BREGENZ, Keroldus, Ulrich V ?, Ulrich III, Ratbert, Ulrich I, Gerold d. Ä) was born ~1237. He died ~1285 in Frauenfeld, Thurgau, Switzerland.

He had the following children:

+ 172 M i. **Eberhard BÜRGLEN** was born ~1265.

Twentieth Generation

159. **Johannes II. von ESPASINGEN** (Johannes I.von KRAHEN/CRAGIN, Bertold von KRAHEN, Hermann III. von KRAHEN, Heinrich I. von STETTEN, Hermann I. v STETTEN V. ESPASINGEN, Hermann HIRSCHECK D.J., Hermann HIRSCHECK D.Ä, Heinrich v HIRSCHECK D.Ä, Hermann HIRSCHECK, Hermann v. HIRSCHECK D.Ä I, Adalbert v. WINTERTHUR V. KYBURG, Liutfried v. WINTERTHUR, Ulrich V v. BREGENZ, Keroldus, Ulrich V ?, Ulrich III, Ratbert, Ulrich I, Gerold d. Ä) was born ~1233. He died ~1270.

Johannes resided 1263 in v. Espasingen. He resided 1266 - 1270 in v. Schwandorf.

He had the following children:

173 M i. **Heinrich von ESPASINGEN** was born ~1236. He died Apr 1273.

Heinrich resided 1273 in v .Espasingen.

+ 174 M ii. **Johannes III.von ESPASINGEN** was born ~1236 and died ~1273.

The Swabian Connection – Expanded Edition

161.   **Heinrich V. von FRIDINGEN** (Heinrich IV von FRIDINGEN, Heinrich III. von FRIDINGEN, Rudolf I. von FRIDINGEN, Heinrich I. von STETTEN, Hermann I. v STETTEN V. ESPASINGEN, Hermann HIRSCHECK D.J., Hermann HIRSCHECK D.Ä, Heinrich v HIRSCHECK D.Ä, Hermann HIRSCHECK, Hermann v. HIRSCHECK D.Ä I, Adalbert v. WINTERTHUR V. KYBURG, Liutfried v. WINTERTHUR, Ulrich V v. BREGENZ, Keroldus, Ulrich V ?, Ulrich III, Ratbert, Ulrich I, Gerold d. Ä) was born ~1243 in Germany. He died ~1281.

Heinrich was employed Vogt 1273 - & 1288 in Friedingen. He was employed Vogt 1280 in Krahen, Germany.

He had the following children:

+   175   M   i.   **Heinrich VI. der CRAIGER** was born ~1260 and died ~1297.

      176   M   ii.   **Rudolf IV. der FRIDINGER** was born ~1270. He died ~1289.

162.   **Rudolf III. von FRIDINGEN** (Heinrich IV von FRIDINGEN, Heinrich III. von FRIDINGEN, Rudolf I. von FRIDINGEN, Heinrich I. von STETTEN, Hermann I. v STETTEN V. ESPASINGEN, Hermann HIRSCHECK D.J., Hermann HIRSCHECK D.Ä, Heinrich v HIRSCHECK D.Ä, Hermann HIRSCHECK, Hermann v. HIRSCHECK D.Ä I, Adalbert v. WINTERTHUR V. KYBURG, Liutfried v. WINTERTHUR, Ulrich V v. BREGENZ, Keroldus, Ulrich V ?, Ulrich III, Ratbert, Ulrich I, Gerold d. Ä) was born ~1247. He died ~1299.

Rudolf resided 1267 in v. Krahen. He was employed Vogt 1275 & - 1298 in Freidigen, Germany. He was employed Hapburgish Burgvasall Bussen 1291 in Bussen, Germany.

He had the following children:

+   177   M   i.   **Heinrich VII. FRIDINGEN** was born ~1275 and died 1321.

163.   **Konrad II. von FRIDINGEN** (Heinrich IV von FRIDINGEN, Heinrich III. von FRIDINGEN, Rudolf I. von FRIDINGEN, Heinrich I. von STETTEN, Hermann I. v STETTEN V. ESPASINGEN, Hermann HIRSCHECK D.J., Hermann HIRSCHECK D.Ä, Heinrich v HIRSCHECK D.Ä, Hermann HIRSCHECK, Hermann v. HIRSCHECK D.Ä I, Adalbert v. WINTERTHUR V. KYBURG, Liutfried v. WINTERTHUR, Ulrich V v. BREGENZ, Keroldus, Ulrich V ?, Ulrich III, Ratbert, Ulrich I, Gerold d. Ä) was born ~1241. He died ~1281.

Konrad was employed Vogt 1271 in Friedingen, Germany. He was employed Vogt 1280 in Krahen, Germany.

He had the following children:

+   178   M   i.   **Burkhard I. FRIDINGEN** was born ~1255 and died ~1310.

172.   **Eberhard BÜRGLEN** (Eberhard BÜRGLEN, Heinrich BÜRGLEN, Berchtold BÜRGLEN, Berthold von STETTEN V. BÜRGLEN, Hermann I. v STETTEN V. ESPASINGEN, Hermann HIRSCHECK D.J., Hermann HIRSCHECK D.Ä, Heinrich v HIRSCHECK D.Ä, Hermann HIRSCHECK, Hermann v. HIRSCHECK D.Ä I, Adalbert v. WINTERTHUR V. KYBURG, Liutfried v. WINTERTHUR, Ulrich V v. BREGENZ, Keroldus, Ulrich V ?, Ulrich III, Ratbert, Ulrich I, Gerold d. Ä) was born ~1265.

He had the following children:

      179   M   i.   **Arnold BÜRGLEN III** was born ~1285. He died ~1324.

      180   M   ii.   **Ulrich BÜRGLEN** was born ~1290. He died ~1338.

      181   M   iii.   **Eberhard BÜRGLEN**.

Twenty-First Generation

174.   **Johannes III.von ESPASINGEN** (Johannes II. von ESPASINGEN, Johannes I.von KRAHEN/CRAGIN, Bertold von KRAHEN, Hermann III. von KRAHEN, Heinrich I. von STETTEN, Hermann I. v STETTEN V. ESPASINGEN, Hermann HIRSCHECK D.J., Hermann HIRSCHECK D.Ä, Heinrich v HIRSCHECK D.Ä, Hermann HIRSCHECK, Hermann v. HIRSCHECK D.Ä I, Adalbert v. WINTERTHUR V. KYBURG, Liutfried v. WINTERTHUR, Ulrich V v. BREGENZ, Keroldus, Ulrich V ?, Ulrich III, Ratbert, Ulrich I, Gerold d. Ä) was born ~1236. He died ~1273.

Johannes resided 1273 in v .Espasingen.

He had the following children:

    182 M   i.   **Werner SCHWANDORF** was born ~1258. He died ~1288.

    183 M   ii. **Johannes IV. SCHWANDORF** was born ~1258. He died ~1288.

    184 M   iii. **Heinrich SCHWANDORF** was born ~1258. He died ~1288.

175.   **Heinrich VI. der CRAIGER** (Heinrich V. von FRIDINGEN, Heinrich IV von FRIDINGEN, Heinrich III. von FRIDINGEN, Rudolf I. von FRIDINGEN, Heinrich I. von STETTEN, Hermann I. v STETTEN V. ESPASINGEN, Hermann HIRSCHECK D.J., Hermann HIRSCHECK D.Ä, Heinrich v HIRSCHECK D.Ä, Hermann HIRSCHECK, Hermann v. HIRSCHECK D.Ä I, Adalbert v. WINTERTHUR V. KYBURG, Liutfried v. WINTERTHUR, Ulrich V v. BREGENZ, Keroldus, Ulrich V ?, Ulrich III, Ratbert, Ulrich I, Gerold d. Ä) was born ~1260. He died ~1297.

Heinrich resided 1280 in der Crager. He was employed Vogt 1296 in Friedingen, Germany.

He had the following children:

    185 M   i.   **Gotfried von KRAHEN** was born ~1277. He died ~1307.

                   Gotfried married **Katherina von BODMAN**. Katherina died 1307.

    186 F   ii. **Agnes von KRAHEN** was born ~1280. She died 1323.

                   Agnes married **Jakob MARSCHALK**.

177.   **Heinrich VII. FRIDINGEN** (Rudolf III. von FRIDINGEN, Heinrich IV von FRIDINGEN, Heinrich III. von FRIDINGEN, Rudolf I. von FRIDINGEN, Heinrich I. von STETTEN, Hermann I. v STETTEN V. ESPASINGEN, Hermann HIRSCHECK D.J., Hermann HIRSCHECK D.Ä, Heinrich v HIRSCHECK D.Ä, Hermann HIRSCHECK, Hermann v. HIRSCHECK D.Ä I, Adalbert v. WINTERTHUR V. KYBURG, Liutfried v. WINTERTHUR, Ulrich V v. BREGENZ, Keroldus, Ulrich V ?, Ulrich III, Ratbert, Ulrich I, Gerold d. Ä) was born ~1275. He died 1321.

Heinrich married **N von. HOMBURG?**.

They had the following children:

+   187 M   i.   **Heinrich VIII FRIDINGEN** was born ~1306 and died ~1347.

+   188 M   ii. **Rudolf V. der Jung? FRIDINGEN** was born ~1294 and died 1352.

+   189 F   iii. **Anna FRIDINGEN** was born ~1301 and died ~1349.

+   190 M   iv. **Ulrich FREIDIG** was born ~1304 and died ~1356.

178.   **Burkhard I. FRIDINGEN** (Konrad II. von FRIDINGEN, Heinrich IV von FRIDINGEN, Heinrich III. von FRIDINGEN, Rudolf I. von FRIDINGEN, Heinrich I. von STETTEN, Hermann I. v STETTEN V. ESPASINGEN, Hermann HIRSCHECK D.J., Hermann HIRSCHECK D.Ä, Heinrich v HIRSCHECK D.Ä, Hermann HIRSCHECK, Hermann v. HIRSCHECK D.Ä I, Adalbert v. WINTERTHUR V. KYBURG, Liutfried v. WINTERTHUR, Ulrich V v. BREGENZ, Keroldus, Ulrich V ?, Ulrich III, Ratbert, Ulrich I, Gerold d. Ä) was born ~1255. He died ~1310.

He had the following children:

| 191 | M | i. | **Burkhard II. FRIDINGEN** was born ~1288. He died ~2-1330. |

Burkhard was employed Domherr 1318 - 1330 in Konstanz, Germany.

| + | 192 | M | ii. | **Johann Hans I. von FRIDINGEN DER KRAYGER** was born ~1290 and died ~1335. |

Twenty-Second Generation

187. **Heinrich VIII FRIDINGEN** (Heinrich VII. FRIDINGEN, Rudolf III. von FRIDINGEN, Heinrich IV von FRIDINGEN, Heinrich III. von FRIDINGEN, Rudolf I. von FRIDINGEN, Heinrich I. von STETTEN, Hermann I. v STETTEN V. ESPASINGEN, Hermann HIRSCHECK D.J., Hermann HIRSCHECK D.Ä, Heinrich v HIRSCHECK D.Ä, Hermann HIRSCHECK, Hermann v. HIRSCHECK D.Ä I, Adalbert v. WINTERTHUR V. KYBURG, Liutfried v. WINTERTHUR, Ulrich V v. BREGENZ, Keroldus, Ulrich V ?, Ulrich III, Ratbert, Ulrich I, Gerold d. Ä) was born ~1306. He died ~1347.

Heinrich was employed wirter=farmer 1346. He resided 1346 in Weinzinsen.

Heinrich married **Ursula**. Ursula died 1346.

They had the following children:

| 193 | F | i. | **Ursula FRIDINGEN** died ~1395. |

Ursula was employed Nonne=Nun in Feldbach. She was employed Nonne(Nun) 1395 in St. Agnes, Schaufhausen, Switzerland.

+	194	F	ii.	**Margaret FRIDINGEN** was born ~1328 and died Mar 1371.
+	195	M	iii.	**Heinrich IX. FRIDINGEN** was born ~1330 and died Apr 1395.
+	196	M	iv.	**Ulrich #? FRIDINGEN**.

188. **Rudolf V. der Jung? FRIDINGEN** (Heinrich VII. FRIDINGEN, Rudolf III. von FRIDINGEN, Heinrich IV von FRIDINGEN, Heinrich III. von FRIDINGEN, Rudolf I. von FRIDINGEN, Heinrich I. von STETTEN, Hermann I. v STETTEN V. ESPASINGEN, Hermann HIRSCHECK D.J., Hermann HIRSCHECK D.Ä, Heinrich v HIRSCHECK D.Ä, Hermann HIRSCHECK, Hermann v. HIRSCHECK D.Ä I, Adalbert v. WINTERTHUR V. KYBURG, Liutfried v. WINTERTHUR, Ulrich V v. BREGENZ, Keroldus, Ulrich V ?, Ulrich III, Ratbert, Ulrich I, Gerold d. Ä) was born ~1294. He died 1352.

Rudolf married **N vom STEIN?**, daughter of Berthtold von STEIN.

They had the following children:

| 197 | M | i. | **Elisabeth FRIDINGEN** was born ~1314. He died ~1345. |

Elisabeth was employed Nonne=Nun 1344 in Feldbach.

Elisabeth married **FELDBACH**.

+	198	M	ii.	**Rudolf VI. FRIDINGEN** was born ~1320 and died ~1404?.
+	199	M	iii.	**Heinrich X. FRIDINGEN** was born ~1322 and died ~1396/1408.
	200	M	iv.	**Hans # FRIDINGEN** died ~1417.
	201	M	v.	**Ulrich # FRIDINGEN** died ~1417.

189. **Anna FRIDINGEN** (Heinrich VII. FRIDINGEN, Rudolf III. von FRIDINGEN, Heinrich IV von FRIDINGEN, Heinrich III. von FRIDINGEN, Rudolf I. von FRIDINGEN, Heinrich I. von

STETTEN, Hermann I. v STETTEN V. ESPASINGEN, Hermann HIRSCHECK D.J., Hermann HIRSCHECK D.Ä, Heinrich v HIRSCHECK D.Ä, Hermann HIRSCHECK, Hermann v. HIRSCHECK D.Ä I, Adalbert v. WINTERTHUR V. KYBURG, Liutfried v. WINTERTHUR, Ulrich V v. BREGENZ, Keroldus, Ulrich V ?, Ulrich III, Ratbert, Ulrich I, Gerold d. Ä) was born ~1301 in Zurich, Switzerland. She died ~1349 in After 1349.

Anna married **Gottfried MUELLNER** on 3 Aug 1336. Gottfried was born ~1299. He died 1337 in Before 1349.

They had the following children:

202	M	i.	**James MUELLNER.**
203	M	ii.	**Geoffrey MUELLNER.**
204	M	iii.	**Jakob MUELLNER.**

190.　**Ulrich FREIDIG** (Heinrich VII. FRIDINGEN, Rudolf III. von FRIDINGEN, Heinrich IV von FRIDINGEN, Heinrich III. von FRIDINGEN, Rudolf I. von FRIDINGEN, Heinrich I. von STETTEN, Hermann I. v STETTEN V. ESPASINGEN, Hermann HIRSCHECK D.J., Hermann HIRSCHECK D.Ä, Heinrich v HIRSCHECK D.Ä, Hermann HIRSCHECK, Hermann v. HIRSCHECK D.Ä I, Adalbert v. WINTERTHUR V. KYBURG, Liutfried v. WINTERTHUR, Ulrich V v. BREGENZ, Keroldus, Ulrich V ?, Ulrich III, Ratbert, Ulrich I, Gerold d. Ä) was born ~1304 in Germany. He died ~1356 in After 1356.

Ulrich resided 1323 in Berne, Switzerland. He resided 1340 - 1347 in Aarau, Switzerland. He was employed Mayor 1347 in Baden, Aargau, Switzerland. He was employed Imperial Bishop 1356 in Constanz, Baden-Württemberg, Germany, Holy Roman Empire.

Ulrich married (1) **Adelheid BLUMENBERG** on ~1347. Adelheid was born ~1305 in Germany OR Austria.

They had the following children:

205	F	i.	**Gertrude FREIDIG** was born ~1325.

　　　　　　　　　Gertrude 14 May 1341　Samnung (women religious organization).

Ulrich also married (2) **Ida or Ita** on ~1334. Ida was born ~1305.

They had the following children:

206	F	ii.	**Anna FREIDIGE** was born ~1320. She died ~1360?.

　　　　　　　　　Anna 6 Jul 1334　Samnung (women religious organization), Argau, Switzerland.

207	F	iii.	**Margaret FREIDIG** was born ~1322.

192.　**Johann Hans I. von FRIDINGEN DER KRAYGER** "Hans" (Burkhard I. FRIDINGEN, Konrad II. von FRIDINGEN, Heinrich IV von FRIDINGEN, Heinrich III. von FRIDINGEN, Rudolf I. von FRIDINGEN, Heinrich I. von STETTEN, Hermann I. v STETTEN V. ESPASINGEN, Hermann HIRSCHECK D.J., Hermann HIRSCHECK D.Ä, Heinrich v HIRSCHECK D.Ä, Hermann HIRSCHECK, Hermann v. HIRSCHECK D.Ä I, Adalbert v. WINTERTHUR V. KYBURG, Liutfried v. WINTERTHUR, Ulrich V v. BREGENZ, Keroldus, Ulrich V ?, Ulrich III, Ratbert, Ulrich I, Gerold d. Ä) was born ~1290. He died ~1335.

He had the following children:

208	M	i.	**Rudolf VII. FRIDINGEN/KRAHEN** "Johanniter" was born ~1303. He died ~1372.

　　　　　　　　　Johanniter was employed Comthur 21 Jan 1356 - 4 Feb 1371 in Tobel, Thurgau, Switzerland.

The Swabian Connection – Expanded Edition

Johanniter married **EPPENSTEIN?**.

209 M ii. **Peter I von FRIDINGEN** was born ~1308. He died ~1364.

Peter married **Elizabeth LOMMIS**, daughter of Eberhard von LOMMIS. Elizabeth was born ~1325.

+ 210 M iii. **Johann II d Altere FRIDINGEN** was born ~1302 and died ~1344.

211 M iv. **Ulrich II FRIDINGEN** was born ~1304. He died 1358.

Ulrich was employed Domherr 1336 - 1358 in Konstamz, Germany.

+ 212 M v. **Johann III FRIDINGEN D. JUNGERE** was born ~1311 and died 1350.

Twenty-Third Generation

194. **Margaret FRIDINGEN** (Heinrich VIII FRIDINGEN, Heinrich VII. FRIDINGEN, Rudolf III. von FRIDINGEN, Heinrich IV von FRIDINGEN, Heinrich III. von FRIDINGEN, Rudolf I. von FRIDINGEN, Heinrich I. von STETTEN, Hermann I. v STETTEN V. ESPASINGEN, Hermann HIRSCHECK D.J., Hermann HIRSCHECK D.Ä, Heinrich v HIRSCHECK D.Ä, Hermann HIRSCHECK, Hermann v. HIRSCHECK D.Ä I, Adalbert v. WINTERTHUR V. KYBURG, Liutfried v. WINTERTHUR, Ulrich V v. BREGENZ, Keroldus, Ulrich V ?, Ulrich III, Ratbert, Ulrich I, Gerold d. Ä) was born ~1328. She died Mar 1371 in Switzerland and was buried in St. Johns Chapel.

Margaret married **Goetfried IV von HUNENBERG**, son of HUNENBERG, on ~1370. Goetfried was born 1328. He died 1383 and was buried in St. Johns Chapel.

They had the following children:

213 M i. **Hartmann HUNOBERG GEN WOLF** was born ~1371. He died ~1392.

214 M ii. **John HUNOBERG**.

215 F iii. **Elizabeth HUNOBERG**.

216 F iv. **Anna HUNOBERG**.

217 M v. **Heinrich HUNENBERG**.

218 M vi. **Ulrich HUNENBERG**.

219 M vii. **Hans HUNENBERG**.

195. **Heinrich IX. FRIDINGEN** (Heinrich VIII FRIDINGEN, Heinrich VII. FRIDINGEN, Rudolf III. von FRIDINGEN, Heinrich IV von FRIDINGEN, Heinrich III. von FRIDINGEN, Rudolf I. von FRIDINGEN, Heinrich I. von STETTEN, Hermann I. v STETTEN V. ESPASINGEN, Hermann HIRSCHECK D.J., Hermann HIRSCHECK D.Ä, Heinrich v HIRSCHECK D.Ä, Hermann HIRSCHECK, Hermann v. HIRSCHECK D.Ä I, Adalbert v. WINTERTHUR V. KYBURG, Liutfried v. WINTERTHUR, Ulrich V v. BREGENZ, Keroldus, Ulrich V ?, Ulrich III, Ratbert, Ulrich I, Gerold d. Ä) was born ~1330 in Germany. He died Apr 1395 in Schwaben, Fridingen, Germany.

Heinrich was employed Burggraf (Castle Graf and Winemaker) 1380 - 1395 in Merano, Tyrol, Austria.

Heinrich married **Agatha WESTERSTETTEN**, daughter of Heinrich WESTERSTETTEN. Agatha was born ~1349. She died ~1403.

They had the following children:

220   F   i.   **Hans IV. FRIDINGEN** was born ~1368. She died ~1403.

             Hans married **HORNSTEIN**.

196.   **Ulrich #? FRIDINGEN** (Heinrich VIII FRIDINGEN, Heinrich VII. FRIDINGEN, Rudolf III. von FRIDINGEN, Heinrich IV von FRIDINGEN, Heinrich III. von FRIDINGEN, Rudolf I. von FRIDINGEN, Heinrich I. von STETTEN, Hermann I. v STETTEN V. ESPASINGEN, Hermann HIRSCHECK D.J., Hermann HIRSCHECK D.Ä, Heinrich v HIRSCHECK D.Ä, Hermann HIRSCHECK, Hermann v. HIRSCHECK D.Ä I, Adalbert v. WINTERTHUR V. KYBURG, Liutfried v. WINTERTHUR, Ulrich V v. BREGENZ, Keroldus, Ulrich V ?, Ulrich III, Ratbert, Ulrich I, Gerold d. Ä).

Ulrich married **Margarete WESTERSTETTEN**.

They had the following children:

    221   M   i.   **Konrad #? FRIDINGEN** died ~1421.

198.   **Rudolf VI. FRIDINGEN** (Rudolf V. der Jung? FRIDINGEN, Heinrich VII. FRIDINGEN, Rudolf III. von FRIDINGEN, Heinrich IV von FRIDINGEN, Heinrich III. von FRIDINGEN, Rudolf I. von FRIDINGEN, Heinrich I. von STETTEN, Hermann I. v STETTEN V. ESPASINGEN, Hermann HIRSCHECK D.J., Hermann HIRSCHECK D.Ä, Heinrich v HIRSCHECK D.Ä, Hermann HIRSCHECK, Hermann v. HIRSCHECK D.Ä I, Adalbert v. WINTERTHUR V. KYBURG, Liutfried v. WINTERTHUR, Ulrich V v. BREGENZ, Keroldus, Ulrich V ?, Ulrich III, Ratbert, Ulrich I, Gerold d. Ä) was born ~1320. He died ~1404?.

He had the following children:

+   222   M   i.   **Rudolf VIII. FRIDINGEN** was born ~1348 and died 1418.

    223   F   ii.   **Benedicta FRIDINGEN** was born ~1369. She died 1421.

             Benedicta married **Heinrich von FREIBURG**.

199.   **Heinrich X. FRIDINGEN** (Rudolf V. der Jung? FRIDINGEN, Heinrich VII. FRIDINGEN, Rudolf III. von FRIDINGEN, Heinrich IV von FRIDINGEN, Heinrich III. von FRIDINGEN, Rudolf I. von FRIDINGEN, Heinrich I. von STETTEN, Hermann I. v STETTEN V. ESPASINGEN, Hermann HIRSCHECK D.J., Hermann HIRSCHECK D.Ä, Heinrich v HIRSCHECK D.Ä, Hermann HIRSCHECK, Hermann v. HIRSCHECK D.Ä I, Adalbert v. WINTERTHUR V. KYBURG, Liutfried v. WINTERTHUR, Ulrich V v. BREGENZ, Keroldus, Ulrich V ?, Ulrich III, Ratbert, Ulrich I, Gerold d. Ä) was born ~1322. He died ~1396/1408.

Heinrich was employed Vogte in Fridingen, Germany.

Heinrich married **Adelheid BLUMBERG**. Adelheid was born ~1327. She died 1403.

They had the following children:

    224   M   i.   **Hans FRIDING** was born ~1398 in Wiesholz, Schaufhausen, Switzerland. He died ~1419.

                     Hans resided 1418 in Weisholz, Ramsen, Switzerland.

+   225   M   ii.   **Haintzli/Heinrich FRIDING** was born ~1395 and died Aug 1425.

210.   **Johann II d Altere FRIDINGEN** (Johann Hans I. von FRIDINGEN DER KRAYGER, Burkhard I. FRIDINGEN, Konrad II. von FRIDINGEN, Heinrich IV von FRIDINGEN, Heinrich III. von FRIDINGEN, Rudolf I. von FRIDINGEN, Heinrich I. von STETTEN, Hermann I. v STETTEN V. ESPASINGEN, Hermann HIRSCHECK D.J., Hermann HIRSCHECK D.Ä, Heinrich v HIRSCHECK D.Ä, Hermann HIRSCHECK, Hermann v. HIRSCHECK D.Ä I, Adalbert v. WINTERTHUR V. KYBURG, Liutfried v. WINTERTHUR, Ulrich V v. BREGENZ, Keroldus, Ulrich V ?, Ulrich III, Ratbert, Ulrich I, Gerold d. Ä) was born ~1302. He died ~1344.

He had the following children:

226 M   i.   **Ulrich III FRIDINGEN** was born ~1342?. He died 1362?.

+   227 M   ii.   **Johann V FRIDINGEN** was born ~1343 and died ~1398?.

228 F   iii.   **Margarete FRIDINGEN** was born ~1352. She died `1417?.

Margarete married **Friedrich FREIBURG**.

212.   **Johann III FRIDINGEN D. JUNGERE** (Johann Hans I. von FRIDINGEN DER KRAYGER, Burkhard I. FRIDINGEN, Konrad II. von FRIDINGEN, Heinrich IV von FRIDINGEN, Heinrich III. von FRIDINGEN, Rudolf I. von FRIDINGEN, Heinrich I. von STETTEN, Hermann I. v STETTEN V. ESPASINGEN, Hermann HIRSCHECK D.J., Hermann HIRSCHECK D.Ä, Heinrich v HIRSCHECK D.Ä, Hermann HIRSCHECK, Hermann v. HIRSCHECK D.Ä I, Adalbert v. WINTERTHUR V. KYBURG, Liutfried v. WINTERTHUR, Ulrich V v. BREGENZ, Keroldus, Ulrich V ?, Ulrich III, Ratbert, Ulrich I, Gerold d. Ä) was born ~1311. He died 1350.

Johann married **BALDEGG?**.

They had the following children:

229 F   i.   **Elsbeth von FRIDINGEN** was born ~1330 in Reichenau, Hohenzollern, Wuerttemberg-Hohenzollern, Germany. She died ~1350.

Elsbeth married (1) **Burkard von HOHENVELS** , son of Konrad HOHENVELS . Burkard was born ~1300 in Reichenau, Hohenzollern, Wuerttemberg-Hohenzollern, Germany. He died ~1357?.

Elsbeth also married (2) **Albrecht KLINGENBERG**, son of Heinrich KLINGENBERG "Heintzel" and Margaret VAIHINGEN. Albrecht was born ~1335. He died ~1371.

230 M   ii.   **Heinrich # von FRIDINGEN/FRIDING?** was born ~1329. He died ~1359.

Heinrich married **KLINGENBERG?**.

Twenty-Fourth Generation

222.   **Rudolf VIII. FRIDINGEN** (Rudolf VI. FRIDINGEN, Rudolf V. der Jung? FRIDINGEN, Heinrich VII. FRIDINGEN, Rudolf III. von FRIDINGEN, Heinrich IV von FRIDINGEN, Heinrich III. von FRIDINGEN, Rudolf I. von FRIDINGEN, Heinrich I. von STETTEN, Hermann I. v STETTEN V. ESPASINGEN, Hermann HIRSCHECK D.J., Hermann HIRSCHECK D.Ä, Heinrich v HIRSCHECK D.Ä, Hermann HIRSCHECK, Hermann v. HIRSCHECK D.Ä I, Adalbert v. WINTERTHUR V. KYBURG, Liutfried v. WINTERTHUR, Ulrich V v. BREGENZ, Keroldus, Ulrich V ?, Ulrich III, Ratbert, Ulrich I, Gerold d. Ä) was born ~1348. He died 1418.

Rudolf resided 1415 in Daugendorf, Germany.

Rudolf married **Anastasia von HORNSTEIN**, daughter of Heinrich HORNSTEIN, on 1364.

They had the following children:

+   231 M   i.   **Rudolph IX. FRIDINGEN D. JUNGE** was born ~1368 and died 1442.

232 M   ii.   **Georg I. FRIDINGEN** was born ~1367. He died ~1424.

233 F   iii.   **Dorothea FRIDINGEN** was born ~1397 in Germany. She died ~1501.

Dorothea married **Otto BALDECK** on 1427. Otto died 1428.

+ 234 M iv. **Heinrich XI von FRIDINGEN** was born ~1372 and died 1442.

235 M v. **Johannes or Itelhans FRIDINGEN** was born ~1385.

225. **Haintzli/Heinrich FRIDING** "Haintz/Heinz" (Heinrich X. FRIDINGEN, Rudolf V. der Jung? FRIDINGEN, Heinrich VII. FRIDINGEN, Rudolf III. von FRIDINGEN, Heinrich IV von FRIDINGEN, Heinrich III. von FRIDINGEN, Rudolf I. von FRIDINGEN, Heinrich I. von STETTEN, Hermann I. v STETTEN V. ESPASINGEN, Hermann HIRSCHECK D.J., Hermann HIRSCHECK D.Ä, Heinrich v HIRSCHECK D.Ä, Hermann HIRSCHECK, Hermann v. HIRSCHECK D.Ä I, Adalbert v. WINTERTHUR V. KYBURG, Liutfried v. WINTERTHUR, Ulrich V v. BREGENZ, Keroldus, Ulrich V ?, Ulrich III, Ratbert, Ulrich I, Gerold d. Ä) was born ~1395 in Wiesholz, Schaufhausen, Switzerland. He died Aug 1425 in Wiesholz, Schaufhausen, Switzerland.

Haintz/Heinz resided 1418 in Weisholz, Ramsen, Switzerland.

Haintz/Heinz married **Margarete KELLER OR KLINGER(IN)**, daughter of Walter v HOHENKLINGEN. Margarete died ~1426.

They had the following children:

236 M i. **Peter FRIDING** was born ~1403 in Canton in Northern Switzerland. He died ~1438 in Frutigen, Switzerland.

227. **Johann V FRIDINGEN** (Johann II d Altere FRIDINGEN, Johann Hans I. von FRIDINGEN DER KRAYGER, Burkhard I. FRIDINGEN, Konrad II. von FRIDINGEN, Heinrich IV von FRIDINGEN, Heinrich III. von FRIDINGEN, Rudolf I. von FRIDINGEN, Heinrich I. von STETTEN, Hermann I. v STETTEN V. ESPASINGEN, Hermann HIRSCHECK D.J., Hermann HIRSCHECK D.Ä, Heinrich v HIRSCHECK D.Ä, Hermann HIRSCHECK, Hermann v. HIRSCHECK D.Ä I, Adalbert v. WINTERTHUR V. KYBURG, Liutfried v. WINTERTHUR, Ulrich V v. BREGENZ, Keroldus, Ulrich V ?, Ulrich III, Ratbert, Ulrich I, Gerold d. Ä) was born ~1343. He died ~1398?.

Johann resided 1362 in Krahen, Germany.

Johann married **Margarete HOHENFELS**. Margarete was born ~1350. She died ~1398.

They had the following children:

+ 237 M i. **Hans VI. FRIDINGEN** was born ~1371 and died 1414.

+ 238 M ii. **Konrad III. von FRIDINGEN** was born ~1374 and died ~1448.

239 F iii. **Kunigunde FRIDINGEN** was born ~1381. She died ~1411.

Kunigunde married (1) **Gotz SCHULTHEISS** on ~1410. Gotz was born ~1349.

Kunigunde also married (2) **Heinrich RANDEGG**, son of Heinrich RANDEGG, on ~1400. Heinrich was born ~1365 in Staufen, Freiburg, Baden-Wet, Germany.

Heinrich resided 1401 in Schaffhausen, Switzerland.

240 M iv. **Wilhelm FRIDINGEN** was born ~1389. He died ~1410.

Wilhelm was employed Hauscomthur 1409 in Holland, Germany.

241 M v. **Ital FRIDINGEN** was born ~1386. He died ~1476.

Ital was employed propositas [proposal/proposition] - Monasterii St. Blasii 1407 in Klingnow, Argau, Switzerland. He was employed Propst - Study of Theology 1407 in St. Blasien, Waldshut dist Baden-Württemberg, Germany.

+ 242 F vi. **Elisabeth FRIDINGEN** was born ~1397 and died ~1417.

+ 243 M vii. **Ulrich IV FRIDINGEN** was born ~1386 and died ~1417.

Twenty-Fifth Generation

231. **Rudolph IX. FRIDINGEN D. JUNGE** (Rudolf VIII. FRIDINGEN, Rudolf VI. FRIDINGEN, Rudolf V. der Jung? FRIDINGEN, Heinrich VII. FRIDINGEN, Rudolf III. von FRIDINGEN, Heinrich IV von FRIDINGEN, Heinrich III. von FRIDINGEN, Rudolf I. von FRIDINGEN, Heinrich I. von STETTEN, Hermann I. v STETTEN V. ESPASINGEN, Hermann HIRSCHECK D.J., Hermann HIRSCHECK D.Ä, Heinrich v HIRSCHECK D.Ä, Hermann HIRSCHECK, Hermann v. HIRSCHECK D.Ä I, Adalbert v. WINTERTHUR V. KYBURG, Liutfried v. WINTERTHUR, Ulrich V v. BREGENZ, Keroldus, Ulrich V ?, Ulrich III, Ratbert, Ulrich I, Gerold d. Ä) was born ~1368 in Germany. He died 1442.

Rudolph was employed Comtur/Komthur 1342 - 1358 in Tobel, Switzerland.

Rudolph married **Claranna von TENGEN**. Claranna died ~1399.

Claranna resided in Engen, Baden-Württemberg, Germany.

They had the following children:

+ 244 M i. **Rudolf XI. FRIDINGEN** was born ~1382 and died ~1447.

234. **Heinrich XI von FRIDINGEN** (Rudolf VIII. FRIDINGEN, Rudolf VI. FRIDINGEN, Rudolf V. der Jung? FRIDINGEN, Heinrich VII. FRIDINGEN, Rudolf III. von FRIDINGEN, Heinrich IV von FRIDINGEN, Heinrich III. von FRIDINGEN, Rudolf I. von FRIDINGEN, Heinrich I. von STETTEN, Hermann I. v STETTEN V. ESPASINGEN, Hermann HIRSCHECK D.J., Hermann HIRSCHECK D.Ä, Heinrich v HIRSCHECK D.Ä, Hermann HIRSCHECK, Hermann v. HIRSCHECK D.Ä I, Adalbert v. WINTERTHUR V. KYBURG, Liutfried v. WINTERTHUR, Ulrich V v. BREGENZ, Keroldus, Ulrich V ?, Ulrich III, Ratbert, Ulrich I, Gerold d. Ä) was born ~1372. He died 1442.

Heinrich married **N von WILDENFELS?**.

They had the following children:

+ 245 M i. **Jakob I. FRIDINGEN** was born ~1402 and died 1461.

+ 246 M ii. **Rudolf X. FRIDINGEN** was born ~1412 and died 1466.

   247 M iii. **Heinrich XII. FRIDINGEN** was born ~1421. He died ~1463.

237. **Hans VI. FRIDINGEN** (Johann V FRIDINGEN, Johann II d Altere FRIDINGEN, Johann Hans I. von FRIDINGEN DER KRAYGER, Burkhard I. FRIDINGEN, Konrad II. von FRIDINGEN, Heinrich IV von FRIDINGEN, Heinrich III. von FRIDINGEN, Rudolf I. von FRIDINGEN, Heinrich I. von STETTEN, Hermann I. v STETTEN V. ESPASINGEN, Hermann HIRSCHECK D.J., Hermann HIRSCHECK D.Ä, Heinrich v HIRSCHECK D.Ä, Hermann HIRSCHECK, Hermann v. HIRSCHECK D.Ä I, Adalbert v. WINTERTHUR V. KYBURG, Liutfried v. WINTERTHUR, Ulrich V v. BREGENZ, Keroldus, Ulrich V ?, Ulrich III, Ratbert, Ulrich I, Gerold d. Ä) was born ~1371 in Germany. He died 1414.

Hans resided in Castle Schekenburg In Thalheim.

Hans married (1) **Margaretha GESSLER-ELLERBACH**, daughter of GESSLER, on 1404. Margaretha was born ~1372. She died ~1434.

Margaretha resided 1408 in Aargau Canton, Switzerland (Schenkeneberg Castle). She was employed Burgerin von Brugg 1419 - 1428 in Burgerin von Brugg, Switzerland.

The Swabian Connection – Expanded Edition

They had the following children:

248 F i. **Irenaeus Gretlin? FRIDINGEN**.

+ 249 M ii. **Wilhelm FRIDINGEN** was born ~1390 and died ~1473.

250 F iii. **Elisabeth FRIDINGEN** was born ~1391.

> Elisabeth married **Hans Gramlich von NUSSDORF** on 1417.

251 F iv. **Margarete FRIDINGEN**.

252 F v. **Verena FRIDINGEN** "Vrena " was born ~1406. She died ~1432.

> Vrena married **Wilhelm IMTHURN** .

Hans also married (2) **Elsbeth EPTINGEN**. Elsbeth was born 1385 in Schönau, Baden-Württemberg, Germany/Austria.

238. **Konrad III. von FRIDINGEN** "Hans Konrad" (Johann V FRIDINGEN, Johann II d Altere FRIDINGEN, Johann Hans I. von FRIDINGEN DER KRAYGER, Burkhard I. FRIDINGEN, Konrad II. von FRIDINGEN, Heinrich IV von FRIDINGEN, Heinrich III. von FRIDINGEN, Rudolf I. von FRIDINGEN, Heinrich I. von STETTEN, Hermann I. v STETTEN V. ESPASINGEN, Hermann HIRSCHECK D.J., Hermann HIRSCHECK D.Ä, Heinrich v HIRSCHECK D.Ä, Hermann HIRSCHECK, Hermann v. HIRSCHECK D.Ä I, Adalbert v. WINTERTHUR V. KYBURG, Liutfried v. WINTERTHUR, Ulrich V v. BREGENZ, Keroldus, Ulrich V ?, Ulrich III, Ratbert, Ulrich I, Gerold d. Ä) was born ~1374 in Fridingen, Germany. He died ~1448.

Hans Konrad resided 1418 in Schaffhausen, Switzerland. He resided 1428 in Schaffhausen, Switzerland. He resided 1430 in Ulm, Switzerland. He was employed office man to the Etsch (Teutonic Order's Bailiwick on the Adige) 1439 in Tyrol, Austria. He was employed Stadtvogt @ Castle Haldenstein 1451 in Chur, Switzerland. He was employed Mayer 1457 in Radolfzell, Germany. He resided 1458 in Radolfzell, Germany.

Hans Konrad married (1) **Veronia von FULACH**, daughter of George FULACH, on 1438.

They had the following children:

+ 253 F i. **Margarete FRIDINGEN** was born ~1424 and died ~1461.

Hans Konrad also married (2) **Illegitamate WARTENBURG?**, daughter of N WARTENBURG.

They had the following children:

+ 254 M ii. **Burckhart FRIDINGER** was born ~1423 and died ~1454.

255 M iii. **Jkr. Konrad FRIDINGER** was born ~1420. He died ~1472.

+ 256 F iv. **Anna von STICKEL OR FRIDINGEN** was born ~1435 and died ~1473.

242. **Elisabeth FRIDINGEN** (Johann V FRIDINGEN, Johann II d Altere FRIDINGEN, Johann Hans I. von FRIDINGEN DER KRAYGER, Burkhard I. FRIDINGEN, Konrad II. von FRIDINGEN, Heinrich IV von FRIDINGEN, Heinrich III. von FRIDINGEN, Rudolf I. von FRIDINGEN, Heinrich I. von STETTEN, Hermann I. v STETTEN V. ESPASINGEN, Hermann HIRSCHECK D.J., Hermann HIRSCHECK D.Ä, Heinrich v HIRSCHECK D.Ä, Hermann HIRSCHECK, Hermann v. HIRSCHECK D.Ä I, Adalbert v. WINTERTHUR V. KYBURG, Liutfried v. WINTERTHUR, Ulrich V v. BREGENZ, Keroldus, Ulrich V ?, Ulrich III, Ratbert, Ulrich I, Gerold d. Ä) was born ~1397. She died ~1417.

Elisabeth married **Friedrich WESTERSTETTEN**. Friedrich died 1417.

They had the following children:

257 M i. **Ulrich WESTERSTETTEN**.

243.   **Ulrich IV FRIDINGEN** (Johann V FRIDINGEN, Johann II d Altere FRIDINGEN, Johann Hans I. von FRIDINGEN DER KRAYGER, Burkhard I. FRIDINGEN, Konrad II. von FRIDINGEN, Heinrich IV von FRIDINGEN, Heinrich III. von FRIDINGEN, Rudolf I. von FRIDINGEN, Heinrich I. von STETTEN, Hermann I. v STETTEN V. ESPASINGEN, Hermann HIRSCHECK D.J., Hermann HIRSCHECK D.Ä, Heinrich v HIRSCHECK D.Ä, Hermann HIRSCHECK, Hermann v. HIRSCHECK D.Ä I, Adalbert v. WINTERTHUR V. KYBURG, Liutfried v. WINTERTHUR, Ulrich V v. BREGENZ, Keroldus, Ulrich V ?, Ulrich III, Ratbert, Ulrich I, Gerold d. Ä) was born ~1386. He died ~1417.

Ulrich married (1) **Klara SCHMERLIN THURN**. Klara was born ~1332 in Mals. She died 1 Mar 1406.

Ulrich also married (2) **Anna ROSSHAUPT**. Anna was born ~1385. She died ~1430.

They had the following children:

258   F   i.   **Magdalena von FRIDINGEN** was born ~1410 in Loewenberg, Preussen. She died ~1445.

Magdalena married **Hans Thuring von MUENCH MUNCHENSTEIN**. Hans was born ~1390 in Munchenstein, Switzerland. He died ~ 07 MAY 1449.

Twenty-Sixth Generation

244.   **Rudolf XI. FRIDINGEN** (Rudolph IX. FRIDINGEN D. JUNGE, Rudolf VIII. FRIDINGEN, Rudolf VI. FRIDINGEN, Rudolf V. der Jung? FRIDINGEN, Heinrich VII. FRIDINGEN, Rudolf III. von FRIDINGEN, Heinrich IV von FRIDINGEN, Heinrich III. von FRIDINGEN, Rudolf I. von FRIDINGEN, Heinrich I. von STETTEN, Hermann I. v STETTEN V. ESPASINGEN, Hermann HIRSCHECK D.J., Hermann HIRSCHECK D.Ä, Heinrich v HIRSCHECK D.Ä, Hermann HIRSCHECK, Hermann v. HIRSCHECK D.Ä I, Adalbert v. WINTERTHUR V. KYBURG, Liutfried v. WINTERTHUR, Ulrich V v. BREGENZ, Keroldus, Ulrich V ?, Ulrich III, Ratbert, Ulrich I, Gerold d. Ä) was born ~1382. He died ~1447.

Rudolf married **N. von EMERSHOFEN**.

They had the following children:

+   259   M   i.   **Rudolf XIII FRIDINGEN** was born ~1412 and died ~1473.

     260   F   ii.   **Elsbeth FRIDINGEN** died 1488.

                        Elsbeth married **Albert / Albrecht THUMB**. Albert died ~1483?.

+   261   M   iii.   **Heinrich XIII FRIDINGEN** was born ~1412 and died ~1473.

245.   **Jakob I. FRIDINGEN** (Heinrich XI von FRIDINGEN, Rudolf VIII. FRIDINGEN, Rudolf VI. FRIDINGEN, Rudolf V. der Jung? FRIDINGEN, Heinrich VII. FRIDINGEN, Rudolf III. von FRIDINGEN, Heinrich IV von FRIDINGEN, Heinrich III. von FRIDINGEN, Rudolf I. von FRIDINGEN, Heinrich I. von STETTEN, Hermann I. v STETTEN V. ESPASINGEN, Hermann HIRSCHECK D.J., Hermann HIRSCHECK D.Ä, Heinrich v HIRSCHECK D.Ä, Hermann HIRSCHECK, Hermann v. HIRSCHECK D.Ä I, Adalbert v. WINTERTHUR V. KYBURG, Liutfried v. WINTERTHUR, Ulrich V v. BREGENZ, Keroldus, Ulrich V ?, Ulrich III, Ratbert, Ulrich I, Gerold d. Ä) was born ~1402. He died 1461.

Jakob married **Margarete FRIDINGEN**, daughter of Konrad III. von FRIDINGEN "Hans Konrad" and Veronia von FULACH. Margarete was born ~1424 in Germany. She died ~1461.

They had the following children:

+ 262 M i. **Konrad V. FRIDINGEN** was born ~1442 and died ~1475.

263 M ii. **Jakob II. FRIDINGEN** was born ~1450. He died ~5/1477.

264 F iii. **Barbara FRIDINGEN** was born ~1458. She died ~1480.

Barbara married **Anton EMERSHOFEN** on ~1478. Anton was born 1456?.

246. **Rudolf X. FRIDINGEN** (Heinrich XI von FRIDINGEN, Rudolf VIII. FRIDINGEN, Rudolf VI. FRIDINGEN, Rudolf V. der Jung? FRIDINGEN, Heinrich VII. FRIDINGEN, Rudolf III. von FRIDINGEN, Heinrich IV von FRIDINGEN, Heinrich III. von FRIDINGEN, Rudolf I. von FRIDINGEN, Heinrich I. von STETTEN, Hermann I. v STETTEN V. ESPASINGEN, Hermann HIRSCHECK D.J., Hermann HIRSCHECK D.Ä, Heinrich v HIRSCHECK D.Ä, Hermann HIRSCHECK, Hermann v. HIRSCHECK D.Ä I, Adalbert v. WINTERTHUR V. KYBURG, Liutfried v. WINTERTHUR, Ulrich V v. BREGENZ, Keroldus, Ulrich V ?, Ulrich III, Ratbert, Ulrich I, Gerold d. Ä) was born ~1412. He died 1466.

Rudolf married **STOFFELN?**.

They had the following children:

265 M i. **Veit von FRIDINGEN** was born ~1435. He died ~1478.

266 M ii. **Georg II. FRIDINGEN** was born ~1442. He died ~1493.

Georg was employed Kmtur 1492 in Beuggen, Rheinfelden, Germany.

267 M iii. **Martin I. FRIDINGEN** was born ~1436. He died 1483?.

+ 268 M iv. **Rudolf XI. von FRIDINGEN** was born ~1438 and died ~1483?.

249. **Wilhelm FRIDINGEN** "Guillaume" (Hans VI. FRIDINGEN, Johann V FRIDINGEN, Johann II d Altere FRIDINGEN, Johann Hans I. von FRIDINGEN DER KRAYGER, Burkhard I. FRIDINGEN, Konrad II. von FRIDINGEN, Heinrich IV von FRIDINGEN, Heinrich III. von FRIDINGEN, Rudolf I. von FRIDINGEN, Heinrich I. von STETTEN, Hermann I. v STETTEN V. ESPASINGEN, Hermann HIRSCHECK D.J., Hermann HIRSCHECK D.Ä, Heinrich v HIRSCHECK D.Ä, Hermann HIRSCHECK, Hermann v. HIRSCHECK D.Ä I, Adalbert v. WINTERTHUR V. KYBURG, Liutfried v. WINTERTHUR, Ulrich V v. BREGENZ, Keroldus, Ulrich V ?, Ulrich III, Ratbert, Ulrich I, Gerold d. Ä) was born ~1390 in Fridingen, Germany. He died ~1473.

Guillaume was employed Vogt 1444 in Bregenz, Switzerland. He resided 1455 in Hohenkraken (Castle High Crows in Fridingen, Germany). He was employed Graf (Count/Earl) in Tengen, Germany.

Guillaume married **Anna GRÜNENBERG**, daughter of Johann GRÜNENBERG III and Euphemia KLINGENBERG , on 1434. Anna died ~1471.

They had the following children:

269 M i. **Hans Thüring FRIDINGEN** was born ~1452 in Switzerland. He died 1504.

Hans resided 1482 in Luzerne, Swizerland. He was employed Probst in St. Rlasien in Klingnau. He resided 1491 in Schaffhausen, Switzerland.

Hans married **Veronica HOMBURG**, daughter of Konrad von HOMBURG. Veronica was born ~1455. She died ~1501.

+ 270 F ii. **Ursula FRIDINGEN** was born ~1439 and died ~1513.

271 F iii. **Amalia FRIDINGEN** was born ~1459. She died 1521.

Amalia married **Anton SCHURHAMMER** on 1493.

272 M iv. **Hans Johann VII. FRIDINGEN** was born ~1438 in Switzerland. He died

The Swabian Connection – Expanded Edition

1481.

Hans joined religion to Kehrsatz, Berne, switzerland 1458 in from Sammlungen, Switzerland.

Hans married **Anna Enneli RINGOLTINGEN** "Enneli ", daughter of Rudolph RINGOLTINGEN. Enneli was born ~1428. She died ~1536.

273 M v. **George III. FRIDINGEN** was born ~1459. He died ~1491.

George 1469 Student. He was employed Pfarrer 1471 in Ammerswyl.

274 F vi. **Benedikta FRIDINGEN** was born ~1451. She died ~1483.

Benedikta resided in St. Katharinental.

+ 275 M vii. **Eitelhans FRIDINGEN** was born ~1449 and died ~1493.

253. **Margarete FRIDINGEN** (Konrad III. von FRIDINGEN, Johann V FRIDINGEN, Johann II d Altere FRIDINGEN, Johann Hans I. von FRIDINGEN DER KRAYGER, Burkhard I. FRIDINGEN, Konrad II. von FRIDINGEN, Heinrich IV von FRIDINGEN, Heinrich III. von FRIDINGEN, Rudolf I. von FRIDINGEN, Heinrich I. von STETTEN, Hermann I. v STETTEN V. ESPASINGEN, Hermann HIRSCHECK D.J., Hermann HIRSCHECK D.Ä, Heinrich v HIRSCHECK D.Ä, Hermann HIRSCHECK, Hermann v. HIRSCHECK D.Ä I, Adalbert v. WINTERTHUR V. KYBURG, Liutfried v. WINTERTHUR, Ulrich V v. BREGENZ, Keroldus, Ulrich V ?, Ulrich III, Ratbert, Ulrich I, Gerold d. Ä) was born ~1424 in Germany. She died ~1461.

Margarete married (1) **Stephan von OW/AUW**. Stephan was born ~1435.

Margarete also married (2) **Jakob I. FRIDINGEN**, son of Heinrich XI von FRIDINGEN and N von WILDENFELS?. Jakob was born ~1402. He died 1461.

They had the following children:

+ 276 M i. Konrad V. FRIDINGEN is printed as #262.

277 M ii. Jakob II. FRIDINGEN is printed as #263.

278 F iii. Barbara FRIDINGEN is printed as #264.

254. **Burckhart FRIDINGER** (Konrad III. von FRIDINGEN, Johann V FRIDINGEN, Johann II d Altere FRIDINGEN, Johann Hans I. von FRIDINGEN DER KRAYGER, Burkhard I. FRIDINGEN, Konrad II. von FRIDINGEN, Heinrich IV von FRIDINGEN, Heinrich III. von FRIDINGEN, Rudolf I. von FRIDINGEN, Heinrich I. von STETTEN, Hermann I. v STETTEN V. ESPASINGEN, Hermann HIRSCHECK D.J., Hermann HIRSCHECK D.Ä, Heinrich v HIRSCHECK D.Ä, Hermann HIRSCHECK, Hermann v. HIRSCHECK D.Ä I, Adalbert v. WINTERTHUR V. KYBURG, Liutfried v. WINTERTHUR, Ulrich V v. BREGENZ, Keroldus, Ulrich V ?, Ulrich III, Ratbert, Ulrich I, Gerold d. Ä) was born ~1423 in Germany OR Switzerland. He died ~1454.

Burckhart was employed Vogt=Governor 1453 in Jestetten, Germany (South of Shaufhaussen, Switzerland).

He had the following children:

+ 279 M i. **Friedrich FRIDINGER** was born ~1446 and died ~1488.

256. **Anna von STICKEL OR FRIDINGEN** (Konrad III. von FRIDINGEN, Johann V FRIDINGEN, Johann II d Altere FRIDINGEN, Johann Hans I. von FRIDINGEN DER KRAYGER, Burkhard I. FRIDINGEN, Konrad II. von FRIDINGEN, Heinrich IV von FRIDINGEN, Heinrich III. von FRIDINGEN, Rudolf I. von FRIDINGEN, Heinrich I. von STETTEN, Hermann I. v STETTEN V. ESPASINGEN, Hermann HIRSCHECK D.J., Hermann HIRSCHECK D.Ä, Heinrich v HIRSCHECK D.Ä, Hermann HIRSCHECK, Hermann v. HIRSCHECK D.Ä I, Adalbert v. WINTERTHUR V. KYBURG, Liutfried v. WINTERTHUR, Ulrich V v. BREGENZ, Keroldus, Ulrich V

?, Ulrich III, Ratbert, Ulrich I, Gerold d. Ä) was born ~1435. She died ~1473.

Anna married **Hans Konrad SCHWARZ**.

They had the following children:

280 M   i. **Ulrich SWARTZ** died ~1436.

281 M   ii. **Walter SWARTZ** died ~1436.

282 M   iii. **Conrad SWARTZ** died ~1430.

        Conrad was employed Seschaft 1429 in Fridingen, Germany.

283 F   iv. **Ursula SCHWARZ**.

        Ursula married **WALBURG**.

Twenty-Seventh Generation

259.   **Rudolf XIII FRIDINGEN** (Rudolf XI. FRIDINGEN, Rudolph IX. FRIDINGEN D. JUNGE, Rudolf VIII. FRIDINGEN, Rudolf VI. FRIDINGEN, Rudolf V. der Jung? FRIDINGEN, Heinrich VII. FRIDINGEN, Rudolf III. von FRIDINGEN, Heinrich IV von FRIDINGEN, Heinrich III. von FRIDINGEN, Rudolf I. von FRIDINGEN, Heinrich I. von STETTEN, Hermann I. v STETTEN V. ESPASINGEN, Hermann HIRSCHECK D.J., Hermann HIRSCHECK D.Ä, Heinrich v HIRSCHECK D.Ä, Hermann HIRSCHECK, Hermann v. HIRSCHECK D.Ä I, Adalbert v. WINTERTHUR V. KYBURG, Liutfried v. WINTERTHUR, Ulrich V v. BREGENZ, Keroldus, Ulrich V ?, Ulrich III, Ratbert, Ulrich I, Gerold d. Ä) was born ~1412. He died ~1473.

He had the following children:

284 M   i. **Stefan FRIDINGEN** was born ~1442. He died ~1490.

        Stefan was employed Monch=Monk 1471 in Alpirsbach, Black Forest, Baden-Wurtermburg, Germany. He was employed Propst 1475 - 1477 in Berau, Waldshut, Baden-Württemberg, Germany. He resided 1482 in Wittnau, Baden-Württemberg, Germany. He was employed Propst 1482 in Wittnau, Baden-Wet, Germany.

261.   **Heinrich XIII FRIDINGEN** (Rudolf XI. FRIDINGEN, Rudolph IX. FRIDINGEN D. JUNGE, Rudolf VIII. FRIDINGEN, Rudolf VI. FRIDINGEN, Rudolf V. der Jung? FRIDINGEN, Heinrich VII. FRIDINGEN, Rudolf III. von FRIDINGEN, Heinrich IV von FRIDINGEN, Heinrich III. von FRIDINGEN, Rudolf I. von FRIDINGEN, Heinrich I. von STETTEN, Hermann I. v STETTEN V. ESPASINGEN, Hermann HIRSCHECK D.J., Hermann HIRSCHECK D.Ä, Heinrich v HIRSCHECK D.Ä, Hermann HIRSCHECK, Hermann v. HIRSCHECK D.Ä I, Adalbert v. WINTERTHUR V. KYBURG, Liutfried v. WINTERTHUR, Ulrich V v. BREGENZ, Keroldus, Ulrich V ?, Ulrich III, Ratbert, Ulrich I, Gerold d. Ä) was born ~1412. He died ~1473.

He had the following children:

285 F   i. **Margarete FRIDINGEN** was born ~1438. She died ~1480.

        Margarete was employed Burgerrecht 1468 - 1480 in Strasbourg, Germany.

262.   **Konrad V. FRIDINGEN** (Jakob I. FRIDINGEN, Heinrich XI von FRIDINGEN, Rudolf VIII. FRIDINGEN, Rudolf VI. FRIDINGEN, Rudolf V. der Jung? FRIDINGEN, Heinrich VII. FRIDINGEN, Rudolf III. von FRIDINGEN, Heinrich IV von FRIDINGEN, Heinrich III. von FRIDINGEN, Rudolf I. von FRIDINGEN, Heinrich I. von STETTEN, Hermann I. v STETTEN V. ESPASINGEN, Hermann HIRSCHECK D.J., Hermann HIRSCHECK D.Ä, Heinrich v HIRSCHECK

D.Ä, Hermann HIRSCHECK, Hermann v. HIRSCHECK D.Ä I, Adalbert v. WINTERTHUR V. KYBURG, Liutfried v. WINTERTHUR, Ulrich V v. BREGENZ, Keroldus, Ulrich V ?, Ulrich III, Ratbert, Ulrich I, Gerold d. Ä) was born ~1442. He died ~1475.

Konrad was employed Vogt 1475 in Chur, Switzerland.

Konrad married **METZNERIN?**.

They had the following children:

+   286   M   i.   **Konrad VI. FRIDINGER** was born ~1476 and died 1511.

+   287   M   ii.   **Hans IX. FRIDINGEN** was born 1467 and died 1546.

268.   **Rudolf XI. von FRIDINGEN** (Rudolf X. FRIDINGEN, Heinrich XI von FRIDINGEN, Rudolf VIII. FRIDINGEN, Rudolf VI. FRIDINGEN, Rudolf V. der Jung? FRIDINGEN, Heinrich VII. FRIDINGEN, Rudolf III. von FRIDINGEN, Heinrich IV von FRIDINGEN, Heinrich III. von FRIDINGEN, Rudolf I. von FRIDINGEN, Heinrich I. von STETTEN, Hermann I. v STETTEN V. ESPASINGEN, Hermann HIRSCHECK D.J., Hermann HIRSCHECK D.Ä, Heinrich v HIRSCHECK D.Ä, Hermann HIRSCHECK, Hermann v. HIRSCHECK D.Ä I, Adalbert v. WINTERTHUR V. KYBURG, Liutfried v. WINTERTHUR, Ulrich V v. BREGENZ, Keroldus, Ulrich V ?, Ulrich III, Ratbert, Ulrich I, Gerold d. Ä) was born ~1438 in Fridingen, Germany. He died ~1483? in Switzerland?.

Rudolf 1483 University of Tubingen, Germany. He was employed Hofmeister (später Landkomthur). 1490. He was employed Comthur 1497 in Sumiswald, Switzerland. He resided 1500 in Sumiswald, Switzerland. He was employed Kommenthur zu Sumiswald 1500 in Sumiswald, Switzerland. He was employed Kommenthur zu Hitzkurch, Luzern, Switzerland 1501 - 1501 in Hitzkurch, Luzern, Switzerland. He was employed Comthur (1503,1506,1508,1512,1521) 1503 - 1521 in Koniz, Switzerland. He 1506 Universität Tübingen, Switzerland. He was employed Land Meister/Magistrate 1522 - 1537 in Elsass, Germany. He was employed LandComthur 1525 in Altshausen, Ravensburg, BW, Germany.

Rudolf married **Ottilia EMERSHOFEN** on 1466. Ottilia died ~1490?.

They had the following children:

+   288   M   i.   **Martin II. FRIDINGEN** was born ~1454 and died 1522.

     289   M   ii.   **Georg IV. FRIDINGEN** "Jorg" was born ~1453 in Hochenbürgen, Germany. He died ~1483.

         Jorg resided 1483 in Bussen.

     290   M   iii.   **Johannes "Pre-Reformer" FRIDINGEN** was born ~1458. He died 21 Dec 1534.

         Johannes was employed Superior of the Cistercian Monastery 1493 in Bebenhauser, Germany. He 1481 Universität Tübingen, Switzerland. He 1510 Tubingen, Germany.

     291   M   iv.   **Rudolf XII. FRIDINGEN** was born ~1462. He died ~1536.

     292   F   v.   **Appolonia FRIDINGEN** was born ~1461. She died ~1502.

         Appolonia married **Mark von OW-WACHENDORF**.

     293   F   vi.   **Dorothea FRIDINGEN** was born ~1483. She died ~1529.

         Dorothea married **Anton von LUTERAU**. Anton died 1517.

     294   F   vii.   **Margarete FRIDINGEN** was born ~1476. She died `1495.

         Margarete was employed Nonne=Nun 1495 in Fraeunalb.

+   295   F   viii.   **Magdelena FRIDINGEN.**

270.   **Ursula FRIDINGEN** (Wilhelm FRIDINGEN, Hans VI. FRIDINGEN, Johann V FRIDINGEN, Johann II d Altere FRIDINGEN, Johann Hans I. von FRIDINGEN DER KRAYGER, Burkhard I. FRIDINGEN, Konrad II. von FRIDINGEN, Heinrich IV von FRIDINGEN, Heinrich III. von FRIDINGEN, Rudolf I. von FRIDINGEN, Heinrich I. von STETTEN, Hermann I. v STETTEN V. ESPASINGEN, Hermann HIRSCHECK D.J., Hermann HIRSCHECK D.Ä, Heinrich v HIRSCHECK D.Ä, Hermann HIRSCHECK, Hermann v. HIRSCHECK D.Ä I, Adalbert v. WINTERTHUR V. KYBURG, Liutfried v. WINTERTHUR, Ulrich V v. BREGENZ, Keroldus, Ulrich V ?, Ulrich III, Ratbert, Ulrich I, Gerold d. Ä) was born ~1439 in Switzerland. She died ~1513 in Aarau, Argau, Switzerland.

Ursula married **Johannis Ulrici LUTERNAU**, son of LUTERNAU, on 1454. Johannis was born ~1444 in Germany. He died ~1474 in Switzerland.

They had the following children:

    296   M   i.   **Sebastian LUTERNAU.**

275.   **Eitelhans FRIDINGEN** (Wilhelm FRIDINGEN, Hans VI. FRIDINGEN, Johann V FRIDINGEN, Johann II d Altere FRIDINGEN, Johann Hans I. von FRIDINGEN DER KRAYGER, Burkhard I. FRIDINGEN, Konrad II. von FRIDINGEN, Heinrich IV von FRIDINGEN, Heinrich III. von FRIDINGEN, Rudolf I. von FRIDINGEN, Heinrich I. von STETTEN, Hermann I. v STETTEN V. ESPASINGEN, Hermann HIRSCHECK D.J., Hermann HIRSCHECK D.Ä, Heinrich v HIRSCHECK D.Ä, Hermann HIRSCHECK, Hermann v. HIRSCHECK D.Ä I, Adalbert v. WINTERTHUR V. KYBURG, Liutfried v. WINTERTHUR, Ulrich V v. BREGENZ, Keroldus, Ulrich V ?, Ulrich III, Ratbert, Ulrich I, Gerold d. Ä) was born ~1449. He died ~1493.

Eitelhans married **Margarete von REISCHACH**, daughter of Eberhard REISCHACH. Margarete was born ~1456. She died 1510.

They had the following children:

+   297   M   i.   **Hans Grimmen FRIDINGEN** was born ~1466 and died 1539.

+   298   M   ii.   **Hans Benedict Ernst FRIDINGEN** was born ~1469 and died 1517.

279.   **Friedrich FRIDINGER** (Burckhart FRIDINGER, Konrad III. von FRIDINGEN, Johann V FRIDINGEN, Johann II d Altere FRIDINGEN, Johann Hans I. von FRIDINGEN DER KRAYGER, Burkhard I. FRIDINGEN, Konrad II. von FRIDINGEN, Heinrich IV von FRIDINGEN, Heinrich III. von FRIDINGEN, Rudolf I. von FRIDINGEN, Heinrich I. von STETTEN, Hermann I. v STETTEN V. ESPASINGEN, Hermann HIRSCHECK D.J., Hermann HIRSCHECK D.Ä, Heinrich v HIRSCHECK D.Ä, Hermann HIRSCHECK, Hermann v. HIRSCHECK D.Ä I, Adalbert v. WINTERTHUR V. KYBURG, Liutfried v. WINTERTHUR, Ulrich V v. BREGENZ, Keroldus, Ulrich V ?, Ulrich III, Ratbert, Ulrich I, Gerold d. Ä) was born ~1446. He died ~1488.

Friedrich resided 1476 - 1488 in Walshut, Germany.

He had the following children:

    299   M   i.   **Johannes FRIDINGER** was born ~1464. He died ~1510.

          Johannes resided 1484 - 1490 in Walshut, Germany. He 1484   Student.

    300   F   ii.   **Elizabeth FRIDINGER** was born ~1468.

          Elizabeth married **Johann von HERDIBERG** on 1488.

    301   M   iii.   **Simon von FRIDINGER** was born ~1463. He died ~1493.

          Simon resided 1488 in Berne, Switzerland. He was employed Monastery 1488 in Berne, Switzerland. He was employed Pfarrer 1493 in Muri, Argau, Switzerland.

Twenty-Eighth Generation

286.   **Konrad VI. FRIDINGER** (Konrad V. FRIDINGEN, Jakob I. FRIDINGEN, Heinrich XI von FRIDINGEN, Rudolf VIII. FRIDINGEN, Rudolf VI. FRIDINGEN, Rudolf V. der Jung? FRIDINGEN, Heinrich VII. FRIDINGEN, Rudolf III. von FRIDINGEN, Heinrich IV von FRIDINGEN, Heinrich III. von FRIDINGEN, Rudolf I. von FRIDINGEN, Heinrich I. von STETTEN, Hermann I. v STETTEN V. ESPASINGEN, Hermann HIRSCHECK D.J., Hermann HIRSCHECK D.Ä, Heinrich v HIRSCHECK D.Ä, Hermann HIRSCHECK, Hermann v. HIRSCHECK D.Ä I, Adalbert v. WINTERTHUR V. KYBURG, Liutfried v. WINTERTHUR, Ulrich V v. BREGENZ, Keroldus, Ulrich V ?, Ulrich III, Ratbert, Ulrich I, Gerold d. Ä) was born ~1476. He died 1511.

Konrad resided 1479 - 1489 in Chur, Switzerland. He was employed Mayor 1482 in Chur, Switzerland. He was employed Richter (Judges) & Propst 1502 in Schlanders & Eyre, Italy (Border Of Switzerland).

Konrad married **Felicita ROTENSTAIN** on 1464.

They had the following children:

   302   M   i.   **George FRIDINGER** was born ~1505. He died ~1545.

                     George was employed Vogt 1544 in Hohen Geroldseck, Black Forest, Germany.

   303   F   ii. **Sybilla FRIDINGER.**

287.   **Hans IX. FRIDINGEN** (Konrad V. FRIDINGEN, Jakob I. FRIDINGEN, Heinrich XI von FRIDINGEN, Rudolf VIII. FRIDINGEN, Rudolf VI. FRIDINGEN, Rudolf V. der Jung? FRIDINGEN, Heinrich VII. FRIDINGEN, Rudolf III. von FRIDINGEN, Heinrich IV von FRIDINGEN, Heinrich III. von FRIDINGEN, Rudolf I. von FRIDINGEN, Heinrich I. von STETTEN, Hermann I. v STETTEN V. ESPASINGEN, Hermann HIRSCHECK D.J., Hermann HIRSCHECK D.Ä, Heinrich v HIRSCHECK D.Ä, Hermann HIRSCHECK, Hermann v. HIRSCHECK D.Ä I, Adalbert v. WINTERTHUR V. KYBURG, Liutfried v. WINTERTHUR, Ulrich V v. BREGENZ, Keroldus, Ulrich V ?, Ulrich III, Ratbert, Ulrich I, Gerold d. Ä) was born 1467 in Germany. He died 1546 in Switzerland.

Hans resided 1511 - 1532 in Freyenthurn in Schlanders, Austria. He was employed Landvogt 1525 in Ober & Niederschwaben. He was employed Hofmeister (Steward) 1525 in Constanz, Baden-Württemberg, Germany, Holy Roman Empire. He was employed Landvogt (Governor) 1528 - 1529 in Eggen, near Waldburg, Germany.

Hans married (1) **Brigida STUBEN/STETEN** "Barbara", daughter of Hans STETTEN and Dorothea ROTENSTEIN, on ~1526.

They had the following children:

   304   F   i.   **Dorothea FRIDINGEN** was born ~1505. She died ~1561.

                     Dorothea married **DIPERSKIRCHEN.**

   305   F   ii. **Anna FRIDINGEN** was born 1522.

                     Anna married **Johann Jakob Baron von MORSBURG BEFFORT** on 30 Jun 1545.

   306   M   iii. **Haug FRIDINGEN** was born ~1502. He died ~1560?.

                     Haug married **Ursula von DIEPERSKIRCHEN** on 1551.

   307   F   iv. **Katherina FRIDINGEN** was born ~1503 in Germany. She died 1538.

                     Katherina married **Dr. PRYGION (PHRIGION).** Dr. was born ~1483.

The Swabian Connection – Expanded Edition

He died 1543.

Hans also married (2) **Beatrix GOBERG** on ~1537. Beatrix was born ~1525. She died ~1556.

288.　**Martin II. FRIDINGEN** (Rudolf XI. von FRIDINGEN, Rudolf X. FRIDINGEN, Heinrich XI von FRIDINGEN, Rudolf VIII. FRIDINGEN, Rudolf VI. FRIDINGEN, Rudolf V. der Jung? FRIDINGEN, Heinrich VII. FRIDINGEN, Rudolf III. von FRIDINGEN, Heinrich IV von FRIDINGEN, Heinrich III. von FRIDINGEN, Rudolf I. von FRIDINGEN, Heinrich I. von STETTEN, Hermann I. v STETTEN V. ESPASINGEN, Hermann HIRSCHECK D.J., Hermann HIRSCHECK D.Ä, Heinrich v HIRSCHECK D.Ä, Hermann HIRSCHECK, Hermann v. HIRSCHECK D.Ä I, Adalbert v. WINTERTHUR V. KYBURG, Liutfried v. WINTERTHUR, Ulrich V v. BREGENZ, Keroldus, Ulrich V ?, Ulrich III, Ratbert, Ulrich I, Gerold d. Ä) was born ~1454 in Germany. He died 1522.

Martin was employed Noble Farm Hand 1484. He resided 1502 in Mettenberg, Germany. He was employed Mayer conductor of the temple to Neydlingen 1514 in Neidlingen, Esslingen, Baden-Württemberg, Germany.

Martin married (1) **Margarete von EHINGEN**, daughter of Diepold v EHINGEN.

They had the following children:

+ 　308　M　i.　**George V. FRIDINGEN** was born ~1482 and died 1544.

　　309　M　ii.　**Franz FRIDINGEN** was born ~1504. He died ~1554.

　　　　　　Franz was employed Hauskomthur 1544. He was employed Deutschordenskomthur (Treasurer of the Teutonic Order) 1549 - 1554 in Meinau, Strasbourg, Bas-Rhin, Alsace, France. He was employed Komthur 1549 in Mülhausen. He was employed Hauskomtur 1551 - 1554 in Bacanz. He was employed Deutschordenskomthur 1553 in Meinau. He was employed Comptur 1542 - 1546 in Hitzkireh, Lucerne, Switzerland. He was employed Lietpriester in Hitzkireh, Lucerne, Switzerland.

　　310　F　iii.　**Ottilia FRIDINGEN** was born ~1500. She died ~1521.

　　311　M　iv.　**Dorethea FRIDINGEN** was born ~1499. He died ~1540?.

　　　　　　Dorethea married **Georg / Joerg SCHUTZ / SCHUETZ** on 1520. Georg was born in Eutingerthal/Ittingerthal, Germany. She died ~1521.

　　312　F　v.　**Barbara FRIDINGEN** was born ~1504. She died ~1534.

　　　　　　Barbara was employed Nonne=Nun 1531 - 1534 in Heiligkreuztal, Germany.

　　313　F　vi.　**Catherina FRIDINGEN** was born ~1508. She died ~1557.

Martin also married (2) **N N.**.

They had the following children:

　　314　M　vii.　**Rudolf XV. FRIDINGEN** was born ~1481.

　　　　　　Rudolf 1504　Student.

　　315　M　viii.　**Johann X FRIDINGEN** was born ~1481. He died ~1527.

　　　　　　Johann 1504　Student. He was employed Domherr 1513 in Worms. He was employed Pfarrei 1527 in Dachsel.

295.　**Magdelena FRIDINGEN** (Rudolf XI. von FRIDINGEN, Rudolf X. FRIDINGEN, Heinrich XI von FRIDINGEN, Rudolf VIII. FRIDINGEN, Rudolf VI. FRIDINGEN, Rudolf V. der Jung?

FRIDINGEN, Heinrich VII. FRIDINGEN, Rudolf III. von FRIDINGEN, Heinrich IV von FRIDINGEN, Heinrich III. von FRIDINGEN, Rudolf I. von FRIDINGEN, Heinrich I. von STETTEN, Hermann I. v STETTEN V. ESPASINGEN, Hermann HIRSCHECK D.J., Hermann HIRSCHECK D.Ä, Heinrich v HIRSCHECK D.Ä, Hermann HIRSCHECK, Hermann v. HIRSCHECK D.Ä I, Adalbert v. WINTERTHUR V. KYBURG, Liutfried v. WINTERTHUR, Ulrich V v. BREGENZ, Keroldus, Ulrich V ?, Ulrich III, Ratbert, Ulrich I, Gerold d. Ä).

Magdelena married **Marcus AUW OR OW**, son of Marquadus OW and GUILTLINGEN.

They had the following children:

316　F　i.　**Petronella AUW**.

297.　**Hans Grimmen FRIDINGEN** (Eitelhans FRIDINGEN, Wilhelm FRIDINGEN, Hans VI. FRIDINGEN, Johann V FRIDINGEN, Johann II d Altere FRIDINGEN, Johann Hans I. von FRIDINGEN DER KRAYGER, Burkhard I. FRIDINGEN, Konrad II. von FRIDINGEN, Heinrich IV von FRIDINGEN, Heinrich III. von FRIDINGEN, Rudolf I. von FRIDINGEN, Heinrich I. von STETTEN, Hermann I. v STETTEN V. ESPASINGEN, Hermann HIRSCHECK D.J., Hermann HIRSCHECK D.Ä, Heinrich v HIRSCHECK D.Ä, Hermann HIRSCHECK, Hermann v. HIRSCHECK D.Ä I, Adalbert v. WINTERTHUR V. KYBURG, Liutfried v. WINTERTHUR, Ulrich V v. BREGENZ, Keroldus, Ulrich V ?, Ulrich III, Ratbert, Ulrich I, Gerold d. Ä) was born ~1466. He died 1539.

Hans was employed Vogt 1543 in Herrenburg, Germany.

Hans married (1) **Barbara FULACH**, daughter of Ludovicus? FULACH and Agnes GEMMINGEN, on ~1522. Barbara died ~1550.

Hans also married (2) **Amalia von KNOERINGEN**, daughter of KNOERINGEN. Amalia died 1521.

They had the following children:

317　M　i.　**Bartolomeus FRIDINGEN** was born ~1485 in Fridingen, Hohentwiel, Germany. He died ~1538.

　　　　　　Bartolomeus was employed Leutpriester (Secular Priest) 1537 in Fridingen, Radolpzell, Germany.

298.　**Hans Benedict Ernst FRIDINGEN** (Eitelhans FRIDINGEN, Wilhelm FRIDINGEN, Hans VI. FRIDINGEN, Johann V FRIDINGEN, Johann II d Altere FRIDINGEN, Johann Hans I. von FRIDINGEN DER KRAYGER, Burkhard I. FRIDINGEN, Konrad II. von FRIDINGEN, Heinrich IV von FRIDINGEN, Heinrich III. von FRIDINGEN, Rudolf I. von FRIDINGEN, Heinrich I. von STETTEN, Hermann I. v STETTEN V. ESPASINGEN, Hermann HIRSCHECK D.J., Hermann HIRSCHECK D.Ä, Heinrich v HIRSCHECK D.Ä, Hermann HIRSCHECK, Hermann v. HIRSCHECK D.Ä I, Adalbert v. WINTERTHUR V. KYBURG, Liutfried v. WINTERTHUR, Ulrich V v. BREGENZ, Keroldus, Ulrich V ?, Ulrich III, Ratbert, Ulrich I, Gerold d. Ä) was born ~1469. He died 1517 in Hohenkrahen, Germany (Castle High Crows).

Hans resided in Hohenkrahen = High Crows. He resided 1502. He 1518 University of Wien, Austria.

Hans married **Elsbeth GRAMLICH**.

They had the following children:

318　M　i.　**Hans XI. FRIDINGEN** was born ~1502. He died 1529.

　　　　　　Hans was employed Vogte 1521 in Markdorf.

　　　　　　Hans married **Maria v. MAZEREIN**.

319　M　ii.　**Wilhelm FRIDINGEN** was born ~1502. He died 1529.

The Swabian Connection – Expanded Edition

+   320   M   iii.   **Michael FRIDINGEN** was born ~1502 and died 1529.

Twenty-Ninth Generation

308.   **George V. FRIDINGEN** (Martin II. FRIDINGEN, Rudolf XI. von FRIDINGEN, Rudolf X. FRIDINGEN, Heinrich XI von FRIDINGEN, Rudolf VIII. FRIDINGEN, Rudolf VI. FRIDINGEN, Rudolf V. der Jung? FRIDINGEN, Heinrich VII. FRIDINGEN, Rudolf III. von FRIDINGEN, Heinrich IV von FRIDINGEN, Heinrich III. von FRIDINGEN, Rudolf I. von FRIDINGEN, Heinrich I. von STETTEN, Hermann I. v STETTEN V. ESPASINGEN, Hermann HIRSCHECK D.J., Hermann HIRSCHECK D.Ä, Heinrich v HIRSCHECK D.Ä, Hermann HIRSCHECK, Hermann v. HIRSCHECK D.Ä I, Adalbert v. WINTERTHUR V. KYBURG, Liutfried v. WINTERTHUR, Ulrich V v. BREGENZ, Keroldus, Ulrich V ?, Ulrich III, Ratbert, Ulrich I, Gerold d. Ä) was born ~1482. He died 1544.

He had the following children:

   321   M   i.   **Hugo FRIDINGEN** was born ~1502 in Freiburg, Germany. He died 1568.

   Hugo 1539 & 1540 Freiburg, Germany. He was employed Rentmeister (treasurer) 1567 - 1568. He Universität Tübingen, Switzerland. He was employed Hofmesiter in Tubingen, Germany.

320.   **Michael FRIDINGEN** (Hans Benedict Ernst FRIDINGEN, Eitelhans FRIDINGEN, Wilhelm FRIDINGEN, Hans VI. FRIDINGEN, Johann V FRIDINGEN, Johann II d Altere FRIDINGEN, Johann Hans I. von FRIDINGEN DER KRAYGER, Burkhard I. FRIDINGEN, Konrad II. von FRIDINGEN, Heinrich IV von FRIDINGEN, Heinrich III. von FRIDINGEN, Rudolf I. von FRIDINGEN, Heinrich I. von STETTEN, Hermann I. v STETTEN V. ESPASINGEN, Hermann HIRSCHECK D.J., Hermann HIRSCHECK D.Ä, Heinrich v HIRSCHECK D.Ä, Hermann HIRSCHECK, Hermann v. HIRSCHECK D.Ä I, Adalbert v. WINTERTHUR V. KYBURG, Liutfried v. WINTERTHUR, Ulrich V v. BREGENZ, Keroldus, Ulrich V ?, Ulrich III, Ratbert, Ulrich I, Gerold d. Ä) was born ~1502. He died 1529.

Michael married **Anna HEUDORF** on 1522. Anna died 1549.

They had the following children:

+   322   F   i.   **Agatha FRIDINGEN** was born ~1512 and died 1571.

Thirtieth Generation

322.   **Agatha FRIDINGEN** (Michael FRIDINGEN, Hans Benedict Ernst FRIDINGEN, Eitelhans FRIDINGEN, Wilhelm FRIDINGEN, Hans VI. FRIDINGEN, Johann V FRIDINGEN, Johann II d Altere FRIDINGEN, Johann Hans I. von FRIDINGEN DER KRAYGER, Burkhard I. FRIDINGEN, Konrad II. von FRIDINGEN, Heinrich IV von FRIDINGEN, Heinrich III. von FRIDINGEN, Rudolf I. von FRIDINGEN, Heinrich I. von STETTEN, Hermann I. v STETTEN V. ESPASINGEN, Hermann HIRSCHECK D.J., Hermann HIRSCHECK D.Ä, Heinrich v HIRSCHECK D.Ä, Hermann HIRSCHECK, Hermann v. HIRSCHECK D.Ä I, Adalbert v. WINTERTHUR V. KYBURG, Liutfried v. WINTERTHUR, Ulrich V v. BREGENZ, Keroldus, Ulrich V ?, Ulrich III, Ratbert, Ulrich I, Gerold d. Ä) was born ~1512. She died 1571 and was buried in Kirchzarten.

Agatha married **Felix HOMBURG**, son of Wolf HOMBURG. Felix died 1550.

They had the following children:

   323   F   i.   **Margarete HOMBURG** was born ~1546. She died ~1567.

The Swabian Connection – Expanded Edition

Genealogy of the Austrian Fridinger lineage

(stem table research started by Maria Scheiber 194x)

First Generation

1. **Wolfgang I FRIDINGER** was born ~1460. He died ~1511.

   He had the following children:

   +   2   M   i.   **Erasmus I FRIDINGER** was born ~1485 and died ~1536.

   +   3   M   ii.   **Wolgang II FRIDINGER** was born ~1490 and died ~1529.

Second Generation

2. **Erasmus I FRIDINGER** (Wolfgang I) was born ~1485. He died ~1536.

   Erasmus married **Margarethe SENSLEUTER**.

   They had the following children:

   +   4   M   i.   **Damian FRIDINGER** was born ~1515 and died ~Apr 1568.

         5   M   ii.   **Thomas FRIDINGER** died ~1563.

3. **Wolgang II FRIDINGER** (Wolfgang I) was born ~1490. He died ~1529.

   Wolgang 1509 Universitat Wien.

   He had the following children:

         6   M   i.   **Wolfgang III FRIDINGER** was born ~1546. He died ~1577.

Third Generation

4. **Damian FRIDINGER** (Erasmus I, Wolfgang I) was born ~1515. He died ~Apr 1568.

   Damian resided 1533 in Kriegsdiensten.

   He had the following children:

         7   M   i.   **Sebastian I FRIDINGER** was born ~1548 in Austria. He died ~1573.

                         Sebastian resided 1563 - 1564 in Austria.

         8   F   ii.   **N FRIDINGER**.

         9   M   iii.   **Erasmus II FRIDINGER** died ~1576.

         10   F   iv.   **Julian FRIDINGER**.

                         Julian married (1) **Leonhard MATSCHPERGER**.

                         Julian also married (2) **Wolf EDLINGER**.

   +   11   M   v.   **Andreas I FRIDINGER** died ~1604.

         12   M   vi.   **Hans I FRIDINGER** died ~1604.

         13   F   vii.   **Sofia FRIDINGER**.

Sofia married (1) **Hans ENZENDORFER**.

Sofia also married (2) **Benedict HACKNER**.

14　F　viii.　**Susannah FRIDINGER**.

Susannah married **Achaz MARKGRABER**.

15　F　ix.　**Katherina FRIDINGER**.

Katherina married **N VISCHER**.

Fourth Generation

11. **Andreas I FRIDINGER** (Damian, Erasmus I, Wolfgang I) died ~1604.

Andreas resided in Marktrichter & Hammergewerke In Weyer.

Andreas married **Ester KAMERER**.

They had the following children:

16　F　i.　**Andreas II FRIDINGER** died ~1634 in Regensburg.

Andreas married **Christine WINKLER ZUM WINKLESTEIN**.

+　17　M　ii.　**Sebastian II FRIDINGER** died 12 Nov 1634.

18　F　iii.　**Katharina FRIDINGER**.

Katharina married **N HUEBNER**.

19　M　iv.　**Erasmus III FRIDINGER**.

+　20　M　v.　**Isaak FRIDINGER**.

21　M　vi.　**Wolf IV FRIDINGER**.

22　F　vii.　**Sabina FRIDINGER**.

Sabina married **N ZELLER**.

23　F　viii.　**Ester FRIDINGER**.

24　F　ix.　**Juliana FRIDINGER**.

Fifth Generation

17. **Sebastian II FRIDINGER** (Andreas I, Damian, Erasmus I, Wolfgang I) died 12 Nov 1634 in Krems, Austria.

Sebastian married **Regina**. Regina died 3 Dec 1636.

They had the following children:

25　M　i.　**Hans Ehrenreich FRIDINGER** died ~1634.

Hans resided 5 Jan 1622 in Krems, Austria.

26　M　ii.　**Erasmus V FRIDINGER** died ~1634.

Erasmus resided 24 May 1629 in Krems, Austria.

20. **Isaak FRIDINGER** (Andreas I, Damian, Erasmus I, Wolfgang I).

The Swabian Connection – Expanded Edition

Isaak married **Anna N.**

They had the following children:

    27 M   i. **Hans II FRIDINGER**.

                  Hans resided 5 May 1625 in Krems, Austria.

    28 F   ii. **Anna Katherina FRIDINGER**.

                  Anna married **Peter HORMAYR D.J.**

Stammtable Expanded Lineages

(original by Eberhard Dobler with additions by Jeff Friday)

Table1
Die Herkunft(Origin) die Herren(Lords) von Hirscheck

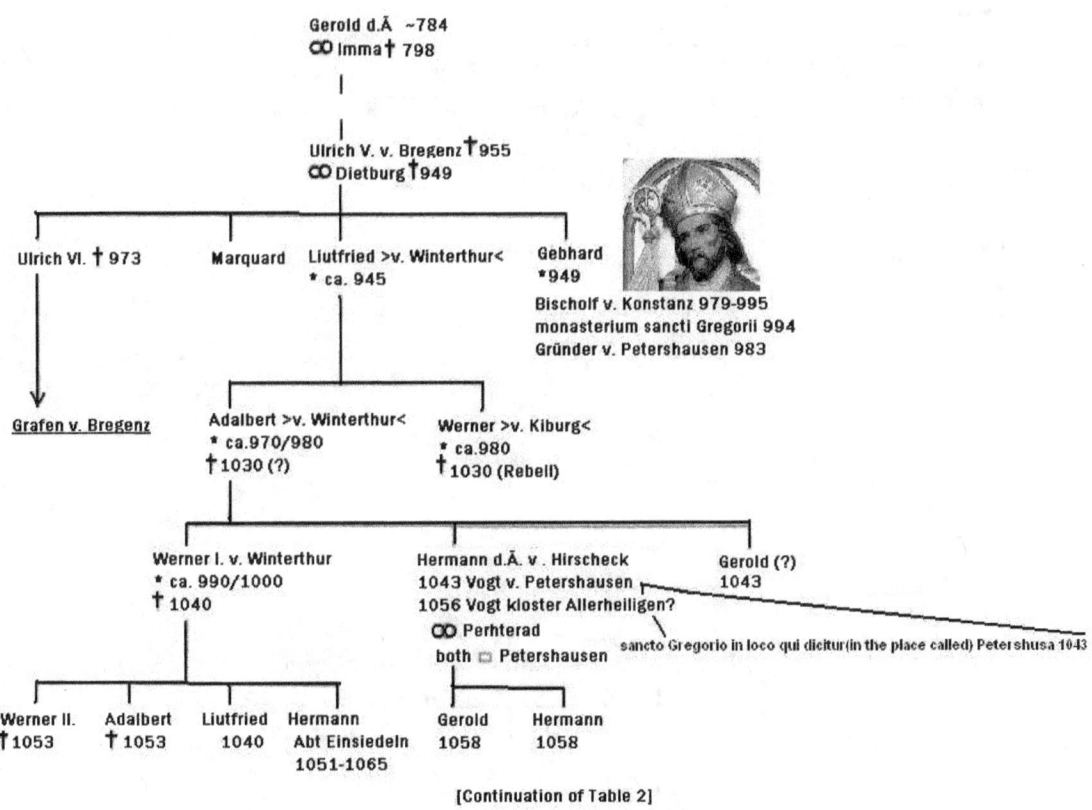

[Continuation of Table 2]

Table2

Die Herren von Hirscheck, von Markdorf, von Annewiler(Andwil)?,von Shussenriet?

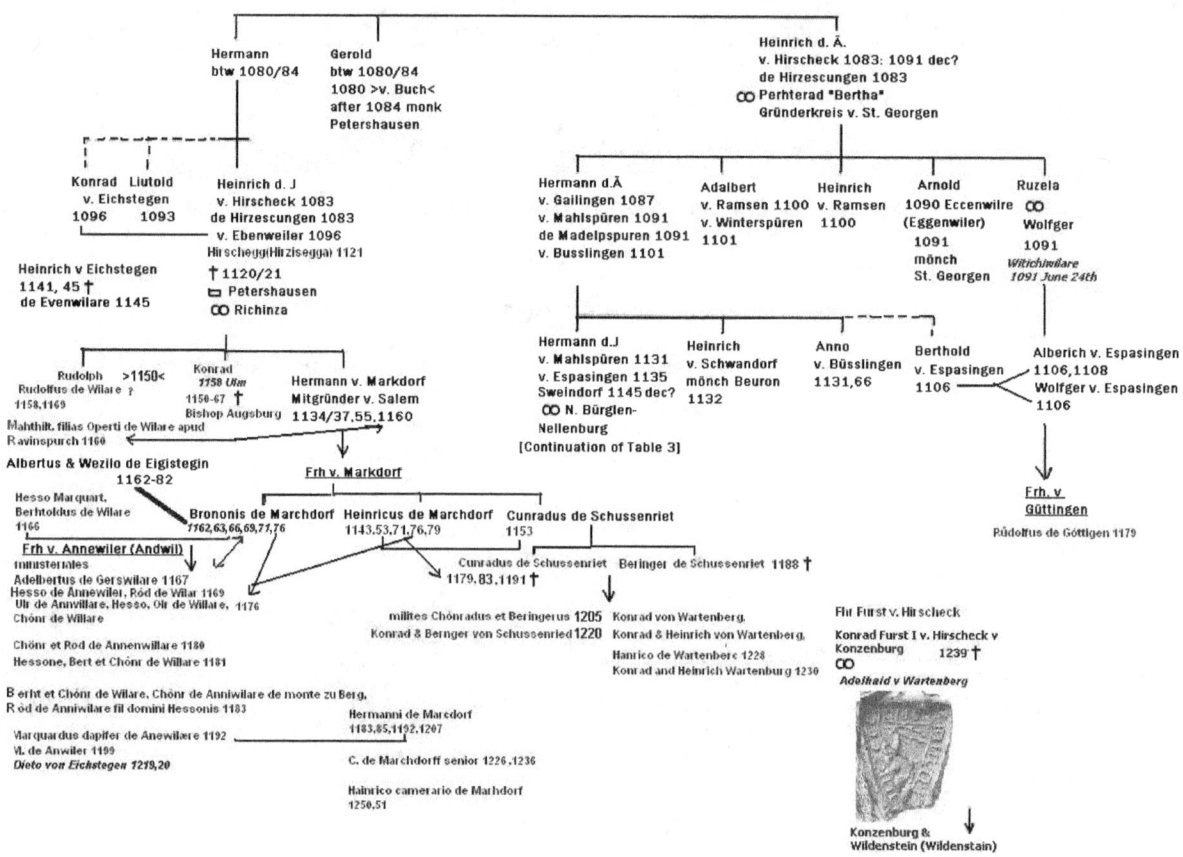

Hermann
btw 1080/84

Gerold
btw 1080/84
1080 >v. Buch<
after 1084 monk
Petershausen

Heinrich d. Ä.
v. Hirscheck 1083: 1091 dec?
de Hirzescungen 1083
∞ Perhterad "Bertha"
Gründerkreis v. St. Georgen

Konrad   Liutold
v. Eichstegen
1096   1093

Heinrich d. J
v. Hirscheck 1083
de Hirzescungen 1083
v. Ebenweiler 1096
Hirschegg(Hirzisegga) 1121

Heinrich v Eichstegen
1141, 45 †
de Evenwilare 1145

† 1120/21
⊏ Petershausen
∞ Richinza

Hermann d.Ä
v. Gailingen 1087
v. Mahlspüren 1091
de Madelpspuren 1091
v. Busslingen 1101

Adalbert
v. Ramsen 1100
v. Winterspüren
1101

Heinrich
v. Ramsen
1100

Arnold
1090 Eccenwilre
(Eggenwiler)
1091
mönch
St. Georgen

Ruzela
∞
Wolfger
1091
Witichiwilare
1091 June 24th

Rudolph   >1150<
Rudolfus de Wilare ?
1158,1169

Konrad
1158 Ulm
1150-67 †
Bishop Augsburg

Hermann v. Markdorf
Mitgründer v. Salem
1134/37,55,1160

Hermann d.J
v. Mahlspüren 1131
v. Espasingen 1135
Sweindorf 1145 dec?
∞ N. Bürglen-
Nellenburg

Heinrich
v. Schwandorf
mönch Beuron
1132

Anno
v. Büsslingen
1131,66

Berthold
v. Espasingen
1106

Alberich v. Espasingen
1106,1108
Wolfger v. Espasingen
1106

Mahthilt. filias Operti de Wilare apud
Ravinspurch 1160

Albertus & Wezilo de Eigistegin
1162-82

Hesso Marquart,
Berhtoldus de Wilare
1166

Frh v. Annewiler (Andwil)
ministeriales
Adelbertus de Gerswilare 1167
Hesso de Annewiler, Rôd de Wilar 1169
Ulr de Annwillare, Hesso, Olr de Willare, 1176
Chönr de Willare

Chönr et Rôd de Annemwillare 1180

Hessone, Bert et Chönr de Willare 1181

B erht et Chönr de Wilare, Chönr de Anniwillare de monte zu Berg,
R ôd de Anniwillare fil domini Hessonis 1183

Marquardus dapifer de Anewillare 1192
VI. de Anwiler 1199
Dieto von Eichstegen 1219,20

Frh v. Markdorf

[Continuation of Table 3]

Brononis de Marchdorf
1162,63,66,69,71,76

Heinricus de Marchdorf
1143,53,71,76,79

Cunradus de Schussenriet
1153

Hermanni de Marcdorf
1183,85,1192,1207

Cunradus de Schussenriet Beringer de Schussenriet 1188 †
1179,83,1191 †

C. de Marchdorff senior 1226 ,1236

Hainrico camerario de Marhdorf
1250,51

milites Chônradus et Beringerus 1205
Konrad & Bernger von Schussenried 1220

Konrad von Wartenberg,
Konrad & Heinrich von Wartenberg,
Hanrico de Wartenberc 1228
Konrad and Heinrich Wartenburg 1230

Fh Furst v. Hirscheck

Konrad Furst I v. Hirscheck v
Konzenburg   1239 †
∞
Adelhaid v Wartenberg

Frh. v
Güttingen

Rûdolfus de Göttigen 1179

Konzenburg &
Wildenstein (Wildenstain)

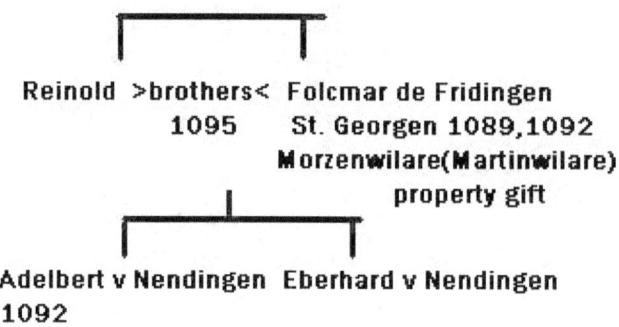

Reinold >brothers< Folcmar de Fridingen
       1095   St. Georgen 1089,1092
                    Morzenwilare(Martinwilare)
                         property gift

Adelbert v Nendingen Eberhard v Nendingen
1092

Table3

Die Herren von Mahlspuren zu Fridingen, von Salenstein, von Reidern

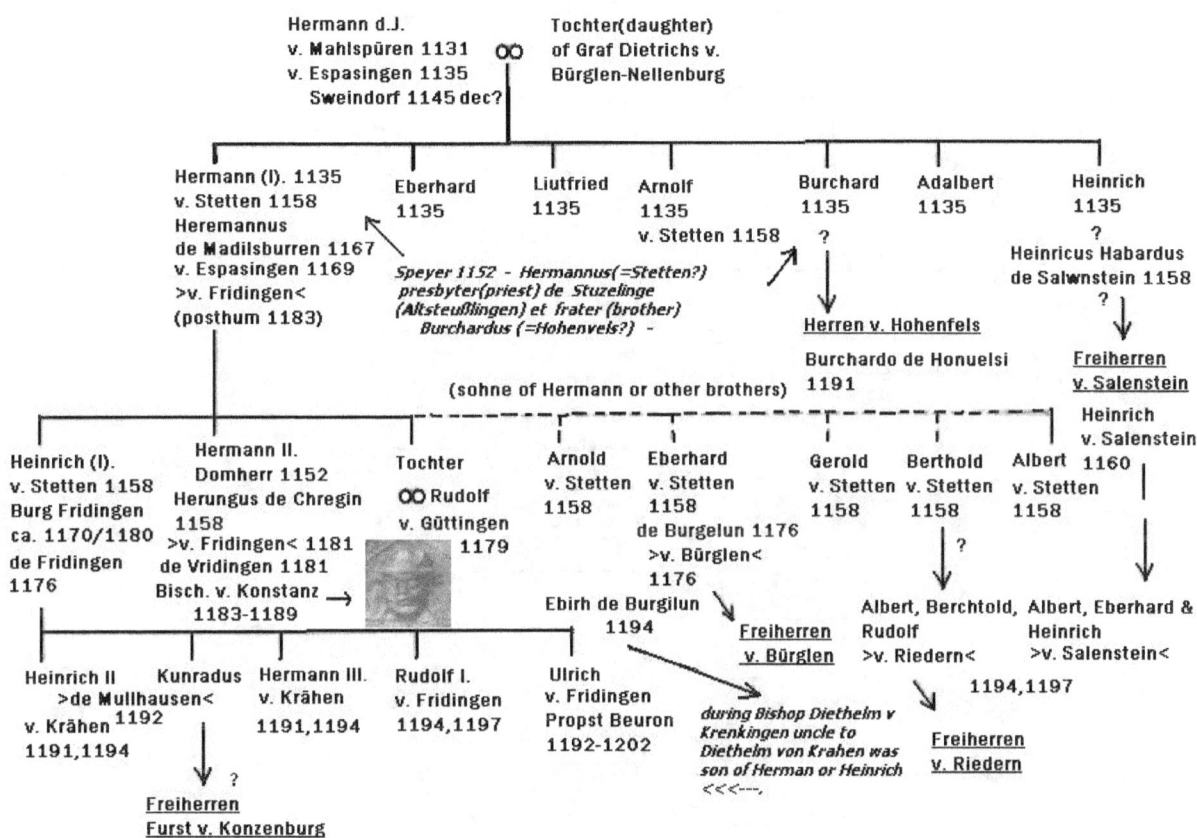

Hermann d.J.
v. Mahlspüren 1131
v. Espasingen 1135
Sweindorf 1145 dec?
∞∞
Tochter(daughter)
of Graf Dietrichs v.
Bürglen-Nellenburg

Hermann (I). 1135
v. Stetten 1158
Heremannus
de Madilsburren 1167
v. Espasingen 1169
>v. Fridingen<
(posthum 1183)

Eberhard
1135

Liutfried
1135

Arnolf
1135
v. Stetten 1158

Burchard
1135
?

Adalbert
1135

Heinrich
1135
?
Heinricus Habardus
de Salwnstein 1158
?

*Speyer 1152 - Hermannus(=Stetten?)
presbyter(priest) de Stuzelinge
(Altsteußlingen) et frater (brother)
Burchardus (=Hohenvels?) -*

Herren v. Hohenfels
Burchardo de Honuelsi
1191

Freiherren
v. Salenstein

(sohne of Hermann or other brothers)

Heinrich (I).
v. Stetten 1158
Burg Fridingen
ca. 1170/1180
de Fridingen
1176

Hermann II.
Domherr 1152
Herungus de Chregin
1158
>v. Fridingen< 1181
de Vridingen 1181
Bisch. v. Konstanz
1183-1189

Tochter
∞∞ Rudolf
v. Güttingen
1179

Arnold
v. Stetten
1158

Eberhard
v. Stetten
1158
de Burgelun 1176
>v. Bürglen<
1176
Ebirh de Burgilun
1194

Gerold
v. Stetten
1158

Berthold
v. Stetten
1158
?

Albert
v. Stetten
1158

Heinrich
v. Salenstein
1160

Freiherren
v. Bürglen

Albert, Berchtold,
Rudolf
>v. Riedern<

Albert, Eberhard &
Heinrich
>v. Salenstein<

1194,1197

Heinrich II
>de Mullhausen<
v. Krähen
1191,1194
1192

Kunradus

Hermann III.
v. Krähen
1191,1194

Rudolf I.
v. Fridingen
1194,1197

Ulrich
v. Fridingen
Propst Beuron
1192-1202

*during Bishop Diethelm v
Krenkingen uncle to
Diethelm von Krahen was
son of Herman or Heinrich
<<<---,*

Freiherren
v. Riedern

?
Freiherren
Furst v. Konzenburg

Table4

Die Edelfrien & Truchsessen von Krähen, von Schwandorf

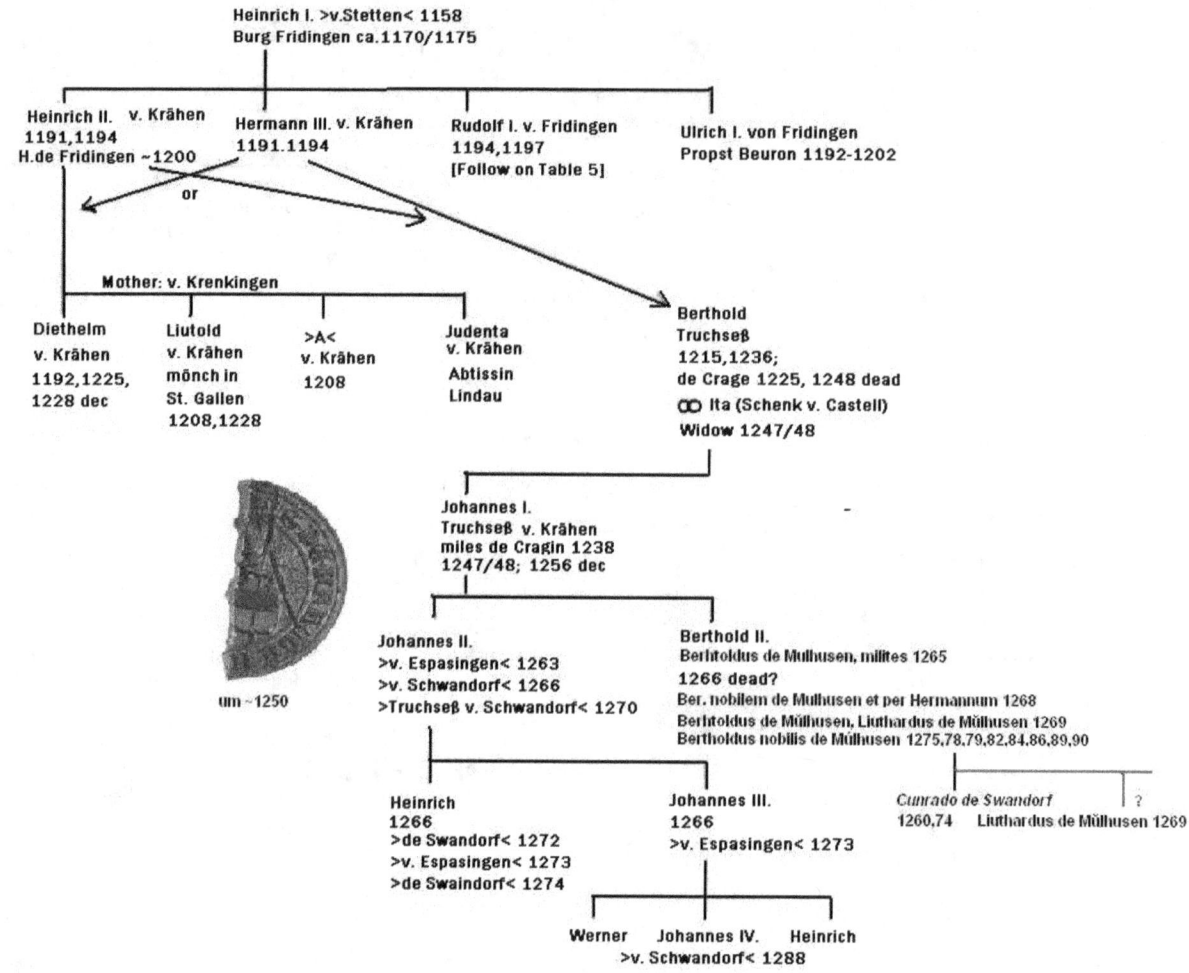

Heinrich I. >v.Stetten< 1158
Burg Fridingen ca.1170/1175

Heinrich II. v. Krähen
1191,1194
H.de Fridingen ~1200

Hermann III. v. Krähen
1191.1194

Rudolf I. v. Fridingen
1194,1197
[Follow on Table 5]

Ulrich I. von Fridingen
Propst Beuron 1192-1202

or

Mother: v. Krenkingen

Diethelm
v. Krähen
1192,1225,
1228 dec

Liutold
v. Krähen
mönch in
St. Gallen
1208,1228

>A<
v. Krähen
1208

Judenta
v. Krähen
Abtissin
Lindau

Berthold
Truchseß
1215,1236;
de Crage 1225, 1248 dead
∞ Ita (Schenk v. Castell)
Widow 1247/48

um ~1250

Johannes I.
Truchseß v. Krähen
miles de Cragin 1238
1247/48; 1256 dec

Johannes II.
>v. Espasingen< 1263
>v. Schwandorf< 1266
>Truchseß v. Schwandorf< 1270

Berthold II.
Berhtoldus de Mulhusen, milites 1265
1266 dead?
Ber. nobilem de Mulhusen et per Hermannum 1268
Berhtoldus de Mülhusen, Liuthardus de Mülhusen 1269
Bertholdus nobilis de Mülhusen 1275,78,79,82,84,86,89,90

Cunrado de Swandorf
1260,74

?
Liuthardus de Mülhusen 1269

Heinrich
1266
>de Swandorf< 1272
>v. Espasingen< 1273
>de Swaindorf< 1274

Johannes III.
1266
>v. Espasingen< 1273

Werner   Johannes IV.   Heinrich
>v. Schwandorf< 1288

The Swabian Connection – Expanded Edition

Table5
Die Frühen(early) Fridinger and Wildenfels(Wildenvels)?

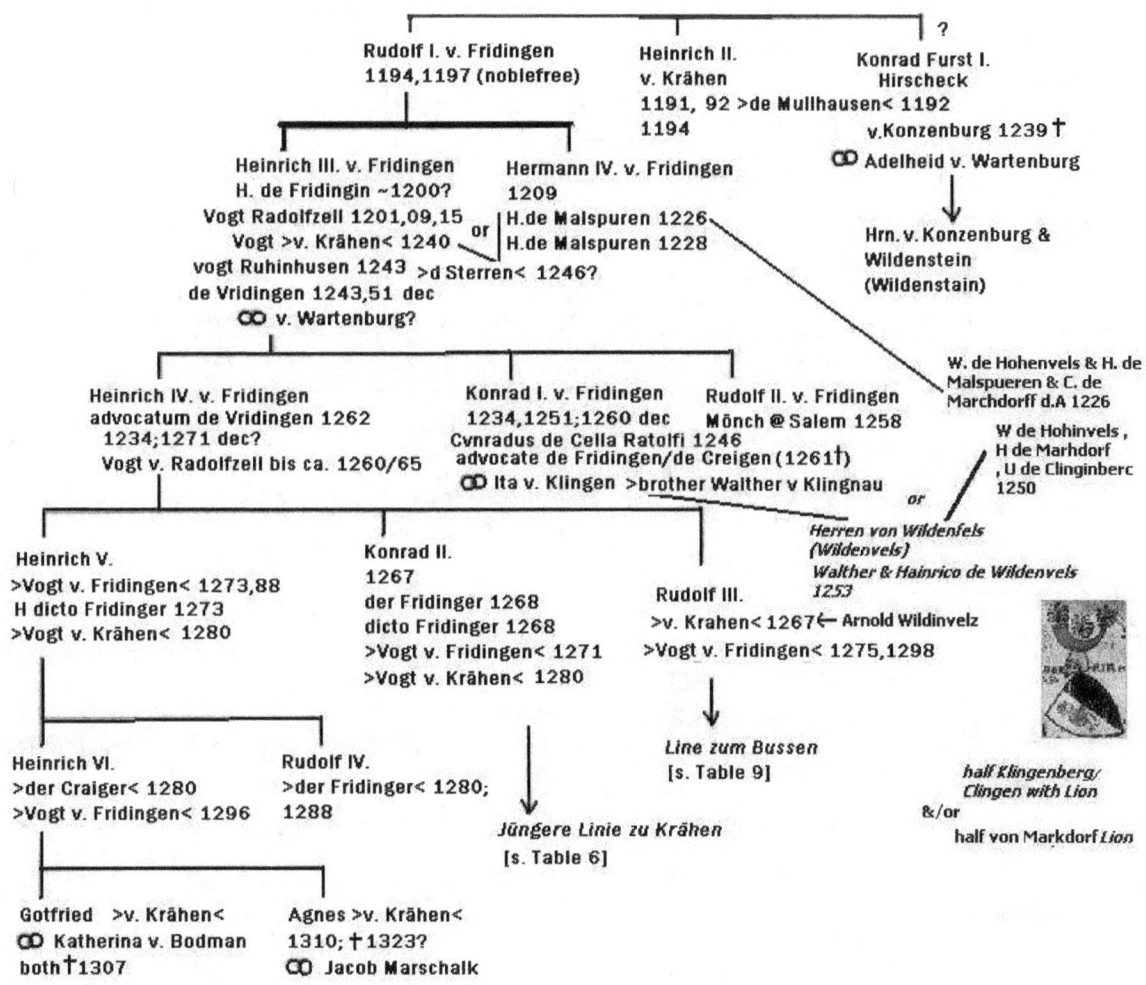

Rudolf I. v. Fridingen
1194,1197 (noblefree)

Heinrich II.
v. Krähen
1191, 92 >de Mullhausen< 1192
1194

Konrad Furst I.
Hirscheck
v.Konzenburg 1239 †
∞ Adelheid v. Wartenburg

?

Heinrich III. v. Fridingen
H. de Fridingin ~1200?
Vogt Radolfzell 1201,09,15
Vogt >v. Krähen< 1240
vogt Ruhinhusen 1243
de Vridingen 1243,51 dec
∞ v. Wartenburg?

or

Hermann IV. v. Fridingen
1209
H.de Malspuren 1226
H.de Malspuren 1228
>d Sterren< 1246?

Hrn. v. Konzenburg &
Wildenstein
(Wildenstain)

Heinrich IV. v. Fridingen
advocatum de Vridingen 1262
1234;1271 dec?
Vogt v. Radolfzell bis ca. 1260/65

Konrad I. v. Fridingen
1234,1251;1260 dec
Cvnradus de Cella Ratolfi 1246
advocate de Fridingen/de Creigen (1261†)
∞ Ita v. Klingen >brother Walther v Klingnau

Rudolf II. v. Fridingen
Mönch @ Salem 1258

W. de Hohenvels & H. de
Malspueren & C. de
Marchdorff d.A 1226

W de Hohinvels ,
H de Marhdorf
, U de Clinginberc
1250

or

Heinrich V.
>Vogt v. Fridingen< 1273,88
H dicto Fridinger 1273
>Vogt v. Krähen< 1280

Konrad II.
1267
der Fridinger 1268
dicto Fridinger 1268
>Vogt v. Fridingen< 1271
>Vogt v. Krähen< 1280

Rudolf III.
>v. Krahen< 1267← Arnold Wildinvelz
>Vogt v. Fridingen< 1275,1298

*Herren von Wildenfels
(Wildenvels)*
Walther & Hainrico de Wildenvels
1253

Heinrich VI.
>der Craiger< 1280
>Vogt v. Fridingen< 1296

Rudolf IV.
>der Fridinger< 1280;
1288

Line zum Bussen
[s. Table 9]

*half Klingenberg/
Clingen with Lion*
&/or
half von Markdorf *Lion*

Jüngere Linie zu Krähen
[s. Table 6]

Gotfried >v. Krähen<
∞ Katherina v. Bodman
both †1307

Agnes >v. Krähen<
1310; †1323?
∞ Jacob Marschalk

The Swabian Connection – Expanded Edition

Table6
Die jüngere(younger) Line zu Krähen

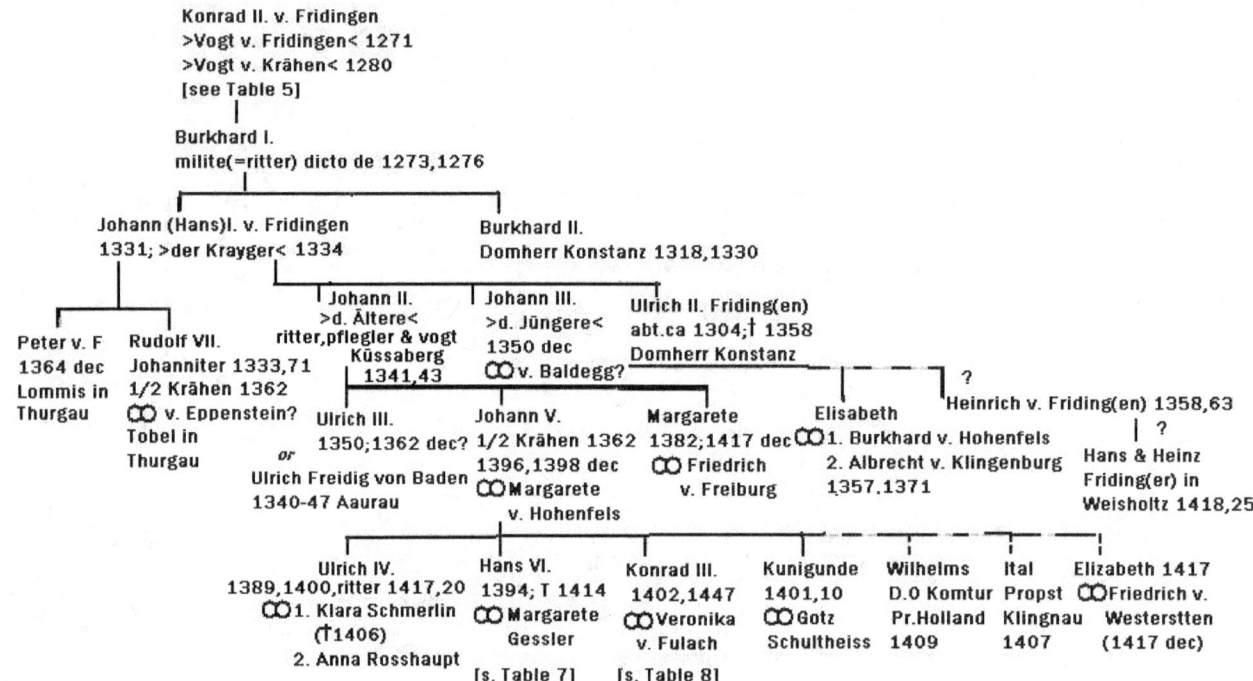

Konrad II. v. Fridingen
>Vogt v. Fridingen< 1271
>Vogt v. Krähen< 1280
[see Table 5]

Burkhard I.
milite(=ritter) dicto de 1273,1276

Johann (Hans)I. v. Fridingen
1331; >der Krayger< 1334

Burkhard II.
Domherr Konstanz 1318,1330

Peter v. F
1364 dec
Lommis in
Thurgau

Rudolf VII.
Johanniter 1333,71
1/2 Krähen 1362
⚭ v. Eppenstein?
Tobel in
Thurgau

Johann II.
>d. Ältere<
ritter,pflegler & vogt
Küssaberg
1341,43

Johann III.
>d. Jüngere<
1350 dec
⚭ v. Baldegg?

Ulrich II. Friding(en)
abt.ca 1304;† 1358
Domherr Konstanz

Elisabeth

?

Heinrich v. Friding(en) 1358,63

or

Ulrich III.
1350;1362 dec?

Ulrich Freidig von Baden
1340-47 Aaurau

Johann V.
1/2 Krähen 1362
1396,1398 dec
⚭ Margarete
v. Hohenfels

Margarete
1382;1417 dec⚭1. Burkhard v. Hohenfels
⚭ Friedrich   2. Albrecht v. Klingenburg
v. Freiburg   1357.1371

?
Hans & Heinz
Friding(er) in
Weisholtz 1418,25

Ulrich IV.
1389,1400,ritter 1417,20
⚭1. Klara Schmerlin
(†1406)
2. Anna Rosshaupt

Hans VI.
1394; T 1414
⚭ Margarete
Gessler

[s. Table 7]

Konrad III.
1402,1447
⚭Veronika
v. Fulach

[s. Table 8]

Kunigunde
1401,10
⚭ Gotz
Schultheiss

Wilhelms
D.O Komtur
Pr.Holland
1409

Ital
Propst
Klingnau
1407

Elizabeth 1417
⚭Friedrich v.
Westerstten
(1417 dec)

Table7

Hans IV of Fridingen and his descendants

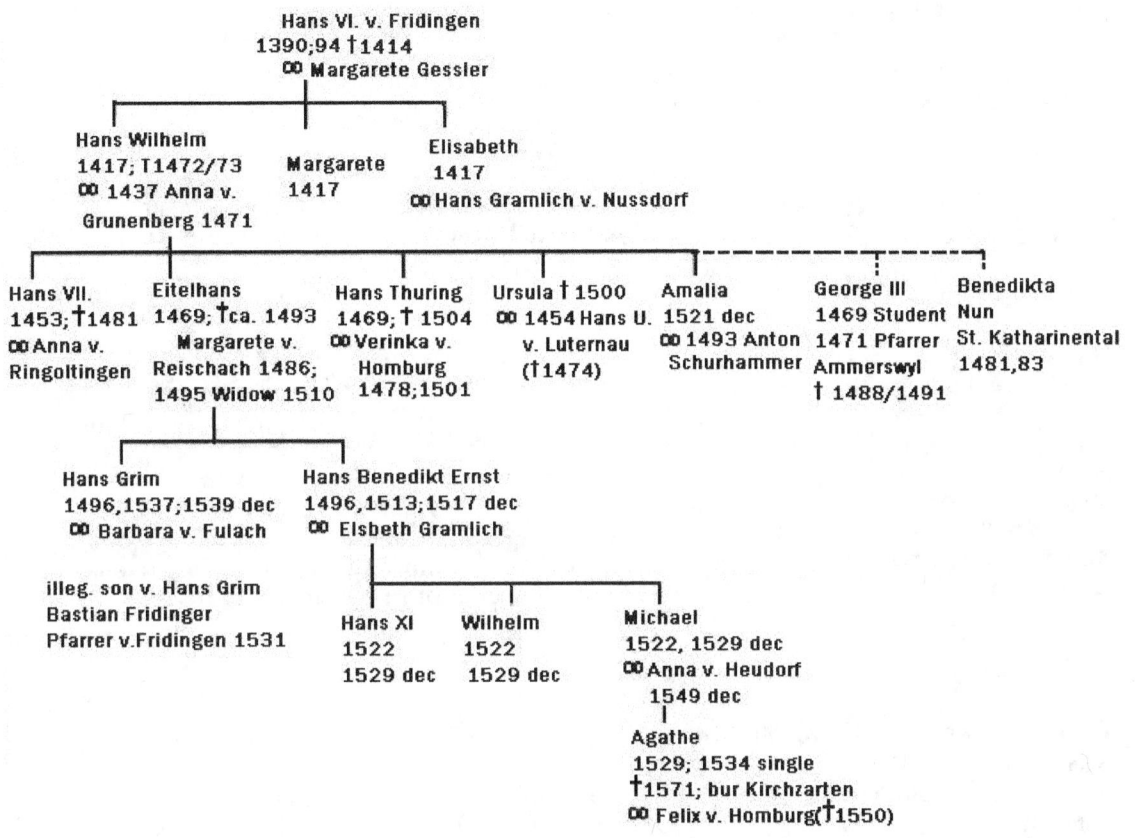

Table8
Die Line Heinrichs XI. & Konrad III von Fridingen

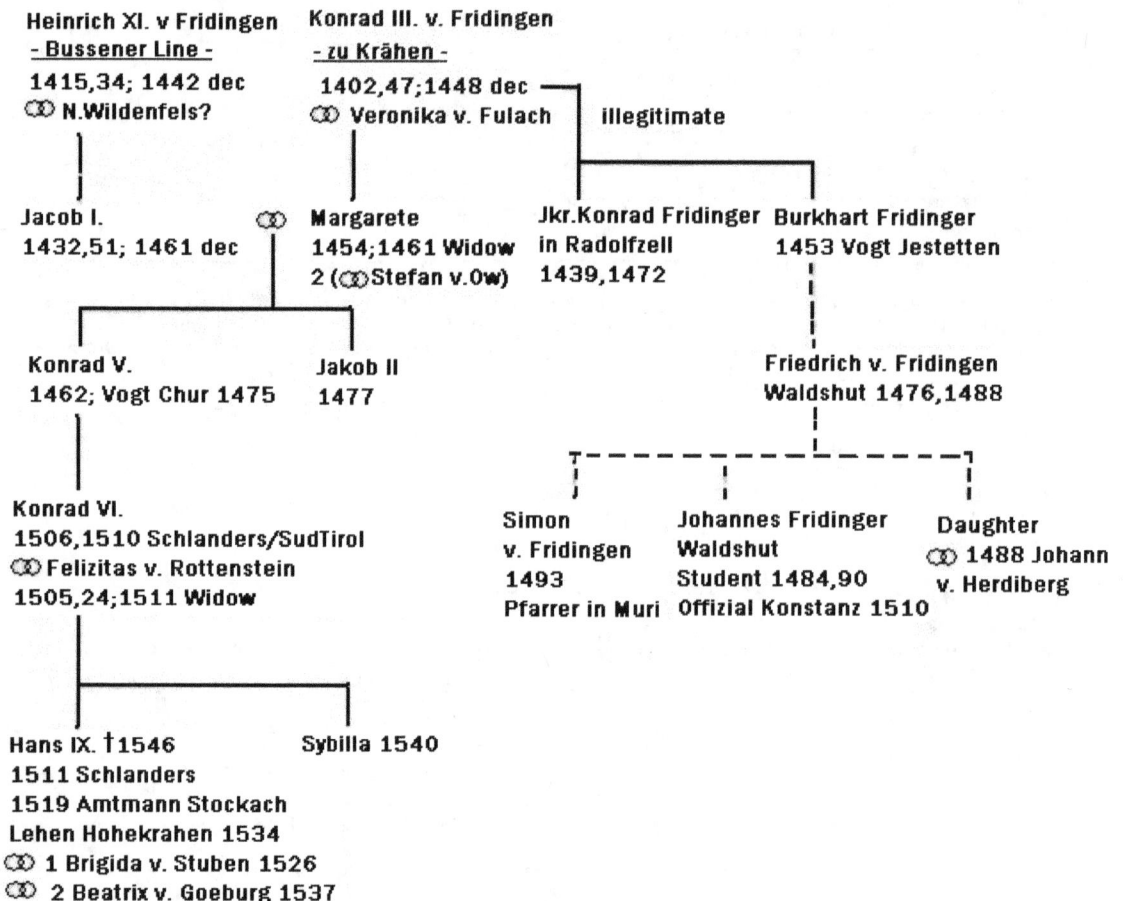

Heinrich XI. v Fridingen
- Bussener Line -
1415,34; 1442 dec
⚭ N.Wildenfels?

Konrad III. v. Fridingen
- zu Krähen -
1402,47;1448 dec
⚭ Veronika v. Fulach   illegitimate

Jacob I.   ⚭   Margarete
1432,51; 1461 dec   1454;1461 Widow
                                 2 (⚭Stefan v.Ow)

Jkr.Konrad Fridinger   Burkhart Fridinger
in Radolfzell   1453 Vogt Jestetten
1439,1472

Konrad V.   Jakob II
1462; Vogt Chur 1475   1477

Friedrich v. Fridingen
Waldshut 1476,1488

Konrad VI.
1506,1510 Schlanders/SudTirol
⚭ Felizitas v. Rottenstein
1505,24;1511 Widow

Simon   Johannes Fridinger   Daughter
v. Fridingen   Waldshut   ⚭ 1488 Johann
1493   Student 1484,90   v. Herdiberg
Pfarrer in Muri   Offizial Konstanz 1510

Hans IX. †1546   Sybilla 1540
1511 Schlanders
1519 Amtmann Stockach
Lehen Hohekrahen 1534
⚭ 1 Brigida v. Stuben 1526
⚭ 2 Beatrix v. Goeburg 1537

The Swabian Connection – Expanded Edition

Table 9

Die Line zum Bussen & Line der Friding(er)

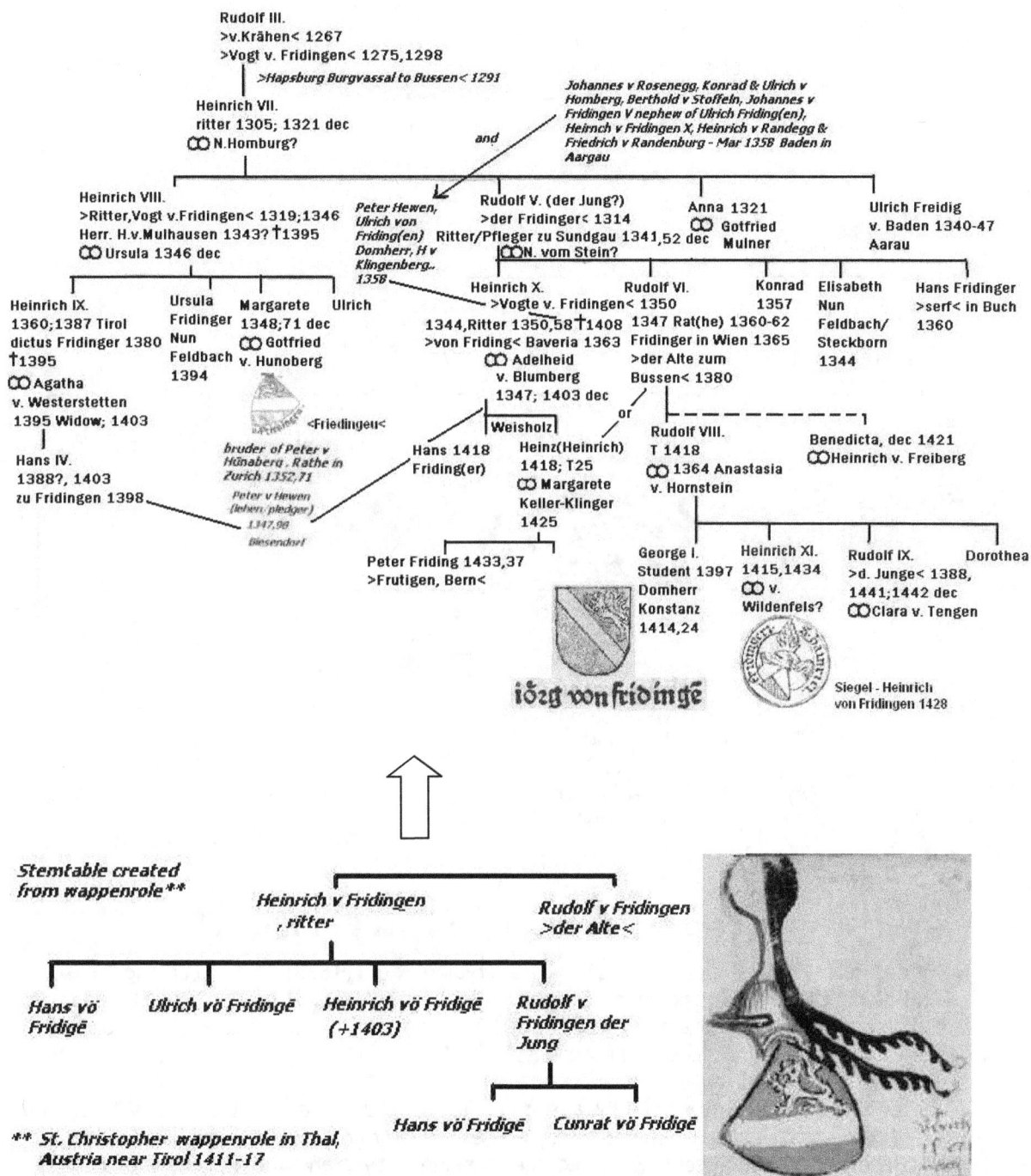

Rudolf III.
>v.Krähen< 1267
>Vogt v. Fridingen< 1275,1298
>Hapsburg Burgvassal to Bussen< 1291

Heinrich VII.
ritter 1305; 1321 dec
⚭ N.Homburg?

Johannes v Rosenegg, Konrad & Ulrich v Homberg, Berthold v Stoffeln, Johannes v Fridingen V nephew of Ulrich Friding(en), Heinrich v Fridingen X, Heinrich v Randegg & Friedrich v Randenburg - Mar 1358 Baden in Aargau

and

Heinrich VIII.
>Ritter,Vogt v.Fridingen< 1319;1346
Herr. H.v.Mulhausen 1343? †1395
⚭ Ursula 1346 dec

Peter Hewen, Ulrich von Friding(en) Domherr, H v Klingenberg.. 1358

Rudolf V. (der Jung?)
>der Fridinger< 1314
Ritter/Pfleger zu Sundgau 1341,52 dec
⚭ N. vom Stein?

Anna 1321
⚭ Gotfried Mulner

Ulrich Freidig
v. Baden 1340-47
Aarau

Heinrich IX.
1360;1387 Tirol dictus Fridinger 1380 †1395
⚭ Agatha v. Westerstetten 1395 Widow; 1403

Ursula Fridinger Nun Feldbach 1394

Margarete 1348;71 dec
⚭ Gotfried v. Hunoberg

Ulrich

Heinrich X.
>Vogte v. Fridingen< 1350
1344,Ritter 1350,58 †1408
>von Friding< Baveria 1363
⚭ Adelheid v. Blumberg 1347; 1403 dec

Rudolf VI.
1347 Rat(he) 1360-62
Fridinger in Wien 1365
>der Alte zum Bussen< 1380

Konrad 1357

Elisabeth Nun Feldbach/ Steckborn 1344

Hans Fridinger >serf< in Buch 1360

bruder of Peter v Hünaberg , Rathe in Zurich 1352,71
Peter v Hewen (lehen, pledger) 1347,98 Biesendorf

Hans 1418 Friding(er)

Weisholz

Heinz(Heinrich) 1418; T25
⚭ Margarete Keller-Klinger 1425

or

Rudolf VIII. T 1418
⚭ 1364 Anastasia v. Hornstein

Benedicta, dec 1421
⚭ Heinrich v. Freiberg

Hans IV. 1388?, 1403 zu Fridingen 1398

Peter Friding 1433,37 >Frutigen, Bern<

George I. Student 1397 Domherr Konstanz 1414,24

Heinrich XI. 1415,1434
⚭ v. Wildenfels?

Rudolf IX. >d. Junge< 1388, 1441;1442 dec
⚭ Clara v. Tengen

Dorothea

iŏrg von friðingē

Siegel - Heinrich von Fridingen 1428

*Stemtable created from wappenrole***

Heinrich v Fridingen , ritter

Rudolf v Fridingen >der Alte<

Hans vö Fridigē *Ulrich vö Fridigē* *Heinrich vö Fridigē (+1403)* *Rudolf v Fridingen der Jung*

Hans vö Fridigē *Cunrat vö Fridigē*

** *St. Christopher wappenrole in Thal, Austria near Tirol 1411-17*

Table 10
Die Line zum Bussen 2

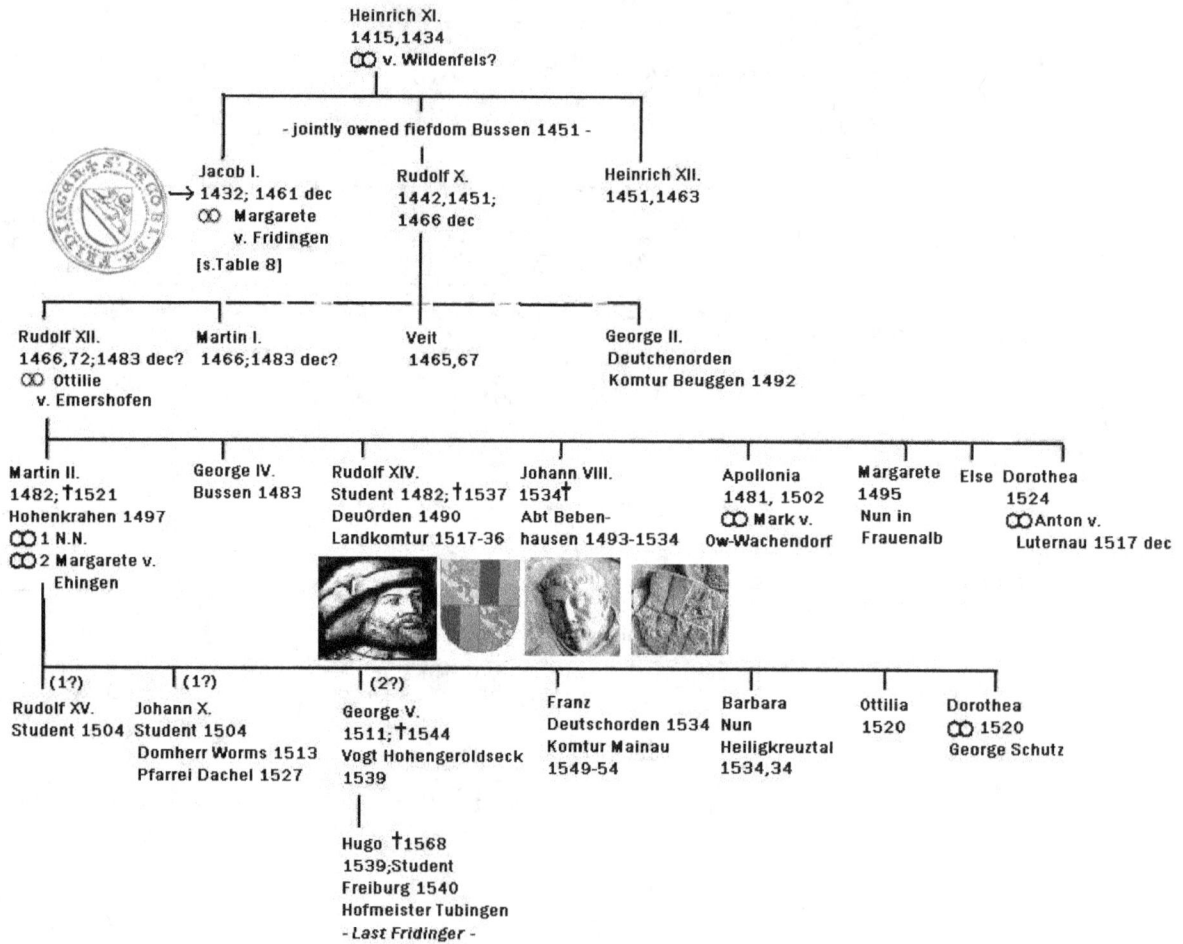

Heinrich XI.
1415,1434
∞ v. Wildenfels?

- jointly owned fiefdom Bussen 1451 -

Jacob I.	Rudolf X.	Heinrich XII.
→ 1432; 1461 dec	1442,1451;	1451,1463
∞ Margarete	1466 dec	
v. Fridingen		
[s.Table 8]		

Rudolf XII.	Martin I.	Veit	George II.
1466,72;1483 dec?	1466;1483 dec?	1465,67	Deutchenorden
∞ Ottilie			Komtur Beuggen 1492
v. Emershofen			

Martin II.	George IV.	Rudolf XIV.	Johann VIII.	Apollonia	Margarete	Else Dorothea
1482; †1521	Bussen 1483	Student 1482; †1537	1534†	1481, 1502	1495	1524
Hohenkrahen 1497		DeuOrden 1490	Abt Beben-	∞ Mark v.	Nun in	∞ Anton v.
∞1 N.N.		Landkomtur 1517-36	hausen 1493-1534	Ow-Wachendorf	Frauenalb	Luternau 1517 dec
∞2 Margarete v.						
Ehingen						

(1?)	(1?)	(2?)				
Rudolf XV.	Johann X.	George V.	Franz	Barbara	Ottilia	Dorothea
Student 1504	Student 1504	1511; †1544	Deutschorden 1534	Nun	1520	∞ 1520
	Domherr Worms 1513	Vogt Hohengeroldseck	Komtur Mainau	Heiligkreuztal		George Schutz
	Pfarrei Dachel 1527	1539	1549-54	1534,34		

Hugo †1568
1539;Student
Freiburg 1540
Hofmeister Tubingen
- Last Fridinger -

Is Friding|Frydig/Fridig s. Fridingen?

How does Peter Friding|Frydig (~1403) or Gwer Fryding|Fridig (1535) relate to Fridingen? Is Friding/Frydig the same as Fridingen? Fridiger/Friding and other variations were used moderately in church legal records between the years 920-1500 as a casual reference to Fridingen/er family. Lets review the clues and research in sections:

1) Peter Friding|Frydig (~1403) is already in Frutigen/Adelboden, Switzerland by 1433 and 1437 – Friding as his written surname and Frydig as the later Frutigesche familie surname. There were only about 400-500 people who lived in Adelboden in 1433 and in that same year 12 independent men began to build the Parish church after being rejected by Bishop of Lausanne @ Interlaken[514]. A northern war in 1415 may have caused Peter to migrate further south - the Swiss Confederation managed to conquer the Lower Aargau, which went partly to Bern in the west and smaller parts to Lucerne and Zurich in the east[515]. Notice there is NO particle "von", attached to his name denoting feudal nobility. In the 15th century the policitcal power in Bern belongs to an

The Swabian Connection – Expanded Edition

upper class which was formed with noble families proceeding from the middle class of the chief town of each state[516]. He is believed to be a lesser/untitled noble, or a 2nd born male, an illegitimate son or voluntary "von" renunciation, descendant of a monch (munk) or simply migrated as many people may not have acquired a Nobel occupation to stay near the familie circle. "There is no clear pattern for use of Surnames, however in most cases Bastards would use a form of their fathers surname without the noble particle "von", indicating they were not regarded as nobles" (Hurwich : 234). The Swiss people and its Confederation were dislodging from their patrician aristocrat's since 1291. Peter was most likely a relative of Ulrich Friding/Fridingen (1304) (Aargau, Switzerland 130km/81 miles from Frutigen) or his cousin Peter Fridingen (~1308) (in Lommis, Switzerland 219km/136 miles from Frutigen) or the Fridinger brothers Hans & Heintz (Heinrich) Friding of Weisholz(near Ramsen), Canton of Shaufhausen in 1418. Fridinger Leibeigene(serf) produced the name Friding. Peter may have known a relative in the War of Sempach 1386 (south of Argau and NNE of Frutigen). If Peter were born about 1380, he would have been too young to fight. Peter may have had a different view of religion (pre-reformation) as to why his location deep into Switzerland near the monstaries at Interlaken, however almost a century goes by until the birth of Gwer Fridig (1535). There were two family feuds (1405/1411) and (1433) that may have caused Peter's flight to Frutigen, Switzerland but probably just social change or that all family members could NOT have led a nobel life. In a Zurich Switzerland archives document for March 22,1411 brothers **Ulrich** (~1379) & **Johann Fridingen** (~1371) dispute was resolved – their names mentioned gebruder/brothers **Friding**[517]. This 1411 dispute may have been the origins of **Peter Friding** (~1403). The 2nd being of Margarete Gessler-Fridngen in 1408-9 living arrangements (after death of her husband Hans) and her son Hans Wilhelm Fridingen in 1440 over the Gessler familie and rights to his mothers side and heir to properties. If you look at the children of Johann V Krahen (~1343) and Margaret Hohenfels (~1350) many of her children had occupations far outside the Hegau area: Wilhelm Fr was in Holland, Germany by 1409, Ital Fr was in Klingnau, Switerland by 1407. February 1332 Johannes Freidinger (~1302) is listed as a frater(brother) in the monastery Frienisberg[518] located in Seedorf, Schweiz 41.9 miles north of Frutigen. In 1380 Heini Freidinger(*Freidig*) (from Freudigen b. Oberburg)[519] is recorded in Fraubrunnen monastery as a farmer[520]. In another book it says Heini Freidinger is established at Grafenried (1.3miles from Fraubrunnen & 41miles from Frutigen) around 1380 (P.Zryd, Grafenried p. 10). Therefore, we would rather back close to the Old German personal name Freido (see Förstemann 2, p. 513, and Socin, p. 223, "the outcast"). . As a surname "**Freidig**" he now lives, for example, the top Simmen valley - the name of ... the Simmen Valley - The name of the hamlet, an Alemannic settlement with the-ingen suffix, with the people of Freido has is phonetically nearer the joy and so firmly naturalized[521]. Hans von Fridingen VI (~1371) was the Steurnmeyern? (Revenue officer?) in Butzberg[522], Aarau, Switzerland in (1409) June 9th. Margaret von Gessler-Fridingen (~1372) was having issues after the death of her husband Hans von Fridingen. She wanted to stay @ Shenkenberg castle in Aargau, Switzerland and was finally awarded (via fief)[523] in 1417. She purchased a house (~1408-9) in Brugg, Aargau, Switzerland to comply with the Bernese. In a Schweiz book[524] it briefly describes Hans Wilhelm Fridingen and the Gessler feude being in Baden (1440) May 21st probably with the refusal of Aaurgau (Jorg and Heinrich) Gessler familie Heritage and other issues continued through (1446) Lindau, (1448) Baden and Lucern (1451) found in Luzern archives. Some where in the relatives of Wilhem von Fridingen generation is where I believe Peter Friding is produced as a second born son or no longer possesing noble rights. Interestingly enough, Peter arrives in Frutigen about 6 years before the Zurich war starts in 1440/43.

Other names appearing in Bern before and after Peter Friding are the following:

Ruff Lugibuhl von Eschy 1430

Peter Rychen(Riechen) von Eschi 1432 (*Eschi*/ Aeschi). Aeschi bei Spiez is located close to the city of Spiez near lake of Thun, Bernese Oberland, in Bern.

Cuno Landbrand v Mulinon 1433. Mülenen is a few miles NNE of Frutigen in Bern.

Ruff Lowenstein 1435, Anthono Schlegel 1435 burger to Bern.

Hensli Bircher 1436 son of Johannes Bircher.

Cuni Schober 1436. Nyclaus (Nicholas) and Peter Schöber, sat in Siebental Dec 1354. Siebental is near Dresden on the other side of Freiding @ Aach, Germany.

Ruffli Weibel 1436.

Christan Grymer 1439. May 1410 Johannes Grymer called Sager is recorded in a Bern fief. Niklaus Grimer, bailiff to Mülenen January 1358 in a Bern record.

[Ryter, Ritter] families are in Frutigen between 1399-1432. Jenni Riter, Peter Riter von Richenbach and Jenni Riter (Wandflu 1952: 79). There are quite a few Richenbachs (Reichenbach in Kandertal, Switzerland, Rickenbach in Thurgovia, Switzerland mentioned in (1040) or Reichenbach near Dresden, Germany). (Johann) Ryter, genannt(called by) von Wildenstein [Hans (Ryter) Wildenstein (II) is in the Bern archives dated (1466) Feburary 16. Ritter DNA matches Fridig haplogroup - see Research..

[Gyseler] Andres Giseler (Gessler?) is in Frutigen between 1404-1439.

[Zimmermann] Hans Zimerman. Jenni (Johann) Zimmermann and brother Konrad (1379) November 29. Many references to others as a Carpenter (Zimmermann). Interesting derivative names found in the same document:

[Zumbrunnen] Cuni zem Brunnen. A Cuni zum Brunnen is from Durrenrot[525] in October 1539. Ulrich zum Brunnen was a citizen of Thun (NNE of Frutigen) in 1367. Vinzenz zum Brunnen from Spiez (south of Thun) in 1426. In other areas Burkhartten zum brunnen (1406) spitalmeister to Constanz (Argovia v8-9 1874: 78).

[Zyrd] Hans ab Ried (1380-1425), Ruff ab Ried 1412.

[Böninger] Johannes Böning (1418). Henmann von Lörrach, Kirchherr to Grenzach, acknowledged Henmann Böning the city of Bern (1390) August 15th (BA : 71353). Johannes Boeninger spitalmeister(Hospital master) in (1372) March 16th and Johann Böninger June 8, 1372. Bern archives: Henmann Böning 1390, Hensli (Johannes) Böniger 1486, 1506, 1521. Johann Böninger 1372.

Note: Boeninger>Boning is another direct evidence to the changing or shortening of names as people began living in Bern. So, if Peter F would have come in as Fridinger would his descendants now be called Friding instead of Frydig?

2) Peter Friding (~1403) or Gwer Fryding | Frydig (~1535) – namesake after whom??

a. **Gwer (Quirin) Fryding {Frydig} (~1535)** could have easily be one of the Fridigerns children who was living in Switzerland. I say this because "Quirin" in Switzerland doesn't appear to be from a German source but a Swiss bordered French name. The name Saint-Quirin[526] (est ~966) is actually (Quirinus=Roman) from Lorraine, France which borders Germany and destroyed during the Thirty years war 1618-48. A few references show first name of "Quirin" being used around 1430's in Cologne and Steinort, Sachsen, Prussia, Germany. Gwer Schöni (~1490) is the 1st recorded "Gwer" found in the Frutigen Berne Archives by June 1520. This indicates to me Gwer's family was already in Adelboden, however just to be sure here are some events around Gwer. There was so much going on shortly before Gwer's birth. Many situations could have occurred for flight(migration) lower into Central Switzerland.

- In 1499 the Swiss siege/Swabian war and in 1512, there was the Fridingen Feude @ Hohenkrahen that would most certainly have made any/all family members flee to Switzerland including that of Hans Benedict Fridingen.

- There is a Gwer Zaller/Zahler born in Frutigen about 1514.There is a Gwer Schöni (~1490) recorded in Frutigen June 29 1520. A Gwer Bächler (~1492) a Landmann to Aeschi also recorded between 1522-1529 in Frutigen. There is also a Gwer Aellig/Elling, Statthalter(Governor) to Frutigen living in Adelboden (1529) whom also has his coat of arms[527] recorded about 1530 as a green oak branch with 2 leaves and an acorn facing upwards. This Gwer appears to be the more probable namesake for Gwer Frydig (~1535).

- In may 1586, Gwer Fryding has a land fief transferred from "Pleiken" {Bleiken bei Oberdiessbach?), Switzerland (43 miles west of Adelboden) or doubtful from Pleicken, Wattwil, Saint Gallen, Switzerland in 1586. I understand having the fief recorded as Fryding indicates the former family name, otherwise if Gwer just showed up in Bern (with no family ties) it would have been recorded as Frydig/Fridig. Only one record could be located for any family in Bleiken Berne

The Swabian Connection – Expanded Edition

Archives – see the following: Ulrich Friding/Freidig (Fridingen) (~1304) and wife Adelheit referenced in the Will of Hartman Weibel[528] at Belliken, in Zurich, Switzerland in May 1347. Bleiken bei Oberdiessbach is 113 miles from Belliken in Zurich. Ulrich could also be the grandfather to Peter Friding (~1403).

b. **Peter Friding (~1403)** some of the following men could be the name sake for Peter:

- May have been named after Peter von Hewen I (~1329-1349) or II (~1364-1414). "Peter Lord to Heuwen gives his consent that Mr. Henry and Ruodolf of Fridingen Gebruder Knight Ms. Adelheid Blumenberg Henry of Fridingen marriage landlady live tithes to Buessendorf and Giltlein to people Hartz received from him as a fief have to give as security for 35 MS Costantzer weight Adelheit retains this good for life to enter into beneficial use Costannts (1347) January 5th at the twelfth evenings at Christmas". Hewen I associated and signed documents together with Johann von Fridingen, Ulrich von Fridingen and Heinrich von Fridingen and records dated March 10 (1358) Baden in Aargau[529].

- Peter von Fridingen (~1308) an uncle or great uncle of Peters father.

- Peter von Hochnegg with Heinrich von Fridingen were both Ritters(Knights) in St .Georgenschild in (1408) June 16th (Meyer 1831 | 166).

- Peter von Hunenberg (~1331-1371) recorded in Kloster Kappel and paternal uncle to Gotfried Hunenberg (1328) who married Margaret Fridingen (~1328) (Woeber | 1893). Margaret's nephew Hans Fridingen IV (~1368-1403) or her 1st cousin Heinrich Fridingen X (~1314) maybe the father or grand-father for Peter Friding. Peter v Hunenberg ritter helped settle disputes[530] between Alten Klingen and the abbess to give Dame Cathedral, and as this fell apart in 1376 (DALP 1828:399).

- Peter Hewen & Heinrich von Mulhausen (Heinrich F VIII?) (1342) Nov 15th church St. Martin in Engen (FU 1885:418). Peter Hewen and Ulrich Fridinge (~1304) recorded in Constanz together (1358) April 14th. Ulrich's siegel stamp recorded as Propst for St. Stephan -
S.VLRICI.DE.FRIDINGE.CN.ECCE.9STANT (=Ecclesiastical) and Peter Hewen
+S.PET.DNI.DE.HEWE.MILIT (=Ritter) vogte to Happerswil. Ulrich was understood to be the brother to Peter von Fridingen (Dobler 1986: 451).

- St. Peter & Paul monastery parish church established in 1200 (in Muhlhausen) were well visited and documenting the Fridingen familie well after 1425. Maria Scheiber documents (pg 310) two single boys named Peter & Paul brothers to Hans v Fridingen around 1490. This period is after Peter Friding, but showing the name Peter being used by the family.

- St.Peter abbey is located in Schwarzwald founded in 1073. Mentioned at least 3 times in Fridingen history in Doblers book.

- Peters in Schaufhausen between years 1339,1372-1403: Peters von Hünaberg 1339 wife Anna Radegg(Randegg). Peter von Torberg/Thorberg 1372. Peter des Fischers v Eglisau 1389 daughter Agness married **Walther dem Keller**. Peter von Falkenstein provost of St. Agnes 1393 mentioned with **Konrad Keller**. Peter Katzenthaler von Rietheim 1394 siegel by Heinrich von Randegg. Peter Löw von Schaffhausen 1394 with Henni Schnider von Beringen. Peter Sarwürker(Sarwürker) 1398 with Wilhelm Zimberman Bürger von Klingnau(Clingenow), Heinrich Sutter(Haini Suter). Peter Ziegler 1401 with **Götz von Hünaberg(<Gotfried married to Margarete Fridingen?**). Peter Ziegler 1401 w/Heinrich v Randegg. Peter Gräppli 1404 to Diessenhofen. Peter II von Wolhusen abbot of Einsiedeln 1376-1386

-Peters outside of Schaufhausen: Conrad (Konrad) **Keller** 1392 Kaplan des Stifts St. Peter to Basel.

3) Uniqueness of the name Fryding/Friding|{Frydig/Fridig} – there is no other etymology of this name for other than Friding/Fryding/Fridiger/Fridinger/Fridingen. No other towns or villages can be shortened to derive this this name other than Fridingen or Freiding/Friding. As I understand "**Friding**" is not Berniche (Canton) in nature/origin but a name shortened or created from another not from an occupation or characteristic as some other serf names were formed. **Friding** is more Southern Deutch (Khegau, Kempten) or Austrian (Tirol) or Northern Swiss (Argau,Basel, Schaufhausen) than from Frutigen (Central Swiss). In Tirol we find the closest variation of all three {Fridingen|Fridinge & Fridige} together which appears about

1411-18 in a 1394-1430 parchment in the Abbey of St. Christopher in Arlberger Thal in Tirol, Austria transcribed men of **Fridingen** as **fridigē** & **fridingē** in Tyrol/Tirol[531]. In Einsiedeln a Weisholz(Canton of Shaufhausen) border document near Ramsen for the **Fridinger** brothers **Hans & Heintz Friding** in 1418. The loss of the n in Fridingen may have occurred since Swiss & Tirol German dialects have gone through the Alemannic **n-aposcope** in phonology (linguistics in sounds), which led to the loss of final –n in words such as Freidig/Fridig/Frydig "Fridingen" (standard German Freidingen/Fridingen). Aposcope {apokoptein} "means *cutting off, away from to cut* is the loss of one or more words from the end of a word, and especially the loss of an unstressed vowel"[532]. Before 1440 the following sex of Fridingen were recorded in Thal, Tirol: Ulrich vö Fridingē (~1386) Hans vö Fridigē, Hans vö Fridigē, Cunrat vö Fridigē (~1384) & Heinrich vö Fridingē (~1330) Agatha Westerstetten of his marital/legitimate housewife. Later noted were two Ministerial men in Constanz: Jorg von Fridingē (Fridingen) (~1453) and Johannes von Fridingē (Fridingen) (~1458) with their coat of arms (wappenschields) in the 1483 book for the Council of Constanz[533].

4) Location of others *Friding(en)/Friding(er)* name variations to Frutigen –

- (Peter Friding ref 1433 Frutigen) or (Gwer Fryding ref 1586 fief "Pleiken" {Bleiken bei Oberdiessbach}, Switzerland in 1586.)
- "Even the sale of the Swiss Good Diethelms to the cathedral chapter of Constance in 1221 was clearly made in the interest remaining in Salem, and without regard to the family. Salem was then purchased by the Bischoskirche in his own near Good. The Episcopal Church itself, but was allowed by canon law to give up this good only if they are also substitutes in other property received. Therefore, in addition to selling his property in Räterschen (in Zurich) Diethelm, Langnau (in Emmethal, Bern?) and Wengi (north of Langnau) and the cathedral, which was the purchase of Salem for other good possible" (Dobler 1986: pg 69). Dobler listed Wengi in the Canton of Thurgau. Wängi is the location in Thurgau. There is another Langnau am Albis, Switzerland in Zurich. Zurich is probably correct as I had not expected ownership in Bern.
- Heinrich Fridingen (~1306) recorded with wife Ursula in Feldback Monastery in 1346 which is 119 miles from Bleiken bei Oberdiessbach, Switzerland. February 1332 Johannes Freidinger (~1302) is listed as a frater(brother) in the monastery Frienisberg[534] located in Seedorf, Switzerland 41.9 miles north of Frutigen and 38 miles from Bleiken bei Oberdiessbach, Switzerland. In 1380 Heini Freidinger [became Freidig] (from Freudigen b. Oberburg)[535] is recorded in Fraubrunnen monastery as a farmer[536]. In another book it says Heini Freidinger is established at Grafenried (1.3miles from Fraubrunnen) around 1380 (P.Zryd, Grafenried p. 10).
- Margaret Gessler-Fridingen (~1382) is living @ Thalheim, Switzerland in Schenkenberg Castle[537] in 1408. Schekenburg is 234 miles from Muhlhausen, Singen, Germany and 288 miles from Frutigen & 136 miles from Bleiken bei Oberdiessbach, Switzerland.
- Ulrich Friding (~1304) vogt to Baden, Argau, Switzerland in 1347.
- Ulrich Friding/Freidig (~1304) and wife Adelheit referenced in the Will of Hartman Weibel[538] at Belliken, Switzerland in May 1347.
- Brüder(brothers) Heinz (Haintzer) F (~1395) und Hans Friding (~1398), beide(both) von Wiesholz located in Ramsen, Switzerland just south from the German border under Singen. Kloster Einsiedeln urkunden[539] 1418. Fridingen @ Singen is only 11 miles from Wiesholz, Ramsen, Schaufhausen, Switzerland.
- Conrad Friding (~1439) appears in a loan via Innsbruck, Austria in 1469.
- Jorg Freiding (~1475) who is a painter from Tirol, Austria in Rattenburg working for Emperor Maximiliian in 1505.
- Heinrich Friding (~1343) near Leuchtenberg, Germany or Wien(Vienna), Austria.
- Sebastian Freyding (~1504) in Untrasried, Ostallgäu, Bavaria, Germany in 1534..
- Christianus Rormeyer Friding (~1534) is a student @ Universität Freiburg in Breisgau, Germany in 1554.
- Werner Fryding/Fridiger/Fridig (~1420) born in Basel Switzerland and now living in Isenthal , Sihl, & Uri, Switzerland by 1443.

- Rudolf von Fridingen VI (~1320) or VIII (~1348) in Baden in Aargau,Switzerland (1364) July 26th.

- Bernische(Canton of Bern) names in the Archives –

6/28/1434 Wilhelm von Fridingen siegler(signed) with wife Anna von Grunenberg and her sister Agnes and Magdelena. Hans Wilhelm Fridingen (~1408) and his wife pays cities of Bern and Solothurn 110 silver marks recorded on a document dated June 15 1434. Also, recorded Agnes and Magdelena received inheritance from Herzogenbuchsee on June 28 1434 believed to be from Albrecht Klingenberg. Euphemia von Klingenburg believed to be the mother of Anna?

5/3/1456 Enneli (Anna) von Fridingen (geb. Ringoltingen) appears again in document with her 1st husband Bernhard von Buttikon and her daughter(?) Margerethas von Buttikon.

5/5/1458 Hans "Johann" von Fridingen and wife Anna von Ringoltingen

1493 Simon von Fridingen (~1463) was the elected decan[540] in Muri,Aargau or Berne and also Munsingen in Berne above Frutigen.

5/1/1500 Rudolf von Fridingen, Komtur to Sumiswald, Switzerland siegler{signed}.

1/10/1509 Rudolf von Fridingen, Landkomtur in Elsass & Burgund, Komtur to Bucken, Komtur to Koniz siegler{signed}..

1/31/1511 Rudolf von Fridingen, Deutchorderskomtur(Teutonic German Order) to Koniz, Switzerland.

3/11/1512 Rudolf von Fridingen, Komtur to Koniz, Switzerland siegler{signed}. Record part of Niedersimmental.

7/24/1516 Rudolf von Fridingen Deutchorderskomtur(Teutonic German Order) to Koniz, Switzerland siegler{signed}.

5/4/1525 Rudolf von Fridingen Landkomtur in Elsass & Burgund document between German Tuetonic Order and Sumiswald siegler{signed}.

5/30/1585 Schultheiss and advice to Berne transferred at **Gwer Fryding** to steer a piece country (1 1/2 Jucharten), " mentioned; at Pleiken", including house and yard on it, to Mannlehen(fief).

5) Lack of Coat of Arms in Frutigen or Adelboden Switzerland between 1433 and 1535 for **Friding|Frydig/Fridig.** – I believe there are a few reasons there has been no coat of arms (wappenschilde) before or during this period.

a. The wappen (COA) was under a slightly different name and in another country (Southern Germany, Northern Switzerland or Austria), hence Fridingen or Krahen in the Hegau, Germany (Swabiche areas).

b. There were only a _few_ coat of Arms (x denotes extinct date) _for Bern_ in the 1340 Zurich wappenrolle (Ringenburg, Kriech/Criech 1475x, Gundelsdorf 1340x, Eschenbach 1309x?, Torberg 1400x, Oltingen 1370x, Nidau 1375x, Schwanden 1308x, and Aarberg 1438x).

c. Typically a wappen (COA) would be carried along to a descendant from someone with a nobility position (Knight, Monch/Munk, Lord etc..). Hence, Peter Friding had become a common Swiss serf. "In the Holy Roman Empire, bastards of Nobles theorectically did not inherit their father's noble status or the right to bear arms unless they were legitimated" (Hurwich : 232). "Some German nobles sought legitimation "by rescript of the Prince in connection" with the grant of their noble status and coat of arms to their illegimate children", however the "untitled nobel Fridingen" familie did not have upper nobility for a Prince. Peter is believed to be a 2nd or 3rd generation serf, so he may never have seen his family arms.

d. Peter probably didn't want to take a chance and thus didn't provide any resemblance of his former familie (COA) to the Swiss Confederacy. The past history is supressed and not carried forward.

- One of the earliest appearances of the actual Friding/Fridig surname was located in Tirol, Austria where find all three names together (**Fridingen, Friding & Fridig**) in a 1394-1430 (abt 1411) parchment in the Abbey of St. Christopher in Arlberger Thal described men of the village of **Fridingen** with (COA) _Blue, Lion over White bend_ as **fridigē** & **fridingē** in Tyrol/Tirol[541]. This location Thal in Austria is 254km from Hohenkrahen,Singen,Germany which is a further distance than to Frutigen Switzerland which is 239km, so it NOT inconceivable that any Fridinger descendants would migrate to Frutigen. Using Hohenkrahen as a starting point, any Northern

The Swabian Connection – Expanded Edition

Switzerland location would have been easy to get to Frutigen. Also, if Gwer Frydig was our progenitor he would have discouraged his surname because of the Swabian war/Swiss war on Hohenkrahen in 1499 & 1512 where quite a few male Fridingen's resided. This suppressed any descendants from making their ancestry known to the Swiss {*Confederation*} that may have been aware of the feuds/wars on the German nobles. The Northern Swiss nobility and Southern Deutchland/Austrian nobility "were being undermined by the Swiss Confederates" and not welcome {*under emperial Reichstag/Parliament*} in central Switzerland when Berne joined the confederation by 1353. Again, backing up the reason to hide your ancestry if living in Switzerland.
- The second appearance for the **Frydig** coat of arms shows up 1564-67 by Heinrich Frydig[542] in the Northern Switzerland/Western Austrian area. This appears to be a personal arms and barely documented on an Oval piece of wood. This is Heinrich (~1540) the son of Conrad and who was related to Verena Fridig (~1489) whose husband Andreas Aschwanden held the arms as Andres fridig in 1555/1560. There is another subtle reference to **von Friding** having a coat of arms in the In the 1888 book "Vierteljahrsschrift für Wappen, Siegel und Familienkunde, Volume 16" von **Friding** is listed on Hohen-Krayen[543]. German: von **Friding auf Hohen Krayen** Jn b. ein w Schrägbalken darüber ein g. Löwe gk H Straußenfederbusch hd: b g. Translated: "**of Friding on High Krayen** Jn b. a w g diagonal bar over it a lion ostrich plume gk H hd: bg". Right below this reference also describes **Fridingen**. There are a few Armorials wappen references to **von Frydinge/Fridinge** and mostly refer to *Fridingische* ministerial men like **Ulrich Friding (Fridingen)** or **Johannes Fridinge(n)** or **Jorg von Fridingē(n)** (~1453) on the German/Swiss border between 1300's and late 1400's, no wappen(COA) deep into the Bern Canton or central Switzerland areas before the 1530's..
- The third appearance doesn't shows up until (1800) in Frutigen as "Frydig". A Bird in between two small fur/pine trees on a rounded Lattice. The next one is "Freidig" in Lenk (1815) with the same form, a brilliant Red Bird standing on a mountain in between two fur/pine green trees. Looking at the coat of arms which are very similar, it appears the later designers of Freidig (1815) knew the two slightly different family surnames were related.

6) Relationships - Anna Spillman marriage to Gwer Fridig in (1553). The earliest record for Spillman in Bern (1250) April 21st for Aarberg, **Chunradus quondam dicti Spilman** & daughter Agnesa for the conventus Frienisperch in Winterswile. There are quite a few Spillmanns in Switzerland in the 1400's. Jenne Spilmann was in Frutigen between 1393-1428. The Bern archives show Antscho Spilmann is in Adelboden before March of 1437. In Berne, Switzerland in 1458, **Hans (Johann) von Fridingen (1438)** and his wife Enneli (Anna), to daughter of the deceased old Schulttheis Rudolf of Ringoltingen, sell at Seckelmeister **Gilian Spilmann** for 187 Rhine. Peter von Hewen (~1358) knew the Fridingen, Seon and Gessler familie, possibly a name sake for Peter Friding.

7) Characteristics of Fridingische men { *of/or like* **Friding(en)/Frydig}**
- Uldaricher/Winterthur/Kyburg/Hirscheck/Fridingen(er)/Krahen/Craege men for the most part reveal a humble and non-spirited personalities albeit their incredible histories of being Knights, Monks, Canons, Kaplans, founders of Villages and Monasteries carrying their COA emblem. As some other families boast their wappenschildes(COA) or Royalty crests, the Fridingen/Krahen are barely mentioned or documented and their Heraldik ancestry is not thrown in the faces of would be guests visiting HohenFridingen, HohenKrahen, Schlatt, Magdeburg (~1378), Dieseenhofen (1419) and Bussen (1483) castles to list a few. The Von Particle attached to their surname barely raised their personal interest in wappenshields(COA's) but rather a smaller personal humble items as a wappenring or Siegelstamp is about as boisterous/outspoken as they got, which was used for occupational documentation. You may think, these images could be like any other Men painted or Drawn at the time, however if you view any of the other images they are distinct and unique in that they are not simply drawn to fill in space as a stick person. Time and Talent were used to be as close

to real appearances. The Codex Manesse (1304-1340) done in Zurich has been the only example showing nearly every noble person that looks almost identical in their facial, hair and body characterstics, otherwise I would have posted Burkart(Burchard) von Hohenfels image with the typical features.

- Rudolph Fridingen (~1445) image in the 1516 Stain glass window in Muenster Church in Bern, Switzerland, he is presented with reddish/orange thin medium long hair and a beard. This struck me as he looked like my father from the 1970's with long thin hair covering the side of his head and large mustache. In a 1900 Berner book by Ludwig Lauterburg[544] a black and white drawing was done {below}, which further brings out the Fridinger character.

Many Friday men including my Grandfather James "Jim" (from a personal statement) and George T Friday (1829) (civil war record) had reddish/orange colored hair. Hansel E Friday (1892) also described as: Short & Stocky with Red Hair and ran the Crawford Young Saw Mill (or aka- Crawford Young Lumber Co. @ Creston, LA). I see this Reddish/Brown hair in my son Zach, now 7 years old. Similar characteristics of DNA often appear in and out of history through relatives. Rudolph actually has a Fridingische facial image common today in the Friding men. Another characteristics are his build and height (about 5'8" tall). The Reddish/Orange Brown hair is known through the Friday family of Natchitoches, LA. We know that DNA characterics can be a higher percentage in one person and limited presence in the next male generation, then all of the sudden re-appear down the line of generations. DNA marker test from a Freidinger male today could confirm slight mutations and same haplotype I1C(now called I2b1) and finally confirm this lost family – no data for comparison as of July 2010, May 2011, Nov 2011, or April 2012. This next record comes the Zimmern Chronical[545] (written between 1497-1566) which can be somewhat contributed to a characteristic or a phase a person may go through in life depending how well things maybe going (or not). Martin von Fridingen (~1454) died in 1521 living through the 1512 Catastrophe @ HohenKrahen which I have yet to thoroughly transcribe and understand. He is recorded as being a noble farm hand in 1484. *Difficult* Transcription: "Bemelter Gabriel dörft probably also therefore a lerman with Martin have started the same came from Fridingen ain geen Costanz times in the growth, he walked up and down in it on how to maintain, however, was very badly dressed, then as the old years before any delicacy of the dresses have taken, but he vermaint, you should never know cheeeeaap and for which he gets in a Sun have were he grüest. The Selbig square one nit of because of poor clothing, and then he Martin was Fridingen, ain unachtpare person why he was modest in ain bad spells Martin> You should cheeeeaap see the Knoepfle who I huet were ', and yet from his so shows the smallest ain guldins Knoepfle he blanchett cord to hang on huet aimer (ZC 1881: 301)."

- After reviewing a black & white drawing (from 13th century) of Diethelm von Krenkingen[546] (~1149) >right> bishop of Konstanz (1189-1206) and uncle of Diethelm von Krahen/Fridingen(~1172). Diethelms von K years as bishop followed Hermann II von Fridingen (~1133) term and bishop of Constanz (1183-1189) <left<. I do see a resemblance to my brother James Bryant F. Diethlem appears to me with a thin frame, small lips & mouth, medium to long nose, small face (less high cheekbone) with dark facial bearding (covering a boyish face) which I have found are some characteristics in Friding men. Robert Henry Friday (1887) also is presented in a photograph with a thin body frame. Diethelm sells Wengi & Langnau Swiss properties in Zurich by 1221.

209

| Rudolf von Fridingen – Stained glass window completed in 1513-1519 | Diethelm von Krenkingen (~1149-†1206) uncle of Diethelm von Krahen/Fridingen (~1172) |

- Johannes Fridingen (~1458) the <u>last</u> Cistertian Abbott @ Bebenhausen, Germany before the reformation is shown to have died of a stroke or apopolexy[547] after 76 years of long life.The only similiarity I see in this image is is height (~5'7"), plumpness of face (sedentary monk), large nose, small lips and the common boyish face well into adulthood. Hans Frydig/John Friday Sr (~1690) from Frutigen who settled in Orangeburg, SC reportly died from an apoplectick fit on Monday June 18th 1759 and interred in the church yard the day after (Salley 2009 : 209). **Note:** apopleptic fits can be caused by a variety of issues, not necessarily the same cause.

- Gotfried von Krahen (~1277-1307) from a votive painting has the typical height , brown hair color and boyish face into adulthood.

The Swabian Connection – Expanded Edition

| Johannes von Fridingen (~1458) abbott @ Bebenhausen. | Gotfried von Krahen d. 1307 votive painting in the Castle Bodmen. |

- Gebhard von Konstanz (949-995) founder of Petershausen in 983 and the son of Ulrich von Bregenz (~920). Liutfried von Winterthur (~945) would have been the grandfather to Hermann and brother to Gebhard. Hermann v Hirscheck (~996) vogt to

Petershausen in 1043 and he was the great-great nephew of Gebhard. A commemorative stamp for his 1000th birthday[548] in 1949 <left<. The choir of the parish church of St. Gordian and Epimachus, Merazhofen, Leutkirch

town in Allgäu Switzerland has a Sculptor[549] of Gebhard created by Peter Paul Metz in 1896 >right>. The boyish face, dark hair with small lips and common fridingishe male in his prime. If you are of Catholic faith, then Gebhard could be your Saint.

8) Surname Adoption – The village at HohenFridingen (near Radolfzell) and HohenKrahen (at Muhlhausen) during the 12th-15th century were very small even in todays standards. Most of the near by areas where full of Nobles, Bishops, and Canons migrating back and forth to Lake Constanz monasteries. The serfs however (limited in numbers) to the Untitled Lords of Fridingen already had their surnames established (Schwarz , Riederer, Drescherin, Batz etc..) before the

The Swabian Connection – Expanded Edition

1430's. Occasionally they used their name in this context "Ulrich Schwarz von Friedingen 1435, Walter Schwarz von Fridingen 1445", Conrad & Adelhaide Drescher son "Hans" the Church Lord to Mulhausen (1368-1389). Adlehaid die Drescher wappen[550] is the same as Fridingen (lacking of lion) dated 1389, Her husband Conrads wappen is similar but with a waffle pattern under the bend. The Drescher family dates to (1273) January 17th in the kloster Herrenalb of whom *Otto der Ältere von Eberstein* owned the rights. November 2nd (1467) Hans Betz[551] von Friddingen & Jean Betz de Friedingen located @ Mulhouse, France bordering Basel Switerland & Lorrach, Germany. Notice their surname really didn't change living in the same village or elsewhere. The Fridinger (~1180/90) family firmly established their surname from about ~1215 through ~1307. The Abbots of St. Gallen Switzerland[552] has surnames beginning by 1077. The only name alterations I've located are ones of the upper nobles or Trustees that occasionally moved to a new locations and hence his family surname would change with the documentations. "From the counts Nellenburg the place came to the family of von **Hirscheck-Konzenberg** of this mountain and from this to the related neighboring lords von **Wartenberg**[553]."

9) Y DNA of Friding | Fridig paralled with other surnames in the Haplogroup –
Proving the parallelled family Haplogroups are from the ancient family lieneages, its obvious that they have a surname origin in Swabia with a Swiss influence just south of Schauffhausen. The Swiss Zimmerman (=Zimbern/Zimbermann), Ritter(=Riedern), Leonberg/Luenberger (=Lowenberg/ Münchenstein), Friding (=Fridingen/Winterthur/aldt Kyburg), Bossart in Wurtemburg and Bosshard familes from Winterthur & later Zurich, Ravensburg in Swabia (=sacristan) Black Forest (=Sacristo) northern Schweiz (=Sigrist/Sacrista/Segrist), Herrenalb in Schwarzwald (=Zehender & Drescher?), Hutto (=Otot/Hotot/Hatto/Hattingen?) moved into Normandie France prior to 1100, Humphrey (=Hundpiss? of Revensburg) or Humfrie/Humphrey from Anneville or Bohun in Normandy prior to 1100 and/or Humpruee in Steckborn, Schweiz

1600's. Wolf (=von Homberg/Hunoberg) from Swabia & Schweiz between 1156-1500's. Possibly more families exists like Tengen, Stoffeln, Strulingen, Pfullendorf, Brunner, Rettig, Ramsen, Fricking(en)?, Schwandorf?, Muenchen?, Nellenberg?, Hewen?, NewHaus?, Steckborn? Etc.. Shown are villages known to have residence or family connections in the Southwestern corner of Swabia(Sveviae) in 1572 drawn by David Seltzlin[554].

10) Two Surname Alternatives – Two surnames comes up as an <u>alternative</u> to Friding|Frydig:

- **First** is the name Fridang/Friding/Fridig (*von Toernlon*) (1450? - ca.1550) in the Canton of Uri. This is Torler Alpes or Tyroler/Tyrol/Torle, Upper Switzerland/Lower Tyrol, Austria. Backing up this Tirol connection is another reference from "Der Landammann in den schweizerischen Demokratien Uri, Schwyz, Unterwalden" which states that "**Heini Fridig** wass Kuenratz sun from torla"[555.] Kuenratz is same as Conrats/Conrad. The brief description appears to be Tirol dialect which if very different German with many possible intonations in the language for similar german words. This Torle location is not Torla Spain, but another word for Torle, Austria (SSE of Kempten, Germany, NNW of Innsbruck, Austria and NNE of Switzerland) or the better location being TURLEN or TOERLEN which is in Knonau in the district of Affoltern in the canton of Zürich, Switzerland[556.] The Uri Fridig's , Werner Fridig(er)/Friding (~1420) is from the Basel area and settled with connections to Uri and Isenthal along with Marti Fridig (~1450) and his children Richi Fridig (~1472), Michael Fridig (~1470) and daughter Verena F Aschwanden (1489) in the the early 1500's. However Peter Friding (~1403) already appeared to have his name established by 1433 and further west into Bern (indicating he came from the Basel, Aargau, and Thurgau etc, however doubtful from Uri) from East to West. Friding (Ulricus de Fridinge 1324, Ulr de Fridinge 1343) was already being used in Constanz NNW of Aargau/Aarau (south of Germany) Ulrich Freidige 4-1331 etc.. Friding|Frydig is shortened from Fridingen/Fridinge { *lat. Fridiger*} in Frutigen by 1433. My belief is these URI Fridig's "Werner" (~1420) was from the Fridinger family from Northern Swiss near Basel, not necessarily from Torla as Heini Frydig/Fridigs father was in the 1450's. Since Uri borders the SE corner of Bern, Peter Friding may have come from there 1st prior to Werner arriving. However this is doubtful Peter F came over the mountains from Uri from the east, but actually more from the Northern Bern via Aargau. "Uri In the whole of Switzerland there is no Canton (unless it be the Vallais) which is more securely fenced in by high mountains on all sides but one[557] than that of Uri or the upper valley (in the Northern part of Uri) of the Reuss" (Methuen 1908:117). Just because the Uri archives/books say the "Uri Fridig's" are from Uri canton does'nt mean the original family has always been there. From the Archives/books perspective the 1440's was a long time ago and they believe many families where already in Uri being dependent on the Empire in (853), however looking at the family it was just the period (1440's) in which this line of Fridigs/Fridings migrated there.

- **Second** is found in the book Alberger Armorial near the Austria border where we find all three {**Fridingen - Fridinge & Fridige**} together in a 1394-1430 (abt 1411-17) parchment in the Abbey of St. Christopher in Thal transcribed the men of **Fridingen** as **fridigē** & **fridingē** in Tyrol/Tirol[558].

- **Third** is the **Friding/Fridinger** lesser noble & serf surname form moving out of Swabian (Bussen & Fridingen) and into Northern Schweiz Cantons (Aargau, Thurgau & Schaufhausen): Prior to 1238 Johannes miles de Craigin (~1217) father Berthold von Krahen (~1185) estate was located @ Tegerwiller (Tägerwilen)[559] & Haiminhovin (Heimenhofen in Allgau or Andwil) in the Canton of Thurgau. Heinrich von Fridingen and his two sons stayed in the area of Richinhusen(Ruhinhusen) in 1243. In 1291, Rudolf von Fridingen became the Hapsburgishe Burgvasall to Bussen, Germany from there the descendant family begins to dominate movement into Northeast corner of Schweiz(Switzerland). Peter von Fridingen (~1308) living in Lommis, Thurgau, Switerland in 1364 doesn't mention any male children but (Eberhard Dobler's research) surprised to find a Fridingen there. The Lommis wappen(COA) appears to be Tengen & fridingeschen in form which is understood to come from the Hirscheck origins. This is can be extended to Ulrich von Frydingen/Fridinge (~1304) and Ulrich F (~1386) and his brother Johannes "Hans" von Fridingen (~1371) . Freidig is listed as a family name between 1331-1378 in Baden, Switzerland. Ulrich Freidig (~1304) was Mayor of Aarau, Baden, Switzerland in 1341. In the same reference Ulrich and wife Adelheit are listed as Freidingen – The Freidig Familiewappen (COA) is located in the City of Baden, Swiss archives. Many surname variations occur for Ulrich in the same canton of (Aargau) Aarau sources[560]: 2x Ulrich Freidige April 8th 1331, 2x Ulrich Freidigo & 1x Ulrichs **Freidigen** July 6th 1334, 1x Uolrich der Freidger Feb 3rd 1340, 4x Ulrich Freidig March 16, 1341, 4x Ulrich Freidig April 15th 1341, 3x Ulrich Freidig December 2nd 1348 (with Johannes Seon{Schienen?}). (1394) May 21st Ursula Fridinger a serf Nonne(Nun) emitted to Kloster St. Agness in Schaufhausen[561] sister of Tiroler Heinrich Fridingen IX. Johannes von Seon

213

appears in Zurich document (March 22, 1411) helping with the dispute between brothers **"Friding"** Ulrich and Johannes von Fridingen "knights" all names Hohenkrahen / Fridingen (Hegau) registered[562]. The brothers Heinz(Haintz/Heinrich) Friding (~1395) and Hans Friding (~1398), both from Wiesholz located near Ramsen, Schaufhausen, Switzerland just south from the German border under Singen. Kloster Einsiedeln urkunden[563] 1418. Heinz(Heinrich) Friding(er) was married to Margaretha Klinger(Keller) before Sept 1425 (STASH:1731) and noted having children in the same records. Fridingen @ Singen is only 11 miles from Wiesholz(=Hegou/Swabia 1094) near Ramsen(=Hegou/Swabia 1106), Canton Schaufhausen, Switzerland.

There is **NO village or town** called Frydigberg/Frydigburg, Frydigland, Frydigdorf, Frydigwalde, Frydigheim, Frydighausen, Frydigbach or Frydigthal to deduce a derivative for Fridig or Frydig. Since, we know Friding definetly came from Fridingen but before Frydig, here we are at discovery and transition of the von Fridingen (Schwabish) to Friding/Fryding (Schweiz) then later Frydig/Fridig (Uri or Frutigische/Adelboden). Although Frydigen is written in a few Swiss records for the Fridingen men in the 1500's is doesn't become a common surname. Rudolph von Frydigen (~1462) in Sumiswald, Switzerland[564] and decribing the Landcomthur in Elsass & Burgundy around 1515 and Lord Franz von Frydigen (~1504) German Order(Deutschordens) and acting head of the house Hitzkirch[565] around 1534. Below is a chart of the possible relative conections to Peter Friding(~1403) or Gwer Fryding/ig(~1535). Some combination of Scenario 3, 4 or 8 are more likely, however all are plausible.

Scenario 1	Scenario 2	Scenario 3	Scenario 4	Scenario 5
Heini Freidinger (Freidig) (~1360) at Fraubrunnen, Switzerland (1380) |? Peter Friding{Frydig} (~1403) in Frutigen, Switzerland by 1433/37 |? unknown sohn |? unknown sohn |? Gwer Fridig{Fryding} (~1535)	Descendant of Hans Wilhelm Fridingen (~1408) | Grandson | Benedict Ernst von Fridingen (~1469) flight to Switzerland in 1512 after feude. |? Sohn Fridingen (~1507) |? Gwer Fridig{Fryding} (~1535)	Hans Fridingen VII (~1438) married to Anna Ringoltingen (~1438) {knew Gillian Spilllmann} |? unknown sohn (~1458) |? unknown sohn (~1478) |? unknown sohn (~1502) | ? Gwer Fridig{Fryding} (~1535) Married Anna Spillman	Ulrich Fridingen (1304) Domherr (Canon) or Cousin of Peter Fridingen (~1308) |? Peter Friding (~1403) in Frutigen 1433/37 | ? unknown sohn (~1458) | ? unknown sohn (~1478) | ? unknown sohn (~1502) | ? Gwer Fridig {Fryding} (~1535)	"Unknown" Ulrich Fridingen (~1382?) cousin to Hans IV (~1368) |? Peter Friding (~1403) in Frutigen 1433/37 | ? unknown sohn |? unknown sohn |? Gwer Fridig{Fryding} (~1535)

Scenario 6 - Konrad von Friding(en) III (~1384) recorded in Klettgau(Cleggow) who has some illegimate children between 1409 and 1423 could very well have been the father of Peter Friding (~1403) who would have been named after a great(?) uncle Peter von Fridingen (~1308).

Scenario 7 – Peter Friding (~1403) younger brother(?) to Hans Wilhelm Fridingen (~1390/1408) familie very active in Brugg & Bruneck (Aarau) Switzerland starting around 1409 through 1469.

Scenario 8 – Peter F (~1403) younger brother or relative to Heinz (Haintz) Friding (~1395) & Hans Friding (~1398) in a 1418 kloster Einsiedeln record, both from Wiesholz located near Ramsen, Schaufhausen, Switzerland.

214

The Swabian Connection – Expanded Edition

In summary with the size of the >von Fridingen< family we know quite a few descendants would escape the noble family lieneage in Swabia/Northern Schweiz and have beginnings else where in Europe (Prague, Austria, and Switzerland). The individual migrations were caused by the dynamics between feudalism, religion, family and competition over occupational resources. Friding surname proves to only come from one family "*von Fridingen*". Peter Friding having appeared in Frutigen Bern (1433 & 1437) had perfect timing (flight for opportunity) as he may have helped construct the Parish Church at Adelboden in the same year. Peter Friding (~1403) or Gwer Frydig/Fryding being in Frutigen/Adelboden their surnames melded into Central Swiss dialects of the period. The DNA haplogroup markers parallelled with other ancient (before 1100 a.d) family groups in this group show a convergence going back to Swabia (Baden-Wurtemburg, Germany) during this renaissance period of monastery and village charters. Using physical (facial/body) characteristics through the ages backs up the research that the path was correct.

Adelboden & Frutigen, Bernese Oberland, Switzerland

The Frydig's/Fridig's were married, born and christened here in Adelboden Valley, Town of Adelboden, Switzerland. The town is situated 1535 meters above sea level. Peter

Friding|Frydig (~1403) , one possible ancestor arrived in Frutigen in 1433. Peter **Frydig** (1618) and Anna Ameler had 4 children who were born in Adelboden; Hans (1646), Barbli (1648), Peter (1649) and Anna (1650). Peter's great grandfather Gwer Frydig settled Adelboden with all the records descending through the Church archives. The Parish church and Adelboden Parish was built the same year Peter Friding (~1403) appears in the neighboring town of Frutigen in 1433.

Parish Church Built 1433 – 579 years old.

Adelboden Valley Swiss History - Switzerland is bordered by Germany to the north, France to the west, Italy to the south and Austria and Liechtenstein to the east. Switzerland was originally inhabited by Celtic tribes who were named Helvetians by the Roman. The establishment of Switzerland is traditionally dated to the Federal Charter dated 1 August 1291. In 1315, takers of the oath, or the Eidgenossen, defeated the emperor's forces and they also defeated a superior Austrian force in 1386. The mountains of Switzerland and Swiss military efficiency proved to be a major obstacle to a conquering army. Adelboden is 1st mentioned around 1409 as "*valle Adelboden*". Historical documents referenced in the Berne archives for the years 1433, 1441, 1469, 1487 & 1488 as

The Swabian Connection – Expanded Edition

significant dates and documents are in a closed inventory with Frutigen. There were only about 400-500 people living in Adelboden in 1433 and in that same year 12 independent men began to build the Parish church after being rejected by Bishop of Lausanne @ Interlaken[566]. Was Peter Friding (~1403) one of these men who appeared in 1433? By 1499 a dozen cantons had joined the Swiss Confederacy. In 1453 it was mentioned as Adelboden alias silva. Adelboden lies in the west of the Berner Oberland, at the end of the valley of the Engstlige river, which flows in Frutigen into the Kander river. Adelboden is a traditional Swiss mountain village on a terrace looking south to the Engstligen waterfalls. The Country has spoken four different languages: German, Italian, Raeto-Romanic and French.

the following cities are located these distances from Adelboden valley Switzerland:

928 miles to Germany in the North

850 miles to Paris, France to the North West

441 miles to Milano, Italy to the South East

223 miles from Zurich, Switzerland to the north, from Zurich an additional 68 miles to Fridingen, Germany.

180.81 miles from Fridingen, Germany to the North.

140 miles to Geneve, Switzerland to the East South East

98 miles to Basel, Germany due North above Bern

34.9 miles from Bleiken bei Oberdiessbach, Switzerland

41 miles to Bern, Switzerland directly North

9.2 miles from Frutigen, Switzerland to the North North East.

Source: Google Maps and km/miles conversion.

Parish Church is in the right middle ground. The current name for the church is the Evangelical Reformed Congregation of Adelboden.

Frutigen Church & Valley in Switzerland

The Reformed Church of Frutigen which was once dedicated to St. Quirinius but is no longer

known under this name: the late Gothic church dating from 1421 was rebuilt in Baroque style between 1726 – 28 encompassing the old parts, after it had been ruined by fire: to the south of the village, the ruins of the Tellenburg which burned down in 1885 and whose remaining walls date back to the 12th century, .

It is certain that for some time after the year 500, when the Franks ruled the old Burgundy Kingdom, Frutigen belonged to France. Until into the 15th century the parish of Frutigen covered an enormous area: Engstligengrund, Kandergrund, Kandersteg and Gasterntal. The original church in Frutigen dates back to the first half of the 7th century. Five further churches were built on the foundations of the first church.

Anyone of the Peter Frydig's (1649) and Anna's children would have been married or christened in the Frutigen Church.

Adelboden is 40 km southwest from Frutigen valley, Switzerland. Peter **Friding [Frydig]** listed in 1433 & 1437 as living

in Frutigen. Peter Frydig (1649) moved to Frutigen by ~1670 and would marry Christina Zuercher in 1672. His son Martin Friday (1689) married Maria Magdelena Dysli on 3-10-1715.

Martin was born and lived in Frutigen. He later moved to Muri , Koniz and later

Stettlen with family before journeying to Carolina in December 1734 and arriving on or about February 5th, 1735.

"The King of Great Britain purchased this Carolina Province of the Lords Proprietors about 1729 and studied to make Agriculture, Commerce and Navigation, flourish there. His Majesty brought in Col Johnson, a worthy Gentleman, to be the Governor thereof; who, at his Departure for Carolina, received Orders and Instruction, but in particular was directed instantly to mark out Places in a proper Situation for building Eleven Towns, viz.
Two on the River Alatamaha, Two on the River Savanna, One at the Head of the River Poupon, Two at the River Santee, One at the River of Watery,One at the Black River, One at the River Wacomau, and One at the River Pedee."

Promotional literature was about to be produced for Switzerland in efforts to attract migration to South Carolina Townships. "In the summer of 1731, Colonel Jean Pierre Purry (born in Newchatel, Switzerland) drew up a little pamphlet in Charles Town, South Carolina, "A Description of the Province of South Carolina..," This promotional-tract literature empacized South Carolina to any other places in the world. After describing the vast wealth of goods and livestock produced by the colony, Purry then spent the better part of three pages explaining the dangers of living in Carolina. He met each of the problems directly climate, sickness, mosquitoes, and rattlesnakes. On Purry's return to Switzerland, his "Description of South Carolina" was published in the Neuchatel newspaper as well as pamphlet form. The pamphlet was disseminated throughout Switzerland, and set in motion what distraught cantonal officials derisively labeled the "Rabies Carolinae" or "Carolina madness". The pamplet was also translated in French, and published in the Gentleman's Magazine, for August, September, and October 1732. "
The entire 4 page document can be viewed on the following *Orangeburgh German-Swiss Genealogical Society* website: http://www.rootsweb.com/~scogsgs/purry.htm or http://www.ogsgs.org/purry.htm

February 28th, 1739/40 Hans Jacob Riemensperger (from Tuggenburgh, Switzerland) distributed another brochure throughout Germany and Switzerland.
http://www.rootsweb.com/~scogsgs/remsb.htm

John Tobbler would later publish another similar description of Carolina in Janurary, 1753 for intention of attracting more settlers from eastern Switzerland.
http://www.rootsweb.com/~scogsgs/toblr.htm

Frydig Marriages – Switzerland 1565-1846

Names	Date	Place	to whom
FRYDIG-			
Abraham FRYDIG...............	07-07-1819	Frutigen, Swit	Susanna ZIMMERMANN
Adam FRYDIG.................	**02-09-1584**	**Hirslanden,Swit**	**Dorothea**
ROSENSTOCK			
Anna FRYDIG..................	10-31-1636	Adelboden, Swit	David EGGER
Anna FRYDIG..................	1660	Swit	Bendicht Klopfenstein
Anna FRYDIG..................	1673	Swit	Christian SENFTEN
Anna FRYDIG..................	1749	Swit	Gwer KURZEN
Anna FRYDIG..................	1749	Swit	Gwer KURZEN
Anna FRYDIG..................	1769	Swit	Peter STOLLER
Barbara FRYDIG..............	1749	Swit	Christen Klopfenstein
[Bertaud] Berchtold Frydig	**04-08-1616**	Adelboden, Swit	**Trini BIRCHER**
[Bertaud] Berchtold FRYDIG...	1625	Adelboden, Swit	Christina AMALER
[Catherine] Catharina FRYDIG	1570	Swit	Clauwi ALLENBACH
[Christian] Christen FRYDIG...	1618	Swit	Vreni GROENER
Christian FRYDIG..............	1651	Swit	Madlen ALLENBACH
Christian FRYDIG..............	1704	Swit	Madle RYTER
[Christian] Christen FRYDIG...	1794	Swit	Elisabeth BACHER
Christina FRYDIG..............	1709	Swit	Rudolf SARBACH
Christina FRYDIG..............	1733	Swit	Niclaus BAERTSCHI
Daniel FRYDIG................	1663	Swit	Anna LIENHART
Daniel FRYDIG................	1710	Swit	Benedicta HILTBRAND
Daniel FRYDIG................	1710	Swit	Benedicta HILTBRAND
[Elisabeth] Elsbeth FRYDIG....	1567	Swit	Christian ZUMKEHR
[Elisabeth] Elsbeth FRYDIG....	1580	Swit	Christian SCHRANZ
[Elisabeth] Elsbeth FRYDIG....	1580	Swit	Christian SCHRANZ
[Elisabeth] Elsbeth FRYDIG....	1610	Swit	Christian HARI
Elisabeth FRYDIG..............	1665	Swit	Hans KLOPFENSTEIN
[Elisabeth] Elsbeth FRYDIG....	1665	Swit	Hans KLOPFENSTEIN
[Elisabeth] Elsbeth FRYDIG....	1671	Swit	Peter SENFTEN
[Elisabeth] Elsbeth FRYDIG....	1675	Swit	Abraham ALLENBACH
[Elisabeth] Lizabeth FRYDIG...	1784	Swit	Peter GROSSEN
Elisabeth FRYDIG..............	1830	Swit	Peter ZURBRUEGG
[Johannes] Hans FRYDIG........	04-05-1562	Frutigen ,Swit	Verena BIRCHER
[Johannes] Hans FRYDIG........	1614	Swit	Margaretha Kammacher
[Johannes] Hans FRYDIG........	1648	Swit	Anna TRUMMER
[Johannes] Hans FRYDIG........	1648	Swit	Anna TRUMMER
[Johannes] Hans FRYDIG........	1659	Swit	Dorothea VON KAENEL
[Johannes] Hans FRYDIG........	06-17-1672	Frutigen,Swit	Anna VIENT
[Johannes] Hans FRYDIG........	01-10-1700	Frutigen,Swit	Barbara SAENFFTEN
[Johannes] Hans FRYDIG........	07-01-1715	Frutigen,Swit	Margreth BOHLER
[Johannes] Hans FRYDIG........	03-28-1738	Frutigen,Swit	Margreth SCHLAEPPI
Johannes FRYDIG..............	03-28-1756	Frutigen,Swit	Catharina STOLLER
Johannes FRYDIG..............	10-18-1802	Lenk Im Simmental,Swt	Susanna BEETSCHEN
Johannes FRYDIG..............	1806	Swit	Verena GLAUS
[Johannes]Johann FRYDIG......	1827	Swit	Sara ROSSER
[Johannes]Johann Peter FRYDIG	1833	Swit	Margaretha SCHNEIDER
[Magdalena] Madlen FRYDIG...	11-10-1716	Lenk Im Simmental,Swt	

[Magdalena] Madlen FRYDIG...	1708	Swit	Hans BOLIERER
[Magdalena] Madlen FRYDIG...	1760	Swit	Jacob SARBACH
[Margaretha] Margreth FRYDIG	05-23-1687	Adelboden,Swit	Peter EGGER
Maria FRYDIG..................	02-02-1809	Frutigen,Swit	Johannes RYTER
Martin Frydig............. Dysli	**03-10-1715**	Frutigen,Swit	**Maria Magdalena**
[Melchior] Melcher FRYDIG.....	04-27-1725	Frutigen,Swit	Margreth FRARY
[Melchior] Melcher FRYDIG.....	01-31-1727	Frutigen,Swit	Christina REICHEN
[Melchior] Melcher FRYDIG.....	11-1776	Frutigen,Swit	Margritha MANI
[Melchior] Melcher FRYDIG.....	12-05-1805	Frutigen,Swit	Elisabeth AMMELER
Peter FRYDIG.................	10-05-1660	Frutigen,Swit	Elsbeth KUNEN
Peter FRYDIG.................	**07-23-1672**	Frutigen,Swit	**Christina ZUERCHER**
Peter FRYDIG.................	10-03-1743	Frutigen,Swit	Elsbeth Waffenschmid
Peter FRYDIG.................	09-22-1765	Boltigen,Swit	Anna BETHLER
Peter FRYDIG.................	10-29-1777	Frutigen,Swit	Catharina DAENZER
Peter FRYDIG.................	05-13-1813	Frutigen,Swit	Catharina ZURBRUEGG
Peter FRYDIG.................	06-18-1846	Frutigen,Swit	Maria GROSSEN
[Quirin] Gwer FRYDIG........	**05-27-1582**	Adelboden,Swit	**Christina Daenzer**
[Quirin] Gwer FRYDIG..........	06-12-1624	Adelboden,Swit	Elsbeth GERMANN
[Quirin] Gwer FRYDIG..........	02-20-1671	Adelboden,Swit	Dichtli BAERTSCHI
[Quirin] Gweer FRYDIG........	10-31-1673	Adelboden,Swit	Barbara BURN
[Quirin] Gwer FRYDIG..........	06-09-1701	Frutigen,Swit	Catharina WAEFLER
[Stephanus] Steffan FRYDIG	11-02-1629	Adelboden,Swit	Barbara DAENZER
Susanna FRYDIG...............	12-1804	Frutigen,Swit	Christian PFISTER
Susanna FRYDIG...............	07-05-1838	Kandergrund,Swit	Gilgen RYTER
Verena FRYDIG...............	12-12-1565	Adelboden,Swit	Hans SENFTEN
Verena FRYDIG...............	06-22-1628	Adelboden,Swit	Clauwi ALLENBACH
Verena FRYDIG...............	1712	Adelboden,Swit	David KUENTIZ

Source: Main International Genealogical Index 4.02—Continental Europe

Frydig Births and Christening's – Switzerland 1557-1950

Names	**Type**	**Date**	**Place**	**Relation**

-FRIDIG-

Anna FRIDIG C		1557	Swit	Fa:Gwer FRIDIG
Anna FRIDIG C		1562	Swit	Fa:Gwer FRIDIG
[Barbara] Barbli FRIDIG C		1560	Swit	Fa:Gwer FRIDIG
[Barthelemy] Bartleme FRIDIG .. C		1591	Swit	Fa:Johannes FRIDIG
[Catherine] Catharina FRIDIG .. C		1607	Swit	Fa:Johannes FRIDIG
[Elisabeth] Elsy FRIDIG C		1593	Swit	Fa:Johannes FRIDIG
[Elisabeth] Elsbeth FRIDIG .... B		1725	Swit	Sp:Georg ALLEMANN
Freni FRIDIG C		1599	Swit	Fa:Johannes FRIDIG
Freni FRIDIG C		1607	Swit	Fa:Johannes FRIDIG
Johannes FRIDIG C		**1558**	**Swit**	**Fa:Gwer FRIDIG**
Johannes FRIDIG C		1588	Swit	Fa:Johannes FRIDIG
Peter FRIDIG C		1601	Swit	Fa:Johannes FRIDIG
[Quirin] Gwer FRIDIG C		**1564**	**Swit**	**Fa:Gwer FRIDIG**
[Quirin] Gwer FRIDIG C		1587	Swit	Fa:Johannes FRIDIG
[Stephanus] Steffan FRIDIG C		1603	Swit	Fa:Johannes FRIDIG

Verena FRIDIG .... B	About	1493	Swit	Sp:Andreas ASCHWANDE
Verena FRIDIG .... M		1560	Swit	Sp:Peter SCHRANZ

-FRYDIG-

Abraham FRYDIG C		1731	Swit	Fa:Melcher FRYDIG
Abraham FRYDIG C		1760	Swit	Fa:Abraham FRYDIG
Abraham FRYDIG C		1774	Swit	Fa:Johannes FRYDIG
Abraham FRYDIG C		1793	Swit	Fa:Melcher FRYDIG
Abraham FRYDIG C		1797	Swit	Fa:Melcher FRYDIG
Abraham FRYDIG .... B		1824	Swit	Fa:Abraham FRYDIG
Abraham FRYDIG .... B		1827	Swit	Fa:Christen FRYDIG
Abraham FRYDIG .... B		1831	Swit	Fa:Abraham FRYDIG
Abraham FRYDIG .... B		1831	Swit	Fa:Johannes FRYDIG
Anna FRYDIG C		1564	Swit	Fa:Hans FRYDIG
Anna FRYDIG .... B	About	1603	Swit	Sp:Niklaus JAGGI
Anna FRYDIG .... B	About	1608	Swit	Re:Carola SCHLATTER
Anna FRYDIG .... B	About	1608	Swit	Re:Carola SCHLATTER
Anna FRYDIG C		1609	Swit	Fa:Gwer FRYDIG
Anna FRYDIG C		1617	Swit	Fa:Berchtold FRYDIG
Anna FRYDIG C		1620	Swit	Fa:Christen FRYDIG
Anna FRYDIG .... B	About	1622	Swit	Sp:Heinrich JAGGI
Anna FRYDIG C		1637	Swit	Fa:Gwer FRYDIG
Anna FRYDIG OR BOLER C		1645	Swit	Fa :Hans BOLER
Anna FRYDIG C		1648	Swit	Fa:Hans FRYDIG
Anna FRYDIG C		1649	Swit	Fa:Steffen FRYDIG
Anna FRYDIG C		1650	Swit	Fa:Peter FRYDIG
Anna FRYDIG .... B	About	1660	Swit	Re:Bertha E. EGGER
Anna FRYDIG C		1679	Swit	Fa:Peter FRYDIG
Anna FRYDIG C		1690	Swit	Fa:Hans FRYDIG
Anna FRYDIG C		1709	Swit	Fa:Gwer FRYDIG
Anna FRYDIG C		1709	Swit	Fa:Gwer FRYDIG
Anna FRYDIG C		1716	Swit	Fa:Gwer FRYDIG
Anna Maria FRYDIG C		1721	Swit	Fa:Marti FRYDIG
Anna FRYDIG C		1745	Swit	Fa:Daniel FRYDIG
Anna FRYDIG .... M		1769	Swit	Sp:Peter STOLLER
[Barbara] Barbli FRYDIG C		1639	Swit	Fa:Steffan FRYDIG
[Barbara] Barbli FRYDIG C		1648	Swit	Fa:Peter FRYDIG
Barbara FRYDIG .... M		1686	Swit	Re:Leo BLOSCH
Barbara FRYDIG .... M		1686	Swit	Re:Leo BLOSH
Barbara FRYDIG .... B	About	1716	Swit	Sp:Christen KLOPFENS
Barbara FRYDIG C		1718	Swit	Fa:Hans FRYDIG
Barbara FRYDIG .... B		1724	Swit	Re:Francis Emil MOSE
Barbara FRYDIG C		1734	Swit	Fa:Marti FRYDIG
Barbara FRYDIG C		1778	Swit	Fa:Johannes FRYDIG
Barbara FRYDIG C		1778	Swit	Fa:Johannes FRYDIG
Barbara FRYDIG C		1792	Swit	Fa:Peter FRYDIG
[Barthelmy] Bartlome FRYDIG ... C		1597	Swit	Fa:Peter FRYDIG
[Benedikt] Bendicht FRYDIG C		1644	Swit	Fa:Steffen FRYDIG
[Bertaud] Berchtold FRYDIG C		**1583**	**Swit**	**Fa:Gwer FRYDIG**
[Bertaud] Berchtold FRYDIG C		1637	Swit	Fa:Berchtold FRYDIG
[Catherine] Catharina FRYDIG .. C		1570	Swit	Fa:Hans FRYDIG
[Catherine] Catharina FRYDIG .. C		1628	Swit	Fa:Gwer FRYDIG
[Catherine] Catharina FRYDIG .. C		1634	Swit	Fa:Berchtold FRYDIG
[Catherine] Trini FRYDIG C		1640	Swit	Fa:Berchtold FRYDIG

[Catherine] Catharina FRYDIG .. C	1752	Swit	Fa:Daniel FRYDIG
[Catherine] Catharina FRYDIG .. C	1756	Swit	Fa:Johannes FRYDIG
[Catherine] Catharina FRYDIG .. C	1766	Swit	Fa:Johannes FRYDIG
[Catherine] Catharina FRYDIG .. C	1778	Swit	Fa:Peter FRYDIG
[Catherine] Catharina FRYDIG .. C	1778	Swit	Fa:Peter FRYDIG
Christian FRYDIG C	1630	Swit	Fa:Berchtold FRYDIG
[Christian] Christen FRYDIG ... C	1646	Swit	Fa:Gwer FRYDIG
[Christian] Christen FRYDIG ... C	1666	Swit	Fa:Hans FRYDIG
[Christian] Christen FRYDIG ... C	1668	Swit	Fa:Daniel FRYDIG
Christian FRYDIG .... B	1671	Swit	
Christian FRYDIG .... M	1754	Swit	Sp:Susanna MARTIG
[Christian] Christen FRYDIG ... C	1767	Swit	Fa:Johannes FRYDIG
[Christian] Christen FRYDIG ... C	1772	Swit	Fa:Johannes FRYDIG
[Christian] Christen FRYDIG ... C	1794	Swit	Fa:Christen FRYDIG
Christian FRYDIG .... M	1818	Swit	Re:Edward BISCHOFF
Christian FRYDIG .... B	1820	Swit	Fa:Christen FRYDIG
Christian FRYDIG C	1846	Swit	Fa:Johannes FRYDIG
[Christian] Christen FRYDIG ... B	1853	Swit	Fa:Christian FRYDIG
[Christian] Christen FRYDIG ... B	1853	Swit	Fa:Christian FRYDIG
Christian FRYDIG .... B	1888	Swit	Fa:Christen FRYDIG
Christina FRYDIG C	1625	Swit	Fa:Gwer FRYDIG
Christina FRYDIG C	1628	Swit	Fa:Berchtold FRYDIG
Christina FRYDIG C	1633	Swit	Fa:Berchtold FRYDIG
Christina FRYDIG C	1635	Swit	Fa:Peter FRYDIG
Christina FRYDIG C	1639	Swit	Fa:Peter FRYDIG
Christina FRYDIG C	1642	Swit	Fa:Steffen FRYDIG
Christina FRYDIG C	1687	Swit	Fa:Peter FRYDIG
Daniel FRYDIG C	1639	Swit	Fa:Gwer FRYDIG
Daniel FRYDIG C	1661	Swit	Fa:Peter FRYDIG
Daniel FRYDIG C	1663	Swit	Fa:Daniel FRYDIG
Daniel Hans FRYDIG C	1673	Swit	Fa:Peter FRYDIG
Daniel FRYDIG C	1705	Swit	Fa:Gwer FRYDIG
Daniel FRYDIG C	1705	Swit	Fa:Gwer FRYDIG
Daniel FRYDIG C	1749	Swit	Fa:Daniel FRYDIG
[Dorothee] Dorothea FRYDIG C	1670	Swit	Fa:Hans FRYDIG
[Elisabeth] Elsbeth FRYDIG C	1577	Swit	Fa:Hans FRYDIG
Elisabeth] Elsbeth FRYDIG .... M	1580	Swit	Sp:Christian SCHRANZ
Elisabeth FRYDIG C	1632	Swit	Fa:Gwer FRYDIG
[Elisabeth] Elsbeth FRYDIG C	1633	Swit	Fa:Gwer FRYDIG
Elisabeth FRYDIG C	1634	Swit	Fa:Gwer FRYDIG
Elisabeth FRYDIG C	1642	Swit	Fa:Gwer FRYDIG
[Elisabeth] Elsbeth FRYDIG .... B	About 1672	Swit	Sp:Hans SCHRANZ
[Elisabeth] Elsbeth FRYDIG C	1675	Swit	Fa:Hans FRYDIG
[Elisabeth] Elsbeth FRYDIG C	1680	Swit	Fa:Peter FRYDIG
[Elisabeth] Elsbeth FRYDIG C	1683	Swit	Fa:Peter FRYDIG
[Elisabeth] Lisabeth FRYDIG ... C	1719	Swit	Mo:Christina FRYDIG
[Elisabeth] Lisabeth FRYDIG ... C	1719	Swit	Mo:Christina FRYDIG
[Elisabeth] Elsbeth FRYDIG C	1737	Swit	Fa:Melcher FRYDIG
[Elisabeth] Elsbeth FRYDIG C	1745	Swit	Fa:Peter FRYDIG
[Elisabeth] Elsbeth FRYDIG C	1749	Swit	Fa:Peter FRYDIG
Elisabeth FRYDIG C	1755	Swit	Fa:Abraham FRYDIG
[Elisabeth] Elsbeth FRYDIG C	1761	Swit	Fa:Johannes FRYDING
[Elisabeth] Lisabeth FRYDIG ... C	1783	Swit	Fa:Peter FRYDIG
[Elisabeth] Lisabeth FRYDIG ... M	1784	Swit	Re:Gottlieb GROSSEN

[Elisabeth] Elisabetha FRYDIG . B	1787	Swit	Re:Gottlieb GROSSEN
Elisabeth FRYDIG C	1788	Swit	Fa:Melcher FRYDIG
[Elisabeth] Elisabetha FRYDIG . B Abt	1790	Swit	Re:Gottlieb GROSSEN
Elisabeth FRYDIG C	1816	Swit	Fa:Christen FRYDIG
Elisabeth FRYDIG C	1820	Swit	Fa:Abraham FRYDIG
Elisabeth FRYDIG .... B	1823	Swit	Fa:Christen FRYDIG
Elisabeth FRYDIG .... B	1823	Swit	Fa:Christen FRYDIG
Elisabeth FRYDIG .... B	1851	Swit	Fa:Christian FRYDIG
[Elisabeth] Elise FRYDIG ...... B	1893	Swit	Fa:Christen FRYDIG
[Elsje] Elsi FRYDIG C	1632	Swit	Fa:Berchtold FRYDIG
Gabriel FRYDIG C	1728	Swit	Fa:Marti FRYDIG
Gilgian FRYDIG .... B	1837	Swit	Fa:Johannes FRYDIG
Jacob FRYDIG C	1665	Swit	Fa:Daniel FRYDIG
Jacob FRYDIG C	1678	Swit	Fa:Peter FRYDIG
Jacob FRYDIG C	1714	Swit	Fa:Daniel FRYDIG
Jacob FRYDIG C	1719	Swit	Fa:Marti FRYDIG
Jacob FRYDIG C	1749	Swit	Fa:Hans FRYDIG
Jacob FRYDIG .... M	1822	Swit	Re:Edward BISCHOFF
[Johannes] Hans FRYDIG C	1568	Swit	Fa:Hans FRYDIG
[Johannes] Hans FRYDIG .... M	1614	Swit	Re:Mary A.K. ROTHLIS
[Johannes] Hans FRYDIG .... M	1614	Swit	Re:Mary A.K. ROTHLIS
[Johannes] Hans FRYDIG C	1617	Swit	Fa:Gwer FRYDIG
[Johannes] Hans FRYDIG C	1620	Swit	Fa:Gwer FRYDIG
[Johannes] Hans FRYDIG C	1626	Swit	Fa:Berchtold FRYDIG
[Johannes] Hans FRYDIG C	1632	Swit	Fa:Steffan FRYDIG
[Johannes] Hans FRYDIG C	1633	Swit	Fa:Gwer FRYDIG
[Johannes] Hans FRYDIG OR BOLER C	1645	Swit	Fa:Hans BOLER
[Johannes] Hans FRYDIG C	1646	Swit	Fa:Peter FRYDIG
[Johannes] Hans FRYDIG C	1662	Swit	Fa:Hans FRYDIG
[Johannes] Hans FRYDIG C	1669	Swit	Fa:Daniel FRYDIG
[Johannes] Hans FRYDIG C	1672	Swit	Fa:Hans FRYDIG
[Johannes] Hans FRYDIG C	1693	Swit	Fa:Hans FRYDIG
[Johannes] Hans FRYDIG C	1702	Swit	Fa:Hans FRYDIG
[Johannes] Hans FRYDIG C	1723	Swit	Fa:Gwer FRYDIG
[Johannes] Hans FRYDIG C	1723	Swit	Fa:Gwer FRYDIG
[Johannes] Hans FRYDIG C	1725	Swit	Fa:Hans FRYDIG
[Johannes] Hans Jacob FRYDIG .. C	1727	Swit	Fa:Melcher FRYDIG
Johannes FRYDIG C	1738	Swit	Fa:Hans FRYDIG
Johannes FRYDIG C	1747	Swit	Fa:Peter FRYDIG
Johannes FRYDIG C	1757	Swit	Fa:Daniel FRYDIG
Johannes FRYDIG C	1759	Swit	Fa:Johannes FRYDIG
Johannes FRYDIG C	1764	Swit	Fa:Johannes FRYDIG
[Johannes] Johann Peter FRYDIG C	1768	Swit	Fa:Johannes FRYDIG
Johannes FRYDIG C	1783	Swit	Fa:Melcher FRYDIG
[Johannes] Johann FRYDIG C	1798	Swit	Fa:Peter FRYDIG
[Johannes] Johann FRYDIG C	1800	Swit	Mo:Barbara FRYDIG
Johannes FRYDIG .... M	1802	Swit	Re:Francis Emil MOSE
Johannes FRYDIG .... B	1822	Swit	Fa:Christen FRYDIG
Johannes FRYDIG .... B	1822	Swit	Fa:Christen FRYDIG
[Johannes] Johann Jakob FRYDIG * B	1826	Swit	Re:Caroline D. STAUF
Johannes FRYDIG .... B	1828	Swit	Fa:Johannes FRYDIG
Johannes FRYDIG .... B About	1832	Swit	Re:Jacob MESSERLI
Johannes FRYDIG .... B	1835	Swit	Fa:Johannes FRYDIG
[Johannes] Hans Christian FRYDI* B	1914	Swit	Fa:Christian FRYDIG

[Johannes] Hans FRYDIG .... B	1919	Swit	Fa:Christian FRYDIG
Lina FRYDIG .... B	1895	Swit	Fa:Christen FRYDIG
[Magdalena] Madlen FRYDIG C	1607	Swit	Fa:Gwer FRYDIG
[Magdalena] Madlen FRYDIG C	1613	Swit	Fa:Gwer FRYDIG
Magdalena FRYDIG .... M	1617	Swit	Re:Francis Emil MOSE
[Magdalena] Madlen FRYDIG C	1620	Swit	Fa:Berchtold FRYDIG
[Magdalena] Madlen FRYDIG C	1621	Swit	Fa:Berchtold FRYDIG
[Magdalena] Madlen FRYDIG C	1624	Swit	Fa:Gwer FRYDIG
[Magdalena] Madlen FRYDIG C	1624	Swit	Fa:Gwer FRYDIG
[Magdalena] Madlen FRYDIG C	1626	Swit	Fa:Gwer FRYDIG
[Magdalena] Madlen FRYDIG C	1629	Swit	Fa:Berchtold FRYDIG
[Magdalena] Madlen FRYDIG C	1667	Swit	Fa:Hans FRYDIG
Magdalena FRYDIG .... B	1762	Swit	Fa:Jakob FRYDIG
Magdalena FRYDIG C	1847	Swit	Fa:Christian FRYDIG
[Margaretha] Margreth FRYDIG .. C	1611	Swit	Fa:Gwer FRYDIG
[Margaretha] Margreth FRYDIG .. C	1615	Swit	Fa:Gwer FRYDIG
[Margaretha] Margreth FRYDIG . B Abt	1670	Swit	Sp:Abraham DURIAN
[Margaretha] Marg. FRYDIG ..... M	1687	Swit	Re:Bertha E. EGGER
[Margaretha] Margritha FRYDIG . C	1776	Swit	Fa:Melcher FRYDIG
Maria FRYDIG C	1756	Swit	Fa:Hans FRYDIG
Maria FRYDIG C	1759	Swit	Fa:Abraham FRYDIG
Maria FRYDIG .... B About	1766	Swit	Sp:Peter ZRYD

-FRYDIG-

Maria FRYDIG .... B About	1766	Swit	Sp:Peter ZRYD
Maria FRYDIG C	1781	Swit	Fa:Melcher FRYDIG
Maria FRYDIG .... B	1785	Swit	
Maria FRYDIG C	1785	Swit	Fa:Peter FRYDIG
Maria FRYDIG .... M	1809	Swit	Re:Samuel RYTER
Maria FRYDIG C	1817	Swit	Fa:Christen FRYDIG
Maria FRYDIG .... B	1836	Swit	Fa:Johann Peter FRYD
Martin FRYDIG C	**06-23-1689**	**Frutigen,Swit**	**Fa:Peter Frydig**
Martin Willi FRYDIG .... B	1950	Swit	Fa:Willy FRYDIG
Martin Willy FRYDIG .... B	1950	Swit	Fa:Willy Oskar FRYDI
[Melchior] Melcher FRYDIG C	1685	Swit	Fa:Peter FRYDIG
[Melchior] Melcher FRYDIG C	1726	Swit	Fa:Melcher FRYDIG
[Melchior] Melcher FRYDIG C	1729	Swit	Fa:Melcher FRYDIG
[Melchior] Melcher FRYDIG C	1755	Swit	Fa:Melcher FRYDIG
[Melchior] Melcher FRYDIG C	1755	Swit	Fa:Melcher FRYDIG
[Nicolas] Niclaus FRYDIG C	1637	Swit	Fa:Peter FRYDIG
[Oscar] Oskar FRYDIG .... B	1896	Swit	Fa:Christen FRYDIG
Peter FRYDIG C	1563	Swit	Fa:Hans FRYDIG
Peter FRYDIG C	1568	Swit	Fa:Hans FRYDIG
Peter FRYDIG C	**1618**	**Swit**	**Fa:Berchtold FRYDIG**
Peter FRYDIG C	1620	Swit	Fa:Gwer FRYDIG
Peter FRYDIG C	1622	Swit	Fa:Gwer FRYDIG
Peter FRYDIG C	1629	Swit	Fa:Gwer FRYDIG
Peter FRYDIG C	1630	Swit	Fa:Gwer FRYDIG
Peter FRYDIG C	1634	Swit	Fa:Steffan FRYDIG
Peter BARTSCHI OR FRYDIG C	1648	Swit	Fa:Gwer FRYDIG
Peter FRYDIG C	**1649**	**Swit**	**Fa:Peter FRYDIG**
Peter FRYDIG C	1665	Swit	Fa:Peter FRYDIG
Peter FRYDIG C	1665	Swit	Fa:Peter FRYDIG
Peter FRYDIG C	1703	Swit	Fa:Gwer FRYDIG

Name			Year	Place	Relation
Peter FRYDIG	C		1708	Swit	Fa:Hans FRYDIG
Peter FRYDIG	B	About	1735	Swit	Sp:Anna BETTLER
Peter FRYDIG	C		1754	Swit	Fa:Hans FRYDIG
Peter FRYDIG	B	About	1768	Swit	Sp:Katharina ZURBRUE
Peter FRYDIG	C		1788	Swit	Fa:Peter FRYDIG
Peter FRYDIG	B		1793	Swit	
Peter FRYDIG	C		1814	Swit	Fa:Peter FRYDIG
Peter FRYDIG	B		1832	Swit	Fa:Johannes FRYDIG
[Quirin] Gwer FRYDIG	C		1566	Swit	Fa:Hans FRYDIG
[Quirin] Gwer FRYDIG	C		1595	Swit	Fa:Peter FRYDIG
[Quirin] Gwer FRYDIG	C		1623	Swit	Fa:Berchtold FRYDIG
[Quirin] Gwer FRYDIG	C		1625	Swit	Fa:Gwer FRYDIG
[Quirin] Gwer FRYDIG	C		1625	Swit	Fa:Gwer FRYDIG
[Quirin] Gwer FRYDIG	C		1636	Swit	Fa:Gwer FRYDIG
[Quirin] Gwer FRYDIG	C		1647	Swit	Fa:Steffen FRYDIG
[Quirin] Gweer FRYDIG	M		1673	Swit	Sp:Barbara BURN
[Quirin] Gwer FRYDIG	C		1675	Swit	Fa:Peter FRYDIG
[Rodolphe] Rudolf FRYDIG	C		1628	Swit	Fa:Gwer FRYDIG
[Rose] Rosina FRYDIG	B		1894	Swit	Fa:Christen FRYDIG
Samuel FRYDIG	B		1829	Swit	Fa:Christen FRYDIG
Samuel Friedrich FRYDIG	B		1889	Swit	Fa:Christen FRYDIG
Sara FRYDIG	B		1838	Swit	Fa:Johannes FRYDIG
[Stephanus] Steffen FRYDIG	**C**		**1628**	**Swit**	**Fa:Berchtold FRYDIG**
[Stephanus] Steffan FRYDIG	C		1636	Swit	Fa:Steffan FRYDIG
[Stephanus] Steffen FRYDIG	C		1705	Swit	Fa:Hans FRYDIG
Susanna FRYDIG	C		1746	Swit	Fa:Peter FRYDIG
Susanna FRYDIG	C		1746	Swit	Fa:Peter FRYDIG
Susanna FRYDIG	C		1756	Swit	Fa:Abraham FRYDIG
Susanna FRYDIG	C		1758	Swit	Fa:Johannes FRYDIG
Susanna FRYDIG	C		1777	Swit	Fa:Melcher FRYDIG
Susanna FRYDIG	C		1781	Swit	Fa:Peter FRYDIG
Susanna FRYDIG	B		1815	Swit	Re:Samuel RYTER
Susanna FRYDIG	B		1815	Swit	Fa:Peter FRYDIG
Susanna FRYDIG	C		1815	Swit	Fa:Peter FRYDIG
Susanna Katharina FRYDIG	B		1847	Swit	Re:Karoline SCHMID
Susanna Maria FRYDIG	B		1891	Swit	Fa:Christen FRYDIG
Verena FRYDIG	C		1574	Swit	Fa:Hans FRYDIG
[Verena] Vreni FRYDIG	C		1623	Swit	Fa:Christen FRYDIG
Verena FRYDIG	C		1691	Swit	
Verena FRYDIG	C		1727	Swit	Fa:Hans FRYDIG
Verena FRYDIG	C		1727	Swit	Fa:Hans FRYDIG
Verena FRYDIG	C		1763	Swit	Fa:Johannes FRYDIG

Source: Main International Genealogical Index 4.02—Continental Europe

Gwer Fridig, ancestral line of Martin Fridig (1689)

Descendants of Gwer FRIDIG : FRYDING

First Generation

1. **Gwer FRIDIG** was born 1535 in Adelboden, Switzerland.

Gwer 30 May 1586 Adelboden, Switzerland.

Gwer married **Anna SPILLMAN** on 1556 in Adelboden, Switzerland.

They had the following children:

> 2 F   i.   **Anna FRIDIG** was born 1 Aug 1557 and was christened 1 Aug 1557 in Adelboden, Canton Bern, Switzerland.
>
> 3 M   ii.   **Johannes FRIDIG** was born 25 Sep 1558 in Canton: Bern: Adelboden, Switzerland and was christened 25 Sep 1558.
>
> 4 F   iii.   **Barbli FRIDIG** was born 28 Jul 1560 and was christened 28 Jul 1560.
>
> 5 F   iv.   **Anna FRIDIG** was born 6 Sep 1562 and was christened 6 Sep 1562.
>
> + 6 M   v.   **Gwer FRIDIG** was born 4 Jun 1564.

Second Generation

6.   **Gwer FRIDIG** (Gwer) was born 4 Jun 1564 in Canton: Bern: Adelboden, Switzerland and was christened 4 Jun 1564 in Canton: Bern: Adelboden, Switzerland.

Gwer resided 30 May 1586 in Adelboden, Switzerland. He 30 May 1586 Mannlehen(?), Switzerland.

> Schultheiss und Rat zu Bern übertragen an Gwer Fryding an der Lenk ein Stück Land (1 1/2 Jucharten), genannt "an Pleiken", samt Haus und Hof darauf, zu Mannlehen.
> Datierung: 30.05.1586 / 09.06.1586
> 5/30/1586 Archiveinheit Obersimmental 39
> Translated: German to English
> Schultheiss and advice to Berne transferred at Gwer Fryding to steer a piece country (1 1/2 Jucharten), " mentioned; at Pleiken" , including house and yard on it, to Mannlehen.
> Dating: 30.05.1586/09.06.1586
> Note: Mannlehen is a 2,343 metre mountain in the Swiss Alps located within the Canton of Berne.
>
> The Magistrate and Council of the city of Bern transfer to Gwer Fryding (living) at the Lenk (localisation, likely within todays village of the same name) a piece of land (1.5 Jucharten = size), named "an Pleiken", including house and farmstead, as personal fief(?). Not sure about the proper translation of Mannlehen: the person receiving it would be a feudal tenant, and this right would be given to the person, not necessarily including the family (sons).(Seelentag, Wolf 9/2009)
>
> Gwer Fridig (1564) list his name on a Mannlehen, Bernese Oberland, Switzerland land record as Gwer Fryding in 1586.

Gwer married **Christina DAENZER** on 27 May 1582 in Adelboden, Switzerland.

They had the following children:

> + 7 M   i.   Berchtold FRIDIG was born 5 May 1583.

Third Generation

7.   **Berchtold FRIDIG** (Gwer, Gwer) was born 5 May 1583 in Canton: Bern: Adelboden, Switzerland.

Berchtold married **Trini (Catherina) BIRCHER** on 8 Apr 1616 in Adelboden, Switzerland.

They had the following children:

> 8 F   i.   **Anna FRIDIG** was born 4 May 1617.

The Swabian Connection – Expanded Edition

| + | 9 | M | ii. | **Peter FRIDIG** was born 16 Dec 1618. |

      10 F   iii. **Madlen I FRIDIG** was born 18 Jun 1620.

      11 F   iv. **Madlen II FRIDIG** was born 8 Jul 1621.

      12 M   v. **Gwer FRIDIG** was born 3 Jun 1623.

      13 M   vi. **Steffan FRIDIG** was born 13 Jan 1628 in Canton: Bern: Adelboden, Switzerland.

      14 F   vii. **Madlen FRIDIG** was born 19 Jul 1629.

      15 M   viii. **Christian FRIDIG** was born 1 Nov 1630.

      16 F   ix. **Elsi FRIDIG** was born 10 Jan 1632 in Canton: Bern: Adelboden, Switzerland.

      17 F   x. **Catherina FRIDIG** was born 26 Oct 1634.

      18 F   xi. **Trina FRIDIG** was born 19 Jul 1640 in Canton: Bern: Adelboden, Switzerland.

Fourth Generation

9. **Peter FRIDIG** (Berchtold, Gwer, Gwer) was born 16 Dec 1618 in Canton: Bern: Adelboden, Switzerland.

Peter married **Anna AMELER** on 1645. Anna was born 13 Dec 1618 in Canton: Bern: Adelboden, Switzerland.

They had the following children:

      19 M   i. **Hans FRIDIG** was born 6 Sep 1646 in Canton: Bern: Adelboden, Switzerland.

      20 F   ii. **Barbli FRIDIG** was born 24 Sep 1648 in Canton: Bern: Adelboden, Switzerland.

 +   21 M   iii. **Peter FRIDIG** was born 25 Nov 1649.

      22 F   iv. **Anna FRIDIG** was born 29 Dec 1650 in Canton: Bern: Adelboden, Switzerland.

Fifth Generation

21. **Peter FRIDIG** (Peter, Berchtold, Gwer, Gwer) was born 25 Nov 1649 in Canton: Bern: Adelboden, Switzerland.

Peter married **Christina ZUERCHER** on 23 Jul 1672 in Frutigen, Switzerland.

They had the following children:

      23 M   i. **Gwer FRIDIG** was born 20 Jul 1675 in Canton: Bern: Frutigen, Switzerland.

      24 M   ii. **Jacob FRIDIG** was born 18 Jun 1678 in Canton: Bern: Frutigen, Switzerland.

      25 F   iii. **Elsbeth FRIDIG** was born 23 Mar 1679 in Canton: Bern: Frutigen, Switzerland.

      26 F   iv. **Anna FRIDIG** was born 16 Sep 1679.

      27 F   v. **Elsbeth FRIDIG** was born 16 Feb 1682 in Canton: Bern: Frutigen, Switzerland.

      28 M   vi. **Melcher FRIDIG** was born 24 Sep 1685 and was christened 24 Sep 1685 in

Frutigen, Bern, Switzerland.

    29 F   vii. **Christina FRIDIG** was born 25 Sep 1687 in Canton: Bern: Frutigen, Switzerland.

+   30 M viii. **Martin FRIDIG** was born 23 Jun 1689 and died 1758.

Sixth Generation

30. **Martin FRIDIG** (Peter, Peter, Berchtold, Gwer, Gwer) was born 23 Jun 1689 in Frutigen, Bern, Switzerland and was christened 23 Jun 1689 in Frutigen, Bern, Switzerland. He died 1758 in before 10-25-1758 Probate Records and was buried in Orangeburg.

Martin married **Maria Magdelena DYSLI** on 10 Mar 1715 in Frutigen, Bern Switzerland.

They had the following children:

+   31 M   i. **John Jacob FRIDIG** was born 18 Aug 1719 and died 1779.

+   32 F   ii. **Anna Maria FRIDIG** was born 1721 and was buried ~ b4 27 Sep 1786.

+   33 M iii. **David FRIDIG** was born 1723 and died 1784.

+   34 M iv. **Gabrial FRIDIG** was born 18 Apr 1728 and died ~1779.

+   35 F   v. **Elizabeth FRIDAY** was born 14 Aug 1731 and died 26 Mar 1824.

    36 F   vi. **Barbara FRIDIG** was born 27 Jun 1734 in Canton: Bern: Stettlen, Switzerland. She died ~1765? in South Carolina.

                       Barbara married **ROMPARTS?**.

+   37 M vii. **John Martin FRIDAY** was born 1748 and died ~1825.

Ships(Voyage) that arrived 1733-1767

Jacob Gallman family from Zurich and others arrived at Charlestown on the ship *William* from London on 5 Feb 1735. Another Dutch Fork source states that the Fridig clan came from Frutigen arrived with them a party of 28 emigrants split off at Basel, a city situated on the Rhine River at the point between Switzerland, German and French Borders. Their intention was to reach a port with a passenger ship and travel down the Rhine to Rotterdam where they could find a ship to sail to Carolina. After four days with no prospects of passage, they changed plans and departed for London. The group was able to obtain passports from Basel and crossed into France. It would take 24 days to reach Calais on the English Channel. They again had to wait another 8 days while the ship was loading a supply of wine. It would take 36 hours to cross the channel. The passage was set on the Ship *William at* a cost of (five guineas) for crossing the Atlantic; first to Braffeidenz' which was New Providence Island in the Bahamas to drop off English Soldiers, pick up provisons and a cargo of lumber; then waiting another 8 days for its departure south along the coast of the new world. The crossing would take a total of nine weeks. Hans Trachsler another Swiss who made the voyage a year after Martin describes the food eaten on the ship. The food was given once each day with a portion of dried beef on Sunday and Tuesdays. Saturday they received a piece of pork and Friday some codfish. The meal for Monday, Wednesday and Thursday was a thin soup of boiled rice, peas and barley. With the meal each passenger was allotted a quart of water and a piece of Zwieback (a biscuit made from wheat). Children under three received no portions and were fed by their parents share. That voyage of Gallmans is described in Jacob Gallman's 1738 letter to relatives in Zurich. Martin Friday and his family arrived at Charleston aboard the ship, William, on or about the 5th of February 1735. The Switzers Petition would immediately be brought Upper House for immediate Passage, Tools and Provision for the settlers.

Ship "William" (1735-1851) arrived in Charlestown, South Carolina on or about (Feb-5-1735) guided by Captain William Vitery.

Ship "Samuel" arrived July 13 1735 in Charlestown, SC – 250 Switzers by Captain Hugh Percy.

Ship "<Unknown> arrive July 17 1735 – 76 took oath & 14 absent.

Ship "St. Andrew" arrived July 20 1735 in Charlestown, SC – 200 Poor Palatines by Captain Peter Robinson.

John **Friday** (1728), son of Hans, stated he had married Susanna Hembright (1732), a Protestant Swisser, who was servant to John Morton, Esq. who came to SC circa 1744 on the ship St. Andrew.

The book *Ships passenger lists (1538-1825)* by Carl Boyer, list Martin Fridig (Friday) b.6-23-1689 d.1758 as an immigrant record arriving in the South Carolina in 1742. The information is listed on page 161 of the Passenger and Immigration Lists from immigration records. The Youn family papers in the SC archives show that David Friday son of Martin (1689) arrived in South Carolina February 5th 1735. The Publication by Boyer, Carl lists Martin **Fridig** in 1742. *Ship Passenger Lists, the South (1538-1825).* Newhall, Calif.: the editor, 1979. 314p. 4th pr. 1986. Reprint. Family Line Publications, Westminster, MD, 1992. It Contains passenger lists mentioned in Lancour, *A Bibliography of Ship Passenger Lists, 1538-1825* (1963), nos. Boyer has indexed ship names, place names, and about 12,000 personal names, with variant surname spellings. Tepper's works, have similar lists.

Note: Martin may have traveled back to Switzerland to receive crowns for land or get additional family members. This date could also be an error in the documenting of immigrant information in 1963.

Arrival of the Switzers - July 19, 1735

South Carolina Gazete *CHARLES-TOWN*, July 19 Saturday 1735.

On Sunday last* arrived here Capt. Hugh Percy in 9 weeks from Rotterdam and 6 from Cowes, with 250 *Switzers* on board, who are come to settle a township on the King's Land in this province upon the Encouragement granted to other Foreigners. Amongst them are Ninety fit to bear arms, and it is not doubted but their feeling in this Province will much contribute to its strength, and by their Industry and Laborious* self's tend to its great advantage; there being in parts of this Province very good Land for Wheat and Corn , they may probably upon proper Encouragement furnish us in time with a good quantity of the necessary and so much wanting Commodity, which now we are obliged on purchase at what rate so ever from out neighbors.

The Province of Pennsylvania*, to which these several years past many thousands (some will say above 70,000) of persecuted* Palatines and Switzers have taken their refuge, is thereby brought in such a flourishing condition, that between the 25th of March 1734, and the 25th of March 1735, from thence is exported Wheat 195,028 bushels*, 1300 Tiercca, Indian Corn 10,464 bushels*, Flour 37,231 Barrels, 1530 Half-barrels; Bread 3232 Pieces, 8474 Barrels, 693 Half-

The Swabian Connection – Expanded Edition

barrels and 681 Qu. Casks."

On Thursday His Honour, the Lieutenant Governor being petitioned by those Switzers that they might be qualified, in order to enjoy the fame, privileges and liberties as those born subjects of the King of England, called a Council, and Directed Tho. Dale, Tho. Lamboll (?) and Henry Gibbes, Esqrs., three of his Majesty's Justices of the Peace, to administer to so many of them as desired it the Oath of Allegiance and to let them subscribe the last* according to a Law made for that purpose when accordingly in the afternoon the same were read to Seventy-six of them then present (some being sick and absent to the number of Fourteen) in the *German* Tongue by an Interpreter sworn* to that purpose*, and having explained to them the meaning of it, and they all being willing to take this Oath, the same was again read in English by one of the aforesaid his Majesty's Justices, and interpreted by those Sentences, which they all repeated, and at the Conclusion subscribed to the aforesaid Oath and test.

They are to settle a Township upon Edisto River, which is thought the best Ground for Wheat, Corn, Hemp and Flax, as also for planting of Vineyards. The Ship St. Andrew, Capt. Peter Robinson, came out the same time with Capt. Percy from Cowes, having on board about 200 Palatines, and is expected here every Day.... Continues...

Note: the letter "f" is used as an "S" and sometimes a "C" during the writing in this period. The correct spelling is indicated inside by a * i.e. laft would be last*. Corrected words are shows as an asterisks *. The original spellings had an "f" used as an "s" in the words.

Arrival of the Switzers - July 26, 1735

South Carolina Gazette *CHARLES-TOWN*, July 26.

On Thursday, His Honor the Lieutenant Governor being petitioned by these* Switzers, that they might be qualified, in order to enjoy the fame Privileges and Liberties as natural born Subjects of the King of England, called a Council, and directed Tho: Dale, Tho: Langboll (?), and Henry Gibbes Esqrs*, three of his Majesty's* Justices of the Peace, to administer to fo many of them as desired* it the Oath of Allegiance and to let them subscribe* (the) Tefs (Teft), according to a Law made for that purpose*, when accordingly in the Afternoon the fame were read to Seventy-fix of them then present*, (some* being sick* and absent* to the Number of Fourteen) in the German Tongue by an interpreter sworn* to that purpose*, and having explained to them the meaning of it, and they all being willing to take this Oath, the fame was again read in English by one of the aforesaid His Majesty's* Justices, and interpreted by those* Sentences, which they all repeated, and at the Conclusion subscribed* to the aforesaid* Oath and Teft.

They are to settle* a Township* upon Edisto* River, which is thought the best* Ground for Wheat, Corn, Hemp, Flax, as also* for planting of Vineyards. The Ship St. Andrew, Capt. Peter Robinson, came out the Fame Time with Capt, Percy from Cowes, having on board about 200 Palatines, and is expected here every Day. Continues...

Note: the letter "f" is used as an "S" and sometimes a "C" during the writing in this period. The correct spelling is indicated inside by a parenthesis. i.e. laft = (last). Corrected words are shows as an asterisk *. The original spellings had an "f" used in the words.

Other ships that arrived in Charles Town, SC: (1719-1859)

Blessing arrives Aug 14th, 1671 by Captain Mathias Halsted in Carolina.
Blessing & Phoenix arrived Dec 13th, 1671 in Carolina.
Pink Elizabeth (1719-1721)
Sloop Elizabeth (1721-1730)
Sloop Louisa (1721-1730)

Anne arrived January 13, 1733. James Oglethorpe was aboard, who departed from England and landed later in Georgia on Feb 12, 1733.

<Ship Unknown> Purry's 150 immigrants from Switzerland arrive December 15, 1732.

William arrived by Capt.William Vitery on February 5, 1735. On board were the Fridig's, Ralph Chapelier, John Ulrick Muller, John Ulrick Beckman, John Frederick Coleman and others.

Samuel arrived July 13, 1735 - 250 Swtizers, 90 fit to bear arms; Melchior Ott was aboard and departed from Switzerland.

July 17, 1735 - 76 took oath, 14 absent.

July 20, 1735 - shipload of palatines arrived.

July 26, 1735 - 220 Switzers headed to Edisto Township.

Prince of Wales arrived Charles Town 1 Feb 1736/7 by Capt. George Dunbar. Geiger/Shellig families.

Eagle arrived in September 1736. Ulrich Buser [Boozer] (1719) & family were aboard.

Prince of Wales arrived Feb 1737 to settle New Windsor Township.

Encouragement arrived in 1740/41. Barbara Akerman.

Ship Rose arrived August 9th 1742 by Capt Andrew Andriss.

St.Andrew by Capt. Brown January 18th, 1744/45. Jacob Geiger & Andrew Buck(Buff) were aboard.

Captain Schirmerhorn from Philadelphia arrived March 2nd 1748. Bennet Hoylet [Hyler] petitioned for land.

Greenwich arrived January 1749/50. Caspar Kuhn (1713) & family were aboard, departed from Switzerland.

Griffin arrived October 17th, 1749. John Jacob Riemensperger, Helpting/Epting, John Adam was aboard, departed from Germany. John George Burkhart also arrived on this ship in 1749.

Neptune arrived in Aug 6th? 1751 by Captain Jed. Hans Rebsome was on board.

Judith arrived before 1751

Ann(e) arrived October 23rd 1751 by Capt. Charles Kennaway w/200 Germans and 100 single artisans from Wurtenberg.

Success arrived December 31st 1751 by Capt. William Isaac.

The Mary arrived 1752. George Kent and George Millander were aboard.

Abel George arrived 1752. James Chesin was from Switzerland.

Edinburgh arrived August 1752 by Capt. Mason from Rotterdam.

Upton arrived Spetember 1st 1752 by Capt. John Gardiner 1500 Germans were aboard with Conrad Emigh/Amick/Emick and John Jacob Frey..

Cunliffe arrived September 1752 by Comm. Joseph Cleales/Cleater from Holland with Palatines)

Snow Rowand arrived October 2nd 1752 by Capt. Arthur Fran/Tran with Michael Bouknight, wife & children; Matthias Wessinger, wife & children; Christian Leytner, wife & children were aboard.

Caledonia arrived December 8th?,1752 by Capt. Alexander Harvie/Harvey. Christopher Dreyer, wife & children were aboard. Anna Sheymeyrin and Michael Hentz were also aboard.

Elizabeth arrived 1752 - Hans (John) Swygert/Swykart and family were aboard.

Anne arrived 1753 by Capt. John Orr from Rotterdam.

John and Mary arrived January 1753 by Capt. Robinson. John Christian Frey and Lourman/Lowman family were aboard.

Elizabeth arrived Jan 31st 1753 by Comm. Thomas Ross from Rotterdam w/319 Protestants to settle in New Windsor Township. Henrick Lybrand, wife and children were aboard.

Priscilla arrived November 1754 by Capt. Thomas Castanack with Hans (John) Martin Swygert and family were aboard.

Captain Crawford and Hereford arrived in 1754

More unspecified German arrivals were in 1756.

The *Britannia* arrived full of Protestants in 1761

Nancy arrived 1761. Johann Henrich Widemann was aboard, departed from Germany.

Britannia arrived October 5th, 1766 with the Heinreck/Henry Guess/Goats.

Britannia arrived from Amsterdam October 17th, 1766 with Andrew Keller.

Hillsborough arrives Thursday Feburary 19th, 1767. William Hanvey was aboard, departed from Belfast, Ireland.

Brigatine *Chichester* arrived from Belfast January 5th 1768. William Reed Master and the Boydes petitioned for land.

Snow James & Mary arrived on January 12th 1768. John Mooore Master from Larne petitioned for land.

Brig *Lord Dunagannon* arrived February 3rd 1768. Robert Montgomery petitioned for land.

Britannia from Newry arrived on September 1st 1767. John Bryan petitioned for land.

Hopewell arrived in Charleston on 6th of January 1773. John Clark "Irish' petitioned for land.

Polly arrived March 1774 from Liverpool, England.

Magna Charta arrived April 1774 from London.

Pallas arrived May 1774 from London.

Carolina arrived May-August 1774 from London.

Mermaid arrived March 1774.

Sloop Benjamin arrived May 1774.

Prosper arrived 1775.

Sloop Commerce arrived August 1775.

Ship Frankland arrived in Charleston on 13 January 1776

Defence arrived October 1776.

Peggy arrived April 1777.

Schooner Margaret arrived in Charleston on 1 January 1820

Brig Angelina arrived in Charleston on 6 January 1820

Brig Columbia arrived in Charleston on 6 January 1820

Schooner Jane arrived in Charleston on 31 January 1820

Schooner Ann arrived in Charleston on 31 January 1820

Brig Mary arrived in Charleston on 3 February 1820

Schooner Eudora arrived in Charleston on 5 February 1820

Ship Java arrived in Charleston on 14 February 1820

Schooner Mary arrived in Charleston on 15 February 1820

Ship Mars arrived in Charleston on 18 February 1820

Brig Eliza arrived in Charleston on 11 March 1820

Ship Montgomery arrived in Charleston on 11 March 1820

Brig Prince Leopold arrived in Charleston on 19 March 1820

Schooner Comet arrived in Charleston on 21 March 1820

Ship Octavia arrived in Charleston on 22 March 1820

Ship South Carolina arrived in Charleston on 27 March 1820

Sloop Lady Washington arrived in Charleston on 4 July 1820

Schooner Mary arrived in Charleston on 10 July 1820

Ship Portia arrived in Charleston on 24 July 1820

Schooner Jane arrived in Charleston on 6 July 1820

Ship Arab arrived in Charleston on 30 July 1820

Brig Christopher arrived in Charleston on 2 August 1820

Sloop Lady Washington arrived in Charleston on 4 August 1820

Schooner Planter arrived in Charleston on 4 August 1820

Schooner Mary Ann arrived in Charleston on 9 August 1820

Brig Catherine arrived in Charleston on 10 August 1820

Ship South Carolina arrived in Charleston on 28 August 1820

Ship Octavia arrived in Charleston on 14 September 1820

Brig Susan arrived in Charleston on 24 September 1820

Ship General Moultrie arrived 1856.

Ship Lodebar arrived 1859.

Other notables were:

Two Brothers arrived Oct 7, 1738 in Savannah, GA by Captain William Thompson. It carried Palatines and the Derrick family. Hans George Picklie and family petitioned for land.
Ship *Anne* would bring James Ogelthorpe and colonists to Yamacraw Bluff, Georgia on February 12, 1733.
Ancona a merchant ship left SC to England on Nov 1740 but was captured.
Europa arrived Dec 4, 1741 at Tybee Island, GA by Captain John Wadham. Jacob Burckhart was aboard.
Friends Good Will arrived in 1750 by Captain Crawford at Cape Fear, NC instead of Charleston, SC.

The Switzers Petition (1735)
(Transcribed by Jeff Friday)

In the upper House of Assembly Wednesday the 5th Feb^{ry} 1734.
Present
The Honble The Lieut Governor

John Fenwick	}
Joseph Wragg	} Esqr
John Hammerton	}

Broad Street Bill Mr Cockran and Mr Jaget from the Commons House brought a Bill for sinking a
Brought   drain in the Broad Street in Charles Town, and for cleaning and Regulating the
said Street read a 1st time in their House.

Read a Petition of **Martin Friday**, Ralph Chapelier, John Ulric Muller, John

Switzers Petn   Ulrick Beckman, and John Frederick Coleman in behalf of themselves and thers, praying they may be released from their Engagements on account of their passage hither, and become settlers in this Province, and the foll^g Message was sent with the said Petition to the Commons House viz^b.

Mr Speaker and Gentlemen
We send you the Petition of Several Switzers, which

Message therein When you have perused, we desire you will appoint a Com^{ee} of your House to Joyn a Com^{ee} of thee Board to consult of Proper means and to relieve the Pet^{or}, and make them usefull to their Province at Settlers therein, which by their Petition they seem inclined to be.

5th Feb^{ry} 1734   Thos Broughton Presd
                                                  Read

next page -------

Read the memorial and acct. thereunto anex'd of the Honble John
Mr Hammerton   Hammerton Esqr. Secretary of this Province for writings etc relating to the
& Mem!   Publick Service and recommended it to the Common House.
                                                 Adjourned

In the Upper House of Assembly Wednesday 4, 5th Feb^{ry} 1734 PM
Present
The Honble the Lieuten^t Governer

John Fenwicke	}
Jos^p Wragg	} Esqr
John Hammerton	}

Writs Signed	The writ chasing three members for the Parish of St. Helena Port Royal, was signed by the Ex^er and the Honble Members of the Majestys Council.
	Mr Blake and Capt Beale from the Commons House acquainted this House that their Com^ee was ready to meet the Com^ee of this House to confer on the subject matter of the Message sent to them this morning.
Com^ee meet On ye Swiss	And the Honble Col. Fenwicke and Jos^p Wragg Esqr went to joyn the said Com^ee.

Adjourned

In the Upper House of Assembly Thursday the 6th Feb^ry 1734.

Present
The Honble the Lieu^t. Govr

The Honble	{ Robert Wright	Joseph Wragg	}	
	{ John Fenwicke	Thos Waring	} Esqr	
	{	Jon. Hammerton	}	

M^r. Manigault and Mr. Jaget from the Commons House brought the following Message vizt.

Honble Gentlemen

This House and debating the Report of the Com^ee of Conference on the Petition of the Swiss lately arrived

Here

next page -------

on the Swiss.	here; agreed to that part of the said Report which related to the Paying the passage of the said Swiss, on their Indentures being assigned to His Excellency the Governor, the better to oblige them to settle in the Township on the South side of Santee River, but to prevent any abuses that may ensue, have Enterd into the Resolution herewith sent you, to which we desire your Honble Concurrence.

<table>
<tr><td>6th Feb^ry 1734.</td><td align="right">By order of the House</td></tr>
<tr><td></td><td align="right">Paul Jenys Speaker</td></tr>
</table>

	Resolved on considering His Majestys 20th Instruction to His Excell^cy the
Resolution on relating to New Settlers.	Governor relating to the Encouragement to be given to Poor Protestants, who are desirous to Settle in this Province, that it is the opinion of this House, that The said Instruction is only to be extended to poor Protestants who are Freemen and not to Covenant Servants, who shall arrive in the Province, and that Such Covenant Servants are not by the said Instruction or by any Engagements the Genl Assembly have enterd into, intitled to any benefit under the same, and that this House will not make any further Provision for any persons that Indent themselves for their Passage, nor for any other Protestants but those that come over and arrive in the Province Freemen.
Report	A Com^ee of both Houses on ye Pet^n of Sev^l Swiss lately arrived.
	Have Examind the State of Appropriated Fund to 29th of Sep^t 1734 and Find good therin only £ 6g:15.g^11r exclusive of Interest due on Publick orders, no such article being Charged in the Debit of the Acco^t which if now placed there,
On the Pet^n of the Swiss.	would make a considerable deficiency on that Fund.
	As to paying the Passages of nineteen of said Swiss the Com^ee are of Opinion that Settling those people altogether in one of the Northern Township may be of great disadvantage in Strengthing the Barrier, therefore recommend the paying the sum of £ 780:10: Currency to discharge their Passage (on Condition that they Settle as aforesaid) and that the Money be raised in the Piece of the

233

next page ----------

Current Year by which means its being made a preced^t for others that may arrive here after will be avoided, nor will the appropriate Fund admit of this additional Expense of paying passage, nor even hold out for defray the Charge of Purchasing Tools and Provisions for all those who may come over on the Encouragement of the said Law.

The Com^{ee} further recommend that Tools and Provisions for one year be provided for all the Swiss now arrived as usual.

And the said Report was agreed to and sent back to the Commons House.

Read a first time and passed with the Amendm^{ts}. a ___

Tax Bill recvd a 1ST time.

Bill for raising the Sum of for defraying the Charges of the Government for one year commencing the 25th. March 1734 and ending the 25th Day of March 1735 and also a Bill for sinking a drain in the Broad Street in Charles Town and for Cleaning and Regulating the

and Y^e Broad Street Bill

the said Street, Read a first time and passed as th amendments.

And sent them both to the Commons House.

Mem of M^r. Abercromby.

Read. The Memorial and Acco^t of James Abercromby by Esqr. Attorney Genl.

Adjourned.

In the Upper House of Assembly Friday they 7th Feb^{ry} 1734.
Present
The Honble the Lieu^t Gov^{nr}

The Hon^{bles}   { John Fenwicke   Robert Wright   }
             { Jos^p Wragg   Thos Waring   } Esq^{rs}

The Hon^{bles} Mr Wragg having produced the Sev^l Indentures of the Swiss mentiond in the Resolution agreed to by this House Yesterday, he deliverd the foll^g acco^t vvz^t.

The

next page

The names of the Swiss, who have not payd their passage
from London to Carolina in the Ship William, William Vitery Master vis^d.

Swiss Indentures Deliverd.

John Mathias and wife	2
Ulrick Speri Smith	1
Jacob Viterling...	1
Jacob Galman and nine Children....................	10
Jacob Spuhl...	1
Herman Christian Dittering & Wife.................	2
Henry Segrist..	1
Henry Walder pr note....................................._1_	
Persons	19

Eighteen passes under Indentures at £6pr Head £   108.0.0
One d^o ft note..   3.10.0
                                   111:10.0
        Exchange 6oo ft C^t   66G:0.0

The Swabian Connection – Expanded Edition

Carolina Currency....   £   780.0.0

Mr. Ouldfield and Col. Gibbs brought the following Message
from the Commons House vist.

Honble Gentlemen.

Thos House hath received Information that Several Persons overseers,
Relating to the   and others who have resided in this Province for a considerable time past, have
Encouragemt   applied for the Encouragement to New Comers for settling the Township by the
to New Comers   Appropriation Law, therefore desire your Honrs will Joyn with us in giving Orders
only.   To the Publick Treasures to take care that no person who is not a New Comers
               shall have the allowance given by the said Law to New Comers only.
               Your Honrs were pleased to Communicate lows? A Letter from Mr. Popple
Mr. Popples Ltr   Secretary to the Board of Trade to His Excy the Governor, we desire your will
               procure us a copy of the Subtance of what His Excy wrote on that Head.
      7th. Febry 1734   By order of the House
                                              Paul Jenys Speaker
                                              Resolved

Source: South Carolina Council Journal – Upper House No 6 Part 1 Nov 7, 1734 – May 26, 1736
Pgs 31-35. Feb 5, 6, 7 1734 Petition of Martin Friday & others.
South Carolina Department of Archives and History

Neighbors of the Fridigs (all variations) 1735-1880

Researching the neighbors of a person can help determine many factors: Arrival of neighbors,
name changes/usage, migrations, associations, family links, relationships, actual physical
locations of residence (i.e., creeks/rivers/streams on a map), street name from the 1910/20
census, places that can be searched for burial/church records by using all the above to cross-
reference information for that period.

Name	Census/Year	District/County, State

Hans Frydig (Lot 398)   1735/36   Orangeburg Dist, SC
His neighbor was Christian (Tapp) Top (Lot 397), Benedict Collard (Koller) (Lot 399), Johannes
"John" (Hans) Meyer (Lot 392), John Orly (Lot 395) and Abraham von Bestall (Lot 396).

Martin Fryday (Lot 11)   2-5-1735/36   Saxe Gotha Township, Berkley Co, SC – Front
St./Santee Rvr. His neighbors were John Jacob Rodey (Lot 13) and Roodie Cooplet (Lot 12).
(SNLP)

Martin Friday   2-07-1736   Saxe Gotha Township, Berkley Co, SC
His neighbors were John Coleman and John Matthews. (SNLP)

Martin Fryday   5-5-1736   Town of Congrees, Berkley Co, SC / Santee
River. His neighbors was Hans Spearly, John Matthews and John Coleman. (SNLP)

Martin Friday   9-10-1737   Saxe Gotha Township, SC / Santee River
His neighbor was Henry Scone. (RG)

Martin Fryday   9-16-1738   Berkeley County, SC

No neighbors with land laid out. (CP)

Martin Friday   2-27-1739   Saxe Gotha Township, SC / Six Mile Creek
No neighbors with land laid out. (CP)

John Jacob Fridig   4-12-1745   Saxe Gotha Township, SC / Santee River
His neighbor was John Matthy east of John.

Gasper/Casper Faust   4-12-1745   Saxe Gotha Township, SC Saluda River W of
Geigers Creek. 200 acres in forks of the Congaree. (CP)
Jos. (John/Jospeph?) Nicholas Junker [Jumper] and Gabriel Friday (1728) witnessed. In 1765
John Friday would be his neighbor.

Martin Fridig   10-18-1746   Saxe Gotha Township, SC
His neighbors were Jacob Thieler and George Hunter.

John Friday (1728)   9-16-1747   Lexington, SC / 12 Mile Creek
His only neighbor was Henry Lockley (Lockly).
Note: This was the son of Hans Frydig (1690) from the Church of Orangeburg.

Martin Friday   4-7-1749   Saxe Gotha Township, SC
His neighbor was Jacob Motte and George Hunter.

Martin Friday   5-1-1749   Saxe Gotha Township, SC
His neighbor was Hans Michael Croft and George Hunter. (SNLP)

John Jacob Fridig   02-26-1750   Saxe Gotha Township, SC / Congaree River
His neighbor was Mary Ann Closman. (SNLP)

John Jacob Fridig   04-24-1752   Saxe Gotha Township, SC / Congaree Creek
His new neighbor was Ann Mary Closman. (SNLP)

John Jacob Fridig   12-5-1753   Saxe Gotha Township, SC / Santee River
His neighbor Samuel Boaker was North West of John. (SNLP)

Hans Fridig   06-05-1753   Saxe Gotha, SC / 12 Mile Crk/14 Mile Branch
His neighbors were Johannes Erhard and Barbara Hussar.
Note: This was Hans Frydig (1690) from the Church of Orangeburg.

John Jacob Fridig   06-27-1754   Saxe Gotha, SC / North Side of Saluda River
His neighbors were John Jacob Geiger, Samuel Boaker "Broakens/Bookter?" and John Matthews.
(RG)

John Jacob Fridig   07-29-1754-3-8-1755   Saxe Gotha Township, SC / Saluda River
His neighbors (across the river) were Barbary Ackerman, John Grangett & Anna Shymerin. (SNLP)
Note: Believed to be directly across the river via reference from Lexington Genealogical
Exchange Map located in Volume 2 Book 4 Spring 1983 p. 186.

Hans Fridig   1-19-1755   Saxe Gotha Townhsip, SC
Note: Thought this was John Jacob, but is actually Hans Frydig (1690) unless the record taker
knew of the name and placed Hans short for John being Johannes.
His neighbors were Johannes Erhard and Barbary Hussars. (SNLP)

John Frydays   11-22-1756   Saxe Gotha Townhsip, SC

The Swabian Connection – Expanded Edition

His new neighbor was <u>Urhart Grober</u> [Gruber]. Other neighbors are Henry Gocklew [Hartley?], George Smith, Godfrey Drayers [Dreher] and Conrad Kinder [Kinler?]. (SNLP)

John Fryday   5-13-1762   Saxe Gotha Townhsip, SC
His neighbors were <u>Godfrey Dreyer</u>, Henry Locklie, Phillip Gruber and Conrad Kinler. (SNLP)
Note: This looks to be the grandson of Hans Frydig (1690).

Jacob Fridig   08-06-1764   Saxe Gotha/Berkley Co/Savany Hunt Creek
His neighbors were Thomas Berry, <u>Henry Gallman</u>, and Anthony Stack. Martin Fridig's land was near and still listed in his name. (SNLP)
Note:
On 9-4-1738 Anthony Stack had 50 Acres surveyed in the Saxe Gotha Township in Berkely County, SC. His neighbors were Thomas Berry and James St. John.

John Friday   2-5-1765   Saluda and Broad River
His neighbors were <u>John Marley</u>, Samuel Rooker, Gasper Faust, Barbara Bome, Jacob Burkit, Gasper Mathias and Jacob Geiger. (SNLP)

John Friday   2-9-1765   Saxe Gotha Township, SC Twelve Mile Creek
His neighbors were <u>Erhart Grober</u>, George Smith, Henry Lachlie [Lockley/Hartley], Godfry Drayer [Drehr] and Conrad Kinder. (SNLP)

Jacob Fridig   2-26-1765   Craven County, SC Saluda River
His neighbors were <u>John Stroub,</u> Joseph Geiger, Barbara Appeals. (SNLP)
Note: Land was originally granted to Peter Klein on Jan 9, 1755.

John Friday   7-3-1765   Saluda and Broad River
His neighbors were <u>John Marley</u> (located north east of John), Samuel Rooker, Gapser Faust, Barbara Rompart, Jacob Berkland [Burghard?], Barbara Bomis and Gapser Matthews. (SNLP)
Note: On 2-18-1764 Henry Weaver had a 100 acre plat (Unrecorded Plat for land not granted) surveyed on the Broad River in Craven County. His neighbors would have been Gasper and Jacob Foost [Faust].

Jacob Fridig   8-17-1765   Lexington, SC Fork of Broad & Saludy
His neighbors were Mary Weaver (Widow), Jacob Geiger and John Conrad Geiger?

Hans Fridig [Jacob!]   08-24-1765   Saxe Gotha Township, SC
His neighbors were <u>Johannes Erhard</u>, Barbara Hussar and Hans George Smith. (SNLP)

John Jacob Frydig   9-19-1765   Berkley Co, SC Saluda Rvr/Congaree Rvr/Broad Rvr
His neighbors were <u>Casper Mathys</u>, and Rachel Matheys. (SNLP)

John Jacob Fridig   3-18-1767   Saxe Gotha Township, SC / Saludy River
His neighbors were John Jacob Geiger, John Mathew and <u>Christian Leiver</u> [Lever]. Samuel Bochens gone by this time. (SNLP)
Note: On 12-15-1752 Thomas Hember had a 300 acre plat surveyed on Cannon Creek of the Broad and Saluda River. His neighbors were Christian Leiver [Lever], Ulrick Sleigh, Henry Gallman and Cornelious Sigler.
On 4-26-1753 Simon Riberhover had a 350 acre plat surveyed between the Broad and Saluda River on Cannons Creek. His neighbors were Christian Leiver [Lever], Cornelious Seigler and Thomas Herber.

David Friday   1-20-1768   Berkley Co, SC Six Mile Creek/Congaree Rvr
His neighbors were Michael Leitner, Egerton Leigh, William Nichol and Ralph Humphreys. (SNLP)
Note:
On 1-13-1767 William Nichols had a plat for 200 acres surveyed on Six Mile Creek of the Congaree River in Saxe Gotha of Berkeley Co, SC. His neighbors were Ralph Humphries, John Troup and David Webb.
On 11-15-1784 Michael Leitner had 300 acres surveyed on Sile Mile Creek in the Orangeburg District. His neighbors were Gabriel Ferdig [Fridig].

David Friday   1-25-1768   Berkley Co, SC Six Mile Creek/Congaree Rvr.
His neighbors were Egerton Leigh, Christopher Leehner, William Nichol and Ralph Humphreys. (SNLP)

Gabriel Fridig   5-5-1768   Craven Co, SC SW side of Broad River
No neighbors with land laid out. (Deed)

David Fridig   9-29-1768   Berkley Co, SC on Mill Creek, S of Congaree Rv
His neighbors were Michael Lights, William Nichols and Jacob Fridig. (RG)
Note: This was a memorial for 300 acres.

David Friday   2-27-1769   Berkley Co, SC Six Mile Creek/Congaree Rvr.
His neighbors were Christopher David Leckner, and William Nicholas. (SNLP)

David and Jacob Friday 5-20-1769   Saxe Gotha Township, SC
Their neighbor was Phillip Pearson, James Berwick and Agness Widle. (SNLP)

David and Jacob Friday 9-15-1769   Saxe Gotha Township, SC
Their neighbor was Agness Widle. (SNLP)

Jacob Friday   5-7-1771   Long Branch Little Saluda River

Jacob Friday   1768,11-2-1771-73   Leesville, SC
His neighbors were John Fairchild, Samuel Gruber (Cooper), Joseph Dill, William Mason, John Dean, Jr and Pierce Butler. (LG)

Jacob & David Fridig   1771   Berkley Co, SC
Brothers lived side by side and their neighbors were Michael Litner, Benjamin Farrar, Edward Southwells and Moses Kirkland (1726). On the other side of Jacob were John Stroupe, Jacob Geiger, and John Shilling.

Jacob Fridig   5-5-1771   Saxe Gotha, SC Congaree River
His neighbors was William Arthur (1731).

Jacob Fridig   05-13-1771   Saxe Gotha/Congaree River/Savany Hunt Creek
His neighbors were Thomas Berry, Jacob Berry, Anthony Stock, Jacob Theiler, Harman Geiger (1738), John Conrad Geiger (1736), Henry Gallman (1743), Martin Fridig and Andrew Moak. (SNLP)

Jacob Friday   11-22-1771   Congaree River (LG)

Jacob Friday   6-12-1772   Saxe Gotha, Berkley Co, SC
His neighbors were Cornelius Duwee, William Arthur, Mathew Lebbecap, Lawrence Charles and Alexander Rose. (SNLP)

John [Jacob] Fryday   6-12-1772   Santee/Saluda River, Saxegotha Township,
Berkley Co, SC
His neighbors were Barbary Romparts, Samuel Rooker, John Marley, Casper Faust, Casper Hensler, Cornelious Dewees, John Bear, John Rolls (1735?), Mary Burkmire, Julius Creed, Leonard Summers, Jacob Tarra, and Marlem Harler. (SNLP)

John Jacob Fridig   9-30-1772   Saxe Gotha Township, SC
His neighbor was Larrance Charles and Gabriel Fridig. (SNLP)

John Frideg   11-24-1772   Colleton Co/St. Pauls Parish, SC Edisto River
His neighbor was John Dean. (SNLP)

John Martin Friday   12-3-1772   Granville Co, SC Buffalo Crk
His neighbor was George Seawright.

Jacob Friday   12-22-1772   NE Congaree River in Berkley CO, Saxe Gotha
Township. His neighbor was William Arthur. (RG)

David Friday   12-1772   Saxe Gotha, SC
His neighbors were John Chestnut, Benjamin Farrar.

Jacob Friday   1-13-1773   Saxe Gotha, SC Congaree River
His neighbor was William Arthur.

David Friday   2-26-1773   Colleton Co, SC Red Bank Creek/Little Saluda
Rvr.
Note: This is a plat for 250 Acres.

Jacob Fridig   3-2-1773   Colleton Co/St. Pauls Parish, Edisto Rvr
His neighbor was Pierce Butler, John Ready, William Mayzek and John Dean Jr. (SNLP)
Note: On 11-24-1772 John Dean had 110 Acres surveyed on the Edisto River in St. Pauls Parish/Colleton County. His neighbors were Jacob Frideg, John Bremar and John Fairchild.
On 8-5-1773 John Dean Jr had a memorial of 100 Acres on the Edisto River in Colleton County/St. Pauls Parish. His neighbors were Jacob Fridig and John Fairchild.

Jacob Friday   9-8-1773   Orangeburg, SC Chinquepin Branch Edisto River
His neighbor was Mary Richards.

[Unknown Friday]   1774   Little Saluda, Fairfield Co, SC
Neighbors were William Brisan, James Huston, Stark, and William Adams.
Note: On 12-3-1772 James Huston had 300 acres surveyed on the Little Saluda River in Colleton Co, SC.

David Friday   8-23-1774   Colleton County, SC
Note: Land grant for 250 acres.

Jacob Fridig   9-13-1774   Colleton county/Saint Pauls Parish/Edisto
river/Saluda river/Elishas creek/Craven county/Fair Forest creek/Ferguson creek/Dutchmans creek/Tyger river
His neighbors were Pierce Butler, Alexander Frederick, John Ready, William Mazyck, John Dean, William Dodd, Whitaker, Daniel Huger, James Brewton, James Wofford, James and Isaac Patens. (SNLP)

Jacob Friday   10-12-1774   Cloud Creek/Long Branch, SC

The Swabian Connection – Expanded Edition

His neighbor was <u>Samuel Gruber</u>. (SNLP)

Note: On 10-29-1772 Samuel Gruber had 350 Acres surveyed at Clouds Creek/Long Branch/West Creek. John Bremar or John Fairchild may have been neighbors; one was the surveyor. The land grant occurred for the 350 Acres on 5-17-1774 and turned into a memorial on 10-27-1774. This location is in the Town of Batesburg, SC.

Jacob Friday   12-20-1774   Orangeburg, SC Chinquepin Branch Edisto River
His neighbors were <u>Ephraim Mitchell</u>, James Mitchell, and Daniel/Dave Hartley. (SNLP)

Jacob Friday   7-12-1775   Orangeburg, SC Edisto Rvr, Chinkapin Creek.
His neighbors were Daniel Hartley and <u>Ephraim Mitchell</u> .(SNLP)

Martin Friday   2-5-1776   Berkley Co, SC Congaree Twnship, Santee Rvr
The neighbors were Roodie Cooplet and James St. John.

Gabriel Fryday   2-3-1782   Boiling Springs Crk/Congaree Rvr/Orangeburg,SC
His new neighbor was <u>Francis Bell</u>. (SNLP)

Gabriel Fridig (d.1779)   1782   Edgefield, SC
Neighbors and Associates were Michael Watson, Arthur Watson, John Hall, Jacob Watson, Daniel Hartle, Sr., Samuel Tomkins (Dead), Benjamin Tutt, Robert Melton, Field Perdue, Thomas Weems, James Buttler, Daniel Shoemat, Samuel Stalmaker, Charles Harrison, Robert Barlow, William Lareymor, James Ferrel, William Cammel, John Johnson, Elijah Bailey, Richard Johnston Sr., Ephraim Prescott (Dead), Ogdon Cockeroft, John Watson, James Buttler, Willis Watson, Jesse Lott (Dead), Robert Stark, Gabriel Fridig, James Roquemore, James Scott, Bentley Stocks, Job and John Red, John Sawyers, Henry Buzbee, John Roberson, James Marlen, John Cook, Thomas Wood, William Thompson, Jesse Porter, Charles Boyl, George Warren, Daniel Shaw, Richard Levins, Coweatling Adams, John Sewgens, Buckner Pilman, John Jones, Gardner Williams, James Barronton, Lewis Watson, Martha Watson, Sarah Lott, Elisha Brooks, John Higgains, John Hartley, James Moore, Edward Pines, Joseph White, John Sawyers, John Watson, Jr., Samuel Stewart, Samuel Wiliams, Christopher Salters, James Harrison, Michael Ward, Howel Johnston, David Gains, Edward Couch, Frederick Hartley, James Warren, James Prichard, and Henley Webb. (EST)

Note: John Odgen Green name may have come from James Cockeroff who was surety for Jacob Green's estate. Jacob was an executor of Ogden Cockroff's will. Godfrey Friday was mentioned as one of three men assigned to appraise the estate of Jacob Green's 1830 will. Ogden Cockercroft has an adjacent line of property on Little Stephens Creek and recorded in Godfrey's land purchase in August 1814 for Edgefield, SC. Frederick Hartley and Gabriel Fridig are mentioned in the 1768 will of Henry Hartley.

John Fridig (1759)   ~3-29-1782   Fairfield/Richland Co, SC
Neighbors recorded in the estate sale of the deceased Elizabeth Rives Chappel (1740). The following people purchased items: John Miles, Hicks Chappel (1759), Timothy Rives, Isaac Love (~1750), Jacob Curry (1758), William Willingham, Henry Gregory, Thomas Hutchinson, Thomas Baker (1755), Barnaby Pope, Col John Winn, James Beard, Laban Chappell (1762), Thomas Jeffreys, Lewis Pope, James Kincaid, Robert Rabb (1742), John Cook, Oswell Ashley, Franeis Brezina, William Daniel, John Fridig, Engal Stockman, Benjamin Busby (~1764) and William Scott. Elizabeth died around 3-29-1782, Richland Co, SC. She was married in 1769 to Henry Chappel (1732). (EST)

Note: Rebecca Chappell (1827) the daughter of John Chappell (1777) married Bennet Proctor who had a child named Mary Proctor in Attala Co, MS after ~1852. Isaac Love married Martha Chappell in 1775 the daughter of Henry Chappell (1732). Robert Busby (1769) who married who married Frances Davisen (1775) had 12 children born in Stewart Co, TN between 1804-1830.

Sherod Busby (~1756) died ~1829 in Giles Co, TN. Sarah Baker (1780) the daughter of Thomas Baker (1755) married Valentine Harmon (1766) who had a child named Henry Harmon (1815) in Knox Co, TN. Mastin Winn Murphy maybe named after the Virginia "Winn" family who moved from Virginia to South Carolina then Kentucky. William Winn (1785) brother Martin Winn (1790) born in Fairfield, SC to Col John Winn (1758) (who married Eleanor Hicks) and John Fridig are recorded in the Elizabeth Rives Chappel (1740) Estate record of 1782 in Fairfield Co, SC. In 1792, a Malachi Murphey is recorded in Camden District, SC along with Green Rives, Peter Foust and others.

David Fridig (1728)   1783   St. John (Paula Inlet, "Spanish" FL)
His neighbors **(in no particular order or location on Paula Inlet)** were Philip Shireman, John Wise, Gaspar (Casper?) Keller, Henry Snell (1766) William Ingraham, John Mulkey, Jacob Sloan, John Chapel (Chappel?), John Keller, Peter Warner, Henry Gally, Adam Cabler, Jacob Whiteman, William Whitman, George Stoughtenmire, Henry Peirgler, William & Thomas Peter (Brothers) and Henry Salley. (CS)

John Friday (1759)   3-10-1784   Fork of Saluda & Broad Rivers
His neighbors were Samuel Rooker, Gasper Foust, Barbara Rompart, Jacob Burland, Barbara Rome, Moses Kirkland and Gasper Mathias.

Jacob Friday   7-18-1784   Congaree River/5 Mile Spring/Bear Branch/6 mile creek, Orangeburg, SC. His neighbor was William Hinson.

Gabriel Fridig   8-21-1784   Orangeburg, SC Long Branch/Congaree Rvr.

Fridig (Jacob?)   10-1-1784   Orangeburg, SC - Chinquapin Creek. N Edisto Rvr. Their neighbors were James Holcomb and Morehead . (SNLP)

John Friday   10-7-1784   Orangeburg Dist, SC Pleasant Garden/Congaree Rvr.

Gabriel Ferdig [Fridig] 11-15-1784   Six Mile Creek/Congaree Creek, Orangeburg District
His neighbors were Michael Leitner. (SNLP)

David Friday   6-22-1785   Orangeburg, SC - Ox Creek
His neighbors were Jacob Gates, Barrel Gant, George Gates, Paul Turquanx and Martin Bleaken. (SNLP)
Note: A George Gates (1723) married a Mary (1731) ~1751 and had 7 children w/one named Christian (1762) who married Elizabeth Ulmer (1775) ~1795. A George Gates (1782) born in SC, migrated to Tuscaloosa Co, AL by 1818 & purchased multiple pieces of Property in Tuscaloosa by 1825.

John Friday   7-1785   Orangeburg, SC
His neighbors were Henry Haim and William Cord.

Gabriel Fridig   2-14-1786   Orangeburg Dist, SC Congaree Creek
His neighbors were Mary Kinsler, Peter Bullett, Ely John Smith, B. Farrir [Farrar] and Joshua Hickmon. (SNLP)

John Friday (*)   2-28-1786   Berkley Co/Charleston Dist/St. James Parish, SC
His neighbors were Francis Cobea and John Days. (SNLP)

Note: On 10-3-1786 Henry Markley had a 152.5 acres plat surveyed at Water of Goose Creek in the Charleston District. His neighbors were George Fushrow, Francis Cobea, Amos Danelly and John Days.

Gabriel Friday   10-17-1786   Ninety-Six Co, SC - Fawn Branch/Lawsons Fork Crk/Pacolet Rvr.
His neighbors were Abraham Markley, Jacob Seigler, John Johnson, John Conners and James Burnett. (SNLP)
Note: Abraham Markley had 150 acres plat surveyed on Bone Branch of the Broad River in Orangeburg Dist, SC. His neighbors were Peter Coogler and Jacob Bookter.

John Martin Friday   12-15-1786   Ninety Six Co, SC - Bufalo Creek Little River
His neighbors were James Coutch and James Collier (1757).
Note: This is John Martin since he received the original Land grant on Bufalo Creek, which is now McCormick Co, SC. James was the son of Cornelius Collier (1720) both born in Virginia.
In 11/23/1784 James Collier had 285 acres on Buffalo Creek 96 District and his neighbors were Lazarus Binton, Bennett Crafton, Michael Deval, Ingivine, Ramsay and Stubbs.
In 3/3/1789 Thomas Lowery has 205 acress surveyed on Waters of Baffelow Creek 96 District and his neighbors were Patrick Calhoun, James Colliers amd Peter Solomon.

J. Friday   4-5-1787   Orangeburg Dist, SC - Broad River
Neighbors were Michael Willer [Wheeler], J Adam Fumer [Fulmer](1753) and Jacob Backter [Bookter].
Note: The SCDAH notes the record as a T Friday "a Transcription Error", but this is actually J. [John] Friday.
On 11-6-1751 John G. [George] Stengly [Stingley] had a 100 acre Land Grant surveyed on Hollins Head Creek.
On 6-30-1785 William Strother (~1750) had a 183 acre plat surveyed on Hollandsheds Creek in Orangeburg District . His neighbors were Jacob Bookman, Joseph Kenly [Kennerly] and George Strother (~1746).
On 3-21-1787 John Adam Summers (1744) had a 1000 acre plat surveyed on the waters of Wateree Creek in Orangeburg District. His neighbors were Wise, George Willer [Wheeler], W. Charles, John Mink, Sligh and Ketsenger.
On 3-23-1787 George Willer [Wheeler] had a 195 acre plat surveyed at Hollensheds Creek in Orangeburg District. His neighbors were William Zeigler (~176x), Jacob Bright and George Shother [Strother].
On 3-27-1787 William Zeigler had a 309 acre plat surveyed on the waters of Hollenshed Creek in the Orangeburg Dist, SC. His neighbors were John Adam Summers, George Willer, John Stingley and Michael Willer.
On 4-15-1788 Michael Willer [Wheeler] had a 260 acre plat surveyed on the waters of Hollinsheads Creek Orangeburg District. His neighbors were Kinerly [Kennerly].
William Strother died ~1822 in Alabama and George died ~1812 in South Carolina.

Samuel Friday (1756-60) 1788   TwelveMile Creek, Lexington Co, Orangebrg, SC
His neighbors and associates were in the German Lutheran Church of Mount Zion were J. G. Bamberg, V.D.M ,Gottfrid Drehr, Leonard Bouch, Mathias Senn, Godfrey Drehr Juner, John Drehr, George Baunecht, John Kleckly, Simon Juninger, Bernhart Muntz, John Glegly Junr., Martin Shiele [Shealy], Georg Fridrick Buch, Sabotian Roff, John Friday (1743), Matthias Wingert, George Michael Wingert, George Wingert, Saml. Friday, John Ruff, Thomas Kenney, and Saml. Rall [Rawl]. (CRCH)
In the 1790 Census page 400 shows John Drehr, Godfrey Drehr and Godfrey Roff. Page 391 shows Joseph Kennerly, Michael and Mathias Wingard. This Joseph was running Weaver Ferry.

Mrs. Fritig(*?)   9/10/1789   Thicketty Creek, Union Co, Ninety Sixth Dist, SC

The Swabian Connection – Expanded Edition

Andrew Gosset had an unrecord plat for land not granted of 78 acres and his neighbors were Babbs (wife of Joseph Babbs?), Mrs. Steen (Eleanor Bogen?) and John Thompson.

William Fridig (1756-74)1790   Orangeburg, SC
His neighbors were John Stack(~1761), John Winright, John Haugabook, Daniel Fisher, John Sharp, John Berry (1756-74) and Joseph Baugman. On the other side were George Pool, Jacob Allman [Hallman] (1756), William Sea [Seay], John Hughs, Henry Slappy [Slappey] (1758) and John Geiger. Another 12 homes down is Marlow Pryor who married Elizabeth Fridig-Arthur. (CS) 100000000
Note:
A William See (1741) married abt ~1761 to a Sophia Poole (1740-50) the daughter of Philip Puhl. In September 1785 William See/Sea married a Elizabeth? Poole sister of George Phillip Poole who were children of Phillip Poole. Nancy Booser [Boozer] and John Tyler witnessed the deed abstract for the Poole and See/Sea family.
On 3-26-1788 John Swigard [Swygert] had a 140 acre plat surveyed on the North Side of Saluda River in the Orangeburg District, SC. His neighbors were George Strothers, John Stack (~1761), and George Bouknight.
An 1813 will of George Pool is made in Richland District with wife Barbara and the following names: Nixon family, William Rivers, and Martin Marshall.
Henry Slappey married Nancy Ann Rutherford (1768) who was from Chatham Co, NC, the daughter of Col. Robert Rutherford. A William Seay (~1777) moved to Knox Co, TN. Michael Seay (~1777) who married Clarissa Jane Clark (~1788) had children born in McNairy 1810 & Rutherford County, TN about 1821. A Jacob Hallman (~1784) married an Elizabeth Weaver (~1784) who had a child named Henry J. Hallman (1812) in Batesburg, SC. Jacob's father also a Jacob (~1733) married an Elizabeth and they had Joseph, Andrew and Henry.
John W Berry (1771) married Sarah Clark (1781) sister to Cornelius Clark.
Thomas Berry has property all the way back when Anthony Stack received acreage back to 1738.

Gabriel Fridig (1752)   1790   Orangeburg, SC
His neighbors were Mary and George Fetner (1768), Thomas Combs, Widow Logy, Samuel Johnston, George Spiller, William Kelly, Joseph Kennerly and 10 more homes down was Michael Wingard and 5 more down was Mathias Wingard. On the other side are John Gregory, Everhart Sweetingburgh [Swittenberg] (1764), John Coon, Benjamin Coon, Fardner {Ferdinand} Adam Minick (1762), George Herring, John Adam Summers, and Benedict Meyer (1761). (CS)
Note:
In 1790 Orangeburg Census John Adam Summers is 7 homes down from Gabriel Fridig. Everheart Sweetingburg is 2 homes down from Gabriel Fridig.
In 12-10-1791 Joseph Kennerly (~175x?) petitioned for an act to be passed establishing a Toll Bridge, setting rates of ferriage that he can charge regarding his purchase of land and building of bridge across the Saluda River at Widow Weaver's Ferry.
William Eberhart Swittenberg married Anna Elizabeth Setzler (1763).

John Friday (1759)   1790   Fairfield, SC
His neighbors were George Ashford (~1723/58), James Hawthorn, John Chappell (1771), David Long , Richard Neelie/Neely (~1742), William Smithwick (~1751), Victor Neely (~1745), Phillip Goats (~1761), William Richardson and Hugh Garmany (1761). On the other side were Joseph Davidson, Andrew Frasier, William Russell, Matthew Smith, James Cameron, Jesse Brown and Joshua Badger (1751?). (CS)
Note: George Goats (~1770) migrated to Giles Co, TN about ~1818 and Sherwood Busby to Giles Co, TN before 1829. John Ashford (1785) the son of George Ashford was in the War of 1812 (3 REG'T (COPELAND'S) West TN MIL) and was married in Wilson Co, TN. Richard Neely's son the Richard II (1785) married Sally Parker (1791) in Bedford Co, TN by ~1807 and resided in Bedford Co, TN. A George Ashford shows up in the 1790 Ninety-Six District Newberry County, SC Census 7 homes down from Alexander Booker [Bookter]. Two David Longs die from Whigs in

243

1779, so possible a David Long Jr above. A Joseph Davidson (1748) was in the 1830 Pike Co, GA census where Godfrey Friday (1801) located then.

Thomas Ammons (1748)1790   Camden District, Fairfield, SC
Living with wife Catherine Friday and children. Their neighbors were Sarah Dunklin, John Cook, Judith Johnson, Burrill Cook, Alex Brunt, Josiah Landrum and Rebekah Grigg. On the other side were Harriss Freeman, Widow Murph, Samuel Richardson, Samuel Boyd, John Harbit, Mary Pearson, M Bennet and John Turner. (CS)
Note: John Turner {from Ireland} married ~1773 Margaret (Mary Ann) Adger (~1762). Burrell Cook married in ~1789 to Mary Pope. John Cook married in 1759 to Mary "Betty" Brown (1742).

Margaret [Beatty] Fridig 1790   North Part of Orangeburg District, SC
Her neighbors were George Boucher/Booker, Sarah Bea, Joseph Patterson (1730), Jacob Howber, Lawrence Fagle, Henry Youngerman, Chirstina Anaminger, James Hunt, John Swycord [Swygert], Henry Summers (1746), Widow Leightner, Henry Swets, Zacheriah Balmer [Bamer?],Matthew Martin and 3 more down was Samuel Hollinshed. On ther other side were Bartley Minick, John Minick, Michael Himmeter, Henry Amick, John Amick, Gasper Momee and Henry Snellgrove. 12 more homes dows is Leonard Lights, George Kelly, Jacob Long and Andrew Kelly. (CS)
Note:
On 5-5-1770 Nicholas Martin has 121 acres surveyed in Craven County. His neighbors were John Haunt, John Kipp, Batholemew Minick, William Saur and Adam Sinier. Batholemew Minick married Mary Magdalena Summer (~1750) sister to Henry Summer.
On 6-21-1775 George Kelly had a 100 acre memorial surveyed on High Hill Creek/Buckhead Creek in Berkley Co, SC. His neighbors were William Kelly and Daniel Kelly.
In 1778 Sarah Bee renounced Thomas Bee to Thomas Hamilton. Sarah Smith (1753) married Thomas Bee Mar 16th 1773, after having 3 children she renounced the marriage.
In 11-12-1784 did a Lease and release Jacob Buchter, John Fridig & Mary Kinscler, widow, both parties of Saxagotha Township, SC, miller by trade, to George Lickes, for Đ100 SC money, 100 acres nearly opposite to the outer limits of Saxagotha Township on north side Santee River adj. land of Thomas Leavas, [sic: Lever], originally granted to Jacob Bushler [Buchter]. John Fridig (X) (LS), Mary Kinsler (X) (LS), Barbaray Fridig (LS), Wit: Nicholas Grub, Jas Stewart. Proved in Orangeburgh District by the oath of Jas Stewart before Jacob Richman, J.P., 12 Jan 1786. Recorded 22 March 1787.
On 2-7-1803 James Sander Guignard had 750 Acres surveyed in the Fork of the Broad and Saluda Rivers in Orangeburg Dist, Lexington, SC. His neighbors were John Rutledge, Bamer, Gabriel Fridig, Peter Braselman, Jacob Seibles and John Nicholas.

John Friday (1743)   1790   Orangeburg, SC
His neighbors were William Rea, William Sanders, John Compty, James Right, and 4 more homes down was Hargrove Arthur (1752). On the other side was Henry Miley, Alexander Gillon, George Barsh [Barah], William Scott, Genl Pinckney. (CS)

Jacob Leaver [Lever]   1790   Orangeburg, SC
Mary Catherine **Friday** (1768) living with husband. Their neighbors were Jacob Wesinger (~1752), Anna Bookmann, John Gossett, John Edings, Margaret Cummerland, John Cummerland and Leonard Bough. On the other side were Anna Margaret Sistrunk, Sherod Busby (~1769), Barbara Keasler, George Lax, Mary Hipp and Martin Jack. (CS)
Note: Mary Catherine **Friday**, [Widow of Jacob Lever] would later marry John Dreher (1765) in 1797 who was living 52 homes down from her via the 1790 Census Record.

William Fiddy(*)   1790   St. Phillips Parish, Charleston, SC

His neighbors were John McQueen, Bennet Taylor, "Austin, Surtliff & Stroble", William Darby, J & J Hargraves, and John Julias Pringle. On the other side were John Smith, Pourie & Kevan, McCally & Davis, John Black, John Hamilton and Edgar Wells. (CS)

Note: "William Fiddy (of the 1790 census) is a known quantity. He's a London merchant who went to Charleston in order to handle some post-war business exchanges. The Citizenship Book in Charleston says "William Fiddy, late a Subject of Great Britain, is become a citizen of this state...9 Aug 1784." He signed his name to legal documents. He was not black/mulatto. William Friday (sometimes Friddy) Senior marked his will with an "FS", and he was definitely mulatto. So two completely different Williams, with no neighbors, relatives, or co-signers of legal documents in common (Imrey, Harriett 2005)."

Gabriel Fryday   2-3-1792   Orangeburg Dist, SC Boiling Springs
Crk/Congaree River
His neighbor was Francis Bell. (SNLP)

John? Fridig   9-27-1794   Cedar Creek Broad River/Camden District, SC
His neighbors were Daniel Frazier, Samuel Alston, Jerry Taylor and George Smith. (SNLP)

Godfrey Fridig   9-27-1794   Camden Co, SC - Cedar Creek/Broad River
Neighbors were Daniel Frazer, Jerry Taylor, William Kirkland, John Fridig, Lewis Haigwood and George Smith.

Frederick Friday (1750-75) 11-6-1794   Newberry Co, SC – Strother Papers
His neighbors and associates were Richard Strother, Mathias Libecap, Alexander Bell, John Hearth, John Raines, John Adam Summers (1744), George Luis, John Kennerly, L. Lunsford, Simon Eleazer, Jacob Eleazer, Isaiah Shirer, Frederick Fryday, Jesse Atwill, Thomas Kennerly, dec. (1795), Francis Higgins, John Hampton, Joseph Kennerly, Alexander Bookter, Jacob Gobson, and Bartholomew Turnipseed. (EST)
Note:
Alexander Booker [Bookter] shows up in the 1790 Ninety-Six District Newberry County, SC Census. Richard Strawther [Strother] is 40 homes away from Alex. Bookter.
Thomas Kennerly died 1795 and his wife Mary would marry a John Malone who sold his Newberry Co Property. Mary's daughter Susan Kennerly (1776-1827) married Jesse Arthur (1771), who witnessed John Malone's will proved on 10 Mar 1802 in Richland Co, SC. Joseph Kennerly was the son-in-law of Anna Maria Fridig/Geiger/Weber/Weaver who was sister to John Jacob Fridig.
In 1790 Orangeburg Census John Adam Summers (1744) is 7 homes down from Gabriel Fridig. Everheart Sweetingburg is 2 homes down from Gabriel Fridig.
In 6-2-1790 Michel Atwell was a neighbor to John Taylor and Henry Weaver at Saluda River at Waters of Holle Creek, Orangeburg Dist, SC.
In 4-19-1793 John Adam Summers was a neighbor to William Sweightemburg at Broad River at Crims Creek, Lexington, SC.

John Fryday (1759)   8-20-1795   Orangeburg Dist, SC Broad River
His neighbors were Sherod Busby and John Fraser. (SNLP)
Note:
On 5-25-1773 Jacob Bookman had a 100 acre plat surveyed in Craven County on Hollins Head Branch of the Broad River.
On 12-26-1784 Jacob Bookman had a 100 acre plat surveyed on Drains of the Broad River in Orangeburg District. His neighbor was Michael Hoke.
On 6-30-1785 William Strother had a 183 acre plat surveyed on Hollandsheds Creek in Orangeburg District . His neighbors were Jacob Bookman, Joseph Kenly [Kennerly] and George Strother.

On 9-26-1789 Sherwood Busby (~1756) had 111 acres surveyed on a Branch of Hollenshed's Creek and Broad River in Orangeburg District, SC. His neighbors were James Kennerley, George Strother, Henry Seastrunk [Sistrunk], Thomas Kennelry [Kennerly] and Jacob Bookman.
On 11-11-1789 John Fraser had 93 Acres surveyed in orangeburg District. His neighbors were Jacob Bookman, Jacob Ellesor [Ellisor/Eleazer], Ponedick Noonamaka, Jacob Purket, Thomas Kennerly and Sherwood Busby.
On 11-11-1789 Sherwood Busby had 371 acres surveyed on Watery Creek of the Broad River in the Orangeburg District. His neighbors were George Harbirt, Adam Somers [Summers], George Freshley, John Busby, John Miller, Tobias Eashler, Anigail Hattawany and Jacob Bookter.

Samuel Friday (1775-84)8-31-1795   Orangeburg, SC - Rawls Creek/Broad Rvr/Saluda Rvr. His neighbors were Isaac Pence, George Werner, Mathias Wesinger, Christian Long/Lang, Michael Wesinger (1744) and John Younginger. (SNLP)
Note: It is believed, Anna Maria Fridig/Geiger/Weber/Weaver gave land to Samuel or allowed his family to live on the land she purchased in 1771-1773. Samuel may have received a parcel of Land after Anna Maria Fridig/Geiger/Weaver death around ~1786 from Joseph Kennerly. Samuel Friday was the Administrator to Hanna Weaver Account Audited after the Revolutionary War on 12-8-1790.
On 11-15-1771 Mathias Westinger [Wessinger] had 150 Acres surveyed in the Fork of the Broad and Saluda River. His neighbors were Leonard Strouler (1754), Thomas Ranseym [Raemy] and Simon Younginger. The same day Leonard Shallor [Shuler] had a plat of 100 acres at Rawls Creek and another 100 acres near Rawls creek on 3-31-1773.
On 3-18-1772 Anna Maria Weaver got a plat of 250 acres on Rawls Creek, Saluda River in Berkly Co, SC.
On 6-18-1772 Mathias Westinger [Wessinger] had 150 acre Memorial plat surveyed between the Broad and Saluda Rivers. His neighbors were Michael Westinger, Simon Younginger (1745), Leonard Shooler [Shuler] and Thomas Ramey.
On 9-26-1772 Thomas Ramey had a 100 acre land grant on Rolls Creek.
On 12-3-1772 Thomas Ramey had a 100 acre Memorial surveyed between the Broad and Saluda Rivers. His neighbor was Leonard Shooler [Shuler].
On 4-15-1773 Hanna Weaver got a plat of 150 acres on Rawls Branch/Saluda River in Craven Co, SC. Her neighbor was W. Winn.
On 5-25-1774 & 10-4-1774 Christian Lang had two plats for 100 acres surveyed in Craven County on the Broad River. His neighbor was Barbara Kisetholf.
About 1776, Leonard Shuler (1754) married Anna "Nancy" Lever (1757) (daughter of Jacob Lever).
On 7-7-1785 William Strother had 196 acres surveyed on 12 Mile Creek of the Saluda River in the Orangeburg District/Ninety Six District. His neighbors were George Strather [Strother] and Samuel Ralls [Rawls].
On 5-12-1787 Michael Lorick had a 77 acre plat surveyed on the Saluda River in the Orangeburg District. His neighbors were William Fleming (1752), Simon Addas, Bernard Hogler/Hyler, Jacob Kelley, John Swigard [Swygert] and Christian Swygard [Swygert].
In the 1790 census page 398 the following neighbors are Flora Youngeninger, Margaret Zimmerlin, Catherine Cootle, Michael Westsinger, Jacob Bookler [Bookter], John Weed, Gollas Souther, Gasper Souther, Simon Younginger, Issac Gossett and Mary Kinnerly.
On 5-29-1790 Thomas Reamey had a 178 acre plat surveyed on Ralls [Rawls] Creek in Orangeburg District. His neighbors were Samuel Ralls [Rawls], Michael Wessinger and John Levers [Lever].
On 5-19-1795 Simon Younginger had a plat of 1.5 acres of "small islands" on the Saluda River River Orangeburg District surveyed. His neighbors were John Younginer (1744) (previous owned islands), Jacob Souber [Souter?], Jonas Beard, John Trayer [Dreher] and Leonard Shooler [Shuler].
Christian Long married Elizabeth Weed and both of their daughters married Amick boys.

The Swabian Connection – Expanded Edition

On 1-31-1800 George Philips had a 497 acre plat surveyed at Willow Swamp Baptist Church (formed from Dean Swamp Baptist Church). His neighbors were James Saunders Guignard, Philip Pence, John Kennerly, Henry High, Christian Long and Michael Hook.
Amos Bank married Catherine Long (1788) daughter of George Long (1758)
Samuel Fleming (1769) was the son of William Fleming and Frances <unknown>.

Friday   3-8-1797   Orangeburg Dist, SC Congaree River
His neighbor was Henry Crick (1745). (SNLP)

Jacob Friday   1797   Orangeburg, SC Chinquepin Branch Edisto River
His neighbors were Ephraim Mitchell, James Mitchell, and Daniel Hartley.

David Fridig   1-6-1798   Edgefield, SC Red Bank Creek 96 District
Neighbors were John Abney, Hughston, A.B Stark, Christopher Martin & Samuel Lewis.

John [Fridig] (1759) 1800   Fairfield, SC
His neighbors were Robert Mcants (~1779?), Henry Inman (~1770?), John Creeks Junr, Burrell Lee Jr (1768?), George Goates (1770), Henry Sykes, Humphrey Gibson, Augustine Williams, Geo Summers (1770?), Garrick [Garrett] Hendrix, Bartholem Turnipseed (1774), and George Ashford (1758). On the other side were Michael Wirey, Mark Busby (~1761?), Alexander Brunt, Jacob Turnipseed (1757) and Harmon Wirey. (CS) Mispelled and listed as John "Firdigg" on the census.
Note:
A Burel Lee was recorded living in the Ninety-Six District prior to October 1787.
George Goats and Sherwood Busby migrated to Giles Co, TN. John Ashford (1785) the son of George Ashford was in the War of 1812 (3 REG'T (COPELAND'S) West TN MIL) and was married in Wilson Co, TN. Robert Busby (1769) had children in Stewart Co, TN by ~1810.

Godfrey Fridig (1770) 1800   Orange Co, SC Windy Hill Creek/Branch, Orangeburg, SC.
His neighbors were Elizabeth Byrd, Johann Peoples (1744/76?), Cornelius Tobin (1759), Elijah Ferds, William Wrotten/Rotten (1770) , Henry Zorn (1759), Thomas Richardson, Moses Cumings, John Jones and and 3 more down was Thomas Draper (1768). On the other side were Robert Jones, Jacob Ridgell and Daniel Metthing. (CS) 01010200100
Note:
On 11-10-1785 Benjamin Byrd (1740/58?) has 100 acres surveyed on Windy Hill Branch Orangeburgh District. His neighbor was John Rivers. A Benjamin Byrd married Elizabeth Allison from NC.
On 7-1795 Cornelius Tobin has a plan of Land surveyed in Beaufort Dist at Stoney Creek. Tobin had thousands of acres surveyed from 1801 to 1805 in Barnwell Co, SC.
On 3-31-1796 Mary Mathaney had 500 acres surveyed on Windy Hill Branch Orangeburgh District – her neighbors were John Jones, William Jones, Benjamin Odom, John Rivers and the Walkers.
On 11-29-1796 Darling Peoples has 222 acres surveyd on Windy Hill Creek, Orangeburgh District.
On 11-7-1797 David Chester had 248 acres surveyed on a branch of Windy Hill Orangeburgh District – His neighbors were Ben Bird and Col Huger.
On 11-7-1799 John Lott had 48 acres surveyed on Windy Hill Creek Orangeburg, SC. His neighbors were William Mathany, Richard Hines and Daniel Odom.
The 1790 census page 263 shows Elizabeth Byrd, John Endley, Moses Cummins, Robert Givens, Benjamin and Caleb Bright. William Roden/Wrotten/Rotton is 14 homes down from Elizabeth. Thomas Drayton is 4 homes down from Elizabeth. Aron and Thomas Richardson are 5 and 8 homes down from Eliz Byrd. John Ridgdell is 21 homes down from Elizabeth Byrd.
On 2009 Google map, this location is South East of Springfield and NE of Barnwell, SC.
William Rotton (1770) married Lydia Lovelace and is living in Edgefield Co, SC.
William is being witnessed on deeds with Jacob Green , the Cockerofts, the Cogburns and the Still family. William Routon shows in Wilkes Co, GA on Abner Reeves will Nov. 6, 1809. Godfrey Friday

also witnessed Jacob Greens will. Godfrey was in Green Co, GA by ~1807 and back to Edgefield, SC by 1814. Jacob, James, John and Noah Hinton were in Wilkes Co, GA by 1805. Lewis Hinton married Mary H. Wooten and in Oglethorpe, GA by 1805. Mary Ann "Polly" Hinton married John T. Wootten. Melissa C. Hinton married Henry P. Wootten. Barsheba Hinton married William L. Wootten and they were living in Wilkes Co, GA. Godfrey Friday would later name a boy Hinton by 1814.

Daniel Friday   1800   Lexington, SC
His neighbors were John Meane, Rueben S Sanders (1776), Joseph Smith, Jacob Seibles (1752) and James Rogers. On the other side were Hargrove Arthur (1733), Samuel and Henry Johnston, James McGowen, Nicholas Hane and five homes down was John Friday. (CS)

John Friday   1800   Lexington, SC
His neighbors were John J Martin, Gerard Berch, Gilbert Pelham, Peter Pluet and six homes down was Daniel Friday. On the other side were Gabriel Friday, Benjamin Stripling, Edward Conyer, Lou Evans and John Bynum. (CS)

Gabriel Friday   1800   Lexington, SC
His neighbors were John Friday, Benjamin Stripling, Edward Conyer, Lou Evand and John Bynum. On the other side were John J Martin, Gerard Berch, Gilbert Pelham and Peter Pluet. (CS)

Frederick Friday (1750-75) 1800   Lexington Co, SC – Zion Church
His neighbors and associates were John Dreher, Martin Heydel, John Geiger, Jacob Sen Jr, Mathias Sen, Leonard Bush, Casper Leephard, Jacob Erhard, John Klegly, Magdalene Tarer, Gasper Lybrand, Barnet Lybrand, George Lykes, Sr., Godfrey Ruff, Jacob Stroup, ???Mathias, Henry Coon, Gotlieb Sox, Jacob Senn, Sr., Danl. Carter, Michl. Drafts, Widow Drafts, Andrew Tarer, ???Montz, Gotlieb Klegly, Michl. Wingard, John Corly, Sebastian Ruff, John Hipp, Thomas Roll, Benjamin Ruff, Godfrey Ruff, Daniel Wingard, Leanard Bugh, Jr,, John Bugh, Andrew Bugh, Frederick Bugh, John Shull, Lawrence Ruff, Philip Fry, Christian Wingard, Philip Tauber, John Mathias, Thos. Derick, Peter Micler, Lorentz Corley, Henry Shull, Valentine Coon, Jonas Mathias, Wm. Senn, Frederick Bush, Abrhm. Geoger, Jr, Abrhm. Geiger Sr,Godfrey Cromer, Andrew Cromer (1751), Geroge Wingard, Benjamin Wingard, Ehterl Davis, ???? Coogle, John Oxner, Christian Long, Wm. Friday, Frederick Friday, David Kennerly, M. Leber, Saml. Bookman (~1766), George Gross, George Likes, Jr, John Nichols, Jacob Nunemaker, Jacob Younginger, Stepehen Hoke, Christ. Sharp, John Beard, James Smith, John Byner, Christian Shultz, John Mathias, Gasper Souter, M.B. Stark, Sebastian Youginger, John Stark, John Kleckley, Frederick Tarer, Christian Caufman. (CRCH)

William Fridig (1756-74)1800   Lexington, SC Forks of the Saludee & Broad
His neighbors were Barbara Miller (1756-74), Rachel Dreher, George Wheeler (1762), Ulrich Myers Jr (1770), Thomas Frick Sr, Thomas Monk, Thomas Frick Jr, Mathias Quattelbum (~1736) and Thomas Gibson.. On the other side were Susannah {Unknown} Waysinger , James Calk, Elick Jenkins, Barruck [Baruch] Snellgrove (~1775), Mathias Yantz [Younce] , Francis Coon, John Anger, John Lygthner [Leitner?] and Jacob Begley Jr. (CS) p.333 000200110100 Living with Brother same age range? This brother may have been Lewis Friday (d. 1821).
Note:
Susanna Wessinger was the wife of Jacob Wessinger (~1755). Baruch Snellgrove (1775) the son of Edward Snellgrove (1740) is reported to have married Mary Elizabeth Williams/Northrop. Gabriel Fridig (1752) and Edward Snellgrove witnessed and Edgefield Deed in November 1788. On 3-13-1774 & 5-7-1774, George Wheeler had a 100 acre land grants surveyed in Craven Co, SC. By 9-23-1774 George had a 100 acre memorial surveyed between the Broad & the Saluda Rivers in Craven County, SC

In 1778, a 300 acre tract on Camping Creek was sold with land described as having being previously owned by Barbara Miller who transferred the tract in 1778 to her son, George Henry Wirts. This record (Bullow & Bullow to Wheeler- *Newberry Deeds O-51)* provides evidence that Anna Barbara Miller (1728) was the widow of George Henry Wertz and had remarried John Miller after the death of her husband Wertz (palmettoroots.org 2004)

On 3-29-1787 Thomas Frick has a 158 Acre Plat surveyed on the Waters of Stephen Fork/Creek, near Camping Creek of Orangeburg District. His neighbors were Jacob Shumpert, Ulrick Miers and William Haring.

On 5-12-1787 Michael Lorick had a 220 acre plat surveyed on Ragnerses Creek on the Saluda River in Orangeburg Dist. His neighbors were Jacob Snider (~1747?), Mathias Wesinger, Adam Metts and John Comerlander.

George Wheeler married Barbara Addy (1768) about ~1787.

On 3-29-1789 George Strother had a plat surveyed on the waters of the Saluda River in the Orangeburg District. His neighbors were John Gartman and John Stingley.

On 9-14-1789 Nathaniel Busby had a 95 acre plat surveyed on Hollinsheds Creek in the Orangeburg Dist, SC. His neighbors were Needham Busby, William Sigler [Zeigler?], George Whealer and George Strothers.

On 11-2-1789 Francis Coon had a 156 acre plat surveyed on Camping Creek and the Saluda River in Orangeburg District, SC. His neighbors were Spencer Wilson, Henry Amick, Jacob Felmoner and Henry Summers.

The 1790 Census shows William Calk (father of James?), Mathias Wysinger (father of Susannah?). John Derrick Jr has Solomon Roberts and Susannah Sea as neighbors.

George Wheeler is shown with the following neighbors: Jacob Rugleman, William Rawls, Jacob Booser [Boozer], Barbara Shoots [Shotts?], George Phillip Hook, George Spencer, Eost Metts, Phillip Gartman, George Kymer, Anythony Sea, George Dreher, Godfrey Earhart, and six more home down is Daniel Gartman, Elizabeth Taylor, John Jenkins, John Kennerly and 15 more homes down are John Fridig and William Rea. On the other side are Uldrick Mayer, Bartholemew Gartman, John Gartman Sr & Jr, James Galtzer, David Leasley, John Sea and Gabriel Miller (~1760?).

In the 1790 Census James Calk's neighbors are (skipping a few household's between) Thomas Gibson, Esther Elmore, Thomas Monk, William Calk, Thomas Pickley, John Derrick Sr, John Swicord [Swygert], Mathias Wysinger [Wessinger], John Laboult, John Stack, Christian Swycord [Swygert], Michael Lorick, Jacob Harman, John Derrick Jr, Susannah Sea and 7 & 9 more homes down are Elzy Linzay (~1775) [Lindsey] and Samuel Weaver. Jackson/Elzy Lindsey married Ellon/Evelyn Malone (rootslady@rootslady.com).

A Samuel Weaver (1759) from Virginia married Nancy Hutson (1767) and migrated to White Co, TN by ~179X.

In the 1790 census Jacob Wessinger (~1755) neighbors are Mary Catherine **Friday** (1768) living with husband Jacob Leaver. Their neighbors were Jacob Wesinger (~1752), Anna Bookmann, John Gossett, John Edings, Margaret Cummerland, John Cummerland and Leonard Bough. On the other side were Anna Margaret Sistrunk, Sherod Busby (~1769), Barbara Keasler, George Lax, Mary Hipp and Martin Jack. (CS)

Note: Mary Catherine **Friday**, [Widow of Jacob Lever] would later marry John Dreher (1765) in 1797 who was living 52 homes down from her via the 1790 Census Record.

On 5-3-1791 John Miller had a 100.5 acre plat surveyed on the Broad River in Orangeburg Dist Lexington Co, SC. His neighbors were John Fulmer Sr, Martin Yetter, Eberhart Sweetenberg, Thomas Long and John Folmer [Fulmer].

On 2-16-1793 Uldrick Moyer Sr had a 140 plat surveyed on the water of Stephens Creek in Lexington County of Orangeburg. His neighbors were Andrew Moyer, Michael Moutz, Christian Barbara Shoemake and Thomas Frick.

On 2-16-1793 George Wheeler had a 65 acre plat surveyed on Camping Creek of the Saluda River in the Orangeburg District.

On 5-31-1793 John Miller had a 110.5 acre plat surveyed on the waters of the Borad River in Lexington County/Orangeburg District,SC. His neighbors were John Folmer Sr., Martin Yetter, Eberhart Sweetenburg, Thomas Long and John Folmer.

About ~1795 James "Jim" Calk married Susannah Jenkins. Their son Elijah Calk (1770) married Mary Younce (1758) and migrated to Clarke Co, AL & Wayne Co, GA.

On 5-28-1796 Alexander Jenkins had a 290 Plat surveyed on the Saluda River in Orangeburg District. His neighbors are John Gregory, Jacob Fulmer, Quaddlebum [Quattlebum], Freeman Snelgrove and Archy Dunbar.

On On 3-29-1802 George Mayer had a 131 Acre plat surveyed in the Fork of the Broad and Saluda Rivers and Stephens Creek in Orangeburg Dist. His neighbors were Ulrich Mayer, Thomas Frick, Thomas W Waters and George Whealer.

Samuel Fridig (1756-74)1800   Lexington Co, SC - Forks of Saludee & Broad Rvr
His neighbors were John Stinley[Stingley](1756-74), Christian Swicord [Swygert] (1779), John Swicord Jr [Swygert] (~1773), Leonard Lights, George Wise Jr, John Wise (1742), Christian Harman (~1765), Andrew Kelly (1752), George Wise, John Smith (1770), George Kelly, Jacob Lorick, Jacob Hamiter, Mary Comerland, Isaac Pence, Jacob Roach, Mathias Younginger, Jacob Peckley, Andrew Weed (1764), Thomas Smith (1768) and 2,3, & 5 homes down are Thomas Roll [Rawls], John Weed, and John Comerland. On the other side were John Metz (1750?), John Coogler (1748) and Catherine Coogler. (CS) p.345 300100001001

Note:

On 11-9-1771 George & Andrew Kelly had each a 100 plat surveyed between the Broad and Saluda rivers.

On 7-2-1772 George & Andrew both again had a 100 acre Memorial plat surveyed between the Broad and Saluda rivers.

On 10-1-1774 Andrew Kelly had a 100 plat surveyed on the Saluda River in Colleton Co, SC. Andrew Kelly (1752) married a Mary and moved to Dallas Co, AL about ~1832.

On 6-21-1775 George Kelly had a 100 acre memorial surveyed on High Hill Creek/Buckhead Creek in Berkley Co, SC. His neighbors were William Kelly and Daniel Kelly.

In Feb 1785, Leonard Leytz [Lightsey] and Phillip Gartman witnessed a lease and release from Hans Ullrick Seydelers to George Kelly of 100 acres on the north side of the Saludy River on Bear Creek.

On 3-29-1785 George Strother had a 25 acre plat surveyed on the Waters of the Saluda River in Orangeburg Dist. His neighbors were John Gartman and John Stingley.

On 5-15-1786 Joseph Metza [Metz] had 80 acres surveyed for Michael Craps on the waters of High Hill Creek on the Saluda River in Orangeburg District. His neighbors were Michael Craps, Thomas Smith and Swicord [Swygert].

George Wheeler married Barbara Addy (1768) about ~1787.

About ~1786 John Meetze (1766) married Regina Coogler (1764). They lived on the Meetze branch of High Hill Cr. between Irmo and Ballentine, SC, and are buried in a family cemetery now under waters of Lake Murray (Nichols, Carls).

On 3-27-1787 William Zeigler had a 309 acre plat surveyed on Hollinshed Creek in the Orangeburg District. His neighbors were John Adam Summer (1744), George Willer [Wheeler?], John Stingley and Michael Willer [Wheeler?] (1755-65). Michael Wheeler married Katherine [Unknown] and their daughter Rosannah (1792) married John Christian Rister (1811).

On 5-10-1787 George Wise had a 112 acre plat surveyed on Beards Creek at the Saluda River in the Orangeburg District. His neighbors were George Myers and Jacob Bigley.

On 5-12-1787 Michael Lorick had a 77 acre plat surveyed on the Saluda River in the Orangeburg District. His neighbors were William Fleming, Simon Addas, Bernard Hogler, Jacob Kelley, John Swigard [Swygert] and Christian Swygard [Swygert].

On 5-24-1787 John Weed had 144 acres surveyed on a Branch of High Hill Creek of the Saluda River in the Orangeburg Dist. His neighbors were Nimrod Hambrick, John Sayboyle [Seible], George Boughnit, Peter Braselman, Jacob Seibell [Seible] and John Comerland.

The Swabian Connection – Expanded Edition

On 5-25-1787 Thomas Smith had a 60 acre plat surveyed on the Branch of the Saluda River in Orangeburg. His neighbors were Jeremiah McCartee, Christian Swigard [Swygert], Jacob Bagley and John Comlander.

On 3-29-1789 George Strother had a plat surveyed on the waters of the Saluda River in the Orangeburg District. His neighbors were John Gartman and John Stingley.

In the 1790 census John Stingerley Jr & Sr [Stingley] lived side by side. Their neighbors were Elizabeth Snellgrove, George Gartman (1762), Michael Craps and Nicholas Sea. The Jacob Pickley Jr family was 14 household's down. George Gartman married Anna Barber (1762) abt ~1775. Nicholas Seay (d~1817) married Margaret Snellgrove about ~1777. Also, a Nicholas Sea (1765) married a Maragaret "Peggy" Snider of which they had a child named Ruhama (1812) born in Lumberton, Robeson Co, NC. Nicholas (1765) migrated and died ~1829 in New Orleans, LA. Nancy Seay (1777) is reported to have married John Gartman (1777).

In the 1790 census James Calk's neighbors are (skipping a few household's between) Thomas Gibson, Esther Elmore, Thomas Monk, William Calk, Thomas Pickley, John Derrick Sr, John Swicord [Swygert], Mathias Wysinger [Wessinger], John Laboult, John Stack, Christian Swycord [Swygert], Michael Lorick, Jacob Harman, John Derrick Jr, Susannah Sea and 7 & 9 more homes down are Elzy Linsay and Samuel Weaver.

On 5-8-1790 George Wise had another 190 acres survyed in the Fork of the Broad and Saluda Rivers with Thomas Pickley and Malakiah Helen as neighbors.

On 9-13-1792 Jacob Pickley had a 100 acre plat surveyed on a Branch of High Hill Creek of the Saluda River in Orangeburg District, SC. His neighbors were Woolrick Hiller.

On 4-8-1795 Jacob Pickley had a 23 acre plat surveyed on High Hill Creek Orangeburg Dist at the Saluda and Broad Rivers. His neighbor was George Wise.

On 2-4-1797 Jacob Kelly (1748) had a 51 Acre plat surveyed on High Hill Creek Lexington County and Orangeburg District. His neighbors were Thomas Bigley and Thomas Pickley.

On 2-7-1798 John Metz had a 244 acre plat surveyed Near Pen Branch Edisto River in the orangeburg District. His neighbors were Mrs. Askew, George Hartzog, and Christopher Metz.

About 1798 George Wise Jr married Mary Margaret Kelly (1776) daughter of John George Kelly. George's son Joseph (1807) married Sarah Rachel Cayce; they moved to Attala Co, MS.

George Wise Sr married Anna Barbara Buckle [Bickley]. Sophia Jane Wise (1768) married John Stingley (1756-74) and she moved to Sallis, Attala Co, MS.

Samuel Friday (1775-84)1800   Lexington Co, SC - Broad River

His neighbors were John Swicord Jr, Barnett Highler/Hyler [Hoyler] (~1761-d.1825), Jacob Lorick, Isaac Pence, John, Michael & Mathias Wessinger, Andrew Weed, George Philips and Ulrick Coogler (1776). On the other side was Nancy [Lever] Shewler [Shuler](1757), Samuel Fleming (1775-84), Rebecca Labolt, George Likes [Leitze] (1774), Henry Coon, Michael Boughneit, George Boughneit, Dorothy Pickley, John Dreher, Thomas Raimey, Jacob Pickley, Philip Varner, Tenor Huffman, Elizabeth Dagan, Margaret Simmerly, Jacob Younginger & Jacob Rouch. (CS) p.269 301000001001

Note:

On 4/7/1751 Barnett Hoylet had 300 acres plat surveyed in the Fork of Broad and Saluda rivers. Neigbors were Martin Chazmyer, Jacob Hinkey, George Hunter and John Pearson.

ON 6/17/1772 Leonard Shooer [Shuler] has a memorial of 100 acress surveyed between the Broad and Saludy Rivers. His neighbors were Thomas Ramey, Mathias Wasinger, and Simon Younginger.

On 6-18-1772 Mathias Westinger [Wessinger] had 150 acre Memorial plat surveyed between the Borad and Saluda Rivers. His neighbors were Simon Younginger, Leonard Shooler [Shuler] and Thomas Ramey.

On 12-3-1772 Thomas Ramey had a 100 acre Memorial surveyed between the Broad and Saluda Rivers. His neighbor was Leonard Shooler [Shuler].

About 1776, Leonard Shuler (1754) married Anna "Nancy" Lever (1757) (daughter of Jacob Lever).

Andrew Weed (1764) is reported to have married Mary Grey (1769) in 1786.

251

The Swabian Connection – Expanded Edition

On 4-22-1785 Thomas Rough had a 125 acre plat surveyed on High Hill Creek in Orangeburg Dist. His neighbors were B. Hiler [Highler], Thomas Smoks, Michael Lorick and ORR Beard.

On 5-12-1787 Michael Lorick had a 77 acre plat surveyed on the Saluda River in the Orangeburg District. His neighbors were William Fleming, Simon Addas, Bernard Hogler [Highler], Jacob Kelley, John Swigard [Swygert] and Christian Swygard [Swygert].

On 3-26-1788 Mary Ann Hipes [Hipps?] had a 68 acre plat surveyed on Youts Branch of the Saluda River in Orangeburg Dist. Her neighbors were George Likes, Lennard Shoolan [Shuler], Godfred Driker [Dreher] and Jacob Levan [Lever].

On 3-26-1788 John Swigard [Swygert] had a 140 acre plat surveyed on the North Side of the Saluda River in Orangeburg District. His neighbor were George Strothers, John Stack and George Bouknight.

The 1790 Census shows John Laboult with neighbors William Calk (father of James?), Mathias Wysinger (father of Susannah?). John Stack, Christian Swycord [Swygert] and Michael Lorick are 4-5 household's down from Laboult. John Derrick Jr has Solomon Roberts and Susannah Sea as neighbors.

On 9-14-1794 John Swicord Jr [Swygert] had an 18 acre plat surveyed on the Saluda River. Neighbors were Barnard Hyler [Highler] (d.1825), T Hall and Michael Lorick.

On 5-19-1795 Simon Younginger had a plat of 1.5 acres of "small islands" on the Saluda River River Orangeburg District surveyed. His neighbors were John Younginer (previous owned islands), Jacob Souber [Souter?], Jonas Beard, John Trayer [Dreher] and Leonard Shooler [Shuler].

On 6-1-1797 Jacob Bookter had a 232 acre plat surveyed between the Broad & Saluda Rivers in the Orangeburg Dist. His neighbors were Michael Lorick and Tobias Geiger.

On 1-31-1800 George Philips had a 497 acre plat surveyed at Willow Swamp Baptist Church (formed from Dean Swamp Baptist Church). Neighbors were James Saunders Guignard, Philip Pence, John Kennerly, Henry High, Christian Long and Michael Hook.

William Friday (1774-84)1800   Lexington Co, SC Broad River – Dutch Fork

His neighbors were John Derrick (1755-74), John Malone (~1758-1802), Zachariah Bamer [Balmer] (1756-74), Esther Lorick and Philip Homamer (174X-55). On the opposite side were John Nicholas (1756-74), Robert Bookman (1756-74), Jacob Kelley (1756-74), James Turner (1774-84), Thomas Rives (1786), Paul Naites (1774-84) and Jacob Ellisor [Eleazer] (1756-74), John Oneal (1774-84), Barbery Swicord [Swygert], James Roll [Rawls] (174X-55), Benjamin Smith, John Norton, Sherod Busbie [Busby] (~1756), Nathaniel Busbie (~1728), George Hewitt, Adam Amick (1769?), Rachel Fraser, Micajah Busbie (~1767), Robert Busbie (~1769), Michael Hoke (174X-55) and James Dailey. (CS) p.267 01200100101 living with Mother born (1756-74)

Note:

This location was thought to be High Hill Creek, but is actually east of that and south of Holinshead creek on Bookman's Creek. Bookman Creek is located today in Richland Co, SC just north of the Lexington County line.

Busbie was actually spelled Busby. Robert Busby died in 1829 Stewart Co, TN; Nathaniel (~1728) died in Lexington Co, SC about 1803; Micajah (~1769) died ~1845 in Henderson Co, TN. Sherod (~1756) died ~1829 in Giles Co, TN.

On 3-4-1773 Jacob Terrick [Derrick] had a 75 acres Memorial Plat surveyed on High Hill Creek of the Saluda River from a chain of title to a grant to John Ragnous on March 8, 1763.

In July 1775 John Malone, John Flinn and Henry Wheler [Wheeler] witnessed a Lease and Release from John Wheeler and wife Sarah of Camden District, Craven County, SC to Robert Dearington for 300 acres on Rafting Creek. A John Wheeler (1743/6) married a Sarah Haworth and died in Rutherford Co, TN? in 1802.

In 1782, Timothy Rives (father of Thomas Rives) was an "executor of will" and was recorded in the will/estate sale of his sister Elizabeth Rives Chappell (d. ~1782). John Friday (1759) of Fairfield County purchased items at this estate sale.

On 11-8-1784 Michael Hoke had a 100 acre plat surveyed at Bookman's creek, near Nicholas Creek and later owned by John Derrick in 1802.

The Swabian Connection – Expanded Edition

On 12-26-1784 Jacob Bookman had a 100 acre plat surveyed on Drains of the Broad River in Orangeburg District. His neighbor was Michael Hoke.

On 4-11-1787 Timothy Reeves [Rives] had a 106 acre plat surveyed near the Congaree River in the Camden District. His neighbors were Uldrick Beard, John Compty, Henry Sistrunk and Thomas Taylor.

In 1788 Jacob Buchter [Bookter], Jacob Buckman [Bookman], Robert Bockman [Bookman], Jacob Ellesar [Eleazer], Gabriel Miller and others signed the German Lutheran Church of Bethlehem on Faust's Ford in Orangeburg Dist, Lexington Co, SC.

On 8-17-1789 John Kennerley had a 385 Acre plat surveyed at Turkey Cock Branch/Broad River in Orangeburg Dist. His neighbors were John Nicholas, Michael Hook, Jacob Bookter and Jacob Illeasor [Ellisor/Eleazer].

About 1790, John Malone sold his Newberry Co Property and later married Widow Mary [Unknown] Kennerly, wife of the late Thomas Kennerly. Mary's daughter Susan Kennerly (1776-1827) married Jesse Arthur, who witnessed John Malone's will proved on 10 Mar 1802 in Richland Co, SC.

In the 1790 Census shows Anna Margaret Sistrunk (wife of Henry Sistrunk) is listed a Ret. Her neighbors are Jacob Leaver, Jacob Wessinger and Anna Bookman. On the other side are Sherod Busby, Barbara Kessler, (5-8 down) were John Beard, Jacob Earhart, Jacob Tarar [Tarrar] and Anna Shuler (1750?).

A John Nichols in 1790 Census neighbors are Henry Cook, Thomas Martin, Godfrey Drehr, and John Geiger. On ther other side are Michael Hoak [Hoke], William Steugner, Thomas Ralls [Rawls] & 4 more down is Adam Amick.

Also in the 1790 Orangeburg Dist Census, Jacob Leaver [Lever] w/wife Mary Catherine **Friday** (1768). Their neighbors were Jacob Wesinger (1752), Anna Bookmann, John Gossett, John Edings, Margaret Cummerland, John Cummerland and Leonard Bough. On the other side were Anna Margaret Sistrunk, Sherod Busby (~1756), Barbara Keasler, George Lax, Mary Hipp and Martin Jack.

Note: Mary Catherine **Friday**, [Widow of Jacob Lever] would later marry John Dreher (1765) in 1797 who was living 52 homes down from her via the 1790 Census Record.

On 5-16-1797 Jacob Kelly had a 38 acre plat surveyed on Bookmans Creek Orangeburg District near the Broad river. His neighbors were Joans Beard and James Turner.

On 2-2-1800 James Sander Guignard had 1000 Acres surveyed on Ralls [Rawls] and Kennerly Creek at the Broad & Saluda Rivers in Orangeburg Disat, Lexington, SC. His neighbors were John Marley, Joseph Kennerly, Philip Pence, George Philips, Michael Hook, Peter Braselman, Jacob Seible, John Nicholas, Barnes, Fridig, Lee Hard, John Rutledge and Wofford.

On 2-7-1803 James Sander Guignard had 750 Acres surveyed in the Fork of the Broad and Saluda Rivers in Orangeburg Dist, Lexington, SC. His neighbors were John Rutledge, Bamer, Gabriel Fridig, Peter Braselman, Jacob Seibles and John Nicholas.

A James Rawls was a private under Capt. John Crane and Capt. James Cook, Col. Thomas Williamson, 2nd Regt., Volunteer Mounted Gunmen, 28 September 1814-27 April 1815 in Stewart Co, TN. George Friday (1787) was also in the same county in the War of 1812.

John Martin Friday   1800   Lexington Co, SC

His neighbors were Barbara Monts, Thomas Derrick and Charles Corley (1742). On the opposite side were Michael Drafts (1771), Barnet Lybran, Leonard Lytes, Thomas Roll (1762?) and Andrew Tarrar (1778). Three additional homes down was John Geiger's place. Ten more down from John Geiger's was Catherine Lever's home. (CS) p.266 300101001001

Note:

On 10-19-1784 George Drafts did a Lease & Release to John Berry.

In the 1790 Census Leonard Lights neighbors are John Leibrandt, Hannah Dunbar, Mary Steele, William Nichols and 8 down is Henry Snellgrove, and another 7 down is Margaret Fridig. On the other side is George Kelly, Jacob Long, Andrew Kelly and Jacob Fulmer Sr. Also in the 1790 a John Drafts has neighbors who are William Fulmer, John Fulmer Jr, Sr, Lewis Coursey and 7 homes down is George Derrick. On the other side are Frederick Archy, Godfrey Roof, John

Painter, George Tuner, the Blackley's, John Geiger, John Drehr, Godfrey Drehr and 3 & 4 more down are John Nicholas and Michael Hoak [Hoke].
Michael Drafts married Catherine Corley before 1808. About 1812, Thomas Rawl married Barbara Corley (1773). Barnett Lybrand is reported to have married Marjorie Gestman.
On 2-8-1816 Gabriel Frideg [Fridig] had 997 acres surveyed on Bickleys Branch in Lexington Co, SC for David Shotts. David's new neighbors were Johnathan Taylor (1777), Cornelious Clark (1786), Turpin and Brazelman. Cornelious Clark (1786), son of Gregory Clark, married Nancy Lee. Nancy Clark (~1795) sister of Cornelious, married Dave Shotts (~1790). Rachel Clark (1787) sister of Cornelious married Johnathan Taylor (1777). Andrew Tarrar married Catherine Corley, who was first married to Michael Drafts. Ann Derrick married John Drafts then Lawrence Corley. Barbara Mayer Monts (1746) daughter Catherine Monts married William Thomas Derrick. Michael Drafts (1775-84) was the son of George Drafts (d. ~1784). John W Berry (1771) married Sarah Clark (1781) sister to Cornelius Clark. Thomas Berry had property all the way back when Anthony Stack received acreage back to 1738.

Elizabeth Prior [Friday]   1800   Lexington, SC
Her neighbors were Martin Hook, John Smith, Samuel Mashburn, Lavina Sanford and Samuel Aldridge. On the other side were Jesse Arthur, Robert Stark, John Bynum and Lou Evans. Another 3 homes down was Gabriel Friday. (CS)

Fridig   2-24-1800   Orangeburg Dist, Lexington Co, SC Rawls Creek/Kennerly Creek/Broad & Saluda River
His neighbors were James Sanders Guignard, John Marley, Joseph Kennerly, Phillip Pence, George Phillips, Michael Hook, Peter Braselman, Jacob Seible, John Nicholas, Barns, Lee Hard, John Rutledge and Wofford. (SNLP)

Friday   1-27-1801   Orangeburg Dist, SC Long & Congaree River
His neighbor was Henry Crick. (SNLP)

Peter Fridig   12-10-1802   Georgetown/Charleston/Colleton/Marion District
Notes: Leonard Dozer (1751) just a had a 100 acre plat surveyed 9-1-1802 at Little Reedy Creek and Reedy Creek Bay in the Marion District.
Stephen Laurence just had 420 acre plate surveyed 6-7-1802 at Port Royal Island/St. Helenas Parish in the Beaufort District.
John G Guignard (1751) was treasurer of the upper division at Columbia.
Jacob Drayton (1762) and died in 1806. Jacob was the Circuit Solicitor of the State and Eastern Circuit. He was the son of William Drayton (1732) Royal Chief Justice. Jacob had 640 acres surveyed on Little Jenistee/Generostee Creek in the Ninety Six District on 6/10/1784.
William Drayton has plat surveyed recorded the day before at the same location. (RLC)

Gabriel Fridig   1-20-1803   Orangeburg, SC Congaree & Saluda River/ Kennerly's Creek.
Neighbors were James Sanders Guignard, Alexander B. Starke, Mary Kinsler, Richard Hampton, Jacob Bowie, John Marley, John Rutledge, Michael Leitner, and Peter Coogle. (SNLP)

Gabriel Fridig   2-7-1803   Lexington/Orangeburg Dist, SC Fork of Broad & Saluda Rivers
His new neighbor was James Sanders Guignard. Other neighbors were John Rutledge, Bamer, Peter Braselman, Jacob Seibels and J. Nicholas. (SNLP)

John Fryday   5-3-1806   Lexington Dist, SC Boiling Springs Crk/Beaver Dam Crk
His new neighbor is Michael Lee. Other neighbors are William Taylor and Sepastion [Sebastian] Ruff. (SNLP)

The Swabian Connection – Expanded Edition

Friday   9-22-1806   Orangeburg, SC Clouds Creek/West Creek/Saluda Rvr. The neighbors were <u>Shadrack Ward</u>, Dillie, John Fairchild, William Taylor, Nathan Norris and George Akins. (SNLP)

Frederick Friday   1808/9   Capt Thomas P. Lovetts District, Screven Co, GA other neighbors in the same county that defaulted on taxes were John Beard, Hezekiah Vicory [Vickery?], John Scott and James Smith. (TXL)

Godfrey Friday   1809   Jenkins District, Greene Co, GA
His neighbors, associates and commrades were Jacob Autrey, Samuel Ansley (1774), John Austin, Johnathan Burgess (1794), David Brewer, John Barnett, William Bird, Allen Booles, Thomas B. Burford, Bledsoe Brockman (~1781) married Elizabeth Landrum (1785), Bevin Booles, Benjamin Boon, William Burford, William Booles, Samuel Beavers, Joseph Bays, Charles Culbehouse, Robert Crutchfield, Duke Cole, Robert Cisnea, James R. Daniel, Drury Davis, John R. Daniel, William Daughtie, William Davis, Phillip Edmondson, Elijah Evans, Richard Feeman, Zachariah Fears, Joel Forrester, Aquilla Greer (1799), John D. Graftenreed, William Gutery, Leonard Greer (1786), William Greer (1790) married Rebekah Ammons (1790), Richard Garrett, Marbury Greer, Joseph Goodwin, William G. Grimes, Lemuel Greene (1785) son of William Green (1764), Thomas A. Gibbs, William Harwell, John Hodges, Thomas Head, Travis Hammock, Cadar Holt, Williamson Harris, Thoms Harwell, George Hunt, William Irby, Daniel Irby, Abraham G. Jackson, John P. Jones, James Jarrell, Thomas Lackey (1780), James Lowery (1783/8) son of Charles Lowery (1765), Jesse Leavins (~1789)?, John Lewis, David Lindsey, William May, Anderson McElroy, Matthew Kinnee, John Mayfield, Anderson C. Middlebrook, John McNealy, Alexander McAlpin, William W. Moore, Joshua Martin, Ransom Meadows, Daniel Meadows, James Mitchell, Charles Morris, Samuel Nelms, Harrison Oneal, George Oneal, George Owen, George Pitt, Thomas Pinkard, Hardy Phillips, Nathan Penington, Lazarus Pierce, John Phillips, Heny Payne, Edmond Pierce, Richard Park, Davis Rollins, Alexander N. Robinson, Daniel Reed, William Redd, Frederick Randle, William Rowland, Martin Slaughter, David Sayers, George Shaw, William H. Swinney, Ezekiel Stanley, Jacob Sayers, Henry Swendal/Swindall (1778), William Thrift, Isham Took(e) (1782/5), Samuel Thompson, Leonard Tuggle (1795) married Nancy Hensley, James Towns, Willis Towns, Abner Veazey, Jese Wilson, Levi Webb (1789), Silas Wilson, William Waters, Alexander Walden, Joseph Welbourn, Dempsey Wilkerson, Josiah Watts, Cordy T. Wilburn, Jubal E. Watts and Washington Whitlock. (TXL)

<u>Martin Friday</u>   11-09-1809   Orangeburg, SC Goodland Swamp S Edisto Rvr. His neighbors were <u>Friday Arthur</u>, Benjamin Buzbee, Salley, Jesse Pitts, William Walker, Johnston, William Young [Yon?], Gideon Jennings. (DEED)

George Friday   1810   Stewart Co, TN
His military comrades & neighbors were Josiah Askew, Wm Alsup, Samuel Alsup, Elish Askew, Wm Anders, Nicholas Brewer (1783), Thomas Brewer, Lewis Brewer (1778), George Berry, Thomas Berry, William Berry, Levi Buchanan, John Chambers, Wm Cormack (1785), J. Chambers, Rueben Elliot, Gideon French, Thos. French, Frederick Gross (1765), John Hendley, John Hendrix, Lewis Jackson, John Jackson, Wm. Largent, Wm. Largent (1785), John Lyndsey, Jas. Largent, Drury Mathews, B. [Benjamin?] Murphy (1791), Geo. McDaniel, Jas. Miller, Jas. Massingale (1785), Thos. Massingale, John Massey, Hilliary Morris, Daniel Oglesby (1785), Wm. Outlaw, John and Edward Rogers. (CS)
Other names under Woodsfolks: George, John G, John Lindsey, Robert, Spicer (~1792), Thomas, Thomas B and Washington Brown, Johnathan Been/Bean (1781), Charles Burress, William Burress, John Burris, John Burrus, Hiram Chappel, Thomas Gates (1793), William Green, Joseph and William Lindsey, John Lockey [Lockley?], Jeremiah Stephens (~1781), James R. Talbot (1794), John Talbot (~1791?) Rueben Todd (1780/6), Henry Grigg [Gregg] (~1790/2) and Joseph Miller.

The Swabian Connection – Expanded Edition

Note:

In the 1790 Ninety-Six District – Edgefield Co, SC page 66 "transcriptions" on the first column, Elisha Stevens (son James would marry Hinton Friday's daughter), William Bryant, William Largant [Largent], (a William Largent (1785) was in the same regiment as George Friday. Godfrey's (1770) daughter Abbie (1805) would marry a William Green (1779-1805). An Alexander Bean is in Edgefield, SC is very near the above mentioned.. A James Miller (1774)(son of James Miller (1750))was from this area and also had a sister named Rebecca Miller (1797).

In the 1790 census, some of the familiar neighbors where Godfrey Fridig (1770) would live are in order skipping the un-recognized are Elisha Stephens, William Bryant, James Miller, William Dean, William Morris, William Largant [Largent], Moses Clark, William Miller, David Miller, John Stephens, William Green, William Clark, William Clark Jr,The Youngblood's, Alexander Bean, John Bledsoe, and William Odum.

In 1791 a John Lindsey is living next to William Largent in the Ninety Six District, SC.

The 1800 census in Orange Co, SC for Godfrey Fridig (1770), list one boy born 1785-1790. The first son of Godfrey, also a Godfrey was record being born in 1800-1. In 1810, there is no census record for Godfrey, but he is recorded in Jenkins District of Greene Co, GA 1809 Tax List. Later the census only shows his know sons. George Friday was in Tennessee by 1810.

By the 1820 Stewart Co,TN Census the following people were still in the county: Wm Alsup, Lewis Jackson, John Lindsey, William Largent (family from Edgefield & Newberry Co, SC), Nicholas and Thomas Brewer, Gideon French, J. Cormack, Seth Outlaw.

There is a Benjamin and Elijah Brown, Wm. Linessey [Lindsey?] in the county by 1820 who are names that are names in the Friday ancestry. The Largent's come from Edgefield, Ninety-Six & Craven Counties of South Carolina.

Also, in Battalion 3 Woodfolk's Company are George, John G, Lindsey, Robert, Spicer, Thomas, Thomas B and Washington Brown, Johnathan Been/Bean (1781) (family from Newberry,SC), Charles Burress, William Burress, John Burris, John Burrus (intermittently used as Burroughs), Hiram Chappel, Jesse Jenkins, John G Jenkins (1793?), Joseph and William Lindsey, John Lockey [Lockley?], Jeremiah Stephens (~1781), James R. Talbot, John Talbot (Thomas and John Talbot in Tuscaloosa by 1830 living very near the Friday's), Rueben Todd (1780/6) (lived by Elizabeth Fridy/Fraley in 1820 Rutherford Co, TN).

A William Burress (1785) lived in Lawrence Co, TN. His daughter Nancy married Probate Wiggs (1807). Ansel Tolbert (1770) married Mary Richardson Burress (1784) the daughter of John Burress (1758).

In 1820 Wilkes Co, GA census John Murphy (father of Rebecca Murphy) has neighbors Patience, William and Gabriel Todd. Also, there is a William Berry. John Talbot was the guardian of a John Hendricks. John Todd (~1760) widow ~1803 Elizabeth of Wilkes County could also have married a Fridy/Friday, then divorced before 1820.

Friday Arthur   1810   Lexington, SC
His neighbors were Capt. John Quatellbaum, Henry Geiger, Jacob Cover, Thomas Wingard (~1783), James Rogers, John Sharp, Abraham Taylor and 14 more homes down is Christian Swygert. On the other side were Henry Amons [Ammons] (1795?), John Wing, Capt. John Hart (1758). (CS)
Note: This Henry Ammons maybe the son of Catherine Friday, daughter of Gabriel Fridig (1728)

Gabriel Friday   1810   Orangeburg, SC
His neighbors were William Kinsler, John Senn, Widow Carter and Jacob Seen Jr. On the other side were Phillip Fry, George Monty, John Monty, Molly Davier, Jacob Sharp, Michael Wise and John Baugh. (CS)

M [Martin] Friday   1810   Lexington, SC
His neighbors were William Yawn [Yonn], The Judy's, William Sally, The Martin's, Haysworth's, Chavas and the Hutto's. On the other side were John Haynsworth, Ann Bolan, The Argoe's., Brigman's and the Hall families. (CS)

The Swabian Connection – Expanded Edition

David Friday (1766-84)   1810   Lexington, SC
His neighbors were Jacob Chapman, Alex Bolan Stark, Charles Pener, Widow Baugh, Mathis Younginger, Mathias Coogler and Uriah Coogler (1776). Five, Six and Seven more homes down from Uriah were George Sykes, John Stack and Christian Wessinger. On the other side were Michael Wheeler [Willer?] (1755-65), George Holdawanger, John Presley (Peesley), Lazaris Miller and Capt. Jacob Linder. (CS)
Note: Michael Wheeler married Katherine [Unknown] and their daughter Rosannah (1792) married John Christian Rister (1811).

David Friday (Fridy)   1810   Fairfield, SC
His neighbors were William Kincaid, William Kennedy, Samuel Kennedy, Joseph Richardson and John Sightnes. On the other side were William Kennedy Jr, Christian Sythe, David Freeman, James Atkins, Robert Martin and Stephen Gibson. (CS)

D^0 Friday (1766-84)   1810   Orangeburg Co, SC
His neighbors were Wm Cooper, Bruer, Jn Turner, BJ Corbet, G Dyches, Lt Gardner and John Corbet. On the other side were J Baker, R Posey, JN Gibson, Ann Collum, Dickes, J Fannin, N Posey, G Brown, M Tyler, R Tyler, Th M Adams, Thomas Youn, G Rushton, Huckaboy [Huckaboo]. (CS) Pg. 168 000100010001
Note: other neighbors were Gardner, Gibson, Harper, Henry, Holbac, Huckaby, Jones, Martin, McCoy, Michum, More, Poe, Posey, Pou, Rambo, Rourk, Rushton, Thompson, Turner, Tyler, West and Your.

Henry Friday   1810   Richland, SC
His neighbors were Nancy Swygert and James Thompson. On the other side were Julian Stringer, Alan Collins, William and John Rawlermaw, and David Strickling. (CS) Pg. 305
Note: other neighbors were Berry, Chavis, Collins, Depaker, Easton, Evans, Frost, Goodwyn, Griffin, Gurr, Halliday [Holliday], Harris, Hays, Howard, Joiner, Likes, Martin, McLemore, Mcullah, Mings, Otley, Rawlinson, Sanders, Strange, Strickling, Thompson, Turner, Whitmore and Wood.

John Friday (1743)   1810   Lexington, SC
His neighbors were James McGowan, Thomas and James Oliver, John & Widow Bookman, Peter Jumper, Joseph Strother (1755), George Brice and Samuel Rambo (~1783). On the other side were Charles Spires, Jeremiah Ables, Nicholas Hane, Mathias Senr, Charles Holman and Henry Weaver. Samuel Rambo was the brother to Daniel Rambo (1785) who is living 4 homes down from Samuel Berry Friday in 1830 Lexington Co, SC.(CS) Pg. 76a

Gabriel Fridig   4-27-1810   Lexington Dist, SC Saluda River

Gabriel Friday   1810   Lexington Co, SC
(CS) Pg. 171

David Friday (1775)   1811-13   Barnwell Co, SC
His neighbors were Elisha Chavis, George Keadle, John Keadle, Thomas and John Newman & Noel Turner (1764).

Martin Friday (1783)   1-13-1813   Orangeburg, SC Goodland Swamp S Edisto Rvr
His neighbors were Lewis Jones, Gideon Hutto, Joseph Rushton, Friday Arthur and Martin Salley. (SNLP)

David Friday   1-18-1813   Barnwell Dist, SC Savannah Rvr/Silver Bluff
His neighbor was John Cofer, Thomas Newman, John Turner, Noel Turner, John Fryer, John Hart and John Newman. (DEED)

257
The Swabian Connection – Expanded Edition

Note: On 1-14-1814 George Keddle had a 760 acre plat surveyed in Barnwell District. His neighbors were Thomas Newman, John Fryer, John Cofer, George Turner, William Patterson and Sampson Griffin.

David Friday   5-15-1813   Orangeburg Dist, SC Edisto River
His neighbor was Robert Garvin, James Smith and James Garner Sr.

John Gabriel Friday   9-13-1813   Lexington, SC Spring Branch Congaree River
His neighbors were Elisha Daniel and John Harsey.

Gabriel Friday   12-6-1814   Lexington Dist, SC Broad River/Saluda River
His neighbors were Robert Stark, William Kinsler, and Alexander B Stark.

John Frydy [Friday]   1-9-1816   Lexington Dist, SC
His neighbors were Jeremiah Edwards and Johnathan Taylor. (SNLP)

Gabriel Frideg   2-8-1816   Lexington Dist, SC - Bickleys Branch
Surveyed for David Shotts (~1790) by Gabriel. David's neighbors are Johnathan Taylor (1777), Cornelious Clark, Turpin and Brazelman. (SNLP)

Gabriel Friday   7-6-1816   Lexington Dist, SC Six Mile Creek
His neighbors were Michael Leitner, William Kinsler, Richard Hampton and William Sims. (SNLP)

Gabriel Fridig   5-10-1817   Lexington Dist, SC
His neighbors were Robert Stark, William Kinsler, John Rutledge, Daniel Delaney, Mary Kinsler, Richard Hampton, Bartlett, Peter Coogle, Michael Leightner, John Marley and Jacob Bonie Whitticks. (SNLP)

Emanuel Friday   10-27-1817   Lexington Dist, SC Congaree River/Congaree Creek
His neighbor was Gabriel Friday.
Note: Emanuel had a plat for 600 acres and 10 acres surveyed at the Congaree River the same day.

Elizabeth Fridy (1755-74)1820   Rutherford Co, TN
Here neighbors are John Bean (1761), John Newman (1754/1802), and Rueben Todd (1780). On the other side are William A. Liddon (1795), Shadrack Ferguson (1769-80), Thomas Furgeson (1798), Sally Massy, Kesiah Woods and John Gregory (1765). 7S (CS) 0101001110106001200301
Note: This Elizabeth maybe a Puckett, wife of Caleb Fraley and daughter of Drury Puckett. Rueben Todd (born in Wilkes Co, GA) married Jean Russel then Jemini Todd. Rueben Todd has a sister named Elizabeth Todd and their father was named Benjamin. Sally Woods Massy was the wife of Drewry Massey. William Abram Liddon (son of Benjamin Liddon (~1770)) married Mary White Davis (1800). John Hogan Bean (1765) married Jane McFarland (1782). John Todd (1760) had a daughter and wife named Elizabeth. Elizabeth (1760), wife of John (1760) was a widow by 1819. John Gregory married Elizabeth Neal (1771); they settled in Virginia by 1837. John Newman (1754) has a daughter named Elizabeth. All of the following people above have a tie to Virginia or North Carolina. There are seven Brown families in Rutherford Co, TN via the 1810 Census and many more by 1830. Shadrack Ferguson (1769-80) & Thomas Furgeson (1798) were brothers (Feldman, Steph Carson 2005). Thomas Brown (1785-94) is living beside Thomas Ashley (1766-84) "born in SC" in Rutherford Co, TN as recorded in 1810 census. John Todd (~1760) widow ~1803 Elizabeth of Wilkes County could also have married a Fridy/Friday, then divorced before 1820.

Frederic Friday   1820   Marion Co, MS

The Swabian Connection – Expanded Edition

His neighbors were William Phillips (1801) , Rueben Wright, William Pervis and Campbell Ivy. On the other side were Lewis Williamson, William Yarbrough, Thompson Phillips (1795), Daniel Blue and Hope H Lenoir. Frederic is working in agriculture. 1S (CS) 00000013000010000000000000

Friday Arthur   1820   Lexington Co, SC
His neighbors were John McCreless , Thos K Poindexter, Jacob Bell, Henry Kaiser, Jacob Kaminer (1789), Jacob Kelly, Jesse Arthur, Amos Banks and 6 more homes down was Thomas Rall. On the other side was Gregory Clark, David Hernab? and George Eigleburger. (CS)

Gabriel Friday   1820   Lexington, SC
His neighbors were Coonrad Shull and Andrew Browner (sp?). On the other side were William Daniel, Nicholus Hook, Jacob Chup, Margaret Senn, David Senn, William Senn, Mark Huggins, Uriah Carter, and three homes down from there were Frederick and Andrew Baugh. (CS)

Martin & David Friday   1820   Orangeburg, SC
His Neighbors were James Fanning, Charles Brickle, Elizabeth Bird, Jacob Barrs, Thomas Edwards, Elizabeth Harley and two more down were Daniel and John Stroman. On the other side were David Friday, Benjamin Culler, Phillip Jackson, Charles Hall and Richard Williams. (CS)
Note:
Martin   00001010010080040305022
David   20001000100002000000000001

Martin Fridy   1820   Orangeburg, SC
His neighbors were were John Salley, John M Sally, Jacob Stroman, James Brown, Nelley Hutto, Hue Philips and Gidion Hutto (1773/1808). On the other side were George Salley, Shadrack Pundles, Thomas Gray, John Hoan(sp?), Catherine Bell and Sarah Hutto. (CS)
10001000010080041204202

John Friday   1820   Lexington, SC
His neighbors were Jesse Sharp (1802), William Drennen (1775-94), Henry Shull, Mathias Senn, Nicholas Hayne, James Cayce, William Kinsler, Louis Pou, Henry Seibels, and 3 additional homes down was Mary Arthur. On the other side were John Patton, Sarah Seibles (1769), Randolph Geiger, Catherine and Margaret Corkman. (CS)

David Friday (1775-94)   1820   Lexington, SC   Sandy Run, SC?
His neighbors were Jacob Souter, Samuel Kennerly, Nancy Geiger, Peter Jumper, Harman H Geiger (1797), Nancy Wise, John Fannon, James Spires and William Pool. On the other side are John Matthias, Sarah Mathias, Lewilla Snyder, Samuel Leaphart, Jacob Huffman, and Enoch Storie [Story]. Six more homes down was John Swygert who the family was familiar and close. (CS)

Henry Friday (45+yrs)   1820   Richland, SC
His neighbors are unknown. (CS) Pg. 13 02100110101030000

David Friday [Fridy]   1820   Fairfield, SC
His neighbors were Lubin/Labin Chappell, Joseph Kennedy/Romedy, Thomas Marshall, Christian City/Citz, Silas Ruff, Thomas Richason and Abner Brown. On the other side were John Chappell, Sythe "Ilett" Richarson, Nathan Cook, Henry W Hood, James Elkins, Sarah and Gracy Pear(e)son. (CS) Pg. 66

David Friday (1775-94)   1820   Orangeburg, SC
His neighbors were Mier Poosey [Posey] and William Pool. On the other side were John Ott, Joseph Riddy, David Cook, Casin Howel, Ott Jones, George Smith, Jonathan Wright, Daniel Howel, William Cannady, Rachel Riddy and Joseph Fanning. (CS) 2000100000101

The Swabian Connection – Expanded Edition

David Friday   5-5-1820   Orangeburg, SC Burkelow Creek S Edisto Rvr/N Edisto Rvr. His neighbors were <u>Nehemiah Posey</u> and Kinching. (SNLP)

Godfrey Fridig   1820   Edgefield Co, SC
His neighbors were Sarah Elmore (1775-94), Luke Elmore (1794-1804), Elisha Stevens Jr and Henry Clarke. On the other side are William Green (1794-1804), Thomas Dean (1775-94), Martin Sriddum and Jacob Adams. (CS) 201001020010200000000
Note:
Aquilla Ann Stevens was the daughter of James Stevens (1785) who married Hinton Friday (1814) son of Godfrey (1770).
On 11-12-1784 Allen Hinton had a 150 acre plat surveyed at the water of Stevens Creek in the Ninety-Six District. Allen is still there by August of 1786.
In the 1790 Ninety-Six District – Edgefield Co, SC page 66 "transcriptions" Elisha Stevens (son James would marry Hinton Friday's daughter), William Bryant, William Largant [Largent], (a William Largent (1785) was in the same regiment as George Friday. Godfrey's (1770) daughter Abbie (1805) would marry a William Green (1779-1805). An Alexander Bean is in Edgefield, SC is very near the above mentioned.. A James Miller (1774)(son of James Miller (1750))was from this area and also had a sister named Rebecca Miller (1797).
In the 1790 census, some of the familiar neighbors where Godfrey Fridig (1770) would live are in order skipping the un-recognized are Elisha Stephens, William Bryant, James Miller, William Dean, William Morris, William Largant [Largent], Moses Clark, William Miller, David Miller, John Stephens, William Green, William Clark, William Clark Jr,The Youngblood's, Alexander Bean, John Bledsoe, and William Odum.
other neighbors were Adams, Burt, Clark, Dean, Elmore, Fortner, Gales, Glazier, Green, Harbley, Hart, Halloway, Lang, Lowry, McClymore, McManus, Miller, Mims, Norris, Odum, Pardue, Parkman, Presley, Stevens, Stiddum, Thomson, Trotter, Walton, White, and Youngblood.

William Friday **(*)**   1820   Chester Co, "Charleston Neck", SC
His neighbors were Benjamin F Dunkin (1792) and J Simpson. On the other side were Joseph Carpenter, John Linfser (sp?) and Sarah Pennington. Two more homes down was Sarah R Purcell, Ann Prentice, Elvin Deuter, J.G. (Johann George) Happoldt (1769), John Gates and Edward O'Neal. (CS)

<u>Martin Friday</u>   11-29-1821   Orangeburg, SC
His neighbor was still Henry Salley. (DEED)

A. Friday   12-10-1821   Lexington, SC – Congaree Creek/River
His neighbors where <u>Joseph Lybrant</u>, Jonathan Taylor (1777), David Ciser, Joseph Jones and John Bayles. (SNLP)

<u>Martin Friday</u>   11-29-1821   Orangeburg, SC
His neighbor was still Henry Salley. (DEED)

Friday   2-8-1823   SW of Scouter Creek, Wolf Branch and Congaree Creek, Lexington Dist, SC
The immediate neighbors were Johnathan Taylor (1777) and Christian Rall [Rawl] (1784). To the North was Terpin and Wadsworth land. (SNLP)
Note: Kathryn Celia Rawls (1810) , daughter of Christian would marry Andrew Jacson Berry by 1830.

Friday   3-28-1823   Lexington Dist, SC Congaree Creek
The neighbors were <u>Christian Rall</u>, S. Wadsworth, Terpin, John Hart, Jonathan Taylor (1777), and Jones. (SNLP)

The Swabian Connection – Expanded Edition

Gabriel Friday   7-31-1823   Lexington Dist, SC Congaree Creek/River
His neighbors were <u>Rachael Sarah Honold</u>, Wadsworth, Turping, Elizabeth S. L., Jonathan Taylor
(1777) and Savid Honold. (SNLP)

David Friday   11-22-1824   Orangeburg, SC Burkelow Creek S Edisto Rvr/N
Edisto Rvr. His neighbors were <u>Cassin Howell</u>, Nehemiah Posey, James Head and John Ott.
(SNLP)

Rueben Friday   1824   Lexington District, SC Saluda River
His neighbors and associates were Friday Arthur, M. Hook, Jacob Wessinger, John Mathias, John
J, Swicard [Swygert], Jacob Nunnimaker Jr, Michael Lorick, Samuel Leaphart, John Mets, Jacob
Mets, Joseph Chupp, Samuel Mets, Frederick Derick, Godfrey Derrick, David Lauerman, Abraham
Stock, George Likes, John Smith and Uriah Carter. (PETN)
Note: Inhabitants of Lexington district, counter-petition asking that they not be made to remove
fish nets from the Saluda river, and that a commissioner be appointed to superintend the opening
of the river.

Sally [Unknown] Friday 3-29-1825   Lexington Co ,SC Rocky Creek/Saluda River
Her neighbors were <u>John Gartman</u> (1777), Jacob Site, Dennis G Hays (1790?), Mrs. Poindexter,
Jacob Ralls [Rawls], Henry Weaver and David Boozer (1786). (SNLP)
Note: The current day location is near Edgefield in Lexington Co, SC south of the Saluda river on
the far western edge of Lexington, just west of Hollow Creek where Henry Weaver Jr. owned
land. Part of Rocky Creek is actually in Edgefield (modern Saluda Co) and close to Cloud's Creek.
On 5-12-1823 David Boozer and Daniel Rall had 370 acres surveyed on 12 Mile Creek in Lexington
Dist, SC. His neighbors were Drafts, Corley, Thomas Derrick, Brazilman, George Kraps and
Dempsey Coward.
A Sallie Boozer (1796) married John Cappleman (1773) had a son named Daniel (1822) and she
died in 1830. Dennis Gregory Hayes (1790) married Martha C Mitchell (1800).
Jacob Ralls [Rawls] was still there by 5-7-1827 when William Hendrix and John Kyser (~1767)
purchased 28 acres on Rocky Creek. John Kyser married a Barbery Gartman in 1804.
John Gartman was on Rocky Creek by 6-16-1810 when he purchased 68 Acres. John Gartman
married Nancy Seay (1777) about 1798 who was the daughter of Nicholas Seay. Elizabeth
Gartman (1782) married John Jacob Rawl (1776) about (~1799). John Jacob Rawl (1776) also
married Sarah "Sallie" Corley (1802) about (~1838) and both died in Coweta Co, GA. Christian
Rawls (1784) is reported to have married Nancy Ann J Hendrix (1787) in 1809 Lexington Co, SC.
Rebecca "Sally Rawl (~1808) daughter of Jacob Rawls and Sallie Corley married Frederick
Harmon (1804) and had children after 1831. David Boozer (1786) married a Catherine Rawl
(1792) about 1810 in Lexington County, SC. Sophia Schneider Kyzer (1780) married Henry
Weaver (1780) and show up Tuscaloosa Co, AL before 1839.
Mrs. Poindexter maybe Thomas Kennerly Poindexter's mother or Wife; Elizabeth Jane Kennerly
who married Joseph Poindexter. Thomas Kennerly married a Jones? Then married Mary Ralls-
Poindexter in Edgefield, SC on 8 Dec 1811. A Sarah "Sallie?" Weaver (1778), daughter of Henry
Weaver is reported to have married Captain John Quattlebaum (1774). Andrew Jackson Berry
(1811) married Kathryn Celia Rawls (1810) the daughter of Christian Rawls (1784) brother to the
above Jacob Rawls (1776). Samuel Berry Friday (1802) son Rueben Friday (1828) was issued
guardianship citation to Amanda (1842), Sarah E Berry (1844), Daniel and Louisa Berry (1833) in
arms after Andrew & Kathryn Rawls Berry were struck by lightning in 1855 Attala Co, MS.

George Friday   1830   Tuscaloosa, AL
His neighbors were H (Henry C.) Hendricks, J Pennington, J T Sandford, John Poe (1784), Simeon
Pugh (177X), Thomas Ellard, James Gaunn?, Lewis Pate, J.B. Jones, Augustus Beel, Jane Skinner,
John Leopard, W.W. Neel, Luke Durden, H [Henry] Parker & Wm Snider (~1782). On the
otherside were Jesse Jenkins (1790-1800) , J W Beel, James Gray, Susan Reddin and M Jackson.
(CS) 1110101000000220001

The Swabian Connection – Expanded Edition

Note: Tignal Pugh was issued 79.96 acres on 1-4-1831. Henry C Hendricks was issues 40.25 acres on 10-1-1835. Thomas Ellard was issued 80.29 acres on 11-1-1830. John Tolbert (1st listed as Talbert, 2nd as Tolbert) was issued 40.1 acres on 10-14-1834 and 10-21-1834. A John Tolbert is listed in the 1790 census for Abbeville, Ninety-Six District, SC. George Friday was issued 40 acres on 10-21-1834. Jesse Jenkins was issued 40 acres on 9-20-1839. Jacob Lindsey was issued 39.96 acres on 10-14-1834. James Lindsey was issued 40.1 acres on 10-1-1835. Andrew Pennington (1799?) was issued 40.19 acres on 11-4-1834. John Poe was issued 80 acres on 4-30-1824. William B Hendricks (1808) was issued 40 acres on 10-16-1834 just 5 days before George Friday was issued his property.

Thomas Friday   1830   Tuscaloosa, AL
His neighbors were James Lindsey (1780-90), Jesse Snider (1802), Aaron Shannon, Deannah Canvendish, Andrew Codell, H.F. Bell, Jarod Bell, Spencer Griffin, Elizabeth Tolbot/Tolbert (1780-90), Lorenzo D. Vance (1806), Benjamin Lee, Samuel Stedman (1750-60), Samuel Johnson and David Denton (1797). On the other side were William Johnson (1790-1800), James M Bush (1800-10), Bird Carridyne (1800-10) and Thomas Hicks (1790-1800). (CS) 100001000000000001
Note:
All of the following neighbors are living near Thomas Friday more/less than 1 mile away: Henry Webb was issued 39 acres of land on 10-1-1835. In the 1860 census James Lidsey [Lindsey] (1795) is living beside William R Bell (1829) born in South Carolina. A John Tolbert purchased 40.1 acres by 10-21-1834. James Lindsey was issued 40.1 acres on 10-1-1835. Samuel Stedman was issued 80.49 acres on 9-1-1825. Samuel Johnson was issued 79.94 acres on 10-1-1834. William B Hendricks was issued 40 acres on 10-16-1834 north of Thomas near George Friday's property. Isham Parker had 39 acres issued on 11-4-1834. Thomas & William Pate had 159 acres issued on 3-20-1837. Thomas Friday had his 39 acres issued on 11-7-1837 and 9-20-1839.

Friday Arthur   1830   Lexington Co, SC
His neighbors were Col. Henry Arthur, James Casey, John J Seibles (1752), Martha Jumper, John Threewits, William Drennan (1780-90), Ian? Geiger, and Isham Leach (1804). On the other side was West Merchant, John Schull, Mary Arthur and Alexander Bell. (CS)
Note: a William E Drennan (1813) married a Cynthia E [Unknown](1818) and had sons named John Friday Drennan (10-25-1842 - 4-29-1846) and Campbell Bryce Drennan (11-10-1838 - 12-9-1843) who are buried in the Washington Street Methodist Church Cemetery in Columbia, SC. William Drennen (1775-94) is two doors down from John Friday (1743) via the 1820 Census.

David Friday   1830   Barnwell Co, SC Hollow Creek
His neighbors were George Turner Sr, Noel Turner (1764), Jacob Foreman, George Turner, John Cosser and Mrs. Smith. (CS)

Samuel Friday (1802)   1830   Lexington Co, SC Black Creek/North Edisto River (N Leesvile)
He had 3 children and his neighbors were James Williamson, Thomas Shultz, Henry Sea (~1793), Levi Williams, John Caughman, George Holman, Jacob Rilly?, Martin Librand, John Vanzant, Jacob Drafts, James Calk.
On the other side were Matthias Hatfield, John Kinard, George Dunlap, Daniel Rawls, David Kiser, John J Crapp (1803), George Caughmato?, George Gartman (~1800), Elias Taylor (1807), Christian Kizer [Kyzer] (~1740) and Daniel Rambo (1785). Two more homes down was Jesse Harmon, David Harmon, George Sawyer and John Ruff. (CS)
Note:
5-18-1772 James Williamson had a 200 acre plat memorial surveyed on Black Creek on Craven Co, SC. His father was Benjamin Williamson.

The Swabian Connection – Expanded Edition

9-10-1810 Daniel Rambo purchased a 1000 acre platt on Black Creek. His neighbors were father Laurance Rambo (~1750), and William Williamson.

3-2-1812 David Seegress for Godfrey Oswalt a plat for 657 aces on Black Creek. His neighbors were George Levingston, Harden Griffin, William and John Berry.

George Gartman had 139 acres surveyed by John W Seay on 1-14-1826. George married Hepsibah Seay.

John Berry was a neighbor with 306 acres by 6-24-1822 on Big Black Creek. This record is for Samuel Berry Friday (1802). David Kyzer (1800) {son of Christian (~1740) moved to Bibb Co, AL and purchased land by 10-1-1835.

"Samuel Friday bought land on "waters Blk Creek" in 1823 from William Taylor." "Black Creek was mentioned infrequently, but was a briefly-used name for a creek of the North Edisto River connected to Lightwood and Hell Hole Creeks just below Leesville." "The headwaters of the Hollow Creek system (of the Saluda) are just above Leesville (Imrey, Harriet 11-2007)".

William Taylor (1776) died in 1823 and his will was probated in 1825.

Henry Seay (~1793) son of Nicholas Seay married Sarah Sally Fulmer (1794).

A William See (1741) married abt ~1761 to a Sophia Poole (1740-50) the daughter of Philip Puhl. In September 1785 William See/Sea married a Elizabeth? Poole sister of George Phillip Poole who were children of Phillip Poole. Nancy Booser [Boozer] and John Tyler witnessed the deed abstract for the Poole and See/Sea family.

A William Seay (~1777) moved to Knox Co, TN. Michael Seay (~1777) who married Clarissa Jane Clark (~1788) had children born in McNairy 1810 & Rutherford County, TN about 1821.

Nancy Seay (1777) is reported to have married John Gartman (1777).

Daniel Rawls (~1780) son of Jacob Rall (1752) married Mary Ann Lorick (1790).

David Friday (1780-90)   1830   Lexington Co, SC
He lived with 7 children beside Samuel and Michael Leaphart (1795), Lewis Metz, Jonas Mathias. Hebrew, Andrew Geiger, Elizabeth Geiger, Samuel Hufman, Thomas Butler, Joseph Airhart and Emanuel Sistrunk. (CS)

On the other side were Meredith Wise, Michael Lorick, Elizabeth Daniels, John C Martin, Michael Wise, Levi Williams, John Caughman, George Holman and Jacob Kelly (1780-90). (CS)

Note: On 11-14-1818 Jacob Gable had his 170 Acre plat surveyed on 12 Mile Creek/Saluda River in Lexington Co, SC. Emanuel Seestrunk [Sistrunk], David Kleckley, George Lephart, Likes and Samuel Kennerly were his neighbors.

On the other side were Meredith Wise, Michael Lorick, Elizabeth Daniels, John C Martin, Michael Wise, Levi Williams, John Caughman, George Holman and Jacob Kelly (1780-90). (CS)

Henry Friday   1830   Richland Co, SC
His neighbors were Nathaniel Parrot, Simon Martin, Lewis Richardson and Thomas Parrot.
On the other side were Charles Ellis and W.G. Burdell. (CS) Pg. 407
Note:
On 8-19-1793 William Cason had a 274 acre plat surveyed on Rocky Branch in Camden District, Fairfield Co, SC near Dutchman's Creek. His neighbors were William Miller, Henry Poole, Brayd and Thomas Parrott.

On 12-24-1828 Wesley Parrot had a 300 Acre plat surveyed on Colonels Crk/Wateree Rvr in Richland Dist, SC. Simon Martin, Jacob J Faust, John Rabb and Jesse Killingworth were his neighbors per Survey.

Peggy Friday (1760-70) 1830   Fairfield Co, SC
Their neighbors were John Lightner, Barbara Kennedy, William Ashley and Susan Freeman.
On the other side were Christian Freshley (1780), John Watt, Limon Cockrell, Henry Edrington and Robert Blakley. (CS) Pg. 397 000011000000000010001

Milley Friday(1790-1800)1830   Fairfield Co, SC
Their neighbors were John Lightner, Barbara Kennedy, William Ashley and Susan Freeman.

The Swabian Connection – Expanded Edition

On the other side were Christian Freshley (1780), John Watt, Limon Cockrell, Henry Edrington and Robert Blakley. (CS) Pg. 397 0100000000000010001

Gabriel Friday (1752)   1830   Lexington, SC
His neighbors were his stepson William Kinsler, Dudly Leeman, James Wilkinson and the Taylors. On the other side were Catherine Hook, Nicholas Hook, John M Swycord [Swygert] (1808), Jacob Sears and Jacob Hook. (CS)

William Friday (*)   1830   Chester Co, "Charleston Neck", SC
His neighbors were George McClain, James Carpenter, John Loudser, John Gates, Sarah Remmington, E. D. Happoldt, P. Newton, and two more homes down was Elizabeth Happoldt (1776). On the other side were James Gillett, Peter Duvall, Louisa Johnson, Frank Capers and Thomas Coon. (CS)

Godfrey Friday I & II   1830   Edgefield, SC
Father and Son lived beside William Green, Benjamin Stevens, Jeremiah Bucklatter, Robert Burnett, James McCrary, John McCrary, John Johnson, Alexander McCrary and Barbara Hughs. On the other side were George Mcmanus, Elisha Stevens, Mathias Stevens, Elizabeth Stevens, David Hart and Aaron Green (1798). (CS) 00011001000001 – II 30001000000001
Note: Aaron Green (1798) married Demaris Baker (~1802), daughter of Thomas Baker (~1774).

David Friday   9-8-1830   Barnwell District, SC Hollow Creek
His neighbors were George Turner Sr, Noel Turner, Jacob Foreman, George Turner and John Cosser and Mrs. Smith. (SNLP)

John Fredi (1790-1800) 1830   Conecuh Co, AL
His neighbors were _____ A Weldon, James Thompson Jr and James May. On the other side was William Frenurum?, Isham Moore, Robert Smitre? and Carmon Jones. Pg. 90
02000100000000110001 (CS)(*)

Godfrey Friday (1801)   1-10-1834   Little Stevens Creek Branch of Savannah River - Edgefield, SC
His neighbors were Berryman Baker (1799), William A Strother (1811) and Benjamin Frazier (~1785). (Deed)
Note: William Augustus Strother (1811), the son of George James Strother (~1791) married Nancy Coleman (1816). Ben's son William Frazier (1804) married Eliza Ann Cantelou (1814).

Friday   9-10-1836   Orangeburg Dist, SC Turkey Branch/Tampa Branch/Muddy Branch/ North & South Edisto River
His neighbors were James Sharp, Gleeton, J. Hutto, G. Hartzog. (SNLP)

Thomas Friday   1837   Tuscaloosa, AL
His new neighbors were Thomas and William Pate south of his property.

David Friday   2-21-1838   Orangeburg, SC Cedar Creek/S Edisto Rvr
His Neighbors were John Ott's, Joshua Prothro and, Evan Prothro. (SNLP)

Rebecca Ann Beardon   1839   Tuscaloosa, AL
Rebecca Friday married Reuben Bearden in 1836 and Austin Hood who married them is to the Southwest and West of their property.

George Friday (1787)   1840   Tuscaloosa Co, AL
(CS) 010000010000001200001 pg. 205

264

Thomas Friday   1840   Tuscaloosa Co, AL
(CS) 111001000000031000010 pg. 205

Henry Friday   1840   Tuscaloosa Co, AL
(CS) 200010000000022001000 pg. 205

Milley Friday   1840   Fairfield Co, SC
(CS) 00010000000000001001

Godfrey Friday (1770)   1840   Edgefield Co, SC
His neighbors were William H Green (1780-90), Alexander McCrary (1778), John McCrary, Barbary Hughs, Esther Meeks, Stephen Stalnaker and Tho A Ingram. On the other side is Elizabeth Stevens, John Jo Still and Peter Ouzts (1803). (CS) 00100000100000001000001
Note: Peter Ouzts (1803) married ~1824 to Lucinda Lowery (1808) the daughter of John William Lowery (~1760).

Godfrey Friday   1840   Pike Co, GA
His neighbors were Elizabeth Carson, Seward Haris?, James Dismuke (1770-80) and John Hitchcock. On the other side were James Biggum, John P Clegg (1792), George Pothos, Barton Alford and Daniel Tillery. (CS)

Milley Friday   1840   Fairfield Co, SC
(CS) Pg. 156 00010000000000001001

Gabriel Friday   1840   Fairfield Co, SC
His neighbors were John Barker, Mary Brown, X Hargood, X Smart and Lewis Thompson. On the other side were John Jarod, X Ashford, X Evans and X Watt. (CS) Pg. 158 00000010-

Daniel H Friday (1813) 1840   Lexington, SC
His neighbors were Anna [_____] Friday (1780-90), Patrick Neice, Benjamin Hutto (1789), Martin Hutto (1812), William Hutto (1796), Dice Mixon (1810-20) and and P.J. Starns. (CS)

Martin Friday (1780-90) 1840   Orangeburg, Orange Co, SC
His neighbors were William Yon (1770-80), Jeremiah Hainsworth (1760-70), Henry Young, Robert Argrove, Effa Yon, Martin Argrove, William H. Corbett (1810-20) John Brown, Elizabeth Sally, John Corbett, Martin Bolen (1790-1800) and John A Sally. The Corbett, Fanning's and more Yons lived further down. On the other side of Martin lived Jacob Stroman (1791), Redick Sojourner (1791), Elisha Tyler (1790-1800), John Wolfe and Henry Smoke (~1805). (CS) 100010010000000001-0
Note:
In the 1790 Census Jery Hainsworth neighbors are John Sally, John Daily, Mary Adams, Joseph Cootterry, William Pugh, and Martin Sally. On the other side is George Kelly, Henry Varnadore, Wittenhal Warner, Phillip Wolf, Martin Dickson and 8 more down is Benjamin Odum, Leven Collins and Uriah Odum. Martin Bolin married a Mary Posey. Reddick Sojourner married Levicia Salley (1791), daughter of Ann Friday who married Henry Salley. Jacob Stroman married 3x w/first marriage to Ann Milhaus [Millhouse]. Henry Smoke married Rachel McMichael and Susannah Pearson.

T.A Friday   1840   Edgefield Co, SC
His neighbors were George Free, John May, Sarah Strone, and John Faulkner. On the other side were Sarah Dew, Tempy Bryant, Robert Byrant and Bartley Sanders. (CS)

David Friday (1775)   1840   Lexington Co, SC

His neighbors were Kindred Hydrick, Isaiah Howell, Pleasant Huckaby and Robert Garvine. On the other side was Nehemiah Posey Jr. (1775), Jacob Kitching, Joshua Prothro, Joseph Douglas, Edmund Prothro, Mary Head and Frances L Walker. (CS) 0011100010000000100101

William Friday (*)   1840   Chester Co "Charleston Neck", SC
His neighbors (in no particular order) were Thomas Gates, Henry Grines, Albert Happoldt (1805-10), C.D. Happoldt (1803?), Henry Houchin, Eams Johnson, Louisa Johnson, Mary M Lindsor, Peter H. Marchant, Grace Mitchell, Mary Nelson, Betsey North, John O'Neale, Patrick O'Neale, Thomas Ohion, Rose Pendell, Charles P Schirer, Alexander Wilson, and Benjamin Wreden. (CS)

Lee Fryday   1840   Perry Co, AL
His neighbors were Absalom Autry, R.B. Cook, Daniel Terry, Andrew Bell, Seaborn J Fuller, Johnathan Glaze, John Mitchell , Thomas McCaine, John M Melson, James Bell, R.C. Sanderson, William Gay, Alfred Fuller and Levi Martin. (CS)

Samuel Friday (1802)   1840   Bibb Co, AL
His neighbors are Jeremiah Stickey, Oliver Abstance, Jennings Abstance (1808), Riley Kellerman , Reason Hinton (1780-90) and David Reid. On ther other side is Frederick Joice, Berryman McDaniel (1788), James Gray, Elizabeth Bobers, James Kimball and James Bromitt.
(CS). 122001121001
Note: transcribed as Sanl. Finiary. Census shows Saml. Friday. Berryman McDaniel married Sarah Mayfield (1797) of whom were from Fairfield, SC.

Godfrey Friday   1-18-1847   Edgefield Co, SC Pen(n) & Stevens Creek, Little Saluda, Savannah River, Little Creek.
His neighbors were John C Allen, A.B. [Allen] Addison, Charlotte Peterson, John Bledsoe, Mark Mathews, John C Harris, Ann McCreary, Theophilus Hill, Alexander P Keinard, Josiah Howell, Evans Permenter, Henry C Turner, David Crain, James Lowry, John Smyley, Benjamin Stevens, George J Strothers, B.W. Bledsoe, Joseph Sanders, and John Adams.

Martin Friday   3-5-1849   South Edisto Rvr/Goodland Swamp/Cowford Lake Orangeburg Dist, SC
His neighbors were Joseph Duncan Allen, J. H. Morgan and Jacob Stroman. (SNLP)

Saml [Samuel] Friday   1850   Bibb Co, AL
His neighbors were James Wright, John McKee (1804), Gideon N Thompson (1824) and William C "Columbus" Davis (1809). On the other side were his son Lemuel Friday (1825), Nehemian P Vernon (1809), John W Keadle (1815) and Wiley Fields (1804).
Note: Gideon married Temperance Camp (1822). William C Davis (1809) married his 3rd wife Mirande Frances Myers/Berry in 1860 Nacogdoches, TX. John McKee was born in Anderson, SC and he purchased land in Tuscaloosa Co, AL by 1823. James Wright was in the same county by 1823. John W. Keadle married Jurelia Baker (1825).

Rebecca Friday-Bearden 1850   Tuscaloosa Co, AL
She is living w/husband Rueben Bearden and neighbors are James Lindsey, Thomas Beam, Jesse P. Daniel (1789), John Findley, Goyne and Daniel Hitchcock. (CS)
Note: This James Lindsey (1795) married a Lydia who had 3 sons (Major, James & John) one daughter Melissa (1837) who married John Skelton (1831). This James Lindsey may be the same person who was in George Friday's Woodfolks regiment in Stewart Co, TN during the War of 1812.

George Friday (1787)   1850   Tuscaloosa Co, AL

His neighbors were William Friday (1819) Jeptha Friday (1827) and Isham Parker (1805) [Minister Baptist Church]. On the other side was Larkin Griffin (1791) [Louisa Ludlow (1820) w/son David (1848) living in the Griffin home],Nancy Goodson (1790) & Richard Jordan (1812). (CS)
Note: Nancy [Richardson] Goodson was born in Virginia, married to Benjamin Goodson (1790) in Smith Co, TN in 1813 and children born in White Co, TN between 1831-37. Benjamin was in the War of 1812 in the TN volunteers (Clarke, William T - 2003). A James Clake Griffin (1769) married a Sophia Chase (1770) and had a daughter named Rebecca Griffin (~1798). James father Richard Griffin (1734) had a son named William (1762) who had a son named Larkin Griffin born ~1792. William (1762) died (1819) in Robertson Co, TN. Isham Parker (1805) married Sarah Pate (~1804).

William Friday (1819)   1850   Tuscaloosa Co, AL

Jeptha Friday (1827)   1850   Tuscaloosa Co, AL

Henry Friday (1760)   1850   Dublin Beat, Perry Co, AL
His neighbors are Samuel Wiley (1788), Richard Parker (1801), William C Card (1810) and Jmaes Harris (1818). On the other side were Charles Terry (1790), Anderson W Davis (1810) and John T Wilson (1783). (CS)

Henry Friday (1812)   1850   Oktibbeha Co, MS
His neighbors are Green B Stallings (1805) from NC, John McDowell (1769), Allen Maldin (1802), Albert C Miller (1832), David A Walton (1814) from TN, and Hardy Kennedy (1806). On the other side was William P Pullen (1803) from Virginia, David Montgomery (1788) from Fairfield Co, SC, Paul Valentine (1803) from NC, Benjamin S Thomas (1822), Hugh Bell (1789) and William Waker (1806). (CS)

D. H Friday (1813)   1850   Orangeburg, SC
His neighbors were Levisa Gaunt, Israel Gaunt (1797), David Niece, E. Niece and Patrick Niece (1785). On the other side was Rusell Gunter (1784), Rivers Gunter (1799) Aaron Christmas (1803), H.W. Millhouse (1825) and William B Jones (1818). (CS)
Note: Rivers Gunter was Joshua Gunter's father and Polly Gunter's grandfather (Risinger, Dana 2004)!!!!

Elizabeth [Brown] Friday1850   Attala Co, MS
Her neighbors were Lucinda Brown (1780), Major Brown (1800), Thaddius Wigley (1822), Joab Scarborough (1826) "Dept Sheriff" and Hosea Crowder (1813). Six more homes down were John (1819) and Nancy Suddeth (1833). On the other side were Archer "Archibald" Lindsey (1805), John Mangrum (1825), Thomas Reynolds (1800), P.M. Ray (1795), and Jas "James" F. Lowery (1810). (CS)
Note: Thaddeus Wigley (1822) married Nancy Hansbrough (1825) about 1849 in Leake Co, MS. Thomas J Wigley (1794) (uncle of Thadeus) born in Virginia married Ann J. Brown (1798) who was born in Georgia. Thomas was in the war of 1812 under Captain James Green and found at the Battle of New Orleans. John Salamon Mangrum (1825) married Mary Lindsey? and moved to Attala Co, MS about 1844 around the same time the Friday's migrated.

Emmanuel Friday   1850   Attala Co, MS
His neighbors were Joseph Shuler (1811), George Stingiley (1794), B. "Barbara" Derrick-Stingiley (1799), and W.C. Dubard (1822). On the other side were A.G. Anderson (1805), S.C. Clark (1817) and Henry Brown (1805). (CS)

David Friday (1800)   1850   Lexington, SC
He and Margaret (1790) neighbors were Lewis Meets [Meetze] (1800) and Jonas Mathias (1782). On the other side was Andrew Geiger (1798) and Samuel L Lorick (1812). (CS)

The Swabian Connection – Expanded Edition

Anderson Friday (1811) 1850   Edgefield, SC
His neighbors were Bennett Nobles (1805) with Joseph (1800) & Elizabeth Williams (1815) living with the Nobles. The John Goff (1810) household was full with family including the Smella and Hicks. On the other side was Rebecca Youngblood (1793) & children, Evans (1790) & Caty Pressley (1780), Charles (1829) & Elizabeth Kennerly (1830), James (1829) & Margaret Roberson (1830). (CS)

Anderson Friday (1811) 1850   Edgefield, SC
His neighbors were Bennett Nobles (1805) with Joseph (1800) & Elizabeth Williams (1815) living with the Nobles. The John Goff (1810) household was full with family including the Smella and Hicks. On the other side was Rebecca Youngblood (1793) & children with Evans (1790) & Caty Prepley (1780) in the same household. Further down was Charles (1829) & Elizabeth Kennedy (1830), then James (1829) & Elizabeth Roberson (1830), (CS)

Magila Friday (1832)   1850   Fairfield Co, SC
She is living with Phillip Pullig (1792 and family. Her neighbors were Jacob Bookman (1800), Mary A McCants (1800). Five more homes down was Nathan Mann (1790), then John R Kenneday (1820). On the other side was John B Jenkins (1803), Daniel Scott (1800) and Jeremiah McCartha (1814). (CS)

Martin Friday   6-10-1852   South Edisto Rvr/Goodland Swamp Orangeburg Dist, SC
His neighbor was Daniel C. Larey. (SNLP)
Note: Martin is deceased by 6-9-1848, but daughter Ann still living..

Gabriel Friday (1800)   1860   Richland Co, SC
His neighbors were Flora Pettifort (1830), Rueben Smith (1815), William Cook (1827) and Ben Hodge (1820). (CS)
Note: Gabriel is living with Sumter Faust (1826) who is listed as an idiot.

Joseph J Friday (1838)   1860   Titus, TX
He is living with the John Russell (1821) family. Their neighbors were Ambrose Ripley (1835), H.C. Riggs (1824) and David M Smith (1835). (CS)

Daniel H Friday (1813)   1860   Glasscock Co, GA
His neighbors were William Whiter (1813), Elizabeth Hobbs (1810), Richard Hobbs (1831). On the other side were Turner Newsom (1815), Elizabeth Usry (1800) and Samuel Chalker (1818). (CS)

Henry Friday (1815)   1860   Perry Co, AL
His neighbors were Nancy Irvin (1805), Mary Seymour (1796), P. R. Ware (1814), and R.N. Seymour (1826). On the other side were Keziah Stokes (1798) and George Radford (1832). (CS)

Jane [Martha J] Friday-Cabiness 1860   Tuscaloosa Co, AL
Living with husband William R Cabiness and children. Her neighbors are William B Griffin (1834), William C Montgomery (1822) and William Sylivan (1827). On the other side were Thomas J Neighbors (1828), Thos (Thomas) L Wheat (1822) and Reuben Red (1839). (CS)

Leroy Friday (1810)   1860   Dublin, Perry Co, AL
His neighbors were John W. Sanders (1837) and Jauf Summerlin (1813). On the other side were Sampson O'Neal (1810), R. Mitchell (1835), W. H. Gay (1824) and one more house down was John Friday (1808). (CS)

John Friday (1808)   1860   Dublin, Perry Co, AL

The Swabian Connection – Expanded Edition

His neighbors were Benjamin Williams (1784), John B Dugan (1829), S. J. Miller Jr.(1842) and A. H. Burrow (1825). Two more homes down was D. H. Friday (1836).(CS)

D. H. Friday (1836)   1860   Dublin, Perry Co, AL
His neighbor was Alex Barnes (1827). On the other side were Caloin Barnes (1830), A. B. Oden (1812), Burton Paul (1823) and Daniel Terry (1803). Four more homes down Claiborne and Parolee Friday were living with William Gay (1793). (CS)

Claiborne Friday (1839) 1860   Dublin, Perry Co, AL
Lived in the home of William Gay (1793) and wife Lucy (1802). (CS)

Hillard J Friday (1838)   1860   Plantersville, Perry Co, AL
His neighbors were Tomothy Cohwa (1829), Dury Oden (1796) and Anderson Davis (1811). On the other side were Jefferson Ellis (1825), John L. Oden (1825) and S.W. Harvill (1823). Three more homes down was John C. Friday (1837). (CS)

John C. Friday (1837)   1860   Plantersville, Perry Co, AL
His neighbors were S. B. Harville (1830) and Robert R. Peeples (1821). On the other side were Dr. J. H. Phillips (1819), S. A. Duncan (1815) and Isaac Melson (1828). (CS)

Lafayette Friday (1841) 1860   McCrary Dist, Warren, Co, GA
His neighbors were Daniel Swint (1833), Joel Woodward (1828) and Nathan Johnson (1839). On the other side was Malichi Norris (1832), Malichi Williford (1807) and

Aaron Friday (1827)   1860   Oktibbeha, MS
He lived in the home of James H (1821) and Charlotte Steele (1824) and children. Sarah (1837) is his wife and his occupation is a English Teacher. Another ten homes down is a Marlin ("Martin") Friday (1837).(CS)

Marlin ("Martin") Friday (1837)   1860   Oktibbeha, MS
He is living with William Sykes (1833) "Merchant" and his wife Harriet Friday-Sykes (1841) and one child William (1859). (CS)

Samuel Friday (1825)   1860   Oktibbeha, MS
His neighbors are Henry Robinson (1817) and John Walker (1839). On the other side was Charles Nimno (1800) "Postmaster", William Hendon (1835) and Erastus Huntley (1808). (CS)

Reuben Friday (1829)   1860   Oktibbeha, MS
His neighbors were Allen A. Estes (1821), Arthor Skipper (1794) and Daniel Dean (1803). On the other side were Richard Sykes (1831), Irvine Montgomery (1813) and Henry Walker (1824). (CS)

William Friday (1815)   1860   Oktibbeha, MS
His neighbors were David Murphy (1835), William Mckinsey (1827) and Elijah Knox (1810). On the other side were Henry Friday (1815), Holly Murray (1790) and William Clark (1810). (CS)

Henry Friday (1815)   1860   Oktibbeha, MS
His neighbors were Holly Murray (1790), William Clark (1810) and Joe Dickerson (1830). (CS)

Henry Friday (1845)   1860   Oktibbeha, MS
He is living with Nicolus Reedy (1799) ,"Lucinda" (1819) and children. Joseph McGee (1818) and Abram Walker (1810) are neighbors. (CS)

Henry Friday (1815)   1860   Perry Co, AL

His neighbors were Nancy Irvin (1805), Mary Seymour (1796), P. R. Ware (1814), and R.N. Seymour (1826). On the other side were Keziah Stokes (1798) and George Radford (1832). (CS)

George Friday (1787)   1860   Sabine Co,TX
His neighbors were R. R. Burroughs (1829), Louisa J Noble (1821), A. D. (Alfred Davenport) Oliphant (1799) and Joel Halbert (1810). On the other side were J. (Joshua) A. Speights (1819) and Walter Storthers (1806). (CS)

William J Friday (1818) 1860   Tippah Co, MS
His neighbors were Charles Bateman (1814) and on the other side was Jobes Forb (1805). Living with William and family were Gray B Robins (1834) and William Cooper (1836). (CS)

Thomas Friday (1825)   08-31-1867   Little Cedar Creek, Richland District
His neighbors were <u>Elizabeth Metz</u>, David Hamiter, Joseph R Howell, David Gradick and Jesse Wyerick. (SNLP)

Elizabeth [Brown] Friday (1814) 1870   Atlanta, Winn Parish, LA
Her neighbors were the Struce's (Stroud's?). On the other side were J.H. Haddock (1835) and John N Mossley (1813). (CS)

Gabe "Gabriel" Friday   1870   Lexington, SC
His neighbors were Robert McDaniel (1814) and children. (CS)

Thomas Friday   1880   Pickens Co, AL
His neighbors were C. A. & Elizabeth Lancaster, The Stuckey's, Sheridan's, Rhodes and the Noland family. On the other side were John Namner (1840) family and three households of the Clardy families. (CS)

Henry Friday (1814)   1880   Raleigh, Pickens, Alabama
His neighbors were Mrs. M Davis (1845) and Mrs. Jane Cameron (1845). On the other side were Henry Burks (1858) and John Peebles (1823). (CS)

Luinda Friday (1850)   1880   Chilton Co, AL
Her neighbors are Jonah W Frith (1840). On the other side are her family Leroy E Friday (1815), Henry Friday (1840), Joel Friday (1846), Mahalia Price-Friday (1817), John M Seymore (1850) and Luther B. Friday (1842). (CS)

Leroy E Friday (1815)   1880   Chilton Co, AL
(CS)

Henry Friday (1840)   1880   Chilton Co, AL
(CS)

Joel Friday (1846)   1880   Chilton Co, AL
(CS)

Mahalia Price-Friday (1817)1880   Chilton Co, AL
(CS)

Luther B. Friday (1842) 1880   Chilton Co, AL
(CS)

Lemuel D Friday (1826) 1880   Whitefield, Oktibbeha Co, MS

The Swabian Connection – Expanded Edition

His neighbors were Daniel M Harpole (1854), George W. Williams (1830), David Hitchcock (1845). On the other side was Francis Smith (1848), John L Smith (1842) and Joseph McReynolds (1828). (CS)

Laura Friday-Stroud (1848) 1880   Winn Parish, LA
Her and William's neighbors were James Griffin (1843) and John Cuff (1826). On the other side was Allison J. Jones (1854) and James R Spillers (1850). (CS)

Sarah A Friday-Mullins (1844) 1880   Van Zandt, Texas
Her and Samuel's neighbors were Greenville W. Loyd (1822) and Ben F. McCarty (1846). On the other side was Gideon N. Luceford (1846) and Samuel High (1809). (CS)

Mary A Friday-Brown (1840) 1880   Henderson Co, TX
Her and William's neighbors were Elizabeth Grissam (1849) and Mary McCrany (1826). On ther other side was Robert Larance (1823) and Jesse J Jahus (1833). (CS)

Margaret J Friday (1844) 1880   Pleasant Grove, Panola, MS
Living with husband Gray B Robbins and family. Mother Sarah Friday (1818) also in household. Her neighbors were William S Perry (1820), S. Holenger (1847), J.F. Harris (1850) and Peter Merphey (1845). On the other side was W.O. Kishul (1852). (CS)

Gabriel B Friday (1832) 1880   Saline, Howard Co, Arkansas
His neighbors were William Anderson (1842) and Smith Whitten (1857). On the other side were Sims P. Dillard (1813) and Thomas Oddell (1840). (CS)

Berryman Friday (1849) 1880   Warren, Columbia Co, Arkansas
Father Godfrey (1801) is living with family. His neighbors were Bryant A Page (1853) and Daniel J Smith (1816). On the other side were Vinson A Lindsey (1856) and Vinson "Vincent" A Friday (1825). (CS)

Vincent A Friday (1825) 1880   Warren, Columbia Co, Arkansas
Living with mother Rebecca (1810) and sister Rebecca (1848). (CS)

Thomas "George" Friday (1858) 1880   Natchitoches Parish, LA
His neighbor was his father William Fridy "Friday" (1827). On ther other side was Joseph Harper (1845). (CS)

William Fridy (1829)   1880   Natchitoches Parish, LA

William Fridy (Friday) (1827)   1880   2nd Ward, Natchitoches, Louisiana
His neighbors were William Stewart (1833), Randal Woods (1850) and Ed Brewton (1852). On the other side is Thomas (George) Friday (1856) his son, Joseph Harper (1845), Henry Weaver (1829) & Henry Henagan (Hennigan) (1857).

Tabitha (Friday) Wood   1880   Natchitoches Parish, LA
Her neighbors are her Father George Thomas Friday. On the other side two homes down is William Lowrey (1833) and family; another three homes down is Alexander Stewart (1822), his wife Mary Weaver-Stewart with family. (CS)

George Friday (1854)   1880   Grant Parish, LA
His wife and Aurora neighbors are Eliza Williams (1835) and Tim Coleman (1850). On the other side was M. Swafford (1830) and Jeff Hucherson (1857). (CS)

William Friday (1859)   1880   Grant Parish, LA

The Swabian Connection – Expanded Edition

He is living with Altermira (1860) and Alavada Friday (1877) of whom their relationship is unknown/other. Their neighbors were Tom Fletcher (1806) and George Fletcher (1845). (CS)

Wesley Friday (1855)   1880   Lincoln, Louisiana
He was living and working with relatives Daniel L Green (1852) and family. (CS)

* Note: Many records still showed in the various land records names of the landowner's years after being deceased. Birth years have been found by various sources including ancestry.com, online genealogy and family histories web sites.

Legend:

(Deed) = Land Deed

(RG) = Royal Grant

(CP) = Colonial Plat

(CS) = Census Record

(SNLP) = Surveyed Neighbor's Land Plat

(EST) = Estate (note, bonds & receipts)

(CRCH) = Church documents, lists/signatures.

(PETN) = Petition

(TXL) = Tax List or Tax Digest

(RLC) = Reports of Legislative Committe

Underline = Specified Owner Plat who has been surveyed/recorded.

Note: Many recorded (Birth Years) are found by searching http://wc.rootsweb.com database.

Index of Land Grants/Plats in South Carolina (1700's)
(Saxe Gotha, Dutch Fork or various other land grants/plats)

Recorded entries in the SC Department of Archives ---

Name: Date:	Acres:	Entry Numbers:
Hans Fridig 10-04-1735 200 Lot 398. ....Twp. Lot		0009 003 0009 00444 01
Hans Fridig 09-17-1736 200 Surv.22-Oct-1735. Lot 398		0002 005 0034 00522 01

Martin Friday 02-06-1736 approved 9-16-1738 Lot # 11 corners of Front & Bull Streets, but left vacant.

Martin Friday 02-27-1739 100 acres Six Mile Creek w/in Saxe Gotha Colonial Plats Vol 12 Pg 38

Martin Friday 5-11-1739 150 acres in Saxe Gotha

Martin Friday 06-5-1742 Land Grant for 50 acres ajoining his land up the river and 1 town lot in Berkley Co, SC 0002 005 0042 00138 00

Martin Friday 03-13-1744 Plat 100 acres for young child and orphan.

The Swabian Connection – Expanded Edition

Martin Friday 3-12-1745 Plat for 100 acres in SaxeGotha Township   0009 003 0012 00039 01

John Friday 09-14-1747 Plat for 100 acres in SaxeGotha Township   0009 003 0004 00374 01

John Friday 04-13-1748 Land Grant for 100 acres in SaxeGotha Township 0002 003 0042 00292 00

Martin Fridig 09-13-1748 purchased 100 acres from Thomas Browns for two hundred pounds.

John J Fridig 01-09-1755 Land grant for 150 acres on the Saluda River. 0002 005 0006 00258 00

John Jacob Friday 1-19-1755 150 acres opposite (North) side of Saluda or Santee River to Saxe Gotha Township; family of three children. Source: SCCJ, Vol I, 13 March 1744.

Martin Fridig 07-24-1756 purchased 150 acres from Michael Scholuder for two hundred pounds on Chinkapin Creek.

John Martin Friday 3-16-1763 Memorial for 100 acres in Saxe Gotha Township and Berkley County. 0030 002 0006 00052 02

David Friday 04-11-1763 Memorial for two tracts in SaxeGotha Township, One for 100 acres summarizing a chain of title to a grant of Sept 16, 1738 to John Mathews and one for 25 acres summarizing a chain of title to a grant of Sep 16, 1738 to John Colman. 0030 002 0006 00074 00

David Friday 01-20-1768 300 acres on Mill Creek Berkley Co.   0009 003 0009 00218 02

David Friday 08-02-1768 Grant for 300 acres in Berkley Co.   0002 005 0016 00535 00

David Friday 09-29-1768 Memorial for 300 acres on Mill Creek, Berkley Co 0009 003 0009 00218 02

John Jacob Friday 05-07-1771 Plat for 200 acres on Long Branch in Leesville, SC 0009 003 0015 00219 03

Jacob Friday 5-8-1771 50 Acres in SaxaGotha Township, SC on the Congaree River

Jacob Friday 11-2-1771 200 acres in Leesville, SC. 9-3-15-219-3

John Jacob Friday 01-13-1772 Memorial for 50 acres in SaxeGotha Township 0030 002 0011 00106 05

John Martin Friday 12-03-1772 Plat for 400 acres in Granville, Co 000 003 0015 00220 01

David Friday 2-26-1773 Plat for 250 acres in Colleton Co   0009 003 0015 00219 01

John Martin Friday 6-7-1774 land grant for 400 acres in Granville County. 0009 003 0015 00220 01

John Martin Friday 11-04-1774 Memorial for 400 acres Buffalo Creek Granville, County 0030 002 0013 00085 01

David Friday 8-23-1774 Land grant for 250 acres in Colloton County, SC 0030 002 0013 00297 04

David Fridig 1775-77 John Jacob Deed of gift to David Fridig   0007 001 04P0 00118 00

David Friday 2-9-1775 250 acres between Savannah & Saluda river Colleton, Co 0030002001300297 04

Note: The above 18 digits are the SC Dept of Archives Alphabetical Index reference number.

Where the South Carolina Fridigs lived (1735-1870)

Name (Birth)	Date	Location	Source
Martin (1689)	1749	Lived on the road by Fall Creek, Saxe Gotha, SC	SCJ
Gabriel (1728)	1799	Cedar Creek and Broad River, Lexington Dist, SC	BFA
David (1723?)	1750?	Descendants in the fork of the Edisto River.	C&M
David (1723?)	1763	Saxe-Gotha Township, SC	SCA
David (1723?)	1768	Mill Creek Branch S Side Congaree River	C&M
David (1723?)	2-1773	Red Bank Creek of Little Saluda	DDR
John M (1748)	1763	Saxe-Gotha Township, Berkley Co, SC	SCA
John M (1748)	9-1774	Bufalo Creek, Granville Co, SC	SCA
Hans (1689)	1735	Berkley Co, SC	SCA
John J (1719)	6-1754	Saluda River. Near mouth of Kennerly/Geiger's Cr	SCJ
Jacob (1719)	1755-67	Saxe-Gotha Township, SC	SCA
John J (1719)	5-1771	Long Branch Creek, Batesburg-Leesville, SC	LM
John J (1719)	3-1744	opposte Nrth side of Saluda/Santee River to SaxeGotha	SCCJ
John	7-1785	Turkey Hill branch (waters of Edisto) Orangeburg, SC	SCA
John J (1719)	1747	Lived on 12-mile creek.	SCA
John (?)	1800	Fairfield Dist, SC	FC
Hinton (1810)	1870	Gregg Township, SC	SCS
Thoms M (1817)	1870	Tabernacle Township, Orangeburg Dist, SC	SCS
Gabe (1799)	1870	Columbia, Richland Co, SC	SCS
Anderson (1812)	1860	Edgefield Dist, Ridge, SC	SCS
William (?)	1840	Ches, Charleston, SC	SCS
Henry (1760)	1820	Richland Co and Orangeburg, SC	SCS
Martin (1783)	1820-48	Springfield, Orangeburg Co, SC	SCS
Thoms M(1817)	1843	Aiken, SC Orangeburg Co, SC	ES
Patrick A(1842)	3-1864	Graniteville, Edgefield, SC	SCM
George (1787)	1833	Tuscaloosa Co, AL	LP
Fridig's (Jacob?)	10-1784	Chinquapin Creek, Orangeburg Dist, SC	SCA
Godfrey (1801)	1832	Branch of Little Stevens Creek. Edgefield Dist, SC BFA,	SCS
William (1774-84)	1800	Old Bush River Rd/High Hill Crk. Dutch Fork – Lextn,SC	SCS
Godfrey (1770)	1820	Orange Co, SC	SCS
Gabriel (1752)	1800-30	W Columbia, SC	DR
John (1743)	1800	Granby, SC	SCS
Samuel Fridig(1755-74)	1800	Lexington Co, SC Forks of Saludee & Broad Rvr	SCS
Godfrey	1847	Pen(n) & Stevens Crk,Little Saluda,Svnnh Rvr,Little Crk	LS
Samuel Friday(1775-84)	1795	Rawls/Ralls creek between the Saluda and the Broad	LS
Hans (1690)	1735	Near the Crnr of Fenwick St (now Henley) & Middleton	SCA
David Friday (1775)	1820	Near Burculow/Burckalow Creek - Orangeburg, SC	SCA

Legend:

SCA = South Carolina Archives
SCM = South Carolina Marriages
SCW = South Carolina Wills
SCHGM = SC Historical & Genealogical Magazine
FC = Federal Census
SCMAR = SC Magazine for Ancestral Research
JCHA = Journal of the Commons House of Assembly
CBR = Child Birth Record
DR = Death Record
BR = Birth Record
BFA = Bill Friday Archives
C&M = Citizens and Immigrants, SC 1768
SCS = South Carolina Census
SCJ = South Carolina Journals petition for land.
ES = Estate Sale
LM = Land Map
DDR = Deed Record
SCCJ = South Carolina Council Journals
LP = Land Purchase
TR = Tax Roll
FR=Family Record
LS = Land Survey

SC Census Records for the Fridigs 1790-1830

Name	Cens Year	M -10	M 10-16	M 16-26	M 26-45	M 45+	Fm -10	Fm 10-16	Fm 16-26	Fm 26-45	Fm 45+	A F	Dist/Co
Jacob*	1778i												Orngebrg
David	1778i												Orngebrg
Samuel	1788i												Orng/Lex
John	1788i												Orng/Lex
John	1790		2 - U16	2								3	Fairfield
William*	1790		1- 16S+										Orngebrg
Daniel	1800				1								Lexington
Gabriel	1800			1	1			1		1			Lexington
John	1800	2	1			1	4	2	3		1		Lexington
John Martin	1800	3			1		1			1			Lexington
Samuel	1800	3		1						1			Lexington
William	1800		1	2			1			1			Lexington
Godfrey*	1800		1		1		2			1			Orange
Samuel*	1800	3	2		1				1				Lexington
William*	1800			2			1	1			1		Lexington
John	1800	3			1	1				1			Fairfield
David	1810				1								Lexington
David	1810		2	1			1				1		Fairfield
Gabriel	1810				1				1		1		Lexington
Henry	1810	1	2		1		1	1		1			Richland

275

The Swabian Connection – Expanded Edition

Name	Year	C1	C2	C3	C4	C5	C6	C7	C8	C9	C10	Dist/Co
John	1810	1	1		1		1		1		1	Lexington
M	1810				1				1			Orngebrg
Martin	1820				1		1			1		Orngebrg
David	1820			2 18-26	1			1			1	Fairfield
David	1820	2			1							Orngebrg
David	1820	1		1 18-26	1	1	1	1	1			Lexington
Gabriel	1820						1			1	1	Lexington
Godfrey	1820	2		1 16-18			1					Edgefield
Henry	1820		2	1 16-18			1	1	1		1	Richland
John	1820						1		1		1	Lexington
Martin	1820				1		1			1		Orngebrg
William	1820											Charlestn
M Fridy	1820	1			1					1		Orngebrg
Anne	1830											Orngebrg
David	1830	2 <5	1 <10	2 (10-15)				1 (40-50)				Lexington
David	1830											Orngebrg
Gabe O	1830											Lexington
Godfrey	1830	3 <10				1 <30	1 <5					Edgefield
Henry	1830					4 <30						Richland
Martin	1830											Orngebrg
Milley	1830		1 <10									Fairfield
Peggy	1830				1 <30	1 <40						Fairfield
Samuel	1830	2 <5	1 <10		1 <30							Lexington
William	1830											Charlestn
William	1840											Charlestn
Martin	1840	1			1							Orngebrg
Gabriel	1840											Fairfield
James K	1850	3										Richland

Legend:
M = Males
* = Listed as Fridig
Fm = Females
AFm = All Females Including head of families.
-U16 = Under 16
Dist/Co = District or County
Cens Year = Census Year
Orngebrg = Orangeburg Co
i = SC Early Census Index
S=Self

John Friday - 1790 Census - Camden Dist, Fairfield Co, SC. John is one of two male men 16+ plus years of age including heads of families, two male boys under –16, and 3 females including one heads of families living in home.

William Fridig – 1790 Census – Orangeburg Co, SC. William is the only male 16+ plus years in the heads of families.

Gabriel Fridig – 1790 Census – Orangeburg Co, SC. Gabriel is one male 16+ plus years of age including heads of families, two boys under –16 and 2 females including heads of families living in home. 5S.

Margaret Fridig - 1790 Census – Orangeburg Co, SC. Margaret is one of four females including heads of families living in home. 1S.

John Fridig - 1790 Census – Orangeburg Co, SC. John is one of two males plus +16 years including head of families, two males under –16 years of age, and three females including heads of families living in home. 4S.

William Fiddy – 1790 Census - St. Phillips Parish, Charleston, SC. William is one of two males 16+ plus years living in the home. 4S

John Firdig (Fridig) – 1800 Census – Fairfield, SC. John has three males under –10 years of age, one male +45 years of age (Himself), one female under –10, one female plus +45 living in home. 1S.

Samuel Fridig - 1800 Census – Lexington Co, SC. Samuel has three males under –10 years of age, one male (Himself) 26-44 years old, and one female 26-44. 7S. Pg. 345 32010-00100-07

Samuel Friday - 1800 Census – Lexington Co, SC. Samuel three males under –10 years of age, one male (Himself) 16-25 years old, and one female 26-44 living in the home. 1S Pg. 269 30100-00010-01

John Martin Friday - 1800 Census – Lexington Co, SC. John M has three males under –10 years of age, one male (Himself) 26-44 years old, one female under –10, and one female 26-45. 1S. Pg. 266/573 30010-10010-01

William Friday - 1800 Census – Lexington Co, SC. William has one male 10-15, two males 16-25, one female under –10, and one female 26-44 years old in the home. 1S. Pg. 267/573 01200-10010-01

Godfrey Fridig – 1800 Census – Orange Co, SC. Godfrey has one male 10-15, one male (Himself) 26-44, two females under –10, and one female 26-44 years of age living in the home. Pg. 325 01010-20010-00

William Fridig – 1800 – Lexington Co, SC. William is one of two males 16-25. Also there is one female 10-15, two females 16-25 and one female +45 years of age living in the home. Pg. 333/497 00020-01101-00

John Friday – 1800 Census – Lexington Co, SC. John has two males under –10, one male 10-15, one male (Himself) plus +45, four females under –10, two females 10-15, three females 16-25, and one female plus +45 living in home. 6S. Pg. 264/571 21001-42301-06

Gabriel Friday - 1800 Census p. 264 – Lexington Co, SC. Gabriel has one male 16-25, one male (Himself) 26-44, one female 10-15 and one female 26-44 years old in the home. 8S. Pg. 571 00110-01010-08

Daniel Friday – 1800 Census - Lexington Co, SC. Daniel is one male 26-45 years of age living alone in the home. Pg. 571 00010-00000-00

John Friday – 1810 Census – Lexington Co, SC. John has one male under -10 and another male 10-15 years of Age. There is also one female -10, another female 16-15 and wife/mother 45+ years of age. Pg. 76

David Friday – 1810 Census – Fairfield Co, SC. David has two males 10-15, one male (Himself) 16-25, one female under –10, and one female +45 years of age living in the home. 1S Pg. 192

Gabriel Friday – 1810 Census – Lexington Co, SC. Gabriel is 45+ years old and has one female 16-26 plus his 45+ wife living in the household. Pg. 69

M (Martin) Friday – 1810 Census – Orangeburg, SC. Martin has one male (Himself) 26-44, and one female 16-25 living in the home. Pg. 136

Henry Friday - 1810 Census –Columbia, Richland Co, SC. Henry has one male under –10, two male 10-15, one male (Himself) 26-44, one female under –10, one female 10-15 and one female 26-45 years of age living in the home. Pg. 177

John Friday – 1820 Lexington Co, SC. John is 45+ years of age, and has one female 16-26, one female 45+ in the household. Three persons are engaged in Agriculture. 3S

David Friday - 1810 Census – Lexington Co, SC. David is the only male 26-45 living in the home. Pg. 65

David Friday – 1820 Census - Fairfield, SC. David has two males 16-26, one male (Himself) 26-45 years of age, one female 10-16, and one female +45 years old. 5 persons engaged in agriculture. 0S

William Friday – 1820 Charlestown Neck, SC. William Jr? may be the only person in the home. No entries were made to this census other than his name other than "All other free persons". Pg. 73A 000000-00000

Godfrey Friday – 1820 Edgefield, SC. Godfrey had two males under –10, one male 16-18, and one male (Himself) +45 years of age. Additionally there are 2 females 10-16, and one female +45 years of age living in the home. 2 persons engaged in Agriculture. Pg. 125 201001-02010

Henry Friday – 1820 Richland Co, SC. Henry has two males 10-16, one male 16-18, one male (Himself) +45, one female under –10, one female 16-26, and one female +45. Three persons engaged in Agriculture. 0S. Pg. 93 021001-10101

Martin Friday – 1820 Orangeburg, SC. Martin has one male (Himself) 26-45, one female under –10, and one female 26-45 years of age in the home. Eight persons are engaged in Agriculture. Pg. 221 000010-10010

Martin Fridy – 1820 Orangeburg, SC. Martin (same person as record above? – different location) has one male under –5, one male (Himself) 26-45, and one female 26-45 years of age in the home. Eight persons are engaged in Agriculture. Pg. 214 100010-00010

The Swabian Connection – Expanded Edition

David Friday - 1820 Orangeburg, SC. David has two males under −10, one male (Himself) 26-45, and one female 16-26 living in the home. Two persons are engaged in agriculture. Pg. 221 200010-00100

David Friday - 1820 Orangeburg, SC. David (same person as record above – different location with wife) has two males under −10, one male (Himself) 26-45, and one female +45 years of age living in the home. One person is engaged in agriculture. Pg. 216 200010-0001

Mrs. Friddy – 1820 Charleston, SC Pg. 203

David Friday – 1830 Lexington Co, SC. David has two males under −5, one male 5-10, two males 10-15, and one male (Himself) 40-50 years old, one female 5-10, one female 10-15, and one female 30-40 years of age living in household.

Samuel Friday - 1830 Lexington Co, SC. Samuel has two males under −5, one male 5-10, one male 20-30, one female under −5, one female 5-10 and one female 20-30 living in household.

Where the Fridings were & when.

Name (Birth):	Date:	Location:	Source:
Gabriel (1752)	1830	Columbia, SC	Grave, SCA
Gabriel (1752)	1790	Orangeburg Dist, North, SC	FC
Gabriel (1728)	1799	Lexington Dist, SC	BFA
Godfrey (1801)	1832	Edgefield Dist, SC	CBR
Hinton (1814)	1850	Edgefield Co, SC	Census
Anderson (1812)	1850	Edgefield Co, SC	Census
George (1787)	1810-14	Stewart Co, TN	RC
George (1787)	1830	Tuscaloosa Co, AL	FC
Thomas (1805)	1830	Tuscaloosa Co, AL	FC
Thomas (1805)	9-20-1827	Tuscaloosa Co, AL	Marriage
Gabriel B (1832)	1878	Clarksville, TX	CBR
Gabriel B (1832)	1865	Columbia CO, AR	CBR
John Jacob (1719)	5-1771	Leesville, Lexington Co, SC	LM
Thomas M (1817)	1843	Granville Co, SC	ES
John Martin	1763-1774	Granville Co, SC	SCA
Martin (1689)	1758	Saxe Gotha, SC	DR
Martin (1689)	8-18-1719	Muri Bern, Switzerland	CBR
Martin (1689)	1728	Stettlen, Switzerland	CBR
David (1723)	1783	St.John, Paula Inlet, FL	FL Census
David (1723)	3-12-1749	Saxe Gotha, SC	SCW
David (1723)	1760	Cherokee Path	SCMAR
David (1723)	6-13-1760	Saxe Gotha	SCMAR
David (1723)	2-26-1773	Colleton Co, SC	SCMAR
J Jacob Fridig	6-13-1760	Saxe Gotha	SCMAR
John Fridig	1760	Cherokee Path	SCMAR
John Fridig (17xx)	1800	Fairfield Dist, SC	FC
John Fridig (17xx)	1800	Fairfield Dist, SC	FC
Daniel (1750)	1800	Lexington,SC	FC
Martin (1783)	1800's	Springfield,(Graniteville),SC	Home, SCA
Martin (1783)	3-2-1824	Edgefield Dist, SC	SCA
Samuel D	1846	Lexington Dist, SC	SCA

The Swabian Connection – Expanded Edition

James K	1859	Columbia, SC	City Directory
David	1859	Columbia, SC	City Directory
Hager	1816	SC	SCM
Christianna	1819	SC	SCM
Hans Frydig	1749	Orangeburg, SC	SCHGM
John Fridig	1790	Orangeburg Dist, North, SC	FC
William Fridig	1790	Orangeburg Dist, North, SC	FC
Margaret Fridig	1790	Orangeburg Dist, North, SC	FC
William W	1856	Canton, VanZandt Co, TX	CBR
William W (1827)	1-7-1869	Chestnut, Natchitoches Par, LA	2ND Marriage
William W (1827)	1870	Chestnut, Natchitoches Par, LA	CBR
William W (1827)	1853	Henderson Co, TX	1ST Marriage
George T (1856)	12-6-1877	Natchitoches Par, LA	Marriage
Sarah Ann (1844)	8-18-1859	Natchitoches Par, LA	Marriage
Thomas F (1805)	1844	Attala CO, MS	CBT
George (1787)	1833	Tuscaloosa Co, AL	LP
Mary Ann (1832)	8-26-1857	Tuscaloosa Co, AL	Marriage
Jeptha Jackson (1829)	9-6-1850	Tuscaloosa Co, AL	Marriage
Thomas F (1805)	9-20-1827	Tuscaloosa Co, AL	Marriage
Laura (1850)	1-13-1931	Winn Par, LA DR	
Harmon (1870)	1870-1951	Chestnut, Natchitoches Par,LA	BR & DR
Godfrey (1770)	1800	Orangeburg, SC	FC
Patrick A (1842)	3-6-1864	Graniteville, Edgefield, SC	Marriage
Jeptha J (1829)	7-2-1860	Winn Parish, LA	LP
Emanuel (1792)	1835, 1848-54	Attala Co, MS	TR
George (1787)	1810	Stewart Co, TN	TL
L.S. (1873)	1907	Uvalde Co, TX	FR

Legend:
GC = Georgia Census
SCA = South Carolina Archives
SC = South Carolina
ND = No Date
DR = Dead Roll
MCD = Marion County, MS Deed
SCS = South Carolina Census
ARC =Arkanasas Census Record
LR = Land Record
AA = Anals of Alabama
TL = Tax List
RC = Reconstructed Census

Those who went by the name Frydig/Fridig
Pronounced: {Fri-dee/Fry-dee}

Translated from -- Frydig or Fridig "Swiss" to Fridig "Colonial" to Friday/Fridy/Fryday "American".

The following are recorded entries where the name was spelled as Fridig.

Martin Fridig (1689) – son of Peter Fridig.
Source: SC Archives

David Fridig (1735?) – son of Martin Fridig.
Source: SC Archives

John Jacob Fridig (1719) – son of Martin Fridig.
Source: SC Archives and Revolutionary war Index (State Library of SC).

Peter Fridig (d. after 1803) – unknown.
Source: Constable in SC Archives

Godfrey Fridig (1770) – son of Gabriel (1728)
Source: 1800 Orange Co, SC Census & the 1839 William Dubard (1765) Will.
Note: The 1839 Will of William Dubard of Richland Co, SC is the last record of the Fridig name.

Anny Fridig (?) – unknown or wife of Gabriel (1752)
Source: SC Archives

Gabriel Fridig (1752) – son of John Jacob or Samuel Fridig.
Source: Tombstone, SC Archives and Revolutionary war Index (State Library of SC).

Anna "Mary" (Dreher) Kinsler-Fridig (1750) – wife of Gabriel Fridig.
Source: Tombstone and SC Archives.

John Fridig –
Source: SC Archives and Revolutionary war Index (State Library of SC).

Daniel Fridig (1750) – son of David Fridig.
Source: SC Archives

John Martin Fridig (1748) – son of Martin Fridig.
Source: SC Archives and Revolutionary war Index (State Library of SC) & Stub Entries to Indents Issued in Payment of Claims against South Carolina Bk I : by A.S. Salley.

Hans Fridig –
Source: SC Archives and Book of Record Orangeburg Church 1737-1761.

Barbara Fridig – wife of John Jacob Fridig.
Source: SC Archives

Johannes Frydig/Frydig –
Source: Book of Record Orangeburg Church 1737-1761.

Mary Elizabeth Fridig (1748) – daughter of John Friday (1728).
Source: Book of Record Orangeburg Church 1737-1761.

Henry Fryding Jr –
Source: Book of Record Orangeburg Church 1737-1761.

The Swabian Connection – Expanded Edition

Hans George Fridig – Infant son of John Friday (1728).
Source: Book of Record Orangeburg Church 1737-1761.

James Fridig (?) – son of Samuel David Friday-James Knox(1822) or James Kershaw(1877)?
Source: Revolutionary war Index (State Library of SC).

Peggy Fridig – daughter of Gabriel Fridig?(1728).
Source: Bill Friday records.

William Fridig – unknown
Source: 1790 & 1800 South Carolina Census.

Margaret Fridig – wife of Samuel Fridig.
Source: 1790 South Carolina Census.

Gabrial Fridig (1728) – son of Martin Friday (1689).
Source: Bill Friday records, SCA.

Polly Fridig (?) – wife of David Kleckley.

Samuel Fridig –
Source: 1800 Lexington Co, SC Census.

James Fridig –
Source: SC Revolutionary war roll AA 624.

Adam Fridig (?)(*) – Possible Black sharecropper for the Fridig's.
Source: 1870 South Carolina Census.

Milley Fridig (1791) – wife of David Friday
Source: Estate and Chattels Sale (May 1827) of David Friday born (abt 1794).

Gabriel Fridig (1800) – brother of David Friday born (abt 1794).
Source: Estate and Chattels Sale (May 1827) of David Friday born (abt 1794).

Fridig Arthur (1774) – son of Elizabeth Friday and William Arthur.
Source: SCDAH - Senate Committee on Privledges and Elections (12-3-1822) Lexington Dist, SC.

Most Fridig's used the Friday name quite frequently back and forth during the record keeping of title property changes, petitions, tombstones and the sell of personal property. The second to last Friday to use the name Fridig was Gabriel (1752-1830) at his burial place in Columbia, SC. The very last record is Godfrey Fridig (1770) in the 1839 Estate papers of William Dubard (1765). The First Fridig to use the Friday name was either Martin Friday (1689) or John Friday (1690). The Fridig name is mentioned 7(x) in the South Carolina Gazette newspaper for publication years 1732 through 1775, the Gazette of South Carolina for publication years 1777 thru 1780, and the South Carolina & American General Gazette for publication years 1764 thru 1767. In the 1790 census, Gabriel, John, Margaret and William (all of Lexington County) were listed with the name Fridig with the exception of John Friday in the Camden District. Godfrey, Samuel and William were the last to use Fridig in the Lexington, SC Census records.

Today the Freidig (est 1380) name is used in the Simmental Region of Switzerland, which is in the Adelboden area. However, the Frydig name is being used in the Frutigen, Canton Bern, Switzerland where Martin (1689) was born.

The Swabian Connection – Expanded Edition

A literal translation of the name Fridig is peacemaker (Friday, Bill). In the German or Swiss Language, words ending in (ig) are usually pronounced as though they ended in (y) or (ie), hence Fridig becomes Fridy or Fridie, the same as the southern pronunciation of the day of the week, Friday (Friday, Bill 1999). The translation of Friday in Swiss is Friitig. The word Frieden in German is translated to Peace.

Frydig is first documented in the Orangeburgh Citizens Petition in Behalf of Rev. John Giessendanner on May 27, 1749 by Hans Frydig and his Hans Frydig Junr who both signed the petition with many others in the Township of Orangeburg. Frydig is documented 2(x) in SCDAH land records. The first occurrence is on June 4, 1754 for a 150 acre warrant requested by John Jacob Frydig. The second occurrence is for Casper Mathys memorial for 100 acres of land near John Jacob Frydig on Sept 9, 1765.

A spokesperson for the Swiss Federal Archives found the name Frydig (Freidig*) in the Swiss family name book having three places of Origin (Heimatort) "Town of Origin" or *commune d'origine,* of that being from the Bern of Frutigen*, Kandergrund, and Oberwil, Switzerland.

Time Line
724---2012

YYYY-MM-DD

724	- Berthold Ahalolfings ~694 founded Reichenau monastery in Germany.
850	- Erchanger Fridingun mentions in St.Gallen monastery records.
912	- Erchanger & Berthold begin construction on Castle Hohentwiel.
920-10-30	- Erchanger Fridiger contract ends w/St.Gallen monastery.
1089	- Folkmar Fridingen (~1059) is living @ Martinweiler, Germany.
1090	- Fridingen alt-Fridinga established from Reichenau formerly St. Gall.
1200	- Swiss plateau comprised the dominions of the houses of Savoy, Zähringer, Habsburg and Kyburg.
1209	- Bishop Albert Fritingen/Fridingen purchased castle Steinsberg.
1276-01-01	- Burkhart Fridingen purchsed the Salem monastery @ Grundelbuch.
1291	- 3 Swiss states of Uri, Schwyz & Unterwalden unite against agressors.
1351	- Zurich joins the Swiss Federation.
1352	- Glarus and Zug join the Swiss Federation.
1353	- Bern joins the Swiss Federation.
1386	- Battle of Sempach {Meiersholz, Switzerland} Swiss Confederation (Uri, Schwyz, Unterwalden, & Lucern) against Hapsburgs Austrian army.
1409	- first mentioned as Valle Adelboden.
1431	- Margaret Erlbach-Freidingen (~1372) sold castle Shenkenburg
1440-46	- Zurich War: conflict between 7 other cantons.
1460	- Foundation of the first university of Switzerland at Basel.
1481	- Fribourg and Solothurn join the Swiss Federation.
1499	- Swabian/Swiss War: btwn Old Swiss Confedrcy & House of Hapsburg
1501	- Basel and Schaffhausen join the Swiss Federation.
1513	- Appenzell joins the Swiss Federation.
1519	- Swiss Protestant Ulrich Thomas stirs revolt in Switzerland.
1522	- Beginning of the "Reformation".
1535	- Birth of Gwer Fridig Adelboden, Switzerland.
1536	- John Calvin publishes "Institutes of the Christian Religion" .
1541	- Calvin established theocracy in Geneva, Switzerland.

1556	- Marriage of Anna Spillman to Gwer Fridig Adelboden, Switzerland
1558-09-25	- Birth of Johannes Fridig Adelboden, Switzerland
1784-5-5	- Birth if Gwer Fridig Switzerland Adelboden, Switzerland
1565	- St. Augustine, Florida founded.
1582-05-27	- Marriage of Christina Daenzer to Gwer Fridig Adelboden, Switzerland
1784-5-5	- Birth of Berchtold Fridig Adelboden, Switzerland
1616-04-08	- Marriage of Trini Bercher to Berchtold Adelboden, Switzerland
1618-12-13	- Birth of Peter Fridig Adelboden, Switzerland
1648	- Switzerland becomes and independent nation.
1649-11-25	- Birth of Peter Fridig Adelboden, Switzerland
1674	- Accord signed between the Lord Propertors of Carolina.
1682	- South Carolina founded from NC.
1687	- First residents of Natchitoches, Louisiana were Canary Islanders.
1689-06-23	- Birth of Martin Fridig/Friday Frutigen, Switzerland. Son of Peter.
1690?	- Birth of John Friday SR Switzerland
1714	- Natchitoches Parish, LA established for business river district.
1723	- Birth of David Friday son of Martin Fridig Orangeburg, SC
1728	- Birth of John Friday JR Prob.. Lucerne, Luzern, Switzerland
1728-04-18	- Birth of Gabriel Fridig Canton: Bern: Stettlen, Switzerland
1731-08-14	- Birth of Elizabeth Fridig Switzerland.
1731-09	- Colonel Jean Pierre Purry's pamphlet distributed in Switzerland.
1732	- Captain Purry's first party to reach Charleston, SC.
1732-12-2	- 50 Palatines expected.
1733-07-25	- Salzburgers for Purrysburg.
1734-11	- 260 Swiss for Purrysburg arrive at Charleston, SC.
1735 to.	- Saxe Gotha established in 1735 by the Colonial gov't of King George II
1735	- SC Surveyed border to Nrth Carolina & marks pine tree by blazing.
1735-02-07	- Fridig's arrived on the ship "William" at Charleston, SC.
1735-07	- 250 German Switzers arrive at Charleston, SC.
1735-07	- 200 German Palatines arrive at Charleston, SC.
1735-07	- 250 German-Swiss arrive at Charleston, SC.
1736-10	- A large number (170) of German Swiss People arrive at SC.
1735-10-22	- Grant of 200 acres of land to Hans Freydag Orangeburg, SC Township
1737-02 (Toggenburg)	- Above 200 Switzers out of the canton of Tockenburgh
1737	- Rev John U. Giessendanner began work at St. Matthews Lutheran Ch.
1738-11-12	- Voyage of Jacob Gallman 2nd letter to relatives in Zurich,Switzerland.
1740-02-28	- Hans Jacob Riemensperger & Hans Caspar Gallister distribute brochure throughout Germany and Switzerland.
1744	- First reference to the location of Dutch fork between the Saluda and Broad.
1744	- Captain Ham's ship, which brought over some Swiss from Bern.
1744-12	- Capt. Brown's ship with 100 Palatines arrive at SC.
1740-02-02	- Witnesses - Brochure to migrate to SC. Jacob and Martin Fridig.
1741-05-24	- Verena Fridig witness and sponsor to Hans Henry Strauman Baptism
1743-56	- James Glen was royal governor of South Carolina.
1745-04-15	- Easter Service at Church of Orangeburg w/Hans Fridig SR & Wife.
1749	- Start of Friday's Ferry by Martin Friday
1750	- Anglicanism (Anglican Tradition) started in Orangeburg, SC.
1750-12-02	- Baptism of Hans George Fridig Orangeburg, SC
1750-09-30	- Baptism of Johannes Fridig Orangeburg, SC
1750	- Robert, Jacob Geiger sought permission to establish Ferry – Denied.
1752	- Birth of Gabriel Friday in South Carolina.

The Swabian Connection – Expanded Edition

1753-01-16	- Johannes Tobler brochure for attracting more settlers from eastern Switzerland.
1754	- Provincial ferry concession for Martin Friday from Saxe Gotha
1755-7-02	- Treaty of the old Town Saluda with 500 Cherokee Indians.
1759-6-18	- Burial of John Friday Churchyard, Orangeburgh, South Carolina
1759-61	- Cherokee War
1760	- Birth of Henry Friday Orangeburg District, SC
1760	- Expenses/Colonial Services with the War of the Cherokees Indians.
1760	- Orangeburg had nearly 800 residents.
1765	- Birth of Ann Friday daughter of Martin Friday Orangeburg, SC
1768	- Orangeburg Village becomes district seat.
1770	- Birth if Godfrey Friday son of Gabriel
1775	- Battle of Lexington.
1774	- Murder of Loyalist Gabreal Fridig (1728)
1775-1783	- Revolutionary War.
1779-11-19	- SC & Am. Gen. Gazette newspaper calling return John Fridig & others.
1779-12-17	- SC & Am.Gen.Gazette proclamations return of 50 persons or lose land.
1779-12-17	- SC Governor Loyalist List Proclamation of 300+ accused of treason.
1781-02-19	- Battle at Fort Granby, SC.
1781-02-20	- General Sumpter camped at Friday's Ferry on the Congaree River, SC
1781	- Members of American Continental Congress recommend "relief payments" for American POW's released from British captivity at St. Augustine
1781-05-01	- Battle at Friday's Ferry Richland County, SC.
1781	- Battle of Terra Springs, 1 mile east of Lexington, SC.
1783	- Spain reclaimed Florida under the 1783 Treaty of Paris
1784-5-5	- Marriage - Ann Friday & Henry Salley JR East Florida via Paula Inlet.
1784	- SC General Assembly rescinded much of the Confiscation Act
1784-1786	- Greenville, SC formed.
1785	- Lexington County, SC established changing the name from Saxe Gotha.
1785	- Wade Hampton purchased Friday's Ferry.
1785	- Richland County, SC established as part of large Camden Co.
1785	- Newberry and Fairfield Co, SC established.
1786-03-22	- SC Capital approved by Senate & House to move near Friday's Ferry.
1787	- Birth of George Friday in South Carolina.
1788	- South Carolina became a state.
1789-04-20	- is sworn in as the first President of the United States.
1789	- 1789 Thanksgiving Proclamation by George Washinton.
1789-1797	- 1st US President - George Washington.
1790	- 1st US Census South Carolina. William,Gabriel,John,Margaret & William Fridig
1790	- Charleston's last year as the capital of SC.
1791	- George Washington visits South Carolina & Georgia from Spring-Summer.
1791	- Fridays Ferry replaced with a Toll bridge.
1791	- Bill of Rights established 1st – 10th Amendments.
1794	- Frederick Friday listed in Newberry Co, SC Deed records.
1799	- Birth of Gabriel Friday in SC.
1801	- Birth of Godfrey Friday & Nancy Friday – SC
1802	- Birth of Samuel Berry Friday - SC
1802	- University of South Carolina established.
1803	- Birth of Thomas Friday & Rueben Friday – SC
1803	- Louisiana Purchase from France.
1805	- Frederick Friday shows up in GA Land Lottery.

1807	- Natchitoches Parish, LA established.
1808	– Frederick Friday shows on Screven Co, GA Tax List
1805	- Birth of Nancy Tracy Friday – SC wife of Samuel Berry Friday
1810	- Rachal Family show up in Natchitoches, LA Census.
1810	- Henry Friday shows up in Richland Co, SC Census
1811-12-09	- Marion Co, MS established
1812	- John Friday (*) "Muster Rolls" War of 1812
1812	- Swiss Federation claims neutrality.
1812	- Louisiana becomes the 18th State.
1814	- Godfrey friday moves from Greene Co, GA to Edgefield Co, SC.
1815	- Valais, Nechatel and Geneve join the Swiss Federation.
1818	- Birth of William Friday Tuscaloosa, AL
1818	- Tuscaloosa Co, AL established.
1819	- Dutch Bend Pioneers settled via Autauga Co, Al from Orangeburg, SC.
1819	- Migration of Henry Friday & Family to "Dutch Bend" Autaugaville, AL
1820	- Census shows David Friday in the Fairfield District, SC.
1820	- Samuel David Friday Captain of SC Volunteers.
1820-04-20	- Land Patent "Cash Act" for Public lands in the west of the Eastern Seaboard
1825-06-02	- Birth of Simmie Ann Strong in Clarke Co, Georgia.
1825	- Birth of Vincent Friday son of Godfrey (1801)
1827	- A subsequent wooden bridge was built at Fridays Ferry on the congaree river at Columbia, SC.
1827-9-20	- Marriage Certificate State of Ala for Thomas Friday & Elizabeth Brown
1827-10-31	- Birth of William Major Friday Tuscaloosa Co, Ala
1829	- Birth of George Thomas Friday
1833	- Attala, Co, MS established via Land Purchase from the Indians & Kosciusko was the county seat.
1836	- Itawamba Co, MS founded. Rueben Friday shows up in MS tax list.
1836	- Arkansas becomes the 25th State.
1834	- Godfrey Friday(1801) moves from SC with family to Pike Co, GA.
1840	- Birth of Mary Ann Friday & William Friday Chester Co, SC.
1840	- Census Chester Co, SC - William Friday - Charleston Neck
1841-02-24	- Emanuel Friday buys 376 acres of land in Attala Co, Mississippi.
1842	- Birth of George W. Friday Pike Co, GA son of Godfrey (1801)
1843	- Thomas Friday shown 1843-1848 Attala Co, MS Tax lists.
1844-05-02	- Birth of Anssa Ofra Reeves Friday Pike Co, GA
1844-10-01	- Letters in the Kosciusko Post Office, MS. Thomas Friday (1810).
1845-01-15	- Letters in the Kosciusko Post Office, MS. Thomas Friday (1810).
1846-1848	- Mexican-American War – Barkley Friday dies in Mexico in battle.
1848	- Emanuel Friday (1792) on Attala Co, MS Tax Roll
1849	- Godfrey Friday moved Columbia County Arkansas with 14 children.
1849-10-03	- Birth of Berryman B. Friday Lafayette Co, AR
1850	- Census Federal, Lafayette County, AR show Godfrey & Family.
1850	- Orangeburg, SC Tax List & Census show Martin and Thomas M. Friday
1850	- Sallie Friday is listed in Mortality Schedule of Mississippi.
1850	- Friday's listed in Richland, Fairfield, Edgefield & Lexington Co, SC Districts.
1852	- Winn Parish, LA established.
1854	- Birth of Tabitha E Friday Natchitoches Parish ,LA
1854	- Emanuel Friday (1792) on Attala Co, MS Tax Roll
1856-01-02	- Birth of George Thomas Friday Van Zandt Co, TX
1857	- Birth of Laura Friday Daughter of G.T.Friday (1829)
1860	- US Census show Henry & John Friday in Perry, AL

The Swabian Connection – Expanded Edition

1861-1865	- Civil War.
1861-06	- Gabriel Friday enlisted 11th/17th Consolidated Infantry in Benton, AR.
1861	- Lexington, SC incorporated as a town.
1862	- Homestead Act.
1863	- Birth of James Robert Friday son William Friday & Rachel Lindsey
1864	- Winn Parish Tax List, 1864, Winn Parish, LA for Elizabeth Friday
1865	- Birth of John Friday son of William & Rachel Lucinda Lindsey.
1865	- The town of Lexington was virtually destroyed by occupying Union Army forces guarding General Sherman's western flank.
1865-02	- The bridge at Fridays Ferry (at Columbia) was burned by Confederate Soldiers to delay Shermans Union army.
1866	- National Loyalist Convention
1867	- Birth of Minervia Stewart Campti, LA
1869	- Transcontinental Railroad.
1870	- Oktibbeha Co, MS Whitefield P.O. Census index show L. D., Mert & Rueben Friday
1870	- A steel bridge with wood flooring was built at the Fridays Ferry site and was privately owned until 1912. It was dismantled when the current Gervais Bridge was built.
1871	- Birth of Harmon Griffith son of William and Simmie Strong
1871	- Winn Parish Tax List show G.W. & Jeptha J Friday
1871-07-06	- Marriage Contract btwn Tabitha E Friday & William D Wood Natch, LA
1871	- Aiken Co, SC formed.
1873	- Birth of Harmon Griffith Friday son of William & Simmie Strong
1882-09-25	- Marriage of John Friday (1865) & Minervia Stewart (1867)
1887	- Birth of Henry Robert "Bob" Friday, LA
1888	- George Eastman sells cameras for amateur photographers.
1895	- Birth Eula Evaline Friday daughter of G.T. Friday(1856)& Clara Molin.
1895	- Saluda County, SC Established.
1900	- Census, Smith County, TX show Godfrey Friday
1904	- Birth of Lemon Friday grandson of Simmie Strong.
1907	- Louis Stephen Friday operates L.S.Friday Livery Stable in Uvalde Co, TX.
1907	- Oklahoma becomes the 46th State.
1910	- Census, Smith Co, TX Thomas F & Thomas E Friday
1914	- Birth of William Reeves Friday Laneburg, Arkansas
1918-08-01	- Birth of James "Jim" Friday Bienville Parish Saline, LA
1920	- US Census show Thomas F Friday in Smith Co, TX
1924	- Elmer O Friday
1944	- Birth of James R Friday Bossier City, Lousiana
1968	- Birth of Jeff Friday Bossier City, LA
9-9-1973	- 37th Friday Family Reunion in Bossier Parish, LA hosted by Minnie Adams of Wafer Rd.
1973-07-01	- 1ST Family Reunion held at old home place (Della Bunker Archives)
1974-06-30	- 2nd Family Reuinion (from Della F Bunker Archives)
1975	- 3rd Friday Family Reunion (from Della F Bunker Archives)
1977-07-03	- Family Gathering – Louisiana (from Della F Bunker Archives)
1977-08-21	- Friday Family Reunion - Hogan Park, Midland, TX – 105 guests
1978-07-02	- Friday Reunion (from Della F Bunker Archives)
1979-07-01	- Family Reunion (from Della F Bunker Archives)
1980-07-06	- Friday Reunion (from Della F Bunker Archives)
1983-07-10	- Friday Reuion (from Della F Bunker Archives)

1984-06-09 - Friday Reunion – Louisiana (from Della F Bunker Archives)
1999-08-14 - Marriage of Jeff Friday and Robin J (B_____) Marietta, GA
2000-10-21 - Meek-Friday Family Reunion, Magnolia Baptist Church, Saline, LA. hosted by Bobby and Freddie Hood.
2002-03 - 7th Edition Vol 1 Friday "The Swiss Connection" 467 years of Family History.
2002-06-29 - Friday Family reunion hosted by Hugh & Jo Friday in Tuscaloosa, AL UMC.
2002-08 - 17th Edition Vol 1 Friday "The Swiss Connection" 467 years of Family History.
2003-02 - Published Book - Genealogy & History of the Friday's from Switzerland, Colonial and Southern America.
2007-07-07 - Friday Reunion – Fouke Community Center, Fouke, Arkansas
2012 - Friding | Frydig research in the Middle Ages (Mittelalter)

Epilogue

In closing, I would like to urge anyone who has considered researching their family history to pick up a pen, journal, word document, genealogical software to devote some time to the pursuit of their Ancestral knowledge. Doing the added DNA research you can realize your long lost paralell family cousins. The information I have gained is un-imaginable and the places where we have walked is a like a trip in a time machine. The visit to Martin Friday's original land and being near Friday's Ferry was exuberating. Battles were lost, children were born, and history was made. To make the recent or ancient connections Swabian & Schweiz(Swiss) and see the sites of people that were written about over a hundreds of years ago gives a feeling a completeness, discovery, awareness and awe. I hope this inspires other researchers to find more missing stories, documents, photos, and long lost burial places and to further understand these family histories.

About the Author

Born in Bossier Parish, Louisiana in 1968 shortly before man landed on the moon and the year of Dr. M L King's last march. Jeff Friday attended Shorter College of Rome, Georgia at Atlanta, where he earned a B.S. in Business Administration and attended various Computer classes at Kennesaw State University (in Kennesaw) and Dekalb "Perimeter" Colllege in Dunwoody, Georgia. He is working as a Time & Labor Management Implementation Consultant, and has worked as Technical Service Consultant in software, Medical Billing Rep, Collection Agent, Caterer, Newspaper deliveryman, Actor (in motion pictures), Securityman, High-climber window washer, Plumber, Mortgage Loan Originator and a Cook. The son of a Salesman and Benefits Coordinator, he and his wife "Robin" a Teacher, are married with two children living in Georgia.

Photo taken: 1999 in Woodstock, Ga

References

Research Conducted by:

Primary - Jeff S. Friday 2000-2012
Ebehard Dobler 1986 – Berg und Herrschaft Hohenkrahen
Maria Scheiber 1947 – The Familie Fridinger
Frutigen Swiss Archives by Therese Metzger 3-2010
Secondary Swiss/Colonial Research documents: see contributors page and reference interviews, emails etc...

Oral Interviews, mail and email Dialogue – from the (Schweiz) Swiss Connection

Harriet Imrey (email) – 2003-5
Charles Friday – 2002
Mary E S. Friday – 2001-2002
Richard J Friday – 2002
James "Jim" Friday - 1980's
Marilyn Friday – 2002-3
Truman Friday – 2002
Tammy Hayes – 2001
Doris Grande Rose (email) – 2002
Trecia Senecal – 2002
Leo Redmond – 7-2002
Reba Friday – 12-2002
Bruno Steinle (email) – 8-28-2002
Douglas P. Hanke (email) – 1-2003
Peter Gold (email) – 1-2003
Fred Swygert (email) - 2-2003
Jack C Fryday - 3-16-2003
Ruth Stalder – Swiss Federal Archives (email) 7-2003
Jennifer Spencer - NARA (email) 8-2003
Rebecca Kleckley – Kleckley Family (email) 10-2003
Dudley Earl Friday – 3-2004

The Swabian Connection – Expanded Edition

Eddie Friday – 3-2004
Brad Woodward – Anderson Friday Family (email) – 3-2004
Donna Baker – Posey Family (email) – 5-2004
Lalia Garner Jagers – Morning Friday (email) – 5-2004
Benny Barber – F. H. Friday (email) – 5-2004
Bill McDonald – Godfrey Friday Family (mail/email) – 5-2004
Claire Furth - Godfrey Friday/Berryman Baker (email) – 12-2002
Michael Caviness – Martha Jane Friday-Cabiness Family (email) – 8-2004
Bruce A Stewart – Chestnut Cemtery & Stewart Family - 8-2004
Camden Archives and Musuem – 4-2005
Tamara F Quesenberry - (mail/email) – 2005-06
Frances Williams – 6-23-2005
James Munnerlyn (email) – 8-6-2005
Benjean N Rogers (email) – 8-2005
Julie Shepherd – Bearden family (email) – 10-12-2005
Claude T. Friday – Luna L. Friday register (fax) – 12-28-2005
Mrs. Martha Duke – Curry/Burdett Marriage Certificate (email) – 2006
Judy J Davis – John & Mahala Williams-Friday family (email) – 4-2006
Lavinia Nance – Opal Irene Friday-Bailey family (email) - 1-2005
James R. Friday – William Dawson Descendants – (email) - 12-2006
Linda Gail Friday – William Hoyd Descendants (email) – 1-2007
Leo Friday – Elbert Wade Friday Descendants – 2-2007
Martha Hector – Lee Horace Friday family (email) – 5-2007
Kelly Friday Elton – William Thomas Friday family (phone) – 6-2007
Me'chele Kent-Brooks – Thomas W Friday (1911) family (email) – 6-2007
Alla Friday Kelley – William Tom Friday (1869) family (mail/phone) – 7-2007
Sebastian Freidig – own Freidig family descendant from Switzerland (email) – 1-2009
Ron Manley – Lucindas Friday-Kinney & Elder burial (email) – 4-2009
Janet Kelly – William Friday Kelly (~1820) janlynke@aol.com (email) – 10-2004
Dallis Ann Friday Lauffenburger – George S Friday (1909) family twokidstolv@yahoo.com (email/ phone) 08-2009.
Fonda Marie Friday – Edward Brodie Friday (1880) family carolinagal@prodigy.net (email) 11-2009
Gail Friday House – Archie Hugh Friday (1887) descendants (email) – 11-2010
Roelene Taylor trtalor7@hotmail.com (email) – Simmie Strong/William Friday & grsndchildren photo 6/2011.
Gloria "Jean Friday-Avant - ps letter of JRFriday grocery & photo via Wanda Butterfield . 8-2012

Internet Gedcom Data

William T Clarke wtc1129@earthlink.net (Goodson Family History - Rootsweb.com)
Doug Hanke
Multiple wc.rootsweb.com users databases records reviewed – 2000-2010

Historical South Carolina Documents

South Carolina Council Journal – Upper House No. 6 Part 1 Nov 7, 1734-May 26, 1736 Pg. 31-35
Charleston Deed Book T-3
South Carolina Federal Census 1790, 1800, 1810, 1820, 1850
Secretary of State
SC Court of Common Pleas
Accounts Audited of claims growing out of the revolution
Royal Grants Vol. 30
Royal Grants Vol. 42 Pg. 292

The Swabian Connection – Expanded Edition

Royal Grants Vol. 16 Pg. 535
Colonial Plats Vol. 4
SC Land Memorials Vol. 13 Pg. 297 #4
Judgement Roll 1754 Box 37A No. 78A ,1766
Papers of General Assembly
Stub Indents issued in payment of Claims against South Carolina bk. I
Church of Orangeburg "Book of Record"
S.C Department of Archives and History Alphabetical Index
Edgefield Co, SC Census 1850
Estate Sale Record of Nehemiah Posey
General Assembly Petition – Petition of Citizens of Orangeburg District regarding passenger rail rates.
SC Deed Abstracts – See Bibliography.
Youn Family Papers, South Caroliniana Library, University of South Carolina.
No. 36 From Documentary History of the American Revolution, by Gibbes, Volume 3, p. 23
1825 (Robert) Mills Atlas of South Carolina
Lexington Genealogical Exchange
South Carolina Online Records Index
A South Carolina Community, 1740-1990
Newberry Co Estate Abstracts Vol II RR
Abstractions from Lexington Co Will Book A
Marriage & Death Notices Camden, SC Newspapers 1816-1865
State Plats Vol. 33 Pg. 465 #1
State Plats Vol. 32 Pg. 454 #3
State Plats Vol. 33 Pg. 80 #1
State Plats Vol. 18 Pg. 168 #1
State Plats Vol. 11 Pg. 206
State Plats Vol. 43(2) Pg. 395 #3
State Plats Vol. 54 Pg. 488
State Plats Vol. 5 Pg. 155
State Plats Vol. 14 Pg. 279 #1
State Plats Vol. 47 Pg. 126 #2
Index to State Grants 1784-1821 ST659
Accounts Audited of claims growing out of the revolution - RW2733
Papers of the General Assembly.
SCDAH Book T Pg. 478-479
SCDAH Book MM Pg. 242
SCDAH Book PP Pg. 297
Charleston Co Will Vol. 11 Pg. 295-296
SC Colonial Plats Vol. 9 Pg. 218 #2
SC Land Memorials Vol. 8 Pg. 38 #4
SC Land Memorials Vol. 6 Pg. 489 #2
SC Colonial Plats Vol. 4 Pg. 374 #1
SC Land Memorials Vol. 8 Pg. 348 #4
1828 Fairfield Co Estate Records Book H Pg. 204 Lot 48
Edgefield Deed Book 33 pg. 207
1849 Richland Co Estate Records Book L Pg. 95 Box 54 Package 1330
1850 Record of Admissions to the State Hospital
1899 Marriage Certificate for Curry/Burdett by J.M.Friday
Anderson T Friday (1811) Pocket Book dated January 31, 1830

Historical Alabama Documents

Tuscaloosa Co, AL Census 1830, 1840, 1860, 1880

The Swabian Connection – Expanded Edition

Bibb Co, AL Census 1850
Perry Co, AL Census 1860
Judge of Probate Records Tuscaloosa Co, AL 1857
Chilton Co, AL Census 1880
Bureau of Land Management General Land office records
National Archives AL Land Entry Files
Marriage Records of Tuscaloosa Co, AL 1823-1860 pg, 10, 39, 42, 48, 50, 78, 83
Familysearch.org 1880 Census

Historical Texas Documents

Sabine County, Texas Tax Lists 1837-1896 – Texas State Archives Library
Marriage Records Book B
Sabine County, TX - Census 1860
Familysearch.org 1880 Census
Texas Death Records 1890-1976. http://pilot.familysearch.org/ - 2009

Historical Mississippi Documents

1848 Attala Co, MS Tax Roll
1854 Attala Co, MS Tax Roll
1850 Attala Co, MS Census
1820 Marion Co, MS Census
Bureau of Land Management General Land office records "Internet" site
Mississippi Department of Archives and History
Emanuel Friday – Last Will and Testament 1858
Itawamba Co, MS Archives Deed Book 1 "Internet" site
National Archives MS Land Entry Files
Diary of Jason Niles (1814-1894) pg. 33, 61 – Kosciusko, Mississippi – 1961
Familysearch.org 1880 Census

Historical Louisiana Documents

Natchitoches Parish, LA Marriage Book 2 pp.48-47
Natchitoches Parish, LA Census 1860,1880, 1920
Bureau of Land Management General Land office records "Internet" site
Birth Records Sabine Co, LA
Marriage Records of Natchitoches Parish, LA
Church Records of Shreveport, Louisiana
Church Records of Natchitoches, Louisiana
Louisiana Vital Records
West Carroll Gazette
LA Board of Pension Commissioners – Pension Application #721 & 5182

Historical Arkansas Documents

Bureau of Land Management General Land office records online "Internet" site
Beech Creek Cemetery, Waldo, Columbia County, AR Photographs
Lafayette Co, Arkansas Census 1850
The History of Columbia Co, AR. By Netie Hicks Killgore. 1947.

Historical Tennessee Documents

TN Records of Stewart Co Tax Book Vol 2 1810 p.198

The Swabian Connection – Expanded Edition

1820 Rutherford Co, TN Census

Historical Georgia Documents

1870 Dougherty County Census (online)
1860 Warren County Census (online)
1860 Glasscock County Census (online)
1809 Republican & Savannah Evening Ledger 12/30/1809 pg. 2 Col 1
1805 Georgia Land Lottery (online)
1810 Greene County Tax List
Georgia Death Records 1914-1927 http://pilot.familysearch.org/ - 2009
Georgia Research Consortium Militia Record of Capt. Colberts Company [of 139th District of Greene County, Georgia] http://www.georgiaresearch.com/militia_record_of_capt.htm – (online) 2006

National Archives Documents

Tuscaloosa Land Records Vol 33 p.100

Miscellaneous State Records

Online "Internet" Federal & State Census Records

Miscellaneous Records

Notes, Letters, Research, Photographs and Archives of Doris Brown.
Notes, Letters and Archives of Della Bunker.
Notes, Letters and Archives of Marilyn Friday.
Research, Photographs and Archives of Amelia F Ames.
Letters, Photographs and Archives of Gayle Miller.
Letters, Notes and Archives of Margaret Alley.
Notes and Research forwarded from Bill Friday contacts.
Photographs from Clarence Geist.
Notes, Photos, Letters and Archives of Tammy Hayes.
Photos, History, Letters and Archives of Treci Senecal.
Public Record Office (PRO), London, Manuscript Reference CO5, Volume 82.
Archives and Research of David Fridy.
Bibb County Marriage "online"
Research and Archives of Bonnie Roberson-Cooter
Douglas P. Hanke Archives and Research
Ruth Rosenthal archives and Hydrick Family History
David Fridy archives and Research
Peter Gold Research and Archives
Sally Swett Wheeler Research - Archives of David D. Friday History
Fred Swygert - Ships records and Swygert Research
Letters, Research and Archives of Kathie F Peek
Family History Records of Dorothy Spann Dockery
Family History Records of Lillian Dockery Friday
Swiss Family Name Book pg. 279 (located in Swiss Federal Archives)
Sunny Dailey letter to Della Bunker – 5-30-1987
United State Patent and Trademark Office - http://www.uspto.gov/patft/index.html

Historical Site Visit and Research

Cayce Quarry – Old Granby Cemetery, Cayce, SC – 1-2002
Granby Lock – Cayce, SC – 1-2002

The Swabian Connection – Expanded Edition

Fridig Cemetery, W Columbia, SC – 1-2002
Goodland Swamp "Morgan-Corbett" Cemetery, Springfield, SC – 1-2002
Richland County Library, Richland, SC – 2002
Edgefield Historical Society, Edgefield, SC – 2002
Batesburg-Leesville Cemetery, SC – 2002
Cedar Creek Methodist Church, Fairfield Co, SC – 2002
Dawson County, Georgia Libraries - 2002
Forsyth County, Georgia Libraries – 2001-2002
LDS Research Center – 2001-2002
Lexington County Library – 11-2002
Cayce Musuem, Cayce, SC – 11-2002
Black Lake, Creston and Chestnut, LA – 11-2002
Town of Buhl, AL – 3-8-2003
Georgia Federal Archives – 4-14-2005
Georgia State Archives – 4-14-2005

Historical European Virtual Documents

Schaffhausen, Switzerland Archives Website http://www.stadtarchiv-schaffhausen.ch/
Austrian Archives Website http://www.archivinformationssystem.at/
Zurich, Switzerland Archives Website http://suche.staatsarchiv.djiktzh.ch/resultatliste.aspx
Zurich, Switzerland Archives http://www.archivportal.ch/search.aspx
Bern, Switzerland Archives Website www.query.sta.be.ch/detail.aspx
Uri, Switzerland Private Archives http://www.staur.ch/P_Archive/PA_001.pdf
Wurttembergish Urkundenbuch Archives Search Website http://maja.bsz-bw.de/wubonline/
Virtual Monasteries in Europe http://www.monasterium.net/ or http://www.mom-ca.uni-koeln.de/MOM-CA
Landes Archives Baden-Wurtemburg, Germany http://www.wubonline.de/
MO = Monasterium.net(http://www.mom-ca.uni-koeln.de/mom/search) : Charter number
WO = Wubonline.de : Charter number Dates provided by Baden-Wurttemburg Urkendenbuch archive.
MGH = Monumenta Germaniae Historica www.mgh.de/dmgh/indices?q= : Page Number
RI = Regesta Imperii http://www.regesta-imperii.de/regesten/suche.html : Number
AO = Swiss Archives online http://www.archivesonline.org/search.aspx : ID Number
BO = Bayern Online http://www.gda.bayern.de/findmittel
DI = Domherren Konstanz Index http://wwperson.informatik.uni-erlangen.de/cgi-bin/ww-index/LANG=germ/?Index-5722
RW = Rootsweb:database http://wc.rootsweb.ancestry.com/

Bibliography

Burg und Herrschaft HohenKrahen im Hegau. By Eberhard Dobler. 1986

Freiburger Diözesan-Archiv, Volume 29 By Kirchengeschichtlicher Verein fur Geschichte, Christliche Kunst, Altertums- und Literaturkunde des Erzbistums Freiburg mit Berucksi.

Urkundenbuch des Klosters Sankt Blasien im Schwarzwald: von den Anfängen bis zum Jahr 1299, Issue 1
The universal anthology: a collection of the best literature ..., Volume 33 By Richard Garnett, Léon Vallée (i.e. Alexandre Léon), Alois Brand 1899

Allgemeine Weltgeschichte, Volume 94 By William Guthrie, John Gray, Christian Gottlob Heyne, Johann Daniel Ritter, Johann M. Schröckh, Johann Andreas Dieze, Daniel Ernst
Ulmisches Urkundenbuch im Auftrage der Stadt Ulm: Bd. Die Reichsstadt. 1. T. By Friedrich Pressel, Gustav Veesenmeyer, Hugo Bazing. 1900

Commentary to the Germanic Laws and Medieval Documents. By Leo Winer. 1915

Wirtembergisches urkundenbuch: herausgegeben von dem Königlichen, By Württemberg (Germany). Staatsarchiv 1849

Altdeutsches Namenbuch, Volume 1. By Ernst Wilhelm Förstemann, 1856.

Württembergische Jahrbücher für Statistik und Landeskunde, Part 2 By Württemberg (Kingdom). Statistisches Landesamt, Verein für Vaterlandskunde, Stuggart. 1851

Codex diplomaticvs Alemanniae et Bvrgvndiae trans-Ivranae intra fines By Trudpert Neugart. 1791.

Ausgewählte Urkunden zur Erläuterung der Verfassungsgeschichte Deutschlands By Wilhelm Altmann, Ernst Bernheim.

Urkundenbuch der Stadt Braunschweig: 1361-1374 samt Nachträgen By Ludwig Hänselmann, Heinrich Mack, Manfred R. W. Garzmann.

Allgemeines Lexikon der bildenden Künstler von der Antike bis zur, Volume 12. edited by Ulrich Thieme, Felix Becker, Frederick Charles Willis, Hans Vollmer.

Urkundenbuch der Abtei Sanct Gallen, Volume 4, Parts 4-5 By Antiquarische Gesellschaft in Zürich, Historischer Verein des Kantons St. Gallen.

Rudolf Fridingen in Stain Glass Windows in St. Vincent Cathedral.
http://www.orgues-et-vitraux.ch/default.asp/2-0-1750-11-6-1/

University of Tubingen Records: Die Matrikeln der Universität Tübingen, 1477-[1817]
http://www.archive.org/stream/wirtembergisches05wruoft/wirtembergisches05wruoft_djvu.txt

Johannes von Müller sämmtliche Werke, Volume 17. By Johannes von Müller. 1814

Frieding a district of the town of Andechs in Upper Bavaria, Starberg, Germany.
http://de.wikipedia.org/wiki/Frieding. 2010

Die Traditionen des Stiftes Polling, Volume 41 By Friedrich Helmer. 1993

Das Bistum Augsburg: Die Benediktinerabtei Benediktbeuern By Josef Hemmerle

Archiv für die Geschichte der Republik Graubünden, Volume 1 By Theodor von Mohr, Conradin von Mohr.

Zeitschrift für die Geschichte des Oberrheins, Volume 3. 1888
Zeitschrift für die Geschichte des Oberrheins, Volume 37. By Landesarchiv zu Karlsruhe, Badische Historische Kommission, Oberrheinische Historische Kommiss

Die Matrikel der Universität Leipzig: Register By Universität Leipzig, Georg Erler. 1976

The Swabian Connection – Expanded Edition

The Universal Anthology: a collection of the best literature ..., Volume 33 By Richard Garnett, Leon Vallée, Alois Brandl. 1899

Urkundenbuch der Städte Dresden und Pirna: Im Auftrage der Königlich. By Karl Friedrich von Posern-Klett. 1875

Frühneuhochdeutsches Glossar By Alfred Götze. 1967

Neuhart chronicle, vol 4. Fraudheuger. 1988

Festschrift, Volume 20. Friedfertigen. 1858

Academic dictionaries and encyclopedias Friedfertigen
http://de.academic.ru/dic.nsf/dewiki/474150 2010

Zeitschrift für Rechtsgeschichte, Volume 6 By Adolfus Fridericus Rudorff. 1867

Katalog der Gemälde des Bayerischen Nationalmuseums By Bayerisches Nationalmuseum, Karl Voll, Heinz Braune, Hans Buchheit. 1908

Muenchner Wappenrolle Herold http://www.muenchner-wappen-herold.de/generalindex/Generalindex_2008_F.pdf. 2008

Kemptner Wappen und Zeichen Eduard Zimmermann, Kempten, Verlag für Heimatpflege, 1963

Allgemeine Weltgeschichte. By William Guthrie, John Gray, Christian Gottlob Heyne, Johann Daniel Ritter, Johann M. Schröckh, Johann Andreas Dieze, Daniel Ernst Wagner, Ludwig Al. 1801

Indicatore di storia svizzera, Volume 2 By Allgemeine Geschichtforschende Gesellschaft der Schweiz p 285. 1874

Alemannisch South Baden "Sudbaden" http://www.badische-seiten.de/alemannisch/lexikon.php?le=1548 2010

Historisch-geographisches wörterbuch des deutschen mittelalters By Hermann Oesterley. 1883

Altfridingen (Alt-Fridingen) http://www.burgeninventar.de/html/bw/TUTT_big.html 2010
Die Matrikel der Universität Wien, Volume 2, Part 2. 1954

Frederick der Freidige http://www.die-freidigen.de/html/wappen1.html 2010

Walhalla - By Joseph Anselm Pangkofer 1842.

German Teminology. http://de.wikipedia.org/wiki/ 2009

German Translation. http://dictionary.reverso.net/german-english/ 2010

Die gaugrafschaften des almannischen Badens. By Walther Schultze. 1896

Fricke Wappen and Familie History. 2009
http://www.fricke-gernot.de/

The law glossary: being a selection of the Greek, Latin, Saxon, French, Norman, and Italian sentences, phrases, and maxims, found in the leading English and American reports and

The Swabian Connection – Expanded Edition

elementary works: with historical and explanatory notes : alphabetically arranged, and translated into English, for.. by Thomas Taylor. 1866

Akademie Wisershaften Literature Mainz 2009. http://regesten.regesta-imperii.de/
Von der Handschrift zum Buchdruck: Spätmittelalter, Reformation, Humanismus Vol 2 By Horst Albert Glaser, Ingrid Bennewitz, Ulrich Müller. 1991

Kleinere Schriften, Volume 3 edited by Karl Müllenhoff. 1886

Mitteilungen zur vaterländischen Geschichte, Volumes 19-20 By Historischer Verein des Kantons St. Gallen. 1884

Ulmisches urkundenbuch: im auftrage der stadt Ulm, Volume 2. Friedrich Pressel, Gustav Veesenmeyer, Hugo Bazing, Verein für kunst und altertum in Ulm und Obers. 1900

Irkundenbuch der Abtei Sanct Gallen, Volume 6 By Kloster St. Gallen v. 6. 1941
Ortsnamenbuch des Kantons Bern, alter Kantonsteil, Volume 1, Part 1 edited by Paul Zinsli. 1976

Vierteljahrsschrift für Wappen-, Siegel- und Familienkunde, Volume 16
By Herold, Verein für Heraldik, Genealogie und Verwandte Wissenschaft, Berlin. 1888

Wirtembergisches urkundenbuch By Württemberg (Germany). Staatsarchiv

Hicks, Theresa M. "Saxe Gotha Neighbors." 2000.

Imrey, Harriet. Llewelyn Threewits Family. 2009
http://www.palmettoroots.org/Family_Threewits.html

Houseofnames.com. "Switerland: the Early Origins". 2009
http://www.houseofnames.com/xq/asp/sId./kbId.229/title.Switzerland%3A+the+Early+Origins/qx/knowledgebase.htm

Hewett, Janet B. "The Roster of Confederate Soldiers 1861-1865". Volume VI. 1996.

Pearce, Richard / Alicia Patterson Foundation. "An Agreed-upon Tale of Two families". 1975.
http://www.aliciapatterson.org/APF001975/Pearce/Pearce06/Pearce06.rtf

Graham, Paul. K. "1805 Georgia Land Lottery Fortunate Drawers and Grantees". 2004
http://www.1805georgialandlottery.com/bookphoto.shtml

Hicks, Teresa M. "Arrival of the First Fleet and Early Settlers". 2004.
http://www.palmettoroots.org/ShipsFirstFleet.html

Moss, Bobby Gilmer. "Roster of South Carolina Patriots in the American Revolution" Genealogical Publishing Co, Inc. pg. 333. 1983.

Johnson, Faye. " Fairfield Family Histories 1700s-1982". pg. 49-51.

Riggins, Mary H; Petty, Venia F. "Tennessee Records of Stewart County Tax Book Volume 2 pg. 198. 1808-1812".

Attala County Mississippi Cemeteries. 929.3762644. Pg 224,226.

Dallas, Jerry. "Revolutionary War Pension Application of Henry Gragg". File#S10773.

http://ftp.rootsweb.com/pub/usgenweb/sc/military/revwar/pensions/gragg-he.txt

Wiltshire, Betty C. "Attala County Mississippi Pioneers. 929.3762644. 1999.

Schmidt, Steve. "Geographic Encyclopedia". 2000
http://www.placesnamed.com/f/r/friday.asp.

Unknown. "Immigrant Ships Transcribers Guild Charleston, South Carolina." 1999-2002.
http://istg.rootsweb.com/v2/arrivalsv2/charlestonv2.html

SCCJ, Vol I, 13 March 1744 and and Brenda Helen Keck Reed
John Jacob Friday Property Owners of Saxe Gotha & Dutch Fork, SC. 2001

http://www.homestead.com/Weberites/Neighbors.html

18 Sept 1746, SCCJ, and Brenda Helen Keck Reed. 2001

John Friday Property Owners of Saxe Gotha & Dutch Fork, SC
http://www.homestead.com/Weberites/Neighbors.html

A.S. Salley, JR. "The History of Orangeburg County, South Carolina from its first settlement to the
close of the revolutionary war". Bk No. F 277.06.S1. 1898

Gissendanner, Joop. 2000
http://www.xs4all.nl/~sail/orange/block391-400.html

Sakuri, Gail. "Cornerstones of Freedom: The Louisiana Purchase". Childrens Press. 2003.

Richmond County Civil War Regiment "Independent Blues" . 2003
http://ftp.rootsweb.com/pub/usgenweb/ga/richmond/military/civilwar/rosters/cod10reg.txt

Poland, Billie Gene. "History of Bienville Parish VII". 1984.

Holcomb, Brent & Glass, Joihn. "Records of Deaths – Columbia, SC 1875-1877". P.207

Voigh, Gilbert P. "The German & German Swiss in South Carolina." Bulletin of the University of
SC. 1922. P. 49-50.

Logan, John H. "The History of Upper Carolina." S.G. Courtney & Co, Charleston, SC. 1859. p.251-
252.

Gene Jeffries Orangeburg Land Records Hans Freydig. 2001
http://www.logicsouth.com/~genealogy/origin.htm

Thomas P Steele Jr The Steele's of Lexington County South Carolina. 2001
http://www.geocities.com/tsteele.geo/steele.html

Unknown Author Founding of South Carolina. 2001
http://www.richland2.org/rce/founding.htm

SC Historical Society General Sumpter at Friday's Ferry. 2001
http://www.schistory.org/displays/RevWar/archives-online/Gibbes__v__3__p__023.html

Joop Giesendanner Switzerland Citizenship. 2001

The Swabian Connection – Expanded Edition

http://www.xs4all.nl/~sail/orange/b-index.html

Joop Giesendanner Burial of John Friday Senior. 2001
http://www.xs4all.nl/~sail/orange/bur94bur99.html

Rootsweb Muster Rolls Soldiers of the War of 1812. 2001
http://www.rootsweb.com/~nclincol/nclmuster.htm

Gene Jeffries ORANGEBURGH LAND RECORDS and (South Carolina Archives). 2001
http://www.netside.com/~genealogy/landrec.shtml

Gene Jeffries Migration of Henry Friday – Alabama. 2001
http://www.netside.com/~genealogy/alabama.shtml

Gene Jeffries Origin of Name. 2001
http://www.netside.com/~genealogy/origin.htm

South Carolina Historical Association for 1937, Loyalist Proclamations List of 1779. 2001
http://sc_tories.tripod.com/loyalist_proclamations_of_1779.htm

Tony Gallman First Inhabitants of Saxe Gotha, South Carolina. 2001
http://ftp.ev1.net/~jgallman/genealogy/PS05/PS05_153.HTM

Gene Jeffries Brochure for South Carolina 1740. 2001
http://www.logicsouth.com/~genealogy/remsb.htm

SCGEN Cherokee Path. 2001
http://www.scgen.org/path.htm

Arkansas Confederate and Union Soldiers Burial Places. 2001
http://www.couchgenweb.com/civilwar/cem-f.htm

National Park Service - Civil War Soldiers. 2001/2004
http://www.itd.nps.gov/cwss/soldiers.htm

Joop Giesendanner Baptism of Strauman. 2001
http://www.xs4all.nl/~sail/orange/17410524.html

Rootsweb Pleasant Hill Cemetery, Natchitoches Parish La. 2001
http://searches1.rootsweb.com/usgenweb/archives/la/natchito/cemeteries/pleasant.txt

Description of the Province of South Carolina 1732.
http://www.netside.com/~genealogy/purry.htm

Historic Sites in Orangeburg. 2001
http://www.orangeburgsc.net/Quality/sites.html

History of the Town of Lexington, SC. 2001
http://www.lexsc.com/History%20of%20the%20Town%20of%20Lexington.htm

J.G. Braddock Sr, SCIway South Carolina Loyalist. 1998
http://www.sciway.net/hist/amrev/loyalists.html

SC Roots Expenses with War with the Cherokees. 1998

The Swabian Connection – Expanded Edition

http://www.scroots.org/m_184.html

Marita Snyder Martin Friday Marriage references. 2001
http://www.geocities.com/Heartland/Ranch/7943/

Unknown author Deeds of Marion County, MS. 2001
http://dallen1989.tripod.com/Deeds-MarionCo.html

Rootsweb Tuscaloosa Co, AL Marriages 1821-1860. 2001
http://www.rootsweb.com/~aljeffer/tuscal/f.html/

Joop Giesendanner Charlestown, SC Ships 1735. 2001
http://www.xs4all.nl/~sail/orange/ships1735.html

Ken Jones Muster Roll 4th Alabama Volunteer Infantry. 2001
http://www.tarleton.edu/~kjones/4cmstr.html

Unknown Authur, Murdered Loyalist. 2001
http://downloads.members.tripod.com/sc_tories/list_of_murdered_loyalists.htm

Hallman, E.B. "Early Settlers in the Carolina Dutch Fork" Wosford College, 1944 p.30
Martin Friday's home had glass windows.

Buzhardt, Carroll. Edgefield, SC 1850 Census 1999
http://www.rootsweb.com/~scedgefi/1850.txt

Moss, Bobby Gilmer "In the American Revolution" South Carolina Roster, 1985 p.333

Holcomb, Brent H. "SC Marriages 1688-1799" Genealogical Publishing Co, INC. 1983 975.7 Vzhsc

2nd Mass Regiment Original History "Continental Regiment 13" 2002
http://www.2ndmass.org/reghisf1.htm

Muster Roll 7th Infantry Regiment
South Carolina Volunteer Infantry Company F - C. S. A. 2002
http://www.researchonline.net/sccw/rosters/7thcof.htm

Grady L. McFarland. Liberty Chapel Cemetery, Grant Parish La. 2002
http://liberty_chapel_cemetary.homestead.com/files/liberty.html

Morison, Samuel Eliot. "The Oxford History of the American People" 1965.

Lossing, Benson J. Pictorial Field Book of the Revolution". Volume II. Chapter XVIII 1850.
http://freepages.history.rootsweb.com/~wcarr1/Lossing1/Chap50.html

Itawamba Historical Society. Itawamba County, MS Deed Book 1
http://homepages.rootsweb.com/~robfra/deed1.htm

Itawamba Historical Society. Itawamba County, MS Pension List 1926-27.
http://homepages.rootsweb.com/~robfra/pension2.html

Tomlinson, Mona . Big Creek Cem Oktibbeha County, Mississippi 2002
http://www.sturgisms.homestead.com/bigcreek.html

The Swabian Connection – Expanded Edition

In Years Gone By 1834-1984 Dunn's Creek Baptist Church. 1984

1870 Mississippi, Oktibbeha County, Whitefield P.O. Census Index 2002
http://www.sturgisms.homestead.com/1870index.html

Dutch Fork Digest Newsletter, Vol. VII, No. 3, July - Sep., 1992
http://www.dfgensoc.homestead.com/Brittania.html

Eargle, John C. Dutch Fork Digest.
http://dfgensoc.homestead.com/SHIPSLIST.html

Rocker. "Marriages and Obituaries from the Macon Messenger" 1818-1865, 1988.

Clark's, Murtie June. "Loyalists in the Southern Campaign" .VI, 1809.

Die Gemeindewappen des Kantons Sankt Gallen. Edited by the Gemeindewappenkommission des Kantons St. Gallen. St. Gallen, 1947, 28 (+30) p. No ISBN.

Die Wappen der Schweiz, 1st series issued by Kaffee Hag, Zürich, parts 1-4.

Die Wappen der Schweiz, 2nd series issued by Kaffee Hag, Zürich, parts 1,2,4-19.
Baselbiet (several authors) : Liestal, 4th ed. 1996. 287 p. ISBN 3-85673-617-4. Dessemontet, O. and Nicollier, L.F. : Armorial des communes Vaudoises. Lausanne, Spes, 1972.
Gillard, F. : Evolution des armoiries communales de Bex. Schweizer Archiv für Heraldik 89(1975)34-36.

Glutz von Blotzheim, K. : Die Wappen der Bezirke und Gemeinde des Kantons Solothurn. Staatskanzlei des Kantons Solothurn. Solothurn, 3rd ed. 1992, 65 p.

Lapaire, C. : Les plus anciens sceaux communaux de la Suisse. Schweizer Archiv für Heraldik 81(1987)2-8.

Maissen, A. : Wappen und Siegel von Ilanz und der Gruob. Schweizer Archiv für Heraldik 103(1989)9-18.

Mattern, G. : Gersau: a forgotten Swiss canton. ARMA 1328-1332.

Meyer, B. : Die Gemeindewappen des Kantons Thurgau. Huber, Frauenfeld, 1960. +/- 150 p. No ISBN.

Montfalcon, A. De; Martin, P.E. : Armorial des communes Genevoises. Genève, 1925, 18+12 p.

Moos, L. von : Die Entwicklung des Obwaldner und des gemeinsamen Unterwaldner Wappens. Schweizer Archiv für Heraldik 195(1991)200-206.

Moser, A. : Die Wappen der Stadt und des Amtes Erlach. Schweizer Archiv für Heraldik 89(1975)19-33.

Mühlemann, L. Wappen und Fahnen ders Schweiz. Luzern, 1977 and 1997. 164 p.

Sankt Galler Wappenbuch. Buchhandlung am Rösslitor, St. Gallen, 1991. 127 p. ISBN 3-908048-19-9.

Schibli, M. : Die Gemeindewappen des Kantons Aargau. Lehrmitelverlag des Kantons Aargau. 4th edition, 2000. 63 p. No ISBN .

Suter, P. : Die Gemeindewappen des Kantons Baselland. Liestal, 1984, 4th ed., 190 p. ISBN 3-85673-206.

Wandfluh, H. : Siegel, Banner und Wappen der Lanschaft Frutigen. Schweizer Archiv für Heraldik 59(1948)15-22.

Wappenbuch des Kantons Bern. Bern, 1981, 222 p. ISBN 3-292-16100-2.

Wappenbuch des Kantons Graubünden (several authors). Chur, 1982. 212 p.

Ziegler, P. : Die Gemeindewappen des Kantons Zürich. Berichthaus Verlag, Zürich, 1977. ISBN 3-85572-022-3

Ships passenger Lists - 2002
http://olivetreegenealogy.com/ships/index.shtml

Immigrant Ancestor Posting Ship Lists. Palatines to America Index - 2003
http://www.genealogy.org/~palam

Creasey, Sybil. Van Zandt County WWI Draft Registration – 9-2000
http://www.rootsweb.com/~txvanzan/draftcan.htm

Hicks, Teresa M. Arrival of some Ships and Settlers 1751-1756 – 2003
http://dfgensoc.homestead.com/ships.html

Chism, Sue. Passengers to Carolinas - 1774. 11-4-1996.
ftp://ftp.rootsweb.com/pub/usgenweb/sc/ships/1774ship.txt

Tolbert, Sue. "Friday Cemetery – Muskogee, OK". 2001
http://www.usgennet.org/usa/ok/county/muskogee/fridaylist.htm

Texas Death Records 1890-1976. 2009
http://pilot.familysearch.org/

Manley, Ron. Union Church Cemetery, Winn Parish, LA. 4-2009
http://files.usgwarchives.org/la/winn/cemeteries/union.txt

Bibliography (Endnotes)

1 5/30/1586 Archiveinheit Obersimmental http://www.query.sta.be.ch/detail.aspx?ID=56008
2 Relativegenetics.com DNA Marker Report 11/17/2005
3 Federal Department of Foreign affairs
http://www.swissworld.org/en/history/middle_ages/the_territory_expands/
4 Henggeler, Rudolf P.: Consecration of the princely book. Benedictine Abbey of St. Gallus and Otmar to St.Gallen. Einsiedeln 1929th (Monasticon Benedictinum Helvetiae-1)
http://www.sg.ch/home/kultur/stiftsarchiv/geschichte/abtei_st_gallen/aebte.html
5 Eldrid Haggard Aas http://www.eldrid.ch/swgerman.htm 2005
6 A Middle High-German primer: with grammar, notes, and glossary By Joseph Wright Clarendon Press, 1888

7 en.wikibooks.org/wiki/German/Grammar/Alphabet_and_Pronunciation

8 Annuarium Historiae conciliorium Vol 29 W. Brandmuller 1997.

9 Ortsnamenbuch des Kantons Bern, alter Kantonsteil: Dokumentation und Deutung. T. 1. A-F Paul Zinsli Francke, 1976

10 Schriften des Vereins für Geschichte des Bodensees und seiner ..., Volumes 5-6 By Verein für Geschichte des Bodensees und Seiner Umgebung Bodenseegeschichtsvereins., 1874

11 Zeitschrift für die Geschichte des Oberrheins, Volume 17 Kohlhammer, 1865

12 Index zu H.A. Erhard's Regesta historiae Westfaliae. 1861

13 Regesta historiae Westfaliae: Accedit Codex diplomaticus. Die quellen der ... By Franz Friedrich Roger Wilmans, Ludwig Perger. 1847

14 Westfälisches Urkunden-Buch: Die Urkunden des Bisthums Minden vom J. 1201 ... By Heinrich August Erhard, Franz Friedrich Roger Wilmans, Herma. 1898

15 Schleswig-Holstein-Lauenburgische Regesten und Urkunden, bearb. und herausg ... By Gesellschaft für schleswig-holsteinische Geschichte, Schles.1885.

16 Dortmunder Urkundenbuch, bearb. von K. Rübel (und E. Roese). Bd. 1-3, Hälfte ... By Dortmunder urkundenbuch. 1881

17 Urkundenbuch der Stadt Basel Vol 9-10. pg97

18 Hans Jacob Riemensperger brochure translation to attract migration to Saxe Gotha Township, Carolina, in 1740. http://gallman.org/Brochure.htm

19 Alemannisch South Baden "Sudbaden" http://www.badische-seiten.de/alemannisch/lexikon.php?le=1548 2010

20 Publicationen aus den Preussischen staatsarchiven ..., Volume 65 By Prussia. Archivverwaltung S. Hirzel, 1896

21 Quellen und Darstellungen zur Geschichte Niedersachsens, Volume 11 By Historischer Verein für Niedersachsen Verlag August Lax, 1903

22 Weltliches Silber: Katalog der Sammlung des Schweizerischen Landesmuseums Zürich pg 33. Schweizerisches Landesmuseum, Alain Charles Gruber 1977.

23 Uri Urikon http://www.urikon.ch/UR_Uri/UR_Wappen.aspx

24 Uri Suisse Stadt Archives: Fridig (Friding, Fridung, Friden): Typed notes as well as copies of articles (1443-1650). Source: http://www.staur.ch/P_Archive/PA_001.pdf

25 Uri Suisse Stadt Archives: Fridig (Friding, Fridung, Friden): Typed notes as well as copies of articles (1443-1650). Source: http://www.staur.ch/P_Archive/PA_001.pdf

26 Mémoires et documents, Volume 2, Issues 2-3 By Société d'histoire de la Suisse romande. 1841.

27 Der Landammann in den schweizerischen Demokratien Uri, Schwyz, Unterwalden by A. Rosa Benz 1917.

28 Dictionnaire géographique-statistique de la Suisse, tr. et revu par J.L.B. Leresche. Revu pour ce qui concerne la Suisse romande par J.-L. Moratel. 1859

29 Historisches Neujahrsblatt By Verein für Geschichte und Altertümer von Uri, pg45.1894

30 Der Landammann in den schweizerischen Demokratien Uri, Schwyz, Unterwalden By A. Rosa Benz 1917

31 Dictionnaire géographique et statistique de la Suisse, Volume 2 By Markus Lutz. 1837

32 College of Noble Austriae http://www.coresno.com/standeserhoehungen/177-reichsadel/3866-karton124.html

33 Deutsche Studenten in Bologna (1289-1562): Biographischer Index zu den Acta ... By Acta nationis germanicae Universitatis bononiensis, Deutsche. 1899.

34 Albrecht der Schenk von Verthoven http://www.mom-ca.uni-koeln.de/mom/AT-StiAG/GoettweigOSB/1325_II_05/charter#anchor?q=Verthouen

35 Albrect Aidem http://www.mom-ca.uni-koeln.de/mom/AT-StiAZ/Urkunden/1325_XI_17/charter?

36 Regesta sive rerum boicarum autographa ad annum usque MCCC. e regni scriniis fideliter in summas contracta juxtaque genuinam terrae stirpisque diversitatem in bavarica, alemanica et franconica synchronistice disposita curâ Caroli Henrici de Lang Impensis regiis, 1841

303

37 Collectio Constitutionum Imperialum, Hoc est, DD.NN. Imperatorum ..., Volume 3 1673

38 Zurich Switzerland archive. 1411. http://suche.staatsarchiv.djiktzh.ch/detail.aspx?ID=365668

39 Zurich Switzerland archive. 1411. http://suche.staatsarchiv.djiktzh.ch/detail.aspx?ID=365668

40 http://www.klosterarchiv.ch/e-archiv_urkunden_detail.php?id=1756

41 Schaffhauser Beiträge zur Vaterländischen Geschichte, Issues 6-7. 1894

42 Schaffhausen Switzerland Archives Search Engine http://www.stadtarchiv-schaffhausen.ch/SHArchivSuchen.HTM

43 Uri Suisse Stadt Archives: Fridig (Friding, Fridung, Friden): Typed notes as well as copies of articles (1443-1650). Source: http://www.staur.ch/P_Archive/PA_001.pdf

44 Kempten Archives. 1506. http://www.gda.bayern.de/findmittel/pdf/staau_fk-lehenhur_001_2008.pdf

45 Das Verbrüderungsbuch der Abtei Reichenau by Johanne Autenrieth, Dieter Geuenich, Karl Schmid.1979

46 Altdeutsches Namenbuch, Volume 1 By Ernst Wilhelm Förstemann. 1856

47 Chronica der Weitberuempten... Statt Augspurg... Von derselben altem Ursprung... Sampt Abbildung vnd Deutung gedachter Statt alter Monumenten... Auß... Marx Welsers acht Büchern... Gezogen vnd... In vnser teutschen Spraach in Truck verfertigt durch Engelbertum Werlichium Hartmann, Wolffgangus, 1595

48 Berns Ausburger in der Landschaft Frutigen: Wandfluh, Hans 1952.

49 en.wikibooks.org/wiki/German/Grammar/Alphabet_and_Pronunciation

50 Nuovo dizionario geografico universale statistico-storico-commerciale Antonelli, 1828

51 List of Swiss Emigrants in the Eighteenth Century to American Colonies By Albert Bernhardt Faust. 1920.

52 Chronica der weitberüempten keyserlichen freyen und deß H. Reichs Statt Augspurg in Schwaben: von derselben altem Ursprung, schöne gelegene zierliche Gebäwen unnd namhafften gedenckwürdigen Geschichten. Egenollf, 1595.

53 Topographische, historische und statistische Darstellung des Dorfes und Gemeindsbezirkes Melchnau in Seinen Beziehungen zur Vergangenheit, Gegenwart und Zukunft Gedruckt bei Konrad, 1855

54 Heinnrici II, et Arduini diplomata by Holy Roman Emperor (1002-1024) by Harry Bresslau, 1903.

55 Collectio Constitutionum Imperialum, Hoc est, DD.NN. Imperatorum ..., Volume 3 1673

56 Geschichte des Appenzellischen Volkes, Volume 4 By Johann Kaspar Zellweger

57 Irkundenbuch der Abtei Sanct Gallen, Volume 6 by Kloster St. Gallen" for the Abbey @ St. Gallen. 1941.

58 Fridig pronounced Free-dig www.forvo.com/word/fridig

59 Berner Zeitschrift für Geschichte und Heimatkunde Staatsarchiv des Kantons Bern, 1952 or Volkskundlich-soziologische Aspekte der Namengebung in Frutigen Berner Oberland pg35, 1967.

60 Friding pronounced Free-ding http://tts.imtranslator.net/KXvq

61 Frydig pronounced Frew-dee http://tts.imtranslator.net/KXvx

62 Wappenbuch von Arlberger (Abbey of St. Christophe in Arlberger Thal in Tirol, Austria) armorial 1394 to 1430. Otto Hupp Berlin 1937-39. http://bilderserver.at/wappenbuecher/ProfHuppOSPv2_52z2/

63 Fridingē pronounced Free-ding http://tts.imtranslator.net/KWvN

64 Fridigē pronounced Free-dig-Ä http://tts.imtranslator.net/KWvP

65 Historisches Neujahrsblatt By Verein für Geschichte und Altertümer von Uri, pg45.1894

66 Chronik von Meran der alten Haupstadt des Landes Tirol. Wagner 1887.

67 Richental, Ulrich (von) Concilium zu Konstanz Augsburg: Anton Sorg, pg 324 & 404. 2 Sept. 1483. http://tudigit.ulb.tu-darmstadt.de/show/inc-iii-55/0003/thumbs?sid=64c9a6d14e58a520b8245f2555c005d0#current_page

68 Geschichte des Appenzellischen Volkes, Volume 4 By Johann Kaspar Zellweger

69 Wappenbuch von Arlberger (Abbey of St. Christophe in Arlberger Thal in Tirol, Austria) armorial 1394 to 1430. Otto Hupp Berlin 1937-39.
http://bilderserver.at/wappenbuecher/ProfHuppOSPv2_52z2/

70 Volkskundlich-soziologische Aspekte der Namengebung in Frutigen Berner Oberland pg35, 1967.

71 Irkundenbuch der Abtei Sanct Gallen, Volume 6 by Kloster St. Gallen" for the Abbey @ St. Gallen. 1941.

72 Der Geschichtsfreund [Historian Friend], Volumes 77-78.

73 Aegidii Tschudii gewesenen Land-Ammanns zu Glarus Chronicon ..., Volume 2 By Aegidius Tschudi. 1736.

74 Freiburg im Mittelalter: Vorträge z. Stadtjubiläum 1970 Verlag Konkordia, 1970

75 Archivum Heraldicum volume 36-37, pg 62. 1922

76 Deutsches Wörterbuch Volume 1, pg577. 1881.

77 Uri Suisse Stadt Archives: Fridig (Friding, Fridung, Friden): Typed notes as well as copies of articles (1443-1650). Source: http://www.staur.ch/P_Archive/PA_001.pdf

78 Uri Suisse Stadt Archives: Fridig (Friding, Fridung, Friden): Typed notes as well as copies of articles (1443-1650). Source: http://www.staur.ch/P_Archive/PA_001.pdf

79 Der Landammann in den schweizerischen Demokratien Uri, Schwyz, Unterwalden by A. Rosa Benz 1917.

80 Dictionnaire géographique-statistique de la Suisse, tr. et revu par J.L.B. Leresche. Revu pour ce qui concerne la Suisse romande par J.-L. Moratel. 1859

81 Historisches Neujahrsblatt By Verein für Geschichte und Altertümer von Uri, pg45.1894

82 Der Landammann in den schweizerischen Demokratien Uri, Schwyz, Unterwalden By A. Rosa Benz 1917

83 Dictionnaire géographique et statistique de la Suisse, Volume 2 By Markus Lutz. 1837

84 Mémoires et documents, Volume 2, Issues 2-3 By Société d'histoire de la Suisse romande. 1841.

85 Burg und Herrschaft Hohenkrahen im Hegau, by Eberhard Dobler. 1986

86 Grafenried zur Zeit der Dreifelderwirtschaft. By Paul Zyrd. 1942.

87 Fontes Rerum Bernensium   FRB   Volume 10, pg 7.

88 Sprachspiegel, Volumes 21-23 By Deutschschweizerischer Sprachverein. 1965

89 Lexington Co, SC 1800 Census
www.rootsweb.ancestry.com/~sclexing/records/census1800.htm

90 Swiss Federal Archives (email) Ruth Stalder 7-2003

91 en.wikipedia.org/wiki/Apocope

92 Grafenried zur Zeit der Dreifelderwirtschaft. By Paul Zyrd. 1942.

93 Fontes Rerum Bernensium   FRB   Volume 10, pg 7.

94 Sprachspiegel, Volumes 21-23 By Deutschschweizerischer Sprachverein. 1965

95 Ortsnamenbuch des Kantons Bern, alter Kantonsteil: Dokumentation und Deutung. T. 1. A-F Paul Zinsli Francke, 1976

96 Ortsnamenbuch des Kantons Bern, alter Kantonsteil, Volume 1, Part 1

97 Chronik oder geschichtliche, ortskundliche und statistische Beschreibung des Kantons Bern, alten Theils: by Albert Jahn. Stumpfli 1857.

98 Zwischen klösterlichem Ideal und adligen Bedürfnissen : das Zisterzienserkloster Kappel Böhmer, Roland / Niederhäuser, Peter 2006. http://dx.doi.org/10.5169/seals-16586

99 Schweizerisches Urkundenregister, Volume 1 By Allgemeine Geschichtforschende Gesellschaft der Schweiz.

100 Helvetische Kirchen-Geschichten (etc).. by Johann Jacob Hottinger. 1698.

101 Mittheilungen des Vereins für geschichts- und alterthumskunde zu Kahla und Roda, Volume 4. 1894

102 Urkundenbuch der Städte Dresden und Pirna edited by Karl Friedrich von Posern-Klett. 1875

103 50 Weapons That Changed Warfare By William Weir. 2005. **Many books have this same reference.

The Swabian Connection – Expanded Edition

104 History of Christian names By Charlotte Mary Yonge, pg 295. 1884

105 Urkundenbuch der Städte Dresden und Pirna edited by Karl Friedrich von Posern-Klett. 1875

106 Ulmisches urkundenbuch im auftrage der stadt Ulm, Volumes 1-2 By Friedrich Pressel, Gustav Veesenmeyer, Hugo Bazing. 1898

107 Gescghiete der landstandischen verfassung Tirols:Die entstehung und ausbildung der socialen stande und ihrer ..in Tirol. Albert Jager 1881.

108 Urkundenbuch der stadt Aarau - Argovia, Volumes 10-11 By Heinrich Boos. 1879

109 Archeologia e storia della produzione del vetro preindustriale, by Marja Mendera, Università di Siena. 1991

110 Freiburg im Mittelalter. Verl. Konkordia, Freiburg im Breisgau (Germany). 1970

111 Festgabe Adolf Kaegi von schülern und freunden dargebracht zum 30, pg 230. 1919

112 Allgemeine geschichte des freystaats Ury. By Franz Vinzenz Schmid, p92. 1788.

113 Katalog der Gemälde des Bayerischen Nationalmuseums By Bayerisches Nationalmuseum, Karl Voll, Heinz Braune, Hans Buchheit. 1908

114 Die Matrikel der Universität Heidelberg...: T. von 1386 bis 1553 By Universität Heidelberg. 1884.

115 From the communal Reformation to the revolution of the common man By Peter Blickle. 1998

116 Württembergische Jahrbücher für Statistik und Landeskunde, Part 2 By Württemberg (Germany). Statistisches Landesamt, Memminger (v.), Württemberg (Kingdom). 1891

117 Renaissancekultur und antike Mythologie By Bodo Guthmüller, Wilhelm Kühlmann. 1999

118 Kemptner Wappen und Zeichen Eduard Zimmermann, Kempten, Verlag für Heimatpflege. 1963.

119 Die Matrikel der Universität Leipzig: Register, by George Erler. 1976

120 Codex diplomaticus Salemitanus, Urkundenbuch der cisterzienserabtei Salem ... By Salem abbey. 1881.

121 Helvetische Kirchen-Geschichten (etc).. by Johann Jacob Hottinger. 1698.

122 Monasterium.net http://www.mom-ca.uni-koeln.de/mom/CSGXI/6709./charter?q=Frydingen

123 Allgemeine Weltgeschichte, Volume 94 By William Guthrie, John Gray, Christian Gottlob Heyne, Johann Daniel Ritter, Johann M. Schröckh, Johann Andreas Dieze, Daniel Ernst.1801.

124 Frühneuhochdeutsches Glossar By Alfred Götze, pg90.1967.

125 Archeologia e storia della produzione del vetro preindustriale Marja Mendera, Università di Siena. Dipartimento di archeologia e storia delle arti, pg400. 1991.

126 Ulmisches Urkundenbuch im Auftrage der Stadt Ulm: Bd. Die Reichsstadt. By Friedrich Pressel, Gustav Veesenmeyer, Hugo Bazing, pg 697. 1900.

127 Allgemeine Weltgeschichte, Volume 94 By William Guthrie, John Gray, Christian Gottlob Heyne, Johann Daniel Ritter, Johann M. Schröckh, Johann Andreas Dieze, Daniel Ernst, pg400. 1801.

128 Argovia, Volumes 5-6, pg415. 1867.

129 Ulmisches urkundenbuch im auftrage der stadt Ulm, Volumes 1-2 By Friedrich Pressel, Gustav Veesenmeyer, Hugo Bazing. 1898.

130 Archeologia e storia della produzione del vetro preindustriale, by Marja Mendera, Università di Siena. 1991

131 Das Emmenthal nach Geschichte, Land und Leuten By Jakob Imobersteg Huber, 1876

132 Die Heimathskunde für den Kanton Luzern: Neudorf von Melchior Estermann By Joseph. - Bölsterli, Xaver. - Thürig, Melchior. - Estermann, Raphael. – Reinhard. 1875

133 Konstanz record for St. Blasien kloster. State of Archives – Zurich, Switerland. Record for Baden, Switzerland. http://suche.staatsarchiv.djiktzh.ch/detail.aspx?ID=274782

134 Biblisches Wörterbuch enthaltend eine Erklärung der alterthümlichen und ... By Wübbe Ulrich Jütting. B.G. Teubner, 1864

135 Indogermanische Forschungen K.J. Trübner, 1917

136 Urkendenbuch der Stadt Aarau: Mit einer historischen Einleitung, Register und Gloaase, sowie einer historischen Karte. Sauerlander, 1880.

137 Urkundenbuch der Stadt Aarau, herausg. Von H Boos by Heinrich Boos.1880.

The Swabian Connection – Expanded Edition

138 Grafenried zur Zeit der Dreifelderwirtschaft. By Paul Zyrd. 1942.

139 Fontes Rerum Bernensium   FRB   Volume 10, pg 7.

140 Sprachspiegel, Volumes 21-23 By Deutschschweizerischer Sprachverein. 1965

141 Die regesten der ehemaligan sanktblasier propsteien Klingnau und Wislikofen ... By Johann Huber Gebr. Räber, 1878

142 Annales Heremi Dei Parae Matris monasterii in Helvetia, ordinis S. Benedicti Antiquitate religione frequentia, miraculis... auctore R. P. F. Christophoro Hartmanno...1612.

143 Acta Nationis Germanicae: Universitatis Bononiensis ex archetypis tabularii ... By Ernst Friedländer, Carlo Malagola, Università di Bologn. 1887

144 Ulmisches urkundenbuch im auftrage der stadt Ulm, Volumes 1-2 By Friedrich Pressel, Gustav Veesenmeyer, Hugo Bazing. 1898.

145 Wappenbuch von Arlberger (Abbey of St. Christophe in Arlberger Thal in Tirol, Austria) armorial 1394 to 1430. Otto Hupp Berlin 1937-39.
http://bilderserver.at/wappenbuecher/ProfHuppOSPv2_52z2/

146 Richental, Ulrich (von) Concilium zu Konstanz Augsburg: Anton Sorg, pg 324 & 404. 2 Sept. 1483. http://tudigit.ulb.tu-darmstadt.de/show/inc-iii-55/0003/thumbs?sid=64c9a6d14e58a520b8245f2555c005d0#current_page

147 LandesArchives Württembergisches Urkundenbuch http://maja.bsz-bw.de/wubonline/?wub=4654

148 Burg und Herrschaft Hohenkrahen im Hegau, by Eberhard Dobler. 1986

149 Die Matrikeln Der Universität Tübingen. 1877/1906.

150 Fontes Rerum Bernensium   FRB   Volume 10, pg 7.

151 Sprachspiegel, Volumes 21-23 By Deutschschweizerischer Sprachverein. 1965

152 Monasterium.net http://www.mom-ca.uni-koeln.de/mom/CSGXI/6709./charter?q=Frydingen

153 Basel Archives Citizen document. 1537.
http://query.staatsarchiv.bs.ch/query/detail.aspx?ID=826969

154 Acta Nationis Germanicae: Universitatis Bononiensis ex archetypis tabularii Malvezziani. By Università di Bologna. 1887

155 The emblem books of Duke Albrecht VI. of Austria: Ingeram Codex d. Former library Cotta ed. v. Charlotte Mugs & Ortwin Gamber, Vienna, Cologne and Graz; 1986th Yearbook of the heraldic eagle-Genealogical Society; Episode 3, vol 12 born 1984/85, ISBN 3-205-05002-9
http://de.wikipedia.org/wiki/Datei:Ingeram_Codex_101.jpg

156 Saint Gallen Haggenburg Armorial Introduction and edition by Steen Clemmensen from Sankt Gallen Stiftbibliothek (Schweiz) Cod.sang. 1084 http://www.armorial.dk/german/SanktGallen.pdf

157 Freiburger Diözesan-Archiv, Volumes 25-26 By Kirchengeschichtlicher Verein für Geschichte, Christliche Kunst, Altertums- und Literaturkunde des Erzbistums Freiburg Verlag Herder., 1896

158 Das Verbrüderungsbuch der Abtei Reichenau by Johanne Autenrieth, Dieter Geuenich, Karl Schmid.1979

159 Altdeutsches Namenbuch, Volume 1 By Ernst Wilhelm Förstemann. 1856

160 Roberti Turneri Deuonii oratoris et philosophi in academia Ingolstadiensi ...By Robert Turner.165

161 The Universal anthology: a collection of the best literature, ancient mediaeval and modern, with biographical and explanatory notes, Volume 33. By Richard Garnett, Léon Vallée, Alois Brandl. 1899

162 Irkundenbuch der Abtei Sanct Gallen, Volume 6 by Kloster St. Gallen" for the Abbey @ St. Gallen. 1941.

163 Fürstenbergisches Urkundenbuch: Sammlung der Quellen zur Geschichte des Hauses Fürstenberg und seiner Lande in Schwaben, Volume 5. In Commission der H. Laupp'schen Buchhandlung, 1885.

164 Regesta Episcoporum Constantiensium: Regesten zur Geschichte ..., Volumes 1-2 Wagner, 1895

165 Die ritterburgen des Hohgau's, Issues 1-2 By Ottmar Friedrich Heinrich Schönhuth.1833

166 Mitteilungen zur vaterläendischen Geschichte, Volumes 19-20 By Historischer Verein des Kantons St. Gallen. 1884.

167 Zeitschrift für die Geschichte des Oberrheins, Volume 35 By Grossherzogliches General-Landesarchiv zu Karlsruhe, Badische Historische Kommission, Badisches Gene. 1883.

168 Burg und Herrschsft Hohekrahen im Hegau, by Eberhard Dobler. 1986

169 Chartularium Sangallense III, Nr. 1159, S. 168 http://www.mom-ca.uni-koeln.de/mom/CSGIII/Nr_1159_S_168/charter

170 Source: Die Regesten der Archive in der schweizerischen Eidgenossenschaft: Bd., 4. T ...By Theodor von Mohr, Gallus Morel, Friedrich Stettler, Gerold Meyer. 1854

171 Burg und Herrschsft Hohekrahen im Hegau, by Eberhard Dobler. 1986

172 LandesArchives Württembergisches Urkundenbuch http://maja.bsz-bw.de/wubonline/?wub=4654

173 LandesArchives Württembergisches Urkundenbuch http://maja.bsz-bw.de/wubonline/?wub=4654

174 Geschicte der Freiherrn von Bodman Vol 1 pg 57. By Leopold Bodman. 1894

175 Burg und Herrschsft Hohekrahen im Hegau, by Eberhard Dobler. 1986

176 Der österreichische Hussitenkrieg, 1420-1434. pg 33. 1982.

177 State Archives of Zurich ONLINE CATALOGUE (Keyword: Kraey) http://suche.staatsarchiv.djiktzh.ch/detail.aspx

178 Zeitschrift für die Geschichte des Oberrheins, Volume 37 By Franz Joseph Mone, Grossherzogliches General-Landesarchiv zu Karlsruhe, Badische Historische. 1884.

179 Krieger, Albert; Badische Historische Kommission [Hrsg.] Topographisches Wörterbuch des Großherzogtums Baden (Band 2). 1904 http://diglit.ub.uni-heidelberg.de/diglit/krieger1904bd2/0120/ocr

180 Burg und Herrschsft Hohekrahen im Hegau, by Eberhard Dobler. 1986

181 Römische quellen zur Konstanzer bistumsgeschichte zur zeit der Päpste in Avignon, 1305-1378. By Karl Rieder. 1908

182 Prodromus Monumentorum Guelficorum Seu Catalogus Abbatum Imperialis Monasterii Weingartensis: A Potentissimis Illius Nobilissimae Gentis Principibus Fundati, Insigniterque Dotati Etc. Ex Monumentis Domesticis, Aliisque Coaevis Scriptoribus Collectus.1781

183 Uri Suisse Stadt Archives: Fridig (Friding, Fridung, Friden): Typed notes as well as copies of articles (1443-1650). Source: http://www.staur.ch/P_Archive/PA_001.pdf

184 L'Alsace illustrée:ou recherches sur l'Alsace pendant la domination des Celtes, des Romains, des Francs, des Allemands et des Français.1851

185 Wappenbuch von Arlberger (Abbey of St. Christophe in Arlberger Thal in Tirol, Austria) armorial 1394 to 1430. Otto Hupp Berlin 1937-39. http://bilderserver.at/wappenbuecher/ProfHuppOSPv2_52z2/

186 Fürstenbergisches Urkundenbuch: Sammlung der Quellen zur Geschichte des Hauses Fürstenberg und seiner Lande in Schwaben, Volume 5 In Commission der H. Laupp'schen Buchhandlung, 1885

187 Heiligenberg in Schwaben: nit einer Geschichte seiner Alten Grafen und des von ihnen beherrschten Linzgaus. Macklot 1853.

188 Flickinger DNA research Group http://www.familytreedna.com/public/Flickinger/default.aspx?section=yresults

189 Sammlung historischer schriften und urkunden: Geschöpt aus ..., Volume 3 By Max Freyberg Freiherr von. 1830.

190 Sammlung historischer schriften und urkunden: Geschöpt aus ..., Volume 3 By Max Freyberg Freiherr von. 1830.

191 Albrecht Flickinger genealogy web site http://www.flickinger-albrecht.de/3.html. 2008

192 Schriften, Issues 1-4 By Verein für geschichte und naturgeschichte der Baar und der angrenzenden landesteile in Donaueschinge Verein für Geschichte und Naturgeschichte der Baar, 1871

193 Zurich Armorial http://www.armorial.dk/german/Zurich%20WR.pdf

194 Württembergisches Urkundenbuch, Volume 6. 1978
195 LandesArchives Württembergisches Urkundenbuch http://maja.bsz-bw.de/wubonline/index.php?mp=2&fs=true&recherche%5Bsuche%5D%5Bvon%5D=680&recherche%5Bsuche%5D%5Bbis%5D=1299&recherche%5Bsortierung%5D%5B
196 Codex diplomaticus Salemitanus, Urkundenbuch der cisterzienserabtei Salem ... By Salem abbey. 1881
197 Fürstenbergisches Urkundenbuch: Sammlung der Quellen zur ..., Volume 5 By Donaueschingen (Germany). Fürstenbergisches Archive In Commission der H. Laupp'schen Buchhandlung, 1885
198 Zeitschrift für die Geschichte des Oberrheins, Volume 31. W. Kohlhammer, 1879
199 Die Regesten der Archive in der schweizerischen Eidgenossenschaft: Bd., 4. T ... By Theodor von Mohr, Gallus Morel, Friedrich Stettler, Gerold Meyer v. 1854
200 Beschreibung des Oberamts Tuttlingen: mit 3 Tabellen. Bissinger, 1879
201 Zurich Armorial http://www.armorial.dk/german/Zurich%20WR.pdf
202 Württembergisches Urkundenbuch, Volume 6. 1978
203 LandesArchives Württembergisches Urkundenbuch http://maja.bsz-bw.de/wubonline/index.php?mp=2&fs=true&recherche%5Bsuche%5D%5Bvon%5D=680&recherche%5Bsuche%5D%5Bbis%5D=1299&recherche%5Bsortierung%5D%5B
204 Das Land Baden-Württemberg: Regierungsbezirk Freiburg, Kohlhammer. 1982.
205 Nendingen http://www.territorioscuola.com/wikipedia/de.wikipedia.php?title=Nendingen
206 Württembergisches Urkundenbuch, Volume 6. 1978
207 Codex diplomaticus Salemitanus, Urkundenbuch der cisterzienserabtei Salem ... By Salem abbey. 1881.
208 Alemannia, Volume 14 By Anton Birlinger. 1886
209 Codex diplomaticus Salemitanus, Urkundenbuch der cisterzienserabtei Salem ... By Salem abbey. 1881
210 Wirtembergisches Urkundenbuch: herausgegeben von dem Königlichen Staatsarchiv in Stuttgart In commission bei F. H. Köhler, 1871.
211 Wirtembergisches urkundenbuch In commission bei F. H. Köhler, 1889.
212 Beschreibung des Oberamts Tuttlingen: mit 3 Tabellen Bissinger, 1879.
213 Irkundenbuch der Abtei Sanct Gallen, Volume 4, Issues 1-3 By Kloster St. Gallen Huber (E. Fehr), 1892.
214 Das Land Baden-Württemberg: Regierungsbezirk Freiburg. Pg 682, 1982.
215 Schaffhausen Switzerland Archives Search Engine http://www.stadtarchiv-schaffhausen.ch/SHArchivSuchen.HTM
216 Burgen und Schlösser: Volume 43. 2002
217 Zurich Armorial http://www.armorial.dk/german/Zurich%20WR.pdf
218 Württembergisches Urkundenbuch, Volume 6. 1978
219 LandesArchives Württembergisches Urkundenbuch http://maja.bsz-bw.de/wubonline/index.php?mp=2&fs=true&recherche%5Bsuche%5D%5Bvon%5D=680&recherche%5Bsuche%5D%5Bbis%5D=1299&recherche%5Bsortierung%5D%5B
220 Codex diplomaticus Salemitanus, Urkundenbuch der cisterzienserabtei Salem ... By Salem abbey. 1881
221 Canton Luzern Familiewappens. 2010. http://www.staatsarchiv.lu.ch/index/schaufenster/familienwappen.htm?buchstabe=h&wappen=0947.jpg.
222 Codex diplomaticvs anhaltinvs, Volume 1 By Otto Heinema. 1873.
223 Geschichte des ehemaligen Bisthums Lebus und des Landes dieses Nahmens, Volume 1 By Sigmund Wilhelm Wohlbrück. 1829
224 Geschichte des ehemaligen Bisthums Lebus und des Landes dieses Nahmens, Volume 1 By Sigmund Wilhelm Wohlbrück. 1829
225 Römische quellen zur Konstanzer bistumsgeschichte zur zeit der Päpste in ... By Karl Rieder. 1908

The Swabian Connection – Expanded Edition

226 Urkundenbuch der Landschaft Basel, Volume 1 By Heinrich Boos. 1881
227 Burgen und Schlösser: Volume 43. 2002
228 Nomina geographica: Versuch einer allgemeinen geographischen onomatologie By Johann Jacob Egli. 1872
229 Vierteljahrsschrift für Wappen-, Siegel- und Familienkunde , Volume 9 Herold, Verein für Heraldik, Genealogie und Verwandte Wissenschaft, Berlin. 1881.
230 Urkundenbuch der Stadt Basel: Hrsg. von der Historischen und ..., Volume 9 By Basel-Stadt (Switzerland). Staatsarchiv, Historische und Antiquarische Gesellschaft zu Basel.1905.
231 CTS6433=I2A2A1C2A2 via ISOGG http://www.isogg.org/tree/ISOGG_HapgrpI.html
232 FTDNA understanding Haplogroups http://www.familytreedna.com/understanding-haplogroups.aspx
233 FTDNA Genetic Distance Markers. 2010 http://www.familytreedna.com/genetic-distance-markers.aspx?testtype=37
234 Britam.org Haplotype I. 2010 http://www.britam.org/Questions/Y%20Haploroup%20I.html
235 Distribution of European Y-Chromosome DNA haplogroups by country in Percentage Feb 2012. www.eupedia.com/europe/european_y-dna_haplogroups.shtml
236 Das ehemalige Frauenkloster Tänikon im Thurgau Buchdruckerei Berichthaus, 1906
237 Die Regesten der Archive in der schweizerischen Eidgenossenschaft: Bd., 4. T ... By Theodor von Mohr, Gallus Morel, Friedrich Stettler, Gerold Meyer v. 1854
238 Monasterium.net 1291 http://www.mom-ca.uni-koeln.de/mom/CSGIV/1291_VI_15.1/charter?
239 Urkundenbuch der Stadt Basel: Hrsg. von der Historischen und ..., Volume 9 By Basel-Stadt (Switzerland). Staatsarchiv, Historische und Antiquarische Gesellschaft zu Basel.1905.
240 Monasterium.net 1296 http://www.mom-ca.uni-koeln.de/mom/CSGIV/1296_III_20/charter?
241 Zeitschrift für die Geschichte des Oberrheins, Volume 31. W. Kohlhammer, 1879
242 Vierteljahrsschrift für Wappen-, Siegel- und Familienkunde, Volume 9 By Herold, Verein für Heraldik, Genealogie und Verwandte Wissenschaft, Berlin. 1881
243 Die Regesten der Archive in der schweizerischen Eidgenossenschaft: Bd., 4. T ... By Theodor von Mohr, Gallus Morel, Friedrich Stettler, Gerold Meyer v. 1854
244 Die Regesten der Archive in der schweizerischen Eidgenossenschaft: Bd., 4. T ... By Theodor von Mohr, Gallus Morel, Friedrich Stettler, Gerold Meyer v. 1854
245 Irkundenbuch der Abtei Sanct Gallen, Volume 4, Issues 1-3 By Kloster St. Gallen Huber (E. Fehr), 1892.
246 Die Miller von und zu Aichholz: Eine genealogische Studie, Part 1, Volume 1 By Franz X. Woeber Gerold & Co., 1893
247 Vierteljahrsschrift für Wappen-, Siegel- und Familienkunde , Volume 9 Herold, Verein für Heraldik, Genealogie und Verwandte Wissenschaft, Berlin. 1881.
248 Heildelberg Archives on Loewenburg: http://digi.ub.uni-heidelberg.de/diglit/kindlervonknobloch1898bd2/0533/ocr?sid=7b2919bf8ffccf4ec97149e8c89615d8
249 Die Aargauer Gessler in Urkunden von 1250 bis 1513 [ed.] von E.L. Rochholz edited by Ernst Ludwig Rochholz. 1877
250 Urkundenbuch der Stadt Basel: Hrsg. von der Historischen und ..., Volume 9 By Basel-Stadt (Switzerland). Staatsarchiv, Historische und Antiquarische Gesellschaft zu Basel.1905.
251 Die Regesten der Archive in der schweizerischen Eidgenossenschaft: Bd., 4. T ... By Theodor von Mohr, Gallus Morel, Friedrich Stettler, Gerold Meyer v. 1854
252 Kloster Fraubrunnen http://de.wikipedia.org/wiki/Kloster_Fraubrunnen
253 Urkunden für die Geschichte der Stadt Bern und ihres frühesten ..., Volume 1 By Karl Zeerleder. 1853
254 Urkundenbuch der Abtei Sanct Gallen, Volume 4, Parts 1-3 By Antiquarische Gesellschaft in Zürich, Historischer Verein des Kantons St. Gallen.1899
255 Landesarchive Baden-Wurttembergisches Online Indexes for St. Gallen Monastery. http://www.wubonline.de/
256 Die Matrikel der Unversität Heidelberg ..By Universität Heidelberg.1893.

257 Conrad Grünenberg's Wappenbuch ~1500. http://www.armorial.dk/german/Grunenberg.pdf

258 Geschichte der Stadt Radolfzell am Bodensee By Peter Paul Albert. 1896

259 Fürstenbergisches Urkundenbuch: Sammlung der Quellen zur ..., Volume 5
By Donaueschingen (Germany). Fürstenbergisches Archive In Commission der H. Laupp'schen Buchhandlung, 1885

260 HegauRitter Wildenstein caste History: http://www.hegauritter.net/Wildenstein.html

261 Zimern Nobles by Wikipedia. http://de.wikipedia.org/wiki/Zimmern_%28Adelsgeschlecht%29

262 Zimmerman record http://www.mom-ca.uni-koeln.de/mom/DE-BayHStA/KUPassauNiedernburg/24/charter?

263 Urkundenbuch By Ludwig Schmid 1862

264 Das Koenigreich Wuerttemberg: Bd.Schwarzwaldkreis By Wuerttemberg. Statistisches Landesamt. 1905

265 Fürstenbergisches Urkundenbuch: Sammlung der Quellen zur ..., Volume 5 By Donaueschingen (Germany). Fürstenbergisches Archiv In Commission der H. Laupp'schen Buchhandlung, 1885

266 Geschichte des appenzellischen volkes, Volume 1 By Johann Caspar Zellweger. 1830.

267 Schaffhausen Switzerland Archives Search Engine http://www.stadtarchiv-schaffhausen.ch/SHArchivSuchen.HTM

268 Zeitschrift fur die Geschichte des Oberrheims Volume 26. G Braun 1883.

269 Geschichte der grafen von Zimmern: ein beitrag zur geschichte des deutschen ...By Heinrich Ruckgaber.1840.

270 Sammelband mehrerer Wappenbücher - BSB Cod.icon. 391, [S.l.] Süddeutschland (Augsburg ?), um 1530 http://daten.digitale-sammlungen.de/~db/bsb00007681/images/index.html?seite=154&fip=193.174.98.30

271 Darvin Martin Blog: BeforeSwtizerland http://beforeswitzerland.blogspot.com/2010/10/martin-yoder-and-zimmerman-all-one-big.html

272 Ancestry.com forum by Lee Lybarger. 5-2005. http://boards.ancestry.com/surnames.leuenberger/8/mb.ashx

273 Rootsweb.com Post for Lybarger family. By Pat Smith. Nov 1, 2001. http://wc.rootsweb.ancestry.com/cgi-bin/igm.cgi?op=GET&db=:1670239&id=I7584

274 Directory of family associations. By Elizabeth Petty Bentley. Genealogical Pub. Co., pg. 204. 1996

275 Lybarger Linkages Newsletter, by Lee H. Lybarger. 2005. http://home.comcast.net/~j_lybarger/fall_2005.htm

276 Email from Carol from Swiss Leuenberger FTDNA website

277 Katalog der Bibliothek des Reichstages, Volume 5 By Germany. Reichstag. Bibliothek, Eduard Blömeke, Dr. Johannes Müller (Oberbibliothekar) Druck von Trowitzsch, 1899.

278 Ysearch.org Reeder DNA results: http://www.ysearch.org/search_view.asp?uid=RJCSU&viewuid=55HJG&p=0

279 Regesta Episcoporum Constantiensium: Regesten zur Geschichte ..., Volumes 1-2 Wagner, 1895

280 Friedrich Riederer Spiegel der wahren Rhetorik (1493) Herausgegeben von Joachim Knape und Stefanie Luppold. 2008http://www.harrassowitz-verlag.de/dzo/artikel/201//002/2058_201.pdf?t=1228389416

281 Burg und Herrschaft Hohenkrahen im Hegau, by Eberhard Dobler. 1986

282 Furstenburgisches Urkendenbuch: Sammlung der Quellen zur – Volume 5, 1885.

283 Regesta Episcoporum Constantiensium: Regesten zur Geschichte ..., Volumes 1-2 Wagner, 1895

284 Schaffhausen Switzerland Archives Search Engine http://www.stadtarchiv-schaffhausen.ch/SHArchivSuchen.HTM

285 Burgen, Adelssitze und Wehrbauten im Linzgau. http://www.andreas-utz.info/inventar.htm

286 Ingeram Codex 98 Von Jungingen http://commons.wikimedia.org/wiki/File:Ingeram_Codex_098.jpg

The Swabian Connection – Expanded Edition

287 Brunner Genealogy and Brunner Family History Information.
http://www.geni.com/surnames/brunner
288 Rumisperchwird also von Brunner http://www.wubonline.de/wubpdf.php?fs=true&id=647
289 Römische quellen zur Konstanzer bistumsgeschichte zur zeit der Päpste in Avignon, 1305-1378. Karl Rieder. Verlag der Wagner'schen Universitätsbuchhandlung, 1908
290 Die Miller von und zu Aichholz: Eine genealogische Studie, Volume 2 By Franz X. Woeber. 1898.
291 Schriften des Vereins für Geschichte des Bodensees und seiner ..., Volumes 3-4 By Verein für Geschichte des Bodensees und Seiner Umgebung. 1872.
292 Zeitschrift für die Geschichte des Oberrheins, Volume 47 By Grossherzogliches General-Landesarchiv zu Karlsruhe, Badische Historische Kommission, Karlsruhe.1893.
293 Berner Zeitschrift fur Geschichte und Heimatkunde Staatarchiv de Kantons Bern, 1952.
294 Schweizerisches Geschlechterbuch, Volume 2
295 Das Jahrzeitenbuch der Leutkirche von Aarau By Jakob Hunziker Sauerlaender, 1872
296 Aar: the old term for Ger. Adler
http://docs.exdat.com/docs/index-73268.html?page=77
297 Abtei Einsiedeln http://www.klosterarchiv.ch/download/05_04_24_aemterverzeichnis.pdf
298 Dreyfacher Ehrenkranz St. Meinradi das ist Einsidlische in drey Theil verfaßte Cronick. Worinnen entworfen wird: Erstlich der Ursprung der Capellen, Zweytens der Anfang und Wachsthum deß Benedictiner Gotteshauses. Drittens 405 Wunderwerck, welche durch die Einsidlische Gnaden-Mutter geschehen seynd Meinrad Eberlin, 1723
299 Frohburg (Adelsgeschlecht) http://de.wikipedia.org/wiki/Frohburg_(Adelsgeschlecht)
300 Staats- und Rechtsgeschichte der Stadt und Landschaft Zürich, Volumes 1-2 Orell, Füssli, 1856
301 Zeehender wappen in Zurich http://www.chgh.net/heraldik/z/ze/zeender.htm
302 Markus Zehnder wappen from Canton of Thurgau , Switzerland
303 Feast of St. Michael Archangel http://en.wikipedia.org/wiki/Michaelmas
304 The Feast of St. Michaels http://www.feastofstmichael.com/history.html
305 Geschichte des Appenzellischen Volkes, Volume 4 By Johann Kaspar Zellweger
306 Neues preussisches Adels-Lexicon: Oder genealogische und diplomatische Nachrichten von den in der preussischen Monarchie ansässigen oder zu derselben in Beziehung stehenden fürstlichen, gräflichen, freiherrlichen und adeligen Häusern, Volume 1 Gebr. Reichenbach, 1836.
307 Württembergische Quarterly Journal 12 (1889), S. 138.
308 Actensammlung zur Geschichte der Zürcher Reformation in den Jahren 1519-1533 J. Schabelitz, 1879
309 Zurich wappenrolle for Bosshard http://www.chgh.net/heraldik/b/bo/bo08.htm
310 An American Dictionary of the English Language: Exhibiting the Origin ... By Noah Webste J.B. Lippincott, 1857
311 Notes and Queries Oxford University Press, 1875
312 http://home.arcor.de/bertrams/ueberau/herren_hoefe.htm
313 http://www.aumann-auman.de/
314 Burgen, Adelssitze und Wehrbauten im Linzgau. http://www.andreas-utz.info/inventar.htm
315 Das Bistum Bamberg, Franken und das Reich in der Stauferzeit. Der Bamberger Bischof im Elitengefüge des Reiches 1138-1245
316 Die ritterburgen des Hohgau's , Issues 1-2 Ottmar Friedrich Heinrich Schönhuth 1833.
317 Monumenta boica, Volume 7 1766 Bavaria, Germany
318 Members of Parliament: Parliaments of England, 1213-1702 By Great Britain. Parliamen
319 Die Bäuerlichen Familiennamen des Landkreises Oschatz. Isolde Neumann. 1970
320 Geschichte des Egerlandes (bis 1437) ...: mit unterstützung der Gesellschaft ... By Heinrich Gradl. 1893
321 Urkunden-Buch der Familie Teufenbach: im Auftrage des Mähr. Landes-Ausschusses By Vincenc Brandl.1867.

322 Standhaftigkeit der altwürttembergischen Klosterfrauen im Reformations-Zeitalter By Konrad Rothenhäusler 1884

323 Fredirech Humpis Waltrams Epitagh with Fridngen wappen ancestry. http://commons.wikimedia.org/wiki/File:Pf%C3%A4rrich_Epitaph_Friedrich_Humpis_Ahnenprobe_links_4.jpg

324 Germaniae Topo-Chrono-stemmatographicae sacrae et profanae Pars Altera: Görlinus, 1662

325 The New Schaff-Herzog Encyclopedia of Religious Knowledge: Embracing Biblical, Historical, Doctrinal, and Practical Theology and Biblical, Theological, and Ecclesiastical Biography from the Earliest Times to the Present Day, Volume 4,1909.

326 Codex diplomaticus Saxoniae regiae Giesicke, 1891

327 Pueschel wappen http://www.konrad-chile.de/Escudos/thmPueschel01.jpg

328 Feudal Cambridgeshire CUP Archive

329 The Battle Abbey Roll: With Some Account of the Norman Lineages, Volume 1 J. Murray, 1889

330 Annuaire du Département de la Manche , Volumes 42-45 J. Elie, 1870

331 Mary (Humphrey) Warner" by Genevieve Tylee Kiepura in "The American Genealogist," Vol. 26: 153-156, 218-219.

332 Libri confraternitatum Sancti Galli augiensis fabariensis By Kloster St. Gallen, Abtei Reichenau, Abtei Pfäfers. 1884

333 Die Christliche Sagengeschichte der Schweiz By E. F. Gelpk. 1862.

334 Directorium Diplomaticum oder chronologisch geordnete Auszüge von ..., Volume 1 By Ludwig August Schultes. 1821.

335 Geographisches Lexikon der Schweiz, Volume 2 By Charles Knapp, Maurice Borel, Victor Attinger, Heinrich Brunner, Société neuchâteloise de géographie. 1904.

336 Paul Willimksi http://www.hattingen-baden.de/Hattingen%20-%20Geschichte.htm

337 Zur Geschichte von Hettingen http://www.hohenzollerischer-geschichtsverein.de/userfiles/files/HZ-Heimat/HH_026_1976_ocr.pdf

338 Mitteilungen, Volumnes 39-40 1906

339 Albert Hugh Smith, English Place-names Elements, 2 volumes, Cambridge, 1972.

340 Albert Hugh Smith, English Place-names Elements, 2 volumes, Cambridge, 1972.

341 François de Beaurepaire, Les noms des communes et anciennes paroisses de la Seine-Maritime, éditions Picard 1979. p. 92.

342 Feudal Cambridgeshire CUP Archive

343 Winchester in the early Middle Ages: an edition and discussion of the Winton Domesday Frank Barlow, Martin Biddle Clarendon Press, 1976

344 An armorial of the army of invasion of Flanders 2.06-9.10.1297 http://www.armorial.dk/french/CPF_Ost-de-Flandre.pdf

345 Willement's roll of arms http://www.armorial.dk/english/WIL_PreEd.pdf

346 Some Feudal Coats of Arms from Heraldic Rolls 1298-1418: Illustrated with 830 Zinco Etchings from Effigies, Brasses and Coats of Arms, Joseph Parker J. Parker & Company, 1902

347 Dictionnaire de la noblesse, contenant les généalogies, l'histoire & la chronologie des familles nobles de France, l'explication de leur armes, & l'état des grandes terres du royaume On a joint à ce dictionnaire le tableau généalogique, historique, des maisons souveraines de l'Europe, & une notice des familles étrangères, les plus anciennes, les plus nobles & les plus illustres La veuve Duchesne, 1770.

348 The Present State of Great Britain and Ireland: In Three Parts. The I. Of South II. Of North Britain, III. Of Ireland. ... Also the Present State of His Majesty's Dominions in Germany. A. Bettesworth, G. Strahan, J. Round, J. Brotherton, W. Mears, and J. Clark, 1723 - 51

349 http://en.wikipedia.org/wiki/Clan_Home

350 http://www.baronage.co.uk/2003b/colding-1.html

351 Mémoires de la Société des antiquaires de Normandie, Volume 23. 1858.

352 Dictionnaire De La Noblesse: Contenant les Généalogies, l'Histoire & la Chronologie des Familles Nobles de France. 1776.

353 Genealogy of the Page Family in Virginia: Also a Condensed Account of the Nelson, Walker, Pendleton and Randolph Families, with References to the Byrd, Carter, Cary, Duke, Gilmer, Harrison, Rives, Thornton, Wellford, Washington, and Other Distinguished Families in Virginia Richard Channing Moore Page, Jenkins & Thomas, printers., 1883.

354 Families of Western New York: Excerpted from Genealogical and Family History of Western New York - A Record of the Achievements of Her People in the Making of a Commonwealth and the Building of a Nation. William Richard Cuttor 2009.

355 http://www.edmundchandler.com/Documents/coatofarms.html

356 The Fairs of Medieval England: An Introductory Study, Volumes 72-74

357 La science heroique, traitant de la noblesse, de l'origine des armes, de leurs blasons, & symboles ... avec la genealogie succincte de la Maison de Rosmadec en Bretagne: le tout embelly d'un grand nombre de figures en taille douce, sur toutes ces matieres Gabriel Cramoisy, 1644

358 Reallexikon der germanischen Altertumskunde, Volume 25 By Johannes Hoops Walter de Gruyter, 2003

359 http://deeds.library.utoronto.ca/charters/01180075/Hughes

360 History of the Penrose Family of Philadelphia. Josiah Granville Leach, George Hoffman Penrose private circulation, 1903

361 Colonial And Revolutionary Families Of Pennsylvania By John W. Jordan 2004. p660

362 http://www.yfull.com/tree/I-CTS6433/ Feb 2015

363 Conrad Grünenberg's Wappenbuch ~1500. http://www.armorial.dk/german/Grunenberg.pdf

364 Mittelater – Moyen Age – Temp Medieval. Journal of the Swiss Association castles. Basel, Switzerland. Jahrgang, 2006/1, März 2006
http://www.burgenverein.ch/publikationen/mitteilungen/2006/pdf/1_06%20Mittelalter.pdf

365 Aarau, Switzerland archives. http://www.stadtkirche-aarau.ch/jo/index.php/das-innere/grabplatten

366 Zuricher Wappenrolle notes. http://www.armorial.dk/german/Zurich%20WR.pdf

367 Wappentafel der Bischöfe von Konstanz, Mitte 19. Jh. von Franz Xaver Stiehle (bis zum Spätmittelalter Fantasiewappen; später teilweise unzuverlässig, im Mittelalter bei Amtsträgern in Doppelfunktion teilweise mit anderen Bistums-/Abtswappen angereicherte Schilde)
http://upload.wikimedia.org/wikipedia/commons/5/5b/Wappentafel_Bisch%C3%B6fe_von_Konstanz_F_X_Stiehle_19Jh.jpg

368 Codex diplomaticus Salemitanus, Urkundenbuch der cisterzienserabtei Salem ... By Salem abbey 1881.

369 Denkmäler aus der feudalzeit in lande Uri: (Das kätschen von Attinghusen.) Heinrich Zeller-Werdmüller. 1884

370 Codex diplomaticus Salemitanus, Urkundenbuch der cisterzienserabtei Salem ... By Salem abbey 1881.

371 Kemptner Wappen und Zeichen Eduard Zimmermann, Kempten, Verlag für Heimatpflege, 1963

372 College of Noble Austriae http://www.coresno.com/standeserhoehungen/177-reichsadel/3866-karton124.html

373 Siegel und Wappen des Adels und der Stadte des Kantons Argau By Walther Merz. 1907

374 Wappen der löbl. Bürgerschaft von Winterthur J. J. Siegfried, 1855

375 Zuricher Wappenrolle 1335/1345 http://www.vikinganswerlady.com/ZurichRoll/
http://www.silverdragon.org/HERALDRY/ZurichRolls/zroadt2v_files/ZROA07.GIF

376 Zurich wappen rolle http://de.wikipedia.org/wiki/Z%C3%BCrcher_Wappenrolle

377 Schaffhauser Beiträge zur Vaterländischen Geschichte, Issues 6-7, 1894.

378 Family von Bodman –Alt-Bodman Castle http://fr.wikipedia.org/wiki/Famille_von_Bodmann

379 Wappen der löbl. Bürgerschaft von Winterthur J. J. Siegfried, 1855

380 Wappenbuch von Arlberger (Abbey of St. Christophe in Arlberger Thal in Tirol, Austria) armorial 1394 to 1430. Otto Hupp Berlin 1937-39.
http://bilderserver.at/wappenbuecher/ProfHuppOSPv2_52z2/

The Swabian Connection – Expanded Edition

381 Richental, Ulrich (von) Concilium zu Konstanz Augsburg: Anton Sorg, 2 Sept. 1483
http://tudigit.ulb.tu-darmstadt.de/show/inc-iii-55/0324

382 Saint Gallen Haggenburg Armorial Introduction and edition by Steen Clemmensen from Sankt Gallen Stiftbibliothek (Schweiz) Cod.sang. 1084 http://www.armorial.dk/german/SanktGallen.pdf

383 Wappen deutscher Geschlechter, überwiegend aus Südwestdeutschland - BSB Cod.icon. 312 [S.l.] Süddeutschland 16. Jh http://daten.digitale-sammlungen.de/0000/bsb00001651/images/index.html?fip=193.174.98.30&id=00001651&seite=43

384 Wappen deutscher Geschlechter, überwiegend aus Südwestdeutschland - BSB Cod.icon. 312 [S.l.] Süddeutschland 16. Jh http://daten.digitale-sammlungen.de/0000/bsb00001651/images/index.html?fip=193.174.98.30&id=00001651&seite=43

385 Die Wappenbücher Herzog Albrechts VI. von Österreich: Ingeram-Codex d. ehem. Bibliothek Cotta; hrsg. v. Charlotte Becher u. Ortwin Gamber; Wien; Köln; Graz; 1986. Jahrbuch der Heraldisch-Genealogischen Gesellschaft Adler; Folge 3, Bd. 12 Jg. 1984/85; ISBN 3-205-05002-9

386 Saint Gallen Haggenburg Armorial Introduction and edition by Steen Clemmensen from Sankt Gallen Stiftbibliothek (Schweiz) Cod.sang. 1084 http://www.armorial.dk/german/SanktGallen.pdf

387 Wappenbuch von Arlberger (Abbey of St. Christophe in Arlberger Thal in Tirol, Austria) armorial 1394 to 1430. Otto Hupp Berlin 1937-39.
http://bilderserver.at/wappenbuecher/ProfHuppOSPv2_52z2/

388 Richental, Ulrich (von) Concilium zu Konstanz Augsburg: Anton Sorg, 2 Sept. 1483
http://tudigit.ulb.tu-darmstadt.de/show/inc-iii-55/0403/image?sid=4980b74504a00fa95e4e6f0abcdea121#current_page

389 Wappen deutscher Geschlechter, überwiegend aus Südwestdeutschland - BSB Cod.icon. 312 [S.l.] Süddeutschland 16. Jh http://daten.digitale-sammlungen.de/0000/bsb00001651/images/index.html?fip=193.174.98.30&id=00001651&seite=43

390 Julius Kindler von Knobloch: Oberbadisches Geschlechterbuch, Band 1. 1898
http://de.wikipedia.org/w/index.php?title=Datei:XIngeram_Codex_101b-Alt_Frydingen.jpg
http://commons.wikimedia.org/wiki/File:Ingeram_Codex_101.jpg

391 Anton Tirol wappenbuch Süddeutschland Ende 15. Jh. – 1540 http://dfg-viewer.de/show/?set[image]=137&set[zoom]=default&set[debug]=0&set[double]=0&set[mets]=http%3A%2F%2Fdaten.digitale-sammlungen.de%2F~db%2Fmets%2Fbsb00001649_mets.xml

392 Siehe auch Leopold Stierle: Herren von Friedingen, die das Wappen Alt-Friedingen geführt haben, Zeitschrift für Hohenzollerische Geschichte 36 (2000).

393 Die Edlen von Friedingen Streiflichter aus der Geschichte eines süddeutschen Adelsgeschlechts, by Rene Moeri.
http://www.zwingliana.ch/index.php/zwa/article/download/784/695-1-PB.pdf

394 Deutsche Studenten in Bologna (1289-1562): Biographischer Index zu den Acta ... By Acta nationis germanicae Universitatis bononiensis, Deutsche. 1899.

395 Ingeram Codex 94 http://commons.wikimedia.org/wiki/File:Ingeram_Codex_094.jpg

396 Richental, Ulrich (von) Concilium zu Konstanz Augsburg: Anton Sorg, 2 Sept. 1483
http://tudigit.ulb.tu-darmstadt.de/show/inc-iii-55/0003/thumbs?sid=64c9a6d14e58a520b8245f2555c005d0#current_page

397 Wappen deutscher Geschlechter, überwiegend aus Südwestdeutschland - BSB Cod.icon. 312 [S.l.] Süddeutschland 16. Jh http://daten.digitale-sammlungen.de/0000/bsb00001651/images/index.html?fip=193.174.98.30&id=00001651&seite=43

398 Grünenberg, Konrad: Das Wappenbuch Conrads von Grünenberg, Ritters und Bürgers zu Constanz - BSB Cgm 145, [S.l.], um 1480 [BSB-Hss Cgm 145] http://daten.digitale-sammlungen.de/~db/0003/bsb00035320/images/index.html?seite=246&fip=193.174.98.30

399 Wappenbuch von Arlberger (Abbey of St. Christophe in Arlberger Thal in Tirol, Austria) armorial 1394 to 1430. Otto Hupp Berlin 1937-39.
http://bilderserver.at/wappenbuecher/ProfHuppOSPv2_52z2/
400 Codex Sammlungen Inventory. Rudolph von Fridingen quartered Wappen Schilde.
http://codicon.digitale-sammlungen.de/inventiconCod.icon.%20391.html
401 Archivum heraldicum, Volumes 36-37 By Schweizerische Heraldische Gesellschaft. 1922.
402 Family Crests (Frydig & Freidig) State Archives of Bern Switzerland Falkenplatz #4. Provided by Christoph Nicklaus
403 Frieding (Andechs) http://de.wikipedia.org/wiki/Frieding_(Andechs)
404 Albrecht der Schenk von Verthoven http://www.mom-ca.uni-koeln.de/mom/AT-StiAG/GoettweigOSB/1325_II_05/charter#anchor?q=Verthouen
405 Albrect Aidem http://www.mom-ca.uni-koeln.de/mom/AT-StiAZ/Urkunden/1325_XI_17/charter?
406 http://www.klosterarchiv.ch/e-archiv_urkunden_detail.php?id=1756
407 Beiträge zur Erforschung steirischer Geschichte, Volume 33 By Historischer Verein für Steiermark, Historische Landeskommission für Steiermark.
408 Mittheilungen, Volumes 42-46 By Historischer Verein für Steiermark. 1894.
409 http://en.wikipedia.org/wiki/Gerold,_Prefect_of_Bavaria
410 http://de.wikipedia.org/wiki/Udalrichinger
411 http://fmg.ac/Projects/MedLands/SWABIAN%20NOBILITY.htm#GeroldUdalrichingerMImma
412 Uldaricher familie http://de.wikipedia.org/wiki/Udalrichinger
413 Casus Monasterii Petrishusinsis Monumenta Historica
http://www.mgh.de/dmgh/add/bsb00000887_00656
414 Casus Monasterii Petrishusinsis Monumenta Historica Index
http://www.mgh.de/dmgh/add/bsb00000887_00656
415 Freiburger Diözesan-Archiv: Zeitschrift des Kirchengeschichtlichen ..., Volume 2 By Kirchlich-Historischer Verein der Erzdiöcese Freiburg, Kirchengeschichtlicher Verein für das Erzbistum Freiburg Herder, 1866
416 Jahresbericht des Historischen Kreisvereins im Regierungsbezirke ..., Volume 34 By Historischer Kreisverein im Regierungsbezirke von Schwaben und Neuburg. 1869
417 Quellen und forschungen zur geschichte Schwabens und der Ost-Schweiz
 By Carl Borromaeus Aloys Fickle Schneider, 1859 - 104 pages
418 Theodor Ilg 2008 http://www.michael-buhlmann.de/Geschichte/gesch_rez_i.htm
419 Freiburger Diazesan-Archiver Volumes 32-33 pg 155
420 Quellen zur Schweizer Geschichte Allgemeine Geschichtforschende Gesellschaft der Schweiz 1883.
421 Beschreibung des Oberamts Tuttlingen: mit 3 Tabellen. Bissinger, 1879
422 Beschreibung des Oberamts Tuttlingen: mit 3 Tabellen. Bissinger, 1879
423 Nendingen http://www.territorioscuola.com/wikipedia/de.wikipedia.php?title=Nendingen
424 Quellen zue Schweizer Geschichte, Volume 14. 1894.
425 Monasterium.net http://www.mom-ca.uni-koeln.de/mom/CSGXI/6709./charter?q=Frydingen
426 Zeitschrift für die Geschichte des Oberrheins , Volume 37 G. Braun, 1884
427 Destroyed or inaccessible dances of death in Switzerland: 2011
http://www.totentanz-online.de/laender/verzeichnis-ch-zerstoert.php
428 Zuricher Wappenrolle notes. http://www.armorial.dk/german/Zurich%20WR.pdf
429 Wappentafel der Bischöfe von Konstanz, Mitte 19. Jh. von Franz Xaver Stiehle (bis zum Spätmittelalter Fantasiewappen; später teilweise unzuverlässig, im Mittelalter bei Amtsträgern in Doppelfunktion teilweise mit anderen Bistums-/Abtswappen angereicherte Schilde)
http://upload.wikimedia.org/wikipedia/commons/5/5b/Wappentafel_Bisch%C3%B6fe_von_Konstanz_F_X_Stiehle_19Jh.jpg
430 Wappentable Bishops of Konstanz.
http://upload.wikimedia.org/wikipedia/commons/5/5b/Wappentafel_Bisch%C3%B6fe_von_Konstanz_F_X_Stiehle_19Jh.jpg

431 Burg und Herrschaft Hohenkrahen im Hegau, by Eberhard Dobler. 1986

432 Codex diplomaticvs Alemanniae et Bvrgvndiae trans-Ivranae intra fines dioecesis Constantiensis: cev fvndamentvm historiae eivsdem dioecesis Trudpert Neugart Typis San-Blasianis, 1795

433 Regesta Episcoporum Constantiensium: Regesten zur Geschichte ..., Volumes 1-2 Wagner, 1895

434 Römische quellen zur Konstanzer bistumsgeschichte zur zeit der Päpste in ... By Karl Rieder

435 Freiburger Diözesan-Archiv, Volumes 7-8 By Kirchengeschichtlicher Verein für Geschichte, Christliche Kunst, Altertums- und Literaturkunde des Erzbistums Freiburg Verlag Herder., 1873

436 Kleinere Schriften: bd. Abhandlungen zur deutschen litteraturgeschichte. 1873 S. Hirzel, 1873

437 Römische quellen zur Konstanzer bistumsgeschichte zur zeit der Päpste in ... By Karl Rieder

438 Friedrich Riederer Spiegel der wahren Rhetorik (1493) Herausgegeben von Joachim Knape und Stefanie Luppold. 2008http://www.harrassowitz-verlag.de/dzo/artikel/201//002/2058_201.pdf?t=1228389416

439 Die Mittelalterlichen Architektur- und Kunstdenkmäler des Cantons Thurgau Johann Rudolf Rahn, Ernst Haffter, Robert Durrer Eidgenössische Landesmuseum-Comission, 1899

440 Regesta Episcoporum Constantiensium: Regesten zur Geschichte ..., Volumes 1-2 Wagner, 1895

441 Friedrich Riederer Spiegel der wahren Rhetorik (1493) Herausgegeben von Joachim Knape und Stefanie Luppold. 2008 http://www.harrassowitz-verlag.de/dzo/artikel/201//002/2058_201.pdf?t=1228389416

442 Ridern (1939) Durschen in the Canton of Glarus wappen http://www.ngw.nl/int/zwi/r/riedern.htm

443 Regesta Episcoporum Constantiensium: Regesten zur Geschichte ..., Volumes 1-2 Wagner, 1895.

444 Die Regesten der Archive in der schweizerischen Eidgenossenschaft: Bd., 4. T.] Die Regesten der Benedictiner-Abtei Disentis im Canton Graubünden. Druck und Verlag von G. Hitz, 1854

445 Paul Willimksi http://www.hattingen-baden.de/Hattingen%20-%20Geschichte.htm

446 Zeitschrift fur Wuttemburgische Landesgeschicte Volume 25 BY w. Kohlhammer 1996.

447 Württembergische Vierteljahrshefte für Landesgeschichte, Volumes 8-9 pg 345 W. Kohlhammer, 1899

448 Die Zähringer – Herzöge im hochmittelalterlichen Schwaben http://baarverein.de/mediapool/94/943479/data/bibliothek/Andere_Dateien/Buhlmann_2009_Zahringer.pdf

449 Hohenzoller Heimat http://www.hohenzollerischer-geschichtsverein.de/userfiles/files/HZ-Heimat/HH_010_1960_ocr.pdf

450 Zur Geschichte von Hettingen http://www.hohenzollerischer-geschichtsverein.de/userfiles/files/HZ-Heimat/HH_026_1976_ocr.pdf

451 Mitteilungen, Volumnes 39-40 1906

452 Quellen zur Schweizer Geschichte By Allgemeine Geschichtforschende Gesellschaft der Schweiz 1883.

453 Codex Diplomaticus Alemanniae Et Burgundiae Trans-Iuranae Intra Fines ... By Trudpert Neugart Typis San-Blasianis, 1795

454 Quellen zue Schweizer Geschichte, Volume 14. 1894.

455 Regesta Episcoporum Constantiensium: Regesten zur Geschichte p 248, Volumes 1-2 Wagner, 1895

456 Aarau, Staatsarchiv Aargau, AA/3116: http://www.e-codices.unifr.ch/en/saa/AA3116/269v/medium

457 Casus Monasteriuss Petrishusensis http://www.dmgh.de/de/fs2/object/display/bsb00000887_00654.html?sortIndex=010%3A050%3A0020%3A010%3A00%3A00

458 Heiligenberg in Schwaben: nit einer Geschichte seiner Alten Grafen und des von ihnen beherrschten Linzgaus. Macklot 1853.

317

459 Das ehemalige Frauenkloster Tanikon im Thurgau by Johann Rudolph Rahn, Johann Nater.1906.

460 Monasterium.net http://www.mom-ca.uni-koeln.de/mom/CSGVIII/1364_XI_30/charter?q=Friedingen

461 Deutche Reichstagsakten: Auf Veranlassung und mit Unterstusung Volume 9. J.G Cotta 1887.

462 Anzeiger für schweizerische Altertumskunde, Volumes 17-20 By Antiquarische Gesellschaft in Zürich, Schweizerisches Landesmuseum.1887

463 Jahrbuch für Münchener Geschichte, Volume 2 By Karl von Reinhardstoettner, Karl Trautmann J. Lindauersche Buchhandlung (Schöpping), 1888

464 http://www.ngw.nl/int/zwi/p/ponto.htm or www.pont-en-ogoz.ch

465 Casus Monasteriuss Petrishusensis
http://www.dmgh.de/de/fs2/object/display/bsb00000887_00654.html?sortIndex=010%3A050%3A0020%3A010%3A00%3A00

466 Regesta Episcoporum Constantiensium: Regesten zur Geschichte der Bishcöfe von Constanz, von Bubulcus bis Thomas Berlower, 517-1496, Volumes 1-2 Wagner, 1895

467 Codex diplomaticus Salemitanus, Urkundenbuch der cisterzienserabtei Salem, herausg. von F. von Weech. 1881 Salem Abbey

468 http://www.ebersbach-musbach.de/gemeinde/aeptissin_anna_saal.html

469 Zeitschrift für die Geschichte des Oberrheins, Volume 31. W. Kohlhammer, 1879

470 Fürstenbergisches Urkundenbuch: Sammlung der Quellen zur ..., Volume 5 By Donaueschingen (Germany). Fürstenbergisches Archiv In Commission der H. Laupp'schen Buchhandlung, 1885

471 Die Regesten der Benedictiner-Abtei Disentis im Canton Graubünden L. Hitz, 1854

472 Kleinere Schriften: bd. Abhandlungen zur deutschen litteraturgeschichte. 1873 S. Hirzel, 1873

473 Bern Archives von Heidegg http://www.query.sta.be.ch/detail.aspx?ID=43861

474 Rerum Germanicarum veteres iam primum publicati scriptores VI: In Qvibvs ... By Johann Pistorius Peez, 1726

475 Historische Zeitschrift, Volumes 53-54. 1885

476 Die Regesten der Benedictiner-Abtei Disentis im Canton Graubünden L. Hitz, 1854

477 Fürstenbergisches Urkundenbuch: Sammlung der Quellen zur ..., Volume 5 By Donaueschingen (Germany). Fürstenbergisches Archiv In Commission der H. Laupp'schen Buchhandlung, 1885

478 Fürstenbergisches Urkundenbuch: Sammlung der Quellen zur ..., Volume 5 By Donaueschingen (Germany). Fürstenbergisches Archiv In Commission der H. Laupp'schen Buchhandlung, 1885

479 Das Württembergische Urkundenbuch Online - Landesarchiv Baden-Württemberg
http://www.wubonline.de/

480 Schiller: Schwäbische Heimatjahre (Im Vaterhause ; Auf der Fürstenschule ... By Jacob Mino Weidmann, 1890

481 Württembergisches Adels- und Wappenbuch: Im Auftrag des Württembergischen ... By Otto von Alberti, Friedrich Gaisberg-Schöckingen (Freiherr von.), Albert Botzheim (Freiherr von.), Württembergischer Geschichts- und Altertumsverein W. Kohlhammer, 1898

482 Württembergisches Adels- und Wappenbuch: Im Auftrag des Württembergischen ... By Otto von Alberti, Friedrich Gaisberg-Schöckingen (Freiherr von.), Albert Botzheim (Freiherr von.), Württembergischer Geschichts- und Altertumsverein W. Kohlhammer, 1090

483 Swiggers son Gottschalk 1058
http://fmg.ac/Projects/MedLands/GERMAN%20NOBILITY.htm

484 Casus Monasteriuss Petrishusensis
http://www.dmgh.de/de/fs2/object/display/bsb00000887_00654.html?sortIndex=010%3A050%3A0020%3A010%3A00%3A00

485 Quellen zur Schweizer Geshichte 1883.

486 Sex of Gundelfingen http://www.historisches-lexikon-bayerns.de/artikel/artikel_45553

487 Fürstenbergisches Urkundenbuch: Sammlung der Quellen zur ..., Volume 5 By Donaueschingen (Germany). Fürstenbergisches Archiv In Commission der H. Laupp'schen Buchhandlung, 1885

488 Württembergisches Adels- und Wappenbuch: Im Auftrag des Württembergischen ... By Otto von Alberti, Friedrich Gaisberg-Schöckingen (Freiherr von.), Albert Botzheim (Freiherr von.), Württembergischer Geschichts- und Altertumsverein W. Kohlhammer, 1898

489 Heilger Anno von Steuslingen http://www.feuerwehr-altsteusslingen-briel.de/Altsteusslingen-Dateien/Infos/St_Anno.htm

490 Codex diplomaticvs Alemanniae et Bvrgvndiae trans-Ivranae intra fines ... By Trudpert Neugart Typis San-Blasianis, 1795

491 Fürstenbergisches Urkundenbuch: Sammlung der Quellen zur ..., Volume 5 By Donaueschingen (Germany). Fürstenbergisches Archiv In Commission der H. Laupp'schen Buchhandlung, 1885

492 Fürstenbergisches Urkundenbuch: Sammlung der Quellen zur ..., Volume 5 By Donaueschingen (Germany). Fürstenbergisches Archiv In Commission der H. Laupp'schen Buchhandlung, 1885

493 Die Kultur der Abtei Reichenau Scientia-Verlag, 1970

494 Fürstenbergisches Urkundenbuch: Sammlung der Quellen zur ..., Volume 5
 By Donaueschingen (Germany). Fürstenbergisches Archiv In Commission der H. Laupp'schen Buchhandlung, 1885

495 Fürstenbergisches Urkundenbuch: Sammlung der Quellen zur ..., Volume 5
 By Donaueschingen (Germany). Fürstenbergisches Archiv In Commission der H. Laupp'schen Buchhandlung, 1885

496 Kleinere Schriften: bd. Abhandlungen zur deutschen litteraturgeschichte. 1873 S. Hirzel, 1873

497 Kleinere Schriften: bd. Abhandlungen zur deutschen litteraturgeschichte. 1873 S. Hirzel, 1873

498 Zeitschrift für die Geschichte des Oberrheins , Volume 37 G. Braun, 1884

499 Markdorf Wappen History http://www.ngw.nl/int/dld/m/markdorf.htm

500 Quellen zur Schweizer Geschichte, Volume 3 1883

501 Quellen zur Schweizer Geschichte, Volume 3 1881 Switzerland

502 Fürstenbergisches Urkundenbuch: Sammlung der Quellen zur ..., Volume 5 By Donaueschingen (Germany). Fürstenbergisches Archive In Commission der H. Laupp'schen Buchhandlung, 1885

503 Zeitschrift für die Geschichte des Oberrheins, Volume 31. W. Kohlhammer, 1879

504 Die Regesten der Archive in der schweizerischen Eidgenossenschaft: Bd., 4. T ... By Theodor von Mohr, Gallus Morel, Friedrich Stettler, Gerold Meyer v. 1854

505 Richental, Ulrich (von) Concilium zu Konstanz Augsburg: Anton Sorg, 2 Sept. 1483 http://tudigit.ulb.tu-darmstadt.de/show/inc-iii-55/0003/thumbs?sid=64c9a6d14e58a520b8245f2555c005d0#current_page

506 Deutche Reichstagsakten: Auf Veranlassung und mit Unterstusung Volume 9. J.G Cotta 1887.

507 Richental, Ulrich (von) Concilium zu Konstanz Augsburg: Anton Sorg, 2 Sept. 1483 http://tudigit.ulb.tu-darmstadt.de/show/inc-iii-55/0044

508 Wappenbuch von Arlberger (Abbey of St. Christophe in Arlberger Thal in Tirol, Austria) armorial 1394 to 1430. Otto Hupp Berlin 1937-39. http://bilderserver.at/wappenbuecher/ProfHuppOSPv2_52z2/

509 Die Ministerialen der Zähringer in Burgund By Matthias Storm.2007.

510 Das Württembergische Urkundenbuch Online - Landesarchiv Baden-Württemberg http://www.wubonline.de/

511 Burg und Herrschaft Hohekrahen im Hegau, by Eberhard Dobler. 1986

512 Castles & Places in Baden-Wurtemburg. Castle Rock High Crows in Hegau. Frank Buchali. http://www.burgen-web.de/hohenkraehen.pdf

513 Burg und Herrschaft Hohenkrahen im Hegau, by Eberhard Dobler. 1986

514 Village Church in Adelboden http://www.ref.ch/data/78/downloads/1723_baf5e3b4a0e3e831cd2741eeb10c1847.pdf

515 Canton Aargau (AG) General Information http://kunden.eye.ch/swissgen/kant/agallg-e.htm
516 en.wikipedia.org/wiki/Swiss_Nobility
517 Zurich Switzerland archive. 1411. http://suche.staatsarchiv.djiktzh.ch/detail.aspx?ID=365668
518 Fontes rerum Bernensium: Bern's Geschichtsquellen, Volume 6. In Commission der Dalp'schen Buchhandel (K. Schmid), 1891.
519 Grafenried zur Zeit der Dreifelderwirtschaft. By Paul Zyrd. 1942.
520 Fontes Rerum Bernensium   FRB   Volume 10, pg 7.
521 Sprachspiegel, Volumes 21-23 By Deutschschweizerischer Sprachverein. 1965
522 Die Segesser zu Mellingen, Aarau und Brugg, 1250-1550 K J Weiss 1884.
523 Swiss Castles www.swisscastles.ch/aargau/schenkenburg_d.html
524 Chronicon Helveticum – Gessellschaft der Schweiz pg 49. 1968
525 Kirchliche und soziale Zustände in Bern unmittelbar nach der Einführung der Reformation (1528-1536) Gustav Grunau, 1906
526 Saint Quirin http://de.wikipedia.org/wiki/Saint-Quirin
527 Aellig/Ellig coat of arms 1530 in Bern. http://www.query.sta.be.ch/detail.aspx?ID=432563
528 Zurich Archives "Will of Hartman Weibel" 5/10/1347. http://suche.staatsarchiv.djiktzh.ch/detail.aspx?ID=274782
529 Fürstenbergisches Urkundenbuch: Sammlung der Quellen zur Geschichte des Hauses Fürstenberg und seiner Lande in Schwaben, Volume 5 In Commission der H. Laupp'schen Buchhandlung, 1885
530 Die Schweiz im ihren Ritterburger und Bergschlössern J. Dalp, 1828
531 Wappenbuch von Arlberger (Abbey of St. Christophe in Arlberger Thal in Tirol, Austria) armorial 1394 to 1430. Otto Hupp Berlin 1937-39. http://bilderserver.at/wappenbuecher/ProfHuppOSPv2_52z2/
532 en.wikipedia.org/wiki/Apocope
533 Richental, Ulrich (von) Concilium zu Konstanz Augsburg: Anton Sorg, 2 Sept. 1483 http://tudigit.ulb.tu-darmstadt.de/show/inc-iii-55/0003/thumbs?sid=64c9a6d14e58a520b8245f2555c005d0#current_page
534 Fontes rerum Bernensium: Bern's Geschichtsquellen, Volume 6. In Commission der Dalp'schen Buchhandel (K. Schmid), 1891.
535 Grafenried zur Zeit der Dreifelderwirtschaft. By Paul Zyrd. 1942.
536 Fontes Rerum Bernensium   FRB   Volume 10, pg 7.
537 Schloss Schenkenberg in Thalheim. http://www.swisscastles.ch/aargau/schenkenberg_d.html
538 Zurich Archives "Will of Hartman Weibel" 5/10/1347. http://suche.staatsarchiv.djiktzh.ch/detail.aspx?ID=274782
539 http://www.klosterarchiv.ch/e-archiv_urkunden_detail.php?id=1756
540 Freiburger Diözesan-Archiv , Volumes 70-71 Verlag Herder., 1950
541 Wappenbuch von Arlberger (Abbey of St. Christophe in Arlberger Thal in Tirol, Austria) armorial 1394 to 1430. Otto Hupp Berlin 1937-39. http://bilderserver.at/wappenbuecher/ProfHuppOSPv2_52z2/
542 Archivum Heraldicum volume 36-37, pg 62. 1922
543 Vierteljahrsschrift für Wappen-, Siegel- und Familienkunde, Volume 16 By Herold, Verein für Heraldik, Genealogie und Verwandte Wissenschaft, Berlin. Page 37. 1888
544 Neus berner Taschenbuch Ludwig Lauterburg. KJ Wyss 1900.
545 Zimmerische chronik, Volume 2 By Froben Christof Zimmern (Graf von), Johannes Müller, Wilhelm Wernher Zimmern (Graf von) J. C. B. Mohr, 1881
546 Bischof Diethelm von Krenkingen (Bischof von Konstanz 1189-1206). Kolorierte Federezeichnung, Mitte 13. Jh. Codex traditionum Weißenaugiensis. Kantonsbibliothek St. Gallen. Kopie des Freiherrn Joseph von Laßberg, um 1830. http://upload.wikimedia.org/wikipedia/commons/2/2b/Diethelm_von_Krenkingen.jpg
547 Orden Online: Johannes von Fridingen http://www.orden-online.de/wissen/j/johannes-von-fridingen/

548 Gebhard von Konstanz Commeratvie Stamp. http://www.austria-lexikon.at/af/Wissenssammlungen/Briefmarken/1949/Hl_Gebhard

549 Scupltur of Gebhard von Konstanz http://commons.wikimedia.org/wiki/File:Merazhofen_Pfarrkirche_Chorgest%C3%BChl_rechts_Gebhard.jpg

533 Württembergisches Adels- und Wappenbuch: Im Auftrag des Württembergischen AltertumsvereinsKohlhammer, 1898

551 Cartulaire de Muhouse Volume 3 by Zavier Mossman 1885.

552 Henggeler, Rudolf P.: Consecration of the princely book. Benedictine Abbey of St. Gallus and Otmar to St.Gallen. Einsiedeln 1929th (Monasticon Benedictinum Helvetiae-1) http://www.sg.ch/home/kultur/stiftsarchiv/geschichte/abtei_st_gallen/aebte.html

553 Das Land Baden-Württemberg: Regierungsbezirk Freiburg. Pg 682, 1982.

554 Swabian Map 1572 by David Seltzlin http://en.wikipedia.org/wiki/File:Seltzlin_map_1572.JPG

555 Der Landammann in den schweizerischen Demokratien Uri, Schwyz, Unterwalden By A. Rosa Benz 1917

556 Dictionnaire géographique et statistique de la Suisse, Volume 2 By Markus Lutz. 1837

557 The Alps in nature and history by William Augustus Brevoort Coolidge Methuen, 1908.

558 Wappenbuch von Arlberger (Abbey of St. Christophe in Arlberger Thal in Tirol, Austria) armorial 1394 to 1430. Otto Hupp Berlin 1937-39. http://bilderserver.at/wappenbuecher/ProfHuppOSPv2_52z2/

559 Die Regesten der Archive in der schweizerischen Eidgenossenschaft: Bd., 4. T.] Die Regesten der Benedictiner-Abtei Disentis im Canton Graubünden. Druck und Verlag von G. Hitz, 1854

560 Urkendenbuch der Stadt Aarau: Mit einer historischen Einleitung, Register und Gloaase, sowie einer historischen Karte. Sauerlander, 1880.

561 Ursula Fridinger Nonne @ St. Agness Shauffhausen http://stash.sh.ch/index.aspx?guid=11cce1549f724903a2b83a004282e0d0

562 Zurich Switzerland archive. 1411. http://suche.staatsarchiv.djiktzh.ch/detail.aspx?ID=365668

563 http://www.klosterarchiv.ch/e-archiv_urkunden_detail.php?id=1756

564 Das Emmenthal nach Geschichte, Land und Leuten By Jakob Imobersteg Huber, 1876

565 Die Heimathskunde für den Kanton Luzern: Neudorf von Melchior Estermann By Joseph. - Bölsterli, Xaver. - Thürig, Melchior. - Estermann, Raphael. – Reinhard. 1875

566 Village Church in Adelboden http://www.ref.ch/data/78/downloads/1723_baf5e3b4a0e3e831cd2741eeb10c1847.pdf

www.ingramcontent.com/pod-product-compliance
Lightning Source LLC
Chambersburg PA
CBHW080407290526

45791CB00008BA/2176